RELIGION, CONFLICT AND RECONCILIATION

CURRENTS OF ENCOUNTER

STUDIES ON THE CONTACT BETWEEN CHRISTIANITY AND OTHER RELIGIONS, BELIEFS, AND CULTURES

GENERAL EDITORS

REIN FERNHOUT
JERALD D. GORT
HENRY JANSEN
LOURENS MINNEMA
HENDRIK M. VROOM
ANTON WESSELS

VOL. 17

Religion, Conflict and Reconciliation

Multifaith Ideals and Realities

Edited by

Jerald D. Gort
Henry Jansen
Hendrik M. Vroom

Amsterdam - New York, NY 2002

The paper on which this book is printed meets the requirements of "ISO 9706:1994, Information and documentation - Paper for documents - Requirements for permanence".

ISBN: 90-420-1460-1 (Bound)
©Editions Rodopi B.V., Amsterdam - New York, NY 2002
Printed in the Netherlands

Contents

Preface	ix
Part I: Defining the Parameters	1
Religion, Conflict and Reconciliation JERALD D. GORT AND HENDRIK M. VROOM	3
Religious Reconciliation: A View from the Social Sciences ANDRÉ DROOGERS	11
The Nature and Origins of Religious Conflicts: Some Philosophical Considerations HENDRIK M. VROOM	24
Part II: Perspectives on Conflict and Reconciliation	35
Hindus and Muslims in Bengal: Is Religious Experience a Unifying Factor? VICTOR A. VAN BIJLERT	37
Religious Conflict and Hindu Tolerance CORSTIAAN J.G. VAN DER BURG	51
Liberation Theology in South India S. GANGADARAN	60
Divided Families and Social Conflict: Comparing a Greek Tragedy and an Indian Drama LOURENS MINNEMA	68
Buddhist Thoughts on Conflict, 'Reconciliation' ... and Religion MICHAEL MCGHEE	85
Theological Preparation for Reconciliation in Judaism TZVI MARX	93
Three Models of Reconciliation: A Christian Approach CEES VAN DER KOOI	104
Religion, Conflict and Reconciliation Ecumenical Initiatives Amidst Human Brokenness and Community Division JERALD D. GORT	117

Can the Children of Abraham be Reconciled: Ishmael and Isaac
in the Bible and the Qur'an ANTON WESSELS   134

Isaiah Berlin: Teleological Thinking as a Cause of Conflict
CONNIE AARSBERGEN   145

The Road to Sainthood: Reconciliation in Graham Greene's
The End of the Affair HENRY JANSEN   154

Secular Saints: The Possibility of Reconciliation
Without Transcendence DESIREE BERENDSEN   164

Women in Engaged Buddhism
CLAUDIA ROMBERG   176

Islam, Gender and Reconciliation: Making Room
for New Gender Perspectives TIRZA VISSER   186

Part III: Case Studies of Conflict and Reconciliation   195

Interreligious Conflict and Reconciliation in Indonesia
AGUS RACHMAT WIDYANTO   197

A Pillar of Social Harmony: The Study of Comparative Religion
in Contemporary Indonesia during the New Order HERMAN L. BECK   216

Religious Reconciliation as a Challenge of Governance:
India at the Start of the Twenty-First Century
CHAKRAVARTI RAM-PRASAD   231

Islam and Muslims in India: Problems of Identity and Existence
ASHGAR ALI ENGINEER   239

Processes of Reconciliation in India
SWAMI AGNIVESH   251

Reconciliation in Practice: Indian Experience
ANDREAS D'SOUZA   260

Religion, Conflict, and Reconciliation in Sri Lanka
NALIN SWARIS   270

Truth and Reconciliation in Post-Apartheid South Africa
PIET MEIRING   279

An Islamic View of Conflict and Reconciliation
in the South African Situation FARID ESACK   290

On Playing Reconciliation in a Situation of Racist Conflict
TON VAN PROOIJEN   298

Seeds of Conflict: Christian-Muslim Relations in Tanzania
FRANS WIJSEN and BERNARDINE MFUMBUSA   316

Religion, Conflict and Reconciliation in Rwanda
JAN VAN BUTSELAAR   327

Religion, Conflict and Reconciliation in Bosnia Herzegovina
DONNA WINSLOW   340

Peace, Reconciliation and New Religious Movements
REENDER KRANENBORG   356

Part IV: The Papers and the Discussions: Reaping the Harvest   365

Why Do Religious Groups Become Involved in Conflicts?
ANDRÉ DROOGERS   367

The Meaning of Reconciliation
VICTOR A. VAN BIJLERT   372

A Blueprint for the Process of Peace and Reconciliation
JOSIEN FOLBERT   377

Views of Conflict and Reconciliation
KAREL STEENBRINK   385

Index of Names   391

Index of Subjects   395

Contributors   403

Preface

The Interdisciplinary Research Group on the Encounter of Religious Traditions (IRGERT), in operation for nearly two decades within the Faculty of Theology of the Free University in Amsterdam, has organized and hosted a number of medium-sized international and interreligious conferences and workshops throughout the years (including 'Dialogue and Syncretism' 1988, 'On Sharing Religious Experience' 1990, 'Human Rights and Religious Values' 1993, 'Holy Scriptures in Judaism, Christianity, and Islam' 1995) and has published several volumes in its academic series *Currents of Encounter*.

The book in hand, the seventeenth to appear in this series, consists of a collection of thirty-five essays dealing with the potential and actual, very often ambiguous role that religion plays in situations of conflict and processes of conflict-resolution. Thirty of the compositions included here were originally presented as discussion papers at the most recent IRGERT workshop, entitled 'Religion, Conflict, and Reconciliation,' held from March 30 to April 2, 2001 at the convent of Our Dear Lady of Eem, Amersfoort, the Netherlands, and four, written subsequently and making up the final section of this collection, consist of synopses of some of the main lines of thought and argumentation which emerged from the workshop papers and discussions.

In addition to these thirty-four essays consisting of case studies of, theological views on, and general questions regarding religion, conflict, and reconciliation, attention is drawn to the position paper, immediately following this preface, which was sent beforehand to the participants with a view to clarifying some of the prominent issues and questions involved in the workshop theme: In what way do religions contribute to the rise and/or resolution of conflict? Is the effectuation of interhuman reconciliation possible in the absence of religion? Is it possible in the presence of religion?

Finally, the editors of the present symposium would like to express their deep appreciation to the Netherlands Organization for Academic Research, the Department of Global Ministries of the Uniting Protestant Churches in the Netherlands, the Van Coeverden Adriani Foundation, and the Netherlands School for Advanced Study in Theology and Religion, without whose generous financial support neither the workshop nor this publication would have been possible.

The Editors
Jerald D. Gort
Henry Jansen
Hendrik M. Vroom

Part I

Defining the Parameters

Religion, Conflict and Reconciliation

Jerald D. Gort and Hendrik M. Vroom

> Humans are by and large incorrigibly religious.... Whatever the wishes of the cultured despisers of religion, as a species we yearn to see things whole and sacred. We insist on telling a cosmic narrative and locating ourselves somewhere in it. Something primordial wants assurance that we are supported by the same powers that brought earth into being and threw sun and stars into orbit. And something wants to name with the name of God "the fathomless mystery that surrounds the burning mystery of own lives."
>
> Rasmussen 1996: 178; quotation from Johnson 1993: 10

> Marx and Ludwig Feuerbach, in stressing that God is an erroneous idea of humanity, ignored the fact that God is a necessary idea, deeply rooted in all human beings.
>
> Van der Bent 1991: 662

But what is the role of religion in situations of hostility? Can and does it contribute to understanding and rapprochement or is it merely and usually a source of friction and contention? In this symposium we wish to reflect on and discuss a number of questions that come immediately to mind or need to be raised in connection with the theme: Religion, Conflict, and Reconciliation.

For many, religion is synonymous with animosity, violence and war. "Some regard religion as positively harmful—the cause of division, hatred and persecution—and therefore as a relic to be left behind by a world advancing in the direction of a common civilization" (Neill 1971: 517). Ethnicity and religion play a determining role in many of the hotbeds of strife and hostility found throughout the world, which is not really that surprising considering the fact that religion and culture are so closely interwoven. Conflicts between ethnic groups often have a religious component. In situations of this kind, religion seems to be Janus-faced. In times of prosperity and peace religious leaders speak in terms of harmony and compassion, and believers accept each other across denominational and religious boundaries. As soon as tension rises, however, religion presents another face: people dedicate themselves to a 'sacred cause' and offer their lives in the defense of interests endorsed by faith and stamped with a religious seal of approval. Sacred writings often teach the love of peace and compassion, but in times of war religious adherents are very adept at finding other scriptural references which they claim justify bloody confrontation with people of other faiths or even with those of a different persuasion within their own religion. "Every religion carries within it the germ of its own degeneration or perversion" (Sundermeier 1991: 857). Because of the involvement of religious organizations and groups in war, hatred and malice, nonbelievers often call for the abolition of all religions. The existence of social evil as a consequence of religious belief forms one of the main arguments in the case made against religion by its critics.

The fact that various groups within a pluralist society each appeal to an extraterrestrial authority presents a significant problem. Because each religious denomination appeals to an authority which is not recognized by others, religion can very easily become a factor in conflict. Religious claims to truth, it is often averred, are inherently conflictive. May people appeal to the will of God to justify what they do or do not do. As the classical question in the discussion regarding the relation between religion and ethics has it: Is that which is good what the gods will or is the will of the gods that which is good? Must we do what God says because God says it, or may, and must God's will, too, be judged according to the norm of that which is good? Is something good or does it become good because God wills it, or does God will it because it is good? What is the highest norm: God or that which is good? In Plato's dialogue on this theme Socrates remarks somewhat mockingly that the gods all want different things and that it is thus not so very easy to determine what their will is. But let us assume, says Socrates, that there is but one Divinity and that we know what he wills. Are we required to do what the Deity wills *because* he wills it and not because of *what* he wills? Must we obey God's will because it is his will or because we recognize that what he wills is good?

An appeal to the will of God by one party, it has often been pointed out, can prove to be highly dangerous to another group. If during times of ethnic tension the banner of the Cross or the Crescent is lifted above the fray, woe be to those on the other side. The peace-loving attitude of Muslims toward others can, it seems, easily metamorphose into clamors for holy war—such as those that have been fanning the internecine conflict threatening to engulf Indonesia—even though Muslims know full well that the real *jihad* is the battle between good and evil that must be joined and fought out in the heart of each human individual. Christians, too, have regularly harnessed God to their cart, though everyone knows that the Gospel does not teach war but rather love for neighbor. The past millennium "has been a period of Christian division, strife and mutual condemnation. The desire to spread or defend a Christian culture has spawned violence and war, injustice and oppression" (Raiser 1999: 4). Religion can be misused, it is true, but it can also keep people from doing what is wrong and from serving their own selfish interests to the detriment of others. The behavior of religious believers is ambiguous, and religion can be driven in two different directions, that of good and that of evil.

> Religion is not ipso facto "a good thing." Religions and other faiths (chauvinist nationalisms, for example) have been, can be, and are demonic as well as redemptive. The holy destroys as well as saves. Lucifer is dressed out as an angel of light, and what Goethe's Mephistopheles calls "the cruel thirst for worship" can wreak unspeakable horror. The world within, the world of the spirit,

is no sure guide for the world without. It, too, can deceive and defeat.... Religious impulses are as subject to measure by a moral plumb line as anything else that beats in the human breast and issues from human hands. Ben-Gurion's "moral-spiritual energy" of this "mysterious" and "divinely inspired (human) soul" must be judged by its outcomes. "By their fruits you will know them" is the wording from one of Ben-Gurion's ancestors. (Rasmussen 1996: 178-79)

Karl Marx provided a striking characterization of this ambiguity. In the final analysis, he said, religion is bad because it benumbs its adherents and acts as the "opiate of the people." Religion constitutes false comfort and hope. People allow themselves to be lulled into sleep by the sweet promises of their faith and wait for God to make all things new. On the other hand, Marx contended, in situations of exploitation, injustice and poverty, religious faith provides hope that things will be different one day and that the exploiter does not rule this world in an ultimate sense but is subject to a higher power that in due time will straighten what has become so badly bent out of shape. Faith is the rose adorning the chains of oppression; religion is the consciousness of injustice and the longing for justice, love of neighbor and peace. Given this interpretation, it is not as anomalous as it might at first seem that Communism sometimes just let the church be: when the situation improves and the chains have been cast off, it was thought, people will no longer need the fragrance of the roses and the intoxication of the opium provided by religious faith, and religion will simply slip out of the picture. But in far and away the biggest share of cases, Marxist-Leninists did whatever they could to facilitate and hasten the 'demise' of religion. In most Communist situations religious believers suffered greatly at the hands of atheistic authorities and compatriots and in a number of remaining instances continue to do so. During the twentieth century religious adherents have been severely persecuted by the enemies of religion. Nonbelievers prevented believers from living out their faith, forced them to repudiate their religious convictions, or sent them to prisons and concentration camps to die. The atheistic communist regime and system in the Soviet Union created countless millions of victims between 1917 and 1989.

And due to its ambiguous nature, people continue, even now at the onset of the new millennium, to be of two minds regarding religion. Some participants in the debate on religion and culture, even though they themselves are not believers, would not like to see religion disappear because they think that society benefits greatly from it as the conveyer of morality. Immanuel Kant observed that religious faith was good for his servant, Lampe, and Voltaire commented that faith was useful in that it restrained one's staff from stealing the silverware. Fukayama writes that the great moral crisis of the postindustrial era, from around 1965 to the present time, will be overcome because people are social beings by nature. Nonetheless, he assigns an important place to religion in this connection. Religion can play a significant role in the restoration of moral values and the discovery of new ones by giving ritual expression to deep human emotions. Religion is not absolutely necessary, but it also need not be done away with because it can be very useful. Other observers think quite differently about this matter, however. "Faith in a personal God who reveals himself is still rejected as an antiquated superstition that undermines human autonomy" (Van der Bent 1991: 662). In a recent letter addressed to the six billionth citizen of the world, Salmon Rushdie—who was himself condemned and relentlessly hounded by the fanatical ayatollahs of Iran—turned his back on religion. People believe in fairy tales, which are worthless, he writes; religion prevents people from thinking for themselves and taking responsibility for their own lives. Religions cause divisions among people; they encourage hatred and malice and therefore should be abandoned once and for all.

Calls to bid farewell to all forms of faith and to accept hard reality with a view to making room for people to operate under their own steam represent attempts to solve the problem of the ambiguity of religion by simply doing away with religion as such. But those who issue such appeals have completely lost sight of the fact that religion has its own inherent value and that it therefore should not be treated differently than any other aspect of human existence. Let us suppose, for the sake of argument, that religion is in some manner true and that it is also of great importance for human life, even if only as a vehicle for the religio-aesthetic expression of people's deepest thoughts, emotions and aspirations. To be sure, we also need to acknowledge immediately that religion has its potentially bad sides. But this holds for most other things in life as well. Take food, for example. Despite the fact that nowadays a great deal of attention is given to nutritional education and much emphasis is put on wholesome products and good eating habits, there is a growing danger, particularly in the Western world, of addiction not only to alcohol, tobacco, drugs and medicines but also to food. While millions upon millions in our world suffer chronic undernourishment and starvation, large and growing numbers of people in richer countries are struggling with problems of gross overweight and obesity. Yet no one, presumably, would argue that, because of the ills associated with it, eating and drinking should be outlawed.

Another example of something that is part and parcel of human existence and that can serve both good and evil is sexuality. Its capacity for enhancing human mental and physical enjoyment and health is well known and requires no further validation. But at the same time its potential for working iniquity is practically unlimited. The sexual drive can and often does lead to grave harm and unspeakable enormities: aggression, degradation, rape, child abuse, forced prostitution and slave trade. It cannot be doubted that human sexuality has its dark, sinister dimensions, which might well give rise to second thoughts about it. And there are, of course, certain religious orders that would like to see this source of carnal passion, jealousy and maleficence reduced to a few instances of coitus per human life for the sole purpose of procreation. This kind of self-control, it is said, would also contribute significantly to the solution of global overpopulation. For all that, however, nobody in their right mind would argue for the complete cessation of human sexual activity. As with food and sex, the real question with respect to religion is that regarding its use and abuse. Would it not be both feasible and beneficial to complement existing public-education programs on nutritional and sexual matters with information on the subject of wholesome religion, information based on open dialogue and critical reflection and disseminated through schools and the contemporary media, including the internet?

Religions are ambiguous. There can be little doubt about that. They periodically lend themselves to strife but clearly also serve people well; they regularly bring forth good fruit, including teachings regarding human well-being. They are suppliers of images of the good life, the notion that expresses the ideal, the prime idea, the *weltanschauliche* frame of reference used by people to reflect on the moral and practical possibilities of a qualitatively worthwhile, felicitous existence for all. In stark contrast to certain schools and groups that preach the postmodernist dogma that nothing is absolute and everything is totally relative, religions and world views afford visions of the ideal society and purvey firm concepts of probity and decency. They provide answers to the deepest human questions and offer salvific certitudes to people in the midst of the tragedies and unsettling, often terrifying confusions and uncertainties of life. Religions also frequently act as agents of amity and harmony. They tender the spiritual wherewithal for the de-escalation of sectarian tension; they offer moral and practical prospects for easing or resolving situations of contention and for promoting reconciliation, social cohesion and mutually beneficial communal life. They hold out hope, which, according to St. Augustine, "has two lovely daughters, anger and courage. Anger, so that what must not be, shall not be. Courage, so that what must be, shall be" (quoted in Rasmussen 1996: 179). When war ends and the houses lie in ruins and the victims on either side of the conflict are staggering around in a daze, religious organizations and groups are often among the first to bring aid and solace to the former combatants and traumatized civilian population in the form of shelter, food, concern, a sympathetic ear and moral support. They contribute to reconstruction endeavors and are involved in efforts to establish and maintain peace and to foster understanding for the other.

One of the reasons that religions are able to help antagonists achieve reconciliation—which is more a process than an immediate, sudden event—is that they teach people not to look at the world from their own narrow perspective alone but from that of the whole. Zen meditation teaches people to realize that their so-called self ultimately does not exist and that they are but parts of the grand whole to which everyone and everything else also belongs. That insight leads people who internalize it to assume a stance of all-embracing compassion and wisdom, beyond all conflict. The Abrahamic religions teach people that every human being is created equal before God, which implies justice, mercy and love for neighbor. Fukayama states, probably rightly, that it is the merit of religions that they break through the limits of sectarian morality into the realm of the universal.

And in his view, universal morality has come to be so generally accepted throughout the world that it can now be upheld and maintained by governments without the help of religion. It is true that there is wide recognition of a transcultural, comprehensively applicable morality embodied in, among other things, the charter of universal human rights, but the question remains whether the government of a country is the most suitable candidate for the task of looking beyond national interests and imparting universal moral principles to its citizenry. In contrast to governments, the great religions reach across national and political borders. All worldviews, faiths and ideologies that find their sole identification in terms of national or ethnic entities are subject to suspicion that they constitute nothing more than group morality. Resurgent neo-paganism calls for further study in this respect, for in the past it was closely tied to fiercely nationalistic notions such as *heilige Heimat, Blut und Boden*, sacred country, racial purity and hallowed soil.

Because of its universal scope, intent and purpose, religion might well be regarded as a necessary instrument for the achievement of reconciliation. In an account of his experiences as a white Afrikaner member of the South African Truth and Reconciliation Commission, P. Meiring reported that the jurists serving on the commission considered legal action to be the most important and effective means of redressing the injustice suffered by the victims of apartheid who came to testify before the commission. But because the Commission only heard victims who told about relatives who had disappeared or were murdered or who themselves were suffering from the indelible aftermath of torture or assault at the hands of the perpetrators of crimes against humanity under the apartheid regime, the idea of restitution in legal or monetary terms alone simply did not work. It became increasingly clear during the course of the hearings that it is not possible to expiate injustice, abuse and human rights violations with just money and judicial measures. Even if the government, on the recommendation of the Commission, were to grant the victims financial compensation, this would in no way annul or even temper their unutterable loss and pain. Compensation by itself is not capable of effecting reconciliation between communities that were or are at loggerheads and surely not between victims and their tormentors. What was needed to settle the score, to bridge the immense rift between those who suffered and those who inflicted that suffering in South Africa? It soon became apparent that the step toward reconciliation could not be taken without reference to transcendence, Meiring reported, and it was found necessary to look beyond the strictly juridical dimension and to enter into prayer together. By virtue of shared religious faith victims were sometimes able, if asked, to forgive the persecutors and murderers of their husbands and wives, siblings and children. And likewise, a genuine, heartfelt confession of guilt by a torturer or an agent of oppression —an intensely profound process—is very probably not possible absent religion. Religion provides what Zen calls "a bottomless ground" to those who feel the ground sinking away beneath their feet. It offers people security by giving them something to hold on to beyond ordinary reality.

According to John Hick, ideological and religious traditions play a unique role in showing people their place within the totality of things and events and, in this way, helping them to be reality-centered rather than ego-centered. Religious philosophies of life impart knowledge about the entirety of existence and creation. They teach people to recognize and understand the framework in which they live and move and have their being and to discern the purpose and aim of human life. They also transmit stories and rituals that furnish fundamental insight into human, animal and insentient existence here on earth. Religious movements often play a positive role in society. Their universal thrust, which implies that humankind is not the be-all and end-all of existence, makes it possible for them to break through the narrow limits of ethnicity and sectarianism. Faith sometimes inspires people to work tirelessly for reconciliation between individuals, groups and communities and to dedicate their entire lives to service on behalf of others. Believers have often devoted themselves to the well-being of their fellow human beings: Europe north of the Alps was developed largely by monks, who built bridges and roads, cared for the sick and pioneered education. Through the force of their ascetic orientation toward liberation and release of body and mind, *sadhus* (Hindu mendicant ascetics) in India relativize the whole of Indian social life; or put in another way, by virtue of their guiding beliefs and religious way of life, they hold a mirror up to the faces of those who seek their identity and security in the rigid system of hereditary social stratification sanctioned by custom and traditional Hindu belief in India.

Religions direct implicit or explicit criticism against existing social structures and customary life styles and in this way often provide people with a means of escape from situations in which they have gotten bogged down. Religion, thus, often bears good fruit and is probably even indispensable for the realization of peace, harmony and reconciliation in society. In any case, it can be demonstrated on the basis of the classical writings and sacred scriptures of most of the great religions that conflict and hostility do not belong to the heart of their traditions. This means that they have not only the capacity but also the urgent task to seek and foster reconciliation among themselves:

> reconciliation between Christians, Jews and Muslims in Israel and Palestine ... reconciliation between Christians and Muslims in Indonesia, Nigeria, Pakistan, Bosnia and Kosovo, reconciliation between Christians, Muslims and Hindus in India .... (Raiser 1999: 4)

Religions are called to help defuse the disagreements and heal the ruptures that destabilize the planet and diminish our common humanity. No matter how much people from varying cultural and religious backgrounds may differ in their convictions regarding the good life, it is incumbent upon them, for the sake of their own well-being and that of others, to learn to communicate and get along amicably with one another—certainly where they live together in a pluralistic context. As Habermas pointed out, interhuman dialogue is the most important means of forestalling the deterioration and reversal of human advancement.

To sum up, religions provide images of the good life, which by implication also point to what is wrong with life as it is often actually lived by people. These images can and do, of course, vary according to the norms and values of the religions involved. The extent to which religious and ideological views of life diverge or converge is a matter for ongoing investigation, but it is clear that they are ultimately determined by the answer given to the larger question: What is the purpose, the aim of humankind's existence on earth? Because of the images of the good life they project, religions have a great deal of influence on society. If these views of life are used to establish and emphasize ethnic identity, however, the differences between them will lend themselves easily to the generation of sectarianism and conflict. Conflicts between people and groups can be stirred up and aggravated, but they can also be resolved. The supposition underlying this symposium is that religions and worldviews play a significant role in this regard, sometimes as sources or catalysts of social discord, often as agents of human concord. But whether they trigger and fuel conflict or embrace and promote reconciliation, all religions provide images and models of 'the good life' and promulgate teachings concerning what is detrimental to that life.

Bibliography

Johnson, Elizabeth A. (1993). *She Who Is: The Mystery of God in Feminist Theological Discourse*. New York: Crossroad.
Raiser, Konrad. (1999). "General Secretary's Christmas Message." *WCC News* (December).
Neill, Stephen. (1971). "Religion." In: S. Neill *et al.* (eds.). *Concise Dictionary of the Christian World Mission*. London: Butterworth Press.
Rasmussen, Larry L. (1996). *Earth Community, Earth Ethics*. Maryknoll/Geneva: Orbis Books/WCC Publications.
Sundermeier, Theo. "Religion. " (1991). In: N. Lossky *et al. Dictionary of the Ecumenical Movement*. Geneva/Grand Rapids: WCC Publications/Eerdmans Publishing Company.
Van der Bent, Ans J. (1991). "Marxist-Christian Dialogue." In: N. Lossky *et al.* (eds.). *Dictionary of the Ecumenical Movement*. Geneva/Grand Rapids: WCC Publications/ Eerdmans Publishing Company.

Religious Reconciliation

A View from the Social Sciences

André Droogers

Introduction

This paper focusses on the question: under what social and cultural conditions can reconciliation within and between religions take place? An answer to this question is sought in the social sciences. The cumulated theoretical perspectives from the social sciences can be of help om achieving understanding of social conditions. In a more specific vein, the cultural dimension can be illuminated by the reflections and insights belonging to the heritage of cultural heritage. In these disciplines fundamental questions have been raised that are relevant to the study of religion and more specifically to the understanding of the theme of this conference, reconciliation, questions as to how society is organized and functions, how social order can possibly exist and what difference culture as well as religion makes in such matters.

In the course of time, a variety of answers to these questions have been given by the social sciences that may be relevant in the attempt to provide an answer to this chapter's leading question. This diversity corresponds with the history of the disciplines involved and the paradigm shifts that have taken place within them. Confronted with such a broad spectrum and the limited space available, only a very selective summary of pertinent insights from social sciences can be given. Thus, it will be possible only to draw attention heuristically to factors and actors that may play a role in processes of reconciliation, rather than to reach final conclusions. Though this might seem an overly general and cautious approach for a rather concrete and specific question in the study of religion and religions, the suggestion is that a study of reconciliation in religion will profit from even a superficial exploration of the social and cultural context. The importance of such an exercise should not be exaggerated, though. Social scientists have for example been notoriously blind to the spiritual qualities of religion. Besides, society is not something that can be fully made and social scientists are not social engineers.

One pitfall should be mentioned. Reconciliation seems to be basically positive, and conflict has a negative connotation. Yet, just as a conflict can be necessary and healthy, reconciliation may camouflage a socially and morally harmful situation.

First, an indication will be given of the types of questions raised and answers provided witin the social sciences regarding reconciliation, with an emphasis on recent debates. Five crucial dichotomies will be discussed. Subsequently, the implications of these dichotomies for the study of religious reconciliation will be considered.

Reconciliation and the Social Sciences

Reconciliation is not a standard topic in the social sciences. If addressed at all, the theme is couched in other terms. Even then, as a social scientist, one's view of reconciliation depends very much on the paradigm one uses and the presuppositions one embraces.

An obvious way to illustrate this from the history of the construction of theory in social science is to compare the once competing schools of functionalism and (neo-)Marxism that dominated social-science thinking until the 1970s (for overviews see, e.g., Barnard, Harris, Kuper, J.D. Moore). The functionalist presupposition is that order is normal and self-restoring in society, whereas Marxism presents conflict as prevailing, just and necessary. Whereas functionalists had a cyclical view of society as always returning to equilibrium after periods of anomie, Marxists took a linear position, viewing society as the arena in which opposite forces were to engage in a long struggle which would last until proletariat gained ultimate victory.

This means that functionalists would view reconciliation as the ultimate result of social dynamics, once equilibrium and social order had been restored in a predictable and almost natural way. It was supposed to be in the nature of society that, all said and done, competing groups would become reconciled in order to maintain their society and assure its survival despite their differences, more or less as the Cretans of Plutarch's days used to forget their conflicts when confronted with a common enemy (and thus lend their name to the concept of syncretism, see Rudolph 1979). Of course, ideas that legitimate such a united front would accordingly be developed, including those of a religious nature. To the participants it would usually not be clear that these ideas, besides being inspiring, plausible and satisfactory, also serve social functions. In contrast, Marxists would condemn reconciliation as treason to the common cause, as an expression of false consciousness and as an ill-fated attempt to frustrate the inevitable course of history. The social functions of the legitimating ideas needed to be uncovered and made explicit for purposes of unmasking the interests of those in power.

From this comparison it follows that the term reconciliation could easily suffer from hyper-functionalist connotations, which might explain its relative absence from the current social-science parlance. It would be too readily associated with the functionalist discourse, and the question remains whether reconciliation is normal or exceptional.

Though the two schools just discussed can no longer be said to dominate the construction of theory within the social sciences, the insights they stand for cannot be said to have disappeared, and their echoes can still be heard, also in current debates. They represent tenacious patterns of scholarly thought. The comparison between the two, therefore, has more than historical value. For a start, it serves to uncover at least three of the basic dichotomies that have been central to theoretical debates in the social sciences. As we will see later on, at least two others can be added to these three. These dichotomies do not just represent poles in opposition but include a spectrum of relative transitions between the poles. Between reconciliation and conflict various other modes appear. A review of these dichotomies will be helpful in understanding the framework of a view of reconciliation within social sciences, even though such a dualistic way of thinking in dichotomies appears to celebrate contradiction and thereby to represent an absence of reconciliatory thinking in the social sciences themselves. Yet, when understood in a more eclectic way, the extremes cover the alternatives that keep occurring in the relatively incoherent social and cultural reality.

The first set of dichotomues includes those between harmony and conflict, order and anomie, continuity and rupture. People usually view the first pole of these dichotomies as the norm and the second as the deviation. Yet conflict, anomie and deviation are all too common. Changing circumstances, ever innovating self-conscious actors and opposed interests nourish conflict. Reconciliation would appear as promoting harmony, order and continuity, and as a factor against conflict, anomie and rupture.

A second dichotomy that is characteristic of the comparison between functionalism and Marxism is that between cyclical and linear views. The former suggest the universal and predictable repetition of social cycles in a history that repeats itself, disregarding local and temporal circumstances and differences. The latter conveys the notion of idiosyncratic historical change, allowing for uniqueness and ever-changing conditions, a history that is marked by trends and developments. Consequently, in the former reconciliation is an integral and recurring phase of social cycles through time, as in functionalism. In the latter it is almost an impossibility, at most a temporary exception to the usual diversity, strife and struggle, perhaps the once-and-for-all end result of a long-term process, as in Marxism.

A third and related set of dichotomies that has made itself felt in social-science thinking, also outside the functionalist and Marxist schools, distinguishes structure from process, the static from the dynamic. When structure is emphasized, as in structuralism and structural-functionalism, a great deal of attention is paid to the logic of the system and the social scientists focus on the supra-individual dimension. However, when the emphasis is on process, as is characteristic of the so-called praxis approaches (e.g. Bourdieu, Giddens, Ortner), the focus is rather on the questions of what people do with structures, how they are influenced by them, and also how they produce and change them. The concept of power is used in both the structure and the process approaches: in a structure approach to show the power that emanates from the system and in the process approach to show how, on the one hand, people dominate others by manipulating power and, on the other, how they resist domination by using countervailing power. Feminist theory has used both perspectives: making explicit the anchoring of male dominance in social structures and at the same time designing emancipation processes to change power balances.

Within this third set of dichotomies reconciliation could be either a structural given or a provisional result in an otherwise dynamic, vulnerable and ongoing process. In studying reconciliation, it is important to pay attention to the power dimension, since reconciliation can be the result of the wielding of power, either through the structures themselves or through the efforts to erode and replace them. Power, characterized since Weber as the capacity of individuals to influence other people's behavior, despite their resistance (Lemmen, 133; Lukes, 2, 29), is a tool that is neutral in itself and independent of the goal at stake. It can both serve and frustrate efforts towards reconciliation. One reason for which a process may be dynamic is the change of power balances, power never being a unilateral monopoly (Elias, 81). A particular form of power is that of the authorities in a society or a state, especially because they have succeeded in obtaining an exclusive right to the use of violence as a resource to impose their will on other people—even though in practice this right is rarely fully respected by all citizens. Reconciliation can thus be enforced as well as contested by the use of violence, either by the state or its opponents.

There are two other dichotomies that can be added to the above three. The first is that between the individual and the social sphere. Despite their differences, functionalists and Marxists share an emphasis on the autonomous social sphere with its own dynamics and logic over against the influence and power of individual actors. Other approaches in the social sciences, however, have focussed on the individual's role in society and on the dialectics between actor and society. Both are considered to be the product of the other. Individuals play roles in interaction with others, either in maintaining order or in creating conflicts. Therefore a fourth set of dichotomies can be added, namely that between society and individual, group and person, social structure and actor. Accordingly, when studying reconciliation, the role of individuals in stimulating or inhibiting reconciliation in the context of a group or society must receive attention. Are certain individuals vested with the authority to decide for the whole group? What liberty do other individuals have in taking initiatives that deviate from the norm? How much social support do these persons receive? Do they succeed in changing the power relations? What role do the state authorities play in this process?

A second dichotomy that needs to be added is that between society and culture (Barnard, 10-12). This is a rather important dichotomy in cultural anthropology, and it will therefore be discussed in somewhat more detail. It is often a translation of the matter-mind schema that is central to Western thinking (Alexander). Moreover, this dichotomy reflects a disciplinary division of labor between sociologists and anthropologists. Again, both functionalists and Marxists, *bien étonnés de se trouver ensemble*, put much emphasis on the characteristics of society and usually neglect the role of cultural factors. Yet both cultural difference and analogy can play a role in social processes. A great deal can and has been said on the primacy of either society or culture: the social structure as something that characterizes the human being as an animal; culture as that which makes the individual a unique and exceptional animal. The cultural surplus in the human makeup has been labeled in different ways: e.g., the capacity to produce symbols or more generally to produce, pattern and change meanings. Religion is viewed as one of the most striking products of this capacity. A common distinction, with different forms of inclusion and exclusion, is that between culture (singular) as a universal human characteristic (that which is common to human beings, e.g., meaning-making, and distinguishes them from other animals) and culture (plural) as the concrete system of customs, knowledge and meanings that is typical of a particular society or group. In this latter description culture is that which distinguishes groups of human beings from one another or that which the members of a group have in common. Obviously, despite the differences, the one view on culture cannot exist without the other, and the culture of a group comes about through the universal human capacity for culture, just as the human gift for language manifests itself in concrete languages.

But just as one can learn other languages in order to facilitate communication, so one can learn to understand other cultures despite the differences that exist. What is more, from colonial times until the present era of globalization (Bauman, Featherstone, Friedman, Robertson, Tomlinson) contacts between people of different cultures have been increasing. These contacts may, on the one hand, cause a countermovement for the purpose of reinforcing cultural identity. On the other hand, they may facilitate exchange and mixing. In the latter case this does not mean the emergence of a world culture but rather the perforation of cultural boundaries and more than ever an appeal to the general human capacity for culture, simply because people have to maintain themselves in new multicultural contexts in which they were not socialized (Hannerz). They have to speak other cultural languages. The plurality of cultures in contact activates the human capacity for culture in the singular sense of the term. The term 'creolization' has been borrowed from linguistics to refer to this tendency of people to become of necessity increasingly fluent in more than one cultural language (Drummond 1980). With the opening up of cultural boundaries, the autonomy of cultures has been relativized, though much of what has been labeled globalization occurs at the local level—to such a degree that the term 'glocalization' has even been coined (Robertson, 173).

Whereas anthropologists were accustomed to emphasizing cultural relativism, i.e., thinking of differences *between* autonomous and bounded cultures, now differences *within* cultures were also included in this way of looking at cultures (H.L. Moore, 8). At the same time the dynamics of cultural contact imposed themselves as a theme. This brought the internal heterogeneity of cultures, in cluding contradictions, into view. This is currently more visible under the impact of culture contact but was probably present already in the past (Keesing 1994).

This tendency fits well into postmodern discourse, because there too relativization occurs, with the emphasis on the relativity of observation, perception and reporting, as well as of truth in general (Cilliers, Clifford and Marcus, Nencel and Pels, Rosenau, Sarup). Another reinforcement of this trend has come from the growing study of plural and multicultural societies (Eriksen, Jenkins 1997, Turner). For a few anthropologists, these developments have been sufficient to propose abandoning the term 'culture' altogether, because the reality to which the term is supposed to refer—a bounded and autonomous unit—is thought to have become scarce (Brightman, Keesing). Others defend the term as central to the discipline called cultural anthropology. They point to culture, in the singular, as a universal human capacity, at work in a globalizing world.

In any event, culture has comes more and more to be seen as a set of repertoires, with corresponding dispositions and competencies, that are latently available and are activated by individual actors, according to the demands of the situation in which they find themselves. These repertoires may reflect different cultural sources (culture in the old sense of a more or less autonomous whole) and can therefore be multicultural in composition. Since their use is linked to specific contexts, each with its own rules and demands, they need not be consistent and the corresponding forms of behavior are not necessarily coherent. This characteristic is reinforced by the circumstance that these repertoires are not necessarily conscious, especially in routine matters. In this approach the individual level receives more attention, as diversity is most visible there. This has led to an increasing interest in the concept of identity, including references to ethnicity, gender and class, as an expression of a person's positioning and his or her experiencing of culture and cultures and their repertoires (Cohen 2000, Hall and Du Gay 1996, Jenkins 1997, Meyer and Geschiere, Woodward). To the essentialist view of identity as a property that can be lost a more dynamic dimension has been added, emphasizing identification as an ongoing process of identity construction.

The recent debate on culture has implications for the study of reconciliation. Reconciliation has both social and cultural dimensions. It may refer in a social sense to the coming together of formerly opposed groups or persons, but it may also refer in a cultural sense to the coexistence or synthesis of ideas or practices that were previously used as hallmarks of contrasting positions. Where creolization and globalization lead to increasing intercultural contacts, one may find, on the one hand, a reaction of fleeing from uncertainty and confusion and returning to the safety of the former closed and autonomous cultural tradition. This return may be a reinvention of tradition (Hobsbawm and Ranger) for the sake of an explicit identity. Groups will claim the right to maintain their idiosyncratic identity within an otherwise multicultural context. This ideology has been labeled multiculturalism (Turner). But there can also, on the other hand, be a movement towards cultural mixing and some degree of integration and innovation. Where cultural identity is emphasized conflicts may arise and a need for reconciliation. The mere fact that people become conscious of their identity may be sufficient to trigger a movement focussed on identity, even though other people with the same way of life do not opt for such an outspoken position.

However, when people are open to creolization or are forced by economic or political conditions to adopt an open attitude, different cultures, including their differences, are given public space and even contradictions can be easily accepted. The capacity of people to operate in more than one cultural setting, nourished by a new relativism both internally and externally, diminishes in a striking way the chance for conflicts to emerge. In their personal identity people succeed in living with opposing cultural tendencies, even to the point that these differences are no longer perceived as such. This is sometimes facilitated by the circumstance that contradictions may remain unconscious and implicit. People may then feel they share a common interest as long as explicit conscious questions about details are not raised (Cohen 1985). Whatever the situation, when dealing with conflict and reconciliation people use their cultural repertoires to attach meanings to persons, ideas, rituals, objects etc.

The five dichotomies that were discussed above have deeply influenced the construction of paradigms in the social sciences, including cultural anthropology. Though the abundant number of options offered by the dichotomies seem to confuse more than that they help, the paradigms, when taken together, set the framework for the understanding of social reality and thus of reconciliation. In view of the diversity in the debate, not only the topic but also the approach chosen may contain elements of reconciliation. Though the proponents of the different paradigms often claim to have the final answers, the paradigms' value is much more heuristic. The paradigms draw attention to possibilities that must be verified in concrete cases. Together they can be translated into a checklist of questions that can be raised. Though not discussed in a systematic way, the issues raised so far will guide the quest for an answer to this paper's central question. In the case of reconciliation this list could include the following items:

> To what degree does reconciliation reflect an inherent tension between conflict and harmony?
> What are the structural and the processional dimensions of reconciliation?
> How are cyclical and linear tendencies related with respect to reconciliation?
> How specific and local or how universal and global are the processes that produce reconciliation?
> How lasting or how provisional is reconciliation?
> How do structures and actors interact in the praxis of reconciliation?
> What power processes are characteristic of reconciliation praxis?

What are the dynamics and inner logic of the cultural context and how do they influence reconciliation?
What is the role of creolization and globalization in reconciliation?
What repertoires are relevant to reconciliation and how are these related to tradition?
Do implicit elements become explicit and *vice versa* and how does this influence conflict and reconciliation?
How do actors construct their identities and to what degree does reconciliation occur in and through this process?

Reconciliation and Religions

The framework described in the preceding section and the checklist of questions to which it gave rise, though not necessarily applied as systematically as just presented, can serve when we now focus on reconciliation in the field of religion. Before this is done, a few precautionary observations must be made. When studying religion from the point of view of the social sciences, it may complicate the practice of research that not only the scholar but the believer as well develops a view on society. The religious view may not correspond to that of the social scientist. In contrast to the scholar' position, the believer's usually has a spiritual and a moral dimension. A religion's followers present and promote a blueprint for authentic religious experience and the ideal society. Social scientists may, on the other hand, discover inevitable and striking differences between ideal and practice. An example is the difference in views on hierarchy and power. A confessed equality of all believers may mask social differences. With regard to the topic of this paper (reconciliation), similar contrasts between professed intentions and actual behavior may occur. Though some of the paradigms that have been used in the social sciences draw attention to the ultimate and decisive domination of order and harmony, thus coinciding with religious beliefs on full reconciliation, other approaches will point to actors and factors that frustrate efforts towards reconciliation or will even defend its impossibility.

Keeping these remarks in mind, the general views developed in the previous section can now be applied to the case of reconciliation in religion. The basic dualities in the five dichotomies discussed above, coupled with the questions in the checklist, will orient our discussion. The heuristic approach adopted above will be applied here as well. The following inventory of aspects and dimensions that may occur is meant to be used and tested in concrete cases, as, for example, described in the other case studies prepared for this book.

Reconciliation in religious matters presupposes opposition between groups or individuals representing differing beliefs, narratives, rituals, ideals, ethics and social practices. Reconciliation puts an end to strife and adversity. The degree to which a reconciliation is reached may vary from a full merger of parties, convictions and practices via peaceful coexistence to an armed peace, a cold war, with the continuous possibility of returning to the situation of conflict. The conflict may be presented as a religious one, but social, cultural, economic and political dimensions will most likely not be absent and may even form the real basis of the conflict. Religion will be used here to legitimize or even hide non-religious goals and interests. Yet religious convictions will play a role, whether that of legitimizing reconciliation as a value or that of justifying conflict as a religious demand or even as a holy war. Linear views of the history of the world, moving towards an eschatology, could work in favor of both reconciliation and conflict.

In social-science approaches that emphasize the structured nature of society, reconciliation—whether between religions or within one particular religion—will most likely be explained from the needs of the social system, either those of society as a whole or those of the religious group in particular. In order to maintain the system and safeguard society in case of an external or internal threat, internal religious factions will overcome their differences and competition, seek reconciliation and will unite against the common enemy. Religious justification of non-religious interests, including those of the social system, could reinforce such a process. Power is viewed as vested primarily in social structures and the established religious and secular authorities that represent them. These persons may wield their power to promote religious reconciliation, but they may also decide to use their power to prevent any reconciliation.

Process approaches on the other hand, of which the praxis approaches are an example, view religious reconciliation first of all as an interplay between actors, structures (both social and symbolic) and events. The term 'repertoires' may be used instead of structures, in which case the structural context is translated into available patterns for behavior and thinking. Other concepts that are used in praxis approaches are habitus (Bourdieu), model (D'Andrade and Strauss), schema (Strauss and Quinn) and figured world (Holland et al.), more or less with related meanings, referring to contextualized repertoires. Attention is paid in these approaches to the role of power and violence to differing extents. In the context of religious reconciliation, the question then is: What sets of meanings do actors use when they try to make sense of events that together form the process? How they submit themselves to these events? But also: How do they provoke them, with or without the exercise of violence? As far as the use of repertoires is concerned, the question is: Which persons, i.e., which secular or religious leaders, have the power to determine which sets of meanings and actions are to be dominant and to what degree are other people free to follow alternative patterns? These models of and for reflection and behavior, whether dominant or recessive, represent values that may either serve reconciliation or impede it. The collective experience of a group or society serves as to remind one of what may happen, how events may develop and what scenarios are possible. Where reconciliation does not occur, new conflicts may arise. But there is in fact, as we already saw, a whole spectrum of possibilities, including peaceful coexistence, an attitude of live and let live or a latent ambiance of tension. The idea of repertoires, as well as that of creolization, points to the circumstance that people are not necessarily consistent in their positions. With regard to religions this practice differs from the ideal of systematic reflection on beliefs and convictions articulated by the leaders of a religion or as, e.g., summarized in scholarly textbooks on the world's religions, sometimes literally focussing on (sacred) texts.

As far as reconciliation is concerned, this room for variation suggests that official and popular views may differ and that this may work both in favor and against reconciliation. The efforts of the leaders may be frustrated by silent or open resistance from believers, just as believers may see their preferences frustrated by their religious or secular leaders. It has been suggested in the same vein that people who seemingly conform to some cultural ideal may very well possess a mood of resistance and opposition (Scott).

In more than one case such differences of opinion have led to the rise of new religious movements that may in time have become established religions in themselves, including some of the world religions. Failed reconciliation may stimulate religious life because it nourishes countermovements. It is important to note the role of individuals and the way they wield power resources, either as leaders of such movements or as repressing authorities. These resources include personal charisma as well as exclusive experiences with the sacred, such as visions and trance. Moreover, the events that form the history of such an episode may be shown to have their own consequential domino-like dramatic logic, seemingly without the expressive intervention of the actors involved. The dialectics of society and actors suggest that actors are not always able to direct events and circumstances—the theme of many successful novels in world literature.

Though contact between cultures, including the religion with which each may be identified, is as old as humanity, the increasing number of contacts in recent centuries and decades has greatly added to people's religious repertoires, making ideas, rituals and practices available to them that were previously inconceivable. This must have led to situations in which reconciliation became an issue. The attention recently given to syncretism is an expression of this trend, since syncretism is one way of reconciling ideas and rituals from different religious sources. At the same time the social structures have been subject to erosion, with the consequence that social control and the exercise of power do not function as was the case traditionally. Absolute truths lose their plausibility and come to be understood as relative. The mass media open possibilities of influencing believers that escape their leaders' control—unless of course these selfsame leaders seek to control mass media as a strategic means to reinforce their dominance over their believers. Simultaneously, because social control has diminished and the traditions are losing impact, individuals are challenged to maintain their identities. They will have to position themselves in the religious market, which means that they have the option to reconcile seemingly diverse views or to stick to good old-time tradition, perhaps not in its original form but at least as they think it was. This may be accompanied by some form of isolation or even an hostile attitude towards outsiders, as occurs in forms of fundamentalism, diminishing the chances of reconciliation.

In considering the role of repertoires it is important to be conscious of the fact that they may contain explicit ideas about conflict and reconciliation. These ideas may be related to the maintenance of the religion's identity, defending the uniqueness of that religion. They may also represent a religious view that argues in favor of an open attitude towards people of other faiths, even though this does not lead to a self-effacing attitude. In any case, there may be some form of a logic at work that justifies the attitude taken. Religious lay movements such as Hassidism, Arya Samaj or the Muslim Brotherhood may arise precisely because of an explicit popular self-defense against what is experienced as a threat to what is considered to be most sacred—especially if the established clergy do not seem to take the defense of this identity seriously. In shifting their loyalty, people position themselves within the context of transformations that they see occurring. In doing so they may appeal to ideas and values that are part of collective memory but have not been emphasized by the leadership. The new movement addresses the issues by making use of a neglected sector of the religious repertoire. This sector may contain ideas about reconciliation, but it may also contain ideas about the defense of identity. Obviously, this defense of identity may involve non-religious factors such as ethnic, linguistic, economic or political aspects—also because the events that provoke religious reactions most probably reflect these aspects. Religion may serve, as was observed above, both as a model of and as a model for the social context.

Conclusion

In this paper we argued that the social sciences offer a framework for the understanding of the social and cultural conditions under which reconciliation between and within religions may take place. It was suggested that a number of basic dichotomies that have marked theoretical thinking in the social sciences, though not developed for the study of religion (let alone that of religious reconciliation) could serve to map those conditions. These dichotomies refer to harmony and conflict, cyclical and linear models, structure and process, individual and society, society and culture. They should be used as heuristic devices to be tested and complemented in concrete case studies.

Bibliography

Alexander, Jeffrey C. (1990). "Analytic Debates: Understanding the Relative Autonomy of Culture." In: Jeffrey C. Alexander and Steven Seidman (eds.). *Culture and Society: Contemporary Debates*. Cambridge: Cambridge University Press. Pp. 1-27.
Barnard, Alan. (2000). *History and Theory in Anthropology*. Cambridge: Cambridge University Press.

Bauman, Zygmunt. (1998). *Globalization: The Human Consequences.* Cambridge: Polity Press.
Bourdieu, Pierre. (1977). *Outline of a Theory of Practice.* Cambridge: Cambridge University Press.
Brightman, Robert. (1995). "Forget Culture: Replacement, Transcendence, Relexification." *Cultural Anthropology* 10: 509-46.
Cilliers, Paul. (1998). *Complexity and Postmodernism: Understanding Complex Systems.* London and New York: Routledge.
Clifford, James, and George E. Marcus (eds.). (1986). *Writing Culture: The Poetics and Politics of Ethnography.* Berkeley: University of California Press.
Cohen, Anthony P. (1985). *The Symbolic Construction of Community.* London: Tavistock.
———. (ed.). (2000). *Signifying Identities: Anthropological Perspectives on Boundaries and Contested Values.* London and New York: Routledge.
D'Andrade, Roy, and Claudia Strauss (eds). (1992). *Human Motives and Cultural Models.* Cambridge: Cambridge University Press.
Drummond, Lee. (1980). "The Cultural Continuum: A Theory of Intersystems." *Man* 15: 352-74.
Elias, Norbert. (1976). *Wat is sociologie.* Utrecht/Antwerp: Het Spectrum.
Eriksen, Thomas Hylland. (1993). *Ethnicity and Nationalism: Anthropological Perspectives.* London and East Haven Ct: Plutro Press.
Featherstone, Mike (ed.). (1994). *Global Culture: Nationalism, Globalization and Modernity.* London: SAGE.
Friedman, Jonathan. (1994). *Cultural Identity and Global Porcess.* London: SAGE.
Giddens, Anthony. (1984). *The Constitution of Society: Outline of the Theory of Structuration.* Cambridge: Polity Press.
Hall, Stuart, and Paul du Gay (eds.). (1996). *Questions of Cultural Identity.* London: SAGE.
Hannerz, Ulf. (1992). *Cultural Complexity: Studies in the Social Organization of Meaning.* New York: Columbia University Press.
Harris, Marvin. (1969). *The Rise of Anthropological Theory: A History of Theories of Culture.* London: Routledge & Kegan Paul.
Hobsbawm, Eric, and Terence Ranger (eds.). (1983). *The Invention of Tradition.* Cambridge: Cambridge University Press.
Holland, Dorothy *et al.* (1998). *Identity and Agency in Cultural Worlds.* Cambridge, MA/London: Harvard University Press.
Jenkins, Richard. (1996). *Social Identity.* London and New York: Routledge.
———. (1997). *Rethinking Ethnicity: Arguments and Explorations.* London: SAGE.
Keesing, Roger H. (1994). "Theories of Culture Revisited." In: Robert Borofsky (ed.). *Assessing Cultural Anthropology.* New York: McGraw-Hill. Pp. 301-12.
Kuper, Adam. (1983). *Anthropology and Anthropologists: The Modern British School.* London: Routledge & Kegan Paul.
Lemmen, M.M.W. (1990). *Max Weber's Sociology of Religion: Its Method and Content in the Light of the Concept of Rationality.* Hilversum: Gooi en Sticht.
Lukes, Steven (ed.). (1986). *Power.* Oxford: Blackwell.
Meyer, Birgit, and Peter Geschiere (eds.). (1999). *Globalization and Identity: Dialectics of Flow and Closure.* Oxford: Blackwell.
Moore, Henrietta L. (ed.). (1999). *Anthropological Theory Today.* Cambridge: Polity.

Moore, Jerry D. (1997). *Visions of Culture: An Introduction to Anthropological Theories and Theorists*. Walnut Creek: AltaMira.
Nencel, Lorraine, and Peter Pels. (eds.). (1991). *Constructing Knowledge: Authority and Critique in Social Science*. London: SAGE.
Ortner, Sherry B. (1984). "Theory in Anthropology Since the Sixties." *Comparative Studies in Society and History* 26: 126-66.
Robertson, Roland. (1992). *Globalization: Social Theory and Global Culture*. London: SAGE.
Rosenau, Pauline Marie. (1992). *Post-Modernism and the Social Sciences: Insights, Inroads, and Intrusions*. Princeton: Princeton University Press.
Rudolph, Kurt. (1979). "Synkretismus vom Theologischen Scheltwort zum religionswissenschaftlichen Begriff." In: *Humanitas Religiosa: Festschrift für Haralds Biezais zu seinem 70. Geburtstag*. Stockholm: Almqvist & Wiksell. Pp. 193-212.
Sarup, Madan. (1988). *An Introductory Guide to Post-structuralism and Postmodernism*. New York: Harvester Wheatsheaf.
Scott, James. (1985). *Weapons of the Weak*. New Haven: Yale University Press.
Strauss, Claudia, and Naomi Quinn. (1994). "A Cognitive/Cultural Anthropology." In: Robert Borofsky (ed.). *Assessing Cultural Anthropology*. New York: McGraw-Hill. Pp. 284-300.
———. (1997). *A Cognitive Theory of Cultural Meaning*. Cambridge: Cambridge University Press.
Tomlinson, John. (1999). *Globalization and Culture*. Cambridge: Polity.
Turner, Terence. (1993). "Anthropology and Multiculturalism: What is Anthropology That Multiculturalists Should Be Mindful of It?" *Cultural Anthropology* 8: 411-29.
Woodward, Kathy (ed.). (2000). *Questioning Identity: Gender, Class, Nation*. London/New York: Routledge, in association with The Open University.

The Nature and Origins of Religious Conflicts

Some Philosophical Considerations

Henkdrik M. Vroom

Introduction
Why is it that so many religious traditions are involved in conflicts? In this paper we will first comment on the seriousness of this question and then deal with the usual answer (from the religious side) that the use of religion is a misuse that rests on a misunderstanding of religion. The question is whether religion itself includes elements that lead to conflicts. In the second section we will analyze this in relation to Christianity by inquiring into the reasons for its frequent intolerance and involvement in conflicts. The root of the problem lies in the identity of religious traditions itself, which we deal with in the third section. In the fourth we will look at the idea that conflict should always be avoided and give reasons why religion has such a strong influence on humans that it is, indeed, inclined to be misused.

It has often been said that truth claims and especially ideas as to the exclusivity of a religion are sources of conflict. The opposing idea is that all conflict is caused by the misuse of religion. Both ideas are one-sided. Let me start with religion as a source of conflict. In a volume on hate and religion Hijme Stoffels, an expert on right-wing Protestantism, argues that claims to unique and exclusive truth lead to intolerance, hatred and thus to conflict. The idea of exclusivity stimulates antithetical behavior between groups of people and this in turn leads to rejection, exclusion and conflict. It is not plausible, indeed, that an antithetical attitude between people will contribute to reconciliation between different groups. Exclusive beliefs stimulate the formation of groups which identify themselves over against other denominations. Therefore, right-wing orthodoxy can easily become a source of conflict. "Without hate no orthodoxy," Stoffels says (1994: 63). On the other hand, we should not forget that the societal context determines whether or not the development of religious groups is accompanied by hatred and threats. It makes a difference as to whether a group is a small minority, a majority and whether or not it has strong relationships with the ruling elite.[1]

Orthodoxy bases its absolute claims upon divine authority, be it a holy scripture or a immediate divine revelation, and its leaders often see themselves as

---

[1] See the *dhimmi* status of Jews and Christians in the Arab world (Khoury 1982: 82ff.) and the Amish as another example of a peaceful traditional religious minority.

capable of judging other people without feeling any need to justify this view. Other Christian ideas are contested as false and other religions as pseudo-religions (cf. Kuyper 1904: III, 445ff.). Because one lives in a sinful and blind world, the need is felt to resist the temptations of the evil one, isolate themself and exclude those members who fall into sin and heresy (cf. Stoffels 1994: 63). Such movements and especially such leadership is apt to become involved in conflict. Stoffels mentions seven strategies which orthodox groups can use when they encounter other groups, varying from the mobilization of the membership and attack, via a kind of propaganda war, to softer forms like negotiation and dialogue. Being powerful can help one win, whereas the price for peace and harmony can be a loss of identity (Stoffels 1994: 64).

It is debatable whether the claim to uniqueness necessarily ends up in conflict, but as one of main arguments of the critiques of religion, it should be taken seriously. A usual line of defence is that such conflicts do not emerge from religions but from its misuse or misunderstanding. Christian faith furthers love, mercy and justice and therefore does not lead to conflict. On the contrary, Christianity helps to bring people together and to become reconciled. Does Buddhism not help people detach themselves from involvement with evil and to live in peace? For what reason, then, could religion be an incentive to conflicts between groups or nations? However, some Buddhist groups are involved in civil war and Hindu fundamentalists are at war with Muslims and Christians, even though Hinduism teaches that all religious paths lead to the divine on the invisible top of the mountain. People from various religious schools should tolerate and accept one another.[2] Some say that all children of Abraham are militant and a potential danger to other people. Although Muslims may claim that the small *jihad* is the struggle against unbelievers and the more difficult *jihad* the fight against one's own heart and that the Prophet has said that there should be no force in religion, there are too many reports on violence to leave it at that. References to Israel are also ambiguous. For decennia the state of Israel has not been able to end the conflict with the Palestinians peacefully, although one should realize that Israel's militant attitude cannot be understood without taking into account the centuries-old persecution of Jews in a 'Christian' Europe. Even if the religious ideals are often peaceful and beautiful, the dark reality prohibits one from blaming others for all religious violence. In order to try to find the root of intolerance we now proceed to the question of whether Christianity is inherently intolerant and open to conflict.

---

[2] See in this volume, e.g., the contributions by Swaris, Engineer, Van Bijlert and Van der Burg.

Is Christianity in Itself Intolerant?

In church history force has often been bound up with religion. Nobody less than Augustine himself explained Luke 14:23 ("compel people to come in") in a way that has had disastrous consequences (see Ricoeur 2000: 39). Eternal salvation cannot be reached without faith in Christ. And does not love for our neighbor require that we take pains to help our neighbor as best we can? Now the soul's eternal salvation is the best they can have, so we should not foster their possession of worldly goods if such hinders them from eternal salvation (so Thomas Aquinas). Eternal bliss has priority over temporal goods and the well-being of many over that of a single person. It follows that the church, on the basis of her responsibility for eternal salvation, should ban those heretics who endanger salvation and leave them to the worldly court so that they can be removed from this earth (Thomas Aquinas, *Summa Theologica* II-II.11.3). This religious insight gained flesh and blood in the Inquisition. One of the most hard-hitting metaphors stems from the inquisitor Salamances: "the heretic is a most infectious animal: therefore he must be punished before the virus of impiety breaks out and spreads outside."[3] The commandment to love clearly entails preventing one's neighbor from being infected with wrong ideas, even if this requires the impediment of his earthly well-being (Schmidt-Leukel 2000: 183). This rule follows from two premises: (1) eternal salvation has priority over temporal salvation and (2) the salvation of many takes precedence over that of a single person. Because both insights are beliefs, intolerance and persecution followed from the content of faith and are not a straightforward misuse of religion by other powers.

Two remarks may be added here. Such persecution is possible only if a religious community cooperates with government. In most cases such a bond between state and religion requires a majority position, because if a religious group forms a minority such persecutions will not be possible. We also need to distinguish between intolerance and persecution on the one hand and hate on the other. Hate does not follow from Christian ethics as the banning of heretics clearly did. Extinction from infectious persons does not necessarily require hatred—one has to love his enemy—although one can ask whether it makes much difference to the persecuted if they die under loving hands.

The sting of exclusivism does not lie primarily in right doctrine and its truth claims but in a specific doctrine: *extra ecclesiam nulla salus* (Denzinger and Hünermann 1965: no. 802). The kernel of the problem is the exclusive admission to salvation to those in the church and not primarily the truth claim, although both are closely related. It is important to see that in religion truth is nearly everywhere lived truth and not doctrine as such. Insight into truth requires that people follow the rules of a tradition. Therefore, every religious group needs

---

[3] In: Perry Schmidt-Leukel 2000: 184; Simancas, *De catholicis institutionibus liber*, Rome 1575, Tit. II, n.17.

some space to be able to live according to its beliefs and therefore every religious group needs to create its own atmosphere under penalty of loss of its identity. If religious groups do not have the possibility for finding their place in society, they can choose isolation and live outside the mainstream of a culture, as the Amish in the USA do or as the Rechabites did in the old Israel (Jeremiah 35).

From this it follows that the problem does not lie in the truth claims as such. Sometimes in Christianity true doctrine has been understood as a precondition for inheriting eternal life, but, because not everyone can learn all doctrines by head, nuances have been added so that the doors of heaven will not be closed to the simple and mentally handicapped persons. So, admittance to eternal happiness is not dependent upon explicit assent but on belonging to the community of saints, of which people become members through baptism. The exclusivity has been reallocated from true doctrine to the true church, the validity of baptism and the right administration of sacraments. Because people are included in the body of Christ through baptism, everyone could partake in salvation, including those who are not as intellectually gifted. So the questions of truth and salvation were dependent on membership in the church, as we find in the classical phrase *extra ecclesiam nulla salus*. The medieval church administered eternal salvation and mediated in the distribution of God's grace and salvation. The classical text to support this view is that Jesus told Peter that he would be given the keys of the Kingdom of heaven, which made Peter the leader of the earliest church and the predecessor of the popes: "I will give you the keys of the kingdom of heaven, and whatever you bind on earth will be bound in heaven, and whatever you loose on earth will be loosed in heaven" (Matthew 16:19). Thus, the church as a body was given a role to play in the administration of salvation. This idea has been worked out in the various circumstances in which the church existed. In Hellenism and in Roman culture the organization of the church became more strict. Heretics were persecuted with the aid of emperors. Doctrine was developed under the influence of Greek philosophy and, at the end of the sixteenth century, after the Reformation, a quite elaborate body of Catholic doctrine had come into being. People were required in principle to approve of this doctrine, under penalty of being excommunicated (*anathema sit*).

The conclusion is that the idea of the church as the mediator of salvation provided an incentive for intolerance within the church. The church preserves the truth, mediates grace and owns the keys of the Kingdom of heaven. Therefore, a church community necessarily makes judgments about true belief and right practice and for that very reason also about competing worldview traditions and their ideas.

The identity of a group—every religious group—brings with it the need to draw lines, whether they are drawn sharply or more loosely. Communities can therefore be more or less tolerant or antithetical. People can respect others, talk, listen and learn or refuse to give account of their own beliefs and to listen to others. The measure of tolerance and conflict can vary considerably. Lack of respect for others and refusal to encounter others and engage in cooperation and dialogue will lead to tension. Conflicts arise when religious groups try to fight other groups openly with words and forbid their members to associate with those who belong to other confessions. However, violent conflicts do not follow necessarily from the regular task of preserving their identity and the 'conflicts' which inevitably will arise from this, although there is no sharp line between disciplinary conflicts and behavior which leads to violence.

Christianity is not necessarily intolerant over against people with other opinions and practices. Jesus associated with tax collectors and prostitutes and mocked his own religious leaders who thought themselves able to demarcate clearly the line between those who were virtuous and those who were not. The distinction made by the Reformation between a theology of the cross and a theology of glory is relevant here. A *theologia gloriae* is the idea behind a triumphalistic church which thinks that it possesses the truth. A *theologia crucis*, however, is the idea behind a church which acknowledges that everything it does is a fallible human attempt and realizes that it does not possess the truth. Rather, the church only testifies to the truth and to him whom has been called a servant of people, whose mission it was to love God above all, his neighbors as himself and to reconcile God and humans and humans with one another.

On this basis it may be said that Christianity should not be involved in violent conflicts but always help to improve relations between people. However, this does not undo the fact that even among the most influential church fathers and popes there have been those who ordered people to be killed for their heresies or divergent ideas and/or practices. Even if many Christians today consider this to rest on a misunderstanding of Christianity, it is a fact that the tradition as such produces conflict. The reason of this is the distinction between what belongs to the tradition and what does not—a distinction present in every tradition.

Identity and Conflict

Internal intolerance in one form or another is a characteristic of every group that unites people for a certain end. External intolerance begins when a group tries to make other people accommodate themselves to its rules. External intolerance can result in religiously motivated conflicts such as the forced baptism of Jews and persecution of people with diverging opinions. Actually every group, religious or secular alike, will try to organize itself in such a way as to be able to realize its goals. Depending on the cultural context, this can have minor and major consequences. An example of a contextual adaptation are the Saturday services of a Nepalese church, because in Nepal it is the Saturday and not the Sunday which people have off and services should be held on a day of rest. Thus the church accommodates itself to its culture, while preserving its identity by forbidding its members to participate in Hindu rituals, thus avoiding the conflicts that arise from that practice. A more serious problem arises when a Christian community argues for establishing a theocracy or an Islamic state institutes *sharia* as its law or a state considers itself founded on Hinduism.

Because religious traditions are not theories about concrete objects in reality but pass on insights into reality, ways of life and moral rules which all together give form to life in community, they can influence people's lives deeply, although most of them will not determine all aspects of life. Therefore, religions are interwoven with cultures, just as secular worldviews influence lifestyles as well as architecture, as is clearly visible in the former Communist architecture.

Cultures and religions are dynamic and are always included in contextual processes of change. They do influence one another, as minorities take over customs of the majority or refuse to do so and choose isolation over adaptation. When the group's lifestyle and its differences with the contextual culture are stressed conflicts can easily arise. In circumstances in which the various groups are equally powerful or a group feels that it has been injured, such conflicts can easily lead to violence, as described in some of the case studies in this volume. Only religious traditions which do not organize groups could not take part in conflict.

This rather trivial conclusion brings the critics of religion to the well-known advice that religion should be abandoned. However, this rests on a neglect of the role of worldview traditions. If these traditions would cease to exist, conflicts would not disappear but evolve along other lines. Worldview traditions and especially religions teach people how to live and how to relate to other people. They preach the giving of alms, justice, honesty, solidarity and other virtues on which the quality of a society depends, although they do not stimulate exactly the same virtues. Traditions and culture determine privileges and responsibilities. Every culture needs such worldview traditions which explain who people are and how they should live. If religious traditions do not fulfill this need, secular traditions will.

Dependent upon circumstances, groups will or will not accentuate their own identity. Ethnic and religious minorities can choose to accommodate themselves to the prevalent culture or to isolate themselves and live on the margins of society. Both strategies are visible in the new immigrant communities in Western culture—fundamentalist groups who stress their own identity as well as people who find their own way in society. Religious traditions are what they are through their heritage, but they are also what they are through their positive or negative relations to culture. Although religious movements can play a role in the processes of reconciliation and peace in society, conflicts between them are inevitable.

Is Absence of Religious Conflict Peace?

The next question is whether all traditions are equally inclined to conflict. Is it not true that Buddhism is more peaceful than Islam and does not humanism grant people more personal freedom than Confucian culture? My first thesis is that all traditions engender conflicts, although they are not all of the same sort. My second thesis is that absence of conflict is more often a sign of injustice than of peace.

In relation to 'religion and conflict' it makes sense to distinguish between movements with ideals for society at large and groups who limit themselves to the personal life and community of their members. We can refer to them as society-directed and person-directed movements. The former will try to give form to their ideals in society and because their norms are universal in principle, they will be more quickly involved in conflict with other groups and government. Those traditions which plea for equality, justice for the poor and marginalized and solidarity with all belong to the first category. In other movements which give primary attention to personal development and salvation religion is much more a private affair without clear ideals for society at large. Therefore, the chance for religious conflicts and violence is not as great as in the former.

However, such a division of worldview traditions does not have much value in practical life, as we can see from the example of the wandering *sadhus* who beg for their food. They are part of Hindu society with its many temples and altars on every streetcorner. Also, since the abolishment of the caste system, religion supports the social stratification of society (just as Christianity has done for centuries in Europe). While the *sadhus* have an alternative lifestyle opposed to society, they do not oppose the injustice done to the *dalit*. The Eastern Orthodox Churches under Communist rule, which survived by retreat to their rituals, are another example of a religious community which has survived by concentrating on piety and worship. Every religious tradition has a great many subtraditions which in varying contexts develop different strategies, each with its weak and strong points. Movements which focus on personal development, such as sects and ashrams, can motivate people very deeply to live peaceful and righteous lives but can also isolate them from their family and friends and not allow them to fulfill their obligations to them. Stories of derailed gurus and preachers abound. In this case conflicts do not exist between groups in the population but within families and between individuals. Movements with a strong sense of social engagement can easily become involved in heavy conflict but often play a role in revealing unjust situations, reconciling social conflicts and changing the skewed division of wealth and the global use of energy. Examples of such movements are Ambedkar's Reform Buddhism with its social and political critiques and the northwestern European peace movement with its protest in the 1980s against weapons of mass destruction. The latter resulted in a great many conflicts: in society, churches and many families as well. However, it was exactly in this way that this protest contributed to the peaceful *Umwandlung* in Eastern Europe in 1989.

Different sorts of worldview traditions are involved in different kinds of conflict. In daily life people tend to think of violent conflicts between religious groups, as in the Moluccas between Muslims and Christians, in Sri Lanka between Hindus and Buddhists and in Northern Ireland between Protestants and Catholics—some of these conflicts are dealt with in this volume. However, the term conflict is also used for severe disagreements within a religious community, as in the Anglican Church on the issue of women priests or in India between *dalit* theologians and church leadership. We should not forget that all religious traditions are internally plural, and that this entails conflict. A religious conflict, then, is *a tense division between groups with a religious motivation which cannot be resolved through dialogue and democratic procedures alone.* Depending on one's worldview, one can claim that some conflicts are necessary and cannot be circumvented and hold that absence of conflict is based on acquiescence with oppression and injustice. A traditional patriarchal society may have known only a few incidental conflicts concerning the distribution of privileges and obligations, but who will currently applaud this absence of conflict? Although many Buddhist schools direct themselves toward peace and harmony, a lack of political engagement can support injustice and disharmony indirectly, as other Buddhist groups claim. On the other hand, the Buddhist protest against injustice and violation of human rights can be the cause of conflict, even though it is motivated by *karuna* and esteem for all living creatures. Improvements in society have been realized most frequently via deep conflicts.[4]

Within secularized Western culture it is quite common to criticize religion for its involvement in conflict. However, as stated previously, secularized liberal culture produces its own conflicts. Because liberal capitalism does not deal with the question of how to distribute wealth and energy more equally over the different continents and how to preserve natural balances, by consequence an enormous migration from poorer to richer countries is stimulated, with all the suffering that causes, and in the long run the liberal worldview will on its own be able to prevent ecological crises.

Religious traditions form the deposit of centuries of experience in different situations. Therefore they have a treasury of stories and paradigmatic situations that can be actualized in various circumstances. Sometimes the various lines of approach will seem contradictory, as e.g., two different sayings of Jesus. Jesus not only said: "Do not resist evildoers. But if anyone strikes you on the right cheek, turn the other also" (Matthew 5:39) but also: "Do not think that I have come to bring peace to the earth; I have not come to bring peace but a sword. For I have come to set a man against his father, and a daughter against her mother" (Matthew 11: 34f). Actually, those sayings refer to different situations. In the Jewish Bible as well we are exhorted to love our neighbor as ourselves (Leviticus 19:18) but a false way of speaking about peace is rejected, "They have treated the wound of my people carelessly, saying 'Peace, peace', when

---

[4] Examples: the abolishment of slavery, independence of former colonies, antiracism, emancipation, women as ministers. See Vroom 1999.

there is no peace" (Jeremiah 6:14), because injustice gives the lie to peace. The aim of the Bible is justice with mercy, neighborly love and equality and therefore there cannot simply be forgiveness and the avoidance of conflict but sometimes revolt, prophetic protest and conflict for a just peace are needed. Reconciliation without justice and mercy is a lie (cf. Gort 1992). Such a stress on justice can bring about conflicts. This Christian accentuation of justice and love has been criticized by the Buddhist Masao Abe, who argues for compassion and wisdom instead (Abe 1985: 184). The longing for freedom, equality and justice should indeed be guided by wisdom, and Western culture will have to show more respect for ecological relations in the world and can learn such respect from Eastern traditions. However, because Christianity will always distinguish between God's intentions with creation and the actual situation of the world, tension between the Christian faith and the status quo is inevitable. Such tension can take various forms: either resignation or open conflict.

It seems that we cannot escape all conflict, because some conflicts are justified and the avoidance of conflict often means acquiescence in oppression. Such 'peace' is all too easily compatible with the interests of those who eat the fruits of the status quo. Both secular and religious traditions are dynamic and plural and include subtraditions that accommodate themselves to the prevailing culture as well as subtraditions that oppose it. Both secular and religious traditions can be used to legitimize oppression and ethnicity as well as to criticize it. The form that will be given to a false legitimization of or protest against injustice depends on the beliefs of a religious tradition and its context.

I would like to end this section with some remarks on the reasons why religion can be so powerful, get people into its grip and become a factor in violent conflict. Every religious tradition places human beings in a wider field of relationships in the sense that their own private interests are not the measuring stick for making judgments about the value of things. The world is seen in a wider perspective, e.g., buddha nature, the coming Kingdom of God, or the fulfilment of *dharma* and *karma*. Every classical tradition warns that such goods cannot be acquired by egoistic motives. Therefore it rightly has been said that religion should make people reality-centered instead of ego-centered (Hick 1989: *passim*). This rotation of one's private life—mostly half-heartedly—makes one orient one's life to something greater than onself and derive the meaning of one's life at least partly from living with this goal in mind. Religious traditions teach people how to deal with the impressive experiences they have, such as the birth of a child, friendship in difficult times, amazement about the beauty of nature but also how to react to injustice, sadness, illness, failure and the loss of strength (see Vroom 1989: ch.9). Religious traditions are ways of life and as such they help people undergo these universal human experiences (although they may interpret them in completely different ways). For this reason worldviews are important and especially religious worldviews because they locate people in wider perspectives than secular world views do. If faith is directed to something finite with the suggestion that it is transcendent, religion is changed into its opposite. The most clear example of this is nationalism in which personal existence becomes subordinated to a nation.

Because religion leads to the formation of groups and touches heavily upon the personal lives of people, it is quite understandable that faith can easily play a part in the formation of ethnic groups and that those in power can use religion as a means of gaining power over others. All important things in life are misused in wars and conflict: music, sex, talk and also religion. As long as people eat, there will always be those who are hungry and those who are overweight; as long as people have different gifts, some will enrich themselves at the costs of others; as long as people sexual beings, sexual harassment will exist and as long as people have faith, religion will be misused. It is utterly naive to think that worldview traditions should be abolished because we can do without them.

Some Conclusions

In this contribution we have seen that the role of religion in conflict cannot be considered as misuse only, even if religion is frequently misused. One root of conflict is given with the existence of religious groups themselves. The main source of tension will not be a claim to unique truth but the way of salvation which entails a need to realize a particular way of life, even if this conflicts with other groups in society. When religious groups stress their identity, conflicts may arise, since their identities have to be established in dialogue and confrontation with people of other traditions or those who simply do not believe the teaching of any tradition. Although traditions will change during the processes of exchange and confrontation, the need to preserve their own identity implies that they will draw some lines between their tradition and the other ones. In a plural culture conflicts are inevitable. Conflicts may arise from views and ways of life and from the need to preserve the identity of and as a group. Therefore, theological, cultural and sociological factors will be intertwined in conflict.

This volume deals with case studies of conflicts and processes of reconciliation and the internal possibilities of religious groups to contribute to the establishment of peaceful relations. In this contribution I have discussed the question whether all disagreements or even all conflicts are wrong and defended the view that in a unjust and unsustainable world conflict must arise, either as a protest against how things are or as a consequence of irresponsible human behavior. Conflict can be made fruitful and produce something good if people can become reconciled as well and agree on what is just and wise. Conflicts cannot not be resolved by violence nor by acquiescence with unjust or inappropriate situations. Therefore, the attitudes of those involved in conflicts are most important: honest but not offensive, righteous but not self-righteous, prophetic but ready to be reconciled with the other. Processes of reconciliation require that injustice and inequality in its many forms will be brought into the open. Therefore reconciliation between groups of people are not acts but processes which cannot succeed without wisdom, compassion, love and justice.

Bibliography

Abe, Masao. (1985). *Zen and Western Thought*. Houndmills: Macmillan.
Bible. (1989). New Revised Standard Version. Oxford: Oxford University Press.
Denzinger, Heinrich/Peter Hünermann. (1965). *Enchiridion symbolorum definitionum et declarationum de rebus fidei et morum*. Freiburg i,B.: Herder Verlag. (1991, 37th ed., cd-rom 1997).
Gort, Jerald D. (1992). "Liberative Ecumenism: Gateway to the Sharing of Religious Experience Today." In: J.D.Gort et. al. (eds.). *On Sharing Religious Experience*. Amsterdam/Grand Rapids: Rodopi/Eerdmans. Pp. 88-195.
Hick, John. (1989). *An Interpretation of Religion*. Houndmills: Macmillan.
Khoury, A. (1982). *Toleranz im Islam*. Munich: Chr. Kaiser Verlag.
Kuyper, Abraham. (1904). *Encyclopaedie der heilige Godgeleerdheid*. 2nd ed. Kampen: Kok.
Lefebure, Leo D. (2000). *Revelation, the Religions, and Violence*. Maryknoll: Orbis Books.
Ricoeur, Paul. (2000). "Toleranz, Intoleranz und das Nicht-Tolerierbare." In: Rainer Forst (ed.). *Toleranz. Philosophische Grundlagen und gesellschaftliche Praxis einer umstrittene Tugend*. Frankfurt/New York: Campus Verlag. Pp. 26-44.
Schmidt-Leukel, Perry. (2000). "Ist das Christentum notwendig intolerant?" In: Rainer Forst (ed.). *Toleranz. Philosophische Grundlagen und gesellschaftliche Praxis einer umstrittene Tugend*. Frankfurt/New York: Campus Verlag. Pp. 177-213.
Stoffels, Hijme C. (1994). "God haat de zonde, maar heeft de zondaar lief. Angst en walging in hedendaags Nederlands orthodox protestantisme." In: Wim Haan en Anton van Harskamp (eds.). *Haat en religie*. Kampen: Kok. Pp. 61-74.
Vroom, Hendrik M. (1989). *Religions and the Truth*. Transl. Johan Rebel. Amsterdam/Grand Rapids: Rodopi/Eerdmans.
———. (1999). "Can We Change the Fatherhood of God? The Hermeneutics of Change in the Tradition of the Interpretation of the Bible." In: Marcel Sarot and Gijsbert van den Brink (eds.). *Identity and Change in the Christian Tradition*. Frankfurt a.M.: Peter Lang. Pp. 219-40.
———. (2000) "Religious Pluralism and Plural Society." *Studies in Interreligious Dialogue* 10: 197-223.
Ward, Keith. (2000). *Religion and Communion*. Oxford: Oxford University Press.

Part II

Perspectives on Conflict and Reconciliation

Hindus and Muslims in Bengal

Is Religious Experience a Unifying Factor?

Victor A. van Bijlert

Hinduism and Islam in Bengal

For at least ten centuries Bengal has witnessed the flourishing of different religious traditions on its soil. Situated on the fringes of the ancient North Indian *Kulturkreis*, Bengal absorbed and fostered non-Vedic Buddhism (until about the twelfth century AD), followed by the reintroduction of caste Hinduism. From the early Mughal period onward many Eastern Bengali tribals and lower caste Hindus converted peacefully to Islam. Thus Bengal ended up having a predominantly Muslim population in its eastern half and a predominantly Hindu population in its western half.

For many centuries this has simply been a fact of life with no strong political implications. Only after the British hegemony and the introduction of colonial 'modernization' did this well-known reality gain political importance. On a pan-Indian scale the verifiable existence of a sizeable minority of Muslims and a large majority of Hindus in India proved to be of a highly explosive nature. In 1947 this fact became the foundation of new nations carved out of the British Indian empire. Within less than forty years—from the beginning of the twentieth century to independence—Hinduism and Islam seemed to have turned into aggressive nation-building forces.

Where Muslims and Hindus had lived as next-door neighbors in Bengal for centuries, now they had become enemies and needed the protection of separate national homelands. It is fair to point out that the demand for a protected homeland was mainly put forward on behalf of the Indian Muslims. It was for this reason that Pakistan was created in 1947. Its west wing covered the western part of the Punjab, Sind, Baluchistan, the Northwestern Frontier Province and bits of Kashmir; while its east wing comprised the whole of East Bengal. The Muslim-Hindu dividing line cut right across Bengal, breaking it neatly in two (as once before in 1905). In 1971, the east wing of Pakistan became the independent nation state Bangladesh. Thus, it seems that Hinduism and Islam in Bengal were a source of tragedy and deep trauma. Are these religious traditions necessarily hostile to each other?

In what follows I will discuss this issue at the level of socio-political mobilization and the 'counting of noses'; and at the personal level from the point of view of Vedanta as a set of values of Indian modernity. The latter is a necessary corrective to the popularly held view that Hinduism and Islam are incompatible. In this article Islam and Hinduism will be sometimes used as a shorthand for Muslims and Hindus and their respective cultures and histories.

When I speak of Vedanta, I mean primarily the philosophy preached by those who have lived and realized the spiritual goals of Vedanta in modern times and who propagated it as a gospel of Indian modernity. Among them, Swami Vivekananda (1863-1902) and Sri Aurobindo (1872-1950) were great communicators reaching wide audiences in India and abroad. Their personality and writings were sources of inspiration for young Indian revolutionary nationalists. The Vedanta thought promulgated in the late nineteenth century fostered the values and ethics of Indian modernity and national empowerment. Since Vedanta was in the last analysis derived from the Upanishads and the *Bhagavadgita* (the famous scriptures of Hinduism) it is tempting to subsume it simply under Hinduism. But many important nineteenth-century thinkers constantly emphasized the need for reform and modernization of Hinduism on the basis of Vedantic thought and realization. Although they spoke from inside the Hindu tradition, they were critical of much in it.

Bengali Hindus and Muslims under the Census

According to the historian Richard Eaton, in Bengal massive conversion to Islam took place during the Mughal period (from the mid-sixteenth century onwards). The converts were tribal people and low-caste Bengalis. They had been organized by *pirs* (Islamic holy men) to clear the jungles in East Bengal. The cleared land was made fit for the cultivation of rice. Often these holy men were subcontractors in the service of a Hindu landholder. The latter often acted as civil servants for the Mughal empire, especially as tax and rent collectors. The eastern part of Bengal was thus 'colonized' only a few centuries ago. By contrast the western part of Bengal had already been settled more than 1500 years earlier. Hence it had been exposed to Brahmanic and Buddhist influences for a long time. That the east of Bengal was inhabited mainly by Muslims and the west mainly by Hindus was known. As to the reasons for this remarkable distribution, different explanations have been proposed. Eaton discusses and criticizes them all (Eaton 1997: 113ff.). The Muslim majority in Bengal was first clearly demonstrated and measured precisely in 1871 when the first census of the whole of India was taken. Since that time it has haunted colonial, nationalist and communist politics. It is no exaggeration to say that the census reports created the Hindus and Muslims as fixed categories and crystallized the caste system. These reports probably contributed much to large-scale pan-Indian caste and communal politics, with often dire consequences. From the point of view of the British Empire, the census enabled administrators to conveniently measure, count and divide the Indian Empire into groups and grouplets whose worldviews and customs were now authoritatively recorded and fixed forever in mutually exclusive categories. In fact, the census can be said to have been the midwife of communalism on a national scale. This is because communalism is not entirely the product of British policy. It did exist before, but through the census it acquired national importance. Suddenly upper caste Hindus became aware of the fact that in the province of Bengal proper the Hindus were slightly outnumbered by Muslims. Two groups antagonistic to each other could now be counted and properly defined and understood. Muslims were one homogeneous group, Hindus formed another group. Irrespective of social standing or economic interests these two groups would forever remain apart, because their essence (Hinduism or Islam as the case may be) prevented mixture or unity or grouping along shared interests other than 'religious' ones. Communalism was born: the 'ism' of defending one's own religious community and being suspicious of the other community.[1]

Let us first look at the categories involved. Especially the Hindu category baffled the census takers. They were faced with the following problem: whom to include in the category and whom to exclude? Obviously Christians, Muslims, Buddhists, Jains, Sikhs, animists, and atheists would be excluded. What remained would then be Hindus of all sorts and descriptions. In his *Report on the Census of Bengal, 1872*, H.Beverley, Inspector General of Registration, wrote as follows:

> The word 'Hindu' is used ... in a two-fold sense, implying a distinction of race as well as of religion. The old meaning of the word comprehended nothing more than an Indian origin.... All who were not Muhammadans were Hindus. But a finer distinction was probably intended to be made in the census tables, the term Hindu being applied to those only who profess the Hindu religion, and all aboriginal tribes, and even several of what we have hitherto been accustomed to regard as Hindu castes, however low in the social scale of Hinduism.... It is difficult ... to separate the pure Hindu from the low castes which have adopted some or other form of Hinduism. The problem can only be satisfactorily solved by a clear definition of what we mean by Hinduism, and no one has ventured as yet to lay down any such definition. (Ch. III: 129)

It seems that Beverley regarded Brahmanic orthopraxis to be the high standard of Hinduism. The others, tribal peoples and low castes, more or less deviated from Brahmanic norms, but as long as they did not explicitly belong to another world religion, they were to be counted as Hindus. The problem of definition remained. Ten years later, J.A. Bourdillon of the Bengal Civil Service reiterated the question:

---

[1] For a useful discussion of communalism in the context of colonialism, see Pandey 1999: 6-22.

> "What is a Hindu?" ... [T]he question has often been asked before and since without eliciting any satisfactory reply. No answer, in fact, exists: for the term in its modern acceptation denoted neither a creed nor a race, neither a church nor a people, but is a general expression devoid of precision, and embracing alike the most punctilious disciple of pure Vedantism, the Agnostic youth who is the product of Western education, and the semi-barbarous hillman, who eats without scruple anything that he can procure and is as ignorant of the Hindu theology as the stone which he worships in times of danger or sickness. Writing of the same subject ... Sir Alfred Lyall [says that] ... the religion of the non-Mahomedan population of India [is] "as a tangled jungle of disorderly superstitions, ghosts and demons, demi-gods and deified saints; household gods, tribal gods, local gods, universal gods, with their countless shrines and temples, and the din of their discordant rites; deities who abhor a fly's death, those who still delight in human victims, and those who would not either sacrifice or make offering—a religious chaos throughout a vast region never subdued or levelled (like all Western Asia) by Mahomedan or Christian monotheism.

Bourdillon wrote this in the 1881 *Report on the Census of Bengal* (71, § 178). This rather lengthy statement shows in all its vigor and self-assuredness the late nineteenth-century colonial view of the large majority of the Indian population. The British tendency to look down upon 'primitive' and 'incomprehensible' people and to feel more akin with Islam (after all, the immediate predecessors of the British were the Muslim nobles from Central Asia and Afghanistan) is also neatly expressed. These prejudices remained a feature of some sections of the British colonial administration until independence.

The differences between Hinduism and Islam are not only based on British colonial misrepresentation, lack of sympathy or the inability to understand. Hinduism, unlike Islam, does not have a single standard code of religious authority. Islam has the Qur'an, but Hinduism has a wealth of more or lesser sacred scriptures. Something of a pan-Indian Hindu canon can be found in the nineteenth century among urbanized and highly educated Bengali Hindus. It consisted of the classical scriptures of Vedanta: the Upanishads and the *Bhagavadgita*. We will return to the Vedanta later. One possible way of looking at Hinduism is to interpret it as a social institution, rather than as a set of dogmas and doctrines. The dynamics and bewildering multiplicity of Hinduism are understood as the creative and complementary opposition between life in the world and the sphere of renunciation of the world (coupled with Brahmanization and Sanskritization). From the sphere of renunciation originate all ultimate values and religious authority. The institution of renunciation (practised by both monks and saintly householders) is at least a phenomenon that encompasses almost all manifestations of indigenous Indian religiosity throughout the ages (see Dumont 1960 and Heesterman 1985: 26-44). But this perspective was not yet available to the British census takers.

It should be clear by now, that there were (and to some extent still are) huge difficulties in defining Hinduism and Hindus. But once the existence of the category Hindu(ism) had been fixed, it set Hindus off against what they were not, i.e., Muslims. Consequently a problem of enormous magnitude emerged which still remains largely unsolved. In Bengal the ratio between Muslims and Hindus tilted towards the former. On a pan-Indian scale, Muslims always formed a considerable minority. The Hindus were always in the majority. The pan-Indian ratio was the basis of all communal political arguments and demands. These mostly centered on the rights of the Hindu majority and the protection of the Muslim minority. Hindu majoritarianism and Muslim minoritarianism have remained the prime feature of communalism down to the present.

Communalism

My contention here is that communalism and communal conflict between Hindus and Muslims is a *modern* phenomenon and a problem intricately linked with the onward march of statist modernity itself. As we have seen, the categories themselves were created for and by the census. This in turn became a major administrative tool. The resulting antagonisms between Muslims and Hindus are not primarily a religious but a political, psychological and socio-economic problem.[2] Consequently, reconciliation between Muslims and Hindus is only possible on the level of personal interaction and on the basis of truly inspired religiosity. On the level of society, the mutual hostility between Muslims and Hindus can only be resolved by revolutionary changes in society itself and in state governance.

Much bad blood and mutual suspicion go back to the beginning of the twentieth century. This is not to say that there never were any conflicts between groups of Hindus and Muslims in the pre-colonial period. Nor is it true that communalism was something the British administrators were keen to promote secretly in order to keep the population divided against itself so that Empire might survive. But whatever divisions were at hand, the British simply utilized them in order to uphold imperial paramountcy. The conflicts in pre-colonial times, however, had never assumed pan-Indian significance nor involved a nation-wide participation. The most dramatic and incredibly violent outcome of communalism was the partition of British India at independence in 1947. The new countries India and Pakistan were the direct result of nationalist aspirations in the 1920s and 1930s. The Islamic homeland of (undivided) Pakistan would have been an unthinkable phenomenon at the time of the Delhi Sultanates in the fourteenth century, of the Mughal empire in the sixteenth century or even the Bengal Sultanates between the thirteenth and the early seventeenth centuries.

If we accept the proposition that communalism is a modern reality with no deep roots in distant history, we still need to understand its origins. Peter Heehs, in a survey of scholarly explanations of communalism, distinguishes four types:

---

[2] For an excellent overview of the different interpretations of communalism and its origins, see Heehs 2000: 124-42.

political, socio-economic, cultural and essentialist. The political explanation points to an alleged British imperial maxim: "keep the Hindus and Muslims apart as much as possible!" Some British political decisions seem to lend credence to this theory. The first partition of Bengal in 1905 into a Muslim east and Hindu west was ostensibly for administrative purposes. But the hidden agenda of the British Government was to break the backbone of the revolutionary nationalist movement whose Hindu protagonists came largely from eastern Bengal. The creation of a Muslim majority in the east Bengal province would boost Muslim interests and prevent them from merging with the interests of the Hindu nationalists. The subsequent creation by the British administration of separate electorates for Muslims and Hindus (allegedly to safeguard minority interests), was another instance of the 'divide and conquer' policy.

The proponents of the socio-economic explanation of communalism—a position favored mostly by Indian Marxists—contend that poor Muslim cultivators of the land were exploited by upper caste Hindu landlords and that the competition for government jobs under the British Raj always gave the better educated Hindus the advantage over ill-educated Muslims. The cultural explanation holds that Hindus are by nature divided into many castes and groups and therefore cannot accommodate the egalitarian Muslims. The more extreme form of the cultural explanation is the essentialist one which claims that Hindus and Muslims simply are what they are: violent, given to oppressing the other, aggressive, etc. (Heehs 2000: 125-26). Heehs points out the weaknesses of these explanations, offered mostly by historians (with the exception of the essentialist view, which is hardly held by serious historians). According to Heehs, explanations from the disciplines of anthropology and psychology provide more useful insights: scapegoating and demonizing the other and the incompatibility of 'final values' (Heehs 2000: 132-34). Heehs pleads for an interdisciplinary approach to the problem in order to find acceptable and plausible solutions (Heehs 2000: 136). The major deficiency in all these explanations is their implied tendency to essentialize and homogenize the Hindus and the Muslims. This I would call the trap of 'census modernity'. It is a dangerous trap, for it implies that somehow a group of religiously inspired people who among themselves are all equal and share many vital interests is necessarily at odds with other religious groups.

A moderate 'Marxist' explanation to the effect that the real causes of communalism are socio-economic and always result from social inequalities and social injustices seems to be the most plausible. Religion is a convenient marker of identity, but it can hardly be the real cause of the violence manifested in a communal riot, for example. Religious identity can in fact veil a very real issue of class struggle or, more commonly, a struggle between rival local holders of power. Communal riots seldom happen spontaneously but almost always require thorough preparation. If communalism were the only cause of political violence in South Asia, we would probably not find violence absent religious involvement.

But this is far from true. In some Indian states political violence is almost endemic (the same is true of certain areas in Pakistan and Bangladesh).

For instance, the recent spurt of violence (at the beginning of 2001) in western Bengal between followers (better: hired thugs) of the CPM (Communist Party of India Marxist) and the Trinamul Congress, shows all the signs of communal violence but no religious conflict was involved here. Nor was there even any evidence of a battle between the ideology of Marxism and a lower middle class ideology. Violent clashes between adherents of both parties continued in some district towns (notably Garbeta and Keshpur). Strongman politics, gross abuses of power, social injustices flagrant inequalities and elitism were then and continue to be the breeding ground for all kinds of political violence. Religion is not the cause of conflict; in a potentially explosive situation it only defines who is friend and who is foe.

Moreover, massive violence (regardless of its alleged source of inspiration!) has a logic all its own. It breeds more hatred and mutual distrust, reinforced by the memories of past violence. Thus a spiral of violence, revenge and counter-violence occurs. Most of the violence affects innocent people. This reinforces the tendency to demonize the opponent and boosts demands for revenge.

Vedanta as Modern Hinduism: And What about Islam?

I have stated above that reconciliation between Hindus and Muslims may be possible on the level of personal interaction and on the basis of inspired religiosity. This requires a mindset that is different from that of the opportunistic politician or local strongmen. It requires conviction and strongly held personal moral and spiritual values.

The importance of spiritual values for the individual within modern society had already been recognized by Bengali Hindu intellectuals in the nineteenth century. Their concept of indigenous modernity hinged on this issue. Challenged by British dominance in Bengal since 1757 and dissatisfied with 'traditional' Hindu practices and customs, urban Bengali savants throughout the nineteenth century were seeking a canon of Hindu spirituality and ethics that could replace tradition and would still strengthen Hindu identity. In other words, urban Bengali Hindus were trying to define a Hindu modernity that would be a viable answer to the challenges of both tradition and growing Western hegemony. Rammohun Roy (1774-1833) was the founding father of this intellectual quest. He found his answer in a rational and liberal interpretation of the Vedanta (especially the classical Upanishads). He set the modern trend among urbanized Hindus of regarding the Vedanta as the fountain of Indian spirituality and Indianness *par excellence*.

Bankim

Vedanta was also taken up by the influential Bengali novelist and essayist Bankim Chandra Chatterjee (1838-1894). Bankim especially advocated modernizing re-readings of the Bhagavad Gita as the prime source for Indian nation-building. Bankim wrote many novels in Bengali. In his essays he discussed the social, political and religious issues of his time. In his later years he was motivated by a strong urge to define and modernize Hinduism for his urban compatriots.

In a series of "Letters on Hinduism" written in English, Bankim tries to answer the vexing question of "What is a Hindu?" A Hindu cannot be merely a "native of Hindusthan" (Bankim Rachanavali 1969: 228)[3] for there are Muslims in India who are not Hindu. Therefore one ought initially to assume that a Hindu is "a person who professes the Hindu religion" (228). Bankim shows how many different and opposing forms of Hinduism may exist like Vaishnavism, Shaktoism and Tantrism. 'Religion' is not the same as the indigenous term *dharma*: "To the Hindu, his relations to God and ... to man, his spiritual life and his temporal life ... form one compact and harmonious whole ... All life to him was religion" (230-31).

Aware of the census reports, Bankim notes that the Europeans had subsumed too many things under the single term Hinduism, from social polity, codes of ethics, folklore, to popular observances (233-35). Bankim maintains that this was a distortion of facts although much "rubbish of ages" had indeed crept into Hinduism. This rubbish has to be removed, "exterminated before Hinduism can hope further to carry on the education of the human race" (235). "But reformed and purified, it [i.e., Hinduism] may yet stand forth before the world as the noblest system of individual and social culture available to the Hindu even in this age of progress" (235).

Bankim gives his own general definition of religion: "... in theory a philosophy of life; in practice ... a rule of life. It includes our beliefs, and the principles of our conduct founded upon those beliefs" (237). And he once more affirms: "the substance of Religion is Culture" (238). Bankim asks "Why do we worship God?" and answers: "Worship is a means to culture as an end, and we worship Him, because to worship Him is to promote our culture" (264). He develops this further in the following statement which reveals his mind on contemporary world religions and how they should change:

> ... religion in its broadest and most legitimate sense is culture. If this be true, the most perfect religion is that which supplies a basis for the most complete development of culture. It follows from this that no religion which refuses to recognize the highest possible ideal in a perfect personal Being, like the religion of Humanity, can be a perfect religion. Nor can a religion which does not comprehend in it a religion of Humanity, as both Christianity and Hinduism un-

---

[3] The following page numbers in the text refer to this work.

doubtedly do, be a perfect religion, for the perfection of our moral feelings depends in a large measure upon our conduct towards (our) fellow men. - [A] religion which excludes nature-worship is an imperfect religion. - [T]he absence of this—in Christianity and Mohammedanism, serves to develop narrowness and bigotry, and to harden the sterner virtues into cruelty and fanaticism. Hinduism alone contains within it all these elements of worship. (264-65)

We need not rush to conclusions about Bankim's stance regarding Christianity and Islam. To his mind also Hinduism in its 'rough' form contains 'rubbish' and needs to be reformed and purified. The essence of such purified (read: modernized) religion is an interiorized process of spiritual purification, shorn of outward rituals and practices that have become meaningless. If religion is 'culture', the most practical and easily accessible form of culture is purification of the mind, for this requires only will power, not social standing.

In his Bengali essay "Chittashuddhi" (Purification of the Mind), Bankim argues that the essence of Hinduism consists in purification of the mind which entails three things: (a) control of the senses, (b) mental non-attachment to the objects of the senses and renouncing egoism, (c) devotion to God.

> The essence of Hinduism (*hindudharma*) is purification of the mind; I entreat those who wish to investigate the true essence of Hinduism to pay special attention to this fact. There is no more essential fact which has penetrated into Hinduism than this one.... If there is purification of the mind, all doctrines/ opinions (*mat*) are pure, in the absence of purification of the mind, all doctrines are impure. Whose mind is impure has no religion. ...
> It is not so that the purification of the mind is the essence only of Hinduism, it is the essence of all religions. It is the essence of Hinduism, it is the essence of Christianity, it is the essence of Buddhism, it is the essence of Islam, it is the essence of atheistic Comteism. He who has mind-purification is the best Hindu, the best Christian, the best Buddhist, the best Muslim (*musalman*), the best Positivist.... (Bankim Racanavali 1361: 259)

Obviously in this view of Hinduism it is not impossible to meet other world religious traditions, provided there are Muslims (or Christians) who could agree that purification of the mind and the centrality of human consciousness as part of a larger consciousness constitute an essential part of modernized religion. This view need, of course, not clash with ultimate values held by Muslims or Christians willing to enter into dialogue. In the realm of spirituality centering around consciousness—a prime concern indeed of the philosophy and spiritual disciplines of the Vedanta—there may well be opportunities for reconciling different religious traditions. This Vedantic view, at least, could be a basis for sympathetic dialogue.[4]

---

[4] On this possibility from a Christian point of view see Chethimattam 2000.

Sri Ramakrishna

Sri Ramakrishna (1836-1886) was a contemporary of Bankim. Whereas Bankim was primarily an intellectual, Sri Ramakrishna—acting as temple priest in the temple of Dakshinewar in north Calcutta—was a seeker for and realizer of the mystical vision. During his lifetime Sri Ramakrishna had followed the many Hindu paths to God and found always in the end the ultimate experience of his chosen Deity, the Goddess Kali. After having practised the ways of Tantrism and Vaishnavism and realized their supreme goals, Sri Ramakrishna was initiated into non-dual Vedanta by the itinerant monk, Tota Puri who had come to Dakshineswar sometime in 1864. After his initiation, Sri Ramakrishna began to practise Vedantic meditation and quickly experienced the ultimate state of consciousness called *nirvikalpa samadhi* (the deepest concentration without conceptualizations). Not long after this Sri Ramakrishna wanted to try other paths. The first non-Hindu path he attempted to practise was Sufism, into which he was initiated by a recent Hindu convert to Islam, Govinda Ray. For three days Sri Ramakrishna tried to dress and eat as a Muslim, reading the Namaz and repeating the name of Allah. Then he received a vision of a bearded man, followed by the experience of merging with Brahman without attributes. This again is the supreme goal of Vedanta. All these events are recorded by an immediate disciple of Sri Ramakrishna, Swami Saradananda (1865-1927) in his Bengali work *Ramakrishna Lilaprasanga*.[1] I quote the following comment made by Swami Saradananda on Sri Ramakrishna's practice of Sufism from the English translation:

> From the event mentioned above [i.e., that Sri Ramakrishna only ate Muslim food and did not even want to see Hindu Deities], it becomes clear how sympathetic the Master's mind became towards other religious communities after he had attained perfection in the Vedantic discipline. It also becomes clear how, by having faith in the Vedantic knowledge alone, the Hindus and the Mohammedans of India may become sympathetic towards one another and develop brotherly feeling. Otherwise, as the Master used to say, "There is, as it were, a mountain of difference between them. Their thoughts and faiths, actions and behaviour, have remained quite unintelligible to each other in spite of their living together for so long a time." Does the practice of Islam by the Master ... indicate that the said difference would some day disappear and both the Hindus and the Muslims would embrace one another in love? (300)

There are interesting differences between Bankim and Sri Ramakrishna. Bankim constructs a 'Protestant' form of Hindu values and ethics. Bankim's Hinduism is based on rejection of later 'accretions'. He never advocated renunciation of the world; rather, his Hinduism serves among other things as a gospel of social progress, self-improvement and Indian nation-building. Sri Ramakrishna's concept

---

[1] For the details of Sri Ramakrishna's practice of Islam see the English translation of this work: *Sri Ramakrishna the Great Master*, Vol.I, 294-302.

of Hinduism on the other hand, is entirely founded on renunciation of the world. Both Bankim and Sri Ramakrishna, speaking on the level of Hindu spirituality, embrace Islam and Muslims. For both, Hindu spirituality in its highest form is identical to Vedanta. But for Sri Ramakrishna, Vedanta means giving oneself totally up to God. Social progress and modernity do not form part of this quest for the ultimate.

Swami Vivekananda

It was left to Sri Ramakrishna's most prominent immediate disciple, Swami Vivekananda, to work out the modernizing aspects of Vedanta on the basis of its spirituality. The other important figure in modern Vedanta was Sri Aurobindo who—inspired by Sri Ramakrishna and Vivekananda—emphasized the emancipatory political inplications of modern Vedanta. As in Bankim's thought, nation-building formed an important part of both Vivekananda's and Aurobindo's teaching. This included the acceptance of Islam in India. Let us first look at Swami Vivekananda.

In a lecture delivered in Boston, Swami Vivekananda proclaimed the universality of Vedanta. Vedanta has no quarrel with any other religious tradition:

> ... in India,... philosophies and systems arose, built around certain persons—such as Buddhism.... They each have a certain leader to whom they owe allegiance, just as the Christians and Mohammedans have. But the Vedanta philosophy stands at the background of all these various sects, and there is no fight and no antagonism between Vedanta and any other system in the world. (Vivekananda 1999: vol. 1, 388)

Moreover, Vivekananda stated: "I accept all religions that were in the past, and worship with them all ... I shall go to the mosque of the Mohammedan ... Not only shall I do all [this] ... but I shall keep my heart open for all that may come in the future" (Vivekananda 1999: Vol. 1, 374). In Vivekananda's view of modern Vedanta there was no and ought to be no real conflict between different religious traditions.

Communalism was already known in Vivekananda's times. In 1896 he was reported to have made the following comment:

> [The] Vedantic spirit of religious liberality has very much affected Mohammedanism. Mohammedanism in India is a quite different thing from that in any other country. It is only when Mohammedans come from other countries and preach to their co-religionists in India about living with men who are not of their faith that a Mohammedan mob is aroused and fights. (Vivekananda 1999: Vol. 5, 310-11)

Indian Muslims were deeply influenced by the indigenous Indian ethos, according to Vivekananda, and any rioting was caused by outside interference. This seems to imply that Hindus and Muslims in principle can live together peacefully.

Vivekananda did not subscribe to the theory that in India Islam was introduced by the sword. Lower caste Hindus had voluntarily converted to Islam in order to escape oppression at the hands of the powerful and the rich. In a letter from 1894 Vivekananda observed:

> Why amongst the poor of India so many are Mohammedans? It is nonsense to say, they were converted by the sword. It was to gain their liberty from the ... zamindars [big landowners] and from the ... priests, and as a consequence you find in Bengal there are more Mohammedans than Hindus amongst the cultivators.... Who thinks of raising these sunken downtrodden millions? A few thousand graduates do not make a nation, a few rich men do not make a nation ... Ninety per cent of our people are without education—who thinks of that? (Vivekananda 1999: VI. 8, 330).

Vivekananda's remarks about Indian Muslims seem to be an echo of remarks made twenty years earlier by H. Beverley in the *Report on the Census of Bengal, 1872*:

> When ... the Musalman conquerors of Hindustan invaded the lower delta with the sword and Koran ... [w]e can imagine that very little persecution was required to change the faith of [the] miserable helots of Bengal. ... In Bengal ... the great mass of the people embraced the faith of Muhammad simply to escape from their ignoble position under the Hindu system (138)

It matters little that this explanation may be wrong, as Richard Eaton (1997) shows in his study on Islam in Bengal. What does matter in this connection is the fact that many accepted the above-mentioned census report. Vivekananda expressed similar views in order to criticize orthodox upper caste Hindus for their lack of sympathy for the poor. Vivekananda wanted these upper caste and middle class Hindus to convert to Vedantism and help build the nation. The process of nation-building had to include the downtrodden Muslims as well.

Sri Aurobindo

The matter of nation-building was taken up by Sri Aurobindo (or Arabindo Ghose as he was called in British intelligence reports). From the late nineteenth century onwards, Sri Aurobindo was active in political journalism and in behind-the-scenes organization of the first stirrings of Indian revolutionary nationalism. In the first decade of the twentieth century Aurobindo had become the symbol of cultural and political resistance to Western colonial domination. Inspired by Bankim and Vivekananda, Aurobindo developed a Vedantic concept of national regeneration and political emancipation. Like Vivekananda, Aurobindo also included the Indian Muslims in his concept of nation-building. Aurobindo wrote an article entitled "'Swaraj' and the Musulmans" for the *Karmayogin* which appeared on June 19, 1909. In it he rejected the British decision to create separate electorates for Hindus and Muslims but insists that

We must strive to remove the causes of misunderstanding by a better mutual knowledge and sympathy; we must extend the unfaltering love of the patriot to our Musulman brother, remembering always that in him too Narayana dwells and to him too our Mother has given a permanent place in her bosom. (Sri Aurobindo 1996: 390)

Reconciling religious differences would, in Aurobindo's opinion, be possible only on the basis of a deeply realized unity and universality. In the same issue of the *Karmayogin*, in an article called "The Ideal of the *Karmayogin*," he postulates the possibility of a universal religion in the future: "The religion which embraces Science and faith, Theism, Christianity, Mahomedanism and Buddhism and yet is none of these, is that to which the World-Spirit moves." In fact this is a new kind of "wider Hinduism which is not a dogma or combination of dogmas .... [I]n this Hinduism we find the basis of the future world-religion." This new and wider Hinduism embraces all other religions and even adopts all their sacred books as its own:

> This *sanatana dharma* (eternal religion) has many scriptures, Veda, Vedanta, Gita, Upanishad, Darshana [the philosophical schools of classical Hinduism], Purana, Tantra, nor could it reject the Bible or the Koran; but its real, most authoritative scripture is in the heart in which the Eternal has His dwelling. (Sri Aurobindo 1996: 385)

Concluding Remarks

Is reconciliation between Hindus and Muslims possible on the basis of Vedantic religious experience such as Aurobindo suggests in the passages cited above? Aurobindo is obviously speaking here on the level of personal experience. His Vedantic realizations were a private affair. When formulated in journalistic writing, they did, however, stir large audiences. We will return to the personal perspective presently. On the level of the state the answer must be different. Only a strong but ethically solid secularism on the state level can prevent violent clashes. The state can only remove the socio-economic sting from organized religions by ensuring universal social equality and impartial justice. Political organization along religious lines, need not be a cause for worry, provided the organization is responsible and uses religion only for moral and ethical guidance. In fact, one could wish that moral and ethical guidance and the interiorization of genuine values (as taught, for instance, in the *Bhagavadgita*, the Qur'an or the Upanishads) would inspire all politicians and policy makers. This is not a wholly utopian proposal. Modern Vedantic values and ethics have already been developed and implemented with some success in the management of the corporate sector in India (see Chakraborty 1995).

At the level of the individual person, acceptance, forgiveness, tolerance and sympathy can be fostered and learned. A genuine acquaintance with the values taught in the above-mentioned scriptures would help towards that end. The modern Vedantins referred to above all held that every person can overcome his or her present distrust, hatred, misunderstanding, anger and a host of other diametrical opposites of human virtues. This capacity lies within everybody. It is not limited by the adherence to any particular religious tradition. But the realization of acceptance, tolerance, forgiveness, and unselfishness is not an object of discursive thinking or argumentation. It is a feeling. All it takes is the will to develop it.

Bibliography

Aurobindo, Sri. (1996). *On Nationalism: Selected Writings and Speeches*. Pondicherry: Sri Aurobindo Ashram. 2nd ed.
Bankim Racanavali. (1361, Bengali Era). *Dvitiya Khanda*. Calcutta: Sahitya Samsad.
Bankim Rachanavali. (1969). Edited by Shri Jogesh Chandra Bagal. Calcutta: Sahitya Samsad. English works.
Chakraborty, S.K. (1995). *Ethics in Management: Vedantic Perspectives*. New Delhi: Oxford University Press.
Chethimattam, John B. (2000). "Vedanta as a Method for Interreligious Theology." In: *Vedanta: Concepts and Application*. Calcutta: The Ramakrishna Mission Institute of Culture. Pp. 187-203.
Dumont, Louis. (1960). "World Renunciation in Indian Religions." *Contributions to Indian Sociology* 4: 33-62.
Eaton, Richard M. (1997). *The Rise of Islam and the Bengal Frontier, 1204-1760.* Delhi: Oxford University Press.
Heehs, Peter. (2000). *Nationalism, Terrorism, Communalism: Essays in Modern Indian History*. New Delhi: Oxford University Press.
Heesterman, J.C. (1985). *The Inner Conflict of Tradition: Essays in Indian Ritual, Kingship, and Society*. Chicago and London: The University of Chicago Press.
Pandey, Gyanendra. (1999). *The Construction of Communalism in Colonial North India*. New Delhi: Oxford University Press.
Saradananda, Swami. (1996). *Sri Ramakrishna the Great Master*. Transl. Swami Jagadananda. Mylapore, Madras: Sri Ramakrishna Math.
Vivekananda, Swami. (1999). *Complete Works of Swami Vivekananda*. Mayavati Memorial Edition. Calcutta: Advaita Ashrama. 8th reprint, subsidized edition.

Religious Conflict and Hindu Tolerance

Corstiaan J.G. van der Burg

Introduction

On December 6, 1992, a mob of Hindus burst through the cordon around the heavily guarded Babar mosque in Ayodhya, a Hindu place of pilgrimage in the northern Indian State of Uttar Pradesh, and in a few hours destroyed this four-century old Muslim monument. Even then the Hindus did not stop and the unrest continued, for no sooner had the news of the immolition spread than riots broke out everywhere in northern and central India, lasting for days and costing the lives of hundreds (mostly Muslims). Only after this wave of violence and bloodshed was over, did the police and the army take action. After the event a number of Hindus denounced the incident but maintained that the Indian Muslims had asked for it themselves, e.g. by not adapting to the Indian situation. Although this affair was not an isolated incident, it was the most bloody in a long chain of similar events taking place in the whole of India since the 1980s.

This picture of Hindus losing themselves in violence and destruction contradicts the popular perception of Hinduism as a spiritual, non-violent and tolerant way of life. Moreover, Hindus display ambivalence in their attitude towards Muslims: the same Hindus who blame them for not adjusting to circumstances view tolerance as an outstanding characteristic of Hinduism.

The topic of Hindu tolerance highlights the need to reconsider the basic terms we use to talk about Hinduism and to question common assumptions which have been built into our knowledge of Indian civilization (Van der Veer 1996: 5). This article will focus in particular on the development of Hindu-Muslim relations inside India as a nation state.

Tolerance and Inclusivism

The German Paul Hacker (1913-1979), the first Western Indologist who analyzed the Hindu use of 'tolerance', was surprised to find that the notion of 'tolerance', or 'putting up with' in the usual sense of the word, i.e., tolerating divergences to a certain extent, hardly existed in India. For him, the religious policy of the Buddhist king Ashoka (3rd century B.C.) was *the* example of officially instituted administrative tolerance (Halbfass 1988: 410) and as such an exception to the rule. Although he gives some more examples, his general conclusion was that if something like 'tolerance' existed in Hinduism, it was in the shape of what he called *inclusivism*, which was evident in Neo-Hinduism in particular. According to Halbfass

The central and pervasive element in Hacker's definitions and exemplifications of "inclusivism" is the practice of claiming for, and thus including in, one's own religion or world-view what belongs in reality to another, foreign or competing system ["die Praxis, das Fremde unterordnend dem Eigenen anzuschliessen (Hacker 1978: 386)]. It is a subordinating identification of the other, the foreign with parts or preliminary stages of one's own sphere. It is not considered to be a process of additive annexation; nor is it a form of syncretism or eclecticism. The other, the foreign, is not seen as something that could be added to, or combined with, one's own system; instead, it is something a priori contained in it. Hacker provides a variety of examples which show that there are various types and modifications of inclusivism. Time and again, he refers to Tulsidas, the *Bhagavadgita*, and Radhakrishnan's universalized inclusivism, and he suggests a deep affinity between non-dualism and inclusivism. (Halbfass 1988: 411)

The examples which Hacker cites are taken primarily from the religious mythology and poetry of traditional Hinduism (e.g. *Bhagavadgita* 9: 23: "Those devotees likewise who, endowed with faith, offer worship unto other Divinities: they, o son of Kunti, offer service, [albeit] not in the prescribed mode, unto none but Myself" (Belvalkar 1959: 43)), as well as from Neo-Hinduism (e.g. Radhakrishnan: "The *Vedanta* is not a religion, but religion itself in its most universal and deepest significance" (Radhakrishnan 1968: 18)). This latter statement, says Halbfass, "summarizes Radhakrishnan's attempts to derive the 'tolerance' and 'inclusiveness' of Hinduism from the metaphysics of Advaita Vedanta." Hacker called this "The most comprehensive application which the principle of inclusivism has ever found" (Halbfass 1988: 409; Hacker 1978: 601).

Although references to classical Indian philosophy are less frequent and conspicuous, Hacker himself suggests according to Halbfass (1988: 413)

> that the practice of inclusivism can be traced back to the late Vedic hymns, as well as to the Brahmanas and Upanishads; he does, however, not explain all instances of "identification" in the Brahmanas and early Upanisads as inclusivistic. As one very significant case, which prepares or anticipates later non-dualistic inclusivism, he mentions the *tat tvam asi* and the doctrine of being (*sat*) in the sixth chapter of the *Chandogya Upanishad*.... It is, however, obvious that the inclusion and subordination of earlier speculations and of competing concepts is only one side of the "inclusivism" which we find in the *Chandogya Upanishad*. What seems to be more important is the subordinating and reductive "identification" of cosmic and physical phenomena, or occurrences of everyday life. The sun, the moon, fire, and so forth, are traced back to being itself; they are explained as being contained in it, as emanating from it, and as ultimately identical with it. The inclusivistic neutralization of all doctrines and concepts by subordinating them to the doctrine of pure, absolute being, and the reductive explanation of all phenomena by tracing them back to this one being cannot be separated.... The "form" or pattern of thought is basically identical: The phenomena are traced back to the fundamental cosmological principle *sat* in the same manner in which all specific concepts and teachings

are reduced to the all-encompassing doctrine of pure being. (Halbfass 1988: 414)

Although Hacker himself did not (cf. Halbfass 1988: 411) explore the undeniable connections between 'inclusivism' and the pervasive hierarchization of Hindu society, it is evident that these connections play a role in his definition of inclusivism. Louis Dumont, on the other hand, who gave the classic description (1972) of the 'homo hierarchicus', referred somewhat casually to the theme of tolerance, noting that the heterogeneity which excludes one group from other groups is the very basis for its integration into the total hierarchical system, i.e., its qualified recognition and toleration.

Hacker claims that inclusivism is a typically, even exclusively Indian phenomenon. To what extent, if at all, can this claim be justified? Hacker himself asks the question whether the use and assimilation of Greek concepts in early Christian thought provide an analogue. In this particular case, we may accept his negative answer (cf. Halbfass 1988: 415).

Tolerance as a Critique on 'Secularism'

Up to now we have looked at 'tolerance' in terms of pure religious inclusivism. We should not, however, entertain illusions about the existence of such a *Reinkultur* in the 'lived reality' of India. For although it is present in many phases in the historical development of post-traditional Hinduism, it appears in different shapes and with many additions to Hinduism.

In fact, Indian pluralistic society is unthinkable without the notion of 'tolerance' as a societal ideal. This at least is revealed in the thinking of the social psychologist Ashis Nandy. He thinks that the secular ideology of "no preference and no interference in religious matters" which since the post-Independence days of Nehru has dominated Indian society should be done away with. In Nandy's opinion (1990: 84-85), there has always been in India a tolerant and syncretist "popular culture" and a "popular religion." It seems as if Nandy is projecting the modern 'multiculturalist' utopia not only upon the precolonial past but also upon the traditional rural society. In his view, the common individual is not a backward religious fanatic but a tolerant syncretist. It is the modernizing and secularizing state that has destroyed traditional syncretism (Nandy 1990: 88) and forced people to become united into separate, competing groups. This is certainly not entirely unfounded. In the colonial period the introduction of the democratic vote resulted in the mobilization of religious communities along with a sharpening of symbolic boundaries. Even today political leaders in India play an important role in the escalation of religious conflicts, only for electoral gain. But to say, as Nandy does, that the common person is essentially syncretist contradicts the fact that those involved in religious violence or who vote for religiously tinted nationalist parties are not misguided by political leaders but act on their own accord.

Moreover, his views on the precolonial period appear to be biased, considering the innumerable instances of religious violence the historical sources mention (Björkman 1988; Chandra 1984; D'Cruz 1988; Gaborieau 1985; Gold 1991a and 1991b; Kakar 1996; Thapar 1992). That it is not the modernizing secularizing state that is the source of violence is demonstrated by the fact that the Nehruvian period after Independence was not characterized by extreme religious strife.

A more thorough examination of Nandy's reasoning reveals that to him the true syncretist spirit of India appears to be essentially Hinduistic. He thereby denies, in fact, Muslims for example the right to have their own religion and argues that they should consequently realize their Hindu essence. So, in fact, his views are not essentially contrary to what inclusivism concludes on the basis of historical evidence (cf. Van der Veer 1993: 15-16).

In order to share or argue against these conclusions we must now take a closer look at Hindu-Muslim relations in India.

Hindus and Muslims

If we want to understand the difficult coexistence of Hindus and Muslims—of which the horrendous massacres of December 1992 are an exemplary reflection—we need to distinguish between more or less immediate causes and underlying circumstances. To acquire insight into the underlying circumstances we need to explain terms like *religious nationalism* and *communalism*.

Which phenomena are indicated by these terms? To answer this question we need to explore the backgrounds of nationalism and communalism in the colonial period (up to 1947). We can divide this period into the nineteenth century Hindu 'renaissance', with its political implications, and the religious and political developments in the first half of the last century. It is important to realize that the developments in the religious outlook do not stand alone but are 'supplemented' by nationalist and communalist ideologies.

Before we describe these periods in more detail, we must explain the notion of communalism. Having the broad meaning of 'the care of a community's wellbeing', it could be more specifically circumscribed as 'the politically or socially assertion of a group's common characteristic', which has in itself nothing to do with politics or society. Put differently, when a group has a certain cultural feature, like a common ethnic descent, a religion or a language, then such a group also has, according to communalistic ideology, a common interest in other fields, e.g. social, political or economic. So, communalism promotes a group's interests in those fields where this interest is, in fact, not so evident (cf. Chandra 1984; d'Cruz 1988; Panikkar 1999). That Indian communalism gained ethnic and religious features—and did not gain characteristics based on estate or class differences—in modern democratic India can be explained on the basis of a set of factors, some of which we will elucidate.

The arrival of the British as a colonial power in India (end of the eighteenth century) means for the Hindus the end of Muslim dominance that lasted six centuries: the fall of the Mughal empire. The 'dishonesty' of Muslim rule still evokes the need for revenge with some Hindu groups, which means a serious threat to the coherence of Indian society. We find this theme recurring when Hindus at the present time elucidate their stance towards Muslims.

Under British colonial rule between the end of the eighteenth century and 1947 Hindus and Muslims were repeatedly played off against each other, due to the 'divide and rule' policy of the British. Therefore political Hinduism, resulting from the need for its own identity as a reaction against the threat of Western colonial dominance, had found corroboration for its aspiration to get rid of all remnants of the Islamic presence in the subcontinent.

Although it is not possible to mention one specific historical event marking the rise of Hindu nationalism as a special form of communalism, one can state that the wave of religious renaissance and reform in the latter half of the nineteenth century carried the germs of anti-Muslim activism which grew and flourished so abundantly in the decennia to come.

Hindu nationalism in its militant form rose in the middle of the nineteenth century among the urban literate middle classes as a reaction to British colonial dominance. The first movement was the Brahmo Samaj, the 'Society of [Believers in] the Godhead', founded in 1828 in Calcutta by Raja Ram Mohan Roy. Striving after a 'humanistic Hinduism' the movement was very much against the immolation of widows, which in its turn caused a reaction from the side of conservative Hindus who cherished such practices. In the same period more reform movements were established, such as the Arya Samaj, the 'Society of the Nobles', founded in 1875 by Svami Dayanand Sarasvati. He wished to reform Hinduism from within in order to counterbalance the British presence, particularly in its intellectual and socio-economic aspects. The Arya Samaj can be called reformist indeed because its motto was: "Back to the Vedas (the oldest documents of Divine revelation); back to the old values and social institutions of the earliest Vedic times." It is important to know that right from the start this movement cherished a peculiar and clearly defined image of the 'enemy'. The Muslims should first do away with practices unacceptable to Hindus, such as eating beef, and then be brought back into the fold of Hinduism because their ancestors had at the time been forcibly converted to Islam. Svami Dayanand succeeded in elevating the Vedas above all other authoritative Hindu scriptures, rendering them into "the Book" *par excellence*, an infallible foundation and solution for all the world's problems.

Although Svami Dayanand was not able to bring about a great wave of reform—his message was too elitist and perhaps too modern (the denial of brahmins' authority, opposition to the caste system) and although his movement was going to stay marginal, his ideas appeared to have much influence on the subsequent religious nationalism and communalism.

Hindutva

Only towards the end of the nineteenth century did the Hindus start to turn against the Muslims politically. That was when the British played the Hindus and Muslims off against each other as separate electorates, as they were alternately privileged by the colonial rulers. In this way they were more and more reshaped into interest groups, characterized by religious difference. Communalism entered politics. On the basis of religious differences both groups endeavored to win the favor of the government in several fields at the cost of the other community.

Most of Hindu ideology and the accompanying religious symbolism—which is still in use, albeit in a more militant shape—dates from the period of the 1920s and 1930s of the last century. In 1923 Vir Savarkar published his book *Hindutva* ('Hindudom'), one of the writings that contributed most to the development of communalist ideology. This book is a glorification of *Blut und Boden* nationalism aiming at the reinstatement of the Hindu nation which once existed during the Golden Age of King Rama, the ideal monarch and, as such, the Ramayana hero. This nation will encompass the whole of *Bharat*, the motherland India, where one people will live: one in blood, history, religion, culture and language.

In order to realize this ideal Hindu nation of *Bharat Mata*, 'Mother India', Hedgewar founded the RSS, the *Rashtriya Svayamsevak Sangh*, the 'National Volunteer Corps', in 1925. where, in tens of thousands of local branches all over the country and abroad, volunteers were trained in a semi-military way to serve as useful citizens of the future Hindu state. The RSS' cultural division is the VHP, the *Vishva Hindu Parishad*, the 'World Hindu Assembly', which has branches wherever Indians live for religious, cultural and social activities. Hindu ideals are also central to the VHP, so much so that Hinduism is seen as the oldest religion in the world and Sanskrit as the mother of all languages. If we dismiss these statements as pseudo-scientific, then we do not understand their hidden meaning. Although the ideals of these movements may finally be economic and political, science and religion do not only serve as disguises and rationalizations of the proper purposes. In this connection religion is extremely useful as an organizing principle and as an instrument for mass mobilization, whereas religiosity—the strong emotional commitment to religious matters—is in many ways tapped in order to serve the aim of India's re-Hinduization. In short,

> [T]he politics of Hindutva is primarily engaged in defining the nation as Hindu through a process of cultural homogenization, social consolidation and political mobilization of the majority community and at the same time, by stigmatizing the minorities as aliens and enemies. (Panikkar 1999: xxx)

Viewed from this perspective it is understandable that the complete religious artillery should be correctly positioned, particularly against that which is seen as the major threat to Hinduism and an impediment for the foundation of an ideal Hindu state: the Muslim minority. Nineteenth-century Arya Samaj gave rise to *shuddhi*, 'purification', the attempt to win the descendants of Islamic converts back to Hinduism. The Muslims have long been accused of conspiring against the Hindus and of bringing about the fall of Hindu India with foreign help. In this connection the attempt of the Bharatiya Janata Party, the 'Indian People's Party' (BJP), to 'liberate' the birthplace of the God-king Rama should be seen as a carefully orchestrated scheme to deliver a blow to Islam and not as a riot that got out of hand.

Final Remarks

In view of the historical developments one can in all fairness ask oneself whether the aggression against Muslims which continues up to the present could be caused by a genuine fear of an Islamic danger, of a kind of state within a state. In all objectivity, there have been few grounds for this fear right from the start of Independence. It started so well, from Independence onwards, in spite of the fact that the old British colonial policy of divide and rule had been continued. The initial secularism had been formally adopted by the Indian administration, including the ideals of liberty, equality and respect for human dignity. However, after the founding of Pakistan as a separate Muslim state, the minority position of the Muslims in India (125 million over against 850 million Hindus) has merely been given extra confirmation socially, economically, politically as well as religiously. This only determined their fate since the fall of the Moghul empire. Discriminated against or lagging behind, it is in any case a fact that the Muslims as a group never were a social economic threat to the Hindus and therefore do not deserve to be a target of discrimination and aggression.

The underlying cause for this aggression lies somewhere else, as may have become clear from the developments described. Added to these is the social economic slump which has paralyzed India for many years. It was precisely in the 1990s, when India was badly in need of economic reforms after the fruitless efforts of the successive Gandhi administrations to save the country economically, that India lacked the political stability needed to implement these reforms. This economic stagnation as well as the political unrest hit the vulnerable middle class in particular. This middle class had developed successfully economically in the 1980s, but that was the end of this growth.

> [T]he mid-1970s to the late 1980s was characterized by a sustained decline in poverty ratios in both rural and urban India[. I]n the nineties with the onset of structural reforms and globalization this process has been halted and possibly even reversed.... At the same time, the economic opportunities opened up by liberalization and globalization have considerably increased the incomes of the affluent.... The greater social and political acceptability of the Hindutva in recent times, as Jayati Ghosh suggests, "has had a lot to do with the economic repercussions of a pattern of growth which leaves the vast majority of the population either untouched or even worse off, while generating spiralling incomes and an increasingly flamboyant lifestyle of a minority." [Panikkar 1999: 112] (Panikkar 1999: xxixff.)

So, if the BJP reacts adequately to middle class feelings of economic insecurity for electoral profit, then it is not surprising that precisely these wavering middle classes, searching for ways to defend themselves, find the aggressive message of Hindu nationalists appealing.

In short, social economic contradistinctions and uncertainties are in this way reduced to one paramount difference, namely religion, even ignoring distinctions like class and caste. A social economic crisis was elaborated politically but appeared as a religious clash. And which group was better qualified to be the scapegoat than the Muslims, the weaker section of clearly distinguishable secondrate citizens who for such a long time had been given the short end of the stick? For, next to ethnicity, religion is a powerful mainspring for mobilizing people because both can be applied generally and are capable of arousing extreme emotions.

All this is not to say that the described social economic contrasts could be reduced to a religious controversy, even though the conflicts have become apparent through religious fractures. Analyzing and resolving such conflicts by theological means seems to be even less evident to us. Hindu tolerance (Panikkar 1999: x) presented as inclusivism still seems more likely to be a source of conflict rather than it is a means of settling controversies.

Bibliography

Belvalkar, S.K. (ed. and transl.). (1959). *Shrimad Bhagavadgita*. Hindu Vishvavidyalaya Nepal Rajya Sanskrit Series. Vol. 1. Varanasi: Banaras Hindu University Press.
Björkman, James Warner (ed.). (1988). *Fundamentalism, Revivalists and Violence in South Asia*. New Delhi: Manohar Publications.
Chandra, Bipan. (1984). *Communalism in Modern India*. Delhi: Vikas Publishing House.
D'Cruz, Emil. (1988). *Indian Secularism: A Fragile Myth*. Indian Social Institute Monograph Series. New Delhi: Indian Social Institute.
Dumont, Louis. (1972). *Homo Hierarchicus*. London: Paladin.
Gaborieau, Marc. (1985). "From Al-Beruni to Jinnah: Idiom, Ritual and Ideology of the Hindu-Muslim Confrontation in South Asia." *Anthropology Today* 1 (1985): 7-14.
Gold, Daniel. (1991a). "Organized Hinduisms: From Vedic Truth to Hindu Nation." In: Martin E. Marty and R. Scott Appleby (eds.). *Fundamentalisms Observed: The Fundamentalism Project*. Vol. I. Chicago/London: The University of Chicago Press. Pp. 531-93.
———. (1991b) "Rational Action and Uncontrolled Violence: Explaining Hindu Communalism." *Religion* 21: 357-70.
Hacker, Paul. (1978). "Religiöse Toleranz und Intoleranz im Hinduismus." In: Lambert Schmithausen (ed.). *Paul Hacker. Kleine Schriften*. Glasenapp-Stiftun. Vol. 15. Wiesbaden: Franz Steiner Verlag. Pp. 376-88. Originally published in *Saeculum* 8 (1957): 167-79.
Halbfass, Wilhelm. (1988). *India and Europe: An Essay in Understanding*. Albany: State University of New York Press.
———. (1991). *Tradition and Reflection: Explorations in Indian Thought*. Albany: State University of New York Press.

Kakar, Sudhir. (1996). *The Colors of Violence: Cultural Identities, Religion and Conflict.* Chicago: University of Chicago Press.

Ludden, David (ed.). (1996). *Making India Hindu: Religion, Community, and the Politics of Democracy in India.* Delhi: Oxford University Press.

Nandy, Ashis. (1990). "The Politics of Secularism and the Recovery of Religious Tolerance." In: Veena Das (ed.). *Mirrors of Violence.* New Delhi: Oxford University Press. Pp. 69-93.

Panikkar, K.N. (ed.). (1991). *Communalism in India; History, Politics and Culture.* New Delhi: Manohar.

Radhakrishnan, S. (1968). *The Hindu View of Life.* London: Allen & Unwin. First ed. 1927.

Thapar, Romila. (1989). "Imagined Religious Communities? Ancient History and the Modern Search for a Hindu Identity." *Modern Asian Studies* 23: 209-31.

———. (1992). *Interpreting Early India.* Delhi: Oxford University Press.

Van der Veer, Peter. (1994). *Religious Nationalism: Hindus and Muslims in India.* Berkeley: University of California Press.

Liberation Theology in South India

S. Gangadaran

Introduction

Saiva Siddhantha Philosophy arose as a protest movement against certain forms of Vedic ritualism that hold to the supremacy of rituals. Some Vedic schools, especially *Purva Mimamsa*, maintain that rituals, and not the grace of God, function as the sole factor in release. The Saiva Siddhantha system, on the other hand, emphasizes the grace of Siva as the primary factor in all God's activities. There are some important features of Saiva Siddhantha which may be considered to be liberating factors. These liberating factors are relevant in cases of conflict between religious traditions and conflicts between different groups in society. It will be argued below that God has created the world through love and therefore that he wants people to love one another, to overcome their conflicts and become reconciled with one another. In this contribution I will deal with some of the main causes of conflicts, relevant in south India, between rich and poor, men and women, and humankind and the natural environment. I will also deal with religious conflicts both within the Hindu culture and between religious traditions.

The Concept of Liberation in Saiva Tradition

The *Taittiriya Upanishad* informs us that human personality includes physical, vital, mental, intellectual and blissful aspects. These are accepted in the Indian tradition and the Saiva Tamil tradition follows this general Indian tradition, enriching it by providing its own specific contributions on this issue. The physical body is the first sheath of the human personality and therefore the physical well-being of a person is to be nourished, since the physical being is a vehicle of God. Vital air plays an important part in maintaining the physical well-being, and the importance of mental well-being can not be overemphasized.

The intellectual and blissful aspects are higher aspects and need to be ascribed more importance. This does not mean that the physical and other aspects are to be neglected as has sometimes happened in history. We should not allow people to be cheated with respect to these physical aspects in the name of religion. The well-being of the individual in this world is as important as the well-being of the individual in the world to come. The point to be noted here is that even though we need to develop social and cultural aspects of human beings in a significant manner, economic factors of development must not be ignored or neglected. Thus, liberation in Saivism is explained as liberation from bondage and the attainment of the bliss of Lord Siva.

Human Beings as Makers of Their own Destiny

Saiva Siddhantha believes that the essential character of human beings is freedom. The law of *karma*, as understood in Saiva Siddhantha, helps human beings understand the significance of freedom. This law is to be understood from two perspectives. The first perspective informs us that the past actions of a being determine his/her present situation. This is only one aspect of the law of *karma*. The significant aspect of the same law states that future actions are determined by one's present actions. This second aspect of this law is only an extension of the first. Just as one's present state is determined by one's past, so one's future is shaped by one's present actions.

God is the one who administers the law of *karma*. Saiva Siddhantha believes that actions in one's present life are the result of actions in one's previous life. Wealth, poverty, happiness, unhappiness, high social status and low status are all determined in the womb. But even though these are determined, our responses towards these events are not.

The purpose of the five acts of God is to make us responsible beings. Saiva Siddhantha informs us that the activities in this birth (*prarabdha*) are only part of the total *karma* (*sancita*) of a person. If a person has learned to make proper responses meaningfully in a consistent way, then a fresh *karma* (*agamya*) may not arise. The duty of a responsible being is to act in such a way that his present actions do not lead to fresh *karmas*. If a person has learned this lesson by making use of the inner light provided by God, then he need not worry about that part of *karma* (*sancita*) which has not yet begun to bear fruit for him. For example, the total *karma* of a person may be 7000-fold, whereas another's may be 700. If we learn to act in such a way that a fresh *karma* is not produced, i.e., if we are responsible in our responses to the already determined actions (*prarabdha*), then God comes to our rescue and destroys our total *karma*.

Freedom from Caste Oppression

We must distinguish Hinduism from Vedic religion. Vedic religion emphasizes the four divisions of color (*Varna*) and of stages (*Asrama*). The student stage, the householder stage, the stage of preparation for renunciation and the renunciation stage are the four which are common to all human beings. But the division according to color is as follows: 1) the learned and the wise, 2) the valiant who protect the land, 3) the business people who engage in commerce and 4) the working people who ensure the maintenance of the land through labor. When the Aryan race came into contact with the pre-Aryan race, this division of people according to stage and color was adopted by the Indian people. This may have served its purpose in history in enabling all shades of people to be 'absorbed' into society. This 'absorption' is also sanctified by certain passages of scripture, such as the *Purusha Sukta*.

This system works as long as there is mobility among the groups in society. The incident of Satyakama Japala mentioned in the Chandogya Upanishad shows that there was mobility among the various groups of society. Problems arise when human selfishness enters the system. The son or daughter of the learned and wise should have the required qualifications for occupying that position. If the son or daughter does not have the capacity for succeeding in his or her father's position, he or she should surrender that position to someone from another group who is qualified. If the father insists that his son or daughter occupy the position of the learned in spite of his or her not having the required capacity, then eligible persons from other sections cannot occupy that position. As a result, disturbances in society arise.

The *bhakti* system, especially Saiva Siddhantha, arose as a protest against caste oppression in society. The Saiva saints of the seventh century A.D. emphasized the gracious nature of Siva: everyone is equal in the eyes of Lord Siva. If a person expresses genuine love for Siva, he or she has to express his or her love in concrete terms. If a person truly loves God, his or her love of God should be manifested in the love of his or her neighbors. If a person does not love his or her neighbor, this implies that he or she does not love God. This love between people implies that, from a Hindu perspective, they will strive for reconciliation.

The Conception of God in Saiva Siddhantha

Saiva Siddhantha states that reason may be of help with respect to understanding God. But reason alone cannot be sufficient for understanding the reality and significance of God's acts. Saiva sages who have experienced God give us certain suggestions as to how we may approach the supreme Being. Tirujnana Sambandar cautions us not to indulge in excessive inquiry. At the same time, Saiva Siddhanthin does not neglect the importance of reason. We need to understand that inquiry is necessary. Excessive inquiry, however, may not give us the desired result.

God acts through his *sakti* with which He is integrally associated. *Sakti* has the nature of an unlimited desire (*iccha*), pure knowledge (*jnana*) and an unlimited freedom to act (*kriya*). The important factor regarding the five acts of God through his *sakti* is that bestowing grace is God's primary act. The first four activities are for the purpose of bestowing grace.

> Do not by arguments and examples, indulge
> In *excessive* enquiry. Our Lord is a blazing Light.
> Ye who wish to be rid of great sorrow live with your mind fixed on Him.
> Come, ye holy ones, unto the Lord.
> Tirujnana Sambandar, Tiruppasuram, 3.54.5 (Tiruvalluvar, Tirukkural, 339)
>
> Direct your thinking as far as it can go
> Express the truth as best as you can

> Even if denied our Lord verily exists,
> Seek ye the good well-tried path.
> Tirujnana Sambandar 2.36.10 (Tirumular, Tirumanthiram, 2103)

God creates because He loves. Protection, destruction and concealment are all expressions of grace. The destruction of the body has the aim of wiping out the fatigue of birth and death. Death is not simply to be seen negatively as mere deprivation of life. Tiruvalluvar says that death is like sleep and birth after death is like waking after a refreshing sleep.

The question now arises: In what sense is this death or destruction a spiritual rest or renewal of life? The destruction of the body is effected so that the fatigue of birth and death may be relieved and that only the soul remain. Therefore, as a kind of rest and preparation for experiencing new *karma*, death indicates the involution of the soul with the world. This is a gracious act from both cosmic and individual points of view. If involution serves the ripening of *karma*, re-creation serves the eventual ripening of spiritual darkness.

The work of deluding the soul is for a certain period of time aided by the concealing power of God. This is really the power of Siva which hides from souls the true nature of objects in the world, so that by experiencing them the maturation of spiritual darkness may be effected. Its function, though characterized by the negative aspect, is actually positive. The soul that mistakenly thinks that the objects of the world yield pleasure concludes finally for itself that the pleasures derived from them are evanescent and therefore not worthwhile. We must understand clearly what the purpose behind the act of obscuration is: obscuration is effected by God to veil the nature of the soul as intelligent and bring about indifference to the fruits of actions, good and bad, by first making them engage in action (or, as one commentator puts it, to avoid the avoidance of *karma*). Grace is the granting of release, since all activities are expressions of his grace and there is no ground for attributing cruelty to Siva.

The Nature of Grace in Saiva Siddhantha

Saiva Siddhantha holds that God's grace is the basis for all religions in the world. Tirujnana Sambandar, one of the leading saints of Saivism, criticized the views of Jainism and Buddhism in the tenth verse of almost every decad of his poems. In the decad sung at Tiruirumboolai he says that Siva's grace is the basis of the views of Jainism and Buddhism. Even though Siva's grace is the source of all religions, religious views are distorted when these arise via the medium of human beings who become selfish and so distort the teachings of the original master. In some cases we may say that they are right in what they affirm but wrong in what they deny of other religions.

The function of the concealing power of God is to make us grow. The grace of God is at work in all religions and we need to respect and understand his work in them. If we realize that God is also present in other religious traditions, we will not be involved in interreligious conflicts but, on the contrary, attempt to establish peace between the adherents of different religions.

Reinterpretation of Scripture

This is one of the ways in which we can prevent religious conflicts. Hindu theology of religions itself implies a strong tendency toward harmony among religious traditions. "Reality is one; sages call it by various names" (*Ekam sat, vipra bahuda vadanti*). When we consider the different gods in various cultures and also in Indian culture, we need to distinguish one salient feature in the Indian system. Indra, Varuna, Agni, Soma, Rudra are some of the gods mentioned in the Rigveda. We also come across many gods in Greek and other cultures.

We need to consider the significance of the statement "Reality is one" when we think about the many gods mentioned in the Rigveda. The sun god, appearing under different names according to different cultures, was everywhere regarded as the god of justice and of a successful human social order. As such, the god had a special affection for the poor. As far as I know, there is no mention of Reality being one in other cultures. The idea of Reality as one determines the view of ultimate Reality in Indian culture.

The spirit of this statement has been understood and practised in Indian culture. For example, Sankara understood this spirit and applied it in his time after a gap of a thousand years. At the time of Sankara, Vedic deities were not worshipped. Instead, Siva, Sakti, Ganapati, Gaumara, Surya and Vishnu were worshipped. Sankara observed that Reality is one, whether it is worshiped as Siva, Sakti, Ganapati, Gaumara, Surya or Vishnu. The spirit of the Rigvedic dictum was preserved and imparted through Sankara's writings.

It is my opinion that Gandhiji received his inspiration from the Rigvedic dictum and Sankara's use of this dictum. It was his custom to arrange for the reading of texts from three major religions, Hinduism, Islam and Christianity, during his daily evening prayers and maintained that Rama, Allah and Jesus are various expressions of the same Reality. Gandhiji was courageous enough to include even the God of Christianity and Islam in explaining his philosophy of God. We can thus understand the universal nature of Indian culture in dealing with the concept of God. It is a pity that attempts are now being made to distort the pluralistic notion of God, which is the spirit of Hinduism. This may be called the 'communalization' of Hinduism. In this way Hinduism becomes another exclusivistic religion, with also the attendant dangerous consequences of religious conflicts between Hindus and Muslims and tension between Hindus and Christians. I agree with those Hindu scholars who urge us to be careful to retain the pluralistic notion of God in our culture.

If everyone fully understood the spirit of his/her own religion, harmonious living would not be impossible. In the seventh century A.D. Jainism was the dominant religion in the Pandian kingdom, practised by the king and most of his subjects.

According to the *Periyapuranam*, one of the canonical writings of Saivism, Jains were very strict with respect to their religious tenets. Accordingly, if a Jain happened to see a person with sacred ash, he would, according to Jain beliefs, become polluted. If a person heard that someone had seen a person wearing sacred ash, he would also become polluted by hearing about it. The Pandian king Nedumaran was a practising Jain and his wife Mangayarkarasi was a Saivite. Saivites used to wear ash for purifying the heart. The whiteness of sacred ash denotes the purity of the heart. As a devoted wife, the queen would not want to pollute her husband by allowing him to see or hear about her wearing of the sacred ash. At the same time, as a daughter of a Chola king who was by tradition a Saivite, she wanted to practise the Saiva religion. It is therefore said that she wore sacred ash on her breasts. This shows that living in harmony as husband and wife is possible if the adherents of the conflicting religious views respect each other's religion.

Tirujnana Sambandar considers God to be the support of the helpless, even though He does not depend on others for His support. He uses the phrase "Arravarku attra Sivan" (Tirujnana Sambandar, 3.120.2). The term *arravar* denotes those who have no support in this world, such as widows, orphans, etc. Lord Siva supports these people and at the same time he does not need support from any quarter. This is conveyed by the term *attra Sivan*. In many of his poems Tirujnana Sambandar represents God as revealing justice. This is figuratively expressed by the image of God riding on a bull, whereby the bull represents justice. It is also mentioned that God does not choose a horse or an ornamental elephant as His vehicle. He rides only on the bull. This reaffirms the fact that God reveals and supports justice. This also implies that we can reach God only through righteousness. We cannot bypass righteousness and reach the feet of God.

God, who is just, is also characterized by compassion. Cruel things are done in the name of justice. In Saiva mythology Siva gives half of His body to His consort Uma, who represents mercy or compassion. Justice is the primary character of God. According to Saivism true justice finds fulfillment in compassion or mercy.

Ecology

Saiva temples had their origin under the shade of trees. In Kanchepuram the Siva temple must have begun with a linga under a mango tree. In the Madurai Meenakshi temple complex, the beginning of the Siva temple is the linga under the Kadamba tree. In the same way we can trace the history of all Saiva temples to their natural background. Temple gardens are important in Saiva temples. It is a tradition in the temple to use only flowers taken from the temple garden. The temple tanks are also necessary and water from this tank is to be used for temple purposes. The devotees are also required to wash their hands, feet and body before worshipping God. Thus, taking care of nature is one of the main concerns of Saivism.

Status of Women

Women are the protectors of the Saiva religion. Karaikkal Ammayar is one of the chief of the Saiva saints in enunciating the way of devotion. Among the images of sixty-three saints, Karayakkal Ammayar is the only one who has the privilege of being represented in a sitting position. Her decad of poems is called 'The First Decad', implying that she is the foremost leader among the Saiva saints. With regard to music too, she is one of the important people who made use of music for the propagation of devotion. We may say that the present day carnatic music is the gift of Karaikkal Ammayar's poems. In the case of Appar, one of the four important saints of Saivism, it was his sister Thilakavathiar who was responsible for his spiritual development. Thus women are the staunch supporters of Saivism even today.

Conclusion

The grace of God, human beings as the makers of their own destiny—these are some of the common points between liberation theology as explained by Christian philosophers and the philosophy as explained by the Saiva philosophers. Christian philosophers think that the appropriate way to change oppressive structures in society is to make use of scriptural paradigms. In South India Swami Agnivesh and Kundrakudi Adigalar are attempting to change oppressive structures. The result depends on the responses to these saints effected by the common people. We have not yet achieved that aim. We believe that by the grace of God we are moving towards the goal of removing the oppressive structures of our society, ensuring the total liberation of human beings. Because God has created the world out of love, people should love God and the creation he has made and therefore become reconciled with one another and their natural environment.

It is said that God is both just and at the same time compassionate. Insofar as his justice requires that he punishes wrongdoing, the question arises as to how that is compatible with his compassion. How can a compassionate or merciful God also be strict and impartial in administering justice? God's compassion is conveyed by such descriptions as the help of the helpless, i.e., *arravarku arra Sivam*. Siva himself has no support. He has no father or mother. But he is the father and mother of all and sees to their spiritual welfare. His merciful nature is also represented by the depiction of Siva as united with *sakti* in a single figure, half male and half female.

Siva is also represented as riding on a bull. This signifies that he regulates what happens to each individual with impartial justice, according to their *karma*.

Siva is also represented as riding on a bull. This signifies that he regulates what happens to each individual with impartial justice, according to their *karma*. How they respond to their experiences is not determined but lies within the responsibility of each person. Because Siva regulates the operation of *karma*, he is the embodiment of justice.

The operation of *karma* and compassion come together in the following way. When, in his present life, an individual acts consistently with a sense of responsibility, the Lord in his compassion will annul not only the *karma* pertaining to this birth but all the *karmas* accumulated from previous births as well, however much that may be. In this way God is seen to act with compassion, without transgressing the requirements of his justice.

Bibliography

Clothey Fred W. and J. Bruce Long (eds). (1983). *Experiencing Siva*. Lucknow: South Asia Books.
Devasenapathi, V.A. (1966). *Saiva Siddhantha*. Madras: University of Madras.
Lohfink, Norbert F. SJ. (1987). *Option for the Poor*. Berkeley: Bibal Press.
Mahadevan T.M.P. (1974). *An Invitation to Indian Philosophy*. New Delhi: Arnold-Heinmann Publishers.
Santa Ana, Julio D. (ed.) (1975). *To Break the Chains of Oppression*. Geneva: WCC.
Sarvarpalli Radhakrishnan and Charles A. Moore (eds) (1967). *A Source Book in Indian Philosophy*. Princeton: Princeton University Press.
Sivaraman K. (1973). *Saivism in Philosophical Perspective*. New Delhi: Motilal Banarsidas.
Tirujnana Samabandar, Appar and Sundarar. (1953). *Tevaram Adangan Murai*. Madras: Saiva Siddhantha samajam.
Tirumular. (1976). *Tirumandiram*. Tiruvavaduturai Adhinam.

Divided Families and Social Conflict

Comparing a Greek Tragedy and an Indian Drama

Lourens Minnema

Introduction

"Let us be reconciled! Are we not all members of one united human family?" The idea of 'a united human family' is a pleasing thought for its speculative users. But is the idea very helpful when it comes to solving social conflicts? Do its users take the historical roots of this idea into account? Were similar ideas already prevalent in the classical literature of Greece and India? These are some of the issues which should be raised before embracing a utopian idea like 'one united human family'. One way of pointing out the problematic character of this idea would be to compare two classical narratives which have been and still are considered full of philosophical implications by Western and Indian philosophy. From the Western tradition I have chosen Aeschylus' *Seven against Thebes,* one of the Greek tragedies, a genre which is taken seriously by pre-Christian and post-Christian philosophy; from the Indian tradition I have chosen the *Bhagavadgita*. I shall be focussing on these classical narratives dealing with social conflict in order to raise two critical questions directed at contemporary users of the concept of 'a united human family'. My aim is to stimulate a specified use of this notion instead of a speculative one.

The Plots of the Narratives

In the chapters of the *Mahabharata* preceding the chapters which constitute the *Bhagavadgita* the conflict between two related clans claiming their right of succession to the same throne has escalated, so much so that a 'civil war' has become inevitable. The two armies are already in place on the battlefield in the first chapter of the *Gita*. This battlefield of the Kurus is called the "field of *dharma*" or "of righteousness." This qualification interprets the battle as the universal battle between good and evil, between the just and the unjust. The Kaurava clan, led by its king Duryodhana, are the unjust, because they have cheated during the dicing game with Yudhisthira, the noble king of the Pandava clan who is nevertheless too weak to protect his kingdom and family from falling into the hands of Duryodhana whose lust for power has proven to be uncompromising and inconsiderate of the consequences for others. Both the villain Duryodhana and his opponent on the battlefield, the noble hero Arjuna, have received the support of their negotiator Krishna, a neighboring king of Dwaraka: Duryodhana has been given the support of Krishna's army, while Arjuna enjoys the advice of Krishna as his personal charioteer, friend, counsellor and teacher. Just when the two armies are about to start fighting, Arjuna takes up a position between them and surveys the situation. Realizing that relatives, teachers, and friends on both sides will be the victims of this morally ambiguous and disastrous slaughter and that he himself will have to kill some of his own family members and teachers, Arjuna suddenly becomes so distressed and depressed that he refuses to fight. Krishna, however, tries to persuade him to fight by arguing mainly that it is Arjuna's caste duty as a warrior to do so and, above all, that, cosmically speaking, Arjuna's immortal self can neither die nor be killed but is identical to the supreme Self. Eventually, Krishna convinces him by revealing himself as the supreme Self of the universe and by pointing out that a cosmic and therefore inevitable fate is about to take its course according to Krishna's plans. Arjuna is expected to act in accordance with his duty but to do so in a detached way, through knowledge of and devotion to the supreme Self.

The classic Greek playwright Aeschylus wrote a tragedy called *Seven against Thebes*. Its dramatic plot contains elements which are comparable to important elements in the dramatic plot of the *Bhagavadgita*. Two armies oppose each other. The leader of the attacking army, Polynices, king of Argos, is the brother of the leader of the defending army, Eteocles, king of Thebes. Having already selected six other Theban army commanders to oppose six of the seven army commanders at the city gates, Eteocles suddenly finds out that the seventh opponent is his very own brother. He cries out, lamenting the curse upon his family (ll. 653-55). Eteocles and Polynices are the two sons of Oedipus, king of Thebes, who killed his father Laius and married his mother Jocasta.

According to William G. Thalmann (1978), this moment constitutes the pivotal turning point of the dramatic plot. The central shield scene (ll. 369-76) paves the way for the shift from the first section centred on the city's survival, to the third section centred on the family's destruction, from the war between two cities to the fratricidal conflict between two brothers.

> The danger to Thebes comes not only, and not even originally, from the foreign army, but from within her own ruling house. Eteocles and Polynices are heirs not merely to civil power but to a curse which afflicts their family. ... The general movement of the *Seven* is toward a restoration of equilibrium in the context of the city. That is accomplished by the narrowing of the conflict *from* war between Argos and Thebes *through* the fight at the city gates between the Argive chiefs and the Theban champions *to* the climactic fratricidal duel between the two brothers. *The Seven Against Thebes*, then ... portrays the effect

of a family curse and thereby examines the problem of inherited guilt. (Thalmann 1978: 7)[1]

Again, he writes:

... in spite of the most energetic and well-intentioned efforts to the contrary, *the curse will be fulfilled*. Not only the sudden break, but the ring composition itself stresses the change. ... In the first epirrhematic scene, the chorus are in panic and Eteocles attempts to calm them. In the second, these roles are reversed: Eteocles is seized by a kind of mad desire, and the chorus, though themselves still agitated, try to dissuade him. ... In the first stasimon, the chorus fear for the city and for themselves. In the second stasimon, the concern has largely shifted, and narrowed, from the city to its ruling family. (Thalmann 27-28)

Thalmann continues: "the battle *in itself* does not matter very much, for it is the result—the outward manifestation only—of the curse" (Thalmann 1978: 29) and "The movement from the first section of the play to the third is not so much toward a change in circumstances as toward a recognition of the situation for what it really is" (Thalmann 1978: 30). The shield scene presents the decisive moment of insight into what is actually happening: faced with a family curse instead of an enemy attack, Eteocles can only let the situation take control of him.

According to Thalmann, the play is about Eteocles bearing the burden of inherited guilt, not about Eteocles assuming personal responsibility for the duel and the working out of the curse, even if the chorus calls his eagerness to fight his brother a savage desire (Thalmann 1978: 148).[2] Martha C. Nussbaum does not agree:

---

[1] Thalmann 1978: 1: "... Aeschylus's treatment of the myth of the house of Laius ... revealed the progress toward fulfillment of an inherited curse. This fundamental, organizing pattern may, in the last analysis, be called the plot of the Theban trilogy. The dramatic *praxis* was the suffering of three successive generations because of the curse. Cf. also p. 59: "... the more comprehensive theme of madness ... is used in the play to link all the stages of the family curse.... Laius's error was due to *atè* resulting from the curse. Oedipus in turn was in a rage when he cursed Eteocles and Polynices .... The madness of war is but an external sign of a mental imbalance within this family which has infected the whole city.

[2] Cf. Hutchinson 1985: 149-50: "Eteocles is decided at once, and does not waver .... To ask about his freedom of choice is to ask about the causes which maintain him in his resolve. He is assuredly impelled by the Erinys, and in that sense he has no freedom. But the question does not seem fruitful. Eteocles is not insane like Heracles.... The Erinys works both against and through his real personality, a personality which is vividly felt in this scene. We watch the interaction of the human and the divine, not so much intrigued by the philosophy as compelled by the fact.

... he now discovers that the seventh opponent is this same brother. At first he cries out, lamenting the curse upon his family (lines 653-5). He then pulls himself up short, declaring that "it is not fitting to weep or grieve" (line 656): for against this brother's unjust violence he will station an appropriate champion, himself: "... Leader against leader, brother against brother, foe against foe, I shall stand against him...." This reasoning looks peculiar: the category of brother does not seem to work the way the other two do, towards justifying Eteocles' decision. He appears to be missing something if he feels no pull in the opposite direction, no tension between his civic and military obligations and his duties as a brother. (Nussbaum 1986: 38)

Nussbaum points to the fact that tragedy is not only about making decisions but also about "how it *feels* to be in that situation" (Nussbaum 1986: 32):

Tears, and not the refusal of tears, would appear to be the more appropriate response.... The Chorus of Theban women, themselves mothers of families, feel this strangeness, reproaching their king not so much for his decision—or at any rate not only for his decision—but, far more, for the responses and feelings with which he approaches the chosen action.... Eteocles, having already shifted, like Agamemnon, from horror to confidence, now replies with an Agamemnon-like inference: "Since it is clear that the situation is controlled by a god, it is appropriate to go quickly" (lines 689-90). Constraint gives license to eagerness. Again the women respond by blaming his enthusiasm: "Too ravenous is the desire (*himeros*) that goads you on to accomplish a man-killing that bears bitter fruit, shedding blood not to be shed" (lines 692-4). Eteocles' reply grants that he does indeed feel a passionate desire for fratricide ... he simply tries to explain the desire's origin. (Nussbaum 1986: 38-39).

Eteocles blames the desire on the workings of his father's "dark curse." The chorus does not accept this as exonerating Eteocles from responsibility for the desire. For they immediately reply: "But still, don't *you* stir yourself up" (l. 697).

From the perspective of Nussbaum, Eteocles should be blamed and is blamed by the Chorus for his fratricidal passion, like Agamemnon at Aulis. Bernard Williams argues that her reading is a moralistic distortion: "rather than telling him what [Agamemnon] should have felt, we should be prepared to learn what was involved in getting through it" (Williams 1994: 135).

The scene in the ... play, *Seven against Thebes* ... is sometimes called the Decision of Eteocles, but it does not in fact present a decision: Eteocles knows from the beginning that he is going to face his brother at the last of the seven gates and kill him. He recognises, too, that all this is coming about because of the curse that Oedipus laid upon them. What he does is to resist the Chorus's attempt to dissuade him, and in the course of that he comes to a better understanding of the reasons there are for facing his brother: justice, shame, honor. He also recognises a rising passion of destructive anger and understands that this itself is a result of his father's curse. The Chorus tells him that he need not, all the same, press forward, and makes various attempts to persuade him not to go to the battle, their final words being "Do you want to shed the blood of your own brother?" To this Eteocles replies with his last words in the play: "When the gods decree it, you may not escape evil" (718-19). Eteocles' growing consciousness of the curse, of his situation and his reasons, and his refusal to take what he sees as a cowardly retreat perhaps do earn him the title that he has been given of 'der erste "tragische" Mensch der Weltdichtung.' But ... there is some obscurity in the relations of Eteocles' *ethos* to his *daimon*. The difficulty does not lie between the inner and the outer, between Eteocles, other motivations and the external force of Oedipus's curse: there is no inherent problem in that. It is to be found rather in his recognising this necessity, and the way in which his recognising it affects his motivation. How are we to read his last line? It seems to express a recognition of that necessity. At the same time, it might be taken to express a reason for his decision to go out and fight. But if that is what it does, there is a puzzle about what exactly his decision can be.... In fact, this obscurity is not forced on us by what Eteocles says. His words need not be read as involving immediate fatalism, because they need not be taken to present the gods' necessity as itself one of Eteocles' reasons. He has given his reasons; what he last expresses is the necessity of the situation in which these must be his reasons. The working of supernatural necessity does not in general involve immediate fatalism or anything like it. Sometimes, as in Agamemnon's case (and on the suggested reading, Eteocles' is similar), the necessity presents itself to the agent as having produced the circumstances in which he must act, and he decides in the light of those circumstances. In other cases it shapes events without presenting itself at all. (Williams 1994: 136-37, 139)

The Moral Dilemma

As in the *Bhagavadgita*, the issue at stake in the *Seven against Thebes* is, in the first instance, a conflict of loyalties which poses a moral dilemma: the simultaneous necessity and impossibility of choosing between the family code not to kill a relative and the warrior code not to neglect one's duty. Eteocles faces the same dilemma as Arjuna does in the *Bhagavadgita*. Whereas Eteocles is struck by the necessity of acting, Arjuna is struck by the impossibility of acting. Their spontaneous response is exactly the opposite: Eteocles is eager to fight, whereas Arjuna is eager not to fight. In both cases, this spontaneous eagerness is considered too strong an emotional response. Eteocles, in the opinion of the Chorus, should recover from his madness and respect the family values, whereas Arjuna, in the opinion of Krishna, should recover from his depression and honor the warrior values.

The arguments brought forward by the Chorus to convince Eteocles are very different from those Krishna advances to convince Arjuna. This difference relates primarily to their respective roles. The relationship between Eteocles and the Chorus is, from the perspective of Eteocles, a relationship between the king and the people whose security he is obliged to guarantee; from the point of view of the Chorus, it is a human relationship between emotional beings sharing the same basic family values. The relationship between Arjuna and Krishna is, from the point of view of Arjuna, a relationship between a pupil and his teacher, whereas for Krishna, it is also a relationship between a human being and God. Arguments among humans are open to dispute, arguments of divine teachers addressing human pupils are not, in principle, open to debate, at least not the decisive ones. In fact, this is precisely one of the arguments Eteocles uses against the Chorus: one cannot go against the gods. In Eteocles' view, there is no room for choice or debate with the Chorus, since the gods have already decided otherwise. The gods, having cursed his family, plead guilty anyway. The Chorus does not take this view as a religious insight but as an unconvincing excuse to cover up an evil desire. It insists that the actual debate is not with the gods but with the Chorus and that it is, more particularly, about the difference between sane and pure feelings of brotherhood over against an insane and impure desire to kill without consideration for 'significant others'. In both cases, the Greek gods—aside from the Erinys, Apollo and Ares especially (Thalmann 1978: 54-55)—are not part of the solution of how to act but part of the problem.

In the *Bhagavadgita* Lord Krishna is the ultimate solution of how to act. According to Angelika Malinar, Krishna represents ideal kingship and teaches it to Arjuna as an alternative to both ascetic renunciation and unrestrained rulership. Unrestrained rulership is represented by Duryodhana (in the Udyogaparvan) who sacrifices family ties to self-interest in power by force. Since Krishna advocates sacrificing the family ties to the warrior's duty of exercising authority by the use of force, the illegitimacy of Duryodhana's position is all but self-evident. Duryodhana claims that his traditional role of royal performer of the ritual sacrifice automatically bestows upon him the authority of the gods, and it is the warrior's duty to stick to his consecrated task of defending his territory by all means. Uncompromising steadfastness, after all, is the prime value of a warrior (Malinar 1996: 77-78), and the one value Arjuna fails to display. Arjuna's argument that the goal of warriorship does not make sense if the means of war destroys the very family to which it is supposed to offer the fruits of victory and that this insight should lead to a peaceful refusal to engage actively in war comes close to embracing institutional asceticism (abstaining from all [ritual] action by becoming an ascetic). Indifference is not necessarily the alternative to Duryodhana's warrior value of steadfastness or to Arjuna's fairly ascetic value of renunciation, because indifference concerning the outcome of the war is an ambiguous value which can express both Duryodhana's self-interest without consideration for others or for his own life and the disinterest of heroes and ascetics. The *Bhagavadgita*, moreover, implicitly disqualifies Duryodhana's self-interest as a form of blindness and explicitly disqualifies Arjuna's disinterest as a form of confusion. Neither of them links action to knowledge in the proper way, neither of them escapes the problem of guilt. Neither of them succeeds in distancing himself from the entanglement of his (immortal) self with the result of his (temporal) actions. Action is linked up with blindness or confusion because it is linked up with desire. Similarly, in the case of Eteocles, action is linked up with rage because of his claim that it is driven by his father's curse (or by a recognition of the cruel inevitability of having to commit a crime). One seemingly crucial (but ultimately not decisive) value both *Seven against Thebes* and the *Bhagavadgita* propose as an alternative, according to Hutchinson and Malinar respectively, is self-restraint or self-control. This interpretation requires closer investigation.

According to G.O. Hutchinson (1985: 148-49), Eteocles' resolve contains three aspects: mad desire (l. 715), a warrior's honor (l. 717), and resignation (l. 719). A fratricidal act is morally worse than feelings of shame at being thought a coward. Eteocles' utterances are so written as to demonstrate that his decision is wrong. He maintains a tone of self-control by referring to external causes such as divine power, the curse, and a warrior's duty to fight. He attempts to minimize the *daimon* that is raging in him by rationally defending his irrational decision. Contrary to Eteocles' rational and resolute character and contrary to his presentation of the matter—the audience sees him as a man driven by a furious desire. His natural self-control is horribly distorted. In the first section of the play, Eteocles was rendered distinctive by his contempt for wild emotion, by his own self-control and by his warm admiration for moral excellence, whereas the boasting Argives and Polynices are presented as eager for blood, war and destruction (Hutchinson 1985: XXXV). Eteocles' comparative self-control now partly covers furious passion, whereas the passion and horror of the Chorus are now not irrational (as in the first section) but proper and right. It is Eteocles' suppression of these feelings of horror (ll. 656f., 696) which is irrational and wrong. The moral contrast, for that matter, between Eteocles and his wicked brother Polynices, who falsely claims to act rightly and in accordance with the will of the gods, is not simply annulled: Eteocles is still right in his morally sincere and legitimate determination to defend the city.

John Gibert offers a different framework of interpretation:

> Aeschylus established the pattern with some of his principal characters, for whom the straight path leading to decision (if it should be called by that name) includes at most a little hesitation. The ordeal, however, continues in the moment *after* the character's course has been irretrievably set. The feeling which now comes to the fore is not guilt or regret, but something more like full awareness (in each character's case for the first time in the play) of the rejected alternative. In the report of the chorus (*Agamemnon* 184-257), Agamemnon is swept away by the horror of killing his daughter and never again capable of sound thinking (220-1: *tothen to pantotolmon phronein metegnoo*). Clytemnestra realizes that she has been an instrument of the curse on the house of Atreus and apparently fears its continued effects (*Agamemnon* 1448-1576). Eteocles seems, to the chorus at least, to go completely mad, and he also recognizes the working of his father's curse (*Seven Against Thebes* 653-719). (Gibert 1995: 29)

Williams, as we saw above, stresses Eteocles' capacity for recognizing necessity and for attuning his reasons accordingly; Eteocles does not become mad but furious. Self-control is not the issue; recognition of necessity is.

The *Bhagavadgita,* according to Malinar, draws its notion of self-restraint from the yogic concept of physical and spiritual self-discipline in combination with the samkhyistic concept of cosmic self-acting nature (*prakrti*). The real enemy in the war appears to be one's own desire, that is to say, the desire to relate to the fruits of one's actions as if these are the desirable fruits of one's desirous actions. Arjuna should come to realize that he is not the real agent of his actions, but that cosmic nature itself is acting through his actions, regardless of what Arjuna does or intends to do. This cosmic activity is thought of as a cosmic sacrificial process in the sense that the energy spent is necessary to guarantee the maintenance of the metabolic universe. Participation in this cosmic sacrifice would imply active participation in its purpose of upholding the universe while dissociating oneself from the self-interested desire to relate to the results of one's actions. This is exactly what Krishna is doing as the legitimate (dharmic) and independent (yogic) Lord of the universe. He reveals himself to Arjuna as the ideal self-restrained ruler upholding the universe by acting purposefully according to his royal duty without desiring any personal gain (results) from his sacrificial activity. Devoting one's actions to this self-detached king of the universe becomes the purest and most liberating duty a human being can fulfill. Dispassionate self-discipline benefitting the well-being of the community (*lokasamgraha*) becomes a core value of the warrior code. The conflict of loyalties (between the *kuladharma,* family duties, of a relative and the *svadharma,* caste duties, of a warrior) is transcended by being loyal to the one legitimate ruler of the universe.

In one respect, Malinar's approach to the *Gita* is fairly problematic. In a personal comment Jan Heesterman writes:

> I do not entirely agree with Angelika Malinar. Krishna is not the ideal king. One may even wonder whether India knows such an ideal king. Even Rāma was, as a king, not able to be ideal. More than elsewhere, in Indian civilisation kingship is dubious. A king, that is, lacks transcendent authority because he is and is supposed to be fully worldly. Krishna, however, is both above and outside the cosmos, and simultaneously encompasses the cosmos—a form of doing the splits of which only he, not the king, no matter how ideal, is capable.

Chakravarti Ram-Prasad comments similarly:

> Malinar's view of Krishna as the ideal king is highly problematic. First, there is the larger question of the very centrality of kingship in classical Indian thought, with mainly Western writers over-stressing it (as if kingship were not to a certain extent important to practically all pre-modern Christian culture). But even if we set that aside, Krishna is not to be so easily ascribed ideal kingship—compared to Rama; and this is certainly so within the tradition. His origins are as a princeling of a small state; his primary base, even after the establishment of a city-state in Dvaraka, is in the lowly cowherd clan of Yada-

vas; at no time does his formal intervention in the affairs of the cousins amount to royal action; it is as emissary, as cousin to both parties, and, elusively, as a transcendental presence, that he appears in the Mahabharata.

Similarity

A comparison of the two narratives reveals several similarities and differences, two of which I would like to reflect on briefly. The first point of comparison is a similarity: in both cases, there is no actual[3] return to the traditional family code or to family values as such. In the case of *Seven against Thebes*, the price paid for saving the city is the destruction of the family through the violation of the family code. Not Eteocles but the Chorus, that is to say, non-kin, defends the kinship system and its value of basic solidarity. In doing so, the members of the Chorus not only undermine their self-interest in a political system which protects its citizens regardless of family ties. They also empathize and sympathize with Eteocles in his capacity as the close relative of Polynices, thereby themselves crossing the border between kin and non-kin. Empathy and sympathy become values which transcend the limits of family solidarity.

In the case of the *Bhagavadgita*, there is no return to the traditional family code either. According to Malinar and von Stietencron (Malinar 1996: 2-3, 69, 86), Duryodhana represents a new concept of power and rulership which is based on territory instead of family. The traditional kinship system of government by ruling royal families is replaced by territorially based centralized states. This new development had started in the fourth century B.C.E. in Magadha, following the Persian example of the Achaemenides. Politically speaking, a kingship based on external expansion was much more powerful than its predecessors as long as it focussed on external enemies. The unrestrained urge for expansion brought about a moral crisis, however, as to the kingship's legitimacy. At the latest, this crisis must have occurred when the expansion turned inwards. Self-restraint and self-detachment were now proclaimed the new warrior values which could transcend the new habits of unrestrained rulers without returning to the old family values of a ruling family system. According to Romila Thapar, in the case of lineage systems, authority is based on genealogical relationships (Thapar 1984: 10).

> Political stability often lies in the open frontier which makes migration possible so that tensions within the clans can be eased by the migration of some. Territorial sovereignty or the delineation of boundaries do not play a central role. Lineage becomes the legal sanction. (Thapar 1984: 11)

> Variations in forms of government are recognized both in the differentiation between monarchies and chiefdoms as also within the latter category. The possibilities of alternatives may account in part for the insistence on kingship as the

---

[3] A distinction should be made between the propagated or implicit message and the cultural meaning of the ways in which the drama actually unfolds and functions.

DIVIDED FAMILIES AND SOCIAL CONFLICT   77

legitimate form of government in the *rājadharma* sections of the Manu *Dharmaśāstra* and the *Mahābhārata* which date to the period after the establishment of the state. (Thapar 1984: 116)

The breaking away of the segment of the clan was possible if there was enough land and other resources available in the vicinity. With the increase in numbers of *gana-sanghas* and kingdoms this became more difficult since in the case of the latter erstwhile frontier zones would have been claimed, protected and defended. The need to expand access to resources both in terms of fertile land and busy trade routes encouraged the conquest of neighbours. But the conquest of neighbours was through a systematic campaign as that between Magadha and the Vrjji confederacy, and not through sporadic raids.... Whereas the lineage system profited by intermittent raids and warfare the state system required a limitation on locations given to warfare—the fields of battles and of campaigns —with a substantial area of stability and peace. This was necessary to prevent the disruption of agriculture and trade. Neighbours were therefore envisaged in a network of either hostile or friendly alliances .... (Thapar 1984: 129)

Many of the narrative sections of the *Mahābhārata* represent the period just prior to the emergence of state systems.... Political institutions are as much kin-based as social relationships, the major ritual remains the *yajña* in various forms, and a pastoral-cum-agrarian economy is evident, with an emphasis on clan holdings rather than the breaking up of land into private holdings. The succession of the Kuru realm is among the *rājanya* lineages and this is firmly maintained even though neither of the contenders are [*sic*] actually related by blood to the Kuru lineage. The genealogical ... lineage links were regarded as essential to the narrative.... Post-Vedic society is clearly depicted in the didactic sections of the text where the existence of the state is taken for granted [and] monarchy is described as the ideal system .... A characteristic of lineage society which is noticeable in the *Mahābhārata* is the resort to migration to ease tension and conflict, particularly in relation to political power. Thus the Pāndavas build a new capital at Indraprastha .... In terms of the confrontation between non-state and state system, the *Rāmāyana* encapsulates the conflict more clearly and is essentially a statement in favour of the monarchical state. (Thapar 1984: 132-33).

What might have been an inter-tribal conflict over succession takes on the dimensions of the end of an epoch. This is precisely what it is; the end of the epoch of *kshatriya* chiefships .... The intrinsic sorrow of the battle at Kurukshetra is not merely at the death of kinsmen but also at the dying of a society, a style, a political form. The concept of the present as Kali-yuga combines a romanticization of the earlier society with the sense of insecurity born of a changing system .... (Thapar 1984: 140-41)

In my view, it is within the epic genre in general and tragic reinterpretations of epic narratives in particular that the history of world literature reveals a sociopolitical and moral shift from kinship systems of government to non-kinship systems, crossing the borderline of the family as the basic organizational form of society. The epic genre contains many stories about ruling families trying to cope with infighting because of rival claims to succession to the throne: for example, the story of the rivalry between Yudhisthira, the lawful successor living in exile, and his cousin Duryodhana, the unlawful king in the *Mahabharata* epic or the story of the rivalry between Sunjata, the lawful successor living in exile, and his half-brother Dankarantuma, the unlawful king in the West African *Sunjata* epic. As its underlying critical message, the ruling family as the main political institution is often depicted as the main source of political and moral instability, not just incidentally but structurally, although not necessarily intentionally. Besides, the 'disunited family' can simply be a subject which functions as a very helpful narrative ploy for developing a convincing plot, as in the Germanic *Nibelungenlied*. One should keep the difference between history and legendary myth in mind and, likewise, the legitimizing function of epics for certain dynasties. However, where the borderline between kinship systems and non-kinship systems is actually crossed, the family code is still considered a primary source of norms and values, although it is not restored as such. Instead, the family has become too extended a network to unite the state and the state has come to encompass too many territories and citizens to communicate a natural feeling of basic unity. This process of increase in scale, complexity and differentiation had an impact on power concepts and feelings of solidarity alike. Eli Sagan, who demonstrates the transformation process from "band society" (kinship) into "complex society" (state) in Buganda, Tonga, Tahiti and Hawaii, records:

> We see how fragile, how dependent on individual leadership the centralized state in complex societies was. Dissolution was an ever-present possibility. Although the centralized state was an invention of advanced complex societies, a stable state, one in which the possibility of dissolution was remote, was another, equally difficult achievement, one beyond the power of most complex societies. ... We are talking of an expansiveness of ideas and feelings. The feeling of pathos, for instance, is crucial to all great epic poetry. In Homer's *Iliad* this feeling ripens because we care for both sides of the war. Homer, in fact, takes no sides. (Sagan 1985/1986: 80-81)[4]

The transition from family structures organizing the state into broader non-kinship structures was accompanied by an extension and transformation of family values into broader sociopolitical values. However—and this is the first point I would like to make—these advanced complex societies were not as advanced as our global society. And if the epic and tragic poetry of classical Greece and India marked a crucial transition, it did so without proclaiming all human beings on earth to be full members of the same united human family. One wonders, then,

---

[4] Cf. Thapar 1984: 62: "The fear of anarchy is frequently alluded to which is not surprising in a society moving towards complex stratification." On Odysseus' pity of Ajax, see Williams 1994: 72.

to what extent it would be helpful to turn to the notion of the family when faced with social conflicts on a global scale. In the past, the notion was not necessarily a very helpful one in solving real conflicts precisely because the notion meant something specific. Instead, such a humanist appeal to unity among humans in general is likely to come into conflict with the notion of the family. Varadaraja V. Raman comments:

> Clearly, the humanist attitude is neither new, nor confined to a particular civilization. This is not surprising since humanism is an expression of the natural affinity of human beings, an intra-species bond which tends to become hazy and weakened when local affiliations are formed, only because these latter provide the security that comes from closeness and family ties. (Unpublished conference paper)

Difference

The second point of comparison between the two narratives is difference with regard to the solution to the social conflict.

In the Greek case, the conflict between the two brothers is, in the play itself, explicitly interpreted in terms of division, arbitration, and reconciliation but in a tragic sense. It is presented as a dispute over property claims asserting one's right of inheritance. The real inheritance, however, turns out to be their father's curse. The process of allotment is used as an image for the duel between the two brothers but in accordance with their father's curse (Thalmann 1978: 62-79). The lot suggests an arbiter. At the climax of the conflict this informal mediator appears to be the iron of the brothers' swords. This iron is called a "resolver of quarrels" (l. 941) and is associated with Ares, the god of war. "The purpose of the lot should be to apportion the property; indeed, the word for 'arbiter' used in the *Seven*, *datètès* (line 945), literally means 'one who divides'." (Thalmann 1978: 75). The division which results is not one of property, as would be expected, but of the brothers' bodies: they are pierced by the sword. The iron, in the capacity of arbiter, performs its particular kind of division, of equitable distribution. The brothers have been "conciliated with the aid of iron" (*dièllachthe*, ll. 884-85; cf. l. 767), and Ares is called a "reconciler" (*diallaktèr*, l. 908). He accomplishes a tragic reconciliation of sorts when the brothers are united in death, sharing the same piece of land: a common grave (ll. 937-39). 'Death' is their 'share', their 'fate'—three meanings of the same Greek word: *moira*.

Yet, the use of violence has not brought about a real solution because, in the meantime, the emotional ties and Eteocles' emotional incapacity to deal with these ties have become the real problem, while reason has become increasingly incapable of guiding the emotions. The social conflict turns into an inner conflict. Emotions become the problem, and reason offers no solution. Worse still, there is no solution. Instead, Eteocles' simultaneous need and inability to face his situation emotionally (and to act accordingly) is emphasized. To 'face' one's situation 'emotionally' means: to see, to know one's situation by turning to one's feelings as a legitimate source of knowledge.[5] This is a legitimate source of knowledge, it is true, but, I would add, not just of one's situation and role but of the human condition in general as being ineluctably finite, as being inescapably mortal. In the final analysis, radical finitude and mortality are emotionally recognized as the common fate of all human beings. That does not sound like a solution. But it is this emotional recognition which, in fact, enables breakthroughs in solving social conflicts. Not the ability to defend 'the united human family' but an emotional recognition of the human inability to do so can unite the human family. This is exactly what takes place in Homer's *Iliad*, when Achilles and Priam become reconciled (cf. Redfield 1994: 214-18). A similar sense of loss generates a sense of shared suffering and of shared vulnerability; this disarming recognition of a common weakness generates a much greater willingness to compromise and to be reconciled than a position of strength and gain. In general, thus, the decisive value enabling a breakthrough in the tragic conflict is a shared knowledge of one's own and the other's human finitude and mortality. There is no solution to the social conflict without consciously realizing the depth of the inner conflict.

The *Bhagavadgita* offers a very different concept of mortality and a fairly different solution to the conflict. The use of violence does not bring about the solution in the Indian case either. The real problem consists of Arjuna's desire not to act and his confusion on how to act. Krishna reminds Arjuna of the immortal-

---

[5] According to Nussbaum, Eteocles has made it his lifelong aim to dissociate himself, in imagination and feeling, from the family that bore him, regarding himself first and foremost as a citizen. He speaks of his fellow citizens as direct descendants of mother Earth, without biological parents. "If he is able to solve the dilemma of brother-killing without pain, it is because he has resolutely refused to acknowledge the existence of families and their importance in human life. Consistency in conflict is bought at the price of self-deception" (Nussbaum 1986: 39). (Thalmann (1978: 42-50) offers a different interpretation of the Earth imagery but would agree with the tenor of Nussbaum's argument (see p. 49).) The Chorus blame Eteocles for wanting to see and feel only one part of the social conflict. Allowing these feelings would turn the experience of suffering into a source of knowledge, of understanding the social conflict more fully, of acknowledging that there is no way out, and of recognizing that the best the agent can do is to bear his suffering as the natural expression of his goodness of character (Nussbaum 1986: 45-50). Aeschylus does not offer a solution to the conflict but "has indicated to us that the only thing remotely like a solution here is, in fact, to describe and see the conflict clearly and to acknowledge that there is no way out ... and to think about his case as showing a possibility for human life in general" (Nussbaum 1986: 49-50). Secondly, Aeschylus shows us that the pain and remorse resulting from our commitments are part and parcel of human goodness itself: "If we were such that we could in a crisis dissociate ourselves from one commitment because it clashed with another, we would be less good" (Nussbaum 1986: 50). Nussbaum's interpretation of Agamemnon is criticized by Williams (1994: 134-35).

ity of the self and identifies his individual self or soul (*atman*) with the eternal Self ruling the universe. This argument of Krishna is not open to debate,[6] whereas warrior values are freely debatable. Mortality is intrinsically bound up with differentiation and individualization. Inasmuch as the individual soul is individual, personal, specific, it is mortal or, rather, it becomes mortal. The process of individualization acting upon the eternal self moulds its form, not its character. Its character remains immortal but, the more the self takes shape, the more mortal its manifestation becomes. 'Being born' does not mean 'becoming mortal' but 'becoming even more mortal than the subtle body of the endlessly wandering soul has become already before entering the coarse material body.' The soul itself is only immortal to the extent that it remains in contact with *Brahman* outside the cycle of lives, deaths, and rebirths. This contact takes the form of absolute knowledge or yoga liberating the *atman* from mortality, that is, from individuality. Arjuna is taught not to identify with his family nor with the social conflict as such but, instead, to concentrate on the inner conflict between his mortal feelings of desire and the immortal Individuator[7] acting out his universal program of destroying and renewing the universe. Feelings are a source of ignorance and blindness, not of absolute knowledge. The real enemy in the war appears to be not one's own desire but one's own ignorance. Accepting the human condition means accepting the fate of the universe by distancing oneself from one's individual or family goals while simultaneously devoting oneself to the Lord of the universe by doing one's social duty. The decisive value enabling a breakthrough in the conflict is not self-constraint but self-knowledge, i.e., knowledge of one's own immortal self. In the final analysis, radical infinity and immortality are spiritually realized as the common destiny of all human beings. That sounds like the ultimate solution. But is the Hindu concept a solution for the Greeks if the Greek concept explicitly excludes immortality as part of the solution while the Hindu description of self-knowledge disqualifies Greek self-knowledge as a form of ignorance? How should one—and that would be my second point—unite or reconcile two fundamentally different or even conflicting ideas of a united human family?

Aeschylus' tragedies had come to represent 'classical' Greek culture almost immediately in the third century B.C.E when Hellenism in Alexandria decided to codify the memorable past (Assman 1992: 277-80) and all the more so when Romanticism turned to tragic heroes with whom the upper bourgeoisie could identify (Schlaffer 1973). The *Gita*, however, did not emerge as significant even to brahminical commentators until 700-800 years later and was not a powerful

---

[6] I am indebted to my colleague Corstiaan van der Burg for this insight, which he conveyed to me personally.

[7] The term 'Individuator' is proposed by Ramesh N. Patel (1991: 130) as a contextually accurate translation of *Purusha*.

presence in Hindu culture until modern times. Nowadays, outside academic circles, the *Gita* is considered representative of 'classical' Indian culture. This characterization of Aeschylus' tragedies and of the *Gita* as 'classics' of their respective cultures has become part of modern Western and Indian self-understanding and, as such, part of intercultural communication.

These cultural reconstructions of cultural heritages complicate matters considerably. The designation 'classical' implies a concept of culture that imagines cultures to be timeless, stable, coherent, homogeneous, codifiable, and exemplary for at least a crucial period of time—their 'classical' period. Whereas classical Greek culture would stand for mortality, finitude, the historical fate of humankind and limited knowledge including emotional knowledge, classical Indian culture would stand for immortality, infinity, the transhistorical destiny of humankind and absolute knowledge excluding emotional knowledge. The Greek tragedy and the Indian drama discussed in this essay could in that case then be presented as strikingly similar, in that they share the same conflicts and in that both of them are very 'classical' examples of their respective cultures. But they could just as easily be presented as strikingly different, since they are very 'classical' examples of the extent to which the norms and values of their respective cultures differ. This is particularly evidenced by the fact that they offer entirely different solutions to similar social conflicts. The differences between these two presentations will become respectively less distinct or, on the contrary, more distinct, depending on whether the comparative juxtaposition is being introduced into Hindu culture, which tends to be most impressed by the radical unity in the diversity of things,[8] or into Western culture which tends to be more impressed by radical difference in the alterity of cultures (Rouland 1988). While secular humanists like Isaiah Berlin would stress the insurmountable cultural gap between the Western value system and the Indian one, religious humanists like Nilima Sharma do not hesitate to bridge the gap by stressing that both the *Gita* and "the existential humanism of the twentieth century" (especially Sartre) are primarily concerned with "man's effort to realize the potential greatness of humanity," and are therefore in "close rapport" (Sharma 2000-01: 94-96).

One way of dealing with the issue of alternative approaches to cultural differences consists of separating an ideological level of aspirations inspired by diverging worldviews from a practical level of attitudes and practices motivated by a

---

[8] Michaels 1998: 19-21: "Die kohäsive Kraft, die die Hindu-Religionen zusammenhält und sie gegen fremde Einflüsse widerstandsfähig macht, bezeichne ich als 'identifikatorischen Habitus'.... Anders als Max Weber ... und anders als Louis Dumont ... stelle ich nicht die Kaste, das Individuum oder die rituelle Reinheit in den Vordergrund, sondern den Familienverbund als Deszendenzgruppe.... Hinter allem steht für mich der identifikatorische Habitus: die Festlegung einer Identität durch ihre Gleichsetzung mit etwas anderem."

converging willingness to find solutions to shared conflicts: diverging spiritualities and ideologies, converging moral attitudes and cooperative practices. Another way of dealing with the issue is offered by the introduction of a culture concept which focusses on the transient, unstable, incoherent, heterogeneous, improvising, and exceptional aspects of cultures (cf. Ewing 1991; Strauss and Quinn 1994; Keesing 1994; Brightman 1995). If cultures are much more fragmentary than a homogeneous concept of culture allows one to imagine, then cultural boundaries are more fluid and intercultural exchange is transformed into *multi*cultural exchange. Acceptance of a heterogeneous concept of culture would mean that an Indian drama is not or is no longer representative of Indian culture as such and that an heir to ancient Indian culture is not bound to reproduce his or her heritage. He or she may be acquainted with ancient Greek culture to the same extent as is its Western heir. His or her fragmentary worldview is an incomplete puzzle and, by making multicultural comparisons the 'worldviewer' becomes a puzzler who discovers new ways of putting pieces together. Such discoveries may be very confusing if located on the battlefield of existing multicultural and multireligious social conflicts. Things become less confusing if the 'worldviewer' has had time to prepare for this battlefield by analyzing the discordant and reconciliatory potential of the worldviews involved. But there is no recipe for this: there are no established patterns which conflicts and reconciliations follow. One can have a worldview stressing alterity or one emphasizing unity. But neither of these worldviews as such can guarantee that a reconciliation with one's enemy, one's destiny, one's God or humanity is brought closer by stressing one of them. Some proposals, however, are just too superficial to be of any help and I consider the notion of 'one united human family' to be one of them.

Bibliography

Assman, Jan. (1992). *Das kulturelle Gedächtnis. Schrift, Erinnerung und politische Identität in frühen Hochkulturen*. Munich: C.H. Beck.
Brightman, Robert (1995). "Forget Culture: Replacement, Transcendence, Relexification." *Cultural Anthropology* 10: 509-46.
Ewing, Katherine P. (1991). "The Illusion of Wholeness: Culture, Self, and the Experience of Inconsistency." *Ethos* 18: 251-78.
Gibert, John. (1995). *Change of Mind in Greek Tragedy*. Göttingen: Vandenhoeck & Ruprecht.
Hutchinson, G.O. (1985). *Aeschylus: Septem Contra Thebes*. Oxford: Clarendon Press.
Keesing, Roger M. (1994). "Theories of Culture Revisited." In: Robert Borofsky (ed.). *Assessing Cultural Anthropology*. New York: McGraw-Hill. Pp. 301-12.
Malinar, Angelika. (1996). *Rājavidyā. Das königliche Wissen um Herrschaft und Verzicht. Studien zur Bhagavadgita*. Wiesbaden: Harrassowitz Verlag.
Michaels, Axel. (1998). *Der Hinduismus. Geschichte und Gegenwart*. Munich: C.H. Beck.

Nussbaum, Martha C. (1986). *The Fragility of Goodness: Luck and Ethics in Greek Tragedy and Philosophy.* Cambridge: Cambridge University Press.
Patel, Ramesh N. (19910. *Philosophy of the Gita.* New York: Peter Lang.
Redfield, James M. (1994). *Nature and Culture in the Iliad: The Tragedy of Hector.* Expanded Edition. Durham/London: Duke University Press.
Rouland, Norbert. (1988). *Anthropologie juridique.* Parts I-II. Paris: Presses Universitaires de France.
Sagan, Eli. (1985/1986). *At The Dawn of Tyrrany: The Origins of Individualism, Political Oppression, and the State.* New York/London: Alfred A. Knopf, Inc./Faber and Faber.
Schlaffer, Heinz. (1973). *Der Bürger als Held. Sozialgeschichtliche Auflösungen literarischer Widersprüche.* Frankfurt a/Main: Suhrkamp.
Sharma, Nilima. (2000/2001). "Concept of Existential Humanism in the Bhagavadgita." In: Shashi Prabha Kumar and Ranjan K. Gosh (eds.). *Spirituality, Science, and Technology: World Philosophy Conference. Platinum Jubilee Celebrations of the Indian Philosophical Congress.* New Delhi: PHISPC.
Strauss, Claudia and Naomi Quinn. (1994). "A Cognitive/Cultural Anthropology." In: Robert Borofsky (ed.). *Assessing Cultural Anthropology.* New York: McGraw-Hill. Pp. 284-300.
Thalmann, William G. (1978). *Dramatic Art in Aeschylus's 'Seven against Thebes'.* New Haven/London: Yale University Press.
Thapar, Romila. (1984). *From Lineage to State: Social Formations in the Mid-First Millenium B.C. in the Ganga Valley.* Oxford: Oxford University Press, 1984.
Williams, Bernard. (1994). *Shame and Necessity.* Berkeley: University of California Press, 1994.

Buddhist Thoughts
on Conflict, 'Reconciliation' ... and Religion

Michael McGhee

Introduction

After the repression, after the terror and intimidation, after the violence and the atrocities, when the present tyranny is overthrown and the settlement reluctantly accepted—enmity and hostility linger on, murderous resentment, the desire to revenge past wrongs .... These are powerful and consuming emotions that determine the form of a person's subjectivity, that determine a collective *inter*subjectivity, from which it is difficult for individuals to free themselves, even generations later. They are among the conditions that make it difficult to end the conflict at all, and that will help to precipitate further conflict. They quietly smoulder on in people with long and precise memories, ignite again when external and interior conditions meet. These interior conditions include a dark and unexamined *eros* for violence and self-immolation, an *eros* kept alive by heroic stories and histories of injustice and maybe heightened by fusion into the local soteriological tradition. And this is just to talk about the *victims* of injustice. The perpetrators, on the other hand, may well flourish in conditions of conflict, enmity and hostility. There is a fierce pleasure in brutality *or* a cold indifference in pursuit of further goals, often represented in mystical language, surrounding, say, nation or territory. In either case we have a subjectivity shaped by strong impulses, well-guarded at its frontiers from alien intrusion.

All these things give a feeling of *life*, and they are difficult to give up, even to *think* of giving up, since they form the conscious identity of those who are invited to contemplate the thought. Another thing that brings victims and perpetrators together, however, is the striking human tendency to register the enemy as other than human. It seems to be easier to do harm to others if you have the (linguistic) resources to avert your gaze from the perception of them as fellow beings. Perhaps this is evidence of unconscious recognition of the terrible truth of what we do, and even a ground of hope in that case. This does not imply that there is a *primal* "perception of others as fellow beings." That is a(n emotional) perspective learnt slowly through cooperation and collaboration, a narrow circle that can be widened to include the 'other'—but only through some transformation of the (inter)subjectivity that is historically founded on enmity.

But what has this to with the notion of 'reconciliation'? One sceptical thought about the procedure of this symposium is that the *aftermath of violence* has nothing to do *per se* with any such notion. It is at least arguable that 'reconciliation' is often irrelevant just because the conditions for the application of that term have never been in place. Reconciliation is a process that goes on between individuals or within a community *where a former harmony has broken down*. Enemies can only be reconciled if they were once friends. In the aftermath of violence between communities or classes, then, the issue is not reconciliation but an initial building of trust and making some form of community a possibility in the first place. But since community can also break down ... there are no permanent repairs.

But if 'reconciliation' is not always the appropriate notion, it does belong within a family of notions that have some application to the context of conflict and its aftermath—overcoming resentment, forgiveness, etc—so for the purposes of this essay perhaps 'reconciliation' can stand for the whole family. In any case, it is quite clear that an absolute condition of 'reconciliation' is that the settlement is just and accepted. But it does not follow that there is nothing in the new arrangement to feed further resentment. 'A just and lasting settlement' usually means that nobody gets exactly what they want and everybody gets a lot of what they do not want. So perhaps what we call 'reconciliation' takes generations if it is in the public domain, and a lifetime in the private, if it is achieved at all. And it cannot be stage-managed nor reduced to a brief public encounter. It is an area of self-deception. Perhaps the real point is that 'reconciliation' is a limiting concept that determines an indefinite process that has its own rewards but also has a function, that of making future conflict less likely.

Dependence

So, after the settlement there is still alienation, hostility and enmity. This for some of us will be felt as *itself* a burden and oppression. For others there is apparently no oppression of spirit at all, only the apparent flourishing of the unjust, who seem to prosper and grow fat under such conditions. How are we to make sense of this?

Perhaps all we can do is cautiously test a hypothesis or, better, put our trust in a possibility, that is at least sometimes confirmed in experience: that in those who flourish in injustice some aspect of the soul is dormant or, at worst, at some point stifled and now dead. So what are the conditions under which some people are insensible of the burden and others profoundly aware? One answer that I shall try to explore here relies upon a notion of human subjectivity as constituted by formations that may have the appearance of permanence and totality but in fact arise in dependence upon conditions.

In introducing this notion I invoke the Buddhist doctrines of 'dependent arising' and of *anatta*, the idea that there is no fixed and permanent self. What *appears* permanent and fixed, to be the thing itself, in fact depends on conditions. The two doctrines stand in the relation to each other of general principle and particular application. The doctrine that there is no fixed self but only contingent formations is an application to a particular case of the principle that things arise in dependence on conditions, and all the forensic and diagnostic work of Buddhism lies in finding out what these are and changing them if necessary. And here I want to introduce a third notion, that of *dukkha*, which is variously translated as 'suffering' or 'unsatisfactoriness'. There are various forms of *dukkha*, but perhaps the most crucial is a kind of unease of the mind that intimates the awakening of a dormant sensibility. The intolerable burden that I mentioned earlier may be felt at first only as a small disturbance, as something not quite 'right', until, by a long series of transitions, it becomes dominant in consciousness.

But this idea of something becoming dominant in consciousness needs to be distinguished from the idea of consciousness being *dominated*. There is a negative connotation to the latter that carries an implication of oppression, the idea that one's consciousness cannot be fully itself, cannot develop, cannot billow out into full sail, while it is *constrained*. It is the sense of this constraint and a kind of prereflective uneasiness that starts to be felt in the experience of *dukkha* or 'unsatisfactoriness'. It seems that the mediating notion is that of the domination of consciousness by particular thoughts and motivations that in some sense *oppress*.

So let us work this out a little by way of an example or two that I have taken from a recent book on Buddhist ethics by Peter Harvey (2000: 247):

"He abused me, he beat me, he defeated me, he robbed me", the enmity of those who harbour such thoughts is not appeased.
"He abused me, he beat me, he defeated me, he robbed me", the enmity of those who do not harbour such thoughts is appeased.
Enmities never cease by enmity in this world; only by non-enmity (i.e., loving-kindness) do they cease. This is an ancient law. (*Dhammapada* 3-6)

What is striking about this passage is that it makes a series of *empirical*, that is to say, testable, claims about the conditions under which enmity may be appeased. It is not appeased in those whose minds remain dominated by certain resentful thoughts, thoughts, in other words, that determine the form and direction of powerful negative emotions. Now the characteristic illusion that accompanies such domination, and this is the pragmatic force of the *anatta* doctrine, is that it seems to be *the very form* of the mind itself. But then the *Dhammapada* goes on to represent an entirely different frame of mind. As so often in Buddhism, something positive is here presented by means of a negation, the idea of a consciousness *not* dominated by the resentful thoughts that reinforce the spirit of enmity. It is as though we all already know and are familiar with what is negated, that it is the normal form of human experience, and we can hardly represent an alternative except by the use of a negation sign as signalling something unfamiliar and other. First there was enmity, and now there is something new, let us call it 'non-enmity', first there was 'harm', now there is the possibility of 'non-harm', first there was 'intoxication' now there is 'non-intoxication'. Of course Buddhism *does* have positive terms to represent the alternative, but the use of the negation sign is itself an intriguing representation of the awakening to what is new and unfamiliar.

But what is the nature of the transition, from harboring resentment to *not* doing so? How is one to free one's mind from such thoughts, and why would one be *motivated* to do so? It is not a straightforward matter of the will, a matter of suppression, say, though on occasion suppression and an act of will may be called for. It is rather a matter of starting to allow one's mind to dwell on other kinds of thought than resentful ones. This depends upon the presence of *interludes*, of moments when the thoughts and feelings that nourish enmity are silent. The transition from resentment to non-resentment is only possible in moments when, rather than forming one's subjectivity, the spirit of enmity can become an object of attention, from a point of view that finds it unsatisfactory. This point of view or attitude is a delicate plant, easily smothered in its earlier stages of growth. Now the text refers to 'non-enmity', which Harvey rightly glosses as "loving-kindness" (*metta*). What is needed, in other words, is not the willed suppression of a set of thoughts, an unmotivated and indifferent absence but an opposing spirit to fill the mind, against which the spirit of enmity will surely contend and before which perhaps it may finally flee.

The empirical claim is that the nurturing of the opposing motivating thoughts of 'non-enmity', and the actions that are their expression, amounts to the nurturing of a new and unfamiliar formation of mind. Harvey (2000: 147) also quotes a passage from a story in the *Vinaya*:

> my parents were killed by a king, but if I were to deprive the king of life, those who desired the king's welfare would deprive me of life and those who desired my welfare would deprive these of life; thus enmity would not be settled by enmity. (*Vinaya* I.348)

These reflections are presented as considerations in favor of bringing enmity to an end on the part of someone who desires that this should be so, even though he also wants to revenge his parents' death. In other words, the elimination of enmity already has a motivational role within a mind that is beginning to find enmity 'unsatisfactory'. We can easily imagine, though, that in another mind these reflections would not favor the ending of enmity: the prospect of enmity might be contemplated with indifference or even with satisfaction. Considerations in favor of one course of action or another need particular dispositions to weigh with. If it is a truth that enmity is not settled by enmity, then one and the same truth presents itself differently according to the mind that contemplates it. My suggestion is that the sense of *dukkha* is an intimation of the new, transformed mind of non-enmity, is its earliest intervention.

But the 'ancient law' that 'enmities never cease by enmity' but only by non-enmity has to be treated with circumspection. Non-enmity can only be achieved within oneself, within the individual. Achieving this within oneself is a necessary but not sufficient condition of bringing about the cessation of enmity. One's ending it within oneself does not end it in the other.[1] It takes both parties to bring about the cessation of enmity. And this brings us to the issue of reconciliation and religion.

Reconciliation and Religion

The first thing to say is both obvious and striking, that there is indeed such a thing as 'reconciliation', that human beings *have* undergone a process that has issued in enemies being 'reconciled'. This is worth saying because 'reconciliation' can appear subjectively impossible whether one is trying to reconcile enemies or is oneself one of those to be reconciled. Some people know the realities of the process better than others do, because they have undergone the determinate ordeals that bring reconciliation about, or have been the witnesses thereof. If this were not true then our discussion would be in vain. That there are such people is a source of hope, that what may seem impossible might not be, and it can strengthen our faith in the stories of enmity, of discord, and of the reconciling of enemies, that we read or hear within the literatures of our traditions. But their authenticity as practical wisdom has always to be tested, against contemporary experience. But contemporary experience also has to be tested against the literature, in a cautious to-ing and fro-ing that is not quite a circle.

But, strictly, this has nothing to do with religion. It is an independent human reality that can however be *incorporated* into a religious tradition, which can then be *one* of the public repositories of such wisdom as we have gained about the overcoming of enmity. The point of this is to underline the thought that it is not *religion* that gives us 'reconciliation', but that the processes of 'reconciliation', the sense of its urgency and importance, have sometimes entered into and enriched the formations of religion. The best of religion needs the phenomenon of 'reconciliation', but the need is not mutual.

But we have been invited at this symposium to reflect upon how religion is 'implicated' in conflict, and how it may 'contribute' to the process of 'reconciliation'. The invitation raises the question whether what we call 'religion' is one and the same phenomenon in both cases. There are, of course, reasons for saying that they are not, and the religious among us may thus quite properly seek to distance themselves from what is done 'in the name of religion'. But maybe a more radical answer says that they are a single phenomenon, implying that religion is a complex whose possibilities of public expression and self-understanding reflect the realities of the trajectory of self-transcendence that it serves to make available to its 'adherents'. Another way of saying this is to claim that the spiritual state of the 'adherents', reflected in their dispositions and expressed in their actions, determines their appropriation of the religion, and this latter may in turn, in its particular embodiments, either reinforce that state, or provide the

---

[1] I am grateful to Dr Robert Morrison for insisting on this point.

route towards transcending it. There seem to be such possibilities in all the major traditions, aspects of which beckon or attract very different states of mind, precisely those states of mind that provide the conditions for conflict *and* the conditions for 'reconciliation'. The important question, though, is: What can be *done* with our states of mind? What this question registers is the fundamental perception that even our own states of mind can be troubling to us, can be unsatisfactory or *dukkha*, and if that is our implicit claim then we must also ask: Unsatisfactory from what point of view? The answer I have given refers us to a contrary state of mind, one that struggles for expression against the odds, that seeks the overcoming of enmity. There is a profound human interest involved in matters of conflict and the possibility of reconciliation, and this interest permeates religion itself. Religious traditions *can* give us the means, though only of course because people have discovered and set them out and can do so again, of movement from the unregenerate state to the regenerate, from a state of greed, hatred and delusion to compassion and insight, and we can be arrested or fixated at any point on the trajectory, and so can what is embodied in place and time of a particular tradition.

There is hardly an accidental or contingent relationship between the states of mind that give rise to conflict and hostility or to the processes of reconciliation, on the one hand, and the manifestations of religion, on the other. It is not as though, unhappily, religion happens sometimes to reinforce and encourage communalism, say, and sometimes, happily, happens to encourage the spirit of reconciliation. It is, rather, all the other way around. Religious possibilities are themselves the product of these forces, which enter and determine religion quite independently of 'religious belief', so that even the theistic traditions may be radically reinterpreted in the light of these independent human realities, can even be seen to develop along the same arc as the trajectory from the spirit of conflict to the spirit of reconciliation.

Forgiveness

So Buddhism works in the light of a general principle, that phenomena arise in dependence upon conditions. But templates of this kind need to be applied to particular realities, and we have to work out in detail the forms of interdependence. So what account can we give of the conditions upon which 'reconciliation' depends, and of those to which it gives rise, especially since, as we have already seen, the overcoming of the spirit of enmity *within oneself* is not by itself enough? There is a couplet by the English poet William Blake that seems apposite here: "Mutual forgiveness of each vice/ Such are the gates of paradise." These lines give us much of the truth about 'reconciliation', and they include the insight that there is something more profound and joyful in a life lived in the spirit of reconciliation, than there is in a life lived before ever reconciliation was needed. The same thought is to be found in one of Blake's aphorisms: "without forgiveness there is no friendship." At first sight this is a strange saying, since we surely have friends we have never needed to forgive, who have never needed to forgive us. But maybe the point is that where genuine forgiveness has been needed and then been achieved our experience and *conception* of friendship are enlarged. We are brought into a more abundant life.

Forgiveness seems to be an essential aspect of reconciliation, but it entails that there has been wrongdoing, that some harm or injury has been done. Now, *some* forms of conflict are merely *disputes* that need to be *resolved*, and this can be done amicably, without the *hostility* or *enmity* that call for 'reconciliation'. It is, fundamentally,wrongdoers and their victims who need to be 'reconciled'. Sometimes the wrongdoers are also themselves victims and the victims wrongdoers. The proper moral outrage that victims of injustice feel can sometimes give them the illusion that they are themselves virtuous, but former victims can also become wrongdoers when their own turn comes around.

The readiness of one person or one party to forgive the other is not enough for reconciliation, however. Reconciliation seems to require at least that forgiveness is genuinely offered and genuinely accepted. These are both difficult and painful processes, though the nature of the ordeal is different in each case. The one who forgives, and *offers* forgiveness, must undergo a revolution of attitude. That is to say, it is necessary to overcome the spirit of resentment, revenge, vindictiveness, the pleasure in at least the imagination of the punishment of the wrongdoer. The ideal limit is the disappearance of the negative spirit entirely, but there are many transitions before that transformation is achieved. But there is a breakthrough when the resentment is no longer strong enough to affect the demeanor of the former victim towards the wrongdoer, who may be forgiven even if they do not repent. None of this is without the danger of illusion, though, since one may believe that one has forgiven another just because one has repressed one's resentment.

Perhaps it is even more difficult to come to the point of *receiving and accepting* forgiveness. The doctrine of *karma* seems applicable here as an empirical reality: actions have consequences, not just for others but also for oneself. To accept forgiveness also requires that we forgive ourselves, and the process involves acknowledgement or confession and remorse. It requires us meekly to accept the blessing of our former victim, and to accept and understand the refusal of that blessing, if that should be the outcome. And here is the karmic effect: remorse seems to involve a painful re-enactment. We have to relive the harm with the compassion that the harm naturally attracts, to relive it through the eyes of the victim and then live on in the knowledge that one is the person who performed this deed, the person capable of performing it. Here is a suffering of the wrongdoer that may at first only assuage the spirit of vindictiveness in the victim, but it may also make forgiveness easier since this suffering also attracts the spirit of compassion, and compassion can bring about the retreat of resentment.

We *may* be informed of these truths, if indeed they are such, by the various religions of the world, but only because *they* were first informed by the native experience of human beings, undergoing the ordeals of life, and finding within themselves the resources to respond. But these resources come as a kind of revelation. There is a kind of grace of nature here, since our *temptation* is to identify ourselves with the mind that we found ourselves with. So that the mind that awakens in us seems like a gift, like a reality that stands over against us even as it seems to support us. Perhaps this is a perspectival illusion.

Bibliography

The Dhammapada: The Sayings of the Buddha. (2000). Transl. John Carter. Oxford: Oxford World Classics.
Gyatso, Tenzin (the Dalai Lama). (2000). *Ancient Wisdom Modern World: Ethics for the New Millennium.* New York: Little, Brown.
Harvey, Peter. (2000). *An Introduction to Buddhist Ethics: Foundations, Values and Issues.* Cambridge: Cambridge University Press.
Journal of Buddhist Ethics. Online journal: jbe.gold.ac.uk.
McGhee, Michael. (2000). *Transformations of Mind: Philosophy as Spiritual Practice.* Cambridge University Press.
———. (2001). "Moral Philosophy and 'Buddhist Ethics'." *Contemporary Buddhism* 1.

Theological Preparation
For Reconciliation in Judaism

Tzvi Marx

Renewal after Breakdown

The power of renewal, of *teshuva* and the promise of reconciliation, of *kappara*, has throughout been a catalyst for Jewish optimism and hope. The refusal to concede the finality of failure, of weakness, of suffering, of goals unachieved has characterized the Jewish people through its rocky history in its striving to become "a holy people, a kingdom of priests" (Exodus 19:6). To reflect on this as a Jew means to do so in the company of others—to be engaged by the reflections of our predecessors in wrestling with moral dilemmas. Prophets, scholars, poets, philosophers, theologians and mystics have left a record of their reflections. This literature is our common heritage, a shared language that makes our disagreements intelligible.

These last three generations have been uniquely privileged to shape a Jewish nation in its land. They are also uniquely and unspeakably tragic in having experienced the Holocaust and the continuing trauma of its aftermath. These two factors together make this period of Jewish history singular. The directions that we must take are therefore as yet uncharted. The unity and disunity of this people confronting these challenges both in Israel and the *diaspora* is complicated even more by postmodernity.

Yet the same power to persevere, to renew body and spirit, individually and collectively, to fight cynicism and indifference, to dare to hope that improvement is possible, is the same precious gift that contemporary Jews, like their forebears, have inherited from their prophetic and rabbinic tradition and, like them, through learning and deeds, contribute it to the general store of human hope.

Failure and Rehabilitation

Failure is the problem and rehabilitation is the project of the Yom Kippur Fast Day. The greatest defeat by which the human being can be confronted is the discovery of his own moral weakness. Faced with the realization that too often he lacks the capacity to live up to his values and commitments, it is an easy road to despair, cynicism and a loss of long term purpose. How much easier it is to decide that he is simply not capable of realizing his best intentions! He may comfortably retreat into accepting his shortcomings and rationalizing his moral weakness as built-in. He thereby guarantees that he will rehearse these failures repeatedly and eventually lose any initial sense of guilt or shame ("mitoch she'hutra na'aseh lo ke'heter" (Talmud Yoma 86b)). It is to escape these uncomfortable sensations (that signal moral capability of which he has fallen short) that reinforces the inclination to dismiss the moral enterprise. "Nothing ventured, nothing lost" is the psychological inverse to the achievement incentive suggested by the aphorism "nothing ventured, nothing gained!"

But there is more to the project of Yom Kippur! It is not only about the failure of achievement in moral goals. It is also about the failure in relationship in religious goals. We have failed to live up to the expectations of Another with Whom, in covenant, certain obligations were undertaken. It is also about damaged relationships with people whom we befriended, loved or simply did business with.

The word *chet* (sin) has in it then the connotation not only of personal failure but also of failed relationship. Judaism is rich in its vocabulary for failure. The Yom Kippur liturgy has the worshipper chant these confessional lines (*vidooi*) individually and collectively twice in every one of the services: that is, once in the silent *Amidah* (standing prayer) and once in the *chazzan*'s (prayer leader's) repetition. This comes to eleven times if one includes the confession in the afternoon *mincha* service preceding the last meal before Yom Kippur.

"Ashamnu, Bagadnu, Gazalnu, Dibarnu doofi ... Titanu." There is a failure word for every letter of the aleph-bet:

> We have: become guilty, betrayed, robbed, spoken slander, caused perversion, caused wickedness, sinned wilfully, been violent, falsely accused, counseled evil, been unfaithful, scorned, rebelled, provoked, turned away, been perverse, acted wantonly, persecuted, been obstinate, been wicked, corrupted, been abominable, strayed, led others astray. (Art Scroll Siddur translation: 277)

So in facilitating rehabilitation, it is not only about one's motivation to strive again for moral goals despite the experience of failure but also about the possibility of re-entering into relationship. How does one create faith in oneself to bear the brunt of this challenge? How does one reinforce the trust in the Other to accept one's human identity with all its limitations so that one may be moved to reach for more than one thought possible on the basis of past performance? How can one mend broken friendships, retrieve hurt love, rebuild trust in our social context?

There is an interdependence working here which makes this project so difficult. In the first place we need to believe in ourselves—that we are capable of being entrusted with commitment and values. In the second place we need to believe that others can genuinely have their faith in us restored despite our having disappointed or even betrayed them. In this we must also believe in the capacity of others—whether God or human beings—to forgive. Believing in ourselves, is dependent on believing in the trust of others. At the same time, the trust from others is dependent on our capacity to learn to trust ourselves.

Belief in the human capacity for goodness after failure is illustrated by the chasidic rabbi, known as the Grandfather of Shpoles. During the High Holy

Days it was his custom to speak to God in his room for an hour or two in a language which is not typical of prayer books:

> Don't think of man's sins, I beg of You. Think rather of his good deeds. They are fewer, I agree. But You must admit, they are more precious. Believe me, it isn't easy to be good in this world. And if I didn't see with my own two eyes that man, in spite of all obstacles, is capable of kindness, I would not believe it. And so I ask of You: don't be harsh with your children; rare as it may be, it is their kindness that should surprise You. (From Wiesel 1982)

Teshuva *and* Kappara

The rehabilitative aspect of Yom Kippur can be summed up in two words: *teshuva* and *kappara*. *Teshuva* from the root word *shuv* (return) denotes a change of direction from the path of failure to renewal. But this is no simple reversal, no retreat backwards along the misguided path from which one came, no mere returning to the starting point, erasing one's footsteps, as if one had never left. That simple kind of change would have been grammatically expressed in another form: *shiva* (returning). *Teshuva* connotes rather a circling around in search of a new path, a blazing of a new unprecedented trail, a determined cutting down of thick internal obstacles that block the way, in the quest for a renewal of that former sense of confidence and trust but chastened by the sharp awareness of one's vulnerability to failure.

This linguistic nuance was stressed by the master talmudist Rabbi J.B. Soloveitchik on the basis of its use to describe the prophet Samuel's pastoral 'rounds' (*ve'savav*) in the region "of Bethel, Gilgal, and Mizpah. There he acted as judge over Israel" after which "he would return to his home in Ramah "u'teshuva'to haRamata'"(I Samuel 7:17). His return (*teshuva*) was roundabout (*savav*): he circled round, it was not a mere linear backtracking. This same grammatical form also connotes the annual cycle of time (*teshuvat ha'shana*) (II Samuel 11:1; I Kings 20:22). The heavenly spheres circle back to their starting points but not by backtracking (from Soloveichik 1980: 59).

Oddly, in this sense the way back may appear to be an even further distancing from one's starting point than simply turning around. Paraphrasing one of the fathers of gestalt psychology, Kurt Lewin, the shortest spiritual (he would have said psychological) distance between two points is often the seemingly longer and more circuitous path. A person is to a large extent a product of his biography and experience. His experience of 'undoing' (sin) cannot be undone; it can only redirected, reintegrated into the new whole of moral existence that he struggles to attain. In the effort to find himself, he cannot dismiss who he was, but must bring his old identity into a new gestalt, and in this newer context redefine the old elements of his life, both the good and the bad. *Teshuva*, in the Judaic process of self-renewal, takes account of this complexity. The Lord does not desire the death of the sinner but for him to turn from his misguided course (*shuv'o midrachav*) so that he may live a moral life (from the Yom Kippur Ne'ilah liturgy adducing Isaiah 55:6; Ezekiel 33:11; 18:23, 32).

The second key word, *kappara*, usually translated as atonement, can be understood from two perspectives, covering up and transformation (*tahara*, lit. purification), that are suggested in the morning's Torah reading (Leviticus 16:1-34). Aaron the high priest suffers the death of his two sons Nadav and Avihu. What a trauma! He was literally stunned into silence (Leviticus 9:2-3). Aaron was Moses' "spokesman to the people" (Exodus 4:16), his steady and trusted partner, characterized by the rabbinic sages as "a lover of peace" (Ethics of the Fathers 1:12). More, than anyone, Aaron could have expected his life to follow some reasonable pattern. All this was shattered in one instant. In recognizing that tragedy and failure threatens continued faith in the meaning of life and morality, a remarkable set of instructions is offered on how to pick up the pieces of one's life (Leviticus 16:2-33). And these are immediately preceded by the recalling of Aaron's tragedy (v. 1) as if in connection to it.

As was said, *chet* or sin (the failure to live up to one's ideals or commitments) and death are crises which nurture disillusionment and loss of hope. The discovery that things do not always work out as one would have wished is a hard challenge for every human being to reconstruct his world of meaning, but this time unarmed with the simple trust that good intentions necessarily lead to good consequences.

How is one to recapture the sense of worthwhileness in life, its beauty and meaning? How is one to find again the energy for creativity, for wonder and motivation? Two possibilities for renewal are suggested in the declaration, "For on this day atonement (*kappara*) shall be made for you to purify you (*tahara*) of all your sins" (Leviticus 16:30). This verse addresses the dilemma of living with a flawed past in a renewable present. The negative effects of one's past must be carefully handled to neutralize their deadening influence on the possibility for new beginnings.

In its root *kappara* (atonement) means 'covering over' and 'pacifying' (see Brown *et al.* (BDB) 1977: 497). That is how the ark cover comes to be called *kapporet* (Exodus 25:17). This dimension of renewal relies on neutralizing the further impact of failure by bounding it, by limiting its negative influence. The residue of that influence continues, however, to exist as a feature of one's memory and self-awareness. There is no 'magic bullet' cure here that makes it simply disappear.

Another dimension of renewal is offered in *tahara* which means 'purifying' (BDB: 372). Here the reality of the past is anulled by being transformed. It becomes unrecognizable in the psyche of the person because it is absorbed in a larger framework of self-development. It may actually become a positive motive force in energizing new directions for the constructive development of personality.

Daily Temple Offerings (He-lambs) as Symbols

Two ways of handling crisis and renewal are reinforced in the ritual controversy between Shammai and Hillel over what the *kevasim* (he-lambs) symbolize. They are the *karban tamid*, daily Temple offerings (Numbers 28:3). According to Shammai "they suppress (*kovshin*) the sins of Israel" in the spirit of the prophet Micah (7:19): "He will take us back in love by covering up (*yichbosh*) our iniquities." Hillel objects since what is suppressed will eventually resurface. Rather, "they launder their sins, rendering Israel like a new born babe, free of all sin." This is in the spirit of the prophet Jeremiah (4:14): "Wash (*kivsi*) your hearts clean of wickedness." Hillel connects *kevasim* to the word *m'chabsin* (launder), linking the letter *samech* of *mechabSin* to the similar sounding letter *sin* of *kevaSim*. (Source: Pesikta d'Rav Kahana, 6; see Kanovitz: 30).

These two ways of handling human failure reflect an awareness that in motivating renewal we can not disregard the fact that the person carries with him his moral biography. If we want him to succeed, he must be helped in 'failure management'. Depending on the particular crisis and personal situation or stage, *kappara* or *tahara* aspiration may be the more suitable. The more minimal 'cover-up' (*kappara*), a kind of compartmentalization of psychic energies, may at times be more effective in energizing that person to get beyond his immediate moral paralysis. At other times the more radical 'shake-up' *tahara*, a kind of integration, is more appropriate for the person to feel cleansed of whatever it is that is getting him stuck.

The message of Yom Kippur and its elaborate rituals so poignantly described is that we are never stuck. Whether or not we want to believe that this is so may depend in part on what other alternatives we have and to the extent that we can shake off that feeling that "there is nothing new (possible) under the sun" (Kohelet 1:10).

Choosing One's Lot (Or: Don't Let Fate Get One's Goat)

It is more than humorous that Yom Kippur*im*, A Day of Atonement*s*, is playfully read as Yom *Ke*-Purim, A Day *like* Purim. The latter expresses the experience of life as fate, the arbitrary product of a lottery, like the day chosen by Haman to destroy the Jews of Persia. *Pur*, meaning 'lot' (Esther 9:26), symbolizes seemingly arbitrary events. Lots play a key role too on Yom Kippur in the Biblical cultic drama. Though this cult is no longer actual (since 73 C.E.), we still draw from it contemporary lessons.

Among other offerings, two are designated for the ritual of atonement. "Aaron shall place lots upon the two he-goats, one marked for the Lord and the other marked for Azazel" (Leviticus 16:8). Azazel is a hard and rough mountain where the goat was dashed to pieces (Yoma 67b). The Mishna of Yoma (chapters 1-4) describes the preparatory process.

> Seven days before Yom Kippur, the high priest was removed from his house to the cell of the counselors ... bringing court elders to read before him the order of the day ... so that he may become familiar with the service ... saying to him "we adjure you not to change anything of what we said to you." ... If he sought to slumber, young priests would snap their middle finger before him ... keeping him amused (all night) until the time for the (morning) sacrifices.

Priests to assist the high priest were chosen by lot for the different parts of the service. There were altogether five services; the high priest changed his garments five times and washed his hands and feet ten times (bYoma 32b). Before he could perform the atonement ritual on behalf of the community, the high priest had first to seek atonement for his own failures.

> He made confession saying "I have done wrong, I have transgressed, I have sinned before Thee, I and my house, O Lord! Forgive the wrongdoing the transgressions, the sins which I have committed and transgressed and sinned before Thee, I and my house."

And only then could he approach the two he-goats whence "he shook the urn and brought the two lots. On one was inscribed 'for the Lord', and on the other: 'for Azazel'... a thread of crimson wool was tied on the head of the he-goat which was to be sent away" to Azazel. The dashing of the he-goat upon the rocks was a dramatic acting out of sins being fragmented into insignificant particles.

Importantly, there is nothing to distinguish the goats that could have given a clue as to each one's destiny. Ideally, they had to be "alike in appearance, in size, in value" (Mishna Yoma 6:1). The fate of these animals—whether as an offering to God or as a scapegoat to Azazel—is purely by chance.

To claim that the one's life is out of one's hands and is rather the result of forces beyond one's control is easy. "One is born and one dies against one's will" (Ethics of the Fathers). Furthermore, "whatever happens, it was designated long ago and it was known that it would happen; as for man, he cannot contend with what is stronger then he" (Kohelet 6:10), that is, his fate.

It is against this view of one's life, as predominantly a product of chance, that Yom Kippur addresses itself. The scapegoat, itself randomly selected, is the medium of liberation, carrying away human guilt over past failures. These guilt 'blemishes' are barriers that prevent people from believing in their power to begin again. Preceding the scapegoat's fatal journey to the wilderness, the priest made confession for the house of Israel. Recalling their iniquities, he pleaded for divine atonement, holding God to His promise that "on this day shall atonement be made for you" (Leviticus 16:30, Yoma 66a).

New Age and Yom Kippur

One recognizes this aspiration resonating in the New Age jargon about creative "waves in the human energy systems" in one New Ager's intense struggle "to be more loving, to believe in yourself, to forgive, to have compassion, and to release pain and negativity." This is what the program of Yom Kippur is about. For Rabbi J. Soloveitchik, the greatest instruction of Yom Kippur is that the "future that imprints its stamp on the past and determines its image" rather than that the past unalterably determines human destiny. "The future transforms the thrust of the past" because one's past is actually indeterminate and can take more than one future direction. It awaits the choices made in the future to determine what the past meant (Soloveitchik 1983: 115).

This is a reversal of the uni-dimensional common sense notion of time as linear. In the words of a New Ager "we move from linear time to a more intuitive time." Under the guiding hand of positive acts, past sins are accounted as merit and achievement (Yoma 86b). The past is thereby transformed by what comes after.

What greater symbolic protest against chance and fate than that Jews on Yom Kippur ritually transcend the ordinary biological processes by abstaining from food and drink, washing, oiling their bodies, conjugal relations, and they walk barefooted (wearing no leather shoes). By giving testimony to freedom, choosing life and renewal, and refusing to become life's victims, they decide that Yom Kippurim is *not* like Purim after all.

"In the seventh month, on the tenth day of the month, you shall practice self-denial; and you shall do no manner of work ... for on this day atonement shall be made for you to cleanse you of all your sins; you shall be clean before the Lord" (Leviticus 16:29-30). Besides various labors which are prohibited on Yom Kippur (as on all the festivals), there is a special mandate on Yom Kippur connected to the process of atonement: self-denial (*inooi*)! Some translate it as 'self-affliction'. The Mishna (Yoma 8:1) spells out these five afflictions or forms of self-denial. Since the Biblical mandate is to "afflict your souls," perhaps one "must sit in heat or cold in order to suffer?" ask the Sages. Not so! Just as the prohibition "you shall do no manner of labor" is observed passively, so too the engagement in self-affliction is to be passive, i.e., some form of self-denial (Talmud Yoma 74b). The sabbatical aspect and the afflictive aspect of Yom Kippur are linked; hence one may learn from one to the other.

One can sense from all this that the *inooi* (denial) of Yom Kippur seems in some way to be a further extension of Shabbat. In what sense is this so? For one thing, Shabbat charges people to cease activities in the creative realm only (*melekhet makhshevet* (thoughtfully designed activity)), while Yom Kippur extends the restrictions as well to the survival realm on the biological level. On the Shabbat humans are directed to demonstrate mastery over their creative, voluntary capacities by containing them; on Yom Kippur they must extend this over some of their biological and instinctive functions as well.

To what end is this drama played out? On Shabbat humans step out of history and function only within nature as a creature, as a passive particle of creation; on Yom Kippur they steps out of nature as well, by transcending some of its ordinarily legitimate claims upon them. On Yom Kippur humans attempt for a day to become timeless beings, not bound by their past. On Yom Kippur time works for humans. "It is a Day of Atonement, to make atonement for you before the Lord your God" (Leviticus 23:28). As Maimonides puts it (Mishneh Torah, Laws of Repentance 1:3), "'atzmo shel yom kippurim mechaper'—the essence of the Day of Atonement atones for the penitent." According to Rabbi Judah Ha'Nasi the day is so effective as to facilitate atonement even for non-penitents (Yoma 85b). The quality of this sacred time works in favor of human beings, laundering even their unknown transgressions, gaining time for them to try again.

Yom Kippur in this vision is not a 'time' machine but a 'time-less' one. It defies our ordinary logic of history. We are ordinarily bound by our past, by the decisions we have taken, by our oversights as well as by our malice. In this day we are taken in by the two-faced nature of time, as enemy and as ally.

As our enemy, for "man comes from dust and ends in dust ... he is like the pottery that breaks, the grass that wither, the flower that fades, the shadow that passes, the cloud that vanishes, the breeze that blows the dust that floats, the dream that flies away" (from the High Holiday Liturgy following "U'Netaneh Tokef" prayer). As our ally, the cleansing, purifying, atoning nature of this day liberates us from the logic of time. We are enabled to enter a new reality where *kappara* eliminates (by transforming) our past.

Reinforcing us in making this transition from a time-dominated to a timeless, free reality is the role of the afflictions (denials). Our manifold activities, creative and instinctive, root us in history and biology, i.e., in time processes. In that wonderful fascinating oasis of timelessness, the Day of Atonement, for 25 hours everyone is the same age. We become somehow united with one another, concerned for one another's welfare, extending this caring to the uttermost bounds of existence. The loss of this sense of time is sadly felt to be ebbing away in the last minutes of Yom Kippur as the *chazzan* chants during the final *Ne'ilah* prayer: "Open for us the gate of prayer even at the closing of the gate, even now that the day has declined" (Hymn: "P'tach lanu sha'ar").

Reconciliation through Conflict Resolution

The Torah reading in which the Yom Kippur service is described, and its sequel, calling Israel to become a holy people (Leviticus 16-20), links two themes: reconciliation (ch. 16) and conflict resolution (19:17-18).

Reconciliation
Yom Kippur beckons with its promise of purification from guilt and its hope for renewal in one's relationship with God—"for on this day shall atonement be made for you to purify you of all your failures" (Leviticus 16:30). The Hebrew word *chet* ('sin') fundamentally means 'failure'. This process is however absolutely dependent upon sober and honest self appraisal and criticism—"and he shall confess all the sins of the Israelites" (v. 21).

Conflict Resolution
This honesty in confronting failure, weakness, guilt and anger and the readiness to accept responsibility for one's own role infuses reconciliation as well in interpersonal relations. Note that the instruction to "love your neighbor as yourself!" comes as a climactic conclusion to a sequence of instructions that begins with "you should not hate your brother in your heart" (Leviticus 19:17-18). It is this hiding of one's negative feelings towards others, feelings that may well be justified, that could be a

source of revenge when power balances shift in one's favor. Instead, one should openly express one's objections towards another's resented behavior: "you shall surely rebuke your fellow man" (v. 17). This allows for an airing of negativity (Maimonides, Mishneh Torah, Laws of character Traits 6:6). Perhaps there has been a misunderstanding which the other is willing to concede, had he only been aware of it, and had it not been concealed from him by the injured party.

Sinful Dishonesty
Dishonesty in the name of civility is accounted as sinful for the one who keeps silent: "you should not sin on his account" (v. 17. commentary of Nachmanides). Honest communication allows for correction by the perpetrator and at least allows for the catharsis of emotion by the victim.

This candor is illustrated by the chasidic Rabbi Levi-Yitzchak of Berditchev who once offered God a bargain: "We shall give you our sins and in return, You will grant us Your pardon. By the way, you come out ahead. Without our sins, what would You do with Your pardon?" (From Elie Wiesel's "Souls on Fire"). This subtle reproof clearly demonstrates how much Rabbi Levi wanted to remain in the relationship despite his pique with God.

Criticism, not Humiliation
Criticism must not aim to humiliate the perpetrator. The public shaming of anyone ("malbin p'nei havero ba'rabim") is considered a cardinal sin in general. In this case it also undermines reconciliation and is in itself a source of 'sinning' by the 'victim' (Sifra, Kedoshim 2:4). The role of victim and victimizer can easily be interchanged in the context of reconciliation wrongfully construed. This is another way to interpret "you should not sin on his account" (Rashi on Leviticus 19:17).

Ultimately, you will not have the need "to take vengeance nor bear any grudge." Note the subtlety in the difference between "not taking revenge"—that is not to behave in the same negative way—and "not bearing a grudge"—that is not to act self-righteously in not taking revenge (Talmud Yoma 23a).

Both behavior (revenge) and feelings (grudge) need to be addressed in conflict resolution with reasonable expectations. If you can thereby come to "love your neighbor as yourself"—this is conflict resolution at its best. But loving is impossible without honest communication about one's grievances in the relationship.

Timing
The wise king Solomon may be right when he says "there is a time for silence and a time for speaking" (Kohelet 3:7), but he was only talking about timing, not repression. One needs to choose the good moment and the good way to initiate a critical dialogue (Talmud Yebamot 65b). Communication is not synonymous with merely speaking. Indeed, Cain spoke to his brother in the sense of making speech noises, but the hiatus in the text—it does not report what he said—suggests that he did not actually communicate anything (Genesis 4:8). Should we be surprised by the ensuing violence?

Mediation

Sometimes a third party is helpful—those two brothers could have used a good family counselor. Thus the Bible directs a couple, caught in a tense marital crisis and frustrated in their ability to communicate, to seek the help of the priest (Numbers 5:15). As a skilled spiritual guide he might help them break through their communication block. Love means there is no shame in admitting that sometimes "a person cannot alone extricate himself from his imprisonment" (Talmud Berakhot 5b).

Prophetic Critique: Isaiah 57:14-58:14

The capacity for reconciliation that is promised in the Torah resonates through the Yom Kippur rituals, but it can not be superficially or merely ritualistically construed This is the message which the prophet Isaiah brings to Yom Kippur as "his" *haftarah* is read in the morning.

By 10.30 in the morning in most synagogues on Yom Kippur people have been fasting, piously abstaining from food and drink for sixteen hours with another nine to go. If they are traditional, they have carefully washed their fingers only below the knuckles and merely rubbed some drops of water into their eyes to clear them of the night mucous. They have foregone their usual body care with oils and lotions. Needless to say, they have not engaged in marital 'activity'. And they stand long hours in the synagogue wearing the less comfortable non-leather footwear. In most modern communities it also means that they have paid good money to reserve seats for themselves and their families for the 'privilege' of 'afflicting themselves' (Leviticus 16:31) in fulfillment of God's *mitzva*. Imagine, after all this, the feelings of the worshippers confronted by the prophetic rebuke against all their best efforts!:

> Is such the fast I desire, a day for men to starve their bodies? Is it bowing the head like a bulrush and lying in sackcloth and ashes? Do you call that a fast, a day when the Lord is favorable? No, this is the fast I desire: to unlock fetters of wickedness, and untie the cords of lawlessness, to let the oppressed go free; to break off every yoke. It is to share your bread with the hungry and to take the wretched poor into your home; when you see the naked, to clothe him, and not to ignore your own kin. Then shall your light burst through like the dawn and your healing spring up quickly. (Isaiah 58:5-8)

These words of Isaiah are like a sharp needle deflating one's sense of piety, of achievement, of purity and morality. To his question "is this the fast I desire?" one is tempted to answer: Yes! You ordered this! Look to Leviticus Chapter 16 and to the Talmud tractate Yoma, all eighty eight folios! If the prophet is right, we ought to end this charade of symbols and role-playing and engage only in the ethical reconstruction of society, calling for the giving of *tzedaka* in the place of Yom Kippur fasting, the offering of shelter to the needy in the pace of abstaining from leather footwear, showing solidarity with the widow, orphan, and stranger in the place of confession and prayers!

The prophet has in earlier harangues made his view clear. He is not against ritual and symbolic actions. What he earlier (chapter 1) claims is that what God "cannot abide" is "assemblies with iniquity" (v. 13) that is, piously approaching God while "hands are stained with crime" (v. 15). If you "wash yourselves clean; put your evil doings away from My sight, cease to do evil; learn to do good; devote yourselves to justice; aid the wronged, uphold the rights of the orphan; and defend the cause of the widow" (v.16-17) then the Lord offers to "reach an understanding: Be your sins like crimson, they can turn snow-white; be they red as dyed wool, they can become like fleece!" (v. 18).

Rituals and symbols are meaningful when matched by the ethics and morals they are meant to represent. The quest for personal piety and spirituality must be a quest for justice and righteousness too. Together, the personal and social realities together have to be the objects of *teshuva* (repentance) and *kappara* (atonement). To ignore the human being in the quest for God, says the prophet, to "fast in strife and contention" (Isaiah 58:4), is to render the spiritual quest grotesque and to make a parody of God. Better an impious honesty than a pious hypocrisy! Reconciliation must be based on truth if it is to be long-lasting: "Justice and well-being [can] kiss" when "truth springs from the earth" (Psalm 85:11-12).

Bibliography

Brown F., S.R. Driver and C.A. Briggs. (1977) *Hebrew and English Lexicon of the Old Testament*. Oxford: Oxford University Press.

Kanovitz, Israel. *Bet Shammai ve'Bet Hillil: Osef Shel Mámareihem*.

Scherman, N. (ed.). (1988). *The Complete Art Scroll Siddur*. Brooklyn: Mesorah Publications.

Soloveitchik, Joseph B. (1980). *On Repentance*. Transl. P. Peli. Hebrew Original: Al Hete-shuva. (1974). ed. P. Peli. Jerusalem.

———. (1983). *Halakhic Man*. Transl. L. Kaplan. Philadelphia. Hebrew Original: *ish Halakha* (1944).

Wiesel, Elie. (1982). *Souls on Fire*. Westminster: Random House.

Three Models of Reconciliation

A Christian Approach

Cees Van der Kooi

Introduction

The term 'reconciliation' has frequently been used over the last decade for various programs within a social and political context. Generally, the term refers to a way of proceeding towards the restoration of mutually amicable relations between individuals or sections of a population. One can easily think of examples on the international political scene and these hardly need to be mentioned explicitly. In most cases the problem is not that the parties involved do not realize the necessity of restoring relations. The problem is rather the uncertainties regarding the implications of the way towards reconciliation: what are the stations and intersections on the road to reconciliation? The content of reconciliation as a concept remains quite vague. Minimally, reconciliation means simply the cessation of a situation of conflict and disrupted relations between individuals or groups. In a more positive and objective formulation, reconciliation involves doing justice to different groups politically, socially and economically, and giving them adequate access to the good life, education and development.

At the very outset of this contribution it should be made clear that the broader, social use of reconciliation is not the primary aspect on which I will be focussing here. My primary goal is to explore the theological content of the concept of reconciliation. This restriction is not at all meant to suggest that reconciliation has nothing to do with economic, social and political aspects of human relations. The opposite is the case. The presupposition behind the Christian concept of reconciliation is, however, that a real and comprehensive restoration of mutually amicable human relations has its ground and motive in the reconciliation of God with humankind. This restoration and healing of the relation between God and humankind has definite, immediate implications on the social, economic and political levels[1].

A second remark I wish to add immediately concerns the location of the doctrine of reconciliation in Christian theology. In the Western Latin tradition reconciliation in particular functions as a central concept that points to the core of salvation. It needs to be stressed, however, that the church does not have any official dogma of reconciliation similar to the dogma of the Trinity or the Christological dogma of the

---

[1] For a fine example see Assefa 1994.

unity of Christ as one person in two natures. The only thing that is articulated in the ecumenical confessions is that "for us as human beings and for the sake of our salvation" (*propter nos homines et propter nostram salutem*) he "came down and became flesh." How his life and death benefit us was not the subject of official doctrinal pronouncements in this period, although in the Protestant churches it certainly became an explicit object of theological debate and a confessional issue. Anyone who surveys the fierceness of the theological debate in Protestant theology readily receives the impression that the doctrine of salvation, soteriology, is completely absorbed by the theme of reconciliation. There are, however, sound biblical and systematic grounds for not accepting that equivalence and arguing that the comprehensive concept of the Christian doctrine of salvation is rather to found in the concept of the kingdom of God. That concept reminds us of the fact that God's intention is for human beings and their world to live and exist under the beneficial sovereignty of God. The notion of 'covenant' may also provide another, more comprehensive term from theological discourse under which reconciliation may be placed: God wants to be our God and he wants us to be his people, and for that reason he sent his son Jesus. We can place the life and work of Jesus within this conceptual framework of covenant and the kingdom of God.

Thus, the background and root of the doctrine of reconciliation is to be found in the Bible. For that reason we must begin with a few biblical-theological notions.

What is the essence of the work of Jesus? He brings people into the saving and wholeness-restoring presence of his heavenly Father. In his words and deeds he puts an end to the separation between people and God. He heals the sick, because illness is the shadow of death. He leads people back to life in connection with and in openness to God. The kingdom of God breaks through around Jesus and the covenant is realized. These are not automatic results of the life of Jesus. Rather, he arouses resistance and is finally crucified. As the risen Lord, however, he appears to his disciples. Because he has been raised by his Father, the disciples become convinced that the relation with God is not broken and that they can participate in the continuing community between the Father and the Son.

From the foregoing it will be clear that reconciliation as a theological concept is subordinate to the theme of the kingdom of God. Reconciliation points to the fact that the kingdom will be completed only through restoration and that this restoration will not be achieved by means of smooth transitions. Along the road to reconciliation we must deal with conflict, opposing interests, reluctance and hidden agendas through which some prefer to maintain a situation of conflict with their enemy in order to sustain the internal unity of a people.

Thus, although reconciliation is not the all-encompassing concept for Christian doctrine, it is nevertheless a concept that functions as a key word in the field of soteriology. It articulates the experience and conviction that the relation between God and humankind has been disrupted. Reconciliation points to the religious or spiritual dimension of human existence. The presupposition is that estrangement in the spiritual dimension has a thoroughgoing effect on everyday life, on mutual human relationships and on the attitude of human beings towards themselves. Viewed from the opposite perspective of achieved reconciliation, the presupposition is that reconciliation between God and human beings has a effect on the relations between individuals and on the way human beings see and experience themselves.

I will elaborate somewhat on the latter. According to Christian doctrine, we all live in estrangement from God, in conflict with our source, the Creator of heaven and earth. This conflict can become visible in the various relations in which human beings participate. It can become reflected (1) in the way people relate to God, turn their back on him or dishonor him by their behavior. The rupture can also become visible (2) in the way people relate to themselves, and/ or (3) in the mutual relations between individuals and (4) in the way people relate to their natural environment. In other words, I am distinguishing among cultic, psychological, interpersonal, social and economic, and finally ecological dimensions of reconciliation. What is at stake in the doctrine of reconciliation is the question of how the relation to God, to our neighbor, to ourselves and to the natural world will be healed and restored. These relations or levels of relations are intrinsically connected with one another, so disruption on one level never exists in isolation from the others. The common assumption in the models of reconciliation that I will discuss in the next paragraphs is that reconciliation between God and humankind is the all-encompassing ground and creates the possibility for reconciliation on the other levels. Each of the models comprehends possibilities for human action that correspond to or are analogous to the way God deals with his children in his creation.

Within contemporary Christianity the doctrine of reconciliation is a frequently discussed or, perhaps one might even say, crucial theme. The reason is clear, particularly in the Western world. What is at stake is the question of what the human race is able to achieve through its own power and initiative. What is at stake is the question of whether human beings are able to realize their own destiny and humanity. How free actually are human beings? In many situations it certainly turns out to be possible for a person to make a decision and take steps toward the resolution of conflict. But what are we to think and to say about the many situations in which good intentions are present in abundance but restoration and healing do not succeed? In these cases we speak of 'hopeless situations', of the irreversibility of guilt and damage. Think of the frustrated relations between victims and perpetrators, the irreversibility of what happened between executioners and the victims they killed.

Each of the three models that will be discussed in the next section point back to the narrative of Jesus Christ. The roots of these three models lie in that history. I will first point to the way in which each of them is rooted in the narrative of Jesus Christ. Subsequently I will discuss how these experiences have been dealt with in the history of piety and theology. The actual goal of this essay, however, does not lie within the field of historical theology. I will present these models as ideal types and will examine them with respect to their usefulness for the present.

Largely following G. Aulén, I distinguish three main models of reconciliation:
a. The Dramatic Model. Reconciliation is the effect of liberation from and victory over the devil and his power. The death of Jesus has catastrophic effects for the devil.
b. What is termed the Objective or Juridical Model. Reconciliation is a kind of atonement and has to do with remission of sins. It is achieved through a sort of satisfaction. The death of Christ clears one of guilt towards God.
c. The Subjective Model. Reconciliation happens when human beings show sincere contrition over evil. The death of Christ is seen as an act of love and brings human beings (as subjects) to a response of love.

In the next section each model be described briefly, followed by a few systematic remarks. The focus will be on the question of what role is granted to the human subject within each model.

Three Models

Salvation as Victory

The dominant model in the early church was the dramatic model, also called the victory model. The devil, the old dragon, is vanquished by Christ the Victor. The human being suffers from illness, transience, the afflictions of life. That is the state of inner and outer conflict in which each person exists. Christ descends to this earth to drive away illness, to break the power of the devil over human existence and to bestow life on human beings. These are the outlines of the framework within which the narratives of the gospel were read in the early church. In his healings and acts of power Christ invades the realm of darkness and liberates people from the bonds of evil. 1 Peter 3:19-20 is an important text in this regard and the confrontation of Jesus with the power of evil is consequently evaluated as a direct victory over the devil. These verses say that after his resurrection Jesus "went and preached to the spirits in prison, who formerly did not obey, when God's patience waited in the days of Noah ..." (RSV). After being raised from the dead, Jesus descended to the underworld and by his invasion liberated the prisoners there from the power of Satan. Due to the disobedience of Adam and Eve in paradise, Satan had obtained power over the human race. According to some in the early church, Satan even had a legal claim on humans. How else could it be explained that, in the narrative of the temptation in the desert, the devil could offer Christ dominion over all the kingdoms of this world in return for one single prostration if he was not really the master of the universe (Schwager 1986: 32-53)?

That human nature which is common to us all is taken hostage by the devil and his henchmen. It is in respect to this that the Son of God descends to the world, assumes our flesh, becomes human. The devil has a deep respect for the Son of God, but when Jesus in the Garden of Gethsemane breaks out in a cold sweat, Satan forgets for a moment with whom he is dealing. When Jesus appears overcome by the situation, the old enemy is deluded into thinking that he is confronting an ordinary human being, ordinary flesh, which he can defeat. He seizes him and kills him on the cross.

On the cross, however, comes the unexpected denouement, rightly called an apotheosis. The devil is tricked. The human flesh of Jesus turns out to be the bait, and Satan takes it. But hidden in the human flesh is the divinity of the Son. As a fish swallows the bait and gets caught on the hook, so Satan is overmastered by the divinity of Christ.[2] Like a fish he is drawn out of his natural element and the human race is no longer dominated by his power. The death of Jesus on the cross defeats the power of the devil, the overwhelming power of death. Since Christ went through death, the power of death has been forever changed.

For centuries the picture of Christ who defeats the dragon was brightly and colorfully painted for the eyes of the faithful. It excited the imagination and was the dominant model. Some remnant of it can be found in the first question and answer of the Heidelberg Catechism. This question asks: "What is your only comfort in life and in death? The answer reads:

> That I belong—body and soul, in life and in death—not to myself but to my faithful Saviour Jesus Christ, who at the cost of his own blood has fully paid for all my sins and has completely freed me from the dominion of the devil; that he protects me so well that without the will of my Father in heaven not a hair can fall from my head; indeed, that everything must fit his purpose for my salvation. Therefore, by his Holy Spirit, he also assures me of eternal life, and makes me wholeheartedly willing and ready from now on to live for him. (transl. A.O. Miller and M.E. Osterhaven)

In these lines we still encounter elements of the victory concept of the early church: he has "completely freed me from the dominion of the devil." Salvation is pictured as liberation and triumph by God. Has this image been exhausted? Not really. Even when contemporary Christians feel somewhat uncomfortable with such a vivid presentation of the state of affairs, it should be acknowledged that such an image expounds contents of the gospel that continue to be relevant and essential. As heirs of the Enlightenment, we modern Christians like to regard ourselves as self-confident and free individuals who make our own choices. Nobody is to have power over us. Is that true or are we dealing here with an active myth? In the last century the banner of individual autonomy has been torn to shreds. More than we had ever recognized that our actions turn out to be dictated by anonymous processes, economic interests and nationalistic sentiments that can be ignited into a murderous firestorm in which one collective flies at another. Those who thought they preserved in their veins the call for freedom of the 1960s have discovered that they are trapped in a web of greed, ambition and anxiety. Addiction is not only found in the forms of alcohol and drug addiction. Our chances of understanding the words cited above from the Heidelberg Catechism increase, however, the more we realize how often we ourselves are trapped in the bondage of processes, anxieties and enslavements.

---

[2] Cf. the example of Cyril of Jerusalem, cited by Schwager 1986: 35.

Against the background of the notion of autonomy the phrase "belong to" is not likely to sound attractive. It smacks of bondage. Perhaps there is only one place, one *topos* where it can be understood in a life-giving way that nurtures identity: in love. The apostle Paul writes in Romans 8:38: "For I am sure that neither death, nor life, nor angels, nor principalities, nor things present, nor things to come, nor powers, nor height, nor depth, or anything else in all creation, will be able to separate us from the love of God in Christ Jesus our Lord" (RSV). The apostle confesses that no power is able to create a permanent fracture between the love of Christ and the human being. That is not a matter of mere academic interest in a world where people fall into the hands of persecutors and torturers, where powers—be they anonymous or infamous—have men and women in their grasp and can cast them into darkness. The Christian church believes that since Christ has risen from the dead, death does not have the power to keep a human being forever out of the reach of the living God. This promise is unshakably rooted in the death and resurrection of Jesus Christ.

The Objective Model
The second model to be discussed is linked historically with the name of Anselm of Canterbury (1033-1109), and in the theological literature is termed the objective or juridical model. The notion that the devil should have a claim on this world made no sense to Anselm. It simply could not be. Is it not written in the Psalms that "The earth is the Lord's and the fullness thereof, the world and those who dwell therein" (Ps. 24:1)?

For that reason Anselm looked for another image to picture the relation between God and humankind. Anselm focussed on the now disrupted good relationship in which God and human beings are supposed to coexist. The conflict concerns the violation of the order between God and humankind and the violation of God's honor. This violation must be atoned for by way of satisfaction or compensation, *satisfactio*. This is often understood as a juridical or forensic way of thinking. I believe that this characterization is too restricted and an inaccurate reflection of what is actually going on. It puts the modern reader on the wrong track because for the contemporary reader 'juridical' means only formal court proceedings and solutions. So, what happened in the Fall? The sin of the human creature offended God's honor and broke God's order. Moreover, God's plan of salvation would fail if the number of fallen angels could not be replenished. Something must be done to restore what has gone wrong. In this context, the words justice and satisfaction are used. It may be that these words sound hard, if not heartless. Merely hearing these words cause a great many people to recoil. Because of the emotional charge these words now carry, such a reaction is underable, but at the same time honesty compels us to say that Anselm should be honored for having given us a sample of extremely contextual theology. He tries to rethink what happened in the incarnation of the Son of God and does so against the background of his own culture.

What he says about humankind's relation to God in terms of order, justice, honor and need for satisfaction if violation occurs needs to be understood against the background of a society in which order and justice were scarce. Order (*ordo*) is not a bourgeois term, to be equated with squeezing out all the creativity and zest from life. Order stands in opposition to arbitrariness and justice in opposition to unlimited retaliation. We approach the inner content of these concepts of order, justice and satisfaction better if we translate them in psychological and social-psychological terms. What has became familiar as the 'juridical' model encompasses, in fact, far more. It explains reconciliation in terms of system theory. Anselm's theology looks at the relation that binds God and humankind in an all-encompassing way. Each member of the system has a unique place in the societal framework. Each member needs to be honored according to the place he or she occupies.

If one does not take others into account, acting as though they do not exist, then relations are disturbed. The world of human beings, the mutual bond which ties them together, begins to totter: a part of the self, of identity, is stolen. In Anselm's terms, our honor is affected, we are shortchanged as persons. It is not right to take honor in Anselm in its personal sense; for him the term has to do with the place someone holds in a framework of relations. According to Anselm, something similar is true for the relation between God and humankind. If human beings do not offer to God the obedience that is due him, than something goes awry in that relation. Human beings, as active participants in the relation between the Creator and his creation, have not fulfilled their obligations. They have not lived up to their responsibilities. At that moment two options are open to God. God can punish humanity, that is, bring the human race to an end. But God's honor prohibits that. He would then not achieve the goal of his work in creation, namely, a humanity that willingly serves Him. Therefore God chooses another way, that is, he chooses to restore the relation. Therefore, he offers the way of compensation or satisfaction. Human beings are offered the possibility of once again becoming subjects.[3] God sends his Son to make compensation possible. Thus God himself facilitates reconciliation. The God-man Jesus Christ is on the one hand a representative of humanity. In Jesus the human race willingly offers the obedience due to God. But there is more. The God-man Jesus Christ does more than He is obliged to do. He lays down his life voluntary and thereby offers a satisfaction that counterbalances the whole weight of the sin of humanity. The voluntary offering of his life creates a 'surplus value' that suffices to compensate for every human slight to God's honor. Therefore the life and death of Jesus is preeminently salvific.

The rethinking of reconciliation as found in the writings of Anselm has had a major influence on Western theology and spirituality. It later became known and labelled the objective or juridical model. We recognize this model in questions 12-19 of the Heidelberg Catechism. The salvation that is obtained at the cross and in the resurrection is explained in terms of justice, wrath and satisfaction. No human being is able to bear the weight of God's wrath in his human flesh. And yet someone of the human race has to do it, as the representative for all fellow-humans. So a human

---

[3] For this interpretation see especially Plasger 1993.

being is needed, one who is truly human and truly righteous (Question 16). At the same time this must be a being who by the power of his divinity is able to bear the weight of God's anger, in order to restore righteousness and life to us (Question 17). The combination of both, a truly human being who represents us and yet possesses divine stature, is found in Jesus Christ, because in his person both natures are united (Question 18). The doctrine of reconciliation found in this catechism rests on the doctrine of Jesus as truly human and truly divine.

It is possible, no doubt, to make critical observations regarding Anselm's concept. In the first place, the concept of justice seems to be quite oriented towards a Roman model of jurisprudence, according to which justice is defined as distributive justice. In the Old Testament and in Paul God's justice is seen as a power that brings salvation. It is primarily a positive concept. That notion almost vanishes in Anselm. In the second place, it is questionable whether the demand for compensation agrees with Anselm's own image of God. Would submission and repentance not suffice?

It must be emphasized, however, that this reflection yields very valuable elements, still useful today. Anselm reminds us that restoring relations will not be easy in many cases. The statement Anselm addressed to his interlocutor Boso is justly famous: "Thou hast not yet considered how great the weight of sin is." On the basis of our own experience we know that forgiveness is a long and often laborious process. It takes considerable effort to restore the proper order to systems of relationships in which individuals coexist with one another and should be enriching one another's lives. Anyone who ignores the disorder or argues that "It isn't all that bad" or glosses things over with the contention that victims should stop complaining and start forgiving, shows too little appreciation for the depth of injury that afflicted people experience. The perpetrator must do something; there must be some form of compensation. When people hurt one another, it is as if they rob one another, as if something is stolen. The injury remains. One can think of marriages that have broken up, leaving the shattered pieces everywhere, of people who have been damaged by their upbringing, of people who were injured because they were violated bodily and spiritually, as in cases of incest and rape. What is necessary in such cases is first of all *acknowledgement*. Acknowledgement is a key word.

Impasse

It is not unusual to find that there is an impasse in the relations between individuals or groups, which in spite of all good will cannot be overcome. This impasse often arises from the absurdity and irreversibility of the injustice inflicted, an attack on life that can no longer be excused as a mistake or as ignorance. That impasse is reached when we encounter what we call an unforgivable act, the root of which appears to have been the sheer lust to kill or do evil. Then even moral discourse falls short and it becomes obvious that some problems can no longer be solved within a moral framework.

In morality a human being deals with him- or herself, his or her own humanity and moral capacity. Standing before the truly unforgivable, the human being as wrongdoer has reached the point where he or she has forfeited all right to go on. At that point the moral order has reached the end of its own capacities. Precisely in encountering unforgivable and absurd evil, it becomes understandable that if there will be any progress, something radically new has to happen, something that both respects the moral order and supersedes and uplifts this order as well.

Guilt can be removed when acknowledgement takes place, and such removal takes place only when God provides a new relation instead of the old one. That is the systematic meaning of objective reconciliation. Wrath, the verdict and its execution are not separate moments but elements in a process that aims at the restoration of life. This reconciliation is objective because, in his relation with his Son, God accomplishes a reality that does not find its origin in the human being but in the relation in which this human has been involved through God's act.

Something like this is found not only in the work of Anselm but also in all modern versions of this model, where in a objective sense the power of guilt or the devil's circle of death and revenge is broken by God. The God who is the fountain of life touches the order in which the unforgivable rules and destroys.

In addition to the objections that have already been raised against Anselm's version of the doctrine of reconciliation I must mention another. It is argued that in the objective doctrine of reconciliation as it appears in Anselm, the Heidelberg Catechism and Karl Barth's version, human agency is expelled. Reconciliation takes place outside of us and is not a sufficiently interactive process.

If one proceeds from the modern individualistic perception of reality, then this is the case. But as soon as one realizes that Anselm and the Catechism reason from humanity as a whole, as a collective with a leader or captain, things become different. Humanity should give something back, do what is fitting and proper. In other words, in his own way Anselm has an eye for the freedom and dignity of the human being. This human being is held responsible, and in this way he is honored as actor. He is not the unresisting victim of a cowardly attack without a will of his own and on the basis of this doctrine of reconciliation he cannot exculpate himself by taking on the role of victim.

The problem is that we, as humans, are not able to repair the relationship. We are not able to put the train back on the track. This is why the incarnation is necessary. The human being who can do this needs the support of divine power or a Divine Power. That is why Anselm and the Heidelberg Catechism turn to the doctrine of Christ as one person in two natures for support. In Christ we encounter a person who by virtue of his divinity is able to bear the verdict of God. The classic doctrine of reconciliation shows an exceptional depth, because it is driven by the notion that God steps in to supply our deficiency. At the same time human beings are not swept away in the atonement but involved in the restoration through the God-man Jesus. In Barth's modern version, the human being is invited to give an answer to that which has been done for him in the event of the cross and resurrection. The accomplished fact of the reconciliation, which ontologically includes all people as fellow human beings of Jesus Christ, dominates this concept. What Barth accomplishes with his concept is that, theologically speaking, there is no other choice than inclusive thinking. The road that must be followed to resolve conflicts can no longer contain any discord or division which we would want to perpetuate. Salvation, peace, indeed any existence in this world, is not possible without that universal dimension.

The Subjective Model
Besides the dramatic and juridical models, a third model can be distinguished. It has entered the history of theology as the subjective model of reconciliation, a not entirely fitting designation. This variant also has its roots in history. We already find it in some form in Augustine, and later on in the Middle Ages, in one of Anselm's students, Abelard (1079-1142). It was adopted by the Socinians in the sixteenth century and has broadened its influence in the liberal theology of the nineteenth century. This is the model that is attractive for many people at the moment, because the central role of the human being is assured at its heart: reconciliation is only accomplished if I, as a human subject, let myself be reconciled and show conciliatory behavior.

The story of the cross is the mirror in which the human can see her own role and repent. Abelard reminds us of the words of Jesus about the woman who was a sinner, after she anointed him with valuable ointment: "Therefore I tell you, her sins, which were many, are forgiven, for she loved much. But he who is forgiven little, loves little" (Luke 7:47 RSV). This vision links up with a verse such as 11 Corinthians 5:20: "So we are ambassadors for Christ, God making his appeal through us. We beseech you on behalf of Christ, be reconciled to God." The focus points towards the change that seeing the life-giving sacrifice of Christ and love brings about in a human being.

In this model, the decisive moment is there to be seized. The initiative for reconciliation and restoration that comes from God seeks a response from human beings. A restored relation is only realized where the human in full freedom repents and shows love in return. It is like the uneven water level in canal locks. The valve is opened and the water streams in, but this does not mean ships in the locks are immediately on the same level. It takes time before the water on both sides reach the same level.

The strong point of the subjective doctrine of reconciliation is that it takes the appeal, indeed, command to reconciliation seriously. God is interactive in his contact with people; he tries to draw us onto the playing field, to involve us. When humans block the passage to reconciliation, something stagnates, petrifies. The power granted to human agency is simultaneously the weakness of the concept. The subjective doctrine of reconciliation has in view situations which can still be turned around and people who can do something about them, people for whom turning around still matters. But what has the church to offer in the case of hopeless situations, when there is nothing left to repair and everything is totally blocked? What if we cannot respond or there is no response to make? It is then that the objective doctrine of reconciliation describes a stunning play by a new player on the field that saves us from absolute despair.

Implications

What is tenable knowledge concerning reconciliation? Before trying to answer this question, we must remember that every model, every model has certain implications. Each of them contains a view of salvation and destruction and leads to ethical consequences. These have been examined in the discussion of the different types of doctrines of reconciliation. This is also the case with the different perspectives on the cross within the New Testament. In the following I limit myself to only two biblical - writers.

Luke

First I want to look at Luke and the Acts of the Apostles. In Luke it is people who bring Jesus to the cross and God is the One who puts injustice right. The injustice was not accomplished without the Sanhedrin, but there is no indication of how God is involved in the wrongdoing of people. This remains vague. The death of Jesus is only a moment in the transition to his glorified condition. In his suffering Jesus is pictured as an exemplary model through which bystanders are moved to repent. While he is hanging on the cross, Jesus prays for his executioners (Luke 23:34). He remains faithful to his last breath, with it entrusting himself to God (Luke 23:4-6). Bystanders are also implicitly summoned to repent in answer to the rehabilitation which Jesus receives because God raises him and shares his glory with him. As a result of the death of Jesus, the bystanders beat their breasts and Peter's listeners ask fearfully what they must do (Acts 2:37). It should be clear that because of these tendencies the gospel of Luke provides ground for the subjective doctrine of reconciliation.

The main impression is that in Luke the death of Jesus as such is not at all a direct and positive factor in salvation. In theological language, the cross does not have any soteriological meaning. Rather, this death has ethical consequences. It makes people anxious about their spiritual state. People must be baptized in the name of Jesus Christ. Only then can they endure the coming judgment that lies in the hands of the glorified Savior. They are called to be part of the new people of God. The ideal of the new people of God is attainable. Indeed, the picture of the ideal congregation is already present in Acts. Those theologians today who prefer this line of testimony above other lines should remind themselves that the consequence of this line is that ethical rigorism which has determined the greatest part of Christian history. The story of Ananias and Sapphira in Acts 5 can be seen as the paradigm of this rigorism.

Paul

In the letters of Paul, the cross and resurrection feature as two moments in one unified salvation history. Paul articulates this history in terms of victory as well as in terms of expiation. That serves as background for the victory model as well as for the objective doctrine of reconciliation. Here too we see ethical implications. The powers of death and sin appear as forces that have been condemned by the cross and have lost their definite legitimacy. From now on Jews and non-Jews have access to the restored relationship with God through Jesus Christ. In the history of the cross God has taken a decisive 'down payment' on His kingdom. The lives of Christians are lived in the shadow of God's acts in the cross and resurrection.

This means their lives take place in the shadow of the judgment God has already spoken. This judgement, however, is not the last word. Paul teaches us that we have to distinguish between the condemnation of powers that took place in the cross event and the fulfilment. The final rescue and glorification of creation still has to take place. It lies in the future. This too will be a judgment. Paul fought tooth and nail to resist groups who thought that the resurrection of Jesus Christ rounded off God's mighty acts. The creation is still sighing, but this is an interim, marked off by a line God has drawn in the sending of his Son and in the future by the Second Coming, the Day of the Lord. The rest of God's acts with this world will take place according to what has become reality once and for all in the history of Jesus.

Concluding Remarks

The comprehensive view of sin as a power provides several perspectives that can point the way toward conclusions. First of all, it can keep us from too much moralism. This may seem strange, because most people generally view sin as a moral issue. They think that in Protestant (and particularly Calvinist) theology the doctrine of total depravity means that the human being is incapable of doing anything good. Sin is identified with moral depravity. This is a serious mistake, even within a Calvinist context. There is a moral dimension present in sin, but this is not its chief dimension. Moral sin is an effect, a visible effect of something deeper. Sin is fundamentally a religious concept. It refers to the ruptured relation with God. It is about an absence in our soul. Anyone who understands the word sin exclusively in terms of good and bad is still on a superficial level. The estrangement is also present when it is not visible. If we approach sin in that way, we split the world into saints and evildoers: one group of bad guys and another group who think they are the good guys, without blemish. The result is that extraordinary forms of evil baffle us, because we cannot conceive of them. The result is that a person or group who does great evil is identified with evil itself. This process fits into a cultural climate where personal integrity and good intentions have become the standard for our self-evaluation. But these standards of personal integrity and good intentions are basically moral standards, and turn out to be insufficient to save us from in fact doing evil ourselves or harming other people or groups. These standards do not save us from actual guilt and damage.

When we take into account the suprapersonal dimension of estrangement, it becomes clear that even our best intentions are not exempt from that estrangement. Furthermore, this theological-anthropological notion of sin as religious estrangement offers another advantage. It is this comprehensive concept of sin in particular that makes it possible to distinguish between the human being and his deeds. Our identity does not coincide completely with our acts, nor does it coincide with our personal integrity; our identity is given to us in the Word as a promise. According to the Pauline letters, our new identity is our being with Christ. It is God's decision to look at us in connection with Jesus Christ. A variety of biblical words point to that relation: sons, children, friends, heirs (Romans 8:15-17).

The outcome of this essay could be the impression that in the final analysis an objective type of reconciliation is preferable to the others[4]. This, however, is not exactly the point I want to make. What I want to stress is the following: dogmatic theology functions as the background debate in many different situations. Thus, dogmatic theology can be of help in these various situations that occur between God and human beings, and between human beings. That means that no model has exclusive precedence. It means rather that in some situations a specific model will be preferable because it leads to a more adequate perception and reaction. It is, however, true that in terms of pure conceptuality the objective model has a more integrative capability. The objective model covers situations and dimensions of life that are absent from or hardly conceived in the subjective model. Particularly in the case of an impasse, of a situation that is beyond repair any more and where all good intentions fall short, an objective concept of reconciliation leads to a view of human life that does not exclude humans from being acting subjects, but also affords salvation from an irreversible isolation and complete identification with guilt. It is the miracle and gift of God that he makes a distinction between act and actor. And when God distinguishes, ossified situations can begin to move again. Those are exactly the dimensions that are implicit in the Exultation of the Cross on Good Friday and in the hymns of Paul Gerhardt.

Bibliography

Assefa, Hizkias. (1994). *Peace and Reconciliation as a Paradigm: A Philosophy of Peace and its Implications on Conflict, Governance and Economic Growth in Africa*. 4th edition. Nairobi: Acis.

Aulén, G. (1931). *Christus Victor: An Historical Study of the Three Main Types of the Idea of the Atonement*. London: S.P.C.K.

Plasger, G. (1993). *Die Not-Wendigkeit der Gerechtigkeit. Eine Interpretation zu 'Cur Deus homo' von Anselm von Canterbury*. Münster: Aschendorf.

Schwager, R. (1986). *Der Wunderbare Tausch. Zur Geschichte und Deutung der Erlösungslehre*. Munich: Kösel. Pp. 32-53.

Van Asselt, W.J. (1999). "Verzoening in veelvoud?" *Kerk en Theologie* 50: 189-204.

---

[4] The integrative function of this model is stressed by Van Asselt (1999).

Religion, Conflict and Reconciliation

Ecumenical Initiatives Amidst Human Brokenness and Community Division

Jerald D. Gort

We are deeply shocked by the misuse of religion by both Christians and Muslims in committing grave acts of violence against humanity. We believe that this is against the essence of both faiths, since both advocate peace and harmony for all peoples, regardless of religious affiliation.

Crisis in the Moluccas

Why do intelligent, capable individuals pray so much and think so little? Can't they see their faith is killing them? Would Muhammad throw stones at Moses? Would Moses retaliate?

Paul Sanche

Lord, make me an instrument of your peace. Oh, Master, grant that I may never seek so much to be consoled as to console; to be understood as to understand; to be loved as to love with all my soul.

St. Francis of Assisi

Lord, give me that pacific mind which spreads Thy peace throughout mankind and knits them all in one.

Charles Wesley

Religion and Conflict

Though up to now it has proven impossible to formulate a completely adequate, universally acceptable definition of religion, generally speaking it can be said to take its rise from a divinely initiated encounter of people with the Holy or the Sacred. The great Dutch missiologist, J.H. Bavinck wrote in a posthumous publication that religion has to do with "man's existential relationships" (Bavinck 1966: 112). It is possible for human beings to be occupied with themselves only and to look no further.

> But as soon as he becomes aware of his relationships, he becomes stupefied and asks: What am I in this great cosmos? What am I, over against the norm, that strange phenomenon in my life that has authority over me? What am I in my life that speeds on and on ...? What am I in the face of that remarkable feeling that overwhelms me sometimes, the feeling that everything must be changed and that things are not right as they are? What am I, over against that very mysterious background of existence, the divine powers? It is in the area of [these] existential relations that man is confronted with the crucial matters of life—and ... religion is the

way in which man experiences the deepest existential relations and gives expression to this experience. (Bavinck 1966: 112)

The human response to the encounter with the Holy usually has both an immediate and a mediate dimension. Subjectively, this religious response assumes the shape of inner feelings of reverential awe, adoration, veneration, worship. Objectively, it is embodied in some concrete form of ritual-cultic and/or conceptual and ethical expression, a few common examples of which are: Holy Scriptures; ecclesiastical, communal and often monastic organization; confessions, theologies and doctrines; narratives and myths; homiletical exhortation and instruction; song, music and dance; gestures and incantations; prayer and meditation; holy meals; offerings and blessings; unctions and rites of ordination, consecration, cleansing and healing; rules for right living, for leading a moral and rewarding existence.

From all accounts, the need for religious experience and articulation in whatever form or fashion appears to be woven into the very fabric of human nature. "No people or tribe is without [religion], however variously it finds expression and even if it has not been specifically identified by name" (Sundermeier 1991: 856). Christians proceed from the biblical teaching that divine *chesed* (Hebrew for loving-kindness, goodness, grace) is an innate component of creation and the creation order: *chesed* is as great as the heavens (Psalm 57:10, 103:11), it is replete in the earth (Psalm 33:5, 119:64), it is everlasting (Psalm 100:5, 106:1). As a revered seminary professor of philosophy of religion, Henry Stob, used to impress upon us: "The entire world and every single human being is ineluctably subject to God's steadfast grace." Being thus in the grip of divine love and favor, people appear to have the need to respond, to commune with the Supreme Being, and it is difficult to imagine how they could do this or even be conscious of Ultimate Reality absent the projicient teachings and rituals of religion.[1] Humans, it would seem, are incurably religious. Moreover, many Christians share the view "that God as Jesus' Father, the Creator, stands behind all religions and that through them God wants to protect human beings in their life and in their humanity. Religions are thus part and parcel of God's work of preservation in the world" (Sundermeier 1991: 856; cf. also Neill 1971: 517-18 and Rahner and Vorgrimler 1965: 329-33).

For the vast majority of the world's population, religion is the stud and stay of life; most people cannot get along without it as a means of coping with existential disquietude and as a medium of faith and hope. Furthermore, religion has it within its power to inspire people and governments to substitute idealism for greed, love of neighbor for ethnic hatred, humanitarian concern for political egotism and economic selfishness, friendship for enmity, irenic deportment for militaristic posturing. Religion, therefore, is of the utmost significance for human beings: in its absence, it may be averred, they cannot truly prosper either personally or collectively.

---

[1] It should be noted here that Buddhism in its original form understood itself as a way of *deliverance* from objective, formal religion. Cf. Rahner and Vorgrimler 1965: 331.

There are those, of course, who espouse a completely different reading of religion. In a recent letter to the editor of *Time Magazine* one Vasudev Parvani wrote:

> The only thing that would [end bloodshed in the Middle East and elsewhere] is the elimination of organized religion. As long as people segregate themselves under various labels like Roman Catholic, Protestant, Muslim, Hindu and Sikh, there will be no peace in this world. (February 12, 2001)

And another skeptic wrote in a British newspaper:

> Religion may not be a disease but it is undeniably an affliction. Far more dangerous than mere weaponry, religions do not, as advertised, produce serenity, compassion and understanding. Far from lifting our eyes to the heavens and making us into loftier, worthier beings, they turn us into monsters?

While sentiments such as the latter may be interpreted as an unwarranted animadversion, the product, perhaps, of a wounded spirit or deep personal disillusionment and anger, it cannot be denied that, in terms of their human, empirical aspect, religions have frequently manifested a protean character with respect to good and evil, exhibiting an anomalous capacity for betrayal of their central teachings, a peculiar propensity for divergence from rectitude and collusion with harmful forces.

> Established religions have often divided people and nations and given rise to tensions and conflicts. They have held up scientific progress, resisted social change, supported the rich and the powerful against the poor and weak, and have often added religious fuel to military conflagrations, making reconciliation more difficult. Of all the wounds human beings inflict on one another, religious wounds are the most difficult to heal. (Samartha 1991: 37)

There are times in which, at the hands of bigots or deluded zealots, religions took on the nature of a Procrustean bed wherein people of other faiths were ruthlessly and sometimes violently forced to fit themselves.

Religions are indeed stamped by tremendous historical ambiguity and it would be a grave mistake to underestimate the critical position religion occupies in human affairs and contexts. Religious convictions and attitudes, on the one hand, and political and economic choices and relationships, on the other, are very often closely related, even—and perhaps particularly—in societies professing allegiance to the canon of a putative separation of church and state. As Paul Marshall recently contended, it would be "absurd to examine a political order without attending to the role of religion" in it, and any analysis of social reality "that ignores religious dynamics should be inherently suspect" (cited in Seiple 2001: 36). And another astute contemporary observer, Joel A. Carpenter, maintains that the world is too permeated by religion "for us to believe that secularization will continue as a dominant narrative," pointing to the fact that "in the field of international relations, conversations have begun concerning

---

[2] Cited from a flyer advertizing the activities and publications of the UK wing of the project entitled 'The Gospel and Our Culture'.

the growing 'religion factor'." Carpenter rightly argues that while the significance of religion may, in the modern era, "have been difficult to accept in the West, where as early as the Peace of Westphalia in 1648 a bargain was struck to keep the all-too-volatile ingredients of religion out of international relations," it is clear that other cultures "have no intention of keeping them out, and [that] contemporary world affairs are shot through with religious dynamics" (Carpenter 2001: 7).[3]

Religions have often played and continue to play a prominent and potent part not only in human well-being but clearly in human strife, dissension and turmoil as well. Religious conflict,[4] which can so easily explode into vicious cycles of retributive violence, is probably the toughest, fiercest and most persistent form of interhuman friction and discord in known human history and certainly in our ever-shrinking present-day world. Interreligious hostility is a species of conflict that poses an exceptionally perilous hazard to human communities and threatens, wherever found, to unravel the fabric of the entire social order not only at the local or national but also the global level.

It is of the utmost importance to realize, however, that religious fanaticism and interreligious ill-will or belligerence do not generally stand alone, but are most commonly catalyzed by powerful determinants external to religion itself.

Rudimentary Agents of Conflict

History demonstrates repeatedly that religion is susceptible to use, or rather misuse, by unscrupulously ambitious persons to attain selfish ends, that religious militancy is usually closely linked with the project of an individual or group seeking to gain ad-

---

[3] Cf. also Carpenter's recommendations: Samuel P. Huntington, *The Clash of Civilizations and the Remaking of World Order* (New York: Simon & Schuster, 1996), and Peter L. Berger (ed.), *The Desacralization of the World: Resurgent Religion and World Politics* (Grand Rapids: Eerdmans, 1999).

[4] Within the context of the argumentation of this essay the concepts of conflict and violence bear a negative connotation. This is not to say, however, that conflict always has to be understood *in malam partem*. In fact, issues of truth periodically call for conflict: sometimes the achievement of liberation and justice depends on its use. One should also distinguish between various types of violence. The kind of random violence glorified in the pre- and post-WW II writings of Georges Sorel and Herbert Marcuse as a means of achieving the ends of the New Left, for example, is and remains totally unacceptable. If violence causes indiscriminate evil, that evil, even if it serves the purpose of a desirable goal, may never be called 'good'. As John Calvin, one of the leaders of the sixteenth century Protestant Reformation, argued, violence in the form of *the application of force to resolve matters of truth* may at times be legitimate and necessary as a means of last resort, provided it is absolutely clear that there is no other way out of an unbearably evil political, economic or social situation and that there is a genuine possibility that its exercise will bring about conditions which are more nearly in conformity with truth and justice.

vantage from or power over others. That is why, in order to grasp fully the role of religion in situations of conflict, it is necessary to distinguish carefully between antecedent or primary and subsequent or secondary causes. Although 'religion' seldom constitutes the essential causal agent of either general interhuman or interreligious hostility, it may and often does serve to inflame existing animosities. "It is not religion *per se*" that gives rise to conflict but rather "its followers with powerful vested interests" who, manipulating "its emotional appeal for their own purposes," are the perpetrators of hostility (Engineer 2001a). In many countries and areas of the present world, conflict between religious groups "is more political than religious, though religious symbols are used" to legitimize it (Engineer 2001b). A protest action or struggle undertaken to redress egregious wrong can be fanned by religious sentiments and loyalties into ugly rampages of bitter hatred seemingly beyond human control. Religion may be and has often been used both to ignite and justify aggression as well as to galvanize and energize response to aggression[5]

It is possible that one might wish to argue for a modification of the thesis that 'religion' is rarely the elemental cause of conflict, pointing to the fact, for example, that there are certain shared holy places in sundry parts of the world which seem by their very existence to inspire and perpetuate interreligious division, hatred and confrontation. But even this is less a matter of 'religion' than of past wrongs, old pain, and human obduracy. Hence, in this case, too, the thesis holds: while the face of religions clearly can and recurrently does become badly blemished and disfigured, it is very often outside factors which cause it to develop this carbuncled complexion. Again, the true underlying causes of human conflict are of a chiefly non-religious nature. A number of the most important of these determinants are outlined in the sequel.

Some of the most salient past and present causes of (potential) conflict are those that fall into the broad category of violations of civil, political, economic, social and cultural human rights: slavery and colonialism; crusading, culture-destroying invasions both old and new; apartheid, casteism and segregation; exploitation and oppression of minorities, women, children, the poor and the helpless; proliferation of arms and crushing external debt in Third World countries; political bullying of weaker nations by stronger ones; gender inequality in North and South, East and West; neglect of victims of epidemic diseases such as AIDS/ HIV; lack of adequate medical care, decent housing, education and employment. And many of these problems are exacerbated by such things as swaggering ethnic pride, unresolved territorial disputes, overpopulation and sweeping corruption.

A second constellation of factors that contribute to present-day conflict are the large numbers of monstrous brutalities, genocides, disappearances, terrorist attacks and other heinous crimes and outrages inflicted on people, coupled with the matter

---

[5] For example, during the time of the Crusades but also at countless historical junctures in various geographical locations on earth both before and after these so-called 'holy wars'.

of the impunity of the perpetrators of these offenses, which, as has been recently pointed out, "is not a new phenomenon. Individuals and groups in power have gone unpunished for serious [crimes against humanity] throughout the history of most of the world's peoples." (Jacques 2000: 5) Of the manifold social pathologies of our time, however, global poverty, world hunger, and rampant racism are arguably among the most nefarious.

Further, interhuman hostility can also be spawned by feelings of innate superiority on the part of those belonging to a given religio-cultural background, coupled with a strong belief in the intrinsic inferiority of other spiritual heritages, which latter are then also often demonized, i.e., turned into victims of what might be termed the 'infidel syndrome'. Some religious adherents seem to be greatly attracted by the temptation to look upon different faiths and religionists *de haut en bas*, and have in fact often exhibited just such a supercilious and condescending air toward other believers and traditions.

Finally, the question may be legitimately raised whether some religions, through their teachings, their theologies, their images of God or the infinite, their anthropologies, or through extravagant, intemperate claims to truth, are not more subject to a sense of primacy, more apt to assume a superior stance, more prone to conflict and violence than others. And indeed, there is no doubt that interreligious conflict can be and in some instances has been and is caused by a clash of ideas, both at the theological-theoretical and practical levels, for example in the area of human rights. Moreover, there is another way in which conflict can result immediately and directly from religion. Religious or moral turpitude has frequently occasioned impassioned criticism and calls to repentance and radical change of direction by prophets ranging from Isaiah through Jesus, Muhammad, Gandhi, to Martin Luther King and Beyers Naudé. Such calls often led and lead to resentful hostility and resistance. It is important not to lose sight of these very real possibilities.

Nevertheless, the violence of injustice remains the most powerful and virulent source of interhuman and interreligious conflict. It is clear that even a superficial analysis of our present-day world reveals a situation shot through with injustice in a host of different shapes and forms. As Robert Schreiter has pointed out, the twentieth century has been characterized by an extraordinary amount of conflict, bloody international, civil and ethnic wars and worldwide patterns of exploitation and domination, all of which has "conspired to make this century surely one of the most violent that humankind has seen" (Schreiter, 10). Indeed, he states, "the times have been so violent that to speak of 'world order' has an oddly oxymoronic ring to it" (Schreiter, 10). And it is instances of human disorder resulting from the abuse of political, military, economic or ecclesiastical power which poison human relations, including those at the level of religion. It is cases of past and present prejudice, arrogance, and oppression that beget abiding malignant effects on local communities and human society as a whole. It is human injustice that underlies most occurrences of human conflict. That being the case, situations of conflict, even though they very often take on a deeply religious hue due to the fact that both the victims and perpetrators of injustice are religious people or are at least closely identified with one or another religion, cannot be resolved without dealing with this primary cause. It is, in short, injustice that will have to be addressed if there is to be any hope for cessation of friction and strife among humans.

Though, as just indicated, situations of inequity and exploitation very often translate into interreligious antagonism and hostility, at their best all the great religious traditions of the world offer ways to deal with the violence of injustice; they can and sometimes do play an important role in attempts to bring about the resolution of conflict and advance the cause of peace, reconciliation, and harmonious coexistence. This also holds for the modern Protestant ecumenical movement, presently embodied in the World Council of Churches (WCC), headquartered in Geneva. Before proceeding to a delineation of some of the ways in which the WCC has been engaged in the struggle for a greater degree of justice and amity in human relations, however, a few preliminary observations are in order.

Four Caveats

Christian Complicity in Injustice and Conflict

A legitimate question may be put as to whether, in view of the centuries-long accommodation of violence by the theology of Christen*dom* created and nurtured in the West and in more recent times the history of the indirect or direct relationships of Christian churches with unjust and inhuman systems, such as mercantilism and colonialism, casteism, slavery and apartheid, *laissez-faire* capitalism and liberal free-market ideology, Christianity can be a credible party to the search for reconciliation. Has its believability in this regard not often "been compromised by its silence and complicity with victimizers in the interest of *Realpolitik*" (Petersen 1992: viii)?

Of course no one, presumably, would want to suggest that Christianity's entanglements with earthly powers of ill are unique in the world. There are many other religious denominations and communities that have been and continue to be involved, sometimes very directly and heavily, in the perpetuation of injustice and human distress. Moreover, Christianity's record in this connection is, like that of the other great religious traditions, by no means entirely negative. Nevertheless, it behooves Christian ecumenical churches to acknowledge at the very outset the fact of their periodic associations, whether conscious or unconscious, with forces inimical to human well-being. And indeed, the modern ecumenical movement is deeply aware that a great deal of egregious injustice has even been perpetrated in the name of or with the explicit or tacit approval of Christianity and the church: against Jews, Muslims, South and North American Indians, black people, women, homosexuals, dissidents and heretics.

Christians and people of other faiths who are guilty of misbehavior in the past or who are allied with exploitative forces in the present must repent, seeking to correct the misconduct in which they were involved by standing in prophetic solidarity with and engaging in sacrificial service among victims of injustice and undertaking any other activities that might lead to the healing of wounds. And in response to these signs and acts of repentance, victims can assume "a 'post-exilic' stance whereby [they] overcome their preoccupation with oppression to become healing agents of reconciliation" through forgiveness and acceptance (Petersen 1992: viii). It is essential, in this connection, not to lose sight of the fact that

> we cannot forgive ourselves for the wrongdoing of our past. Those whom we have injured must do that. ... Repentance can originate from the side of those who have perpetrated violence [of whatever nature], but reconciliation and forgiveness must come from the side of those who have suffered violence. (Schreiter 1992: 21)

And it is important to remember that reconciliation "is, finally, a spirituality or mode of being more than a strategy." Theologically speaking reconciliation "comes upon us like healing" (Petersen 1992: viii).

No Cheap Reconciliation as a Hasty Peace

As stated above, the quest for and restitution of justice is an absolute prerequisite for the resolution of conflict and the restoration of salubrious human relationships. History has seen many who have contended that this quest can best be fulfilled through the employment of force. But though use of the sword may sometimes be necessary to restore justice, even a 'just war' is incapable on its own of resolving conflict and begetting reconciliation. In Greek mythology Ares, the god of war, is called a reconciler, but the only reconciliation he brings about is the tragic unification of contenders in the realm of death.[6] If conflict is to be *truly* resolved, it is of the essence that injustice be unmasked and exposed for what it is wherever it is, in pursuance of which it is imperative for those at the receiving end of ill-treatment and oppression

> to break out of a situation of silence, isolation, fear and falsehood, to know the truth, to recover a shared memory and thus to restore human dignity for victims and accountability for the perpetrators. Without the intentional attempt to create a space where stories of humiliation and suffering can be told, where the truth can emerge and collective remembrance be restored, the search for justice will continue to divide the community rather than reestablish relationships and contribute to a process of healing. (Raiser 2000: vi)

Conflict can never be resolved by papering over reality or covering the perpetration of injustice with the mantle of love.

Ecumenical Christians are fully aware that a simple call for harmony in situations of conflict would constitute what Schreiter has termed a reconciliation which would "trivialize and ignore the sufferings" of victims and call on them "to forget or overlook" what they have experienced, a reconciliation that fails to uncover and confront the real causes of suffering and conflict (1992: 19). If the true sources of "the deeply conflictive realities that create the chasms that reconciliation hopes to bridge," are not "named, examined, and taken away" the only thing that will emerge

---

[6] Cf. L. Minnema, "Divided Families and Social Conflict" in this volume, 68-84.

"is a truce," or "reconciliation as a hasty peace" (Schreiter 1992: 22, 24, 19). It is "the antecedents of reconciliation, namely, the redemption from violence and suffering," (Schreiter 1992: 12) that will have to be pursued if peace and harmony are to be realized.

No Utopian Enthusiasm
The third thing that should be noted here is that for Christians reconciliation is not something that is or can be autonomously set into motion or accomplished by humankind in isolation from divine will and divine action but is, according to the Bible, initiated, activated and ultimately achieved by God in and through Jesus Christ (cf. II Corinthians 5:18-19). In contrast to sentiments held by many in the 1960s and 1970s, contemporary ecumenical Christians are neither naively sanguine about the *human* possibilities of changing society radically for the better nor under the illusion that the world's brokenness can be repaired and its divisions healed by dint of the ingenuity, dedication and exertions of humans alone. As the former General Secretary of the World Council of Churches, Emilio Castro, has recently written, people of his generation who were involved in the ecumenical movement have been "defeated and frustrated," humanly and historically speaking.

> There was on the one hand the whole passion of [the dream of changing] reality ... and on the other hand, even inside the church, there were the stopping forces, the refraining forces, the contradictory forces, and then the powers that were in the world showing themselves to be too powerful for the forces that we could manage or handle at a particular moment. (Castro 2000: 598)

Concepts such as 'one united human family' represent a noble and desirable but, for humans in the present world, unattainable goal. Just as malevolent human behavior and structural evil remain in the end great mysteries, so too is the fact that people are both empowered and able to address injustice but powerless and unable to effect lasting justice and righteousness one of the enduring riddles of human existence. Today, ecumenical Christian optimism regarding the resolution of conflict and the realization of interhuman reconciliation is thoroughly informed by a deep awareness of the profound reality, puissance and tenebrific effects of human sin, pride and egotism. Accordingly, most Christians associated with the ecumenical movement feel called to the discipline of quiet patience.

No Quiescence or Fatalistic View of Human Capacity
Despite this sober realism, however, ecumenical Christian churches know they *must* nevertheless be involved in the struggle against injustice "because of the messages they bear from Christ to be agents of reconciliation" (Schreiter 1992: 12). It is clear from biblical teaching that the correction of unrighteousness and the pursuit of human reconciliation are divine imperatives which take precedence even above religious observance.

> What is to me the multitude of your sacrifices? says the Lord. Bring no more vain offerings. New moon and Sabbath and the calling of assemblies—I cannot endure

iniquity and solemn assembly. Wash yourselves; make yourselves clean; remove the evil of your doings from before my eyes; cease to do evil, learn to do good; seek justice, correct oppression; defend the fatherless, plead for the widow. (Isaiah 1:11, 13, 16, 17)

So if you are offering your gift at the altar, and there remember that your brother has something against you, leave your gift there before the altar and go; first be reconciled to your brother, and then come and offer your gift. (Matthew 5:23, 24)

Because of the clear biblical teaching that they have been entrusted by God with a ministry of reconciliation in the world, Christians are keenly aware that they are called not only to the discipline of quiet patience but to the exercise of holy *im*patience in the form of prophetic action as well. And provided they evince sufficient awareness of and penitence for their past sins and present shortcomings in terms of social, economic and political abuses, Christian churches, as Schreiter rightly argues, *can* be involved in attempts to redress these wrongs.

While for ecumenical churches and Christians attainment of utopia is illusory, they hold that God is the Creator and Sustainer of the world and the Lord of history, which leads them to embrace an essentially positive conception of life on this earth and a cautiously optimistic view of the capacity of humans to work for the salvific transformation of the situations and systems of injustice that deform that life. In the words of Emilio Castro:

If the ecumenical movement has some particular ... vocation, I would say it is to be a movement of people in love with hope. We are to be people who cannot give up, people who still dream that tomorrow belongs in God's ... hands, and that we should be looking, fighting, working for that tomorrow..., knowing that God makes all things new, [trusting] that the power of the resurrection of Christ will be present, shaping, opening the future..., hoping that the promises of the new earth and the new heaven will become a reality. And meanwhile we offer ... our work, knowing that our work in the Lord is not in vain. (Castro 2000: 598-99)

On the basis of convictions such as these, ecumenical churches affirm that it is humanly possible to effect a greater degree of justice among the marginalized and oppressed.

WCC Initiatives: The Search for Justice and Reconciliation

Throughout its history the modern ecumenical movement has understood itself to be participating through its reflection and its various departments and programs in the struggle to overcome the evil effects of human wrongdoing in the world.[7] Notwithstanding or, perhaps better, precisely because of the witting complicity or unwitting

---

[7] This is, of course, not to say that the reflection of the WCC was unflawed or that its programs were always fully effective; there were failures, mistakes, miscalculations, at times there was resistance from some of the member churches.

enmeshment of the church in some of the exploitation and injustice which has afflicted and continues to beset our world, ecumenical Christians consider themselves duty-bound to participate in the attempt to overcome these human scourges, with a view to the settlement of conflict and thereby the creation of conditions conducive to the blossoming of interhuman reconciliation, the realization of *exempla* of peace in the midst of hostility and aggression, models of harmonious coexistence as oases in the desert, enclaves of blessing in the wilderness of persistent human conflict and incendiary fragmentation. Indeed, according to a recent statement by a United Nations official, the WCC has often been in the forefront of the fray, setting world standards for the struggle against injustice. A few of the concrete ways the Genevan ecumenical fellowship has attempted to address some of the sources of social unrest and friction in the world are briefly described below.

Struggle against Injustice
In its efforts to address the causes of interhuman conflict the WCC, through its Commission of the Churches in International Affairs (CCIA), has always been acutely concerned with instances of the lack or the violation of *human rights* in many parts of the world and the need to protect and promote these rights everywhere. The CCIA was "instrumental in effecting the establishment of the UN Commission on Human Rights and took an active part in the composition of the two 1966 International Covenants on Human Rights" (Gort 1995: 207). It was not until the Fifth Assembly of the WCC in Nairobi in 1975, however, that a consensus was reached regarding the content of these rights. It is now generally accepted within the ecumenical movement that they include: a 'first generation' of individual civil and political rights, including religious freedom, a 'second generation' of economic, social and cultural rights, and a 'third generation' of rights to self-determination, development, and freedom from want and aggression (cf. Gort 1995: 205, 223). An awareness of environmental rights has also emerged in recent years. Emphasis is being put on ecological responsibility and the urgent need to halt the injustice of environmental exploitation, first, because humankind has an obligation to husband God's creation, and second, because of the symbiotic relationship between humankind and the environment: when nature suffers, human beings suffer. By the early 1980s it was generally agreed that the modes of ecumenical action for human rights "consist of four main activities: monitoring, advocacy, the building of public awareness, and study" (Gort 1995: 219). It may be safely said that the WCC functions as one of the world's most important watchdogs of human and environmental rights.

From its very inception the ecumenical movement was also engaged in efforts to effect reconciliation between warring peoples, notably in Europe subsequent to the World War I and World War II, and to address the grave injustices inherent in the situation of *refugees* and other uprooted peoples. In the years since the 1970s, during which the refugee problem has escalated greatly, taking on global proportions, "the WCC refugee service [has] developed into a worldwide network of churches and ecumenical partners working closely together for the protection and assistance of refugees," most of whom, it is worth pointing out here, belong to religious traditions other than that of Christianity (Van Hoogevest 1991: 855-56). The 1981 WCC statement on "The Churches and the World Refugee Crisis" argues that refugees, "who are struggling for survival and for the recognition of their human dignity, 'have a natural claim on the churches'" (Van Hoogevest 1991: 855).

In response to the *poverty*, underdevelopment and widespread lack of social justice found in many parts of the world, the Commission on the Churches' Participation in Development (CCPD) and the Ecumenical Development Fund were created in 1970, through which "the WCC engaged in research, education, documentation and publication and provided technical advice and financial support where possible," in pursuit of "three interrelated objectives: justice, self-reliance and economic growth" (VanElderen, 30). After the Nairobi Assembly of the WCC in 1975 the CCPD carried out an influential study on "The Church and the Poor." Further, the WCC Bangkok conference in 1973, whose theme was "Salvation Today," stated that the quest for justice, peace and quality of life is an integral part of Christian mission, and the 1980 conference in Melbourne "described the poor as the criterion for mission work today" (VanElderen 1992: 34). Another important initiative that should be mentioned in this connection is the program on a "Just, Participatory, Sustainable Society," launched in 1975, which focussed attention on, among other things, the use of science and technology by industrially advanced societies "to serve military and economic interests which bring about great suffering [in the Third World]" (VanElderen 1992: 34).

The ecumenical movement also has a long record of condemning *racism*, beginning with the Edinburgh Conference of 1910 and the 1924 book, *Christianity and the Race Problem*, written by one of the outstanding ecumenical leaders of that time, J.H. Oldham. But gradually a "strong sense of the need to go beyond exhortation to action" arose (VanElderen 1992: 31), particularly under the influence of the victims of racial oppression, which led to the establishment of the WCC Program to Combat Racism in 1969. Through this program the ecumenical movement has taken concrete, energetic action in the struggle against various forms of racial discrimination, initially in southern Africa but later in a number of other areas of the world as well, including some southern states in the US.

The most recent addition to this category of ecumenical initiatives is the program dedicated to curbing *violence*, which was launched on February 4, 2001 at a service in the Kaiser Wilhelm War Memorial Church in Berlin, under the title "Decade to Overcome Violence" (DOV). According to the first issue of the WCC newsletter, *Overcoming Violence: Churches Seeking Reconciliation and Peace*, this initiative is an effort through the use of non-violent tactics "to overcome the violence of division in our societies and to respond to the yearning for peace and a life of dignity for future generations." A major issue for consideration here is violence against women and children and the gender inequality and sexism enshrined in law, culture or custom in most parts of the world, which also permeates the world religions, including the Christian church with its historical emphasis on the male perspective. The DOV program has its roots in the earlier reflection and work of the WCC, particularly through its Commission of the Churches on International Affairs, on the complex issue of impunity for perpetrators of human rights violations and crimes against humanity. The DOV also forms the framework within which current work on the matter of judicial impunity is being carried out by the WCC Cluster on Relations, one of the first results of which is the publication already cited above, *Beyond Impunity*, by Geneviève Jacques. Warning "that impunity, with its denial of the verifiable truth and refusal to allow the healing of memories, ticks away like a time bomb in the midst of societies," she reminds her readers that

> the conscience of humankind on the threshold of the third millennium remains haunted by mass and systematic crimes which have escaped judgment and which leave in the memory of the traumatized victims and peoples a permanent scar which time cannot remove, so long as there remains a feeling that a great injustice has not been put right. ... When the present is unworthy of the past, the future will soon take its revenge. (Jacques 2000: 6)

Through its Cluster on Relations the WCC has committed itself, in cooperation with the United Nations and other international and regional agencies and institutions, to the struggle against the severe injustice brought about by impunity. Other relevant foci of the Cluster include globalization and fair trade, good governance, militarization and arms control.

Wider Ecumenism
In recent decades the ecumenical task of constructing building blocks for interhuman reconciliation has come to be understood in terms of cooperative effort with others. Ecumenical Christians came to see the need to live up to the "testimony" of their faith that invites them, obliges them, to stand side by side with all those seeking the same goals (cf. Castro 2000: 596). "In the world there are movements that struggle for peace, for justice and for ecological responsibility. Our task is to put the churches at the service of those movements, to join forces going in the direction of the kingdom of God ..." (Castro 2000: 599).

The wider ecumenism also includes a way of addressing specifically interreligious suspicion and strife, namely the vitally important program of interfaith dialogue, which is specifically directed toward the improvement of relations and the stimulation of cooperation and joint action among the religions. As a recent issue of *WCC News* indicates: "Teaching people to be more sympathetic to believers of other faiths can be a strategy to eliminate violence." Interreligious reconciliation is mediated through a process whereby enemies and strangers become friends who can join hands and work together intimately in a spirit of harmony and trust, a process involving dialogue at four levels.[8]

---

[8] In my view, these levels of dialogue form parts of one whole, similar to the way in which the facets of a precious stone form a single gem.

The first of these is the *dialogue of histories*. This dialogue begins with a serious analysis of past relations between or among the religions involved. What stance have they assumed with respect to one another? And more importantly, what was or is the position they occupy vis à vis each other on the political, social, and economic planes? It is at this level of dialogue that questions of justice and injustice, power and domination, wealth and poverty come to the fore. As already argued, interreligious conflict, division and hatred is very often occasioned by exploitation and oppression via forces and structures with which a certain religion is or has been either rightly or wrongly identified in local, national or global contexts. In such settings the first thing religions and religious believers need to do is engage in a dialogue of histories, which invariably recognizes the victim of injustice as the proper subject and the perpetrator of that wrong as the proper object of any reconciliation that might emerge from this dialogical exchange.

The second tier of discussion among religions is the *dialogue of theologies, philosophies and mythologies*, whose purpose is to remove interreligious nescience and misunderstanding and foster respect and tolerance among people of differing faiths. This level of dialogue offers a means of gaining a sense of the deepest meaning and intention of one another's religious tenets and thus a way of breaking through communalist apprehensions of religion. Moreover, if the parties involved open themselves fully to the divinely inspired truth that enlightens all people of faith, this type of dialogue or comparative theology might yield a new interreligious hermeneutics, an auxiliary tool that could be employed to arrive at a deeper understanding of the divine will for humankind, a fuller comprehension of the sense and significance of life and the world, of injustice, conflict and reconciliation.

It should be obvious from this that participation in a dialogue of theologies by no means requires the adoption of a stance of uncritical relativism or an attitude of detachment with respect to one's own religion. On the contrary, such an attitude, far from being a mark of desirable openness, would seem rather to constitute a sign of infelicitous noncommittal. As Valkenberg has pointed out, this appears to be the case with much of European Christianity at the moment: one notices a certain nonchalance on the part of Western Christians who, in the context of interreligious encounter, "prefer not to talk about faith because it is irrelevant for" them, or who exhibit a "spiritual poverty" resulting from fundamental confusion regarding their faith (Valkenberg 2000: 32). Secure religious identity is the very foundation of authentic interreligious dialogue. In order to have proper dialogue at any level, the partners have to know where they stand. And this knowledge is quickened and enhanced by the proximity of other religions and religious believers: "It is only through encounter with the other that I acquire an idea of who I am" (Valkenberg 2000: 33). For example, the presence of Islam in Europe, as a modern European Muslim leader has observed, can provide the opportunity for Europeans to think about who they are and what they believe (Tariq Ramadan, *Time Magazine*, November 11, 2000). Interreligious reconciliation requires interfaith understanding, and the latter can be achieved only if the partners in dialogue can communicate with each other as committed believers at the spiritual level.

The third stratum of interreligious conversation is the *dialogue of spiritualities*. In the Christian ecumenical view, religious faith itself, in the sense of basic trust in God, acceptance of acceptance by God (cf. Moltmann 1971: 165), is an exceptionally important key to the realization of interhuman reconciliation, because on the foundation of this trust it becomes possible to accept the different other freely and fully. "God is 'for us' and therefore we can and must be 'with one another' and not 'against one another'" (Moltmann 1972: 48).[9] On that account it may be argued that from the Christian perspective interreligious colloquy certainly does not preclude and should definitely include interfaith witnessing to the truth as one has received, perceives, experiences and believes it. In fact, the truth claims of the various religions, based on the authority of holy scriptures and living traditions, would appear strongly to imply an *obligation* to interfaith witness.

At this level of dialogue religious believers would talk together heart to heart about their deepest fears and highest hopes for the future. Their aim would be to effect a peaceful, respectful exchange of truth claims, core beliefs and convictions, existential religious feelings. They would share spiritualities of reconciliation, relate accounts of redemption and sustenance to each other, narratives regarding salvation, i.e., the means whereby the walls of division between God and human beings, human being and human being, and humankind and nature are broken down. They would engage in mutual witness to beliefs in respect of the three elemental questions of human existence: Whence do we come? How ought we to live, and in the presence of what light do we grow and glow? What is our destination? New discoveries about one another's faith convictions may lead the partners in the dialogue of spiritualities to a broader, more inclusive understanding of the *consortium vitae divinae* (participation in the divine life).

The fourth level of interreligious discourse is the *dialogue of life*. There are undeniably real theological and spiritual differences and contextual peculiarities among the religions of the world, but there are also matters and concerns, such as injustice and poverty, which should be and in increasing measure are becoming of high salience to all of them alike. Religion can be of genuinely significant help in the struggle to meet the high goal of addressing the challenges of conflict and ameliorating the manifold situations of human suffering we face in our globalized world. But if religion is to fulfill this potential in any kind of effective way, the various religions will have to join hands and become involved in a sharing of energies, bending their best efforts to the development of collaborative actions of renewal and transformation, i.e., to the establishment of what have been called 'integrative synergies', among themselves but

---

[9] "Gott ist 'für uns,' darum können und sollen wir 'miteinander' und nicht 'gegeneinander' sein."

also between themselves and civil governments along with other secular institutions, visionary movements and moral agencies.

Religion, thus, could make a genuine impact in terms of the resolution of conflict and interhuman reconciliation if the religions, rising above narrow ideological, national or ethnic considerations, would work together as a diaconal ensemble in pursuit of the shared human aspiration to alleviate poverty and injustice at both the global and local level. Broad interreligious solidarity with the poor and the victims of injustice would be a most effective way of engendering conditions favorable to the emergence of interhuman reconciliation.

Concluding Résumé

To sum up: according to ecumenical thought, reconciliation among human beings is not something that can be produced magically like a rabbit pulled out of a hat, but can only be effectively mediated through a complicated process, involving analysis, repentance, and forgiveness. As of late the ecumenical movement has been working with the concept of 'restorative justice' (cf. Raiser 2000: vi) to express the gist of the view that authentic, lasting reconciliation is impossible of achievement absent the following preliminary steps: the stimulation of people's remembrance of what has happened to them in the past; the encouragement of truth-telling and confession of guilt; the liberating redress of wrong; and the transformation of existing structures and relationships that aid and abet the violences of poverty, racism and the many other forms of psychological, political, economic, social, military, and religious oppression which lie at the root of conflict. In brief, justice requires to be sought and served jointly by all persons of good will—certainly including those among them who profess a religion—as the key to the resolution of conflict and hence to harmonious relations among people and religions, for in the globalized, pluralist world in which we presently live, reconciliation is quite simply one of the most important preconditions for the security and well-being, indeed, the very survival of humanity.

Bibliography

Bavinck, J.H. (1966). *The Church Between the Temple and Mosque*. Grand Rapids: Eerdmans.
Carpenter, Joel A. (2001). "The Perils of Prosperity: Neo-Calvinism and the Future of Religious Colleges." Paper delivered at the conference, The Future of Religious Colleges, held at the Kennedy School of Government, Harvard University, October 6-7, 2000; found as an eight-page insert in *Contact: Newsletter of the IAPCHE*, Vol. 12, No. 2, and to be published in a forthcoming volume, *The Future of Religious Colleges*, Grand Rapids: Eerdmans.
Castro, Emilio. (2000). "Memorial Ruth Sovik." *International Review of Mission*, LXXXIX, 355: pp. 595-99.
Engineer, Asghar Ali. (2001a). "The Concept of 'Other' in Islam." *Islam and the Modern Age*.
———. (2001b). "Indonesia: A Country in Conflict." *Secular Perspective*.

Gort, Jerald D. (1995). "The Christian Ecumenical Reception of Human Rights." In: Abdullahi A. An-Na'im et al. (eds.). *Human Rights and Religious Values: An Uneasy Relationship?* Grand Rapids: Eerdmans/Amsterdam: Rodopi. Pp.203-38.

Jacques, Geneviève. (2000). *Beyond Impunity: An Ecumenical Approach to Truth, Justice, and Reconciliation*. Geneva: WCC Publications.

Moltmann, Jürgen. (1971). *Mensch: Christliche Anthropologie in den Konflikten der Gegenwart*. Stuttgart: Kreuz Verlag.

―――. (1972). *Die Sprache der Befreiung: Predigten und Besinnungen*. Munich: Chr. Kaiser Verlag.

Neill, Stephen. (1971). "Religion." *Concise Dictionary of the Christian World Mission*. London: Lutterworth Press. Pp.517-18.

Petersen, Rodney L. (1992). "Foreword." In: R.J. Schreiter. *Reconciliation: Mission and Ministry in a Changing Social Order*. Maryknoll: Orbis Press.

Rahner, Karl and Herbert Vorgrimler. (1965). "Religie." In: *Klein theologisch woordenboek*. Hilversum: Paul Brand. Pp.329-33.

Raiser, Konrad. (2000). "Preface." In: Geneviève Jacques. *Beyond Impunity: An Ecumenical Approach to Truth, Justice, and Reconciliation*. Geneva: WCC Publications. Pp.v-vii.

Reformed Ecumenical Council. (2000). *Crisis in the Moluccas*. Letter to President Abdurrahman Wahid, Mr. Akbar Tandjung, Chairman of the Parliament of Indonesia, and Mr. Kofi Anan, General Secretary of the United Nations, July 26.

Samartha, Stanley J. (1991). *One Christ—Many Religions: Toward a Revised Christology*. Maryknoll: Orbis Books.

Sanche, Paul. (2000). Letter to the editor regarding the situation in the Middle East, *Time Magazine* (November) 2000.

Schreiter, Robert J. (1992). *Reconciliation: Mission and Ministry in a Changing Social Order*. Maryknoll/Cambridge: Orbis Press/Boston Theological Institute.

Seiple, Robert. (2001): "Review of Paul Marshall (ed.), *Religious Freedom in the World: A Global Report on Freedom and Persecution*, Nashville: Broadman & Holman, 2000." *International Bulletin of Missionary Research* 25/1: 36-37.

Sundermeier, Theo. (1991). "Religion." *Dictionary of the Ecumenical Movement*. Grand Rapids/Geneva: Eerdmans/WCC Publications. Pp.856-57.

VanElderen, Marlin. (1992). *Introducing the World Council of Churches*. Geneva: WCC Publications.

Van Hoogevest, Geertruida. (1991). "Refugees." *Dictionary of the Ecumenical Movement*. Grand Rapids/Geneva: Eerdmans/WCC Publications. Pp.855-56.

Valkenberg, Pim. (2000). "De ene God belijden temidden van Moslims en Joden." *Allerwegen* 31/40: 29-33.

Can the Children of Abraham be Reconciled?

Ishmael and Isaac in the Bible and the Qur'an

Anton Wessels

Someone once visited the Church of the Holy Sepulchre (or as the Arabs call it *Qanîsat al-Qiyâma*, The 'Church of the Resurrection') in Jerusalem, when a procession of pilgrims entered. The guide dwelt for a time on a fresco which depicted Abraham's sacrifice of his son. The tourist was suddenly struck by the guide's remark: "According to Jews and Christians it was Isaac whom Abraham was willing to sacrifice, but it was Ishmael." The group of pilgrims turned out to be Muslims. Although the Qur'an leaves open which son Abraham was about to sacrifice, the Islamic tradition by and large holds that it was Ishmael. He is often seen as the ancestor of the Arabs and, because most of the Arabs are Muslims, also as the symbol for Muslims as such. Someone in the group asked the guide: "Why do Jews and Christians say that it was Isaac?" The guide's answer was: "Because Jews and Christians have no place in their heart for Ishmael."

Introduction

On the February 25, 1994, Baruch Goldstein, a Jewish medical doctor from the United States who had only recently immigrated to Israel as a colonist entered the green doors of the mosque of Hebron and opened fire on the Muslims who were prostrated in prayer, their backs turned to him. Goldstein massacred twenty-nine people and left a dozen wounded behind. This fanatic, belonging to some splinter group, intended to undermine the peace process between the Israelis and Palestinians that had been underway since 'Madrid' (1990) and 'Oslo' (1993). He himself was killed shortly afterwards and his grave became a place of pilgrimage for Jewish extremist groups.

The mosque is built on the spot where the cave of Machpela once was, which Abraham bought as a burial site for his wife Sarah (Genesis 23). In this mosque one finds the tombs of the patriarchs and their wives: Sara, Abraham, Isaac, Jacob, Leah and Joseph. Second in importance to the Jews (after the Western (Wailing) Wall), it is also second in importance to Muslims (after the Dome of the Rock).

Around 20 B.C.E. King Herod the Great built a large hall (*haram*) above this cave, which became known as 'The Hall of Isaac'. The chiselled stones still form part of the wall of the stairs that lead to the entrance of the mosque. In the late sixth century a Byzantine church was erected, which included the Hall of Isaac. According to a Frankish report, Jews, who were living in great numbers in Hebron, told the conquerors how they could enter the sanctuary. In turn they were allowed to stay in the city and built a synagogue next to the sanctuary. The veneration of this place by the Muslims has to do with the fact that in the Byzantine period the Jews venerated the tomb of Abraham, as the Greek author Sozomenus from Gaza (c. 440) reports. With the Arab conquest in the seventh century the Christians were expelled and their church became a mosque, but the Jews and their synagogue were allowed to remain. At the time of the Crusades this situation was temporarily reversed, but the Mamluks expelled the Christian knights and built the Abraham mosque (*Masjdjid Ibrahim al-Khalil*) on that spot. The name of this mosque became the name of the whole city. Next to the prayer niche (*mihrab*) in the mosque one finds the pulpit (*minbar*) once presented by Saladin (1191). Until 'The Six-Day War' (June 1967) Jews were not allowed to enter the synagogue. Control of the spot remained in Muslim hands. After the Goldstein incident two separate entrances were made (Hellender *et al.* 1999: 412-13; "al-Khalîl," *Encyclopedia of Islam*).

The three monotheistic religions, Judaism, Christianity and Islam, are all connected with this place where once before in 1929 it was the scene of another massacre in which 80 Jews died. These acts were committed in a place which in Arabic is called *Khalil* ('Friend'), after "the friend of God," a name given to Abraham both in the Bible as well as the Qur'an (cf. Isaiah 41:8; 2 Chronicles 20:7; Daniel 3:35; James 2:23 and Qur'an 4:125; cf. Speyer 1962: 173; also Clement 11:1)

These and similar events raise the question as to whether many conflicts in the world in our time revolve around "the battle for God" (Armstrong 2000)? Are and will the present-day conflicts after the 'fall' of the Berlin wall (1989) and the collapse of Communism, as Samuel Huntington would have us believe, lead to "a clash of civilisations," in particular between the (Western) Christian and the Islamic civilization? With Goldstein in mind, one could raise the question: Does the struggle between Israel and the Palestinians, after all, revolve around a conflict over the inheritance of Abraham (Kuschel 1997)?

Can and should one of the three—whichever one—claim the inheritance of Abraham for itself with exclusion of the other two? Or is there a possibility for the sons (and daughters) of Abraham to be reconciled with one another and return in peace to Abraham's tent?

In this essay I want look at the Bible and the Qur'an to see if they contain potential for conflict or if they offer possibilities for reconciliation between the different claims concerning the inheritance of Abraham. Are the Holy Scriptures themselves, the Bible and the Qur'an, causes for conflict and struggle or do they make an Abrahamitic ecumenism possible? It is important to know if and to what extent a profound (re)reading of Bible and Qur'an, especially in connection with the stories of Abraham and his two sons Isaac and Ishmael could contribute to a reconciliation between the physical and/or spiritual children of Abraham, the father of all believers.

My presupposition is that the holy books—the Old Testament (*Tawra*), New Testament (*Indjil*) and the Qur'an—are in dialogue with one another and must be brought further into dialogue (cf. Wessels 1997). The three books interpellate one another. My argument is that Jews, Christians and Muslims must read and reread not only their own Holy Scriptures but also one another's Scriptures, preferably together.

Abraham and his Two Sons
The Qur'an speaks of two sons of Abraham: Isaac and Ishmael. The earliest references go back to the Meccan period (610-622 B.C.E.). In the Meccan period, it seems, Ishmael is seen as an independent prophet with no connection to Abraham. In the Medina period (after 622) Ishmael is explicitly connected with Abraham. Although Ishmael is reckoned among the patriarchs to whom revelations were given (2:136 (130); 3:84 (78)), Abraham plays the leading role; Ishmael clearly stands in the shadow of Abraham.

Curious as it may seem, because of the significance usually attached by Arabs and Muslims to Ishmael, the 'information' about him in the Qur'an is actually rather limited. That is surprising because Ishmael has received the important role of ancestor of Quraysh, the tribe living in Mecca from whom Muhammad himself stems. In Medina Ishmael emerges from his isolated shadow existence and becomes a privileged son of Abraham. He is mentioned before Isaac (2:133 (132)). Abraham prays that an apostle will emerge from his ranks, i.e., the Arabs (2:129 (123))—i.e. Muhammad himself (Kuschel 1997: 192-93).

According to the Islamic tradition, Abraham did not send Hagar and Ishmael alone into the desert (Genesis 17 and 21) but accompanied them until Mecca. Abraham as well, in addition to Ishmael, has a connection with Mecca in patriarchal times. Jewish interpreters living among the Muslims make this connection as well (Peters 1990: 25). In Mecca Abraham leaves them to their fate, because he has to return to his wife Sarah. Hagar, full of compassion, runs distracted to and fro between the hills al-Safa and al-Marwa with her thirsty child. The small Ishmael scratches in the sand and helps to discover the well Zamzam.

Here we can find the origin of the later ceremony of *Sa'y* (running quickly to and fro along a particular traject) during the pilgrimage *(hadjdj)*. The first Muslims, especially the Helpers *(Ansar)*, were hesitant to walk this route because of its pagan origin. On these two hills were found the idols Isaf and Na'ila, two holy stones, where in the pre-Islamic period people were sacrificed ("Say" and "Isâf/ Na'ila," *Encyclopedia of Islam*).

Ishmael married a wife from an Arab tribe, Djurhum. Arriving for a brief visit, Abraham first meets her when Ishmael is absent. Because this wife does not show him the proper hospitably, Abraham leaves orders for Ishmael to divorce her. On a later visit he meets Ishmael's (second) wife, again in Ishmael's absence. This time he is received with hospitality. On a third visit Abraham ask Ishmael to assist him in the building of the Ka'ba. Ishmael becomes so united with his father, albeit in a subordinate role, that together they build the 'house of God' (2:125 (119) (cf. 2:127-29 (121-23)). After his death, Ishmael is buried close to his mother Hagar in al-Hidjr within the Haram in Mecca. He is seen as the ancestor of the North Arab tribes ("Ismâ'îl," *Encyclopedia of Islam*).

Abraham was the first who practised 'islam', i.e., unconditional surrender to the will of God, in particular by his readiness to sacrifice his own son (Genesis 22) (Küng 1991: 37; cf. Delaney 1998). According to the Qur'anic story (37:99-107 (97-107)), Abraham is commanded in a dream to sacrifice his son. It is striking that the son agrees with the intended sacrifice. On the basis of the Qur'an one is not sure which son is meant, but it was a long time before the Islamic settled on Ishmael. It is true that the average Muslim is of the opinion that it is not Isaac but Ishmael whom Abraham was prepared to sacrifice (Hayek 1972: 54 nt. 2).

On the tenth day of the month of the pilgrimage (*hadjdj*) the sacrifice of Abraham is remembered, which at the same time is celebrated as the great feast (*'id al adha*) in the whole of the Islamic world. The readiness which was shown by Abraham is imitated.

Preference for One Brother over the Other?

What is the relationship between the two sons? According to the Bible and the Qur'an, they are related. But does the Bible not clearly prefer Isaac above Ishmael with all the subsequent tensions? Is the one not elected, as Jews and Christians often claim, and the other rejected? Is the evident dislike of many Jews and Christians for Ishmael and his physical (Arabs) and spiritual descendants (Muslims) not prompted by the Bible itself or even legitimized? Does the problem of animosity not finally lead back to God himself?

Genesis 17 relates that Abraham was promised that his first wife would bear a son. Sarah is already quite old, so this promise does not sound very credible. Abraham himself clearly shows incredulity: "Shall a child be born to a man who is hundred years old? Shall Sarah, who is ninety years old, bear a child?" Therefore he prays: "Oh that Ishmael might live in thy sight!" (Genesis 17:18). Abraham is saying, as it were: "If you have any plans for my descendants, fulfill your promises in any case with my son Ishmael whom I already have." If one listens carefully to Abraham's prayer, one can hear a rather unbelieving request. Be that as it may, God holds firmly to His promise: "No, but Sarah your wife shall bear a son, and you shall call his name Isaac." (Genesis 17:19). God's making of a covenant with Abraham and his son Isaac is not followed by his rejection of Ishmael. God did truly hear Abraham's perhaps incredulous prayer and grants it. Not without reason is his name Yismaël, which means 'God hears', "The Lord has given heed to your affliction" (Genesis 16:11).

One of the reasons why Muslims objected at the time to Salman Rushdie's *Satanic Verses* was because he called Abraham—for Muslims one of the greatest prophets—a 'bastard'. It is good to pay attention to the context in which Rushdie says this. The passage reads as follows:

> In ancient times the patriarch Ibrahim came into this valley [Mecca] with Hagar and Ismail, their son. Here, in this waterless wilderness, he abandoned her. She asked

him, can this be God's will? He replied, it is. And left, the bastard. (Rushdie 1988: 95)

One can wonder if it was not terrible to send this woman and her child into the desert to their certain death. Was that supposed to be God's will? According to the biblical story, it seems that God agrees with Abraham and Sarah's wish to expel Hagar and Ishmael. Although Abraham was not pleased at Sarah's wish, because, after all, Ishmael was his son, God told him to accept her wish and send Hagar and her son away (Genesis 21:8-14). However it may be that Abraham and Sarah abandoned Hagar, God cannot—according to the Genesis story—bear it. Hagar may have fled the first time into the desert because of her proud behavior with regard to Sarah. Nonetheless, the Lord cares for her: he lets her discover a well that saves her. In the Bible this well is called *Lahai Roi* because Hagar said: "I have now seen the One who sees me" (Genesis 16:13). God sees the tears of Hagar and he looks after her, as he looked after Mary, the mother of Jesus: "For he has regarded the lowly state of his handmaid" (Luke 1:48).

Ishmael, Ishmaelites, Arabs

The biblical story about Hagar and Ishmael is written from the experience of Israel living among the different nations. The Bible describes realistically the tensions, contrasts and conflicts which exist and can exist between brothers, family members and peoples.

Ishmael represents the Ishmaelites who in the Hebrew Bible are synonymous with the desert dwellers and Bedouins. They form a covenant of twelve tribes with settlements between the Euphrates and Suez (Genesis 25:18). Most of the tribes are to be identified as traders and nomads with small livestock and camels. In part they were peaceful caravan traders, like the Ishmaelites who bought Joseph from his brothers (Genesis 37:25ff.); in part they were enemies who threatened Israel (Judges 8:24; Psalm 83:7). Some Ishmaelites turn up here and there in Israel (1 Chronicles 27:30) ("Ismael," *Die Religion*).

In the stories in Genesis (16:1-16 and 21:8-21) the Ishmaelites are personified in their ancestor Ishmael, who is presented as the brother of Isaac. According to Josephus, Ishmael is the ancestor of the Arab nation. The rabbis would also later identify the Arabs with the Ishmaelites (Kuschel 1997: 175). In the book of Jubilees, which came into existence between 135 and 105 B.C.E., it is said that Abraham ordered not only Isaac but also Ishmael and his twelve sons (cf. Genesis 25:12-18) and the sons of his other wife Keturah to keep observing circumcision, to avoid adultery and uncleanness and not to intermarry with the Canaanite population. It is said that Ishmael and his sons and one of Keturah's were sent away from Isaac. They settled between Paran and the frontiers of Babylon (Jubilees 20:11-13) (Peters 1990: 24). It is important to note that the idea of the descent of the Arabs from Ishmael was already known and widespread before the coming of Islam. According to Josephus, the

Arabs were circumcised at the age of thirteen because the founder of their race, Ishmael, was circumcised at that age (*Antiquities* 1.12. 2.) (Peters 1990: 25).

The Christian tradition as well made a connection between Arabs and Ishmael before Islam arose. Sozomenus from Gaza writes in his history of the church about 'Saracens', a well-known name for Arabs before and after Islam. This tribe (of Saracens) which descended from Ishmael were originally called Ishmaelites. In order to avoid the accusation of 'bastard' and of being of low descent they called themselves 'Saracens', as if they descended form Abraham via Sarah after all (Peters 1990: 25).[1] As Ishmael was the personification for the Ishmaelitis, so Hagar stands for the Hagarenes, also a nomad people (Psalm 83:7; 1 Chronicles 5: 10, 19, 20; 27:31).

Obviously, in the biblical stories it is first of all made clear that those Ishmaelites and Hagarenes with whom the Israelites fairly often clashed are the descendants of Hagar and Ishmael. In other words, despite the tension and clashes which exist the Israelites are reminded that they are related to them. Ishmael is Isaac's brother and Hagar is also family—she is also Abraham's wife and the mother of Ishmael. All descend from one father.

A Blessing for Both Sons

Yet there remains a difference between the two sons and a difference between the blessings which they receive. Thus, can this tension which has continued throughout history right up until the present be traced back to God in the final analysis? It is true that God made his covenant with Isaac and with Jacob (thus Israel), does that not, therefore, mean discrimination with regard to Ishmael?

It is of great significance to observe that as the life of Isaac was spared (Genesis 22), so also Ishmael was prevented from perishing in the desert. Obviously, not only Isaac but also Ishmael lives under Gods particular protection. By this the Bible expresses that God's grace is not limited to the line Isaac-Jacob (Israel); it also includes the other son of Abraham as well. And since Ishmael stands for the ancestor of a whole people this is not only intended individually but also collectively.

Comparing the blessing for Isaac with the one for Ishmael, one finds that there is not much difference between them. Not only Isaac but Ishmael as well lives as a son of Abraham under the blessing of God. Ishmael will also flourish under God's protection. God will also make him fruitful and numerous and he will become a great nation. Fertility and numerous posterity is also held out for him as the future (Genesis 16:10). "As for Ishmael, I have heard you; behold, I will bless him and make him fruitful and multiply him exceedingly; he shall be the father of twelve princes, and I will make him a great nation" (Genesis 17:20). And I will make a nation of the son of the slave woman also, because he is your offspring' (Genesis 21:13; cf also v. 18) (Kuschel 1997: 172-73).

---

[1] For different interpretations cf. also the article on Saracens in *The Encyclopedia of Islam*.

It is true God makes a covenant with Isaac, but Ishmael also receives the *sign* of the covenant. At the age of 13 Ishmael was circumcised (Genesis 17:23-26; Genesis 17:10; 23-26). Ishmael, the man of the desert, disowned by his father, excluded from the specific history of salvation, still participates in the blessing of God, is clearly loved by God, albeit in a different way from Isaac. While Isaac stayed behind in the country, Ishmael has become the son of the desert (Genesis 21:10) (Kuschel 1997: 173-74). Before the ancestor of the Arab tribes is disowned, he is given the sign of the covenant. Israel can not absolutize its own election. Other children of Abraham also belong to the covenant.

This story, written on the basis of existing tensions that lasted centuries, does not say: They are our enemies because God is on our side and not on theirs. The very peculiar and surprising, liberating message is: This non-Israelite people, sometimes our enemy, is a people blessed by God. There are differences, but they remain children of Abraham, the father of many nations. They all come from one family. God has clearly heard the prayer of Abraham: "Oh that Ishmael might live in thy sight!" (Genesis 17:18). God gives promises to other peoples. Abraham is the father not only of one nation, Israel, but also of the Arabs. The blessing is not limited to the frontiers of Israel.

The Prophet Muhammad and his Appeal to Abraham

Through Keturah Abraham became the ancestor of sixteen proto-Arab groups of nomads. This is still of importance today, according to Hans Küng. Israel felt itself related to the original Semitic Aramaens of the latter part of the second millenium B.C.E. and also with the Semitic proto-Arabs of the first half of the first millennium B.C.E. in northern Arabia and northwestern Arabia. This is what the genealogies express (Küng 1991: 32; cf. references on p. 769).

According to the Qur'an Abraham broke with his fellow citizens, as Muhammad would later break with the Meccans (*hidjra*). Abraham was a community on his own, surrendering (*muslim*) to God, a monotheist (a seeker of God, *hanif*) and did not belong to the polytheists (16:120 (121)). He is seen as the restorer of the original monotheism. This does not mean surrender (*islam*), i.e., being 'Muslim' in its contemporary, sociological sense of the word. The word indicates rather that each religion turns and should turn, after all, on 'surrender to God'. In that sense Abraham is exemplary and those who were with him are called examples for the believers (60:4).

In his discussions with Jews and Christians the Prophet Muhammad appeals to Abraham, who preceded Moses (Judaism) and Jesus (Christianity):

> O People of the Scripture! Why will ye argue about Abraham, when the Torah and the Gospel were not revealed till after him? Have ye then no sense. Lo! ye are those who argue about whereof ye have some knowledge: Why then argue ye concerning that whereof ye have no knowledge? God knoweth. Ye know not. Abraham was not a Jew, nor a Christian; but he was an upright man who has surrendered, and he was not of the idolaters. (3:65-67 (58-60))

The closest to Abraham are the people who follow him and this prophet [Muhammad] and those who believe. (3:68)

Jesus contests with those who pride themselves on the descent of Abraham and derive from it certainty of salvation: "And do not presume to say, 'We have Abraham as our father', for I tell you, God is able from these stones to raise up children to Abraham" (Matthew 3:9). Descent from Abraham is no guarantee of salvation if faith is lacking. The apostle Paul states that Abraham is the father of believers:

> That is why it depends on faith, in order that the promise may rest on grace and be guaranteed to all his descendants—not only to the adherents of the law but also to those who share the faith of Abraham, for he is the father of us all, as it is written, "I have made you the father of many nations." (Romans 4:16, 17; cf. Genesis 17:5)

The covenant concluded with Abraham has believers in view and not his physical descendants.

The Prophet Muhammad makes similar reproaches to Jews and Christians when Jews as well as Christians exclusively, also with exclusion of each other, invoke their election:

> And the Jews say the Christians follow nothing (true) and the Christians say the Jews follow nothing (true); yet both are readers of the Scripture. Even thus speak those who know not. God will judge between them on the Day of Resurrection concerning that wherein they differ. (2:113 (117)

Muhammad represents the claim of others to a share in the inheritance, in addition to Jews and Christians.

Muhammad saw himself as a direct descendant of Abraham: "My Lord! they have settled some of my posterity in an uncultivable valley near unto Thy holy House [namely Mekka], our Lord! ... (14:37 (40)). He also thought that he resembled Abraham (also literally) more than any other prophet. "Look at your friend and you will see Abraham, feature for feature," Muhammad is supposed to have said to his companions (Bukhari t. II 234, Moslim Shaik, t. I, 106; cited by Hayek 1972: 84). It is said that after the nightly journey (*isra'*) Muhammad said: "I have never seen someone who looked more like me than Abraham." Muhammad holds a particular position. His descent via Ishmael goes back to Abraham, the co-founder of the Ka'ba. "In the history of revelation Muhammad by himself means as much as all other prophets from the family of Abraham put together" (Stieglecker 1962: 202). According to the well-known Old Testament scholar Claus Westermann, "Abraham is the father of the religion of Israel as well as of Islam" (Westermann 1986: 258).

Abraham is a true guide for people and the House, i.e., the Ka'ba "And when We made the House (at Mecca) a resort for humankind and a sanctuary ..." (2: 125 (119)). That does not obtain for 'Muslim' in the narrow sense. Abraham, as the original image of Islam, shows the universality of the prophets. In the Qur'an Abraham is not the possession of one faith community alone, not even the 'Muslims'; he is the example of faith for *all* people. As in the New Testament, the idea that physical descent from Abraham would give precedence is completely alien to the Qur'an, since true faith existed already before him.

The people whose leader Abraham is, are the just and the believers, among them there can also be physical descendants. They form a group of believers and have no higher claim than other believers. Faith justifies, not the physical descent of Abraham. (Kuschel 1997: 195, 198-99)

Muhammad's appeal to Abraham in the Qur'an is therefore not meant as a new exclusivism for himself and/or his followers. Nowhere in the Qur'an is it written that Muslims are exclusively the true children of Abraham. Nowhere is the Jewish or Christian claim of being children of Abraham is disputed, as Christians did with respect to the Jews. Muhammad refers, indeed, to the religion of Abraham which existed prior to Judaism and Christianity and is given a new form in Islam after Judaism and Christianity (Kuschel 1997: 201).

Some Muslims did and still often in practice claim an exclusive right to the inheritance of Abraham. There are those who are aggressive with respect to Jews and Christians, take up an defensive, polemical attitude and advocate confrontation with respect to other religions (Kuschel 1997: 270). Although the pilgrimage to Mecca was meant universally, it soon came to be understood exclusively and non-Muslims are not allowed to visit Mecca.

Thus not only are all people of the Book, Jews and Christians, guilty of changing the (meaning of) the texts (*tahrif*) but Muslims themselves as well. The text cited above, that Abraham was neither Jew nor Christian but someone who surrendered to God (*Muslim*) (3: 67 (60)) is directed at Muslims as well. It does not intend to say that Jews and Christians cannot claim descent from Abraham while Muslims can because they are 'Muslim': they also must answer the question as to whether they are true 'Muslims', that is, those who truly believe and surrender in loving obedience to God. The wandering Arabs (Bedouins) say: "We believe. Say: Ye believe not, but rather say, 'We submit, for the faith has not entered into your hearts.'" (49:14).

'Islam' is considered to be the oldest and most authentic religion. Concrete Islam, as it developed in history after Muhammad, is not automatically identical with that authentic and original form but has to strive towards it as well. The Prophet Muhammad falls back on a universal and considered original truth. He understands Abraham as the original image of the true faith, which any person can possess, completely independent of belonging to a particular people or a position in salvation history. The Qur'an is interested in the original authenticity of faith, without rejecting the faith claims of Jews and Christians. As Jesus Christ was both before and after Abraham (cf. the Gospel of John), so was Islam. Islam was present before Muhammad (embodied in Abraham) and appeared again with Muhammad in history (Kuschel 1997: 204-05, 207). In him (Muhammad) the destiny of Ishmael crystallizes and begins anew (Hayek 1972: 192).

What can we say now about the validity of these promises to Ishmael, that he, the son of Abraham and the Egyptian Hagar, would become the ancestor of a great people with twelve princes (Genesis 17:20), the ancestor of the Arabs between Egypt and Assyria (Genesis 25:12-18)? In connection with this Küng states (1991: 76): "Evidently, theological embarrassment already exists in Genesis as to how one is to understand Gods intention for this particular son of Abraham. Obviously God has special plans for Ishmael." According to Michel Hayek, who several decades ago wrote on the 'mystery of Ishmael' (1964), Ishmael was, long before the Hebrew Exodus, the first "voice calling in the wilderness: 'Prepare the way of the Lord.'" Hagar, whose name means 'refugee' is destined by her very name to *hidjra*, the synonym for the Hebrew Exodus (Hayek 1964: 19, 122). The first human tears in the Bible are those of Hagar, the first wife who was rejected, in anticipation of all the humiliated and abandoned women in Islam and the world (Hayek 1964: 215).

Abrahamitic Ecumenism

The Bible tells us that Isaac and Ishmael buried their father together (Genesis 25:9)—an image of the reconciliation between both brothers: they grieved together and they were reconciled together. Nowhere it is said that they saw each other afterwards, although their descendants lived together for centuries, sometimes in conflict but also in peace and in a fruitful symbiosis: in the Middle East, in Spain (Al-Andalus) or in (of all places) Baghdad or the Balkans.

Abraham, as he is depicted in the stories in Genesis, does not advocate exclusivity. Are the three traditions not in conflict with their own origin when they make Abraham exclusively the friend of the synagogue, church or *umma* (Kuschel 1997: 280)? Abraham is presented as intolerant with regard to other religions. He does not cut down the oaks of Mamre, as Boniface did much later with the (Donar) oak in Geizmar. Instead, Abraham builds an altar next to them.[2] There may be differences between Isaac and Ishmael, but neither the latter nor his descendants are rejected by God. The continuing dislike for Ishmael is not legitimized by God in the biblical stories. The inheritance of Abraham cannot be interpreted as belonging exclusively to one descendant—whoever it is. It is faith that matters after all. Differences that exist between the 'three' (Jews, Christians and Muslims) can and should be raised in a dialogue between children of one family, children of one father, who was the friend of God. Not the descendants of Abraham are the believers, but "all who believe are Abraham's descendants" (W. Barnard).

---

[2] He does not travel through the country pulling down altars, as Deuteronomy (12:2-3) commands: "You shall surely destroy all the places where the nations whom you shall dispossess served their gods, upon the high mountains an upon the hills and under every green tree, you shall tear down their altars, and dash in pieces their pillards." See Kuschel 1997: 281.

Bibliography

Armstrong, Karen. (2000). *The Battle for God: Fundamentalism in Judaism, Christianity, and Islam.* New York: Ballantine Books.
Delaney, Carol. (1998). *Abraham on Trial: The Social Legacy of Biblical Myth.* Princeton: Princeton University Press.
The Encyclopedia of Islam. (1997). Leiden: Brill.
Michel Hayek. (1964). *Le Mystère d'Ismael.* Paris: Gallimard.
———. (1972). *Les Arabes ou le baptême des larmes.* Paris: Gallimard.
Hellander, Paul *et al.* (1999). *Israel and the Palestinian Territories.* 4th ed. Melbourne: Lonely Planet.
Peters, F.E. (1990). *Judaism, Christianity, and Islam: The Classical Texts and Their Interpretation.* Vol. I *From Covenant to Community.* Princeton: Princeton University Press.
Speyer, H. (1962). *Die biblischen Erzählungen im Qoran.* Wissenschaftliche Buchgesellschaft. Darmstadt.
Küng, Hans. (1991). *Das Judentum. Die religiöse Situation der Zeit.* Munich/Zürich: Piper.
Kuschel Karl-Josef. (1997). *Streit um Abraham. Was Juden, Christen und Muslime trennt und was sie eint.* Munich/Zürich: Piper.
Die Religion in Geschichte und Gegenwart. 3rd ed. Tubingen: J.C.B. Mohr.
Rushdie, Salman. (1988). *The Satanic Verses.* London: Vintage.
Stieglecker, H. (1962). *Die Glaubenstehren des Islam.* Paderborn: Ferdinand Schöningh.
Wessels, Anton. (1997). "How Do We Live Together with the Scriptures? Living by Scriptures in a Multicultural Society." In: H.M. Vroom and J.D. Gort (eds.), *Holy Scriptures in Judaism, Christianity and Islam. Hermeneutics, Values and Society.* Amsterdam/Atlanta: Editions Rodopi. Pp. 3-19.
Westermann, Claus. (1986). *Am Anfang 1. Mose. (Genesis).* Part 1: *Die Urgeschichte Abraham.* Neukirchen-Vluyn: Neukirchener Verlag.

Isaiah Berlin

Teleological Thinking as a Cause of Conflict

Connie Aarsbergen

Introduction

In this paper we will look at the theme "Religion, Conflict, and Reconciliation" is approached from a liberal-humanistic angle, namely, from the point of view of the Oxford philosopher and historian of ideas Sir Isaiah Berlin (1909-1997). According to Berlin, one of the most important causes of conflict is monist thinking, i.e., the belief that for conflicting ends and values there is only one solution. Closely connected with monism is teleological thinking, the belief that history is moving towards the goal of a state of final harmony where there will be no conflicting values and ends.

In this paper I will begin by giving a description of how Berlin justifies his pluralist and antiteleological views. Furthermore, one of the consequences of views such as Berlin's (with regard to the negative role religions and ideologies play in stimulating conflicts) is that views of the good life are kept out of the public domain as much as possible. An undesired result of this is that a modern Western individual is more and more disconnected from the moral sources that provide motivation and inspiration for positive moral action. In this paper I will also try to correct some of the misunderstandings concerning teleological thinking that lie behind the desire to keep the public domain as neutral as possible.

Berlin's Theory of Values

Before giving an account of Berlin's antiteleological views, I first need to say something briefly about Berlin's theory of knowledge. This theory is based on concepts and categories by means of which people think, act and order the data of experience. The concepts and categories are not given *a priori* but are transmitted through the communities in which individuals live. They change when circumstances in the community change. Certain concepts and categories can have an enslaving or discriminating effect and should therefore be critically examined. For Berlin, the main source of evil is to be found in wrong ideas: they can encourage inhuman behavior. As a historian of ideas but also as refugee from the Russian Revolution (as a child) and a Second World War correspondent, he was strongly motivated to describe wrong ideas that lead to human misery. In his view, two of the ideas most responsible for evil is the belief that in a situation of conflicting values and ends there is one solution or only one set of values that is true (monism) and that in history it is possibile to reach a state of final harmony (teleology).

Berlin is a pluralist (Berlin 1969: 169). There is a plurality of cultures and of individual temperaments. Also, there are many ends which an individual can pursue in his or her life. There are choices among esthetic, ethical and intellectual values. The different ends and values cannot always be combined in one lifetime or in one society. For example, life as an unrecognized but talented artist (outside a welfare state such as the Netherlands) is difficult to combine with family duties. When a judge is too merciful towards a criminal, he is not doing justice to the victim. If a government attempts too much to reduce societal inequalities, this can lead to serious limitations of liberty. Conversely, more freedom is often achieved at the cost of equality.

In order to make the right choices people often manifest a great desire for universal standards of measurement, by means of which they can decide which value or end should receive priority. According to Berlin, however, there are none. People like to believe—both in religion and science—that only one set of values is true. However, pluralism exists not only with respect to values and ends but also with respect to the criteria for deciding which value or end should receive priority. Each community or culture has its own value system. These value systems are not always compatible and can even be contradictory. It is impossible to reconcile these incommensurable value systems by reference to one true system.

All an individual or policy maker can do is to choose among the various incommensurable values or ends. In making that choice one is faced with the responsibility of the consequences of that decision and the sad knowledge that one or more of the cherished values or ends will have to be given up for the sake of another. Choices involve responsibility and this is a burden which many people find hard to bear (Berlin 1969: 114). They seek various ways to avoid this burden. In the realm of science believing that our lives are determined (by, for instance, material or biological factors) can relieve this moral burden. We can no longer blame others or bear the blame ourselves for a world largely outside out of our control. In religions moral dilemmas can be solved by referring to the will of God. God stands for a rational and harmonious order in which all values have their proper place. But in scientific theories influenced by the Enlightenment the world is also understood as harmonious, clear and intelligible, rather than untidy, cruel or purposeless (Berlin 1969: 106-08). The world has an end and a rational person will rank his or her ends and values according to that *telos*. In this fixed order clashes can in principle be avoided. Conflicts and tragedies occur because the correct order and *telos* are not yet known. Religions fill the need for a harmonious world by providing the concepts and categories conducive to finding final answers. Religious believers have difficulty accepting moral dilemmas

---

[1] Berlin wrote primarily for a Western audience and thus has theistic religions mostly in mind.

that would lead to ultimate tragedy—that would subvert the providential order (Gray 1995: 42).

Berlin's Antiteleological View

In religions and secular worldviews the *telos* of humankind is the establishment of an ideal society on earth. On this planet we can work towards a state of final harmony in which there will be no conflict in values. There are ideologists or religious leaders who claim to have special knowledge about this future, about inevitable courses in history leading to it or about the exact nature of the Golden Age that needs to be restored. Marx believed that history would lead to a classless welfare state in which the conflict between equality and liberty on the one hand and individual and group interests on the other would be resolved.

This state of final harmony is an object of intense desire. There is much at stake here and people are willing to pay a high price it demands. Ideologists and religious leaders can take advantage of this desire by justifying cruel acts leading to that goal. For this higher *telos* normal human responsibility is given up so that adherents of a particular worldview can act inhumanly towards others.

Knowledge of the truth with regard to metaphysical, moral and political questions tends to divide humankind into two worlds: the world of the elect and the world of the reprobate (to use traditional Calvinist terminology). Holy wars or wars of extermination against enemies with rival claims are justified by referring to that truth. In the ancient world and in the Middle Ages one of the most important virtues was to defend the truth by all means. People were prepared to die for their beliefs or to kill so that heresies would be uprooted. Because of the influence of Romanticism, Western society has gained an appreciation for the quality of sincerity in belief. It is possible for one to admire the sincerity manifested by adherents of other religions, even if one holds their beliefs to be wrong.

Within Marxism's notion of class conflict, the rival claims were provided by the bourgeoisie and the capitalists. For Berlin, Marxism is even more dangerous than fanatical religious movements. In most religions, if the unbeliever accepts the true faith, he is at least welcomed as a brother. Within Marxism, discussion about the truth with the enemy is regarded as purposeless: the enemy should be eliminated as soon as possible (Berlin 1997: 139).

It should be noted here that, for Berlin, the term 'teleological thinking' is connected with monist thinking, i.e., the belief that there is just one single goal of final harmony in history to which all people must comply. His critique of teleological thinking does not exclude all possibility of developing or improving society, although this should be done in a pluralist way. Berlin's criticism of teleological thinking is largely directed towards at communism and fascism rather than religions. Berlin is not an atheist seeking to abolish all religion. In his work he also shows much respect for (non-fanatical forms of) religion as a way of life. For instance, his biography mentions how much hidden wisdom he had found in the Jewish rituals of burial and mourning when his father died.

Berlin distinguishes between religions that claim to know the will of God and the ones that emphasize the impossibility of human perfection due to the Fall of humankind (Berlin 1978: 153). Intolerance and monism are to be found in the first category. Respect for different views is more likely to be found in the latter category, since it is believed that because of human sin the will of God and the paths leading to final harmony cannot be fully known. Berlin does not specifically mention Christian theologies that believe that the Kingdom of God will be realized not in this world but only in a world to come. He must, however, have had them in mind because such eschatology is often inspired by the awareness of the fallen state of humankind and this world.

If there is too much stress on the Fall in a religion, this can, according to Berlin, also be dangerous. It can justify despotic, non-democratic governments based on the idea that people are evil and incapable of doing anything good. Berlin describes this in his essay on the nineteenth-century conservative Roman Catholic Joseph de Maistre (Berlin 1990).

Berlin objects to teleological thinking on other grounds as well. According to Berlin, a monistic society with just one all-encompassing human purpose cannot put an end to the conflicts within that society (Berlin 1978: 150-51). The (sacred) formulas accepted by that society carry different (perhaps incompatible) meanings for different persons in different situations. This is especially true when vague and general terms are used (such as the fulfillment of the Law of God or the common good, etc.) Furthermore, problems will arise in the secondary ends, the penultimate values for more specific purposes on lower levels. When these subordinate ends come into conflict, it is not possible in most cases to deduce the right approach or answer from the general human goal.

With regard to utopias that are based on a Golden Age in the past, Berlin explains in the following way why the results seldom correspond to the hopes of the religious leaders or human engineers who conducted these social experiments. The makers of the revolution found themselves in each case swept on by the forces which they had released in a direction they themselves hardly anticipated. In plans for human improvement usually only those facts are included which fit neatly into the theories of society, history, political development and change and those facts which are less susceptible to tidy classification are forgotten. Ideologists who look at a past Golden Age usually forget that they are looking at it from a later vantage point and leave out important facts which in their view are too obvious to need mentioning. The revolution usually concentrates upon certain aspect of the upper, public level but inevitably stirs up the lower levels of life, in the obscurest corners of society. The results are byproducts which are largely incalculable. According to Berlin, the more theorists of social programs force the facts into some preconceived mold, the more (violent) resistance they will encounter. The consequences of the experiments are beyond what anybody had desired, planned or expected.

Dealing with Moral Dilemmas

If there is pluralism and, moreover, if there are incommensurable values without universal standards of measurement, how does one deal with moral dilemmas? For Berlin, there are no fixed procedures as to how to solve value conflicts. However, some guidelines can be found in his work.

First of all, a distinction should be made between conflicts among groups (each representing certain incommensurable values), conflicts between an individual and his community (the conflict between personal ends and group interests) and internal conflicts within a personal life.

As an historian of ideas, for all these types of conflict Berlin stresses that the notion of final harmony should be abandoned first. Too many individuals have been sacrificed because of this notion on the altars of great historical ideas. Conflicts of value should be considered as an intrinsic and irremovable element in human life (Berlin 1969: 167).

With regard to conflicts of ends between groups, Berlin's guideline can be found in his writings about Jews as a minority in diaspora (Berlin 1979).[2] If Jews suffer because they are not recognized as a group and feel discriminated against because of their deviating values and ends, they should be able to live in their own country (Jahanbegloo 1992: 85). (This was Berlin's secular motivation for becoming a Zionist. During and after the Second World War, as a war correspondent in Washington and as a friend of Chaim Weizmann, Berlin was active in founding the state of Israel). But in our present multicultural societies, founding new countries for minorities is no longer a practical solution. Berlin later acknowledged that the claims of the Palestinian citizens within the state of Israel were also justified (Gray 1995: 117) but could not provide any advice as to how to deal with this conflict.

What could Berlin's pluralism mean for present-day UN interventions or the endeavors of churches to reconcile conflicting parties? The lack of a universal standard of measurement does not make the peace or reconciliation process any easier. Berlin's pluralism prevents the reaching of a 'solution' through the adoption by the conflicting parties of the value system of a third party who intervenes: this would not show respect for the value systems of the conflicting groups themselves. Berlin's pluralism, however, does not lead to moral relativism. People can recognize when an act is inhuman or insane (Berlin 1978: 166): we know the inhuman when we encounter it. For Berlin there is a "common human horizon" consisting of rules and commandments that have been accepted so widely "and are grounded so deeply in the actual nature of man as they have developed through history, as to be by now, an essential part of what we mean by being a normal human being" (Berlin 1969: 165). Some concepts and categories apply to humankind over such sufficiently long stretches of time that they can be regarded as virtually universal (Berlin 1997: 17). In his view, then, it is possible to condemn certain practices.

---

[2] Cf. also Berlin 2000, a recently discovered essay.

Most of Berlin's work is aimed at value conflicts between individuals and groups and internal conflicts. Berlin does not make such a major distinction between the two. The most probable reason for that is because he is very much aware that it is the community that provides the concepts and categories containing the values and ends from which one is to choose. Although Berlin maintains that the individual is (in the end) free, he is also aware that a person's identity is strongly influenced by his or her community. Even if a dilemma seems at first glance to be very personal (for instance, shall I have a career or a family?), the dilemma itself is very much influenced by the values and ends of the community in which that individual lives.

In trying to resolve a moral dilemma, it is very important, according to Berlin, that personal responsibility not be evaded by referring to the will of God or alternatives such as determinism or inevitable causes in history or life. Berlin is afraid that this will lead to inhuman action. A side effect of this popular 'existentialist' view is that all references to religious or secular moral sources have become suspect.

For Berlin, although conflicts between the ends of individuals and the interests of their societies cannot be avoided entirely, they can be considerably reduced. In his most famous essay "Two Concepts of Liberty" Berlin gives a clear guideline as to how to reduce value conflicts: decisions about giving priorities in conflicting values or rankings in the ends of life should be left as much as possible to the individual. Individuals should be given maximum space to make such decisions themselves.

Positive and Negative Liberty

To reduce the number of value conflicts between the individual and the group, Berlin has a strong preference for negative liberty: freedom from interference by the government, church or community with respect to personal choices. This is freedom 'from'. Berlin is suspicious of all forms of positive liberty: the freedom to live one's life in a certain way. This is freedom 'to' live according to specific ways of life which will lead in the end, it is believed, to even more freedom.

Religions have always offered their adherents ways of life that promise more freedom. The believer should, for instance, liberate himself from slavery to unbridled passions. Ascetics, quietists, Stoics or Buddhists followed (and are still following) these forms of self-renunciation through which the true self could be realized. For Berlin, ascetic self-denial may be a source of integrity or serenity and spiritual strength, but he cannot see how it can be called an enlargement of liberty (Berlin 1969: 139).

But Berlin is more concerned with the political translation of these religious forms of self-realization in the nineteenth and twentieth centuries. There is a political goal—for instance, a just society—which a person would, if she was more enlightened, pursue. Coercion can therefore be justified. The problem with this kind of freedom, according to Berlin, is that it can be given any meaning one wishes.

Closely connected with political theories of self-realization is fanatical nationalism. Before Romanticism, there were already divisions made between higher and lower selves or heteronomous or autonomous selves. Romantic thinkers, such as the German philosopher and poet Johann Gottfried Herder, added the possibility of identification of the individual self with the collective self. There is a collective self that gives meaning and purpose to all its members: my existence is meaningless outside of the larger collective (people, nation) to which I belong (Berlin 1997: 245). According to Berlin, this is again the surrendering of personal responsibility. The road is thus opened for the justification of cruel and inhuman acts.

Consequences of Emphasis on Negative Liberty on the Public Domain

Looking back on his life, Berlin told one of his biographers, Ramin Jahanbegloo, that the strong emphasis on negative liberty had been perverted into a species of *laissez-faire*, which had also led to injustice and suffering. He admitted that his "Two Concepts of Liberty" was deeply influenced by the monstrous misuses of the word 'liberty' in totalitarian countries (Jahanbegloo 1992: 147). In October 1997 the British Prime Minister Tony Blair asked Berlin about the limitations of negative liberty and suggested that "positive liberty had its validity, whatever its depredations in the Soviet Model" (Ignatief 1998: 298). In posing this question Blair must have had in mind some 'paternalistic' measures to prevent poverty and misery due to broken marriages, 'inherited' unemployment, children on the streets late at night and secondary school dropouts. Berlin was already too ill to reply and died a month later.

How could Berlin's concept of negative liberty have been perverted into *laissez-faire* policy? One of the most probable causes is that during the last decades Western liberal governments (like Berlin) have presupposed that individuals have their own moral sources or do not need views of the good life to provide motivation and inspiration for making the right decisions in life. In the 1950s and 1960s most Western individuals still adhered to a religion or secular worldview, but due to secularization and individualism this changed. An increasing number of people are no longer associated with broader communal structures that provide specific views of the good life and want to make the important value decisions themselves. There is also no government assistance, since Western governments are expected to maintain a strict division between the public and private domain. Transgressing that border would mean that preference is given to one of the views of the good life above others, and that could cause conflict with rival ideologies and religions.

In the conflict of values between negative and positive liberty, Berlin prefers a maximum of negative liberty at the cost of positive forms of liberty. But, according to the Canadian philosopher Charles Taylor (1989), this is problematic. The rejection of positive forms of liberty also entails the rejection of the transmission of views of the good life. Moral views and moral sources belong together and cannot be separated. They are essential for the motivation and inspiration for positive action and function as a source of empowerment that becomes lost when one can no longer refer to one's moral sources.

Charles Taylor is not in total disagreement with Berlin. He also acknowledges that there are incommensurable values that cannot be reconciled by reference to one universal set of values as a standard of measurement. But he does not agree with

Berlin's 'solution' of preferring negative liberty alone. How can individuals or policy makers make judgments about the priorities in life if there are no moral sources and no frameworks of the good life? Taylor gives an alternative approach with respect to moral dilemmas. The moral sources should not be hidden in one's private background but should be articulated. The articulation of such sources—especially within the public domain—is needed to make clear what the deeper problems and motivations of moral dilemmas are. But, bearing in mind all past and present religious conflicts, will the articulation of moral sources in the public domain not lead to a sharpening of the conflict instead of resolving it?

Before answering this question, however, why should we not take up Taylor's suggestion and point to Berlin's own moral sources? Berlin is strongly motivated by his desire to avoid human suffering. Human beings should be respected. It is important, in his view, that people be responsible for one another. He values autonomy and pluralism. He acknowledges the importance of the community in conveying concepts and categories. (Berlin is, of course, aware that community values can conflict with individual values (negative freedom).) He has a strong preference for ordinary ways of life instead of 'higher' religious or monastic ways of life, etc. These are values that are part of a (liberal and humanist) view of the good life.

In modern liberal thinking, values such as respect and pluralism are sometimes confused with neutral 'procedural' values. For Berlin, these values are so self-evident that he hardly makes them explicit. But, if we compare these values with those in other worldviews, it will be clear that these values are not neutral but substantive and part of a Western liberal worldview.

The confusion, however does not end there. Ideas of the good life are often mixed up with teleological views. However, within a view of the good life, not all aspects are teleological. Values such as mutual respect, the avoidance of pain and misery, the preference for pluralism and autonomy do not refer to any teleological paths in history but to more prudent considerations or are perhaps motivated by the desire to live as one wishes. Although not teleological, this is also a view of the good life.

A further confusion is that all teleological visions are regarded as potentially dangerous. As Berlin already notes, there are religions without fixed blueprints for final harmony due to a relativization of human knowledge and the human incapacity for perfection. The latter leads to more respect for pluralism.

These misunderstandings still lie behind our reluctance to articulate our moral sources when dealing with a moral dilemma. A consequence is that the connection to views of the good life is lost—views that inspire their followers not to accept moral responsibility and motivate them to positive moral action, both at community and universal level.

A distinction should be made between the fanatical types of teleological thinking and inspirational and peaceful forms of teleology. Examples of the fanatical forms are the instigation of revolutions, Holy Wars or Crusades in order to (re)establish the perfect society or to act according to God's will in history. An example of a modest form of teleology is the Christian belief in the promise of the establishment of the

Kingdom by God, independent of human endeavor. In times of human failure, this belief can motivate one to continue to provide 'foretastes' of that future Kingdom. If we make this distinction, there can be few objections to take up Charles Taylor's suggestion to articulate our moral motivations and to make them public.

Conclusion

On the basis of Isaiah Berlin's philosophy, I have described monism and teleological thinking as one of the main causes of (religious) conflict. Berlin's pluralist thinking leads to a strong emphasis on negative liberty. Furthermore, for the sake of peace in the public domain and in order to avoid paternalism, people have been reluctant to promote forms of the good life. This, in turn, has generated other forms of human misery. In this paper I have tried to show that there are also forms of teleology that do not lead to conflicts or disrespect for other opinions and that views of the good life are not necessarily teleological.

Hopefully this paper and this volume will lead to debates on moral and political dilemmas in which our moral sources are not hidden but articulated and that groups or communities with a specific view of the good life feel less reluctant to transmit their moral sources as a positive example and inspiration for their adherents and those outside the fold.

Bibliography

Berlin, I. (1969). *Four Essays on Liberty*. Oxford: Oxford University Press.

———. (1978). "Does Political Theory Still Exist?" In: *Concepts and Categories*. London: Pimlico.

———. (1979). *Against the Current*. London: Hogarth Press.

———. (1990). *The Crooked Timer of Humanity*. London: John Murray.

———. (1997). *The Sense of Reality*. London: Pimlico.

———. (2000). "Jewish Slavery and Emancipation." In: *The Power of Ideas*. London: Chatto & Windus.

Gray, J. (1995). *Berlin*. London: Fontana Press.

Ignatieff, M. (1998). *Isaiah Berlin: A Life*. London: Chatto & Windus.

Jahanbegloo, R. (1992). *Conversations with Isaiah Berlin*. London: Halban.

Taylor, C. (1989). *Sources of the Self: The Making of the Modern Identity*. Cambridge: Cambridge University Press.

The Road to Sainthood

Reconciliation in Graham Greene's *The End of the Affair*

Henry Jansen

Introduction

Reconciliation belongs intrinsically to the Christian vision. Whether one is talking of reconciliation between God and human beings, God and creation, human beings and creation or between human beings and human beings, one cannot escape the fact that the notion of reconciliation lies at the basis of the Christian religion[1] To understand what basic insights the Christian faith offers for the issue of reconciliation, it is useful to turn not only to systematic treatments but also to narratives told within the tradition, for such narratives reflect the fundamental complexity of life itself (see Vroom 1989 and 1994; Jansen 1995 and 2001).

There is also another reason for exploring the issue of reconciliation in narratives. Most of the essays in this volume deal with the 'big' issues of the day: conflict and reconciliation in Africa, South Africa, the Middle East, the Balkans, etc. These are the issues that quickly and readily capture our attention and as such are analyzed and probed. Narratives, however, concern the lives of concrete individuals and these issues are viewed through the eyes of these individuals. The English poet William Wordsworth once stated that it is the task of poetry to make the ordinary seem extraordinary. This claim could be applied to literature in general and this is important for the issue of reconciliation. For, in the end, it will not be nations and groups that are reconciled with one another. It will not be Christianity and Islam which are reconciled nor different races. In the end it will be this Christian and this Moslem who are reconciled, this Israeli and this Palestinian, this black woman and this white man.

In this essay we will be exploring the question of reconciliation in a novel written by a Christian: *The End of the Affair* (1951) by Graham Greene. In connection with

---

[1] Because of this emphasis the Christian faith has often been seen as a comedy. Although the literary critic Northrop Frye was perhaps the first to do so from a literary point of view (1964: 455), the notion itself is at least to be traced back to Dante's *Divine Comedy* in the Middle Ages. The concept of comedy as applied to the Christian faith was seen as so persuasive in itself that some, such as Paul Tillich (1948: 19-20), saw the Christian faith as exclusively comic, thereby excluding tragedy entirely. Comedy has, as its outcome, generally speaking, reconciliation in view, expressed in the classic forms of a marriage and/or feast that culminates the movement of the work.

the issue of conflict and reconciliation that is the theme of this conference I would like to explore on the basis of this novel two fundamental issues relating to this question. One is the question of change in human beings, since change of heart (repentance, if you will) is seen by many to be virtually impossible. Secondly, in much modern and postmodern thinking on the question of reconciliation, there seems to be almost unanimous agreement that the question of God or, we might say, the question of the transcendent has little or no place in a novel (see the discussion in Gregor 1973: 110-11). With all due respect for literary considerations, it is difficult to understand how one can view the question of reconciliation without taking God into account. In this respect Greene's novel sets one to thinking about questions such as this in an interdisciplinary way—from the point of view of theology and literary criteria—and to seeing how the questions of change and the role of God are interconnected. We will explore the changes in the central character that occur and then discuss how this change is brought about. Before proceeding to this major discussion, however, it will first necessary to deal with some general issues regarding the nature of this novel itself, in order to see better the justification for using such a novel.

The Novel The End of the Affair

Although *The End of the Affair* is an explicitly religious novel, our interest in this novel is not determined by the fact that it can be called a 'Christian' novel in any conventional sense, i.e., a novel with the explicit aim, for instance, of moving people to faith. There are good Christian novels which do this. But this is not the claim here about this novel. Greene is not writing as an apologist for the Christian faith[2] He is writing as a novelist, as a human being, who is exploring certain religious themes. The theme of reconciliation is prominent in this novel and Greene's treatment of it in this novel may help us to get a better grip on the idea of reconciliation from the point of view of Christian faith

The issue of reconciliation is tied to the story line of the novel itself. The gist of the story that is related is one of a love affair carried on for several years (1939-1944) between Maurice Bendrix—from whose point of view the story is told—and Sarah Miles. One night in 1944 Sarah suddenly and unexpectedly puts an end to the affair. This occurs in the following way. During the first V-1 bombing, Maurice goes downstairs to check on his landlady and instead becomes pinned by the front door as a result of a blast. Sarah goes in search of him and, believing him to be dead, prays to the God in whom she does not believe that Bendrix will be allowed to live. If Bendrix is allowed to live, she will believe. When he reappears in the doorway, Sarah is forced to take her vow seriously and puts an end to the affair. The time frame of the novel begins some eighteen months after the affair, when Bendrix attempts to discover who Sarah's new lover is, since she has never told him of her vow. The new

---

[2] One recalls here Graham Greene's remark that he is a novelist who happens to be a Catholic, rather than a Catholic novelist.

'lover' turns out to be God. Sarah dies shortly after this of pneumonia, to which Bendrix has unwittingly contributed. Nonetheless, in the end several of the characters, including Bendrix and Henry, Sarah's husband, become reconciled on several levels.

How this reconciliation is reached has to do, as we suggested above, with the question of repentance or change and the role of God. Both of these are fundamental to the plot of Greene's novel and therefore offer fodder for thinking about these questions. We will thus now turn to the discussion of these two points.

The Question of Change

The ability of human beings to change is one that is contested in contemporary society. Remorse is possible, but repentance is not.[3] Bendrix is a man who at the beginning of the novel was filled with hatred and his hatred was principally directed at Henry and Sarah. The reason for his hating Henry was that Henry was Sarah's husband. He was jealous of Henry's relationship to Sarah. The reason for his hating Sarah was that Sarah had left him, supposedly for another lover.

In general, however, Bendrix is a man who is not successful at human relationships. Even when he is with Sarah, the time that he experiences as the happiest of his life, he portrays a fundamental distrust of her. He cannot quite accept the fact that she loves him. His moments away from her are filled with distrust of and suspicion of her love for him and her commitment to him. Even though there is nothing to complain of in that respect, he nonetheless feels trust only when she is with him. Even those moments, however, contain an element of distrust. When Sarah tells him that she has never loved anyone or anything as she loves him (50), Bendrix knows she is telling the truth. When he makes the same statement to her, however, he confesses that he is the liar and compares himself to the suspicious police officer" "gathering evidence for a crime that hadn't yet been committed" (51).

This suspicion and hatred of others extends to others as well, not only to those who come between him and Sarah but also to those who are trying to assist him. He takes a perverse delight in showing up the ineptitude of the nonetheless sympathetic and respectful detective Parkis from the agency Bendrix has hired to discover Sarah's new lover: Parkis fails to recognize Bendrix as the man whom Sarah met for lunch. Bendrix further shows his disdain for Parkis (78) when he treats Parkis' son, Lance, to not one but two ices, when he knows that Parkis does not like Lance to have ice cream too often.

Another instance of Bendrix' suspicion and hatred of others is to be seen in his reaction to the man Sarah has allegedly been 'seeing'. When Parkis discovers an address that Sarah has been visiting, Bendrix decides to visit the man, Richard Smythe, under false pretences in order to discover more about the man. His first thought on

---

[3] See, for instance, my discussion of Iris Murdoch's use of the terms 'remorse' and 'repentance' in connection with the terms 'grace' and 'forgiveness' in her novels in Jansen 2001: 95ff.

hearing of Richard Smythe (who lives with his sister) is as follows: "I wondered whether Miss Smythe was as convenient a sister as Henry was a husband, and all my latent snobbery was aroused by the name—that y, the final e. I thought, has she fallen as low as a Smythe in Cedar Road?" (75-76). Upon meeting Smythe and unclear as to his profession, he surmises that he might be a Noncomformist minister and takes a certain pleasure in the notion that Sarah might have such a person as lover, for then, he feels her present love affair is not to be taken seriously (82). Here his pain and hurt at being rejected by Sarah clearly emerges as hatred of her as well.

A fundamental problem in Bendrix's character is his egotism (47)—indeed, one might say that it is the root of his hatred and suspicion. Egotism is a fundamental vice which we encounter in other novelists as well—Christian or not[4]. Egotism is often found paired with insecurity and both elements are present in Bendrix's constant depreciation of others. He cannot feel secure in Sarah's love for him and thus continually portrays Henry as a fool who cannot give Sarah what he can. But his opinion of Smythe is also controlled by his feelings of insecurity and egotism—how could Sarah give him up for Smythe, for this man who is so clearly less than Bendrix?

In the process of the novel Bendrix begins to change. Bendrix has, as has already been stated, hated Henry from the start. In the end Bendrix moves out of the solitary, isolated world in which he has lived all his life. This is not the only development in the novel but it is nonetheless, for our purposes, a significant one. Already in connection with Parkis, Bendrix begins to feel something different in his life. At his first meeting with Parkis, after having had his fun in revealing to Parkis that he was the man Sarah had met for lunch, he notices Parkis' dismay at his mistake and Parkis quickly explains that it is the impression that he will make on his son that is the source of his worry. Bendrix begins to ask him about his son and, after Parkis leaves, Bendrix reflects that for ten minutes he had not thought about Sarah. Instead, he remarks, "I had become nearly human enough to think of another person's trouble" (41).

This development in connection with others is also apparent in his relationship to Henry. He began in the novel despising and hating Henry. The first evidence of change in this relationship is when Henry asks Bendrix's help in dealing with a priest who wants to have Sarah buried instead of cremated. Bendrix comments that "... [i]t was odd how close we had become with Sarah gone. He depended on me now much as before he had depended on Sarah—I was someone familiar about in the house" (152). A few lines later he writes: "There had been a time when I hated Henry. My hatred now seemed petty. Henry was a victim as much as I was a victim ...."[5] The

---

[4] See, for instance, the novels of Muriel Spark, Iris Murdoch and more recently, John Irving.

[5] It is true, of course, that Bendrix sees both Henry and himself as victims of God, represented by the priest, but Bendrix himself is so taken up by his hurt and hatred of God at this moment that one must wonder whether his words are as representative of the

relationship between Bendrix and Henry is slowly changing as a result of Sarah's death. Shortly after Sarah died, Henry asked Bendrix to move in with him, to which Bendrix agrees. But this outward change is representative of much more. For this move signifies Bendrix's moving out of his self-imposed isolation in his house and seeing the needs of others. Prior to this he could live alone and indulge himself, but now he finds himself living with someone and being drawn into the struggles and pain of another. Certainly Bendrix is by no means a saint at this stage, but in this move he begins to change and, like Sarah herself, Bendrix learns that he can no longer enjoy sex (171). Self-indulgence begins to give way to a different way of looking at people and life itself.

The most decisive moment in this change comes after Bendrix loses his temper with the priest and says some things about Sarah which he should not have. Coming down later, he looks in at Henry who is asleep and now sees him now as not an enemy but as the first dead and indistinguishable soldier one meets on the battlefield: "just a human being like himself. I put two biscuits by his bed in case he woke and turned the light out" (183). Bendrix has come to see Henry as a fellow human being, as a fellow sufferer. This represents a profound change in Bendrix's character. His hatred of another human being has begun to dissipate and he is able to love, to love selflessly.

What occurs here reflects also on an issue that came to the fore in the discussion at the conference in which the essays in this volume were discussed.[6] When promoting the idea of reconciliation, do we aim for a minimalist or a maximalist approach? A minimalist approach is one in which different groups or individuals are able to coexist and avoid conflict. A maximalist approach is one in which people not only strive to avoid conflict but also to promote a sense of unity, a sense of fellowship. It may be that if one is speaking of reconciliation along racial, religious or national lines, all that one can expect is the minimalist approach—at least as a place to start. When speaking of individuals, however, it is not simply the avoidance of conflict that is the goal but also this sense of unity, of fellowship, with one another as human beings. This recognition of the other as a human being is essential to reconciliation. In order to be reconciled one needs to see the other as a human being, as can be seen in the quote from Cynthia Ngewu at the end of Ton van Prooijen's essay in this volume (314): "This thing called reconciliation ... if I am understanding it correctly ... if it means that perpetrator, this man who killed Christopher Piet, if it means that he becomes human again, this man, so that I, so that all of us, get our humanity back ... then I agree, I support it all." That is the point of reconciliation: getting one's humanity back by granting humanity to the other. Only on this level will reconcilia-

---

true state of affairs. Were they, in effect, "victims" of God?

[6] The international interreligious workshop on Religion, Conflict, and Reconciliation held at Amersfoort, the Netherlands, March 30 – April 1, 2001.

tion ultimately work. It is necessary in Ngewu's case and it is necessary in Bendrix' case.

This change, however, is not something to which Bendrix willingly comes. In the course of the novel Bendrix is continually feeding his hate, nourishing it on what he considers to be Sarah's betrayal of him. But he nonetheless changes. That this change comes about is due to the 'activity' of God in the novel. It is in connection with this further aspect of the question of reconciliation that one finds a major difference with secular, postmodern novelists.

The Role of God

The role of God in this novel has been very much disputed as to whether it is esthetically sound or theologically desirable. The novel includes the issue of miracles, although it does not use the term explicitly. In fact, Greene later regretted this too easy solution, stating that he should have depicted God battering on Bendrix's mind over a number of years (see Donaghy 1983: 63-64). Despite the problems associated with including God in a novel that is not intended to be a Christian novel, one can safely say that Greene's inclusion of this transcendent side of existence is skillfully done. God 'appears' in the minds of the characters (Sarah and Bendrix especially), necessarily entering into the novel as a character whose actions are recorded apart from the other characters' impressions of what God is doing.[7] As such, God is part of the consciousness of the characters—how they think and the responses they make to situations. Here one must also make the point that belief in God is not as such necessary, for both Sarah and Bendrix begin as non-believers and are both forced into belief.

This question is intrinsic, in my view, to the question of change, of whether change is possible. Once we exclude God from consideration, then we are confronted perhaps with the conclusion that people cannot change. If we look at Bendrix, for example, we cannot on the basis of his character be at all optimistic that he will change. At the beginning of the novel he is so filled with distrust and hatred of others that it would be difficult to see how he could change—how he could find it within himself to take the necessary steps to change. Nonetheless, he changes. The question is how such a change comes about.

One of the insights to which Bendrix and we are led is that we are much less in control of events than we like to think. Largely because of events that are beyond his power Bendrix is forced to discover the truth about Sarah. In this whole process he, although he acts, is largely a passive figure. Never is he in control of events as much as he wishes. He is not, as one critic pointed out, an omniscient author but rather the

---

[7] It is also safe to say with Gregor (1973: 111) that the critic who would exclude God entirely from literature must also forget Dante, Marlowe and Dostoevsky. Why God cannot enter into a novel seems to depend upon criteria that are not entirely literary.

opposite (Sharrock 1984: 166). Sarah goes her own way of faith, contrary to his wishes, and when Sarah is on the point of abandoning her vow, Henry and Bendrix have lunch together and Bendrix allows Henry to conclude that he and Sarah were lovers. This causes Henry to go home early before Sarah leaves and without knowing what her plans are, induces her to stay. Sarah is once again forced to put aside her own desire for happiness and deal as a compassionate human being with Henry's need and misery (118-19). A kind of reconciliation occurs here through Sarah's being forced into self-sacrifice for the sake of another. In reading this, one feels that there is something else operative here that goes beyond mere coincidence. It borders on divine guidance.

At one point Bendrix describes himself in the novel as a character in a novel who cannot come to life. In contrast to saints (like Sarah) who have free will, who do the unexpected, Bendrix compares most of us to characters who have no free will, who do nothing unexpected:

> We are inextricably bound to the plot, and wearily God forces us, here and there, according to his intention, characters without poetry, without free will, whose only importance is that somewhere, at some time, we help to furnish the scene in which a living character moves and speaks, providing perhaps the saints with the opportunities for *their* free will. (186)

Bendrix himself, though he does not know it, is being prodded and pushed into sainthood. The examples of this sainthood become increasingly clearer, culminating in his different view of Henry. It is then that he is able to be more than a victim of events around him.

One of the fundamental questions that arise in this context is the credibility of such change. This is quite apparent in the critics' views of Sarah. Some find her development towards sainthood unbelievable, for there is little difference between her love for Bendrix and her love for God (Gregor 1973: 117). Others do find her believable (Donaghy 1983: 65). It may be said that Sarah is not fully successfully drawn as a character perhaps, but there is something more fundamental operative in how she develops as a character that is of essence to our point. It is precisely in the unlikelihood of sainthood that sainthood is often found. That Sarah moves towards sainthood is an example *par excellence* of the mysterious workings of the transcendent in the lives of humans. To look for complete or even adequate explanations on the mundane level is beyond human capacity. We need, as it were, the complete plot and, since none of us are the omniscient authors that we would like to be, it is impossible to explain fully why things happen. The grace of justification and the grace of sanctification often appear as surprises in the lives of people and there are more than we know who have been and are dragged kicking and screaming into faith and sainthood. It is more than simply that other characters provide saints with such opportunities; it is also that these characters need to be saints before they can have any free will. As we know from Sarah's journal, she too has been prodded and pushed by God into sainthood and it is only when she accepts that she is being pushed and prodded that she is able to become the saint she is intended to be.[8]

The presence of God in the novel allows one even more insight into the question of the relationship between free will and our own acting as agents with free will. Theologians and philosophers will be aware of the various solutions that have been offered to resolve the tension between free will and determination. What one sees perhaps in this novel is the complex nature of this problem, in the sense that in one's life the transcendent is always present but that it is not possible to find a resolution to the inherent conflict between the concepts of free will and determination. So much happens *to* rather than *by* us. We are, if not victims of a capricious author, at least passive with respect to much of life. If there is to be change, it cannot and will not occur from within us or even from within the mundane reality of this world and this history. It occurs from without. While perhaps not a distinctly Christian insight into the nature of reconciliation, it is intrinsic to the Christian view of how reconciliation occurs.

This also has a direct bearing on the role of religion in resolving conflict and achieving reconciliation. From the other contributions in this volume, it will be clear how extremely difficult it is to achieve reconciliation between groups involved in conflicts that regularly appear on the front pages of our newspapers. In many of these situations, because of the long history of deep-seated reasons for engaging in conflict (history, land, religion), any attempt at reconciliation—whether maximalist or even minimalist—seems hopelessly futile. Progress is apparently made and, then, one single act can drive the parties back into conflict. Moreover, as Farid Esack's paper shows (290-97), an apparent situation of reconciliation can simply redirect one's anger so that one seeks other conflicts and other victims.

In view of this 'intransigence' of human beings (an important part of Christian doctrine regarding human beings) with respect to reconciliation, the notion of a transcendent being who in some way forces us into reconciliation, may be necessary to achieve any kind of reconciliation. This is, perhaps, one of the fundamental contributions religion can make to resolving conflict and achieving reconciliation. There are two points to make in reference to this. First, Desiree Berendsen has made a strong argument in this volume for a concept of transcendence which is 'this-worldly': a non-supernatural third party (see 164-77). The major question one would want to address to her argument, however, is whether such a secular approach would have enough convincing power to achieve the kind of reconciliation that is needed in view of human intransigence. A secularized view of history and the possibilities for reconciliation may just as easily lead one to abandon the notion of reconciliation altogether, to assume that conflict is part of existence and that it is useless to attempt to resolve

---

[8] Something similar happens to Caroline in Muriel Spark's *The Comforters* (1957), who only through her acceptance of the notion that she is a character in a novel, does she learn to be able to act freely within it.

these conflicts and to become reconciled: it is better, for oneself at any rate, to adopt an attitude of comic distance (see Jansen 2001 on the Dutch novelist Cees Nooteboom). With the idea of a transcendent power, one can take the view that it is one's own religion that leads one to see the 'enemy' as another human being, as one who deserves as much respect as we ourselves do. Is it not religion, in the end, that provides even the possibility of the hope of getting our humanity back?

The second thing that needs to be said here in connection with the role of the idea of supernatural transcendent power is that not even human intransigence is enough to stand in the way of reconciliation. Bendrix is forced to change, as others are forced to change. This change does not, as we saw, come from within the human being him- or herself. It is unexpected and comes from a source outside the human being. The strongest motivation for reconciliation comes in those rare moments of revelation—like Bendrix—when the enemy appears as another human being like ourselves. We are suddenly struck by the fact that the other is our brother or our sister and it is the dawn that brings this revelation (see Esack in this volume, 294-95). Such a revelation is often not desired; we wish, like Bendrix, to hold on to our hatred and to feed our revenge. Such a revelation comes from outside and is forced upon us. One cannot fully account for these developments in terms of biography or history. This notion of 'being forced' into reconciliation raises, of course, the specter of determinism: our lot is not entirely in our own hands. But it also, ironically perhaps, throws open a different door to freedom. One's personal biography and ethnic history itself are not 'closed' but 'open'. We are not trapped in our personal or ethnic histories but through the forcing upon us of this revelation are given the opportunity to enter into a new history. We are free to forge something else out of the new situation in which we find ourselves. We too will be on the road to sainthood.

Concluding Remarks

In this contribution we have briefly—perhaps too briefly—explored the nature of human change with regard to reconciliation and the resolution of conflict. From a theological point of view one can critique the novel for its obvious limitation in conceptual analyses of the problem of reconciliation and the role of God. But, as Gregor points out (1973: 111), Greene did not write a theological treatise; he wrote a novel. And it is in its very limitation with respect to conceptual analyses that it finds its strength. As a novel, Greene's *The End of the Affair* shows how reconciliation takes place, sometimes against the wishes of the protagonists.

Reconciliation requires that a price be paid, that sacrifices be made. One cannot always predict the sacrifices that will need to be made. Moreover, change of heart must often be forced on us. We human beings are hard, stubborn creatures who do not take the road to change easily. To understand that completely one needs the narrative, rather than conceptual analysis. This change is one that is forced, one that in the Christian view of life will always come from outside, from God, from the Transcendent. In writing a novel that incorporates the Christian faith, one must give place to the unexpected, to that which does not fit with mundane expectations and ways of achieving results. This is ultimately the value of Greene's novel to a topic as diverse as reconciliation.

Bibliography

Donaghy, Henry J. (1983). *Graham Greene: An Introduction to His Writings*. Amsterdam: Rodopi.
Frye, Northrop. (1964). "The Argument of Comedy." In: Paul Lauter (ed.). *Theories of Comedy*. Garden City: Anchor Books, Doubleday & Company, Inc. Pp.450-60.
Gregor, Ian. (1973). "*The End of the Affair*." In: Samuel Hynes (ed.). *Graham Greene: A Collection of Critical Essays*. Englewood Cliffs: Prentice-Hall, Inc. Pp.110-25.
Greene, Graham (1951 [1975]). *The End of the Affair*. Harmondsworth: Penguin Books.
Jansen, Henry. (1995). *Relationality and the Concept of God*. Currents of Encounter, Vol. 10. Amsterdam/Atlanta: Editions Rodopi.
———.(2001). *Laughter among the Ruins: Postmodern Comic Approaches to Suffering*. Frankfurt-am-Main: Peter Lang Gmbh.
Sharrock, Roger. (1984). *Saints, Sinners and Comedians: The Novels of Graham Greene*. Tunbridge Wells/Notre Dame: Burns & Oates/University of Notre Dame Press.
Spark, Muriel. (1957 [1994]). *The Comforters*. New York: New Directions Books.
Tillich, Paul. (1948). *The Shaking of the Foundations*. New York: Charles Scribner's Sons.
Vroom, H.M. (1989). *Religions and the Truth: Philosophical Reflections and Perspectives*. Currents of Encounter, Vol. 2. Amsterdam/Grand Rapids: Editions Rodopi/ Wm. B. Eerdmans Publishing Co.
(1994). "Religious Hermeneutics, Culture and Narratives." *Studies in Interreligious Dialogue* 4: 189-216.

Secular Saints

The Possibility of Reconciliation Without Transcendence

Desiree Berendsen

Introduction

The theme of this congress is "Religion, Conflict, and Reconciliation." The assumption for this theme is that religion can be both the cause of conflict and the source of reconciliation. Reconciliation, however, is itself first and foremost a theological term and subject to wide discussion among Christians. In the history of theology several models of reconciliation can be distinguished. In his paper Cees van der Kooi discusses three Christian models of reconciliation. The Western world, although Christian at root, has become very much secularized. Therefore, I want to discuss the possibilities of reconciliation in a secular context: Is reconciliation conceivable absent the idea of transcendence? The central question, thus, is whether it is possible to conceive of reconciliation without reference to any transcendent being as a kind of intermediary. In our post-Christian Western world it would seem to be a necessity of life that reconciliation be possible without the mediation of some transcendent entity—at least if 'transcendent' is taken to refer to that which is beyond being. If it appears to be impossible to reconcile different strains of thought or two sides of an argument without reference to a third transcendent party, then coexistence in a secular society will be very difficult—if at all possible. It seems to be possible to live peacefully in a post-Christian society; thus it would also seem that reconciliation is possible without reference to a transcendent being. Does reconciliation require a third party? Is that third party necessarily transcendent to the other two parties? Is reconciliation between two parties without mediation of a third one conceivable?

In addition to its prominence in theological discourse, reconciliation is also an important notion in law. In present Dutch society law is not theologically grounded, at least not in the first instance. Therefore, legal discourse can be helpful in trying to ascertain the possibilities of reconciliation in a secular context. In this paper I will first briefly mention the three or four models of reconciliation that have played a role in Christian thought, with a view to determining the essence of reconciliation in a theological context. Then we will turn to a legal case, namely the possibility of mediation in punishment and in the restoration of relations. We will try to analyze and describe what the function of reconciliation in this context is. Thereafter I will try to defend the thesis that reconciliation does need transcendence, in the sense of a third party as a kind of mediator, but that this does not imply that (organized) religion is necessary to achieve reconciliation.

Reconciliation in Theology

In his contribution to this symposium Cees van der Kooi, following G. Aulén, distinguishes three models of reconciliation in the history of the church. The first is what he calls the victory model. Reconciliation in this model is a result of the victory of Christ over the devil. The second model is the forensic or objective one. Reconciliation in this model is achieved through the forgiveness of human guilt relative to God subsequent to the effectuation of satisfaction vis-à-vis God. Historically this model is associated with Anselm of Canterbury and Calvin. The third model Van der Kooi distinguishes is the subjective one. Reconciliation occurs when human beings show remorse for wrongdoing and sin. Christ's death in this view is an act of love and leads human beings (the subjects) to love others. This model is associated with Abelard.

W.J. van Asselt distinguishes four models of reconciliation: ransom, sacrifice, substitution and example. The ransom model, which can be traced to Irenaeus, entails that Christ is paid as a ransom to release humanity from evil or the devil. This is what Van der Kooi calls the victory model. The sacrifice model, associated with Anselm and Calvin, views Christ as sacrificed for our sins. This corresponds with Van der Kooi's objective model. Van der Kooi's subjective model is labelled the example model by Van Asselt. The crucifixion of Christ leads to a change in human beings. Van Asselt also associates this model with Abelard. The substitution model is the most juridical one in Van Asselt's view. Van der Kooi's objective model can be seen as a merging of Van Asselt's substitution and sacrifice models. Van Asselt himself sees the substitution model as the organizing principle for the other three. He states that when the substitution model is used as the structuring element of our view of reconciliation, then the limits of the other models can be seen and evaluated.

For our purposes it is important to see that reconciliation in theology always implies in some way restoring the disturbed relation between God and humankind. This is the case even with respect to the subjective or example model, which stresses that Christ's death is an inspiration for human beings to act in a moral way. As is the case with other notions of reconciliation, the initiative in this model lies with God—the only difference being that the human role in reconciliation is somewhat more important in this one than in its counterparts. Of course, it is self-evident that in theological models of reconciliation God plays an important role. Moreover, reconciliation is necessitated by the sinful nature of humankind. In all theological models reconciliation involves the restoration of the relation between God and humankind as it was before the Fall. The starting point is not so much the sins that human beings commit as it is the disturbed relation between God and humankind. Of course, it is because of this disturbed relation that human beings commit sins against each other, but this is a result of the Fall. Reconciliation in theology thus is an affair between God and humankind. If reconciliation between human beings takes place, it is as a result of the restored relation between God and human beings.

A Secular Form of Reconciliation: Reconciliation in (Criminal) Law

First of all it has to be said that although most legal proceedings in one way or another bear reference to a moment of reconciliation and although the word is deeply rooted in the history of law, the term reconciliation occurs almost exclusively in theological literature. We have already seen that in theological discourse reconciliation is always connected somehow with the relation between God and humankind. In jurisprudence the concern is with interhuman relations. Theological reflections therefore cannot be directly injected into legal contexts or translated into terms of philosophical law (Van Roermund 1997: 170). Criminal law is based on ideas of satisfaction, deterrence or retribution. In civil societies criminal law is developed to protect society from revenge. In a way, criminal law is an institutional substitute for revenge. Reconciliation between the offender and the victim of the crime is not a major topic in institutionalized criminal law. Hazewinkel-Suringa's Introduction to the Study of Dutch Criminal Law does not mention the word 'reconciliation' in the index. In another Dutch introduction to criminal law (Van Binsbergen) 'reconciliation' occurs, according to the index, five times in the text. Another Dutch word *zoen* ('kiss,' 'penance'), which is a cognate of the Dutch word for reconciliation, *verzoening*, occurs eight times. All occurrences are in the context of a description of old Germanic and medieval law. Reconciliation was seen as the goal of a vendetta: it was the solemn agreement by which the feuding families ended their vendetta. Reconciliation implied repair of the injustice done (Van Binsbergen 1982: 7). There were crimes, however, for which there could be no reconciliation, such as murder and (high) treason (Van Binsbergen 1982: 8). In the transition from the Middle Ages to modern times, the role of guilt became increasingly more important. As the rural-based society became increasingly an urban-based society, the call for the protection of the society became clearer. From that moment on violation of law and order was seen as a violation of the interests of society or of the authorities. Violation was no longer seen simply as an offence against the private rights of someone or his family but also as a distortion of peace in the city or country. This meant that while people continued to be obliged to seek reconciliation with respect to their feuds on the one hand, the number of instances in which no reconciliation was possible increased on the other. The kinds of crimes associated with the latter could only be punished by the government. In this respect it is important to note that the goal of punishment changed when the definition of violation changed from the offence against private rights to damage to collective interests. Whereas originally the goal of punishment was satisfaction for harm suffered at the hands of an individual or group, the goal later became the protection of society. Harsh measures directed at deterrence were the main means by which this protection was to be achieved (Van Binsbergen 1982: 20).

Thus the thesis can be defended that our legal system is not based on reconciliation but on the protection of society. This is the reason why in criminal law the main focus is not on the relation between the victim and the offender but on the relation between offender and society. The judge's goal is to punish a crime that has been committed, not to restore relations between victim and offender.[1] Theories of criminal law adduce a variety of justifications for punishment by legal authorities (the government), which can be grouped into categories. Of these types of justification, four can be termed classic. The first of these are the so-called 'theories of treaty'. The distinguishing characteristic of which is the idea of a contract which is transferred from the mercantile to the legal sector. It is said that if someone buys something he or she knows what the consequences of the contract of sale are. The purchaser obliges himself to that which by nature belongs to the act of buying. In the same way an offender of a crime accepts that which belongs by nature to a crime, which is punishment (Remmelink 1996: 892). The second type are called 'absolute theories'. The core of these theories is the conviction that the crime itself entails what is required in and justified by the imposition of punishment, apart from the expected practical usefulness. The goal of punishment is retribution or retaliation (Remmelink 1996: 893f.). Opposed to this second category of justification are what are termed relative theories. The relation between the punishment and the crime lies in the goal of punishment. This goal is protection of legal goods and the warding off of injustice. Both the imposition and the threat of punishment are intended to deter one from committing a crime. One of the main goals of punishment in these theories is prevention, both general and special (Remmelink 1996: 899f.). General prevention is the deterrent effect of the punishment on possible offenders. It is hoped that the punishment will lead people to refrain from committing crimes. Special prevention is the effect of punishment on the actual offender: it is hoped that the punishment will keep him or her from repeating the offense. The fourth category combines elements from the absolute and the relative theories. According to this theory, if one holds that the offender, because of his offence, has merited a certain amount of harm, then one must also pay heed to the relative idea that this amount does not have to be imposed more than the maintenance of the legal order demands (Remmelink 1996: 906). Remmelink's *Introduction* holds that this last combination is the best justification for a legal system.

> We thus have a form of justice before us that, although it is only applicable if the protection of society warrants such, joins retribution with special and general prevention, exposes the reprehensibility of the behavior, keeps the norm alive and thereby preserves and enlarges the citizens' trust in the legal order. Nevertheless, it holds open the possibility that the punishment for the condemned entails a *recon-*

---

[1] Cf. the works of the Dutch criminologist Herman Bianchi who argues that criminal justice is no justice at all, because it is not justice for the criminal nor the victim. He has developed ideas aimed at giving reconciliation between victim and offender a place in the justice system again. To reach that goal it is necessary to change the whole of our legal system, because this system is not directed at the reconciliation between victim and offender but at the punishment of the offender. Cf., for example, Bianchi 1984 and 1985.

ciliation, a stimulus to participate again in social life as a decent citizen (Remmelink 1996: 920 (emphasis mine))[2]

Retribution is thus not the final goal of punishment but simply a means. According to this *Introduction*, the final goal is reconciliation—but reconciliation of the criminal with society rather than reconciliation of the offender with the victim. It is striking that we see a structural similarity here between the theological and criminal-law contexts of reconciliation. In both instances reconciliation is a restoration of the relation between an entity that transcends human beings (God, society) and individual humans. In neither of these cases is reconciliation between two conflicting parties at issue. In either case this latter kind of reconciliation can and may be a *result* of the reconciliation between God and the human being or between the human being and the society, but it is not the primary goal. The goal in both cases is restoration of order: the primordial created order that has been destroyed because of the Fall, or the legal order in society.

Mediation as an Attempt to Reconcile Victim and Offender

In the legal process both victim and offender are fixed in specific roles and both run the risk of identifying themselves with these roles. Moreover, the offender runs the risk of seeing himself as a victim too, a victim of the legal system. The victim on the other hand runs the risk of falling into the role of *helpless* victim, because there may be some advantages in playing the role of victim in a convincing way; one can for example acquire privileges through being a victim (cf. Pollefeyt 1999: 40). If the goal is forgiveness, both victims and offender need to undergo an appropriate conversion. The offender has to confess guilt; the victim needs to distinguish between the wrongdoer and his or her wrong deeds. It is impossible for a victim to forgive an offender who does not see him- or herself as guilty. It is just as impossible to forgive if the victim sees the offender as evil itself, not as someone who has done bad things. There is a great deal of truth in Bert van Roermund's comment that the decisive step in reconciliation is made before the process starts. The will to forgive (and in a later stadium to become reconciled) is a precondition for the steps to come; the will to forgive is a phase that precedes the search for truth (Van Roermund 1997: 171). The context of Van Roermund's words is striking: he is discussing the Truth and Reconciliation Committee in South Africa. He cited a sentence in the interim report of the Committee quoting a mother whose son was murdered during Apartheid. She asked: "We want to forgive, but whom do we have to forgive?" (Van Roermund 1997: 170). In the context of this paper I do not want to go into the ins and outs of the TRC[3] but simply show that the attitude of the victim (and the offender) plays an important role in the process of reconciliation. This does not mean that I want to say that victims

---

[2] This quote has been translated from the Dutch by Henry Jansen.

[3] For this see the paper by Piet Meiring in this volume, 279-89.

always have to take the first step and must always be willing to forgive—not at all! I began this paragraph with the observation that both victim and offender have to be converted in order to make reconciliation possible. It can be a liberating experience for a victim to see that it is possible to step out of the role of victim. Moreover, reconciliation is not a simple forgetting of what has been done. As Van Roermund argues, reconciliation provides evidence for the belief that it is impossible for human beings to live with the assumption that absolute evil is incarnated in a specific political system (or specific person, I should add). It might be possible for humanity to live with evil, but it is impossible to live with an absolutized form of evil (Van Roermund 1997: 173). This brings us back to the relation between the victim and the offender, specifically the insight that it is necessary for the victim to see the offender as someone who has done harm, not as harm or evil itself. If the offender were evil itself, he or she would be an incarnation of evil. If we do not want to live with this possibility, we have to distinguish between the person and his or her deeds.

We have seen that criminal law institutions are not organized to reconcile the victim and the offender. If any reconciliation is involved in criminal law it is between the offender and society. We also have observed that this kind of institutionalized law can lead to the fixation of both the victim and the offender in their roles. In the margins of criminal law, however, there are some developments that do take the relation between the victim and the offender into account. Since the 1970s mediation between the offender and the victim of a crime has been occurring quite frequently. Originating in Canada, the idea came to Europe via the United States and the United Kingdom. In Europe in March 1999 there were more than 700 mediation or arbitration projects in operation.

What is mediation?[4] In Belgium two models of mediation exist within the framework of criminal law. The first is legally organized and is called penalty arbitration or mediation (*strafbemiddeling*). This model is used in relatively minor offences. Criminal proceedings cease if the mediation process succeeds. One of the goals of this model is the reparation or compensation of damage to the victim. The second model is called mediation with a view to the restoration of relations (*herstelbemiddeling*). This model is used in more serious cases. This form of mediation occurs outside the judiciary context as such, although its practices and organization are arranged in consultation with the judge and the public prosecutor. In principle, this form of mediation does not have any influence on the criminal proceedings[5].

Both forms of mediation are attempts to bring the offender and the victim together during the legal process. As we have said, the legal system is not organized to reconcile the victim and the offender. Mediation originated from concrete experi-

---

[4] This information is derived from Aertsen 1999: 48-53.

[5] Groenhuijsen (2000: 444) distinguishes between three models of mediation. Two can be identified with the two Aertsen mentions, Groenhuijsen adds a third: a model that sees mediation as an alternative for regular criminal proceedings.

ences and needs of victims and offenders. Victims often need to understand what has happened and why. Victims want offenders to know what the consequences of the latters' deeds are and they may want to make the offender assume his or her responsibilities. Mediation provides the opportunity to ask questions and express expectations directly to the offender (Aertsen 1999: 49). The effect of a personal meeting can, of course, be impressive. The other (the victim, the offender) becomes a living person with a face. Most important are not the concrete results of mediation, but the process and the possibility of active participation in it.

The legal context of mediation is restorative justice. In contrast to the other models of justification of punishment, the restorative justice model is not exclusively directed toward the offender but also toward the victim and society as a whole. The goal of a legal reaction to a crime in this model is to restore relations. A crime is not, as in other models, seen as a violation of rules of the legal authority but as an infringement on persons and relations (Aertsen 1999: 50). The concrete persons involved are once again present in the legal system in this model. It is not the government and the offender that are the actors in the legal process but the victim and the offender. The crime is no longer defined in legal terms alone, but also in its social, personal and moral contexts. The question in the situation after a crime has been committed is not "How can we punish the offender?" but "What can be done to restore the situation?" Restoration is not a side effect but the heart of this approach. The restorative-justice approach is directed toward problem-solving and toward the future rather than at what has happened in the past and punishment. The goal of restoration is not a return to the situation before the crime took place—this is impossible. Moreover, the goal is to find a compensation that is acceptable to each party and to find a new balance (Aertsen 1999: 51 and Bianchi 1985: 162-66). Restorative justice in the USA and Canada first became known through the activities of the so called "victim-offender reconciliation programmes."

It is clear that in this approach, reconciliation has another function than in the legal and theological models we discussed above. Here reconciliation concerns the restoration of relations between people and society has a role in the background. Here reconciliation no longer concerns the restoration of relations with a transcendent entity. Do we here have proof of the thesis that reconciliation without recourse to transcendence is possible? Yes and no. We do have a form of reconciliation in which people were reconciled, conflicts were resolved, without the contribution of an abstract transcendent entity. However, it is clear that in the case of restorative justice as well reconciliation is only possible with the help of a mediator.

The Mediator

What is the function of the mediator in restorative justice? We have already said that the meeting of concrete persons in a situation after a crime has been committed can be an impressive experience. It can be as impressive for the offender as it is for the victim. It goes without saying that this meeting cannot take place without prior organization. One of the most important tasks of the mediator is to create a safe environment in which an authentic meeting can take place. The presupposition of mediation is that the punishable act and its consequences have to be seen as an interhuman situation of conflict that calls for consultation and pacification. When victim and offender are brought together, this is done in the conviction that they will be able to find a solution that is acceptable to both of them.[6] For mediation to be possible it is necessary that the offender of the crime be known and that the offender confesses. When a specific case is selected for a possible case for mediation, both the offender and the victim receive an invitation from the mediator. The invitation is strictly non-obligatory. Neither the offender nor the victim is forced into the process. When both of them accept the invitation, the mediator has conversations with each of them separately. In these conversations the accent is on how the crime is experienced: What has happened? What were the motives? How do the victim and the offender see each other? What were the consequences of the crime? During successive conversations the information from the two parties is exchanged via the mediator. In the next phase, the conversation centers on the theme of satisfaction. What does the one party expect from the other? This can be money or the expression of remorse: concrete or symbolic compensation. When the mediator has spoken to the two twice separately, he or she will determine whether is desirable for the two to meet each other. In the end, in one out of four cases the victim and the offender reach this point (Van Garsse 1999: 56). It is also possible for an agreement to be reached without a direct meeting.

The conversations with the mediator take place at home with the victim or the offender. This is very much appreciated, especially by the victim, because victims often have the feeling that they have not truly been heard during the judiciary process. During the process of mediation the attitude of the parties often changes a great deal. Before this process begins, victim and offender can have a distorted image of each other. It is remarkable that even in cases in which no agreement is reached both parties often feel very satisfied. The parties have a sense that they have been heard and recognized. Moral questions and even reconciliation are brought back in the legal system by this restorative justice.

Reconciliation as Remembering the Past in Order to Open up the Future

We concluded that restorative justice can provide room for taking account of the relation between the victim and the offender of a crime in criminal-law proceedings. Of course, mediation is not a solution for all cases in criminal law. For example, about 95% of penal offences are unsuitable for mediation simply because of the fact that the offender is unknown (Groenhuijsen 2000: 445). In the context of this article we cannot evaluate this; what is important is the fact that a legal system in which reconciliation between victim and offender plays a role is conceivable. What kind of reconciliation is envisaged here?

---

[6] The information regarding the function of the mediator is taken from Van Garsse 1999: 54-59. See also Groenhuijsen 2000: 443.

At this point it would be well to recall the quote we cited earlier from Van Roermund that will to forgive is a precondition for subsequent steps in the process of reconciliation. The goal of restorative justice is to restore relations or even to reconcile the parties. The criminal or offending act has destroyed relationships and has violated people; crimes are seen less as violations of rules. These relationships need to be restored.[7] As we stated earlier, this does not of course mean that the victim is required to or should deny or forget what has been done to him or her. What has to be forgiven is the guilt of the offender. This can only be done when the offender takes up his or her responsibilities for what has been done. If forgiveness is possible, the victim will not be freed from the memories but will be free from the heavy weight of hate and resentment. Forgiveness can give the victim the possibility of reconstructing the past in a creative way such that the remembrance of the crime can be given a productive future (cf. Pollefeyt 1999: 43). Instead of being the passive party, the victim is given an active role which may make it possible for him to create an openness in which he is no longer defined by the role of victim. For the offender, the act of forgiveness can change the guilt into responsibility for the future.

We already mentioned above that forgiving presupposes a conversion on the part of both the victim and the offender. The offender has to confess guilt and ask for forgiveness. The victim must become capable of seeing the offender as someone who has done harm and not as harm itself. The victim can never be forced to forgive; forgiveness cannot be demanded and must be given freely. The offender can only create the conditions on the grounds of which he may be granted forgiveness. Forgiveness is something the victim gives to the offender without feeling obligated to do so. This is not the same as reconciliation. Reconciliation concerns the restoration of the relation between victim and offender with respect to the future, whereas forgiveness is directed toward the past. Reconciliation, however, is not an automatic consequence of forgiveness (cf. Pollefeyt 1999: 45). Although it can be seen as the final step, it might sometimes be impossible because the injustice done is too serious. This will then lead to a dramatic situation of destroyed interhuman relations.

It may seem that mediation and restorative justice are only interested in the victim, the offender and the restoration of their relationship. But this is not true. A crime is never an act without a context. Society as a whole is involved when criminal acts are committed. From the perspective of restorative justice, however, a crime is not in first instance a violation of the rules of society, it is a violation of relations between people and of people in their social environment. This is why the traditional bilateral relationship of the state/criminal justice system and the offender is replaced by a triadic relationship in restorative justice: the triadic relationship between society, victim and offender (Aertsen and Peters 1998: 522). Because a crime is not in first instance seen as a violation of rules but as a distortion of relations that need to be

---

[7] For the differences between retributive justice and restorative justice cf. also the scheme in Wright 1998: 279.

restored, restorative justice can be a means by which the offender can be reintegrated into society.

The key question that remains to be answered, however, is why a victim should want to be reconciled with or even forgive the offender. One of the most important motives we have already mentioned: forgiveness can give the victim the opportunity to grow out of the role of passive victim and to see himself as actively involved in his own life again. From a theological point of view the question of course remains whether it is possible for someone to forgive without having recourse to God who has already forgiven us. It has to be remembered that forgiveness is not a one-way activity from the victim to the offender—the offender must seek and the victim may grant forgiveness. And this two-way direction is even more true for reconciliation. Both the victim and the offender have to be converted before any restoration can take place. Even for the secular context of criminal law there is some truth in the theological models of reconciliation in the sense that reconciliation cannot be reached without outside help. We have seen that in the restorative-justice approach the mediator plays an important role. His role is to create a safe environment in which it will be possible for the victim and the offender to meet each other. The true meeting of victim and offender whereby they truly see each other's faces and look into each other's hearts cannot be arranged by the mediator. He can only create the preconditions for this; the victim and the offender themselves have to experience that the other is a human being too, just like him- or herself.

The question remains: is it possible for two people to meet each other truly without having recourse to any form transcendence? Just as in the section on mediation, the answer here is yes and no. People can meet one another as other *people*, a victim can learn to see an offender as someone who has done harm instead of as evil itself. The offender can learn to see the victim as someone to whom he has done harm. The deed does not have to be forgotten; the deed does not even have to be forgiven, but the *person* can be forgiven and the persons involved can be reconciled. On the other hand, if the question is whether this is a process that concerns just the persons involved, then the answer is no. People cannot be reconciled outside the context of the society in which they live and without other people as mediators and examples.

Authentic Examples: Christ and the Saints of Leiden[8]

One of the theological models that we delineated in the first section of this essay was that of example. The core of this model is that the crucifixion of Christ should lead people to change their lives: Christ's death is an act of love that brings human beings to love one another. His act is seen as an example for human beings. We emphasized

---

[8] I want to thank Jojanneke Drijver, a Dutch radio journalist at the IKON radio for her suggestion of the saints of Leiden (*Leidse Heiligen*) and my colleague Jan Krans for his search on the internet for information regarding these 'saints'.

that even in this model, however, the initiative comes from God. Here the focus is not so much on God but on the role of Christ. In that sense Christ can be called a saint according to Leertouwer's definition. Leertouwer defines a saint as someone who risks his life for the well-being of others or the whole. This definition was given in an interview published in the Leiden newspaper, *Hat Leidsch Dagblad*, in connection with the 'election' of the Saints of Leiden. This election was an initiative of the churches of the city of Leiden together with some shopkeepers. In August 2000 the newspaper published a series in which they gave seven inhabitants of the city the opportunity to vote for their own saints.

The saints these seven persons 'elected' were: Francis of Assisi, Martin Luther King, the athlete Ellen van Langen, Elly Kerkhoff, the director of a socio-cultural training center, Professor Cleveringa, Nelson Mandela, Anton de Kom, a socialist from Surinam, and the physicist Richard Feynman. A soccer player named his grandparents and the soccer player Ronald Koeman. This is not the place to discuss why these particular people were nominated saints. I just want to make some observations. Do these saints have anything to do with Leertouwer's definition of someone who risks his life for the well-being of others or the whole? It is remarkable that authenticity was a keyword in most of the motivations people gave when asked to indicate why they chose certain persons as saints. Courage, being him- or herself, making his or her choices and sticking to one's principles are qualifications that a modern saint should have. Apparently 'being oneself', being authentic, is an important characteristic these days. Someone who has the courage to 'be himself' can become an example for people who find it hard to hold on to their own principles. Some of the saints mentioned were called saints because of their exemplary function—for example Ronald Koeman. Most of the people gave as the reason for their choice that those they 'elected' did what they did not just for themselves. The motivation with respect to Elly Kerckhoff is illustrative in this respect. She is said to have been an inspired woman who did not live long but very intensely. It is said that she always kept her personal interests in the background, even her health was unimportant to her. "Only the other, mostly the one who has less, was central in her life." This woman is truly a saint in Leertouwer's definition.

To the question of why victims should want to forgive the deeds of their offenders and why victims and offenders can be reconciled, we now have somewhat more of an answer. Not only does the search for reconciliation provide the victim and the offender the opportunity to grow out of their judicial roles and open themselves up to a common future, but they can actually achieve it because others have done it before them. People are able to be reconciled with one another because they have seen examples of people who do not just live for themselves.

Concluding Remarks

It is clear that I am convinced of the possibility of reconciliation outside a religious context. It is possible for two people to be reconciled without having recourse to a transcendent reality, although is may be impossible for two parties to be reconciled without the mediation of a third. Of course, a third party is never without his own interests and agenda, but he or she is needed in order to reach reconciliation, because two people or two parties in conflict might not be able to transcend their own positions without the help of a mediatory agent, who is by definition transcendent to both positions, although not neutral. People cannot learn to see others as themselves if they do not learn this from others, from the society in which they live or the religious tradition to which they adhere.

The anthropological suppositions lying behind this conviction cannot be delineated within the limits of this present paper. The only thing that can to be said is that human beings are on the one hand dependent on others; nobody can live on his or her own. On the other hand, people can be held responsible for their acts. We recognize that this responsibility can be heavy. This is one of the reasons why people need examples and other people (saints) who live their lives for us.

Bibliography

Aertsen, Ivo. (1999). "Over goedmaking en bemiddeling bij misdrijven." *Kultuurleven* 66: 48-53.
—— and T. Peters (1998). "Mediation and Restorative Justice in Belgium." *European Journal on Criminal Policy and Research* 6: 507-25.
Bianchi, H. (1984). *New Perspectives on Crime and Justice*. Ottawa: MCC Office of Criminal Justice Ontario.
——. (1985). *Gerechtigheid als vrijplaats. De terugkeer van het slachtoffer in ons recht*. Baarn: Ten Have.
Groenhuijsen, M.S. (2000). "Mediation in het strafrecht. Bemiddeling en conflictoplossing in vele gedaanten." *Delikt en Delinkwent* 30: 441-48.
Pollefeyt, D. (1999). "Vergeving"Een nieuw begin voor dader, slachtoffer en samenleving." *Kultuurleven* 66: 38-47.
Remmelink, J. (1996). *Mr. D. Hazewinkel-Suringa's Inleiding tot de studie van het Nederlandse strafrecht*. 15th ed. Deventer.
Van Asselt, W.J. (1999). "Verzoening in veelvoud?" *Kerk en Theologie* 50: 189-204.
Van Binsbergen, W.C. (1982). *Inleiding strafrecht*. 5th ed. Zwolle.
Van Garsse, Leo. (1999). "Herstelbemiddeling in de praktijk. Ervaringen met bemiddeling tussen daders en slachtoffers." *Kultuurleven* 66: 54-59.
Van Roermund, Bert. (1997). "Recht en verzoening." *Nederlands tijdschrift voor rechtsfilosofie en rechtstheorie* 26: 170-74.
Wright, M. (1998). "Restorative Justice: From Punishment to Reconciliation – The Role of Social Workers." *European Journal of Crime, Criminal Law and Criminal Justice* 6: 267-81.

Women in Engaged Buddhism

Claudia Romberg

Introduction

In comparison to that which obtained in Indian Brahman society at the time of the historical Buddha (565-485 B.C.E.), the ideal of the equality of all human beings in Buddhism included a change of attitude towards women. The patriarchal family system of the Brahman tradition (around 800-400 B.C.E) subordinated women in all aspects of life to men: "Day and night women must be kept in dependence by the males of their families and must be kept under male control.... [A] woman is never fit for independence" (Das 1962: 152). The wives of Brahmans were allowed to assist in sacred rites but were not allowed to study Vedic texts and were considered incapable of attaining salvation. The rigid caste system did not offer any path to salvation along with women could travel independently (see Rau 1957).

With the emergence of Buddhism in ancient India this situation changed. The historical Buddha did not engage in any attempts at social reform in order to change the strict and invincible caste system but tried to create a second world in which these distinctions were no longer relevant. All human (and in the Mahayana tradition even all sentient) beings who had suffered and, having become conscious of that suffering, decided to enter the Buddhist *sangha*, lose their social identity as members of a caste, just as "all great rivers vanish when flowing into the sea." These beings are capable of liberation from samsaric suffering, regardless of their social status or sex. But the fact that no social reform was attempted, neither by the historical Buddha nor by Buddhist communities in later times, shows that there is a certain tension between doctrines that describe ideal circumstances and the actual social situation.

In this essay I will show that no theoretical foundations for any form of discrimination can be found in Buddhism. Although I cannot present solutions for existing injustices, I will point out the theoretical basis for a possible reconciliation of opposing views concerning discrimination in general and the problem of gender in particular. I will illustrate existing tensions on three different levels.

First, I will outline the problems that exist on the level of society. Was Buddhism in its early form a religion open to individuals of all social classes? Was it possible for members of the female sex to enter the Buddhist community and thereby attain salvation? Second, I will describe forms of femininity that are prevalent in Buddhism and answer the question of whether it is possible to attain salvation as member of the female sex. As Diana Paul has pointed out, Buddhism, like Judaism and Christianity, is "an overwhelmingly male-created institution dominated by a patriarchal power structure. As a consequence of this male dominance, the feminine is frequently associated with the secular, powerless, profane and imperfect" (Paul 1985: xix-xx). Male Buddhists created certain images of femininity and, in accordance with these images, established normative rules of behavior for women within the Buddhist community.

Third, I will investigate the possibilities Buddhism offers for a more activist approach toward society and social ethics. Can one draw upon Buddhist teachings in order to overcome social injustices? Does Buddhism formulate certain rights that should be valid in secular society as well? Is reconciliation between existing injustices or discrimination and ideal teachings possible? Is any specifically feminist approach to a socially engaged Buddhism likely to succeed?

Buddhism and Social Problems

Buddhism was not intended to be a religion for the masses. The historical Buddha taught a path to salvation along which each individual could travel. The aim was to overcome suffering and escape rebirth through the practice of meditation and good behavior. But Buddhism was never meant to change society as a whole or to offer salvation by grace.[1] Buddhism teaches a radical responsibility for one's own acts and for the *karma* accumulated by them. By deciding to enter the Buddhist community one makes the first step toward the realization of this salvation. But was everyone allowed to enter the *sangha*? This was not primarily so. Men could enter, but even though women were regarded as capable of attaining salvation they were not allowed to enter the community until the Buddha's aunt and stepmother Mahaprajapati wanted to join. When the disciple Ananda requested this on her behalf, the Buddha reluctantly granted his (not her) request but placed the nuns' order under the control of the monks. The nuns had to obey the Eight Chief Rules (*garudhamma* (Pali)) that made them dependent upon the monks for the proper performance of most of their ceremonies and the authorization of them all. For example, the nuns had to pay reverence to the monks, but the monks were not obliged to acknowledge the nuns in return. Nuns had to spend the rainy season under observance of the monks and were not allowed to admonish the latter. After the institution of the *Vinaya*, the monastic rules, there were 311 rules for nuns whereas there were only 227 for monks.

In this early stage of Buddhism, it was difficult for women for practical reasons to enter the Buddhist order. Men and women had to undergo medical examinations so that no sick people would be admitted. In the case of women, however, their genitalia were to be examined as well (Pitzer-Reyl 1984: 5; Horner 1930: 167).[2] Few members of the community were from the lower social classes. High demands concerning intellectual ability partly restricted illiterate people and especially women from

---

[1] There are, of course, forms of Buddhism that teach 'the power of the other'. For example, Pure Land Buddhism in eastern Asia teaches the reliance of the believer on the grace of the Buddha Amitâbha.

[2] I was not able to find any explanation why such an examination was necessary.

becoming members. The *Therigata*, a collection of poems written by nuns, shows that a large number of the women who entered the *sangha* in the early period of Buddhism were well-educated women from the aristocracy.

This short description reveals that the ideal equality of all human beings was not put into practice on the level of Buddhist society. Women were the victims of discrimination not only in secular Brahman society but in the Buddhist *sangha* as well. Reasons for this can be found in the embedment of Buddhism in the Indian Brahman culture and the different forms of femininity described in the Theravada and Mahayana traditions of Buddhism.[3]

Buddhist Attitudes toward Women

There are basically three general attitudes toward women in Buddhism. The first teaches that female rebirth is a result of negative *karma* accumulated in a past life. This view was strongly influenced by the Brahman background and the general position of women in ancient society. A second view imagines a Buddha to be male and therefore makes male rebirth or a sexual transformation necessary for women. The third view is that gender is irrelevant for salvation in the sense that gender is one of the traits of the ego, which need to be transcended. All three views can be found in Buddhism.

Within the works of the oldest Buddhist literature, the Pali canon and other Hinayana literature that has been transmitted in Sanskrit and classical Chinese, the first view is the most prevalent. The scriptures often speak disparagingly about women. In the *Cullavagga* the Buddha is said to have stated that the Buddhist *dharma* will deteriorate all the more quickly because women joined the *sangha*. The *Anguttara-Nikaya* is very detailed regarding the negative characteristics women are supposed to have and in the *Theragata* women are described as great temptresses and the cause of all suffering. With the development of the *Jataka* literature the position of men and women became very much polarized: being born male was visible proof of one's moral and spiritual superiority. These images were frequently regarded as unalterable and permanent. It is not clear whether these passages are true accounts of the historical Buddha's opinion or whether monks added them later. It is reasonable to state that these descriptions say more about male anxiety and how they were influenced by the cultural standards of their environment—confusing, it seems, objects of perception with their own mental ideas about them—than they do about actual (mis)behavior on the part of women. In order to avoid these fantasies, monks were taught to meditate on women as female corpses, a practice that mirrors the difficulty men had in pursuing the strict guidelines.

---

[3] Please note that neither tradition exists as a homogenous whole but comprises various, sometimes even contradictory, philosophical developments. However, for the sake of convenience I will use these terms in order to refer to the earlier (i.e., Theravada) and the later (i.e., Mahayana) forms of Buddhism with their different goals of salvation.

The fact is that Indian Buddhists believed that women by nature were more deeply involved in worldly existence than men because of female fertility. Motherhood was generally considered a wise and compassionate form of femininity, but mothers with their unconditional love for their children, involving strong karmic bonds, were viewed as the least capable of attaining salvation. Sexuality was also closely associated with women. As the most dangerous samsaric force, strong bodily desire evoked greed for another becoming, for another unredeemed rebirth. The mysterious and destructive form of femininity had to be controlled by the male-dominated Buddhist institution and this is expressed in the Eight Chief Rules and the 311 monastic rules for nuns.

Despite all social and institutional restrictions, the goal for both men and women within this early form of Buddhism was to become an *arhat* (feminine: *arhati*), an enlightened human being who had already escaped the cycle of death and rebirth. Lists in the old Pali canon show that quite a number of nuns became *arhats* and the *Therigata* also speaks of women who became enlightened.

With the development of Mahayana Buddhism in the first centuries C.E. this situation changed. The aim was no longer to become an *arhat* but to become a Buddha, conceived as a male being, the above-mentioned second view. The thirty-two characteristics of a Buddha (*lakkhana* (Pali), *laksana* (Sanskrit)) include the concealed, male sexual organ. This shift made the situation worse, in fact, for women because a doctrinal foundation was laid for the necessity of changing sex before being able to become enlightened. Schuster Barnes suggests that imagining a Buddha as male was due to Hindu influences from the important literary works of the *Mahabharata* and the *Ramayana* that were written at the same time (Shuster Barnes 1987: 121). Within the Mahayana *Prajnaparamita* literature, in the "Perfection of Wisdom Sutras," a (minor) philosophical discussion was begun on whether or not sexual transformation was necessary for women in order to become a Buddha, i.e., to become enlightened. In this corpus it is asserted that all apparent characteristics of beings are illusionary, for everything is in and of itself empty of characteristics. It is only on the level of unenlightened beings that these distinctions exist. Thus, "... if all phenomena are impermanent and insubstantial, then there are no self-existent entities with inalienable and unchanging characteristics such as 'maleness' or 'femaleness'" (Paul 1985: 217). This represents the third attitude. But due to different concepts of femininity prevalent within Mahayana Buddhist literature we find examples of women who attain enlightenment with and without sexual transformation.

A well-known example of a female who changes into a male first and then into a *Bodhisattva*[4] is related in the legend of the daughter of the Dragon King in the twelfth chapter of the Lotus Sutra (*Saddharmapundarika-sutra* (Sanskrit)). This legend

---

[4] The term *Bodhisattva* refers to one who practices the teaching of Buddhism in both otherworldly and secular ways. Instead of becoming a Buddha immediately, this person vows to save all beings and works with compassion for those beings who suffer.

illustrates dramatically that changing from a female into a male—a preconception resulting from the view that women cannot attain enlightenment in their female bodies—is in itself illusionary (Paul 1985: 185ff.) The legend in the Lotus Sutra relates that the *Bodhisattva* Manjushri, known for his great wisdom, praises the spiritual achievements of the eight-year old daughter of the Dragon King. When she appears in front of the Buddha Shakyamuni to profess her faith, the haughty Shariputra reminds her that women cannot realize Buddhahood because they cannot become *Bodhisattvas*. Through her great mental abilities she then transforms herself into a male, immediately becoming a *Bodhisattva*. Since all phenomena, including bodily appearance, are void of innate characteristics, transformation is possible and supports the doctrine of Emptiness (*shunyata* (Sanskrit)).

An example of a female becoming a *Bodhisattva* without sexual transformation is found in the *Vimalakirti-nirdesha-sutra*, admired by the Chinese since the fifth century C.E. and in Japan since the sixth. The basic teaching expounded in the text is the doctrine of Emptiness, stressing that all phenomena are neither coming into nor passing out of existence and are without distinct and innate characteristics, inconceivable, equal and nondual (Paul 1985: 222). Vimalakirti, the main character of the *sutra*, is a man who reaches Buddhahood even earlier than most of the monks in the text. A goddess resides in his house and engages in discussions with the eminent monk Shariputra about the Buddha Dharma. She argues that it is absurd to hold the position of innate distinctions among phenomena. She is finally able to prove that sexual transformation, as a form of discrimination, is counterproductive to understanding the nature of Emptiness.

Both Mahayana stories of a *Bodhisattva* with or without sexual transformation stress the fact that enlightenment is not attained on the basis of gender. Although these stories show that the difference between male and female was still maintained, they stress the fact that the outward appearance, i.e., gender, is not a factor in the attainment of enlightenment and supreme Buddhahood. From the very moment of attainment one can no longer speak of a being with a certain gender but of a *Bodhisattva* who has transcended the worldly, including the aspect of gender. Strictly speaking, a *Bodhisattva* could, philosophically, be considered genderless. However, other adherents of Buddhism obviously did not share this view and the conflict has never been resolved.[5]

Later developments of Mahayana Buddhism, such as Ch'an or Zen Buddhism in China and Japan emphasize that gender is irrelevant to enlightenment. The difference between enlightenment and illusion is one single instance of impeccable thought—and since enlightenment has no visible characteristics, the sex of one who realizes enlightenment is of no importance. In Zen Buddhist literature one often finds

---

[5] Because of an ongoing discussion on the position or 'function' of women within Vajrayana Buddhism, I will not go further into this matter. For a general but recently criticized description of women in Tantric Buddhism, see Shaw 1994.

stories concerning fully enlightened nuns who make fun of monks who cling to sexual distinctions by pointing them to the concept of Emptiness and thereby indirectly making them aware of their discriminatory attitude toward women.[6] In other Zen anecdotes lay women and ordained nuns alike help men to realize enlightenment by using, as Socrates did in Greek philosophy, a maieutic method.[7] In other cases *Bodhisattvas* on the verge of enlightenment are compared to mothers about to give birth—an interesting comparison considering the Theravada view that mothers are the least capable of reaching salvation (Macy 1977: 319-20).

In thirteenth century Japan Dogen Zenji (1200-1253), the founder of the Soto Zen sect of Japanese Buddhism, explains in the chapter entitled "Raihai tokuzui," ('Prostration to Attain the Marrow') of his major work *Shôbôgenzô* ('Storage of the Eye of the Right Dharma')[8] that on the level of enlightenment men and women are completely equal. He writes that one should not discuss man or woman when dealing with a person who has attained *dharma*. Men who do not want to recognize the female capacity for attaining supreme Buddhahood are "stupid people who insult the Dharma" (Dogen 1994: 77). He even admits that all prejudices concerning the inferiority of women are the results of the false association of women with sexual greed:

> Furthermore, nowadays extremely stupid people look at women without having corrected the prejudice that women are objects of sexual greed. Disciples of the Buddha must not be like this. If whatever may become the object of sexual greed is to be hated, do not all men deserve to be hated too?... [I]f we hate whatever might become the object of sexual greed, all men and women will hate each other, and we will never have any chance to attain salvation. (Dogen 1994: 78)

This seems to be the most 'modern' and liberal view on the relation between the sexes that I found in Buddhist texts. By acknowledging hatred, as the result of fear or greed, as the main reason for discrimination against women a first step was made toward the elimination of that mental act. Only respect for life and compassion for all

---

[6] See, for example, the story of the nun Myoshin, Chief of the Business Office, who was not taken seriously by seventeen visiting monks. After having heard their discussion of the parable of the flag moving in the wind, she explains to them the deeper meaning of the flag, the wind and the mind in terms of the concept of Emptiness. See Dogen 1994: vol. 1, 73-74.

[7] See the examples of the Mo-shan Liao-ran and her disciple Zhi-xian or the old woman selling rice cakes and Tokuzan, Master of the Diamond Sutra.

[8] This chapter was probably written around the year 1240. However, Dogen seems to have changed his attitude later when he states that a nun who has served the *sangha* all her life has to bow before a newly ordained monk. This represents the Theravada view. It is not clear whether Dogen actually changed his mind or whether these later texts are apocryphal writings, added during the establishment of a male-dominated Zen Buddhist institution. On the authenticity of Dogen's writing see Heine 1997. For the chapter "Raihai tokuzui," see Dogen 1994: 39-85.

living beings that suffer can remove hatred. Dogen's statement can also be applied to life in secular society, if lay adherents hold to this respect for and compassionate help to others as the basis for a good life. This leads to the third question about the possible relevance of ideal or idealized Buddhist teachings in society.

The Social Relevance of Buddhist Teachings

It is commonly known that philosophical definitions of a certain religion are not always identical with its actual societal manifestation. Since no religion exists without being influenced by the secular world, Buddhism too took forms that did not and still do not necessarily follow from its basic teachings. Historical Buddhist institutions have failed to put certain basic Buddhist teachings into practice. Moreover, in most Asian Buddhist countries the merging of Buddhism with indigenous ideas or the dominant patriarchal structure of society and religious institutions lead to unfavorable situations for women. For example, the theory of *karma* was used in Japan even by Buddhist institutions to maintain the social status quo of the oppressed outcasts (*burakumin*). Under the influence of patriarchal Confucianism in east Asia women who left their home and entered the *sangha* were regarded as failing in their duty towards the family and to bear children. In Thai society women acquire maturity through marriage and childbirth, whereas men do so through renouncing the world and becoming novice monks for a certain period of time.

With the transmission of the Buddha Dharma to the West (late nineteenth century) a new period of Buddhist culture was begun. The striving for so-called 'political correctness', for a non-discriminatory society, for the equality of all human beings and for the implementation of human rights gave rise to a new assessment of Buddhist doctrines. This modern form of Buddhism, commonly called 'Engaged Buddhism', tries to reconcile religious conceptions with social ethics and human rights. Buddhist communities in the West try to adapt traditional Buddhism to modern Western societies.[9] In Asia reform movements were the result of colonialism, Westernization, poverty, foreign invasion, etc.[10] Engaged Buddhism is, in a certain sense, the result of the great tension modern Buddhists felt between theoretical and ideal concepts and the way these concepts have been implemented.

---

[9] Since the 1980s one can observe several reform movements from within the Zen Buddhist sects in Japan as well, led especially by the Buddhologists Hakamaya Noriaki and Matsumoto Shiro, who call themselves "Critical Buddhists." However, no 'activist' approach has yet been formulated by them. I consider the engaged movement of the Vietnamese Zen monk Thich Nhat Hanh as a Western Movement also because he teaches and operates primarily in France.

[10] For example, liberation movements in Asia are TBMSG (Trailokya Bauddha Mahasangha Sahayaka Gana), initiated in the early 1980s by disciples of Sangharashita who worked among B.R. Ambedkar's followers in India, and the Sarvodaya Shramanera Movement led by A.T. Ariyaratne in Sri Lanka. See Queen and King 1996.

As I stated above, I am not seeking solutions for existing, concrete problems of discrimination, but on a theoretical level the following structure can be proposed. First, Mahayana Buddhist sources show that sexual difference is of importance only on a secular level. Philosophically speaking, it is irrelevant because everything is in and of itself empty of characteristics. There is nothing that can be called a distinct self. Yet this doctrine of no-self (*anatman*), together with the doctrine of dependent co-origination does not provide any foundation for notions of autonomous, individual human personalities as a basis for modern human rights and justice.[11] This is one of the reasons for the frequently criticized weakness of Buddhism in terms of ethical concerns.[12] Still, the fact that Buddhism denies the existence of an autonomous, individual self does not necessarily mean that the human person is not important. *Anatman* means that a self is constructed of non-self parts, built by past dispositions and memories, together with present social and other conditions. Similarly, society itself is empty:

> In Mahâyâna thought it is clear that society is empty of selfhood and is constructed of non-society parts, i.e., human persons. Thus society and person are interactive; they are mutually constructive. From a Buddhist perspective, since society and the human person are interactive, it is fundamentally wrong to conceive them as adversial ... the value of the one cannot be finally separated from the value of the other.... Thus, in the end, in Buddhism neither the human person nor society may rightfully dominate, or negate in its behavior, the other. Consequently, it is best to see final importance resting on the values that Buddhism embraces: an end to suffering and the nurturing of awakening in all. Both society and the individual are equally answerable to, should serve and contribute to, these values. (King 2000: 297-98)

Second, cessation of the suffering of all living beings is the foremost aim, as formulated in the *Bodhisattva* vow not to enter nirvana until all living beings are released from pain and evil. Suffering is regarded as an absolute evil. There are two conceptions of the good within Buddhism: first, the elimination of all suffering (as formulated in the Four Noble Truths) and, second, the realization of enlightenment. All forms of Buddhism consider human birth as rare and precious because of the inherent possibility human birth provides for reaching Buddhahood. Mahayana Buddhism asserts that all beings (not necessarily human) carry within them the seed of

---

[11] *Pratiya-samutpada* (Sanskrit); (inter)dependent co-origination implies coming into existence through conditional causation. Since all phenomena come into existence through causation, they lack an essential self (*atman*) and are thus impermanent and void.

[12] Ichikawa Hakugen (1902-1986), for example, states that the ethical pitfall latent in the Zen approach to society derives directly from misinterpretations and false applications of key Buddhist ideas. Cf. Ichikawa 1970 and 1967.

Buddhahood, i.e., 'Buddha-nature'.[13] Therefore no distinction can be made concerning the bearer of this seed, be it male or female.

Third, one can draw several imperatives for social behavior from these basic statements: first, to respect human life as the only possibility for attaining enlightenment and overcoming suffering; second, not to harm others and not to make them suffer even more through inappropriate, disrespectful or discriminatory behavior; third, to help other people, in accordance with the *Bodhisattva* vow, in a compassionate way by all means possible. Traditionally, a sort of social ethics comparable to the biblical Ten Commandments is articulated in the five precepts for lay followers of Buddhism. They are: 1. to abstain from killing; 2. to refrain from taking that which is not given; 3. to abstain from misconduct in sexual acts; 4. to refrain from engaging in false speech; 5. to refrain from using intoxicating drugs. Regarding the above-described mutual constructiveness of society and the individual, these rules again, are not only good for the individual but for society as well. All these rules support the striving of the individual for the perfection of his or her Buddhahood within and help to overcome social injustices.

> All Buddhist social activism is an expression of the compassion for suffering beings that develops more and more as one engages in the process of making real one's embryonic Buddhahood. Suffering beings are suffering beings; Buddhism makes no distinction in that regard between human beings, animals and, for many modern Buddhists, the planet. (King 2000: 307)

With an explicitly feminist Buddhist approach toward enlightenment, sexual difference is categorically emphasized. But this, we have learned from the scriptures, frustrates and is counterproductive to true religious insight and would therefore be a regression. Thus, a reconsideration of the Buddhist doctrine that we all are human beings with the innate possibility of attaining enlightenment is of utmost importance. In this sense it would probably be better to speak of a doctrine of 'equivalence' of the sexes "because equality implies a sense of sameness, whereas equivalence allows for physiological and psychological differences without implying any hierarchy of difference" (Sponberg 1992: 12).[14] The foremost aim of Engaged Buddhism is to put this equivalence into practice. Reforms are likely to succeed in this sense as long as they come from within the tradition, aiming at the realization of particular Buddhist ideas not only on the level of the individual believer but on the institutional level as well. From this latter level the next step toward reforming secular society can and will be made.

---

[13] For a detailed discussion of the concept of Buddha-nature see King 1991.

[14] In this outstanding article Sponberg refers to Børreson 1981. Sponberg prefers to distinguish further between equivalence and inclusiveness, because the latter asserts neither sameness nor a lack of hierarchical differentiation.

Bibliography

Børreson, Kari Elisabeth. (1981). *Subordination and Equivalence: The Nature and Role of Women in Augustine and Thomas Aquinas.* Washington: University Press of America.
Das, R.M. (1962). *Women in Manu and his Seven Commentators.* Varanasi: Kanchana.
Dogen Zenji (1994). *Master Dôgen's Shôbôgenzô.* Transl. by Gudo Nishijima Gudo and and Chodo Cross. Vol. 1-4. Woking: Windbell Publications Ltd.
Heine, Steven. (1997). "The Dôgen Canon: Dôgens's Pre-Shôbôgenzô Writings and the Question of Change in His Later Works." *Japanese Journal of Religious Studies* 24: 24: 39-86.
Horner, I.B. (1930). *Women under Primitive Buddhism: Laywomen and Almswomen.* London: Routledge.
Ichikawa, Hakugen. (1967). *Zen to gendai shisô.* Tokyo: Tokuma Shoten.
———. (1970). *Bukkyôsha no sensô sekinin.* Tokyo: Shunjusha.
King, Sallie B. (1991). *Buddha Nature.* Albany: State University of New York Press.
———. (2000). "Human Rights in Contemporary Engaged Buddhism." In: Roger Jackson, and John Makransky (ed.). *Buddhist Theology: Critical Reflections by Contemporary Buddhist Scholars.* Richmond: Curzon Press. Pp.292-311.
Macy, J.R. (1977). "Beyond Wisdom: Mother of all Buddhas." In: Rita Gross (ed.). *Beyond Androcentrism.* Missoula: Scholars Press.
Paul, Diana Y. (1985). *Women in Buddhism: Images of the Feminine in the Mahâyâna Tradition.* Berkeley/Los Angeles/London: University of California Press.
Pitzer-Reyl, Renate. (1984). *Die Frau im frühen Buddhismus.* Marburger Studien zur Afrika- und Asienkunde. Vol. 7. Berlin: Verlag Dietrich Reimer.
Queen, Christopher S. and Sally B. King (ed.). (1996). *Engaged Buddhism: Buddhist Liberation Movements in Asia,* Albany: State University of New York Press.
Rau, Wilhelm. (1957). *Staat und Gesellschaft im Alten Indien nach den Brâhmana-Texten dargestellt.* Wiesbaden: Harrassowitz.
Schuster Barnes, Nancy. (1987). "Buddhism." In: Arvind Sharma (ed.). *Women in World Religions.* Albany: State University of New York Press.
Shaw, Miranda. (1994). *Passionate Enlightenment: Women in Tantric Buddhism.* Princeton: Princeton University Press.
The Threefold Lotus-Sutra: Innumerable Meaning, The Lotus Flower of the Wonderful Law and Meditation on the Bodhisattva Universal Virtue. (1975). Transl. by Bunnô Katô *et al.* Tokyo: Kôsei Publishing 1975 [14th edition: 1995(14)].
Sponberg, Alan. (1992). "Attitudes toward Women and the Feminine in Early Buddhism." In: José Ignacio Cabezon (ed.). *Buddhism, Sexuality and Gender.* Albany: State University of New York Press.

Islam, Gender and Reconciliation

Making Room for New Gender Perspectives

Tirza Visser

Introduction

A great many conflicts in the world are in one way or another connected with religion. Whether or not religion and differences in faith and truth claims are involved, religion is very often the denominator that justifies all kinds of conflicts. But what about conflicts within one religion or culture, such as the conflict between the sexes? The media in the West depicts the Islamic woman as oppressed and trapped in a particular role in society, leading to the backward position of women in Islam. Although this is not a very accurate description, I agree that in many cases women do not have the same rights and possibilities as men within Islam. Both critics in the West and Islamic fundamentalists refer easily to the Qur'anic texts in order to justify their opinions. The latter group appeal to the notion of the closed gate of *ijtihad* (interpretation), meaning that a renewed interpretation of statements and fragments from these texts is out of the question. Fortunately, other voices have recently been heard who believe otherwise, creating room for a more positive explanation of certain restrictive passages.

It is only recently that the position of women in the Middle East has aroused much interest. Because of that late interest, material on gender studies concerning women in Islam is still limited and I am not in the position to change this in any way. My objective in this paper is to give some brief insight into possible solutions for dealing with the backward position of women in Islam. First, I will give a short historical summary of how women were viewed in the different periods of Islamic history in order to outline the historical development of the gender perspective into what it is today.

Second, I will discuss two possible solutions to the problem. My research showed that a major problem in this area was the androcentric approach. Women are made into objects because they are studied in a male context. I would like to offer a solution using Rita Gross' androgynous model of humanity as contained in her book on feminism and religion (1996). However, Gross' theory is not was not intended for an Islamic context. A second model I will discuss briefly to supplement this is 'Rushdian dialogue'(after the medieval Islamic philosopher Ibn Rushd (Averroes) as presented by the Moroccan philosopher Muhammad Abed al-Jabri (or al-Jabiri, as it is sometimes transcribed). Unlike Gross, al-Jabri did write specifically for an Arabic (and mainly Islamic) context. Although his Rushdian model was not designed specifically for gender issues, I believe it to be of use in this field as well, since he created it as a way of dealing with the problems of modernity.

The History of Gender Perspectives in Islam

Pre-Islamic Arabia

To acquire a complete picture of the development of role models and gender perspectives in Islam it is necessary to look at the pre-Islamic situation. If we go back as far as 6000 B.C.E., agricultural life on the Arabic peninsula had become settled. In the millennia that followed, urban life developed and writing came into use. Information about the role women played in these times can be found not only in archaeological evidence but also in legends and myths. For several periods we also have recourse to legal and religious materials (Nashat and Tucker 1998: 6-7). In the so-called preliterate society, women gained a great deal of prestige because of their important contribution to agriculture. This prestige is underlined by the discoveries of burial places exclusively for women. In Mesopotamia divine powers concerning agriculture were female and in legends from this region women were given important tasks and duties such as the care for a particular product or resource like water. The importance of women is reflected in religious literature, where the role of the different female deities was analogous to the role women played on earth (Nashat and Tucker 1998: 13-18).

With the establishment of the first urban centers in Mesopotamia (c. 3500 B.C.E.), the military sector of society became more important. As a consequence, male power and dominance increased. Husbands and fathers were given full authority over their wives and children, which can be seen in the different laws that were enacted in this period. Women were divided into 'respectable' and 'disreputable' categories, which defined their place in the social hierarchy. Women of the upper class did have the opportunity to participate in the economics and religion of society (Ahmed 1998: 12-16). Dynasties and states followed one another rapidly and the exchange of mores that went with changes in power seems to have led to a decline in the status of women. Women were reduced to pure biological beings, existing only for sexual pleasure and reproduction (Ahmed 1998: 17-18). In the upper classes the veil was introduced, apparently to distinguish decent women from prostitutes. The same was the case with seclusion, which eventually led to the opinion that a woman's place was in the home (Nashat and Tucker 1998: 32-34).

The First Centuries of Islam

In the earliest stages period of Islam two women played an important role. The first, Khadija, was Muhammad's first wife and the one who helped him to believe in the message he received. Khadija was a wealthy widow from Mecca who first hired Muhammad to look after her business and later proposed to him, after which they were married. The second woman is Aisha, Muhammad's most beloved wife and the first among the Muslim women to observe the customs of veiling and seclusion. Aisha became an important source of information about the early Muslim community, since many of the *hadith* about Muhammad's attitude towards his wives and the women of the Muslim community are from her hand. After Muhammad died, Aisha became actively involved in politics, especially concerning the dispute of succession after the third caliph died. The stories of both women show that being good Muslims did not prevent them from playing a role in public life.

The Qur'an makes clear that although men have a higher position than women (2:228), as providers and the ones responsible for financial support, women and men are equal with regard to religious duties, rewards and souls. It is believed that the practices of the society of Muhammad relate only to that particular society at that moment in history. At this point it is interesting to see how different the attitudes towards women could be if one looks at the position of groups such as the Sufis, the Kharijis and the Qarmatians. They all believed that the laws made in the first Muslim society and suitable for that period were not necessarily so for following periods. By allowing women to give spirituality a central place in their lives, the Sufis even challenged the gender perspective of established Islam. Islam does contain an ethical egalitarianism: a different interpretation of the sacred texts of Islam than that proclaimed by the advocates of androcentric Islam. The Qur'anic information, together with the *hadith*, formed the basis of the *sharia*. In the *sharia*, regulations concerning gender were set down in a number of ways. The main characteristic of these regulations is male dominance over the women.

There are three different views regarding gender and the rise of Islam. The first sees the rise of Islam as a very positive thing for women, over against the *djahiliyya* period which is seen as having been very restrictive for women. They were subject to either the tribe or their husband and lacked all basic human rights. The practice of female infanticide strengthens the view of the *djahiliyya* period as a time in which women had no rights at all. Islam is thus seen as a very positive development, introducing marriage, in which the husbands are forced to take some responsibility, and forbidding the practice of infanticide (Tucker 1993: 6-7).

The second view is opposed to the previous one. The rights women had in the *djahiliyya* period were restricted by Islam. In the *djahiliyya* period women could take the initiative in marriage and they could have several husbands. The woman was allowed to retain membership in her own clan after marriage and keep her children with her. She could also divorce her husband. All this changed with the rise of Islam when patrilineal marriage became the only acceptable form of marriage (Tucker 1993: 7-8).

The third view lies between the two extremes of the previous views and minimizes the impact of Islam. Islam took over a great part of the cultural tradition that was practised in that region, especially in Mesopotamia. Under Byzantine and Sasanian rule women did not have many rights in marriage and were required to wear a veil. This was different in pre-Islamic Arabia, in which the tribal structure granted women a relatively large amount of power. They were involved in tribal politics and had their own say in marriage. Women were also recognized as important contributors to the tribes' tradition of oral poetry. The Qur'an text which speaks of spiritual equality between men and women might well be based on this tribal gender perspective. However, by the time of the rise of Islam, the Arab peninsula was changing and tribal values were weakening. Islam expanded with great speed across the borders of Arabia into Mesopotamia, taking over a large part of the Mesopotamian gender perspectives. In the pre-Islamic society of the Middle East, women were considered to be valuable persons within the community. However, with the development of urban societies male dominance became characteristic. When Islam conquered the area, the Muslims took over this attitude towards women and the image of the woman whose humanity was limited to her biological function of reproduction arose (Tucker 1993: 8).

An important period in Islamic history with regard to the establishment of gender perspectives is the Abbasid caliphate (750-1258 C.E.). In this period of 500 years a distinct Islamic culture was developed. Court patronage and the emergence of a group of *ulama* contributed to the shaping of a distinct body of Islamic learning. Veiling and seclusion became standard in this period. Women were no longer allowed to play a part in warfare, as was the case in the age of the Prophet. Nor were they allowed to speak on political issues. At this time, for women of the upper class, the *harim* was instituted, from which women ventured only if they were completely veiled. Although the practice of seclusion and veiling probably dated from Sasanian times, it was during the reign of the Abbasids that Islam itself sought to justify it. Islamic thinkers such as al-Ghazali and Nasir ad-din Tusi wrote in favor of seclusion and veiling. In the historical works dating from this period, women are hardly ever mentioned at all, although it is known that there were women in the *harim* who succeeded in gaining political power. There is not much information on women from the lower classes (Tucker 1993: 9-11; Ahmed 1998: 79-87).

In the twelfth and thirteenth centuries Turkish tribal groups moved into Abbasid territory and took control. One of these groups, the Seldjuks, took over Baghdad in 1055. Already in 1258 they were defeated by the Mongols, who were replaced by the Ottoman Turks during a period when they became weak. The old Islamic empire was reunited under their control. With Turkish rule, the position of women seemed to have changed initially. There are accounts of women participating in tribal councils and even in warfare, albeit occasionally. The role of women in daily life resembled the way women in pre-Islamic Arabia lived, i.e., they had to take care of the animals and the production of the most essential goods. However, once the new rulers were settled they adapted the Islamic way of life, including the old gender perspectives. In the *harim* of the sixteenth and early seventeenth centuries, women did gain more power. This period was called the sultanate of women because of the very obvious and persistent exercise of power by certain women of the palace *harim*. Women in the *harim* were able to acquire wealth and Islamic law made it possible for them to invest this wealth, mostly in *waqf* organizations. In many urban areas over one-third of the *waqfs* were founded by women. This practice was restricted to women of the upper class. Women of the lower classes worked in the margins of many craft industries. Sexual segregation was not absent from the lower class milieu since women and men worked in separate trades. They did, however, meet in the quarters and markets of Ottoman cities, in shared public spaces. In rural areas women and men worked together more regularly, as they were often farmers in a cooperative family unit. These realities were seen and recognized by the ruling *ulama* of Ottoman society and they were apparently willing to adjust the law to social needs, although one would expect them to serve as upholders of an Islamic gender regime.

Modern Views
In the early nineteenth century the societies of the Middle East began to undergo a fundamental social transformation due to Western imperialism. Women from the rural areas and lower-class women suffered from these shifting political and economic patterns. However, one aspect became very important: the emergence of women themselves as a central subject for national debate. The first to treat the subject were male writers mainly from Egypt and Turkey. Issues concerning women were linked with issues concerning national development, nationalism and cultural change. From the West voices were raised to liberate Islamic women, in line with the Western model. Education became important, and accessible to a small number of women. However, the education that was set up for women was aimed mainly at making the women good housewives and mothers, thus following European gender roles. Reformers such as Muhammed Abduh strived for women's liberation as a precondition for the establishment of a modern society, a society in which the European model played a definite role.

The conservative voice of Islam opposed this modernization of women, seeing it as a plot of the West to undermine authentic Islamic culture. It must be said that the Western European attempts to liberate Islamic women were not always welcomed by the female population of Egypt, leading in some cases to a return to veils and non-Western clothing. This can also be seen in Algeria where the response to the French denigration of the indigenous gender system was to promote the veil. The industrialization that was brought to the Islamic world led to difficult circumstances for the women. Their jobs were taken over by machinery and they also lost their traditional jobs of looking after the cattle. This made them fully dependent on the income of the male, since they did not gain access to other kinds of work. Only in the late twentieth century was a feminization of professions visible. For the lower-class women, who were without any education, the possibilities narrowed. Women started to participate in politics as well, fighting for liberation from the colonial powers and participating in nationalist movements. This raises the question as to why, when women's participation was visible and active, so little has changed regarding gender perspectives. The answer might be that changes in the gender system were assumed to follow political changes in a natural way.

Two Different Solutions

A Feminist Approach
This historical overview of the gender perspective in Islam points out that the major characteristic of this perspective is the androcentric approach. According to Gross,

this model has three specific characteristics, the first of which is the amalgamation of the male norm with the human norm. The fact that humanity consists of both women and men, each with their own experiences, seems hardly noted. The danger of fusing maleness with the human norm is that the feminine norm is seen as an exception (Gross 1996: 18-19). The second characteristic is a result of the first one. Because a male point of view is used as the norm of humanity, feminine aspects of religion are ignored.[1] The last characteristic that Gross mentions is closely connected to the previous two. If one accepts the differences between men and women and their experiences, studying religion from a male perspective leaves out a great deal. Women are made objects for men and are only studied in relation to those men and to the degree they are connected to them (Gross 1996: 19-20).

I would like to introduce here Rita Gross' solution of the androgynous, two-sexed model of humanity. This model implies the recognition that humans come in two sexes, both equally human. Besides this, it also recognizes that the biological differences that exist between man and woman are intensified by gender roles and stereotypes. An androgynous model of humanity holds to the conviction that, although there are biological sexual differences, men and women are equally human. An androgynous model will prevent one sex from being preferred above the other or placed at the center of humanity, pushing the other to the margin. This model is opposite to the androcentric one which objectifies women and to the sex-neutral model of humanity in which the existence of cultural-based gender roles is ignored. What is needed is a paradigm shift in the current model of humanity. By introducing the two-sexed model of humanity, Gross believes that not only will scholarship be positively influenced and changed but the model will also leave its mark on the consciousness of people, which will be noticeable in their perception and everyday language (Gross 1996:20-21).

What does this mean for the gender perspective in Islam? The androcentric interpretation of Islamic texts should be replaced by an androgynous reading in order to do justice to women. The differences that can be found in the four Islamic schools of law regarding the rights of women in issues of marriage and divorce and the possession of property suggest that if the Qur'an would have been read by a less androcentric society and, if greater emphasis had been placed on the ethical elements of Islam, laws and regulation regarding women might have been more positive. This was already shown in early history by the Sufis, for example. Unfortunately, mainstream Islam did not follow a reading of the texts that was more positive towards women. A radical rewriting of history from the two-sexed model will probably give a very different overview. Approaching Islamic society from the perspective of the androgyn-

---

[1] Gross is specifically referring to religion, since this is the subject of her book. However, it is my personal opinion that these characteristics are valid for other areas of life as well.

ous model will do more justice to women and make their contribution to this society more visible.

A Philosophical Method: Rushdian Dialogue
In his 1999 article on the clash of civilizations Mohammed al-Jabri provides a solution for dealing with the problems that are caused by the cultural differences between the Western countries and the Arab world. He calls it 'Rushdian dialogue'. It began as an initiative of the governments of Morocco and Spain to improve communication between both nations. Averroes (Ibn Rushd) lived in a comparable situation, in which there were difficult relations between the Arabs, called "I" by Averroes and "other people." Al-Ghazali had begun to propagate against Islamic philosophy, considering it as dangerous and innovative. Averroes reacted by explaining the relation between philosophy and religion. His first move was to make clear the relation between Islamic law and Greek science. After he had done so, he worked on the clarification of the obscurities surrounding the translations of Aristotle. In doing so, he attempted to straighten out the relation between the Islamic "I" and the philosophical "other" (al-Jabri 1999: 75-77). Averroes was also opposed to the practitioners of Law who followed the doctrine of the *batin*, an esoteric movement[2]. In the time of al-Ghazali this doctrine was the ideology of the Fatimids in Egypt, who were the opponents of the Abbasid caliphate (al-Jabri 1994: 36).

Al-Jabri wants to stress the importance of the work of Averroes for modern times by looking at the epistemological principles underlying Averroes' work. The first principle would be "the need to understand the other in his own system of reference" (al-Jabri 1999: 77). Averroes used an axiomatic method for this: dealing with philosophical issues in a philosophical context and religious issues in a religious context. If we look at the situation in the contemporary world, it is clear that the West has difficulties seeing the Arab/Islamic world in its particular system of reference. The method of Averroes would be an excellent way of gaining mutual understanding. In order to create a dialogue, each participating group has to understand and respect the other.[3]

The second principle al-Jabri mentions is the recognition of one's right to be different (1999: 78) and the right to have a different opinion. Averroes used this principle in his discussion on the relationship between religion and philosophy and to clarify how religion and philosophy could coexist. Both are autonomous constructions with their own origins and branches (al-Jabiri 1995: 44). Al-Jabri reacts strongly to Avicenna's syncretism, because this would do injustice to the characteristic features of both disciplines.

---

[2] Al-Jabri (: 36) describes the *batin* as follows: " ... les penseurs ésotéristes qui ont théorisé les doctrines du chiisme ismaélien."

[3] Report of a lecture given by al-Jabri at the conference on "La société civile et le dialogue Euro-Arabe," (December 14-16, 1995), 98.

The final principle which al-Jabri deduces from Averroes has to do with understanding in a tolerant and indulgent way (1999: 78). Here al-Jabri quotes the words of Averroes: "doing justice consists of seeking arguments in favor of one's adversary just as one does for oneself" (1999: 79). Islam is a religion of tolerance and indulgence, as can be found in the Qur'an (al-Jabri 1994: 30).

The main point of the Rushdian method, according to al-Jabri, is that it provides a way of dealing with differences between the West and the Arab/Islamic world, as Islam is the most likely candidate for the role of the 'other' in the post-Cold War era. Al-Jabri feels very strongly about these foundations for a dialogue, since they open the way for human development in modern times (al-Jabiri 1995: 44). Besides the above-mentioned principles, connected with the axiomatic method, al-Jabri refers to other aspects that make the Averroistic spirit adaptable to modern times because of their correspondence with the present: rationalism, realism, and the critical approach. Once again, he stresses that adapting Averroism will mean a rupture with the gnosticism of Avicenna.

What does this mean for gender problematics? What happens if we substitute 'women' for the 'other'? Do the rules of the Rushdian dialogue still prove to be valuable? I believe they do. Beginning with the first principle, the necessity of understanding the other from his—in this case her—perspective will improve knowledge and understanding about the way women live and hopefully create mutual understanding and an opening for fruitful dialogue. As for the second, accepting the fact that women are different and think about things in their own, unique way can only prove to be positive in the relation between men and women. The same is true for the third principle: mutual understanding and toleration. Both aspects will improve women's position in society and perhaps change the prejudiced images of women that exist. Instead of using this model to overcome differences between the West and the Arabic/Islamic world, the Rushdian dialogue could with respect to creating new gender perspectives be used to give the discussion a first impulse.

Conclusion

It is clear that, although Islam contains a hierarchical structure as the basis of relationships between men and women, it also proclaimed in its ethics the moral and spiritual equality of all human beings. In Abbasid times however, sexual hierarchy gained priority over the ethical voice of Islam. This development had a negative effect on the system of law that was created in this period. Despite the different opinions of some marginal groups, the points of view of dominant Islam survived as the sole legitimate interpretation—not because it was the only possible interpretation but because this was the opinion of the dominant political powers of that society. Until the beginning of the nineteenth century, the meaning of gender as laid down by established Islam remained the controlling discourse. With the arrival of Western powers the situation began to change. European rulers used the language of feminism —which they often despised in their own countries—and used the position of women in Islamic society to attack that society. In this way they legitimized Western domination and justified colonial policies. They claimed that veiling stood in the way of progress and civilization and that it was necessary to bring Western values to these undeveloped countries.

However, there is no validity to the notion that progress for women can be achieved only by abandoning the ways of a native androcentric culture in favor of those of another culture. This was not the case with Western liberation of women, but, strangely enough, this is routinely how the matter of improving the status of women is posed with respect to women in Arab society. Change in the gender perspective should happen from within the Islamic society. A rethinking of the Islamic tradition from the perspective of the androgynous model of humanity as described by Gross is perhaps a way of achieving this change in gender perspective. The main point to make about Islam is that, although men and women are not equal, they are certainly both equally human.

Al-Jabri writes of a renewal of Arabic thought. He proposes a rethinking of the Islamic tradition in order to deal with the defects of modernity. He specifically rejects both the interpretation of the Islamic fundamentalists who wish to go back to the old interpretation of Islam—the androcentric interpretation—as well as the modernists who are striving to adopt Western principles of modernization in order to build a modern Islamic society. He refuses the latter view because he believes that Western modernism is built on and out of historical circumstances that are typical for the West and which are not present in the Islamic Middle East. He believes it is wrong to place Western concepts in a non-Western society, even more because he believes that ways toward modernization can be found within Islamic society. Although al-Jabri's main concern is with the problems of modernity in general, I do believe that his approach is valuable for dealing with the problems of the androcentric gender approach. If one can combine his theory of rethinking Islamic tradition with an androgynous model of humanity, society would prove itself to be more positive towards women.

Bibliography

Ahmed, L. (1998). *Women and Gender in Islam: Historical Roots of a Modern Debate*. Cairo: American University in Cairo Press.

Al-Jabri/al-Jabiri, Mohammed Abed. (1994) "Extrémisme et la attitude rationaliste dans la pensée arabo-islamique." In: *L'islamisme: Les dossiers de l'etat du monde*. Paris: 29-36.

———. (1995). *Human Development in the Arab World: The Cultural and Societal Dimension*. Part I. Human Development Studies Series 2. New York: United Nations.

———. (1999). "Clash of Civilisations: The Relations of the Future?" In: G.M. Munoz (ed.). *Islam, Modernism and the West: Cultural and Political Relations at the End of the Millennium*. London/New York: Tauris. Pp. 65-80.

Gross, R.M. (1996). *Feminism and Religion: An Introduction*. Boston: Beacon University Press.

Nashat G. and J.E. Tucker (eds.). (1998). *Women in the Middle East and North Africa*. Bloomington: Indiana University Press.

Tucker, J. (1993). *Gender and Islamic History*. Washington: American Historical Society.

Part III

Case Studies of Conflict and Reconciliation

Interreligious Conflict and Reconciliation in Indonesia

Agus Rachmat Widyanto

Introduction

At present there is a political joke circulating in Indonesia, a cynical joke expressing a sense of bitterness increasingly shared by more and more people. It goes something like this: Sukarno, the first Indonesian president, was commonly regarded as representing the Old Order. His successor, Suharto, assumed a self-congratulatory tone and called his interminable totalitarian regime the New Order. The brief and weak transitory government of President Habibie had neither power nor legitimacy: it was the time of No Order. And finally, as the situation seems to be getting simply more and more chaotic, the current government of President Wahid is rapidly losing all sense of order. His rule is consequently called the era of Disorder.

Unlike its neighboring countries, such as South Korea and Malaysia, which have almost recovered from the Asian economic crisis of 1997, Indonesia seems to be sinking deeper into a crisis of its own doing. On witnessing the constant riots and the destruction of public and private property during the first week of February 2001 caused by Wahid's angry fanatical supporters, who refused to accept the possible impeachment of their spiritual and political leader, Vice-President Megawati lamented the situation by saying that at present Indonesia is facing a critical condition even worse than fifty years ago when it struggled to reclaim its national independence. Back then the people were united and sharing a bright common vision, but now they are internally divided and torn apart by several conflicting visions. And worst of all, the people themselves are fighting one another so fiercely that it seems that they want to destroy national unity.

Similar concerns have been voiced recently by many international organizations and foreign nations. Irritated by the slow financial reforms that have been repeatedly promised by the Indonesian government, and above that also alarmed by the specter of rising brutal communal conflicts both in the cities and in remote Indonesian regions, the World Bank at the end of February said: "Regional unrest, political and ethnic tensions threaten national unity and continue to preoccupy the government" (Cooney 2001). Malaysia and Singapore have already expressed their deep anxiety about Indonesia's present political instability. They even anticipate the worst possible scenario in which there would be a violent national disintegration, spreading across Southeast Asia in a stream of bloodshed, refugees, religious fanaticism and economic disruption. And when the *Nahdlatul Ulama* (NU), the largest Muslim organization with some 40 million members, most of whom are loyal to Wahid, publicly swears that there would be a violent bloodbath if there is any attempt to oust president

Wahid, constitutionally or not, the Indonesian people themselves are suddenly being confronted with the most terrible nightmare they ever could imagine: the prospect of the 'Balkanization' of their own country, in which Indonesia would dissolve into regional chaos and civil war along religious and ethnic lines just as in the former Yugoslavia.

Indonesia is caught in a deep crisis that might well decide the future destiny of its national unity and historical survival as a sovereign nation. At present, news and reports on Indonesia are incessantly crowded with images of political, regional, ethnic and religious strife. In this article, however, we will limit our discussion to just one aspect of that crisis, namely, the phenomenon of religious tension that is becoming much more frequent and violent. Impressed by the sweet memory of the past picture of tolerance and harmony, many people tend to deny the existence of religious tension in Indonesia. What is actually happening, they say, is simply the politicization of religions through the old colonial trick of divide and conquer. Or they say that the religious tension has been co-opted and dissolved into a larger sociological category, such as the general conflict between the majority and the minority.

However, if we are willing to be honest with ourselves and carefully observe the mutual perception of each religious group toward the other, we can readily see that there are indeed indications of religious tension and confrontation. As a group or distinct sociological unit, each religion looks apprehensively towards the others and feels its free existence to be constantly threatened by the maneuvers and movements of the other religions. In brief, there is little mutual trust regarding intentions, so that the relation between different religious communities is still mainly dominated by a hostile image of the other, specifically the disturbing image of Islamization versus Christianization. Hence, although there are indeed other significant factors contributing to the various communal conflicts such as that which have taken place in Ambon and Kalimantan, for example, such conflicts are also strongly charged with religious emotion. The faulty transmigration policy of the government, for example, is interpreted religiously as a political maneuver to 'Islamize' other regions which contain rich natural resources and significant Christian populations with Muslim immigrants from other parts of Indonesia.

Since there is a close connection between religion and politics, we will begin our discussion by first presenting a brief picture of the political conflict that is presently raging in Indonesia. In the next section we will describe Indonesia's religious conflict proper and a way toward possible reconciliation.

The Pattern of the Political Conflict

It is quite difficult to know for certain who is acting against whom in the on-going crisis in Indonesia, since the political scene keeps changing quite rapidly. Those who were still enemies a year ago, such as Megawati and Amin Rais for example, are now trying to achieve a clandestine political marriage. After practically robbing Megawati of her presidency because of her gender two years ago, it is precisely Rais who is now her most active supporter in her bid to replace Wahid so that she may become the first female president of Indonesia. Nevertheless, with a certain unavoidable degree of simplification, we can see a general pattern emerging out of that confusing picture. The conflict is between the following structural forces. On one hand, we have a conflict centered on the political issue of civil supremacy over the former military supremacy. On the other hand, we also have an ideological conflict concerning the foundation of the nation itself: whether it should be based on the past national consensus, namely, the nationalist ideology of the *Pancasila* state (the Five Principles) or be ruled on the basis of the islamic *sharia* (Islamic Law), leading toward the realization of an Indonesian Islamic State.

This twofold pattern of conflict should not be understood in a static sense as being confined to a certain definite social group. Even in the military, for example, we could find opposing tendencies working against each other. The Indonesian National Military (TNI) is divided into the so-called *TNI merah-putih* (the red-white military faction), i.e., the nationalist group, and the *TNI ijo royo-royo* (real green faction), i.e., the pro-Islamic group within the armed forces. The same thing could also be said about the Islamic community in general. That community is also divided into the more nationalistic and the more fundamentalistic factions. For example, Mochtar Buchori, a devout Muslim and prominent member of the DPR (House of Representatives) from the nationalist PDI-P party, says: "What kind of Islam are we going to have as the mainstream? If we are heading for a hard-line Islamic civilization, this country is really going to disintegrate" (cited in: Dahlby 2001: 91). Due to its status as a minority group, the Christian community is mostly nationalistic in spirit, trying to convince the other groups that it is possible to be totally devout Christian people while being totally committed to the nation at the same time (see, e.g., de Jong 1995).

After the downfall of Suharto, one of the paramount reform agendas is the significant reduction of the military role in Indonesia. Besides based on the disgraceful practices of KKN (corruption, collusion and nepotism), Suharto's New Order managed to maintain its power for such a long period by practising two social engineering approaches. The first was the security approach aimed at safeguarding the national unity by repressively applying law and order everywhere. This task to protect the territorial unity and the social cohesion of the nation was the foremost job assigned to the armed forces. As a result, Indonesia was practically ruled by a military regime. From the highest to the lowest layers of society one could find military officers giving minute advice and instructions. Actually, Indonesia was ruled more by order than by law during that period. The most repeated phrase in the political discourse during that period was *atas komando* (under the command), and not that of *sesuai hukum* (according to the law). Whereas law is meant to protect the well-being of the people (*salus populi suprema lex esto*), order is imposed from above to control the people, if necessary by means of intimidation and coercion, so that the power and privilege of the few ruling elite can be securely protected. This was the situation for 33 years at least—perhaps more, since up until the present no serious legal investigation has been conducted concerning the people involved.

The corresponding approach to supplement the above was the so-called prosperity approach: the gigantic task of transforming Indonesia into a modern and prosperous nation through successive PELITA (*Pembangunan Lima Tahunan* = five-year plan phases) modeled after Rostov's theory of gradual stages of economic growth. Officially, this task had to be executed and achieved through the GOLKAR, the then ruling government party consisting mainly of government employees and civil servants working in the public sector, including the armed forces. However, as a matter of fact, PELITA was simply fertile ground for uninhibited corruption, collusion and nepotism. If nepotism primarily referred to the self-enrichment policy of Suharto's family and his crony capitalism of immediate business friends, collusion was the secret and open collaboration between the armed forces and the whole commercial world according to the simple formula of power protecting money and money buying power. This practice of collusion acquired its ideological legitimacy through the doctrine of the dual function of the armed forces (*Dwifungsi TNI*). According to this doctrine, in addition to its professional military function proper, the armed forces also had a social-political obligation to protect the process of national development by taking an active role in all segments of society, including its active participation in the political as well as the economic institutions. As a result, the New Order became a very corrupt and authoritarian regime, since "the cake of the national development" was mostly divided between Suharto's family and the armed forces. Yenni Kwok of CNN gives the following astute observation about the military's involvement in the financial enterprises

> Despite its large role, the military spent only one percent of the budget for military expenses. Hence thus the military largely finances expenditure through a network of businesses and other funds that extend from the capital to the outer regions. (Kwok 2001)

The collapse of Suharto's corrupt New Order gave rise to fresh aspirations for a new democratic Indonesian society. It was be run and managed by a reformed government, that is to say, a government free from the structural sins of KKN and also free from the meddling of the military. Hence, here begins the struggle to build civil supremacy over against the previous military supremacy. That is the first and foremost feature of Indonesia in the post-Suharto's era. The military's seats in Parliament have been reduced to almost half, from 75 to 38, and future plans call for all such seats being abolished by 2009. Moreover, civil society voluntary groups and mass media, which had been severely constrained by the former military regime, are now beginning to flourish freely. For example, in the long autocratic reign of Suharto, there were just three political parties that were permitted to take part in general elections. But now there have already been more than fifty political parties formed freely out of grassroots initiatives.

Liberated from the government's control, the media also enjoy freedom of expression and investigation. As if paying back the old grudges, they now turn their energy to scrutinizing and exposing the scandals and abuses committed by the New

Order, including those committed by the military. In other words, people are starting to breathe in a new atmosphere of freedom. Indeed, according to the well-known Muslim scholar Nurcholis Madjid, one of the most important achievements of the reformation movement is "the freedom from fear. In particular, the fear to express political freedom due to long years of political repression by authoritarian regime" (cited in Anwar 1999: 19). Intoxicated by this new freedom, people are starting to launch lively public debates about the critical issues facing the country, including the discussion about the formerly most taboo topics, such as the possibility for amending or even changing the national constitution altogether as well as changing the political form of the country from the present *Negara Kesatuan Republic Indonesia* (The United Republic of Indonesia) into *Negara Federasi Indonesia* (the Federal Republic of Indonesia). More radical people even go so far as to discuss openly the possible emergence of several smaller independent nations of their own out of the total breakdown of Indonesia. In short, the Indonesian people are beginning to redefine freely the aim, form and foundation of their own nation.

Unfortunately, instead of heading toward a more matured responsible freedom for conducting a democratic life, this newly regained political freedom has a twin darker and more menacing side. It easily turns into a terrible freedom generating disastrous social effects, since it is accompanied also by these two negative social phenomena: the clearly manifest weakness of the central government and the uncivilized freedom displayed by the people themselves. And as we will see later on, religious fanaticism also plays a significant role in this fall from civilized into uncivilized freedom.

Up to now Wahid's government has proved itself to be a weak government lacking in creativity, incapable of providing any workable solutions to several critical problems faced by Indonesia, in particular, financial reform with a view to economic recovery and political reform with a view to regional autonomy. Instead of providing solutions, Wahid is himself entangled in various scandals and problems of his own, the most important of which are the Bulog Gate and the Brunei Gate scandals, involving the alleged misappropriation of some six million dollars. As a result of these scandals he is threatened by possible impeachment.

The weakness of Wahid's leadership manifests itself mainly in the following two troubling phenomena. The first is the ability to act with impunity enjoyed by the transgressors of law and human rights. One of the major demands of the reform movement is to bring to justice those who have been involved in the corrupt New Order of Suharto and those who have committed the crimes against humanity in all parts of Indonesia. But most of those suspected people still remain at large or even enjoy the legal protection given by the government. For example, the charges against Suharto have dismissed on the grounds of insufficient evidence and his current poor state of health. The cases against several senior military officers and police officials have also been dismissed due to the ambiguity of law and order at the time of the events in question. To a certain extent, the provocateurs and the agents of more recent riots and communal conflicts also enjoy such impunity. Forlornly lamenting the stark increase in murder, rape, and other human rights abuses, one ordinary person from Aceh stated: "Anybody can do anything they want" (cited in Dahlby 2001: 83). The same thing can be said of the recent brutal ethnic cleansing of the Madurese in the central Kalimantan (Borneo).

This last example leads us to the second manifestation of the weakness of Wahid's administration, namely, the lack of control by the central government in preventing or resolving the more disturbing events that are taking place not only much more frequently but also much more violently. From one place to another, violent communal conflict explodes without any effective control by the government: Aceh, Ambon, Kalimantan, Lombok, Papua, Sulawesi, and elsewhere. The number of hot spots and unstable provinces increases rapidly. Thus, ethnic conflicts in the remote regions of Jakarta and riots in the big cities are the daily news about Indonesia. For that reason, there are those who claim that Wahid's government has lost credibility and is no longer able to perform the following six reform agendas: bringing an end to the dual function of the military and police, amending the 1945 Constitution, implementing regional autonomy, enforcing the rule of law, empowering the democratic process and institutions, and finally eliminating KKN (corruption, collusion and nepotism) by starting with the trial of Suharto and his cronies (Qodari 2001).

The negative counterpart of the weak government is the uncivilized freedom in which citizens engage toward one another: plundering private property, destroying public infrastructures, mass raping of innocent women, coercively forcing conversion to another faith, and even forced to partake in rituals of drinking fresh human and eating human hearts before being mercilessly beheaded. Under Suharto's New Order, the crimes against humanity were mostly committed by the government against its citizens, helpless victims who were easily manipulated financially by the government and terrorized and tortured by the military. Under Wahid's government, however, we are witnessing crimes against humanity committed for the most part by the citizens themselves, with the convenient miserable inactivity or absence of the government. According to the recent report by the American State Department, human rights' conditions in Indonesia have steadily deteriorated, precisely due to these violent attitudes of its citizens: "The government was ineffective in deterring social, interethnic and interreligious violence that accounted for the majority of deaths by violence during the year" (cited in Reuters 2001). As citizens are more inclined to act and react violently at the slightest provocation, the formerly typical Indonesian attitude of warm hospitality and friendliness is hardly to be seen. Hence, the expression *kebebasan biadab* (uncivilized freedom) has arisen in contrast to *kebebasan beradab* (civilized freedom). Horrified by the phenomenal rise of uncivilized freedom, the voice of nostalgia that wants to return to the past can once again be heard: order is better than disorder. That voice is gaining strength, mostly among the common people who feel abandoned by the new elite which is too much preoccupied with a new distribution of power and privilege among themselves, whereas for many people actual living conditions are simply getting worse.

It is quite interesting to note that religious conflicts have been becoming much more frequent in recent years. It seems that instead of pacifying the latent social tensions that are already present in the society, religion tends to amplify them further so that they finally burst into violent communal conflicts. In other words, the social tensions that are primarily caused by political division and economic jealousy among different groups become highly accelerated if they are filled with religious emotion and interpreted religiously. This religious amplification of the social tensions operates through the horizontal mechanism of communalization and the vertical mechanism of sacralization. Through being interpreted religiously, a trivial accident or a small personal tension between two individuals is quickly transformed into a communal tension involving a large number of people. The conflict between a Christian bus driver and a Muslim passenger in Ambon, for example, rapidly involved the whole city and transformed it into one large firebrand. The criticism directed at President Wahid is also seen as being directed at the *Nahdlatul Ulama* (NU) as a whole. Thus, religious solidarity becomes a very effective carrier and amplifier of social tensions.

Furthermore, religious interpretation tends to sacralize an issue so that it becomes an absolute obligation for the people concerned. By becoming an absolute obligation, it is no longer open to any reasonable considerations—the common sense practice of balancing social costs and benefits—since it now is fully a matter of one's personal conscience directly before God who has a higher law than the law of human beings. With the coming of the *Laskar Jihad* (the Muslim holy warriors) in Ambon, for example, an ethnic strife has been transformed into a bloody holy war that is hopelessly blind to the most obvious fact of being engaged in mutual destruction. Each side is then driven by the unrestrained emotion to commit no less than the complete annihilation (*sikat habis*) of the other: "[I]t was true that the Moluccas were now so tense that *habis,* slang for annihilation, awaited Muslims caught in Christian strongholds and vice versa" (cited in Dahlby 2001: 93). By calling the blood of Akbar Tanjung and Amien Rais (the chairpersons of the House of Representatives (DPR) and the People's Consultative Assembly (MPR) respectively) *halal* (slated to be shed), their political opposition to President Wahid is seen as contrary to God's will and hence —God willing—as needing to be eliminated. Thus, religious language transforms the nature of social tension drastically. It causes it to spread like wildfire to the whole community and elevates the issue into an absolute duty that demands a concrete victim immediately so as to restore the disrupted divine order.

The present crisis of Indonesia is mainly due to the weakness of the central government and the uncivilized freedom of its citizens. There are several theories to explain the cause of this tense situation. There are those who think that it has been ignited surreptitiously yet systematically by the military itself, so that the present government would be discredited and later on the military could defend and reassert the fruitfulness of its doctrine of the dual function of the military much more convincingly to the public at large. The various communal conflicts would then be decoded as unequivocal military signals: "Indonesia's top generals sent a message written in the blood of slaughtered Madurese civilians to President Abdurrahman Wahid last week, 'You do not rule Indonesia, we do'" (Sieff 2001). In other words, the present tension is part of the military's design to increase its political bargaining power considerably with respect to the civil authorities, in particular the reconsideration of the latter's demand for greater accountability concerning military crimes and preventing it from effectively investigating the corruption cases. Others have pointed out that the present crisis is wholly in accord with the sociological trend accompanying any power vacuum within society. As the centripetal forces grow weaker, the centrifugal forces grow stronger. Hence, it is quite comprehensible that at present there are many cases involving separatist movements in the outer regions and transgressions of the law in the cities.

Mohamad Qodary and Roger Baker, however, still point out to another significant factor in understanding the present heightened tension (see Qodari 2001; Baker 2001). According to them, the present social crisis is caused mainly by division within the Muslim community itself. This community itself shows internal rivalry between several competing Muslim factions: one group centered around President Wahid and the other, the greater yet more loosely aggregated group, the Central Axis (*Poros Tengah*), around Amien Rais, the chairperson of the MPR (the People's Consultative Assembly, which is the highest political institution in Indonesia). A quite similar observation is also made by William Liddle, the political scientist on Indonesian current affairs, who states: "Indonesian society is increasingly polarized between Muslims who define their political interests in religious terms and others who do not" (cited in Dahlby 2001: 85).

Mohamad Qodari draws our attention to the amazing fact that whereas former President Habibie was considered to be a friend of Islam, even to such an extent that he was not even perceived as part of the corrupt New Order which he had served obediently for 25 years, President Wahid, on the contrary, is considered by several Islamic factions to be an enemy of Islam (Qodary 2001). That is the reason why the greatest and strongest opposition to Wahid comes largely from Islamic circles: from the various Islamic political parties (PAN, Partai Keadilan, Partai Bulan Bintang etc.), from the Islamic student associations (HMI, KAMMI, BEM etc.) and from other Islamic social organizations (DDII, ICMI etc.). What they demand daily and with a growing degree of persistency is either Wahid's impeachment or resignation.

This public and aggressive resistance to Wahid—conducted in Parliament and on the street—in the name of Islam is quite amazing if we consider the fact that he is the former chairman of *Nahdlatul Ulama* (NU), the largest Muslim organization in the world. Among several other reasons, Wahid has especially incited a wave of political and religious antipathies toward himself by announcing his plan to open trade relations with Israel and to lift the ban on Communism. The first proposal is regarded as demonstrating his lack of personal sensitivity and Islamic solidarity with the Palestinians and thus of being an instrument of Zionism and Western imperialism. His second proposal suffers even worse, since it is judged not only to be a public promotion of atheism but also a political tactic to weaken the Muslim political position by cutting its connection with the *wong cilik* (the poor people). The latter was the traditional social basis of PKI (the Indonesian Communist Party) which once flourished freely in Indonesia until it was literally slaughtered under Suharto's New Order. When Wahid tries to defend his views by stating that the right to one's own personal conviction belongs essentially to human rights as such, he is immediately condemned as being the exponent of Western values that have been imported to Indonesia in order to erode Islamic values.

The situation is getting worse, as there are several Christians occupying key positions in Wahid's administration. Holding cabinet posts are Luhut Binsar Panjaitan (Minister of Industry and Trade), Purnomo Yusgiantoro (Minister of Energy and Mineral Resources), Bungaran Saragih (Minister of Agriculture and Forestry), Sonny Keraf (State Minister of Environment), Manuel Kaseipo (Junior Minister for the Development of Indonesia's Eastern Region), Edwin Gerungan (Chairman of the Committee for the Indonesian Bank Restructuring Agency = BPPN). In conjunction with that fact, several definitely strategic positions in the military intelligence are also held by Christians: Yosmenko (Deputy Intelligence of the Indonesia Defense Force Commander), Arie Jeffre Kumaat (Chief of the National Intelligence Agency = BIN), Tulus Sihombing (Vice-Chief of the Army Strategic Intelligence = BAIS). Seeing this, the Muslim community feels not only that it is underrepresented but also that it is repressed by the Christian community. As Christianity is associated historically with the Western world, the presence of Christians in the government only confirms the suspicion that Wahid is simply the political instrument of the Western world and that Indonesian politics has already been Christianized (see in particular the article, "Tahap Penting"). Hence, despite being a renowned Muslim cleric (*kiai*), Wahid is viewed neither as a friend nor as a partner of Islam. He still sits in the presidency chair due to the fragile support of the Indonesian Democratic Party in Struggle (PDI-P), which under Megawatt's leadership has inherited the nationalistic elan of Indonesia's founding father, Sukarno. But should Megawati look in another political direction or seek another coalition, Wahid—it seems—would soon belong no longer to the future but to the tragic past.

The strong opposition to Wahid reflects an inner division within the Indonesian Islamic community. This division has been commonly formulated as being the opposition between the traditionalist and the modernist Muslims. The traditionalists formulate their mission as "*Indonesianising Islam* whereas the Muslim modernists perceive the issue as problems of *Islamising Indonesia*" (Santoso 1999: 7). These different perspectives manifest themselves politically as the issue of the nation state versus the Islamic state. Belonging to the traditionalist camp, President Wahid basically conceives Islam as a way of life in which humans can shape culture and human personality, in particular, their relationship to the Almighty God (*hablum minallah*) and to one another (*hablum minanannas*). Instead of focussing its attention on the state, Islam should try to permeate civil society in which everything takes place freely and voluntarily according to one's own personal conscience, without any element of force and coercion. Thus Wahid says: "If Islam needs state power to shape people's lives, then it is not a religion anymore. It becomes an authority, and no religion can survive as an authority" (cited in Wright 2001). In that way Islam could reach out toward those of other religions in the spirit of tolerance and solidarity, since it is a peaceful way of life that has no intention of imposing its view on others by power and force.

Wahid's opponents, the modernists, conceive Islam as more than just a way of life. It is a perfect and complete divine guidance embracing all dimensions of life, including the state. In other words, the state is not something that exists beside religion, as if it were a secular domain that coexists in separation from religion as a neutral or profane zone of its own. On the contrary, the state is an instrument for religion to realize its laws and values. Ahmad Sumargono, chairperson of the Crescent Star Party (PBB) remarks succinctly as follows: "For us, Islam is an Ideology with political goals, including Islamic Law" (cited in Wright 2001). The fact of the financial and moral bankruptcy of Suharto's New Order has become historical evidence proving the error and the failure of a purely secular conception of the state. Indeed, the very conception of the secular realm itself, in which there is a separation between state and religion, is seen as a Western notion imported into the Indonesian political discourse by the Christians so as to weaken Islam in order to create a secure public space of their own. In other words, besides the internal tension within the Islamic community itself, there is also an interreligious tension, in particular between Islam and Christianity.

Interreligious Tension and the Process toward Reconciliation

Many people would like to believe that there is no religious tension in Indonesia. Even after the bloody conflict in Ambon and the Christmas bombing of several churches last year, a teacher from Ambon wonderingly said: "We were living previously in peace. We never experienced religious hatred before" (cited in Dahlby 2001: 80). A great mystery has gripped the whole country: Who is the cunning mastermind behind the series of bombings, riots, bloody ethnic cleansing, mysterious murders and violent religious clashes that take place much more frequently in the post-Suharto era? In desperation, since there has never been any adequate explanation or convincing proof concerning the leading actor behind these atrocities, people say that they are the products of a *siluman*, namely, a great evil spirit having neither name nor form of its own. Besides being intended as a cynical criticism of Wahid's administration due to its failure to uncover and catch the evil mastermind, that expression also reflects the deep and widespread anxiety felt by the people at large since, as an invisible demon, a *siluman* can take any form whatsoever and produce its evil effects at any place. We do not know the *siluman* itself, but we do certainly know the multiple and recurring forms of its evil incarnations, namely, SARA (an acronym for *Suku, Agama, Ras, dan Antar Golongan*, i.e., Ethnicity, Religion, Race and Social Classes). Each element of SARA is seen as a centrifugal power, a potential cause for violent conflict that could lead to national disintegration. In other words, people live with the constant sense that something very wrong and terrible might happen at any time, including possible religious conflict, such as a repetition of the Ambon (or the Sampit) tragedy in other parts of Indonesia. As a matter of fact, a rather sporadic reduplication of such tragedy has actually happened in several places in Sulawesi and Lombok. What people most fear is that Ambon is merely a possible pilot project to be expanded later on by the *siluman* into the whole eastern part of Indonesia, traditionally known as the stronghold of the Christian community. Another clear indication that there is indeed an atmosphere of fear embracing Indonesia as a whole can be seen from the unpredictable rate of the *rupiah*, the Indonesian currency, and the deterrence of foreign investors, the IMF and other aid donors to invest their capital, with the result that Indonesia is still struggling with a deep economic crisis due to its own political uncertainty.

One of the indications that a heightened interreligious tension exists indeed between Islam and Christianity is the fact that in the last five years the number of the destruction of religious objects is higher than ever before. Limiting ourselves to just the destruction of church buildings, we can see the following sharp contrast:

> More than 500 churches were destroyed in less than three years only, from 1996 to today [1999]—a very sharp contrast to the less than five similar cases within a time span of more than half century, 1945-1996 (including the five years of physical struggle after the proclamation of independence). (Santoso 1999: 8)

In the last couple of years such cases continue to multiply. Witness the wave of thirty-three bombings on Christmas night last year in eight cities, aimed at Christian churches, in which eighteen people were killed and fifty wounded[4].

It seems that such a sharp contrast should be explained primarily not on religious but on political grounds. It is not so that people lived in peaceful religious coexistence under the New Order, a coexistence that then degenerated drastically into a hostile coexistence under Wahid's Reform Order. In other words, what has changed is not the religious situation but the political situation: from the former enforced stability to the present fluid instability. Just like race and ethnicity, religion has also been used and abused as one of the destabilizing factors in order to achieve a certain political aim. Therefore, in analyzing the phenomenon of religious tension in Indonesia, it would be better to make several subtle distinctions. First, there is the religious tension that has been caused by the politicization of religion. Second, there is a religious tension that arises out of a latent suspicion cherished covertly by each religious community toward one another, particularly concerning the problem of 'Islamization' and 'Christianization'. And finally, there is a religious tension that arises from the confusion or mingling of politics and religion. In analyzing the problem that way, we are also in a better position to determine several ways that could lead toward the process of reconciliation between the religions.

First of all, there is the phenomenon of the politicization of religion. Put in the context of religious tension, this means that, due to its ability to amplify religious

---

[4] See also the website containing the "Report on Church and Human Rights Persecution in Indonesia" (downloaded March 2, 2001): www.fica.org/hr.

emotion and bonds, religion has been used to support or to overthrow a certain power structure. Religious conflict is part of a larger political conflict. Actually, there is no essential difference between the conflict being an intrareligious one, such as that between *Muhammadiyah* and *Nahdlatul Ulama*, or an interreligious conflict, such as that between Islam and Christianity. Being a minority, the Christian community is simply a far easier target than the fellow Muslim community. Since there is enough to indicate that there is a strong coalition that seriously wants to overthrow President Wahid, multiple accidents and conflicts between Islam and Christianity are simply practical means or mechanisms that have been quite conveniently used in order to achieve that political aim. Intoxicated by the great success in overthrowing Suharto, the anti-Wahid coalition wants to make clear to the world the following reasons why Wahid should, like Suharto, be removed from office before finishing his term: his failure to bring economic recovery to Indonesia, his failure to master the violent domestic situation, his failure to gain both wide popular support from the people and effective assistance from the armed forces. Religious conflicts serve best to create such impressions.

What kind of reconciliatory process can prevent and/or overcome this sort of politicization of religion? Directly after the Christmas bombings, a group calling itself FID (*Forum Indonesia Damai* = Indonesia Peace Forum) was formed. It is an interreligious group that was later seen as a model to be imitated by several similar groups working in various places and on various levels of society (SNB, KHAK, etc). The aim of FID is to make people and their local leaders alert to the danger of the politicization of religion so as not to be so easily incited to religious violence by irresponsible provocateurs. Moreover, through the exchange of information and through a joint investigation, this group also wants to expose the real motivation behind the multiple events involving religious conflict and those who actually benefit the most from such conflicts. In addition to trying to unmask as much as possible the motives and agents that draw people into conflict with one another, they also want to allow the victims of religious violence to be seen, so that people can recognize the harshness of human evil and mourn with the victims.

Such a group should attempt—however cautiously—to grow into something more than simply an alert group. It should also become a reflective and prophetic group. Engaging in reflection means having the courage to engage in introspection in order to discover the motivations in one's own religion for provoking either misunderstanding or aggression by other religions. In brief, to be reflective means to be able to recognize one's own faults and weaknesses. For example, based on the segregation case of East Timor, several Islamic factions suspect that there is an international Christian alliance that would like to see the total disintegration of Indonesia. The same suspicion is also directed at Christians living in the eastern part of Indonesia (RMS, OPM). It is quite easy to reject such a suspicion as being groundless and silly. Further reflection, however, might disclose the fact that the approaches and practices of the Christians themselves could be to blame for the growth of such a suspicion. The Church's silence and insensitivity to the crimes against humanity suffered by the

Muslims in Tanjung Priuk, Lampung and Aceh, in contrast to its strong advocacy for the cases of East Timor and Ambon; its close and uncritical relation with the ones in power during the New Order (CSIS, Soedomo, Benny Moerdani etc.) could awaken the suspicion that Christians collaborated with the government in repressing Islam.

In addition to reflection, we should also cultivate a prophetic attitude, namely, the critical awareness that religion can be turned easily into an ideology for justifying anything we want. Instead of serving the living God, we are then serving a dead idol that can be shaped and moved in any direction we want to go. Thus at times there is a *fatwa* (a binding religious instruction) that prohibits women from becoming president. At other times, however, there is almost a *fatwa* enjoining the people to elect and support a woman as president. Religion has been used to motivate people to fight for nationalism against separatism, such as the struggle in which the *Laskar Jihad* in Ambon is engaged. But the same process of religious rationalization has also been used to attempt to change the National Constitution and the *Haluan Negara* (the Basic National Orientation). Prophetic awareness is the consciousness that our relation to God is not only symmetrical but also asymmetrical. We are not only confirmed but also condemned by God for our narrow-mindedness in pursuing our own selfish interests. Seeing the asymmetrical gap between divine intention and human political schemes, the prophetic attitude has the courage to judge it simply as a human deceit instead of the divine concern.

The following question we should pose critically is: Why does religion lend itself so easily to violence? Perhaps, deeply rooted in the makeup of each religion is an unconscious hatred, an enmity toward other religions. Here we are confronted in particular with the ever-haunting phenomenon of Islamization *versus* Christianization. By being placed within such mutual suspicion, a trivial accident can explode into mass and brutal violence. According to Gerry van Klinken, that is exactly what had happened in the Ambon tragedy:

> When a trivial incident occurred at the city's bus terminal, the word flew around each side that "it" [gang war] had started. From here on, events escalated as each side believed only its own version of events. Muslims spoke of halting the "christianization" drive. Christians spoke of Islamic "fanaticism" in Jakarta.... (Van Klinken 1999: 42)

This mutual suspicion is a hidden timebomb, so to speak, that could easily be detonated by almost any incident involving people from the two religious communities of Islam and Christianity.

In addition to often feeling itself to be an easy target for the general social frustration of the masses, the Christian community feels threatened also by the growing power of Islam in Indonesia. That fear is not identical with the minority complex of having to live amid the largest Islamic population in the world. Instead, it is the kind of fear that arises in connection with the observation that something has changed without knowing what it will ultimately bring: the fear of a radical shift. The Christian community feels that gradually but certainly Indonesia has changed and is moving toward Islam. That perception arises through observing the phenomena of the Islamic resurgence and the radicalization of Islam in Indonesia. The Indonesian Islamic revival can be dated back to the foundation of ICMI (the Indonesian Muslim Intellectual Association) in November 1990. Under the chairmanship of Habibie, ICMI proved itself to be the most influential organization in Indonesia. It dominated the intellectual world in the universities and the political world in the government's bureaucracy as well as in the three political parties that were then permitted. It even expanded its influence further into the military as well, causing a split between the Islamic and the nationalistic groups. It was particularly under this growing dominance of ICMI that the policies of the central government were seen through the spectacles of Islamization: placing Muslims in strategic positions throughout the Indonesian social hierarchy and promoting the cause of Islam. In the outer regions, especially in Eastern Indonesia with its significant Christian population, this Islamization is viewed as having its parallel in Javanization, namely, sending Muslims from the crowded islands of Java and Madura to other parts of Indonesia. Hence, the foundation for the present regional tensions was laid. After the fall of Habibie, the influence of ICMI slightly declined, although it is still very much alive, which also explains its current opposition to Wahid. From the very beginning Wahid opposed the idea of the ICMI.

Presently under Wahid, despite the declining influence of ICMI, the aspiration to Islamize Indonesian civil society, if not even the nation itself as a political body, has become stronger than ever. One can even observe the process of the radicalization of Islam through the appearance of multiple militant groups such as the Defender of Islam (FPI = *Front Pembela Islam*), the Army of the Holy War (*Laskar Jihad*), the Indonesian Committee for the Islamic Solidarity (KISDI = *Komite Indonesia untuk Solidaritas Dunia Islam*), the Ka'bah Youth Movement (GPK = *Gerakan Pemuda Kabah*) etc. Parallel to such militant groups, there are also several Islamic militant media such as *Mujahidin, Suara Hidayatullah* and *Sabili*. Driven by the threat of the presence of an international Christian coalition to break Indonesia apart and traumatized by the segregation of East Timor, *Laskar Jihad* sends its army to Ambon and the Moluccas under the pretext of protecting the territorial integrity of the nation. It has also promised to become actively involved in Papua (Irian Jaya) should the separatist movement there become a real threat to the territorial unity of Indonesia. If that were the case, Christians wonder, why had *Lasker Jihad* not yet sent its holy warriors to Aceh? In other words, instead of doing the right thing, *Lasker Jihad* simply makes it worse and more complicated, since it invites regional tension and religious confrontation. The unending conflict in Ambon and the recent turmoil caused by the ethnic clashes between the Dayaks and the Madurese, among others, should be interpreted as a clear warning by the local ethnic power to the national central power in Jakarta about the danger of letting outsiders interfere in local affairs.

On the other hand, the Islamic community finds it impossible to liberate itself from its fear of Christianization. For Indonesian Muslims, Christianization is a complex notion involving several dimensions simultaneously. First of all, it entails the basic intention of Christianity to convert (Islamic) people into Christians. Practically speaking, the essence of Christianity is identified with the twin Dutch words *missie en zending* ('mission'). Besides keeping the horror and trauma of past colonialism still very much alive, those two Dutch words also express the typical Islamic understanding of Christianity as an active, aggressive and triumphalist religion that wants to conquer the world for its faith. At the very least, it is suspected of trying to become the dominant culture in the New World Order—an allusion to Samuel P. Huntington's *The Clash of Civilizations and the Remaking of World Order*.

In brief, it is Christianity, not Islam, that is seen as a militant religion and hence, almost per definition, as something that needs to be resisted. Therefore, all statistical data that show the cumulative increase of the Christian believers will almost always be accepted with social protest and uproar. That is the reason why several censuses on religion almost consistently show the same 'magical' proportion throughout the decades: Islam 87,3%, Protestant 6%, Catholics 3,6%, Hindu 1,8%, Buddha 1%, others 0,3%. In addition, Christianization is also identified with syncretism. Theologically speaking, due to its Trinitarian conception of God and its elevation of Jesus to divine status (committing the unforgivable sin of *shirk* (assigning a partner to God)), Christianity is seen not as a purely monotheistic but a syncretistic religion, containing many pagan elements. Being contaminated by paganism in this way, it has a special affinity with and sympathy for the local and tribal religions, which are not regarded as religions in Indonesia but as cultural heritages. The Christian's concern to cultivate and to protect the local tribes, local cultures, local religions and local people are then seen as syncretistic. Practically speaking, that means that, in defending local cultures, Christianity is viewed as trying to limit the influence of the Islamic culture while creating a missionary field for itself. In that way Christianity is seen as simply manipulating the indigenous culture and people for its own benefit in order to reject Islam's claim to be the greatest religion in Indonesia with its 87% of the total population. And finally, Christianization is also identified with several closely associated ideas: modernization, Westernization and secularization. In this context, the meaning of Christianization has become so broad and vague as to be practically identical with everything opposed to Islam. That virtual identification, however, has a very specific connotation in Indonesia: Christianity is any idea coming from the Western world that weakens Islam, either through penetration (e.g., Human Rights, feminism, separation between state and religion) or through opposition (e.g. monogamy).

It is very difficult indeed to figure out ways to move out of this deep-rooted mutual suspicion towards reconciliation. Perhaps this suspicion will always be present as long as each religion cultivates a missionary elan for converting people and expanding its cultural influence in the society at large. Hence, what we should try to do is devise something like the rules of the game for a civilized or non-violent coexistence. In this way, perhaps the ways and the initiatives toward reconciliation would depend quite a bit on the nationalist movements that are already present and at work within the society. The nationalist groups could act as mediators between the Islamic and the Christian camps, in particular because there are both Muslims and Christians actively engaged in these groups. Their mutual cooperation could act as a model for the possibility of people from different faiths to work and live together for the common good of the nation.

Actually, the heightened tension due to the issue of Islamization and Christianization coincides with the ideological crisis undergone by Indonesian society: should Indonesia continue to enhance its present status as a nation state or move toward the creation of an Islamic state? Even a devout Muslim such as Mochtar Buchori, with many others, acknowledges that such a transition would mean the total disintegration of Indonesia. In other words, the ways toward reconciliation depends on the ability to cultivate the spirit and the national symbols of unity, such as *Pancasila* (the Five Guiding Principles: belief in one God, a just and civilized humanity, national unity, democracy, justice for the people), the common national language and heritage, the common love for the people and the nation. Reconciliation also depends on the ability to uphold the basic foundation of Indonesian society (*Bhineka Tunggal Ika* (diversity in unity)) not only as a national slogan but also as an operational principle for governing the nation—in, for example, forms of regional autonomy and the sharing of power among different parties. In other words, a new political culture based upon the spirit of consensus and cooperation, as opposed to one based on competition and confrontation, still needs to be developed. If the present crisis passes without inciting more violence, it could serve as the catalyst—the lesson in democracy—for the formation of a new historical consensus freely agreed upon by the several power blocs in the new and open Indonesian society, and not imposed from above as in Suharto's New Order.

In addition to trying to look for a new political symbol of unity, each religious community should also apply the reflective and prophetic attitudes to itself. For example, the Christian community might well ask itself why Christianity and Westernization are identified with each other. Perhaps its theological reflection is still Western-oriented, not yet taking Islam seriously enough into account, with the result that it can neither understand nor answer Islamic thinking on democracy, on the relation between the state and religion, on the place of religion in civil society, on the meaning of women's emancipation, etc. As to the Islamic charge on syncretism, the Christian community might ask itself as well whether, in addition to its program of inculturation and political advocacy for the local tribes and customs, it has done enough to nurture the spirit of nationalism and regional tolerance between different ethnic groups or whether it has itself contributed in large degree to the fear of Islamization and Javanization.

This leads us, finally, to a brief discussion of the problem generated by the mixture between religion and politics. Due to the long repressive era of the Suharto's New Order, Indonesian civil society cannot develop properly. Apart from the state's institutions and initiatives, the only free public space available for people to associate themselves for conducting common purposes is provided by the religions. Hence, each religion has its own political party and labor organization, its own school and university, its own financial and bank system, its own intellectual association and charity institution, etc. After the downfall of Suharto's New Order, these multiple religious groups and initiatives surfaced to play decisive roles in the new and free Indonesian society. For example, out of the fifty parties in the last general election, twenty described themselves as Islamic and several others as Protestant, Catholic and Hindu. That is the reason for the symbiotic unity between religion and politics in Indonesia. Such a situation has its positive and negative aspects. The positive side has to do with the development of the political conscientiousness of the people: they have a high degree of political consciousness, willingness to participate in the debate on daily political issues, becoming active and committed to political associations and actions in order to voice their aspirations. Indeed, repressed for such a long period by Suharto's military regime with its depoliticization policies, it is actually religion that keeps the political consciousness of the common people alive and nurtures their aspiration for a new and better Indonesian society. Barred from following other ideologies than the one instructed by the government (the P4 ideology), many people turn to their own religion as the inspiring source for rejuvenating the nation. Thus, for example, Muslims look for their inspiration to the Egypt-based Ikhwanul Muslim Organization and the Christians turn to Latin American-based liberation theology or European political theology.

The negative side of such a situation is twofold. First, instead of becoming the uniting principle, religions become the dividing forces within society. Political aspirations and social movements are split along religious lines and their conflicts and tensions immediately become religious confrontations as well. Religious membership and connections also become the most important conditions for being able to climb the social ladder, resulting in the feeling of being treated unfairly because of religious discrimination. Secondly, the situation robs civil society of mediating groups and agencies. It impoverishes the society's chances and possibilities for providing interreligious groups that could reduce their mutual fear and suspicion of each other. Hence, the way toward reconciliation would seem to coincide with the development of a real civil society in which various voluntary groups are open to people from different faiths and walks of life. Out of that situation a living understanding across religious boundaries might arise: the kind of understanding that is derived not from an intellectual exchange but from familiarity with one another. Hence, instead of becoming exclusive by securing its own interests and promoting its own candidates in its own organizations, religion should promote more the formation of inclusive and voluntary associations in civil society.

Conclusion

Indonesia is at present facing a deep crisis. Due to its close connection with politics, religion has also been manipulated to create a critical situation for the purpose of overthrowing a certain power structure, leading to a heightened interreligious tension. To overcome such a situation, we should not try to depoliticize religion but instead develop something that might be called a political spirituality. First of all, political spirituality means the prophetic awareness about the possibility of turning religion into an ideology to justify our political claims. Instead of providing higher ethical impulses to politics, religion is degraded into a social mechanism for mobilizing people in order to accomplish political goals devised by the leaders. Secondly, political spirituality means the kind of politics that is always open to something higher than just the struggle to obtain and to maintain power. The higher aim of politics is to promote the well-being of the common people. Due to its closeness with the fate of the common people, religion should always challenge politics with the question: What does politics do to the life of the people? Being rooted in the concern for the common people, politics is saved from its Machiavellian character of being an adventure of the few ruling elite to satisfy their personal ambition to power. A brief illustration could perhaps explain this point:

> Gilbert Keith Chesterton said that both economics and politics were a mystery to him until one day when he looked into the eyes of a little girl in a London slum. And then it struck him—the political and economic measures that would be good for that little girl were probably right and the measures that would hurt her were probably wrong. (Cane 1992: 123)

And, finally, political spirituality is the spirituality that is able to break down the circle of violence. Rene Girard has pointed out that violence, including religious violence, is the result of the mimetic desire: the desire to imitate the other in his enjoyment of power and privilege. This desire could only be satisfied by seizing the other's very power and privilege, leading to the reciprocal violence in defending one's own position. Such a violent reciprocity is interrupted only temporarily in the period of mourning after the blood of victims has been shed. The task of religion is to break the circle of that reciprocal violence by inspiring people not to imitate one another but to imitate God whose basic concern is peace and justice.

Bibliography

Anwar, M. Syafi'i. (1999). "Political Violence in Indonesia." *IDF Indonesia Information*, 3.
Baker, Roger. (2001). "Jakarta Evolving Political Landscape." Downloaded February 15. www.stratfor.com.
Cane, Bill. (1992). *Circles of Hope*. New York: Orbis Books.
Cooney, Daniel. (2001). "World Bank: Indonesia Facing Crisis." Downloaded February 23. News.excite.com/news/ap/010223/15/indonesia-economy.
Dahlby, Tracy. (2001). "Indonesia: Religious Zealots and Regional Separatists Force the Issue. Can this Far-Flung Nation Hold Together?" *National Geographic*. 199/3.
De Jong, Kees. (1995). "Honderd procent katholiek, honderd procent Indonesisch." *Wereld en Zending* 24: 22-35.
Kwok, Yenni. (2001). "Men in Uniform and in Parliament." Downloaded February 26. Asia.cnn.com/2001/WORLD/asiapcf/southeast/02/06/indonesia.military/index.html.
Qodari, Muhamad. (2001). "Islamic Groups and the Student Movement." Downloaded February 15. www.thejakartapost.com/detaileditorial.asp?fileid = 20010215.
Reuters News Service. (2001). "Indonesia Human Rights Picture in Tatters." Downloaded February 26. www.nytimes.com/ads/nytcirc/index.html.

Santoso, Aboeprijadi. (1999). Gus Dur's Painful Dilemma: Aspects of Political Islam in Transition." *IDF Indonesia Information*. No. 3 (January 14).
Sieff, Martin. (2001). "Analysis: Army Key to Indonesia's Power." Downloaded March 5. www.vny.com/cf/News/upidetail.cfm?QID = 165114.
"Tahap Penting Menjadi Negara Kristen" (2001). Downloaded February 27. *Majalah Suara Hidayatullah*. www.hidayatullah.com.
Van Klinken, Gerry. (1999). "What Caused the Ambon Violence?" *Against Impunity: Reader for the Human Rights Symposium*. Amsterdam. 11 December.
Wright, Robin Wright. (2001). "Islam's New Face Visible in a Changing Indonesia." Downloaded December 27. www.latimes.com.

A Pillar of Social Harmony

The Study of Comparative Religion in Contemporary Indonesia during the New Order

Herman L. Beck

Introduction

From time immemorial several religions have existed together in Indonesia. Thus, vis-à-vis the religious situation, Indonesian society can be considered to be a pluralistic society. This situation of religious pluralism was not ended by the coming of Islam to Indonesia and its successful spread in this country. However, in 1945, when the Declaration of Independence was being prepared, a heated discussion broke out regarding the question whether Indonesia was to be a pluralistic state with respect to religions or a multireligious one. Advocates of the former aimed at the recognition of several religions existing together in peace and liberty on an equal basis. Their opponents, on the other hand, supported the idea of a multireligious state in which the overwhelming majority of Muslims in Indonesia was officially recognized by the establishment of an Islamic state and the introduction of *sharia*, Islamic Law. In addition to Islam, in keeping with the Islamic law and its stipulations, some other religions were allowed to exist in this multireligious state (cf., e.g., Wawer 1975: 95). Finally, for the sake of the unity of Indonesia, a compromise was reached. It was decided that Indonesia would become a state based on the doctrine of *Pancasila*, which meant that it was neither an Islamic state nor a secularist one![1]

By virtue of the doctrine of *Pancasila*, Indonesia has a limited form of religious pluralism. Since the mid-1970s some five religions have been officially recognized by authority of the state, viz. Islam, Protestantism, Catholicism, Hinduism and Buddhism. However, unofficially, according to the times and circumstances, the government allowed several other religions and religious movements to exist alongside the recognized ones. Theoretically, the five recognized religions are considered to be on a par and are dealt with accordingly. In actual practice, however, some religious groups are assigned a disproportional amount of influence and power by the government. It was this state of affairs that was especially frustrating to Muslims who felt themselves treated as a negligible minority notwithstanding their superiority in num-

---

[1] The doctrine of *Pancasila* consists of five principles that constitute the official philosophy of independent Indonesia: belief in God, nationalism, humanitarianism, social justice and democracy.

bers. In the past these frustrations resulted in outbreaks of violence and they could lead to them again in the future. Because of the explosive character of the situation of religious pluralism and, therewith, its constant threat to the integrity of Indonesian society, the government of the country invests a great deal of time in measures which can help to prevent outbursts (Tobroni and Arifin 1994: 33f.). It promotes and supports any activity in this field. The study of comparative religion is considered to be one of the possible approaches which can contribute to the removal or at least the decrease in the tension between the different religious communities. Although this view was already present during the government of Sukarno, it gained momentum under the New Order of Suharto.

This contribution will focus first on the state of affairs of the study of comparative religion in Indonesia before the establishment of the New Order in 1965-1967. We will then discuss the development of this field during the New Order. Some remarkable analogous developments will become clear between the study of comparative religion, as far as its approaches and its areas of special attention are concerned, and the views of the New Order. Finally, by way of conclusion, it can be stated that the study of comparative religion in Indonesia is closely connected with the opinions and needs of the New Order government.

The Study of Comparative Religion Before the Establishment of the New Order

Scholars of comparative religion in Indonesia are inclined to stress that their discipline forms a part of the Islamic tradition of learning. In fact, in their view, it was practised by Muslims long before Western scholars dedicated themselves to its study (e.g., Ali 1975: 15ff. and 1988: 8). Indeed, even Indonesian Muslims devoted themselves to the study of comparative religion before the twentieth century (e.g., Steenbrink 1990: 41ff.) This view has to be understood as an attempt to refute the criticism of many Indonesian Muslims who consider the study of comparative religion to be a Western discipline with typical Western characteristics. It proved the study of comparative religion to be neither a Western invention nor a typical Western discipline of learning but one typical of the tradition of Islam which can, not to say should, be studied by Muslims (cf. Munhanif 1996: 96). As a result of this view the study of comparative religion was introduced on an unpretentious scale at some institutes of higher learning in the field of religion (see e.g., Daya 1992: 182ff.).

Regarding the contents of the study of comparative religion, it can be stated roughly that, before the establishment of the New Order, this discipline was characterized by an apologetic character. Other religions were studied to reveal their weaknesses and to prove the superiority of one's own (cf. e.g. Munawar-Rahman 1993: 90ff.). A good example of this approach is found in some books by Hasbullah Bakry (1926-). Bakry is a member of the modernist Muhammadiyah movement and was a lecturer at various Islamic institutes of higher learning, e.g. the Perguruan Tinggi Agama Islam Negeri, the State College of Islamic Studies in Yogyakarta. In 1977 he was appointed professor in Islamic Law and the Study of Comparative Religion at the Universitas Islam in Jakarta. In his treatment of the study of comparative religion

Bakry pays special attention to Christianity. He subscribes to the Islamic view in which Christians are considered to belong to the *ahl al-kitab*, the 'people of the Book'. However, through the years they unfortunately lost sight of the truth. Therefore Christians should be brought to Islam, the religion of truth. The study of comparative religion plays, in Bakry's view, an important part in revealing the inadequacy of Christianity and showing the superiority of Islam. For this reason he stresses the meaning of the study of comparative religion for Muslims. They should know where to find the shortcomings of Islam's greatest competitor (e.g. Bakry 1958: 26).

The apologetic use of the study of comparative religion by Bakry has to be understood against the particular background of the time in which he wrote. After the declaration of independance on August 17, 1945, missionary activities boomed. Many, especially young, Muslims lapsed from Islam and converted to Christianity without any knowledge of this religion. In Bakry's view, this kind of conversion could be stopped by comparing Islam and Christianity. A two-track policy had to be pursued by Muslims. On the one hand, Muslims had to be tolerant with respect to Christians; on the other hand, their self-consciousness had to be cultivated by means of the study of comparative religion in order that they become aware of the value of their own religion. A secondary result of this policy could be the conversion of Jews and Christians to Islam (Bakry 1959: 144ff.). Finally, a comparison of Islam and Christianity would reveal that only Islam truly corresponds with the ideology of *Pancasila* because of its doctrine of the unity of God, whereas the Christian doctrine of the Trinity flatly contradicts the official doctrine Indonesian state. Therefore, the Indonesian government should strongly discourage Christian missionary activities (cf. Wawer 1974: 108).

By contrast with Bakry's application of the study of comparative religion which is characterized by its apologetic character, the approach of someone like Abdul Mukti Ali (1923-) is striking by its use of the study of comparative religion as a constructive way to build a harmonious society. However, Mukti Ali shares Bakry's basic assumption that Islam is superior to all other religions, a fact proven by the study of comparative religion (Ali 1975: 38f.). Besides, Mukti Ali claims the Qur'an to be both the starting point and ultimate standard for every Muslim studying comparative religion. The Qur'an should not be considered a literary product like the scriptures of other religions. It is the absolute Truth and the most important source for evaluating and understanding other religions (Ali 1975: 32f.). This Qur'anic approach to other religions, which Ali openly announced at the fourth Dies Natalis of the Institut Agama Islam Negeri (IAIN), the State Institute for Islamic Studies in Yogyakarta on July 12, 1964 and which he published as a booklet in 1965, prompted some Western scholars to label him a *theologian of religions* than a student of comparative religion (e.g. Boland 1971: 206ff.; cf. Steenbrink 1990: 154 and 1993: 233f.). However, Mukti Ali himself consistently speaks of his discipline as the study of comparative religion and he is publicly known as *Bapak Ilmu Perbandingan Agama di Indonesia*, the father of the study of comparative religion in Indonesia (e.g. Ludjito 1990: 17; Ali-Fauzi 1995: 30). At a seminar in celebration of twenty-five years of study of comparative religion at the IAIN in September 1988, Tahir Tarmizi, who has been the Minister of Religious Affairs since 1992, clearly stated that the development of this discipline in Indonesia can not be detached from the figure of Mukti Ali (Taher 1990: 73).

At the time that Mukti Ali presented his views he was a lecturer at the IAIN in Yogyakarta. At this institute he was responsible for the courses in the study of comparative religion at the Fakultas Ushuluddin, the Faculty of Theology. It was Mukti Ali himself who was asked to mould the form and content of this discipline. The fact is, after Mukti Ali returned from his years of study in Pakistan, where he obtained a Ph.D. from the University of Karachi in the history of Islam in 1955, and from a study leave in Canada, where he received a MA from the McGill Institute in 1957, he was appointed to set up the discipline of *Ilmu Perbandingan Agama*, the study of comparative religion, at the IAINs of Yogyakarta and Jakarta (see Damami *et al.* 1993: 25ff.; Munhanif 1996: 92ff.). The IAIN replaced two former institutes of higher learning in the field of religious studies, viz. the Perguruan Tinggi Agama Islam Negeri, the State College of Islamic Studies, which was established in Yogyakarta in 1951, and the Akademi Dinas Ilmu Agama, the State Academy for the Science of Religion, which was established in Jakarta in 1957 (Daya 1992: 185f.; Munhanif 1996: 95). At both institutes the science of religion was given on an elementary level. The curriculum of both institutes was a professional training. It was focussed at the formation of future religious teachers and officials in the field of religion. The same holds true for the education at the IAIN, where great emphasis was laid on social relevance. However, regarding the study of religion in general and the study of Islam in particular, the IAIN aims at a scholarly approach, which is directly linked to social life and issues with which Muslims are faced in society.

The discipline of the study of comparative religion which Mukti Ali set up at the IAIN is, as far as its objectives are concerned, influenced by Wilfred Cantwell Smith, who was the director of his studies at McGill. The study of comparative religion should be the key to a tolerant attitude with respect to believers of other religions. Mukti Ali expressed these objectives in his concept of *agree in disagreement* (Ali 1975: 8). According to Mukti Ali, this concept had to be the central concept of every student of comparative religion, although he never elaborated precisely on its practical application in the field. Indeed, this concept had to be the device of social life as a whole. In Mukti Ali's view, the concept of *agree in disagreement* also implied that every Muslim student of comparative religion had to endorse the idea that the religion he confessed was superior to all other religions (see e.g. Ali 1970a: 23). The Muslim student of comparative religion would easily gain this insight when studying the differences between the various religions. However, the task of the student of comparative religion is much more ambitious. Not only does he need to study the differences between the religions, but his special commission is to discover the similarities between the religions. When adherents of different religions discover the similarities between their religions, they are much more inclined to exchange ideas and to engage in dialogue. The dialogue, based on respect and tolerance of one another, between adherents of different religions is of vital importance for a harmonious coexistence within a single society. Mukti Ali's concept of *agree in disagreement* has become very popular in Indonesia, although sometimes with a different emphasis or interpretation. So, for example, it is stated in a *festschrift* in honor of Mukti Ali's seventieth birthday that his concept of *agree in disagreement* does not at all focus on the certainty with regard to one's own religion but aims at the realization of the togetherness of the Indonesian people as a nation (Dasuki 1993: 66).

The way Mukti Ali organized the courses of the study of comparative religion at the IAIN, in which an approach was chosen to rouse and stimulate a tolerant attitude among the IAIN students with respect to the adherents of other religions and in which his *agree in disagreement* was stressed as the central concept of the study of comparative religion, has to be understood within the context of that time. The end of the Sukarno era was characterized by an increase of tensions between the adherents of the various religions in Indonesia. It is interesting to note the manner in which Mukti Ali puts this situation into words. He postulates the often articulated idea that Indonesians are a peaceable people. Therefore, Muslims and other religious communities used to live a harmonious and peaceful life together. Regrettably, at the beginning of the 1960s this situation came to an end and, ever since, the existence of tensions between the various religious groups has been noticeably felt (Ali 1970b: 39).

Mukti Ali does not go into a full consideration of the possible causes of those tensions. He does not have to do this, because he can assume that it is still fresh in the memory of his public. However, non-Indonesian readers may need some background information. Since 1959 Sukarno pursued a policy based on the ideology of a permanent revolution, known as *Manipol-Usdek* (Ricklefs 1988: 255).[2] After one year this Manipol-Usdek ideology was supplemented by the doctrine of *Nasakom*. Although this doctrine of Nasakom seems to be an attempt by Sukarno to unite nationalists, Muslims and Communists, he actually played the supporters of the different ideologies off against one another (Ricklefs 1988: 256).[3] The modernist-orthodox and traditionalist-orthodox Muslims felt especially excluded by Sukarno's policy. The free rein given to the Communists resulted in increasing influence among Muslims not belonging to the modernist-orthodox and traditionalist-orthodox groups (cf. Bakker 1970: 230).

The growing pressure of Communism, linked to the expanding missionary activities of the Christians, who had since colonial rule played a disproportionally in-

---

[2] *Manipol* is the acronym for *Manifesto Politik*, (Political Manifesto), the ideology of guided democracy. Usdek is the acronym for *Undang-undang dasar 1945, Sosialisme ala Indonesia, Demokrasi terpimpin, Ekonomi terpimpin, Kepribadian Indonesia* (The 1945 Constitution, Indonesian Socialism, Guided Democracy, Guided Economy and Indonesian Identity).

[3] *Nasakom* is the acronym of *Nasionalisme, Agama, Komunisme* (Nationalism, Religion, Communism).

fluential role in Indonesian society, made many Muslims feel threatened and treated as a minority. The appeal of Christianity and communism was ascribed by learned Muslims to the ignorance of their illiterate coreligionists. There was an urgent need for education of the Muslim masses. The Indonesian government of Sukarno could take advantage of this need by establishing the IAIN. Thus it could show its good will and intentions with respect to the Indonesian Muslims. At the IAIN religious teachers and officials in the field of religion were educated to satisfy the needs of the Muslims. Meanwhile the government could supervise the education of loyal religious teachers and officials at this state institute. In addition, by means of the subjects chosen, the government could train Muslims who were convinced of the necessity of the harmonious coexistence of the various religious communities in the country. The study of comparative religion seemed to be the appropriate channel for laying the scientific foundation for this attitude.

The Study of Comparative Religion After the Establishment of the New Order

After Suharto took power from Sukarno during a process which started in October 1965 and ended in March 1967 by the proclamation of Suharto as Acting President, the study of comparative religion in Indonesia was still characterized by its apologetic character, especially when it was considered to be a tool on behalf of missionary activities (cf. Ali 1988: 51). However, the other, more recent trend for crediting the study of comparative religion with the role of promoting dialogue between the various religious communities in Indonesia and for the benefit of the realization of a harmonious life in national unity became increasingly popular, both at Islamic and Christian institutes of higher learning in the field of religion (see Ali 1990a: 11; Bakry 1984: 60; Riberu 1992: 167). Why did this more recent trend, which already began under the rule of Sukarno and in which the apologetic intention of the study of comparative religion was changed to the stimulation of dialogue, develop in an intensified way during the government of Suharto?

After the abortive coup of September 30, 1965, for which the Communists were blamed, chaos ruled the country. Not only had Indonesia almost gone bankrupt in financial and economic respects, but the country was also ind dire straits in social and religious respects. The conversion of many Communists to Christianity, whether or not on the initiative of Christians, to escape persecution and death, caused bad feelings among the Muslims. Besides, the latter reproached the Christians, who intensified their missionary activities since the abortive coup, with abuse of the poverty and ignorance of many illiterate Muslims, urging them to convert to Christianity by promising education, rice and various material goods (cf. Rasjidi 1976: 429ff.). Because of the increasing tensions between Muslims and Christians, the Indonesian people had the feeling of living on a volcano that could erupt at any moment. Suharto was fully alive to this explosive situation and realized that stability was a prerequisite for building up the nation under the New Order. Only after the establishment of stability in Indonesia could the development of the country in the social, economic, political and other fields be taken up. The continuous threat of confrontations between

Muslims and Christians, therefore, had to be put down: stability was also a must in the religious field. Indeed, religion had to be called in for the sake of the socio-economic construction of the country (Boland 1977: 12).

The period of 1965-1969 can be considered to be the stabilization phase of the New Order. Shortly after Suharto was named Acting President by the Provisional People's Consultative Assembly in March 1967 (Ricklefs 1988: 274f.), he took the initiative in getting the leaders of the various religious communities in Indonesia together to confer on the possibilities to ending the religious tensions by joint effort and thus to contribute to the stabilization of the country (cf. Ali 1970b: 42). This consultation, which took place on November 30, 1967, in Jakarta and was known as *Musjawarah Antar Agama*, the interreligious consultation, failed completely. The Muslims were convinced that this failure was due to the refusal of the Christians to accept the proposal which Suharto made in his speech at this meeting. His proposal was based on three pillars: 1. to refrain from any compulsion in religion; 2. to refrain from any missionary activity among people already adhering to a religion[4]; 3. to acquire an attitude of social tolerance in the field of religion. Muslims seemed to be inclined to accept Suharto's proposal for the sake of the stability of the nation, whereas the Christians thought it unacceptable, because they felt they were backing out of their missionary obligation (cf. Gazalba 1971: 15f.).

In spite of the failure of his efforts to stimulate the mutual cooperation of the religious communities in the country by inviting their religious leaders to start an interreligious dialogue and to contribute in that way to social stability, Suharto considered the national situation in 1969 as sufficiently opportune to change his policy focussed on stability to a policy focussed on development. This policy was laid down in *Pelita I*,[5] the First Five-Year plan, for the period 1969-1974, during which all efforts would be concentrated on development. The echo of these social and political developments is recognized in the study of comparative religion. Again, Mukti Ali can be taken as frame of reference. At that time he was not only one of the few academically trained Indonesian scholars of the study of comparative religion but, as Minister of Religious Affairs during the period 1971-1978, he also molded the religious form and content of the policy delineated by Suharto.

Although Mukti Ali's appointment as Minister of Religious Affairs was first of all a political affair which has to be understood in the political situation of that time, his approach as a scholar of comparative religion who stressed the meaning of interreligious dialogue also played an important role in his election to this position (Munhanif 1966: 102f.). Mukti Ali's work between 1965 and 1971 shows that he was meeting the expectations of Suharto and associates regarding the primary responsibility in the field of religious affairs in Indonesia. So, for example, Mukti Ali claims

---

[4] To be understood in the sense of one of the five officially recognized religions in Indonesia.

[5] An acronym for *Pembangunan Lima Tahun* (Five Years Development).

that human beings are religious by nature and the non-religious human being acts counter to his essence (Ali 1970a: 8). Thus, discussions about the existence or non-existence of God are irrelevant. The only relevant discussion is the question whether the god who is worshiped is the true God or a false one. The true God is the one worshiped in the monotheistic traditions. Non-monotheistic traditions detract from God's power and unity (Ali 1970a: 9ff.). This way of thinking fits perfectly with the insights of the New Order that had just dealt with Communism but still feared that it would again become popular and therefore made every effort to prevent it. The discipline of *Pancasila* actually requires one to adhere to a monotheistic religion. Apparently, the findings of the study of comparative religion corresponded to the policies of the New Order government.

Mukti Ali also proved able to apply his theoretical concept of *agree in disagreement* here. As Suharto's efforts failed to put an end to interreligious tensions by a consultation of the religious leaders of the various religious communities in the country, Mukti Ali succeeded in 1969 in bringing together several prominent representatives of various religious communities to carry on a mutual conversation in an unofficial way (Ali 1970b: 43). His basic assumption is that interreligious dialogue does not have to focus on theological issues but on the social-religious issues which are at the center of every religious community (cf. Dasuki 1993: 66). It is the study of comparative religion that supplies the knowledge and understanding of the social-religious issues of the various religious communities. Thus, the study of comparative religion is of primal importance for the interreligious dialogue which has to bring about the stability of society. Let it be noted in passing that Mukti Ali's application of the study of comparative religion differs greatly from the approach of the modernist Muhammadiyah movement of which he is a member. It is more characteristic of this movement to use the study of comparative religion in an apologetic way rather than stressing its meaning for the sake of interreligious dialogue, as Mukti Ali does. The proof of this statement is not only to be found in the already mentioned Hasbullah Bakry but also in the study of comparative religion during a training camp of the Muhammadiyah movement, the so-called Darul Arqam, in the first part of 1970 (see Peacock 1978: 83ff. and Munhanif 1996: 118).

A third theme appearing in Mukti Ali's work during the period 1965-1970 shows another aspect of why the study of comparative religion is believed to be a socially important discipline. Indonesian society was a society in the making. The harmonious coexistence of the various religious communities in the country was indispensable for smooth development. In other words, harmonious coexistence was a necessary condition for good development, whereas chaos was its worst obstacle. That is why Indonesians have to practise learning to live together. Coexistence is made possible by an attitude of mutual respect and tolerance. This attitude is acquired by the study of comparative religion with its concept of *agree in disagreement*, which not only uncovers the differences between the religions but above all reveals what religions have in common (Ali 1970a: 17, 23). The study of comparative religion thus contributes in an essential way to the development of the country.

The last mentioned aspect of the study of comparative religion fits perfectly well with the *Pelita I* program, the First Five-Year Plan (1969-1974), whose purpose was the economic development of the country and stimulated anything contributing to it. After Mukti Ali was installed as Minister of Religious Affairs on September 11, 1971, he turned first to the concept of development. In his view, development had to be a holistic and integral event to which the harmonious coexistence of the various religions in the country, his second area for special attention, could contribute in a significant manner (Damami 1993: 34). Acting on information received from the study of comparative religion Mukti Ali shows the potential power of religion. It motivates and stimulates human beings to do good works in all fields of life. Secondly, religion is creative, i.e., it prompts one not only to work productively but also to work creatively and innovatively. Thirdly, religion sanctifies human life as a whole. Finally, religion integrates. It brings both individual and collective activities into one integrated whole. Religion thus plays an essential and fundamental role in realizing a harmonious social life which is a precondition for every kind of development, including the economic one, in modern times (cf. Boland 1977: 11; Soeroyo, 101f., 105).

The fast economic development of Indonesia had far-reaching effects on social life. The social changes in the pluralistic Indonesian society resulted in "feelings of dislocation, disorientation and relative deprivation," to use the words of Nurcholish Madjid (Madjid 1994: 116), which, in turn, caused social tensions between the various religious communities. This implied that one not only had to look at the importance of religion regarding economic development but also to study seriously the role religion played in social change. A first impulse to this approach was given by Mukti Ali acting as Minister of Religious Affairs by establishing a research department called *Litbang* at his ministry (Steenbrink 1990: 159f.).[6]

After serving as minister Mukti Ali returned to academic life. Since then he stressed the importance of establishing research departments focused on studying the fundamental role religion plays in social developments (Ali 1987: 325). Mukti Ali tried to get research of religions and religious phenomena going by means of the application of the study of comparative religion at both the research departments and the IAINs. The staff of the department of comparative religion at the IAIN Sunan Kalijaga in Yogyakarta was encouraged by Mukti Ali to write survey books on several religions meant for the use of IAIN students. Unfortunately, only two surveys were published: one on Shintoism, the other on Judaism (Daya 1992: 192). Part of the staff of the just mentioned department of comparative religion was also invited to participate in writing a series of textbooks in the field of comparative religion. This series was begun on the initiative of the Ministry of Religious Affairs and was designed for

---

[6] *Litbang* is an acronym for *Penelitian dan Pengembangan* (Research and Development).

the education of IAIN students.[7] This series breathes the spirit of Mukti Ali: the Qur'an and Islam are the touchstones against which the phenomena studied by the comparative religion are to be tested.[8] Joachim Wach's *The Comparative Study of Religion* (1958) was introduced by Mukti Ali at the IAIN as a general introduction to this field.[9] The choice of Wach's book as set reading is understandable. Mukti Ali endorsed many of Wach's views in the field of the study of comparative religion, which he, in his own particular way, adjusted to the Indonesian circumstances. To mention only three examples: Wach's characterization of communism as a pseudo-religion actually implies a condemnation of this ideology, an opinion that is shared by Mukti Ali and fits quite well in the New Order policies (Wach 1958: 37). Secondly, Wach mentions as a fourth criterion of genuine religious experience that it "... issues in action. It involves an imperative; it is the most powerful source of motivation and action" (Wach 1958: 36), which corresponds perfectly with Mukti Ali's idea of the potential power of religion. A third point of contact between Wach and Mukti Ali is found in their stress on the meaning of religion regarding the encounter of God and human beings. This encounter forms the basis of the human encounter (Wach 1958: 31).

It is interesting, in addition to the institutional structures with which Mukti Ali tried to mold the study of comparative religion, to pay attention to the scientific content he gave to this discipline. Even after his term as minister the way Mukti Ali practised the study of comparative religion seemed closely linked to the opinions and policies of the Ministry of Religious Affairs. Thus, what was most striking now was his stress on the importance of the study of comparative religion for leaders of Islamic groups as well as policy makers and other representatives of the government. By means of the study of comparative religion all sides could avoid misunderstandings and mistakes connected with the religious sensitivities of the various Islamic groups in Indonesia. In a tense situation caused by the rapid social changes these misunderstandings and mistakes can easily degenerate into escalations—thus Mukti Ali stated in a public lecture on September 20, 1983 (Ali 1987: 324).

This new theme in the study of comparative religion in Indonesia cannot, in my opinion, be detached from the fact that it was the Muslims who, during the years of the New Order rule, felt increasingly underprivileged and discriminated by the government and started to give voice to their feelings. Their frustrations were not only vented on the adherents of other religions, but now both government and dissenting Muslims were severely criticized in speech, print and deed. Alamsyah Ratu Perwiranegara, successor to Mukti Ali as Minister of Religious Affairs during the years 1978-

---

[7] I know only of *Perbandingan Agama* (1981/1982).

[8] See, for example, chapter V of *Perbandingan Agama*, 213ff.

[9] Wach's book had already translated into Indonesian twice but in a very unsatisfactory way (Steenbrink 1990: 158, esp. 51).

1982, thus propagated a new policy, known as *Tri kerukunan*, threefold harmony. According to this new policy, harmony in Indonesian society was based on three pillars, viz.: 1. the pillar of internal harmony among various factions within a certain religion; 2. the pillar of harmony between the various religions; 3. the pillar of harmony between the various religions and the government (Dasuki 1993: 67; Hofsteede 1992: 126f.; Steenbrink 1993: 235). It is in the first and third pillar that a new theme was now introduced and stressed in the study of comparative religion.

After Alamsyah Ratu Perwiranegara, Munawir Syadzali held sway over the Ministry of Religious Affairs during the years 1982-1992. Contrary to his two predecessors, interreligious dialogue was less stressed in his policy. Actually, the pillar of internal harmony among various factions within a certain religion, the first pillar of his predecessor, was elaborated by Munawir Syadzali in his own particular way in that he fixed all his attention on the promotion of the development of the Islamic community in Indonesia (Steenbrink 1993: 238). If, in his view, the internal situation of the Islamic community would be ameliorated, the interreligious relations and the harmony between the Islamic community and the government would improve automatically. This was the best way to stimulate the national development of Indonesia. In this approach the study of comparative religion can play an important role, according to Tarmizi Taher, at that time one of the senior officials at the Ministry of Religious Affairs, who succeeded Munawir Syadzali as Minister of Religious Affairs in 1992. He articulated the contribution expected from the study of comparative religion for the purpose of national development. The study of comparative religion would broaden the perception of the Indonesian people. It should help to prevent abuse of religion by subversive elements. The study of comparative religion should be focussed on those religious topics that can contribute to found a spiritual, ethical and moral basis on which national development rests (Taher 1990: 95).

At the time that Munawir Syadzali was Minister of Religious Affairs, Mukti Ali was asked in 1988, in celebration of his retirement as a professor of the study of comparative religion and on the occasion of twenty-five years study of comparative religion at the IAIN, to publish a book on the various aspects of this discipline in Indonesia (Ali 1988: VII). In this publication Mukti Ali takes up his favorite, well-known topics. Sometimes he attempts to give life to old issues. Now, for example, he clearly states that dialogue is to be the aim of the study of comparative religion. By promoting dialogue the study of comparative religion contributes to a safe and peaceful world in which the various religious communities live together in harmony (Ali 1988: 67ff.). Students and scholars of the study of comparative religion know that their intellectual and spiritual horizon is enlarged by this discipline, by which they can help to deepen the dimensions of life and culture for the benefit of the community (Ali 1988: 59). Two years later Mukti Ali expressed his opinions even more strongly: the aim of the study of comparative religion is to contribute to the realization of a moral and ethical world (Ali 1990a: 11 and 1990b: 299). Religions, and, thus also, the study of comparative religion, have to serve as a basis for the unity and the peace of humanity (Ali 1994: 10).

These aims of the study of comparative religion, as put into words by Mukti Ali, made him introduce, in addition to his concept of *agree in disagreement*, the concept of *scientific-cum-doctrinaire* in the study of comparative religion as the right method of this discipline. He calls his concept of *scientific-cum-doctrinaire* a synthetic method in which a scientific approach is linked to a particular religious-dogmatic approach (Ali 1988: 64 and 1990b: 299). However, he neither explains how his method works nor elaborates on its application in practice. The only thing he clarifies is that, according to him, the central position of methodology in the study of comparative religion is a product typical of Western culture. In a country like Indonesia it does not make any sense to put too much stress on methodology (Ali 1988: 57). Although Mukti Ali's concept of *scientific-cum-doctrinaire* was immediately accepted by his epigones as very valuable, they still struggled with the question how to evaluate the content of this concept in the right way (Wasim 1989a: 27 and 1989b: 20).

Closely linked to the concept of *scientific-cum-doctrinaire* is Mukti Ali's outspoken opinion that the study of comparative religion should not be science for the sake of science only. He severely criticizes scholars like R.J. Zwi Werblowsky for their search for 'absolute' objectivity. Mukti Ali sides with students of comparative religion like Joachim Wach and Friedrich Heiler who, by means of the study of comparative religion, aimed at the realization of a harmonious co-existence of all religious communities on earth. They were prepared, for the benefit of this goal, to abandon the ideal of 'absolute' objectivity for one of 'relative' objectivity (Ali 1988: 69f. and 1990: 11; cf. Wach, 8). In his publications of this period Mukti Ali claims that the discipline of comparative religion is to be studied for the sake of the *'ibada*, the worship of God (Ali 1988: 72, 1990a: 11 and 1990b: 299). It is interesting to see Mukti Ali connecting the study of comparative religion and the *'ibadat*, the acts of devotions or religious observances, which are the first part of the Islamic Law. First of all the acts of devotions are meant to regulate the relation of the Muslim believer and God. However, the acts of devotions not only address the relation of human beings to God but also enhance the group solidarity the Muslims experience within the *umma*, the Islamic community.

The new approaches and emphases of Mukti Ali in his study of comparative religion show some remarkable correspondences with the views of Munawir Syadzali and his senior official Taher Tarmizi, who gave the Indonesian Islamic community a central position in their policies. The internal development of this community had to be promoted by the removal of the chasm between the various factions within it. Simultaneously, this community had to be founded on a spiritual, ethical and moral base in the benefit of the national development. The study of comparative religion as designed and advocated by Mukti Ali seems to offer the government an outstanding tool in favor of its policies.

Conclusion

By way of conclusion it can be stated that the study of comparative religion in Indonesia can not be detached from the figure of Mukti Ali. From the very beginning he emphasized the social relevance of this discipline as far more important than scientific purity and a well-founded methodology. He based his approach to the study of comparative religion on the way scholars like Joachim Wach, Friedrich Heiler and Wilfred Cantwell Smith studied this discipline. They assigned the study of comparative religion a role of vital importance in stimulating interreligious dialogue and in promoting a harmonious coexistence of humankind. However, the way Mukti Ali adapted the approaches of Wach, Heiler and Smith to the Indonesian situation shows striking similarities with the views of the government and seems to run parallel to its official policies. For the time being, this symbiotic relation will not very likely be ended in the near future.

Bibliography

Abdurrahman *et al.* (eds.). (1993). *Agama dan Masyarakat: 70 Tahun H.A. Mukti Ali.* Yogyakarta: IAIN Sunan Kalijaga Press.
Ali, A. Mukti. (1970a). *Kulijah Agama Islam di Sekolah Staf dan Komando Angkatan Udara Lembang.* Yogjakarta.
———. (1970b). *Dialoog antar Agama.* Yogjakarta.
———. (1975). *Ilmu Perbandingan Agama.* 4th ed. Yogyakarta.
———. (1987). *Beberapa Persoalan Agama Dewasa Ini.* Jakarta.
———. (1988). *Ilmu Perbandingan Agama di Indonesia.* Yogyakarta: IAIN Sunan Kalijaga Press.
———. (1990a). "Ilmu Perbandingan Agama di Indonesia." In: *Ilmu Perbandingan Agama di Indonesia. (Beberapa Permasalahan).* Jakarta. Pp.3-11.
———. (1990b). "Ilmu Perbandingan Agama dan Kerukunan Hidup Antar Umat Beragama." In: *70 Tahun Dr. T.B. Simatupang: Saya adalah orang yang berhutang.* Jakarta. Pp.275-99.
———. (1994). "Religion, Morality and Contemporary Development." In: Burhanuddin Daya and M. Rifa'i Abduh. (eds.). *Religion and Contemporary Development.* Jakarta: Department of Religious Affairs. Pp.3-15.
Ali-Fauzi, Nasrullah. (1995). "Abdul Mukti Ali." *Ulumul Qur'an* 6: 30-31.
Bakker, D. (1970). "Da'wah. Missionaire mobilisatie van de Islam in Indonesië." *De Heerbaan: Tijdschrift voor zendingswetenschap* 23: 226-47.
Bakry, Hasbullah. (1958). *Perbandingan Agama. Jahudi. Nasrani: Bal, Ahmadijah, Animisme.* Yogjakarta.
———. (1959). *Nabi Isa dalam Al Qur'an dan Nabi Muhammad dalam Bybel.* Solo: Ab Sitti Sjamsijah.
———. (1984). *Pandangan Islam tentang Kristen di Indonesia.* Jakarta: Akademika Pressindo.
Boland, Bernard Johan. (1971). *The Struggle of Islam in Modern Indonesia.* The Hague: Nijhoff.
———. (1977). *Godsdienstpolitiek in de Indonesische Republiek.* Leiden: Universitaire Press.
Damami, M. *et al.* (1993). "H.A. Mukti Ali: Ketaatan, Kesalehan dan Kecendekiaan." In: Abdurrahman and Burhanuddin Daya (eds.). *Agama dan Masyarakat: 70 Tahun H.A. Mukti Ali.* Yogyakarta: IAIN Sunan Kalijaga Press. Pp.3-45.

Dasuki, Hafizh. (1993). "Prof. Dr. H.A. Mukti Ali: seorang dosen yang intelek-ulama." In: Abdurrahman and Burhanuddin Daya (eds.). *Agama dan Masyarakat: 70 Tahun H.A. Mukti Ali*. Yogyakarta: IAIN Sunan Kalijaga Press. Pp.61-68.

Daya, Burhanuddin. (1992). "Kuliah Ilmu Perbandingan Agama pada Institut Agama Islam Negeri (IAIN)." In: Burhanuddin Daya and H.L. Beck (eds.). *Ilmu Perbandingan Agama di Indonesia dan Belanda*. Jakarta: INIS. Pp.181-97.

────── and M. Rifa'i Abduh. (1994). *Religion and Contemporary Development*. Jakarta: Department of Religious Affairs.

────── and H.L. Beck (eds.). (1992). *Ilmu Perbandingan Agama di Indonesia dan Belanda*. Jakarta: INIS.

Gazalba, Sidi. (1971). *Dialog antara Propagandis Kristen dan Logika*. Jakarta: Bulan Bintang.

Hofsteede, William C. (1992). "Muslim Initiatives for Harmonious Interreligious Relations in Indonesia." *Studies in Interreligious Dialogue* 2: 123-35.

Ludjito, A. (1990). "Bapak Ilmu Perbandingan Agama di Indonesia." In: *Ilmu Perbandingan Agama di Indonesia (Beberapa Permasalahan)*. Jakarta. Pp.13-17.

Madjid, Nurcholish. (1994). "Islamic Da'wah in Indonesia: the Challenge of Post-Colonialism and of the Social Change in a Plural Society," In: Burhanuddin Daya and M. Rifa'i Abduh. (eds.). *Religion and Contemporary Development*. Jakarta: Department of Religious Affairs. Pp.109-22.

Munawar-Rahman, Budhy. (1993). "Dialog Iman dan Hubungan Agama-Agama." *Ulumul Qur'an* 4: 90-92.

Munhanif, Ali. (1996). "Islam and the Struggle for Religious Pluralism in Indonesia; a Political Reading of the Religious Thought of Mukti Ali." *Studia Islamika: Indonesian Journal for Islamic Studies* 3: 79-126.

Peacock, James L. (1978). *Purifying the Faith: The Muhammadijah Movement in Indonesian Islam*. Menlo Park, California: Benjamin/Cummings Publishing.

Perbandingan Agama. (1981). *Perbandingan Agama*. Proyek Pembinaan Perguruan Tinggi Agama/IAIN di Jakarta. Direktorat Pembinaan Perguruan Tinggi Agama Islam.

Rasjidi, Muhammad. (1976). "The Role of Christian Missions in the Indonesian Experience." *International Review of Mission* 65: 427-38.

Riberu, J. (1992). "Studi Ilmu Perbandingan Agama di Perguruan Tinggi Kristen Katolik." In: Burhanuddin Daya and H.L. Beck (eds.). *Ilmu Perbandingan Agama di Indonesia dan Belanda*. Jakarta: INIS. Jakarta. Pp.165-72.

Ricklefs, M.C. (1988). *A History of Modern Indonesia Circa 1300 to the Present*. Rpt. London: Macmillan.

Soeroyo. (1993). "H.A. Mukti Ali dan pembaharuan pemikiran Islam di Indonesia." In: Abdurrahman and Daya. *Agama dan Masyarakat: 70 Tahun H.A. Mukti Ali*. Yogyakarta. Pp.95-111.

Steenbrink, Karel A. (1990). "The Study of Comparative Religion by Indonesian Muslims." *Numen* 37: 141-67.

──────. (1993). "Indonesian Politics and a Muslim Theology of Religions: 1965 - 1990." *Islam and Christian-Muslim Relations* 4: 223-46.

Taher, Tarmizi. (1990). "Keimanan dan keamanan." In: *Ilmu Perbandingan Agama di Indonesia (Beberapa Permasalahan)*. Jakarta. Pp.71-95.

Tobroni and Arifin, Syamsul. (1994). *Islam, Pluralisme, Budaya dan Politik: Refleksi Teologi untuk Aksi dalam Keberagamaan dan Pendidikan*. Yogyakarta: Sipress.

Wach, Joachim. (1958). *The Comparative Study of Religions*. Edited with an Introduction by Joseph M. Kitagwa. New York/London: Columbia University Press.
Wasim, Alef Theria. (1989a). "Masih lagi: Bagaimana Mendekati Agama?" *Al-Jami'ah: Majalah Ilmu Pengetahuan Agama Islam* 38: 26-38.
———. (1989b). "Prospek Pengembangan Ilmu Perbandingan Agama di IAIN." *Al-Jami'ah: Majalah Ilmu Pengetahuan Agama Islam* 39: 14-21.
Wawer, Wendelin, (1974). *Muslime und Christen in der Republik Indonesia*. Wiesbaden: Steiner.
———. (1975). "Relations of Muslims with other Religious Groups." In: Dietmar Rothermund (ed.). *Islam in Southern Asia: A Survey of Current Research*. Wiesbaden: Steiner. Pp.95-97.

Religious Reconciliation as a Challenge of Governance

India at the Start of the Twenty-First Century

Chakravarti Ram-Prasad

This paper is divided into three parts. In the first part I want to raise some fundamental questions about the role of religion in reconciliation with respect to its most problematic aspect, i.e., when the conflict is itself religious. (But this will also raise the question of what religion can do when the conflict is not religious.) In the second part I will give a brief summary of the nature of social strife in contemporary India, in particular, its religious dimension and the political situation at the turn of the century. In the third I will look at how that political situation, presented in terms of religious conflict, poses challenges to the state's role in managing conflict that involves religion. I will end with a suggestion about how management of religious conflict through the governance of the state has implications for the general contentions made in the first part of the paper about religious reconciliation.

'Religion' and the Varieties of Religious Conflict and Reconciliation: Problems and Potential

The understanding of religion itself is arguably the first issue to be addressed here. Suppose we define 'religion' as follows:

> Religion is a body of doctrine whose main focus and concern is some state that transcends the features of the current life of the one who adheres to those doctrines, where the doctrines describe and prescribe conduct and beliefs in the life appropriate to the attainment of that transcendent state.

The realization of conduct and beliefs will usually occur in a larger context, which we might characterize as 'cultural'. It would then be more difficult to isolate elements of contemporary conflict as primarily religious. In the strict sense of 'religion' above, conflict is religious only if the primary disagreement is over issues of transcendent concern, although, of course, cultural consequences will almost invariably follow (as a result of the implication of religion in wider culture). In that case it would seem that few contemporary conflicts are primarily religious in the strict sense.

Instead, 'religious' conflicts now tend to be religious in a secondary sense: the conflict itself is primarily about material issues of power, institutions, economic wherewithal, political conditions of agency, etc.—in short, about the sustenance of group identities. If the historical determinant of such identity is membership of a religion, then, while the conflict is conventionally 'religious', it is not so in the strict sense. Is the Middle East situation primarily about what constitutes the sacred (e.g., the status of prophets or the possibility of incarnated divinity)? Let us turn then to a wider or looser understanding of 'religion':

> Religion is a collection of referents that people use to identify their membership of a community, where those referents, while containing symbols of transcendence, more generally pertain to an entire range of beliefs, practices, codes and assumptions that help in the identification of membership.

Having made this conceptual point, I will acknowledge the power of conventional usage and proceed to speak of 'religion' and 'conflict' in the wider, cultural sense of group identities articulated through membership in religions.

Even then, the hard question about the role of religion in reconciliation must be preceded by settling whether the conflict is itself 'religious' (in the wider sense) or not. I will now present a taxonomy of the roles of religion in conflict and reconciliation.

1) The conflict is between two religious groups and reconciliation is undertaken by them.

Here it is essential that the claim should not be that one's own religion offers unique resources to resolve the conflict because its teachings provide motivation and strategies for reconciliation. Since the conflict is precisely between different religious traditions, such a claim will simply become another point of conflict, for its implication is a hegemonistic one. It will simply lead to a counterclaim and so it will go on *ad infinitum*. Unfortunately, many claims for the role of religion in reconciliation are of this type, for they express a belief—leading to further antagonism—in the special ability of one's religion to help. Instead, two more promising strategies can be developed.

(i) Mutuality of resources: There can be the attempt to find teachings and directions in both religions that provide a common resource. Then claims for motivation and strategies will proceed from a mutually acceptable nexus: a value that is both Christian and Hindu or Islamic and Jewish. However, it is a moot question in this case as to why religious conflict arises in the first place if there is mutuality of religious resources.

(ii) Introspective clarification: There can be the attempt to direct the resources of one's religion upon oneself and one's coreligionists, without claim to generality. The aim will be to find motivation and strategies for oneself within one's group, so that one can approach the other with the best of intentions but with no implicit assumption of moral hegemony.

2) The conflict is non-religious but between different religious groups and reconciliation is attempted by themselves through religion.

It might be conceivable that, while the conflict is itself not religious, the conflicting groups might take recourse in their own different religions. The worst case scenario is that the conflict then assumes the nature of the situation in type 1, as religious elements are assimilated into the conflict. The most effective use of religion would be as in strategy (ii) of type 1 for introspective clarification.

3) The conflict is between two religious groups and mediation is undertaken by a third party.
I take it as relatively obvious that mediation by a third party is unlikely to be from a religious perspective, since neither of the conflicting parties is likely to want another religion involved, as that would imply that that third religion possessed resources they themselves did not. So, even if the third party were religious, the mediation for reconciliation would have to be religiously neutral, although a religious base for that mediation might convince the conflicting groups about the awareness of religious sensibilities on the part of the third party.

In contrast, if the mediating party were not religious, there might not be any worry about implicit religious claims, but there might be uncertainty about the sensibilities of the third party. It might be thought by the conflicting groups that sympathy for the religious dimension of the conflict was absent in a non-religious mediating party.

4) The conflict is non-religious, but mediation occurs through a religious third party.
In an important sense progress can be made here, provided (i) the conflicting parties agree to the neutrality of mediating party and (ii) they themselves do not object to the importation of religious motivation into the mediating process.

5) The conflict is within a single religious group.
Here, regardless of whether or not the conflict is itself religious, there may be scope for using religion for introspective clarification, so that the shared values of the community are foregrounded in a manner that aids reconciliation. Clearly, the potential of religious processes of reconciliation is at its best in such situations.

The real difficulty with the issue of religious reconciliation is that often the situation is of type 1 (and occasionally 2), whereas the greater scope for religion seems to lie in situations of types 3, 4 and 5 (always granted that it has been established that religion has a chance of affecting any type of reconciliation). Let us now look at the Indian situation, and then consider how the role of state governance might be thought to be imperative in that situation.

The Indian Scene: Religion and Conflict

The subcontinent is home, original or not, to a variety of religions. A range of traditions, the majority (but not all) acknowledging the formal (but only occasionally literal) authority of the Vedic texts, have come to be called 'Hinduism' and together are seen as the largest religion in the state of India. Whether or not there has been or even is an identifiable commonality to 'Hinduism' is a matter of interpretation and dispute. There are also the religions of Jainism, Buddhism and (much later), Sikhism, which were born through particular founders (or a succession of founders) on the subcontinent. Islam was introduced between the eighth and twelfth centuries through both trade and invading armies and subsequently through internal acceptance amongst various groups. By the nineteenth century Islam was the religion (in a range of subtraditions) of nearly a quarter of the subcontinental population. It is the overwhelming religion of the countries of Pakistan and Bangladesh on the subcontinent. It is the religion of about 12-14% of the population of India. Christianity, while having ancient roots, arrived as a major force only in the sixteenth century and now (in various denominations) is the religion of about 3% of the population of India.

There is enough historical evidence to show that there were conflicts involving religion in pre-Islamic India: between Jainism, Buddhism and various strands of Hinduism, and within 'Hinduism' in the sense of conflict between 'sects' or particular strands. In the main, however, religious conflicts were not between political entities like kingdoms. They tended to be state oppression of religious groups, usually unleashed by kings of one persuasion against subjects of another. More rarely, there must have been violence, beyond intellectual disputes, between groups within state formations, as seems likely from the antagonistic tone of surviving religio-social texts.

That past, however, is not directly implicated in the present. The justifications for religion-based conflicts arise from certain readings of the history of the subcontinent after the coming of Islam. In those readings the history of the last thousand years is one of civilizational conflict, between an alien religion and a coherent (if not quite unified) native tradition. To the extent that the interpretation of history is at once the motivation and the justification for conflict, a proper sifting of the historical evidence—focussing especially on the complex, mutually enriching and organically synthesized relationship between Hindu traditions and Islam—becomes an intellectual necessity.

Unfortunately, the development of a modern notion of identity in the nineteenth and twentieth centuries both generated and required simplification of collective memory. It generated simplification through the Indian appropriation of Western Indological categories of religion, culture and politics; it required simplification for the mobilization of a coherent political ideology in response to Western imperial domination. In Islam, the development of a modern identity occurred through a selective amnesia about a common subcontinental culture and a vehement creation of a textually fundamentalized political commonality—and resulted in the campaign for the Islamic state of Pakistan. Within Hinduism, it led to two strategies. The one that became politically dominant at Independence sought to read Hinduism religiously in terms of a possible personal spirituality and culturally in terms of an open space of tolerance within a larger, common, multicultural realm. The other read Hinduism much more sharply, developing a notion of Hindu identity that depended on a pathologized history of conflict and dominance; it, too, had amnesia regarding a common culture.

The former view of Hinduism, among other things, led to the creation of constitutional Indian secularism: the idea that the state was neutral toward the different religions of the polity, while responsible for the protection of all—including religious—minorities. The birth of India and Pakistan through the trauma of Partition problematized the role of religion-based identity from the very beginning: if being Muslim was to be Pakistani, what about being Indian? Could a Muslim be an Indian? The secular dispensation sought, intellectually, to make that question irrelevant.

The history of independent India, however, is a story of social tensions, economic misjudgment and the search for political stability. But these challenges were not and are not religious: social divisions through caste-based conflict, voting and entitlements, economic uncertainty over denying and then attempting to manage globalization and political problems concerning balancing a diverse federal polity in the midst of illiteracy and poverty. These were the challenges that tested the nation-state.

It is out of this nexus that conflict based apparently on religion emerged and Indians have always been attuned to this fact, calling the conflict 'communal'—focussing on socio-political issues—rather than 'religious'. The distinct ideological problematization of communal conflict came through the emergence of a political movement premised on the second idea of Hindu identity described above.

The ideal of Indian secularism, it was argued, neither did justice to the distinct cultural significance of Hinduism nor (more diffusely) recognized the value and influence of religion in Indian public life. The practice of Indian secularism, it was further argued, had been rendered inconsistent through a contrary commitment to minorities that led not to neutrality but to reverse discrimination. This combination of arguments, expressed emotively through a simplified rhetoric of trust betrayed, identity denied and loyalties split amongst Muslims (and other 'religious' minorities) led to the mobilization of certain sections of Hindu society. Amongst those sections, local pressures on access to resources and a resultant sense of economic and political disenfranchisement led to discontent and could readily be parlayed into vote-catching by political parties committed to a 'Hindu' nationalism.

This support could only be garnered by allowing for the psychologically valuable, immediate expression of discontent and the violence that resulted through targeting of Muslims was there for the world to see. Adding to the perception of threat (beyond the transnational loyalties of undeserving Muslims) was the presence of Christians, whose very membership of that religion was seen as a denial of native Hindu culture, since that membership was alleged to be emblematic of a hostile West. So, Christians could also be considered targets.

Such support, however, was not enough for the attainment of political power (which, in India, is without question the attainment of a parliamentary majority). So the political groups concerned with this Hindu-based mobilization sought to do two other things. First, they appealed to the globalized sections of society, which were concerned with economic efficiency in the governance of a liberalizing economy. But for this they needed to reconstitute their appeal at a more non-communal level, emphasizing instead a diffuse nationalism that effectively neutered the bite of their 'religious' appeal. Second, they had to form elaborate alliances with regional and subnational parties with whom they could agree on a common program—which predictably excluded all commitments to any ideology drawing on their favored reading of Hinduism. This multiple strategy was successful and, within a National Democratic Alliance, led the Hindu nationalist Bharatiya Janata Party (BJP) to a governing majority.

It is this situation in which India finds itself at the start of the twenty-first century. And it is in the experience of the constraints and operational possibilities facing this apparently 'religious' power in government that we find some indications towards the management of religious conflict.

Governance of Religious Conflict: The Lessons of Hinduism in India?

It should be obvious, even in this brief account, that Hindu nationalism is hardly a religious nationalism, drawing as it does primarily on political identity, historical interpretations and contemporary resentments. Even the focus of a major tactical controversy, the sixteenth-century mosque at Ayodhya, which was claimed to have been built on a Hindu temple supposed to be the birthplace of the divine Hindu king Rama, was primarily political. Mobilization occurred through appeal to the thought that Muslims had destroyed places significant in Hindu culture. This non-religious reading is supported by the further claim, made by many Hindu nationalist ideologues, that Rama is important as the political exemplar of the ideal 'Indian' ruler and not as a Hindu divinity. But let us now use the wider or looser definition of religion and see communal conflict in India as being religious.

The particular worry, above and beyond any violence that may occur in India, is that there is in government a party whose success had roots in a mobilization based on a pathologizing religious plurality. What are the implications for the management of religious conflict if the instruments of state are in the hands of one of the parties to the conflict? In particular, what happens when that state is neither *de jure* nor *de facto* a religious one?

The extraordinarily rational answer is that, if the state in which this happens is a sufficiently pluralistic democracy, then internal constraints on the management and retention of power work to restrain the scope of religious considerations in governance drastically. This is not an unqualified statement. In particular, it does not imply that conflict arising out of religious identities is easily removed from the polity. Nevertheless, the experience of India at the turn of this century does invite certain judgments about the role of religion in the management of conflict.

What has happened is that the BJP, the dominant party in government, although in a complex and constraining coalition, has found itself not only unable or even unwilling to implement policies arising from religiously-driven ideology but has actually had to adopt policies that are premised on pragmatic values that leave no space for such ideology. The original claim of the BJP and its allies was that, if it came to power, it would treat the unrest of India as a matter of religious difference, in which Muslims and Christians threatened to undermine the integrity of the nation state. In power, a Hindu nationalist government would reinterpret the political space of India—through constitutional amendments if necessary—so that the threats based on difference would be removed through a homogenization of society by native Hindu values (whatever they were).

In power, however, the challenges posed to governance—put simply as (i) managing economic expectations through social development and negotiation of global liberalization and (ii) securing geostrategic stability for the larger sake of achieving (i)—required stepping outside the conceptual boundaries of religious ideology. Dealings in bilateral and multilateral economic and political bodies, with international corporations and national governments, sound economic management and, most immediately, treating the religion-related strategic issue of Kashmir all require suspension of ideology. Securing fair terms, good deals, mutual confidence, these are conflict-resolution aims, but only when religion is either irrelevant or implicated in the conflict. So the BJP-in-government cannot work straightforwardly with the sort of autarky demanded by anti-globalization Hindu nationalists. More pressingly, it cannot represent itself with religionist credentials when it must govern: when Christians are targeted by militant groups who care not for parliamentary power and governance, the BJP-in-government has to respond to it as a law and order problem. When militancy in Kashmir requires new tactics, it must declare unconditional cease-fire as a way of reaching out to potentially amenable (Muslim) groups in Kashmir and winning international diplomatic support. And so it goes on.

This places the governing part of Hindu nationalism in direct opposition to its own non-governing parts: ideologues and grassroots workers within the party, as well as the various related organizations, such as the RSS and the VHP. These people and groups are driven by religious motives; they focus on outcomes uncontaminated by concerns of governance; they would lack any reason to exist if they quitted their religious ideological grounds. Conflict for them exists because of the very fact of religious difference. Doctrinal assertion of groups they oppose—Christian commitment to conversion and Islamic ideals of transnationality are candidates—become reasons for continued conflict.

It is not useful to ask what motivates individual people within the large National Democratic Alliance government to pursue policies that are either neutral to or inimical towards the sort of religion-driven ideology that they or their colleagues once espoused. What does matter is that governance in a pluralist democracy more or less imposes certain restraints which can only occasionally be removed. (This is also to remember that certain policies, while associated with Hindu nationalism—e.g. the decision to conduct nuclear tests, which was almost taken by a series of non-BJP Indian prime ministers over twenty years—were not necessarily alien to India's 'secular' political establishment.) In the case of communal conflict in India, however much many figures in the Indian government might have been implicated in the course of oppositional political mobilization, managing such conflict (for reasons of governance) becomes the overriding imperative for one in power. The most rational response to managing religious conflict seems to be for the managing agent (the state) to treat it as the larger issue of securing peace. From the Indian experience, if this is at all possible, it is only remotely so—and strategically achievable—and then only through a studied neutrality to religious conflict. Where the state colludes in conflict, and this does happen frequently in India, it represents a failure of governance and conflict-management that threatens the government that so colludes. If for no other reason than electoral success, there is sufficient inducement to view governance as a religion-neutral matter.

The powerful lesson to be drawn is that, even if an agent involved in religion becomes a mediating party to religious conflict, its hopes of success lie in evacuating its instrumentality of all religious sensibility. This goes back to the general contention made in part I of this paper: the role of religion in conflict resolution should be viewed with great caution and attempts to involve religion must be treated with circumspection. If anything, rational expectations for success seem to dictate, on the contrary, that mediation in the resolution of religious conflict is most effective when pursued deliberately apart from religious motivation.

Bibliography

Andersen, W.K. S.D. Damle. (1987). *The Brotherhood in Saffron: The Rashtriya Swayamsevak Sangh and Hindu Revivalism.* London: Westview Press.

Appleby, R.S. (2000). *The Ambivalence of the Sacred: Religion, Violence, and Reconciliation.* Oxford: Rowman & Littlefield Publishers.

Boraine, A. et al. (eds.). (1994). *Dealing with the Past: Truth and Reconciliation in South Africa.* Cape Town: Institute for Democracy in South Africa.

Hart, T.A. (ed.). (1989). *Christ in our Place: The Humanity of God in Christ for the Reconciliation of the World. Essays Presented to Professor James Torrance.* Exeter: Paternoster.

Jaffrelot, C. (1996). *Hindu Nationalist Movement in India.* New York: Columbia University Press.

Madan, T.N. (1997). *Modern Myths, Locked Minds: Secularism and Fundamentalism in India.* Delhi: Oxford University Press.

Ram-Prasad, C. (Forthcoming). "Being Hindu and/or Governing India? Religion, Social Change and the State." In: G. ter Haar (ed.). *Fundamentalism and Social Change.*

Islam and Muslims in India

Problems of Identity and Existence

Ashgar Ali Engineer

Introduction

Islam entered India almost immediately during the lifetime of the Prophet Muhammad. It is generally thought that it came into India via the invasion by Muhammad bin Qasim, a young general sent by Yusuf bin Hajjaj, the governor of Iraq during the Umayyad period in the later part of the seventh century A.D. But this is not true. Islam entered India peacefully, through Kerala on the west coast via Arab traders. The region called Malabar in Kerala is an Indianized form of *ma'bar*, which in Arabic means 'passage'. Since the Arab traders passed through that region often it came to be known by that name. The Arabs had, in fact, been trading since pre-Islamic days and then embraced Islam after the Prophet began preaching. They married the local women in Kerala and their offspring spread to different parts of that region. They were later also accompanied by Sufi saints who converted many local people to Islam, mainly from the lower classes. This was therefore the real entry point of Islam into India.

However, as far as northern India was concerned, Islam did enter India through Muhammad bin Qasim's invasion and this has become the sore point in relations between Hindus and Muslims. Qasim's invasion was followed by many others, including those of Shihabuddin Ghauri and Mahmud Ghaznavi. The latter demolished the temple of Somnath, an act that continues to rankle in the memory of upper caste Hindus. This is promoted with prominence in history textbooks, perpetuating the bitter memory of hostility and animosity. Such events are not described in their proper context and are ascribed to Islam's 'hatred of Hindus and Hinduism'. However, such hostile projections are the product of the colonial period from the nineteenth century onward. It is not true that the Muslim rulers simply hated the Hindus and humiliated them throughout their rule. This is a later construction. The Hindu and Muslim rulers had mutual alliances as well as hostilities depending on struggle for power.

In fact, many Hindu rulers had invited the Muslim invaders, including Babar, in order to settle scores with local rulers. Muslim dynasties also fought against one another. When Babar, the first Mughal ruler, invaded India, Ibrahim Lodhi ruled India and Babar was invited into India by the Rajput rulers who were unable to defeat the Lodhi dynasty on their own. Babar is, however, still portrayed in contemporary school textbooks as an invader and strongly condemned for his invasion of India. These constructions and reconstructions of medieval history are made to cater to contemporary political needs. The period between the tenth and the early nineteenth century is often described in these textbooks as the 'Muslim period' and the period prior to that as the 'Hindu period'. Historians maintain that these periods cannot be described in terms of the religious denomination of the ruler as there were serious differences, hostilities and conflicts between rulers who adhered to the same religion. Muslims fought against Muslims and Hindu rulers against Hindu rulers.

It is important to note that neither the Muslim nor Hindu community was homogeneous. Both the communities were highly stratified horizontally as well as vertically. Medieval societies were hierarchical along caste and class lines and the lower rungs of the community did not exactly harmonize with the upper. The upper caste and upper-class Muslims even hated their coreligionists in the lower castes and classes. There was greater harmony between Hindus and Muslims of the lower castes than between lower and upper castes of the same community. Common customs and traditions and mutual influences among these lower castes and classes amply demonstrate this. However, that fact is ignored entirely in the contemporary history books, especially on school levels. These history textbooks have become the breeding ground of communalism and communal hatred between these two communities.

The British rulers initiated this kind of writing of history in order to divide their subjects so that they could rule without serious challenge to their colonial power. They also deliberately or innocently homogenized the two communities by ignoring all differences and treating them as if their interests were uniform. The Indian National Congress, which was an umbrella organization of freedom fighters, wisely adopted the political philosophy of secularism as its foundational philosophy. This organization helped bring the elite of two communities together to fight for freedom. When Mahatma Gandhi appeared, he involved the masses in the freedom movement by championing their causes. He also tried to bring Hindus and Muslims together by taking up religious issues like the Khilafat issue after the First World War, when the British sought to dismember the Turkish empire. The Muslims responded enthusiastically to Gandhiji's call and even the traditional *'ulama* fraternized with him on the issue and supported the Indian National Congress and its concept of secular composite nationalism.

However, soon after the Khilafat movement, serious differences developed between a section of Hindus and Muslims, centered on the power-sharing formula. The Motilal Nehru Committee was appointed to solve the 'communal question', but both Hindu and Muslim communalist leaders opposed its recommendations vehemently and the report consequently drew a blank. Three round-table conferences in the early 1930s also failed to work out any satisfactory formula to resolve the question of power sharing between the two communities. The last attempt to build a political alliance between the Congress and the Muslim League in 1937 also came to naught. After the elections the Congress refused to accept two ministers nominated by the League into its cabinet on the grounds that the League had failed to win a majority of Muslim seats. Muhammad Ali Jinnah, who later became the founder of Pakistan, was furious and vowed to teach the Congress a lesson. He propounded the two-nation theory and sowed the seed of the partition of the country. Partition—justified or not—became the cause of animosity between the two communities in India. The upper caste Hindus never forgave Muslims for this.

It would also be wrong to blame all Muslims for the partition of the country. Indian Muslims were divided on the issue. The lower caste Muslims saw no benefit for themselves in the creation of a 'new homeland' as it would benefit only upper-class Muslims. In fact, a section of lower caste Muslims represented by three Mu'min Conferences demonstrated against the two-nation theory propounded by Jinnah on the March 23, 1940, in Lahore. The Muslim *'Ulama* vehemently opposed it as well and declared their support for the composite nationalism of the Congress and also justified it on religious grounds. This shows clearly that all Muslims were not unanimous on the question of two-nation theory and that the theory was not based on Islam but on the political needs of the Muslim elite. Maulana Husain Ahmad Madani, a prominent theologian and rector of the Darul 'Ulum, Deoband, an important Islamic seminary in India, was in the forefront of the opposition to the two-nation theory and even wrote a book *Muttahida Qawmiyat aur Islam* ('Composite Nationalism and Islam') to refute it. He also undertook a whirlwind tour of India to appeal to Muslims not to be misled by Jinnah and his two-nation theory. This is clear proof of the fact that a section of Muslims strongly opposed the creation of Pakistan. But it is a strange irony of politics that the Indian Muslims as a whole are viewed as guilty of dividing the country and are paying the price for it.

Partition

Partition resulted in human massacres on both the sides of the divide. More than a million people were killed and many more were displaced and cut off from their roots. The ruling classes in Pakistan consisted mainly of the feudal lords, military and bureaucracy and never shared power with the masses. Its Islamic foundation also proved quite fragile and fell apart in 1971 when the Bengali Muslims seceded from Pakistan and formed Bangladesh. The Pakistani ruling elite, led by Z.A. Bhutto, refused to share power with the Bengali Muslims and tried to suppress their legitimate aspirations by sending the army into former East Pakistan. Pakistan, founded as it was on the aspirations of the Muslim power elite, often had to resort to 'Hate India' campaigns to divert the attention of the Muslim masses from their real problems. Pakistan faces great challenges today in the form of ethnic and sectarian conflicts.

Far from solving the communal problem in India, Partition, as pointed out above, aggravated it further. The innocent Muslim masses in India continue to pay a heavy price for the creation of Pakistan. It created hatred in the minds of upper caste Hindus towards Muslims. These Hindus are even unable to distinguish between the interests of the upper-class Muslim elite who created Pakistan and the backward illiterate Muslim masses who were victims of partition. In many communal riots the fanatics raise the slogan *Muslims jao Pakistan aur qabrastan* ('O Muslims, go to Pakistan or the cemetery').

Thus, Partition neither solved the problems of the Muslims in Pakistan nor of those in India. What it did do was shatter the unity of Muslims on the subcontinent. Muslims are now divided into three separate units: India, Pakistan and Bangladesh. Partition was intended to create a homeland for Indian Muslims, but this was far from the case; Indian Muslims are not only divided into three separate sections, but the number of Muslims in India—for whom the Muslim homeland was meant—still remains the highest of all three sections. The Muslim masses in all three countries are facing problems of acute poverty, unemployment and illiteracy. If anyone benefitted from Partition it was the elite Muslims who created the so-called Muslim 'homeland' in the name of Islam.

The Question of Security and Identity

Indian Muslims faced problems of security and identity from day one after India became independent. First, Partition riots made them terribly insecure. Hundreds of thousands of Muslims were killed during the Partition riots in India, just as Hindus were killed in Pakistan. Thus, independence resulted in a great disaster for both Hindus and Muslims in India. Moreover, Indian Muslims were completely confused and did not know what to do. They lost even their sense of confidence. It was leaders of the stature of Maulana Abul Kalam Azad who instilled a sense of confidence and made them proud of their Islamic heritage in India. Maulana Azad's speech from the steps of Jama Masjid in Delhi acted as a balm and had a healing touch. However, Muslims had a difficult time ahead of them in India after Partition.

The Constitution, declaring India a republic, was drafted and adopted on January 26, 1950. The Constitution declared all citizens of India equal in every respect without any distinction made between caste, creed or race. Articles 25 to 30 of the Constitution also gave special religious and cultural rights to minorities. Article 25 thus declares: "Subject to public order, morality and health and to other provisions of this part, all persons are equally entitled to freedom of conscience and the right freely to profess, practise and propagate religion." This article even allows that the "... wearing and carrying of *kirpans* [a weapon] shall be deemed to be included in the profession of the Sikh religion."

Among the cultural and educational rights of minorities Articles 29 and 30 are very important. According to the Article 29:

> (1) Any section of the citizens residing in the territory of India or any part thereof having a distinct language, script or culture of its own shall have the right to conserve the same. (2) No citizen shall be denied admission into any educational institution maintained by the State or receiving State funds on grounds only of religion, race, caste, language or any of them.

Article 30 is also of fundamental importance. This Article is entitled "Right of minorities to establish and administer educational institutions." It says:

> (1) All minorities, whether based on religion or language, shall have the right to establish and administer educational institutions of their choice. (2) The State shall

not, in granting aid to educational institutions, discriminate on the grounds that it is under the management of a minority, whether based on religion or language.

Needless to say, these provisions of the Constitution are of fundamental importance for preserving the religious practices and identities of minority communities based on religion or language and culture. The Indian Muslims and other religious minorities like the Christians, Sikhs and neo-Buddhists highly value these provisions of the Constitution of India. For the Muslims in particular, constituting as they do the largest religious minority, these provisions are of special significance. The Muslims have resisted and preserved—we will discuss this in some more detail in the subsequent pages—their personal laws or *sharia* laws under Article 25, which allows all persons to profess, practise and propagate their religion. However, there are differences among legal luminaries as to whether the state can regulate or legislate with regard to the personal laws in view of Article 25. Muslims of course maintain that the State cannot.

Articles 29 and 30 are also of great importance for the preservation of minority languages and cultures and the Hindu communalists often attack these provisions and want them removed. But it requires a two-thirds majority in Parliament to change the Constitution and hence the Hindutva forces have not yet succeeded in tampering with these important provisions. However, there are violations of these provisions in practice and there are numerous grievances in this respect. But that is another story altogether.

While the incorporation of these articles into the Indian Constitution instilled a sense of confidence among Indian Muslims in the post-independence period, their loyalty to India remained suspect in the eyes of most of the majority community, particularly in northern India. As pointed out before, it is sociologically and politically wrong to homogenize any religious community, but 'Hindus' and 'Muslims' have become political categories since the British period in Indian political discourse, as if they were monolithic blocs without any political, religious, linguistic and cultural differences. Commonality of religion, as the two-nation theory also assumed, does not lead to commonality of politics, nor does it lead to commonality of culture. The north and central Indian Muslims who speak Urdu are distinctly different from Muslims from the south who speak different Indian languages. They have their own political inclinations and compulsions.

The Muslims from the south were indifferent to the question of Pakistan right from the beginning. They did not support Partition with the same enthusiasm as the Urdu-speaking Muslims of northern India. Since the period of British rule, communalism and communal violence remained centered in the north. Even in the post-Partition period the south was relatively free from communal violence until the late 1980s. Until then there were hardly any communal riots in the south, except in Hyderabad which has been center of the Urdu-speaking Muslims and was under Nizam rule. However, after the late 1980s the communal situation deteriorated very quickly in some parts of the south, particularly in the state of Tamilnadu.

Communal Violence

In northern India too there was relative peace between the communities during the 1950s as the entire focus during this period was on the linguistic reorganization of states. In parts of India there were riots on this issue, particularly between Gujrat and Maharashtra, on the question of the inclusion of Bombay. However, an unending cycle of communal violence began in the early 1960s. The first major riot took place in Jabalpur in 1962, shaking the whole country. Jawaherlal Nehru, the first Prime Minister of India, was also thoroughly shaken. He did not expect communal violence on such a massive scale as he thought the communal question was 'resolved' by partitioning the country on communal lines. His illusions were thus shattered. Communalism and communal violence continued, since Partition did not change the communal mindset of some people. It had, instead, aggravated it.

However, Nehru was committed to secular politics. Shaken by the events in Jabalpur, he formed the national Integration Council after the Jabalpur riots and the Chinese invasion of 1962. Unfortunately, however, the Council remained only a paper organization and could not become an active agent in promoting secular values and communal harmony. Most of the Congressmen were communal at heart and had never been as committed to secularism as Nehru had. Many leaders of the Congress were known sympathizers of Hindu communal interests. They were opposed to Nehru's policies both internal as well as external, i.e., his policy of non-alignment. The Jabalpur riots shook Indian Muslims' confidence in Congress as well as in secularism.

It was commitment to secularism that had inspired minorities to stand by the Indian National Congress and thousands of Indian Muslims had supported the Indian struggle for freedom because the Indian National Congress adopted a secular philosophy. Indian secularism, of course, was far from being atheistic or antagonistic to religion, as secularism was in the Soviet Union. Indian secularism guaranteed religious freedom for all and it was this concept of religious freedom that made Indian Muslims feel Islam was safe in India. However, their confidence was shaken with every major communal riot. During the Nehru period as well several large communal riots took place. The situation was greatly aggravated after his death.

Nehru's death in 1964 left a great void, but Indian democracy proved to be vibrant enough to overcome this crisis. Lal Bahadur Shashtri took over as prime minister but did not live long, dying of a heart attack after signing a peace treaty in Tashkant after the 1965 war between India and Pakistan. On his death Nehru's daughter Indira Gandhi became Prime Minister and to strengthen her position she tried to win over minorities by strengthening secular forces in the country. She thus succeeded in winning over minorities who were feeling quite unsafe after a series of communal riots in the country since Jabalpur riot.

However, Indira Gandhi had to face enormous challenges from her opponents both from within the Congress and outside it. The Congress bosses who opposed her split the Congress and Indira's faction became the ruling Congress. To weaken her hold all those ranged against her engineered a communal holocaust in 1969 in Ahmedabad in Gujrat (western India) where the Congress faction opposed to her was ruling. The Ahmedabad communal riots spread to other parts of the Gujrat state and were much worse in intensity than the Jabalpur riots. The Jansangh, which was the Hindu rightist and communal organization, was actively campaigning against Muslims and doubting their loyalty to India at that time. It passed a resolution 'Indianizing' the Indian Muslims—as if they were not Indian enough. Its president in those days was Balraj Madhok, who was known to be extremist in his views. The print media played up the resolution and some papers such as *The Times of India* even supported the resolution in its editorials.

The Indian Muslims were feeling terribly insecure and felt their very existence was in danger. And it was in this suffocating atmosphere that the Ahmedabad holocaust occurred, in which more than a thousand Muslims were killed in Ahmedabad alone. The Ahmedabad riots were followed by equally ferocious communal riots in Bhivandi in 1970. Another communal organization called Shiv Sena came into existence in Maharashtra in the late 1960s and some senior Congressmen of Bombay were supposedly behind it. These Congressmen, who were nursing grievances against Nehruvian leftist policies, lent their discrete support to the Marathi demagogue Bal Thackaray. Thackaray aroused both strong regional as well as communal feelings among the Maharashtrian youth. He was also a staunch enemy of Communists, and it was at his instigation that the Communist activist Krishna Desai was murdered by Shiv Sainiks.

It was Shiv Sena that was behind the Bhivandi riots of 1970. Bhivandi is about 40 miles (60 kilometers) from Bombay and power there lies mostly in Muslim hands. It has a Muslim majority. It is reported that more than four hundred persons, mostly Muslims, were killed in these riots. What was worse and made Muslims even more insecure was the biased role of the police in these riots. In all these riots were instances of the unabashed partiality of the police towards the Hindu side. However, it must be said that only a section of—certainly not all—Hindus took communal positions and showed an anti-Muslim bias. Many Hindus, perhaps a great majority, either remained neutral, took the side of Muslims or fought communal forces in their own community. Shiv Sena in Maharashtra was backed either by communal elements or by those Congressmen who were nursing grievances against Indira Gandhi.

The period between 1970 and 1977 was comparatively peaceful and there were no major communal riots during this period for various reasons. It was during this period that the liberation movement in erstwhile East Pakistan started and Bangladesh seceded from Pakistan through the active intervention of the Indian army. The attention of whole nation was turned to that event. Gandhi's stature was boosted tremendously and she emerged as a great heroine of Indian politics. However, this proved to be quite shortlived and opposition gathered momentum. Jayprakash Narayan, a socialist leader of great stature in Indian politics, launched an anticorruption movement against her and her prestige went down considerably. She also lost an election petition in Allahabad High Court and was unseated. Ghandi declared a state of emergency in 1975 and a large number of opposition leaders were arrested, including Jayprakash Narayan. Most of the Jansangh and RSS (*Rashtriya Svayamsevak*

Sangh: the 'National Volunteer Corps') leaders were also rounded up and there was a complete political vacuum. No one was left to provoke communal violence.

However, the state of emergency was lifted in 1977 and in the ensuing elections Gandhi and her party lost heavily. The newly formed Janata Party formed the government of which the Jansangh was a constituent. The Jansangh ostensibly renounced its communal philosophy and pledged at Gandhiji's *Samadhi* (where his funeral ashes lay buried) to be secular and votary of Gandhian socialism. The northern Indian Muslims who had suffered greatly from the cleansing program during the emergency period voted overwhelmingly for the Janata Party, knowing fully well that the Jansangh was part of it. It was the first and last time that the Muslims voted for the Jansangh in sheer desperation. They expected the Jansangh to reciprocate this gesture towards Muslims but were soon disillusioned. A series of communal riots followed from 1978 onwards. Major riots took place in Jamshedpur, Aligarh and Varanasi in northern India and many innocent lives were lost.

The RSS—which provides ideological direction to Hindu communal forces—was quite unhappy at the Jansangh's renunciation of communalism and embrace of secularism. It believed the latter to be anti-Hindu. The Jansangh members were forced by their RSS mentors not to renounce their RSS membership. All the top leaders of the then Jansangh were also members of RSS. Socialist leaders like Raj Narain in the Janata Party raised this issue (known as the dual membership issue) and asked the Jansangh members in the Janata Party to resign their RSS membership. The RSS made it plain that their members were not to resign and planned several communal riots in Aligarh, Varanasi, Jamshedpur, etc. to display their strength. The Janata Party government collapsed in 1979 as a consequence of this issue and was replaced by the government of Charan Singh, which lasted for only a few months. In the ensuing elections in 1980 Gandhi came back to power, though with less of the popular vote.

After the collapse of the Janata Party, the Janasangh assumed a new *avatar*, now calling itself the Bhartiya Janata Party (BJP) and adopted a moderate posture, still claiming to be committed to 'secularism' and Gandhian socialism. To symbolize its commitment to these ideals, a moderate leader, Atal Bihari Vajpayee was made its president. But this strategy soon came to naught as Gandhi, in order to compensate for her loss of Muslim votes, began to mobilize Hindu votes, adopting Hindu communal postures from behind the scenes. This upset the BJP's apple cart and the party lost ground. They lost heavily in the general elections of 1984 when they received only two seats in Parliament. The BJP was thus forced to rethink its strategy in order to keep its political base intact and attempt to widen it.

Thus it began to resume its earlier aggressive communal postures. Vajpayee was replaced by Shri L.K. Advani, known for his strong Hindutva proclivity, as president of the BJP. In order to compete with the soft communalism of the Congress the BJP adopted the hard Hindu communalism of the early 1980s and even began to question the Nehruvian concept of secularism. A debate took place publicly as to whether Nehruvian secularism, being of Western origin, was at all relevant to India. The BJP, under the leadership of Advani, even dubbed Nehruvian secularism as nothing more than a policy of the "appeasement of Muslims." The only example the BJP could give of the appeasement of Muslims was that of Muslim personal law, under which a Muslim man could have four wives, whereas Hindus cannot—they can have only one. With this the BJP appealed greatly to the Hindu middle class.

The BJP also propagated aggressively the view that Muslims do not practise family planning, that their population is increasing much faster than that of Hindus, that the Muslim population will take over the Hindu population by 2050 and India will become part of Pakistan. The Vishwa Hindu Parishad, a member of the Sangh Parivar (i.e., the Saffron Family, constituting the RSS, the Vishwa Hindu Parishad and Bajrang Dal), took a much more militant communal position on this issue. It distributed pamphlets throughout India showing a Hindu couple with two children and a Muslim man with four wives and a host of children, with the caption: "we five, our twenty-five." Also, after a few Dalit families converted to Islam in Meenakshipuram (Tamilnadu) in 1981, the VHP launched an aggressive movement against conversion to Islam in the same way that it is currently attacking others for conversion to Christianity.

All this greatly communalized the situation in the country and communal riots increased both in numbers and intensity. Naturally, the Muslims began to feel highly insecure and thought their Islamic identity was in danger. Secularism, needless to say, has been a great source of strength for minorities in India, particularly the Muslims. If secularism comes under attack, the minorities feel quite insecure. The militant attack by the Saffron Family on Nehruvian secularism and the VHP campaign against conversion and the myth of the multiplying Muslim population not only weakened Indian secularism but made the Muslims feel politically suffocated. It was under these circumstances that the Supreme Court delivered what has come to be known as The Shah Bano Judgment regarding the maintenance of Muslim divorcees.

The judgment upheld Shah Bano's contention under secular law that she was entitled to maintenance for life and not for only the *iddah* (the three-month waiting period before remarriage after divorce). This judgment, delivered in 1985, was thought to be another attack on Islam and Muslim identity in India. The Muslim leadership across the political parties and sectarian divide united to oppose the Supreme Court judgment and launched an aggressive movement to reverse it. This added to the already aggravated communal situation and went a long way to intensifying the hostility between the two communities.

It was under these circumstances that the BJP launched a new campaign to demolish the Babri Masjid and construct a Ramjanambhoomi temple in its place. The BJP maintained—although without much justification—that Babar, the Mughal ruler after whom the mosque in Ayodhya was named, had demolished the Ramjanambhoomi temple and constructed the mosque. Now that the Hindus were in power, they had the right to demolish the mosque and reconstruct the temple dedicated to Ram and take historical revenge. This, too, greatly appealed to the Hindu middle classes and the BJP, which previously had a narrow political base among the upper caste Hindus, began to expand this base among the middle and even backward caste Hindus in the name of Rama.

The Babri Masjid-Ramjanambhoomi campaign was not only historically unjustified; it launched a frontal attack on Indian secularism. The Muslims began to fear that it was the beginning of the end of secularism in India and that the Sangh Parivar would demolish all historical mosques one after the other and that constitutional guarantees were quite hollow. The Sangh Parivar had prepared a list of 300 such mosques and this was enough to frighten Muslims. Muslims were, furthermore, perturbed by the fact that the ruling Congress government headed by Rajiv Gandhi could do nothing to stop the tide of Hindu communalism. Moreover, Rajiv unlocked the Babri Masjid and allowed Hindus to worship Lord Ram's idol which had been placed there in 1948 by some RSS enthusiasts. This aggressive Ramjanambhoomi movement resulted in a series of communal riots in various parts of India in which hundreds of innocent lives were lost, most of whom were Muslims. The 1987 riots in Meerut and 1989 riots in Bhagalpur sent shock waves throughout India, making Muslims feel terribly insecure.

The Babri Masjid was also demolished by *karsevaks* (voluntary workers) of the Sangh Parivar on December 6, 1992, when Narsimha Rao was the Congress Party prime minister of India. Many secular Hindus also felt that it was a terrible tragedy, and it was not only the destruction of a mosque through political hooliganism but also a terrible blow to Indian secularism. The demolition of Babri Masjid was followed by riots in Bombay, Surat, Ahmedabad, Kanpur, Delhi and several other places. A communal holocaust swept throughout the country. The Bombay riots of 1992 and 1993 were mainly organized by Shiv Sena. These riots in particular had international repercussions: they tarnished the secular image of India.

The Post-Babri Situation

Although, as a result of Ramjanambhoomi movement, the BJP gained tremendous political ground and ultimately succeeded in capturing political power as a major coalition partner, the communal situation eased in the post-Babri demolition period. The decade of the 1980s was the most dangerous communal decade in the post-Independence period. It witnessed the most aggressive form of communalism after the partition of the country. The Sangh Parivar went all out during this period to expand its political base by misusing religious and communal issues one after the other.

However, once it came to power at the center, at the head of the coalition government, it began to downplay communal issues. It wanted to maintain law and order and also wanted to give a message to Muslims that they would be safe only if the BJP was in power. It even promised Muslims a 'riot-free' India in its election manifesto of 1999. Some politicians who made an alliance with the BJP even argued that to ensure a riot-free India one should keep the BJP in power. Hence, these otherwise secular parties legitimized their alliance with this party.

However, it would be naive to think that the BJP could become 'secular' if voted into power. The BJP had been provoking communal hatred in order to gain Hindu votes, but, as a ruling party, it obviously cannot risk provoking communal violence. That would tarnish its political image. As a ruling party, it has to ensure communal peace. But communal peace or the absence of communal violence should not be mistaken for communal harmony. To spread communal feelings is the very ideological basis of Sangh Parivar. If communalism and communal ideology remains alive, communal violence can be incited whenever needed. The BJP does not itself indulge in communal propaganda. The other members of the Saffron family—the RSS, the Vishwa Hindu Parishad and Bajrang Dal—fill this void. The Christian community has also recently come under attack because of conversions.

For the time being, the BJP is being easy on Muslims. It is even following in reverse the polices advocated by Gandhi in the early 1980s. Gandhi, who traditionally depended on minority votes, had tried to switch over to Hindu votes in order to compensate for her loss of popularity among the Muslims. The BJP, which is losing popularity among the Hindus, is now appealing to Muslims to come closer and place their confidence in it. The wooing of Muslims by the BJP can thus be compared with the wooing of Hindus by Gandhi. These are political games which the politicians play in order to achieve power. People of this or that community are used as vote banks and the object of rather than the subject of politics.

Democracy should be an effective tool for the empowerment of people, but it is being used for empowering politicians at the cost of the people. The Congress has always used Muslims as vote bank. The Congress, in its long rule, hardly did anything to solve the acute problems of Muslims. Muslims in India are very poor and backward and their main problems have to do with economics and lack of education. But the ruling parties have done nothing substantial in these fields. Only promises were made. The literacy rate among Muslims tends to be around 35% and among Muslim women it is even more depressing—not more than 18%. Their share in political power and in government jobs is also very dismal. Though the Muslim population is more than 12% (according to the 1991 census) and may reach the 15% level of the census in 2001, the number of Muslim members of Parliament is usually around 5%. In state assemblies it is no different.

Even at the lowest level of government jobs—class three and class four jobs —their share does not go beyond 6-7% and at the level of higher administrative positions like the IAS it is no more than 3-4%. It is true that it is difficult to find qualified Muslims for various jobs and Muslim leaders have also done almost nothing to educate the Muslim masses, but Union and state governments have also done nothing to rectify the situation. They make various promises at election time, but hardly anything, except repeating these promises during the next election, happens. The Muslim grievances are quite justified. They have hardly any share in power as the largest minority in India. The share, if any, is woefully inadequate.

Conclusion

Thousands of Muslims not only participated in the freedom struggle in India and made great sacrifices but also vigorously opposed the creation of Pakistan. They dreamed of a secular India, hoping for the creation of a just society where they would be able not only to follow their religion but also to share power on an equal basis. However, things did not go that way. Although Jawaherlal Nehru was committed to justice towards minorities in independent India, other Congress leaders were not. The majority in the Congress did not share Nehru's commitment. Also, the creation of Pakistan marred to a certain extent the future of Muslims in India. It created powerful prejudices in the minds of Hindus and Indian Muslims were seen as more loyal to Pakistan than to India. A few such instances were generalized in order to reinforce the conclusion which they already had drawn.

The Muslims also did not draw up a proper strategy for their own advancement in secular India. Their leaders, as pointed out before, cared more for religion and identity-related problems than problems related to education and economic progress. These leaders always looked to the past rather than the future. They negotiated deals with political parties—mainly the Congress—to preserve their past heritage rather than build a future for the Muslim masses. It is now dawning on Muslims that, apart from preserving their Islamic identity, they also need to carve out their own niche in a democratic secular India. Although the emphasis is still on building madrasas, more and more secular educational institutions are being built. More and more Muslims are realizing that the education of women is also very important for their progress. A new middle class is slowly coming into existence, which is increasingly championing the cause of modern education. Pressures are also building up from below for certain necessary changes in the status of women, particularly certain necessary changes in the *sharia* law as it operates in India.

Although there is still mass poverty among the Muslims, particularly among the lower caste Muslims, they have turned the corner and many of them are striving for upward mobility. However, they still have far to go and many powerful obstacles to overcome. It is certainly a convoluted way by which progress is made. Even the BJP has discovered that the anti-Muslim tirade cannot yield more results and is negotiating a new political space which is likely to have some place for Muslims, even though this is not easy to accomplish. Its ideological mentor RSS may not allow it to do this. Much will depend on the response of its Hindu voters to this new orientation of the moderate section of the BJP leadership. It will be tested in coming elections.

Whether the BJP forges ahead with its new Muslim policy or not, Muslims have to sink or swim in the Indian political ocean and, from all available signs, it appears that the Muslim masses have decided to swim even if the ocean is choppy. If the future for Muslims is not bright at this moment, it is not dismal either. Given a little more wisdom and a more pragmatic approach, Muslims can succeed in shaping their future in democratic India, even if its secularism is undulating.

Processes of Reconciliation in India

Swami Agnivesh

Introduction

Conflict arises among various religions chiefly because of the emphasis on religiosity rather than spirituality. If we examine the basis of each individual religion we will find that the spiritual basis is the same. Religion defines individual and group identity in terms of differentiation, whereas spirituality does this by integration. From all available indicators, it is exceedingly clear that the time is right and ripe for a major reform initiative.

The need for reform is not confined to a particular age. Reform is a spiritual response to aberrations and no age is free from them. Buddhism was a response to the Hindu world as experienced by Buddha. Christianity was a response to the Jewish world as experienced by Christ and Islam was a response to the Arabic world as experienced by Muhammad. The Arya Samaj, a comparatively new movement in the greater scheme of things tried to address the distortions that vested interests introduced into the Vedic faith. Over the years it too lost its zeal for the reform envisaged by its founder, Swami Dayanand.

Conflict and Conflict Resolution

Life is instinct with conflict. Conflicts emerge from the interplay of competing interests within a framework of power. This makes conflicts endemic to the human situation. Except in a culture of life founded on love and compassion, conflicts cannot be removed from the human situation. Conflict resolution, hence, becomes a central concern in human welfare.

Not all conflicts are necessarily evil. The Indian struggle for freedom, for instance, involved India in a protracted but necessary conflict with the British. The absence of conflict in itself does not prove the presence of peace, for peace is a positive state of being. Change and progress involve conflict: the conflict between the old and the new. To want to avoid conflict is to renounce progress and reform in favor of the status quo. The outcome of indiscriminate avoidance of conflict could be an attitude of compromise dictated by cowardice. This, no less than a habitual indulgence in conflict, corrupts individual and corporate personality.

A majority of conflicts in this world are, however, superfluous and wasteful. As a rule, those who dissipate their energies on peripheral issues tend to dodge fundamental conflicts. They shrink from the defining battles of life. Contrariwise, those who are engaged with serious issues are averse to squandering themselves in petty squabbles and side skirmishes.

Two models of conflict resolution are possible. The first is the martial model. In this model conflicts are resolved by assimilating or eliminating 'the other'. The use of ideological, political and physical force is integral to this model. Its simplistic logic is that conflicts are best resolved by destroying the otherness of the other. The attractiveness of this model is that it avoids the need for dialogue and to alter the outlook of others. It works on a dangerous equation of unity with uniformity. This martial spirit has free access to popular religiosity, especially when the spiritual core of religions is deactivated as in the case of religious fundamentalism.

The second model is the spiritual one. In this approach conflict is not resolved by eliminating 'the other' but by persuading people to embrace an alternate value system or religious tradition. In this model, transforming oneself is deemed the key to reforming others. This model is, however, vulnerable to the presumption of the superiority of one's own doctrinal position and the inferiority of all other alternatives. In that event, what begins as 'dialogue' degenerates into a 'debate' adulterated by coercion. At that point, the spiritual model of conflict resolution is taken over by the spirit of the martial model. The spiritual approach is marked by the ability to coexist creatively with what is different and is free from the insecurity that drives projects of homogenization. The key to the spiritual approach to conflict resolution is the inculcation of the inner strength to celebrate diversity and differences without at the same time losing sight of the distinction between good and evil. To be tolerant to the point of tolerating evil indiscriminately is to create a culture of intolerance: the intolerance of good.

'Establishment ethics' tends to frown upon resistance and the prospect of conflicts. Why the establishment should then initiate and glorify conflicts partial to its own interests is, however, a question that is not to be asked. All through history the religious and political establishments have preached edited versions of morality. In politics and religion, the ruling elites have made every imaginable attempt to foster blind conformity to their own interests, while enjoining the noblest standards of self-transcendence on its followers. All equations of power are vitiated by unilateralism and double standards. It then becomes a spiritual duty to disagree with the presumptions and interrogate the hypocrisy of the establishment, even if this means having to live like Socrates in a state of tension with the establishment.

The spiritual goal cannot be limited to resolving the conflicts that arise from time to time. It must also seek to transcend the very logic of conflict. This calls for a paradigm shift from power to love. Conflicts are endemic to power because power breeds insecurity, which caricatures others as 'enemies' in respect of those who monopolize the fruits of power. Love, on the other hand, insists on the distinction between enemy and enmity. It urges us to see enmity as a spiritual aberration that needs to be rectified and the 'enemy' as a fellow human being who deserves to be set free from the sickness of enmity.

Spirituality is as realistic as it is idealistic. And the realism of spirituality reckons that a wilful abuse of human freedom leads to a hardheartedness that precludes self-reformation. To remain willfully resistant to the call of truth and justice is to activate one's own corruption and eventual destruction. This explains why even in religious scriptures some key moral conflicts are resolved only by the destruction of the agents of evil. The need for this arises in the wake of a total identification of evil agents with evil, so that one cannot be checked without destroying the other. It is hardly safe or fair for anyone, however, to conclude whether or not a given situation has degenerated to this level of irredeemable depravity and to play God in the name of morality.

Secularism and fundamentalism are, though in different ways, ideologies of conflict. Secularism emerged from the tumult of religious wars in Europe at a time when religion had degenerated into doctrinal battlefields on the one hand and political hobbyhorses on the other. This explains, in part, why secularism is inherently suspicious of religion. Historically, it is an ideology that emerged in reaction to the degradation of religion into hate and bloodshed. This negativity explains the attitude of reciprocal intolerance between the followers of secularism and religion. The secular worldview has generated its own brand and brunt of conflicts. Barring the eruption of fundamentalist rashes, religious wars are a thing of the past. The history of the modern world convulses with the violence unleashed by contending economic and political power blocs. Over 120 million people died in direct man-made violence in the last century. An overwhelming majority among them perished in conflicts fomented by politics and economics. Materialism, as the religion of secular humankind, is as productive of conflicts and destruction as religions ever have been.

For all their seeming differences, religious fundamentalism and secularism share a kinship of spirit: the spirit of negativity. While secularism is negative towards religion, religious fundamentalism breeds an attitude of negativity and intolerance among religions towards one another. Religious fundamentalism has as much to do with religion as rock gardens have to do with flowers. Like secularism, it is essentially an offshoot of materialism. What pretends to be an effervescence of religiosity is nothing more than the masquerading of materialistic interests draped in religious fineries. Those who have cared to analyze the hundreds of communal riots in the post-Independence era in India would, for example, readily agree that these conflicts had little to do with religion. They were, instead, contrived by political and economic agent provocateurs.

Whether conflicts emerge from secular or fundamentalist projects, the tragedy is that credulous commoners are misled by their ringleaders into conflictual engagements, spreading the cancer of hate, violence and destruction to the detriment of the nation. Ironically, both groups bank on the religious sentiment of 'devotion'. Patriotism is devotion to one's own country which, in times of war, takes on pronounced religious overtones. But the politicians who egg on the soldiers to die for their country will have no qualms, once the war ends, in filling the country with corruption, making a mockery of the sacrifices made by the armed forces whose praises they are only too happy to sing. Religious conflicts too are skirmishes of devotion, but it is a devotion that excludes an understanding of the true spirit of the religion for which one is fighting. The tragedy is that secularism and religious fundamentalism, like a great deal devised by human beings, are overrun by the spirit of negativity. Conflict is the necessary idiom of negativity.

The spiritual approach to conflict resolution must, hence, go beyond negotiating the peaceful settlement of specific instances of conflicts. It must attend to the cancer of negativity, with its inevitable expressions of hate, alienation and conflict. Negativity is the fundamental spiritual sickness of the human species. Trying to contain instances of conflicts without doing anything to exorcise the given society of the spirit of negativity is, at best, like sticking plaster on festering wounds. The radical approach to conflict resolution must be predicated on fostering a culture of positivity, the culture of love, in the given context.

It needs to be emphasized that conflicts are artificially and deliberately constructed by certain centers of vested interest in any society. They have the means to exploit people's religious and political sentiments, mobilize and misinform the masses, and the money power to invest in creating confusion from which they hope to gain. Faith in the efficacy of violence and cynicism alone concerning the value of peaceful means for problem-solving are injected into the minds of the people. All these prove effective largely because of the absence of an authentic voice that can address the conscience of the people and counterbalance the false propaganda. This lamentable state of affairs results from the escapist attitude that overtakes religiosity in its decline. Religious leaders who can and must play a crucial role in conflict resolution opt out of this challenging responsibility and hide themselves behind the fumes of empty ritualism. It is a proven fact of history that every spiritually enlightened person has an abiding interest in conflict resolution. Peace is the offspring of spirituality.

Conflict resolution must not, in the end, be understood merely as putting out the fire that rages now. To try and resolve conflicts overlooking the demands of justice in the given context is simply to perpetuate conflicts. Most conflicts result from a real or contrived sense of grievance. Unless this aspect of the situation is boldly addressed conflicts will remain endemic. Spiritually valid conflict resolution is peace combined with justice. But justice cannot be practised without a commitment to truth. And truth, in Gandhian thought, is the quintessence of *ahimsa* (nonviolence). History proves that the pursuit of peace, overlooking the claims of justice, is doomed to fail and pave the way for further conflicts.

Towards Healing a Nation

Religion is worthless if it is indifferent to the suffering of the people it is meant to serve. Spirituality is a dynamic and transforming engagement with the world around us and has no room for apathy or escapism. It can empower peoples and nations alike. Spirituality must have something to offer vis-à vis the problems that afflict a people. Here we need to examine only a few illustrative areas.

Disunity
Political schism and disunity plague most societies in the world, especially in Africa and Asia. It is naive to assume that the problem is only in the armed conflicts that

take place. The problem is in our minds and hearts. We allow our minds to be filled with hate. We see others as threats and stumbling blocks. We want to pursue our interests at the expense of the well-being of others. All these are double-edged swords. When these swords begin to cut our own throat, *then* we talk about the need for unity and harmony. It should be kindergarten wisdom that disunity will persist as long as our minds are not detoxified. The spiritual goal is to cultivate a spiritual mental culture. From a spiritual perspective, unity is of utmost importance. But unity has to be seen as part of the commitment to truth, sanctity of life and a sense of mission aimed at maximizing human well-being. Disunity is inevitable as long as vested interests reign. And the task of true spirituality is to transcend selfish goals.

Violence and Disharmony
It is too obvious to escape anyone's notice that even as spiritual discipline declines, violence and destruction mount in a society. This endangers life and liberty. Violence results from two major sources: hate and the inability to cope creatively with differences, both of which are inevitable in the orientation of power. The spiritual strategy for healing this situation is to replace the love of power with the power of love. Love unites, whereas hate divides and scatters. It is of utmost importance to see spirituality as the power to relate to what is different and even seemingly contrary, which is the essence of genuine freedom. Those who are spiritually enlightened transcend stereotypical distinctions and categories that divide people. They work in terms of the essential and endangered humanity of all people. A nation is not safe unless its people are equipped to live with differences. Differences are real and important, and it is dishonest to suggest that they do not exist. But the recognition of differences is not an invitation to be alienated from each other. It is the unspiritual mind that feels insecure in the presence of what is different. But, in coping creatively with differences, we must not abandon the commitment to truth. Truth, however, needs to be enlivened by love.

Justice needs to be seen as a divine concern. Practising justice has to be a spiritual, not legal, commitment. Injustice is inseparable from corruption and untruth. Falsehood is the most universal form of violence. A peaceful and sane society can be built only on the foundation of truth and sanctity. Wherever justice is denied, violence results. This problem will not be solved by increasing the police or paramilitary forces—not even by using the army against one's own people. This malady can be healed only by the antidotes of love, truth and justice.

Violence needs to be seen not only as a series of events but also as being generated within an outlook that makes its outbreak unavoidable. It is like the heat generated by two parts of a machine that are in friction. That friction is written into the logic of selfish human nature. Hence, the solution to this problem can only be a radical one: the transformation of human nature and, consequently, the spiritual regeneration of our society.

It is at this level that the spiritual agenda for building a healthy nation needs to be worked out. But the problem is that those who pride themselves on their pragmatism tend to be impatient with the long-term agenda involved in this approach. People everywhere are looking for short cuts and quick-fix solutions in this age of fast food and instant nirvana. The truth is that all shortcuts are necessarily deceptive and turn out in the end to be avenues of deception and corruption.

The Cornerstones of a Sane Society

Essential to the health and dynamism of every society are:

Resource Management

Spirituality touches our attitude toward the material world and the way we manage resources. We are in a state of trusteeship as far as the resources of this world are concerned. Everything is God-given. Our spirituality in the political and economic spheres of our national life involves the responsibility for ensuring the well-being of all people in managing the resources of the nation. Increasing productivity needs to be matched by the willingness to share the fruits thereof with all in need. The sinfulness of contemporary approaches and systems manifests itself in the exclusion of the people in need from the fruits of development. Until recently this used to happen mainly at the national level. Now, in the wake of globalism, this could become an international reality, unless we are spiritually vigilant.

Acceptance of Responsibility

Stewardship also involves being responsible for the total well-being of the people. It is tragic that in the midst of our political and economic projects and enterprises, we lose sight of the weaker sections of our society. People are becoming increasingly alienated from each other. Those who were once neighbors are becoming enemies. The State can no longer continue to see its role in this context as that of a policeman who keeps people from fighting. The State has to become an active agent for the propagation of life-friendly values. Enabling people to love one another rather than preventing them from fighting and killing one another needs to be emphasized.

Human Worth

Essential to the spiritual outlook on life is the affirmation of the supreme worth of human life. If this is recognized, we shall fight against injustice, poverty and oppression rather than our fellow human beings. The agenda common to healthy religion and constructive politics is the commitment to affirm human worth and to maximize the well-being of all people. All spiritually enlightened initiatives are singularly devoted to this goal. In contrast, it is heart-breakingly ironic that for most people in the world a flag, a territory or an ideology are more important than the lives and well-being of millions of people. If it were not so, over 120 million human beings would not have died by violence caused by humans in the last century. Look at the millions that continue to die either through conflicts or through avoidable famine and starvation. No nation can be healthy and dynamic unless it is committed to honoring human worth and protecting human life. It is necessary to recognize the synergy between development and human worth. The impetus to develop will continue to be absent if a nation is not challenged by this spiritual ideal. Also, if a nation does not develop, it will never discover the full scope of the ideal of human worth. The value attached to a human life varies from one society to another, depending on the extent of its development.

Development with Equity and Compassion
Ironically material development of a certain kind, not less than underdevelopment, could be a source of national disarray. While underdevelopment devalues human life, development understood only as increase in the material circumstances of life soon degenerates into covetousness, consumerism and criminality. Materialistic society will always and everywhere have a criminal fringe. In addition, it unleashes a spirit of competition, which makes people mistake their neighbors for enemies. Many of the communal and ethnic conflicts are, essentially, economic conflicts for the purpose of securing a disproportionate part of the national cake and to disable, if possible, others from sharing national resources. Even where this does not happen in a naked fashion, development that neglects the spiritual and moral aspects of the human situation brings about the impoverishment of human life.

True development must harmonize the material and spiritual nourishment of the human being. It is this wholesome balance that we need to insist on, especially in the wake of globalization. This needs to be seen in the light of the uniqueness of our being as a body-soul continuum. The body cannot be fattened by famishing the soul and *vice versa*. As a matter of fact, one of the major reasons for the growing violence in advanced societies is the exuberance of physical energy (due to enhanced food intake) unmatched and unbridled by moral and spiritual stamina. Violence is often a phenomenon of imbalance. It may seem positive, but it is essentially negative.

Work Culture vs. Corruption
No society can continue to remain healthy and dynamic if it does not evolve and sustain a wholesome work culture. While this is universally recognized, the role of spirituality in this sphere often goes unacknowledged. A healthy work culture is based on two major factors: (1) the commitment to uphold *dharma* in the pursuit of one's vocation and (2) compassion for one's neighbors that makes one want to care and to share. In cultures where this sense of social responsibility is underdeveloped, the work culture also remains embryonic. More seriously, the erosion of the work culture fuels corruption in every society. Work involves spiritual discipline, through which one grows and matures. The alternative is to resort to shortcuts through which the discipline of work is diluted. Corruption is the alternative to work in a spiritually and morally depraved society. Corruption is, more accurately, an antiwork culture in which wealth is idolized. A corrupt society cannot but disintegrate into violence sooner or later, for it must violate love, justice and accountability.

The Attitude towards the Other
A nation is basically a vast human family. Relationships between people are of decisive importance for its character and destiny. What shapes this are the attitudes people hold toward one another. It is here that spirituality can and must play a constructive role. From a worldly and materialistic standpoint that promotes self-

centeredness, others are seen as threats to one's own interests. The spiritual vision celebrates our sense of community and human interdependence. It opens our eyes to the suicidal folly of wanting to thrive at the expense of others. A nation is like a ship afloat on a perilous sea. We shall survive or perish together. Security or well-being can never be selective. Either we are all safe, or we are all at risk. This is the practical wisdom in the practice of love and compassion. To love is to progress together, for love is constructive and active in the service of what is good. The opposite of this is the spirit of hegemony, which seeks to oppress others and reserve all advantages for oneself. It is natural that such an outlook perpetuates and escalates conflicts and cripples the nation. Powerful vested interests are at work in the global arena to foment internal and regional hostilities. One such network is the Global Arms Mafia. It is a pity that Afro-Asian nations that cannot afford to feed their people and educate their children are spending the lion's share of their scarce resources on buying and stockpiling arms. This is aided and abetted by the vested interests within countries. But if the people of this region are to have any quality of life, a radical breakthrough in this area must be achieved.

A Culture of Ahimsa *(Peace)*
This calls for the creation of a culture of peace. The strategic, over against the spiritual, approach to peacemaking is riddled with contradictions. It is, indeed, an aspect of warmongering. That is why the nations of the world clamor for peace and prepare for war at the same time! The outlook that governs the world is based on the paradigm of power. Creating peace on an enduring foundation involves a paradigm shift from power to love. People must be challenged and trained to love one another rather than hate one another. Hate carries a high price for any nation. Love is more profitable than hate!

But hate will seem a more practical and effective strategy to those who are worldly. That is because hate takes less energy than love, though hate results in colossal instances of destruction. It has no energy for anything positive. Hate is a corollary to power. Power has a native genius for the superficial. Power can operate only on the surface of things. Power is powerless in the depths beneath the surface, where spirituality belongs. The only power that works at this level is the power of love. Those who base their life's vision on power exile themselves from the depth that belongs to things. They become, perforce, superficial. What can be controlled and manipulated is the surface. In the depths one can only function in faith and wonder. Awareness of the divine and *bhakti* are depth experiences. Materialism and consumerism are allergic to this culture of depth. They are the play on the surface. The surface is also a domain of restlessness and conflict where peace is a mirage.

This may seem too mystical a strategy for establishing peace in our world of grubby materialism. Exactly! It is foolish to imagine that we can secure the cause of peace by remaining on the foundation of conflict and restlessness. That is where we are today. Spirituality comes with an invitation to shift from this foundation. This does not involve any indifference to things worldly. Rather this enhances the duty to develop everything entrusted to us. But what this outlook changes is the significance we attach to the fruits of our labor and, more importantly, our sense of exclusive ownership as far as the fruits of our labor are concerned. The lust for grasping and grabbing will be replaced by the joy of sharing. The craving for indulgence will give way to the concern for the well- being of all people. Cooperation and kinship will supersede conflict. Without this spiritual revolution, the supreme enterprise of nation-building will rest only on fragile foundations. The destiny of a nation rests, in the final analysis, on the character of its people. And human character can be noble and creative only when shaped and nourished by true spirituality.

Reconciliation in Practice

Indian Experience

Andreas D'Souza

Introduction

Last year I went to the wedding of Hindumati. She was one of the first students to graduate from the tailoring class organized by the Aman Shanti project[1] We had hired Hindumati to assist Asiya Begum, the tailoring teacher. The wedding was arranged in the courtyard of her house and extended into the road, which was cordoned off for the celebration. The bride and groom along with their respective parents and friends sat around the sacred fire under a canopy on a raised platform. The Hindu priest kept reciting verses from the sacred scriptures as he poured *ghee* (clarified butter) and sprinkled incense over the fire. Among those who were present and mingling merrily with the crowd were Hindumati's Muslim colleagues and students.

A year later I went to another wedding. This time it was Asiya who was getting married. Like Hidumati's it was an arranged marriage. This wedding was held in a rented function hall: men were assembled in one section with the groom seated on a throne over a colorfully decorated podium, surrounded by the *qadi* (lit. judge) and the male friends and relatives. In another separate section sat the bride surrounded by her female friends and relatives. Among them were Asiya's Hindu colleagues and students.

Insignificant as it may appear, the mixing of the two communities on the above happy occasions are part of the fruit of our efforts to bring into better relationship the divided community of Sultan Shahi. They are stories of change, not overnight change but change that comes from a long and painful process of healing injured feelings, of creating mutual trust, of rebuilding broken relationships. Ten years back this mixing would not have happened. The elementary school for dropout children in the neighborhood, the tailoring and embroidery classes for young women, the medical clinic and periodic community health camps have attracted Muslims and Hindus over the years and has provided space for healing, for transcending boundaries erected in the name of religion, for building relationships. The project is run from a former Muslim house. The owner sold it to us because he was afraid of the Hindu neighbors and

---

[1] *Aman* and *shanti* are, respectively, the Urdu and Sanskrit words for peace. It is the name of a reconciliation project funded and managed by the Henry Martyn Institute with the cooperation of the local community at Sultan Shahi in the old city of Hyderabad.

moved to a safer place. Situated as it is between the two communities, it has become a neutral ground for interaction, for learning each other's language, culture and religion. It is a small step in our efforts to understand what reconciliation means in practice. The bonds we see developing among Hindu-Muslim children and women and through them among their men is an indication that reconciliation is possible.

In this paper I will narrate a few stories which help illustrate some of programs carried out by the Henry Martyn Institute: International Center for Research, Interfaith Relations and Reconciliation situated in Hyderabad, India. I will refer briefly to the 1990 violent riots as the *Sitz-im-Leben* for the change in focus of the Institute's activities and the revision of its constitution, which became the foundation for its projects aimed at reconciliation. It is my firm belief that reconciliation cannot take place unless our efforts towards it begin with an understanding of the root causes of violence and its endemic and spiral nature. What follows here is a case study of what *reconciliation* means in practical terms as well as a story of my own personal struggle to understand the meaning of reconciliation in a multireligious, multicultural society fragmented by many forces. These few thoughts are offered with the hope that, however difficult and dangerous the demands of reconciliation are, we cannot ignore its call if we wish to contribute to building a just and peaceful society.

From Evangelism to Reconciliation

The Henry Martyn Institute was founded in 1930 as an organ of the church for training missionaries to evangelize Muslims. In the 1960s and 1970s it was also engaged in interfaith dialogue, although it did not give up its evangelistic orientation. In the worsening context of communal misunderstanding and suspicion, of continuing riots often fermented in the name of *religion*, the Institute continues to change its focus, shifting increasingly to interfaith relations and reconciliation. The story of this transformation is already well documented and I will not go into it here (cf. D'Souza 1998). This significant change necessitated a major revision of HMI's constitution and a restating of its goals. Its name also underwent a change from the former *Henry Martyn Institute of Islamic Studies*.[2] These were bold steps, although not everyone has agreed with this change in direction.[3]

---

[2] The change of focus from Islamic Studies to Interfaith Relations reflects the Indian context where Christians are only a small minority amidst people of many faiths, among whom an overwhelming majority are Hindus. We have come to realize that to concentrate only on Muslim-Christian dynamics is socioculturally untenable. The Institute still remains strongly committed to promoting the respectful study of Islam in its academic wing and offers courses on Islam and related languages at various levels.

[3] Christians in India and abroad have criticized the Institute for abandoning its original goal; a partner church has been reluctant to fund programs because they are not 'evangelistic'. One member of the faculty resigned and went to teach in an 'evangelical' Bible College because he felt that the Institute was no longer 'Christian' in orientation.

In the above introductory paragraph I said that HMI's revised constitution became the foundation for its work towards reconciliation. It indeed is a veritable *magna carta*, which defines the primary goal of the Institute to be "an expression of the Church's ministry of reconciliation." The constitution speaks about helping churches fulfill a unique peace-making role, of the need to study and understand Islam and other religions, to work towards the removal of misunderstanding and suspicion, to promote justice and peace, to collaborate with people of other faiths on common concerns. It became the spring board for launching various types of programs to promote reconciliation: work with Hindus and Muslims in the slums, the training workshops in mediation and conflict resolution, the efforts to help empower like-minded groups in Kashmir, Bihar and Manipur, some of the most troubled areas of our country, the women's interfaith journey in which Indian and Canadian women from four different faith backgrounds traveled together to discover what interfaith means from women's perspective.[4] The focus on reconciliation is not a means to an end but an end in itself. A declaration that the aggressive method of proselytism based on an imperialistic reading of the Gospel passage known as "the great commission" (Matthew 28) has to give way to efforts at peace-building, liberating the captives, healing the sick, feeding the hungry, etc. (Luke 4:18).

'Definitions'

My colleagues and I at the Institute have struggled to understand and translate the meaning of the word *reconciliation*. What does this Christian term mean when used as a focus for the life and activity of a Center? From a Christian theological perspective the word refers to the belief that we were once friends of God but that through transgression we became alienated; the sacrament of confession, general or private, and the absolution which follows it brings remission and reconciles us to God by restoring the broken relationship. The Bible, especially Paul, speaks about it in many passages as something already accomplished by God through Christ's death on the cross. Christians are called to be messengers of this 'ministry of reconciliation'. The dictionary definition of reconciliation reflects a Christian understanding. There is first a state of friendly relationship followed by alienation. Reconciliation is the mending or restoring of this broken relationship.

In October 1997 thirty-one women and men from various Indian regions, backgrounds, faiths and commitments met for five days in Orissa for a workshop on "Reconciliation in the Context of Communalism and Casteism from the Perspective of the Oppressed." After much reflection, discussion and struggle, the participants adopted the following as a working definition of reconciliation:

---

[4] A succinct report of the finding of this successful project is published by the Institute and is available on request.

In the context of existing oppression in India, we understand reconciliation as a process of struggle of the people to bring together estranged persons leading towards transformed relationships and structures based on justice.[5]

What does that mean in practice?

In the Aftermath of a Riot

More than ten years ago, in 1990, the old city of Hyderabad was severely affected by riots that lasted almost three weeks. During and immediately after the horrible communal clashes I spent long painful hours in the hospital and on the streets and had seen the consequences of politically orchestrated violence:[6] the mutilated bodies of children, men and women, the burnt houses and shops, the starving crowds confined to their homes during days of curfew. I can still remember the sea of black veiled women surrounding our relief truck, waiting for a little rice, or the long lines of children waiting patiently in the scorching sun for a few biscuits. I listened to agonizing stories of violence and suffering, and wept with more than one of the victims. It was a terrible time.

Mending a broken relationship with God seems much easier than restoring broken trust in the immediate aftermath of a riot. I remember an old couple stretching out their hands in front of me asking, "With whom should we be reconciled? Our only son is gone ...." They were poor, crippled by old age; their son had been killed on the street through no fault of his. Who could bring back that life that was so brutally taken? Who would care for them in their old age? I realized that reconciliation could not happen without addressing the issue of justice. But who can restore justice in a riot situation when the oppressor remains unknown?

Hyderabad has a long history of Hindu-Muslim conflict, which has left indelible scars in the hearts and minds of people. Every fresh riot fuels the anger and hatred and desire for revenge. I experienced the power of hatred in the Osmania hospital during the 1990 riots. Three young men rushed their dying father to the emergency ward. His belly was slit from side to side, intestines spilling out, and a stream of blood marking the passage as his body was carried in. He was declared dead by the surgeon upon arrival. The youngest son coming out of the ward saw a member of the

---

[5] Their attempt to translate the word into their respective languages was less successful, since they found it difficult to convey the dictionary meaning of the word.

[6] This was during the stir resulting from the demolition of the disputed mosque in Ayodhya when tension between Hindus and Muslims was extremely high. It is believed that making use of this situation, a section of the ruling party in Andra Pradesh, of which Hyderabad is the capital, started riots in the old city. Their intention was to create a situation of law and order in the city in order to get rid of the chief minister. Their *modus operandi* was such that it refueled mutual suspicion among Hindus and Muslims, leading to communal violence.

Aman-Shanti Forum doing voluntary relief work in the hospital.[7] The *bindi* on her forehead[8] signaled to him that she was Hindu. Crying "I will kill them," he lunged at her so violently that six police personnel could not contain him. His grief over the death of his father had rekindled anger and hostility in him towards the other community and a desire for revenge. In the heat of that moment no soft talk about reconciliation would have helped. His hostile and violent behavior towards a woman who had nothing to do with the killing of his father is typical of many riots in our cities.

Some members of the Aman-Shanti Forum joined me in trying different programs to bring the divided communities together: one Friday we all fasted and in the evening gathered to break our fast and pray for peace; women from both communities jointly cooked food and around three hundred of us ate together; we started a tailoring unit for Hindu and Muslim women. These were small projects aimed at bringing reconciliation through reestablished relationships. But our efforts seemed totally inadequate: the wounds were too fresh, the hurt too deep. No one was willing either to forgive or to forget the past. I was frustrated and so were many of my friends. It was evident that deep-rooted hatred and desire for revenge cannot be removed without a long process aimed at inner transformation.

My encounter with Vargese opened a small window into the troubled old city. Vargese is a member of the Montfort Brothers, a Catholic religious congregation whose main mission is education. He invited me to Moosa Nagar, a slum thickly populated by Muslims and a few Hindus. Adjacent to it is Kamal Nagar, housing mostly Hindus interspersed with Muslims. The communal tensions there were high, the self-styled leaders exploiting the situation for political and economic gains. Together with Vargese and his organization, *People's Initiatives Network* (PIN), I began efforts to bring the two communities together by organizing projects, such as a school for children and a tailoring center for women. Two Catholic sisters from another religious congregation joined the project. They and Vargese chose to live in the slum. With funding from HMI and organizational support from PIN we started a cycle rickshaw and pushcart cooperative for jobless young men. HMI also funded evening classes for high school dropout children. Vargese, the sisters and I went from door to door raising issues of hygiene, of common programs to alter the condition of the slum, of getting pure drinking water. Brother Vargese was interested in development. My heart was in reconciliation. We put our energies together. *Development for reconciliation* became our goal. With tremendous energy from PIN and collaborative support from HMI, the face of the slum began to change. People were maintaining cleaner sur-

---

[7] The Aman Shanti Forum was a voluntary movement which I helped to organize, consisting of people of various faiths committed to taking action for building interreligious peace. It came into being just prior to the 1990 riots and was very involved in relief work and in post-riot activities.

[8] A *bindi* is a marking which a Hindu woman traditionally applies to her forehead as a sign of being married. Today many women also wear it cosmetically.

roundings; there was less communal tension. After five years of working together, HMI moved on to its own development project in Sultan Shahi, while PIN spread to many other slums along the Musi River. These were years of rich learning: how to transcend barriers of hostility and begin to build relationships. I also learned something about the nature of violence itself.

Spiral Nature of Violence

Violence begets violence. Every act, whether physically expressed, verbally spoken or manifested through a gesture, creates a reaction. The spiral nature of violence was brought home to me as a group of us were driving on a national highway out of Hyderabad. The truck drivers are some of the most dangerous persons on our two-lane roads: they are aggressive and heedless of traffic rules. The unspoken rule is that bigger the vehicle, the greater the rights. It is extremely difficult, even dangerous, to drive on a road used by truckers—especially at night. The tragic consequences of aggressive driving are evident all along the route: broken trucks, crushed smaller cars, upturned lorries with their contents spilt on the road. On this particular drive, two scenes attracted my notice. In the first two trucks lay totally wrecked in the fields on either side of the road. The impact of their head-on collision was so powerful that the vehicles and their contents were thrown to opposite sides of the road. In the second scene a woman's body lay in the middle of the road, her head covered with leaves and the space around her marked with mud bricks. She was a victim of someone's rash driving.

When we who were traveling on that trip discussed these gruesome scenes, I learned that most of the truck drivers do not go through a formal driving school. Instead they learn driving by serving first as a cleaner. They become a driver only after years of humiliating, often abusive and aggressive, apprenticeship under the driver. It seems the suppressed violence of those years manifests itself when the victim himself becomes a driver. Then he bequeaths the same legacy to his own apprentice.

M.G. Akbar, a noted Indian journalist, speaks about the legacy of violence as he describes in a graphic way the aftermath of riots in Jamshedpur, Bihar:

> ... The wounds of the heart festering, and hate oozing from the eyes like malignant pus that will communicate all that it touches.... In the recesses of the hospitals lie the dead, in hideous shapes, and each of them, each man, woman and child, has written a will in the presence of a hundred witnesses, and the will says that each member of the dead person's family receives a legacy of hate, an equal share each; and this legacy has no limits, no boundaries .... (Akbar 1980: 15-16)

Akbar's words confirm what I said above regarding the spiral nature of violence. Whether it be the young man at the hospital or the truck driver on the road or the Hindus and Muslims who killed each other in the riots—all have left a legacy of hate which in turn leads to desire for revenge erupting in more violence. It is like a pebble thrown in the center of a lake. The smallest ripple caused by that stone would create more ripples. This is what I mean by the spiral nature of violence.

To stop violence we must address the inherited tendency towards violence which all of us carry within us. Often we are not conscious of its existence; it manifests itself when least expected. For example, I vent my anger from a frustrating day at office on my spouse or my children or myself. That violence is endemic to all of us seems self-evident. Despite good intentions to remain calm, we often burst out angrily. Such outbursts may not be bad in themselves; even Christ got angry and chased the merchants from the temple. Although anger need not always be suppressed, we should be conscious of how, when and against whom it is expressed. The internal wounds inflicted by even a violent gesture affect the other and are then passed on. Only by taming our own nature can we hope to become true agents of reconciliation.

The roots of conflicts and riots in our cities are to be traced to the endemic, inherited and spiral nature of violence. In the Hyderabad context it is the layers of hurt, unhealed wounds which surface with the least provocation. It may be a small stone thrown on the house of a neighbor, a piece of dirt cast into the courtyard of a temple or a mosque. The deep, festering wounds left by history explode with vengeance and the conflagration takes place.

To change these, to heal centuries-old wounds, we need a process of struggle which is hard and even dangerous.

Interfaith Prayer?

When I took over as Director of HMI in 1992 all of the eight-member team in the organization were Christians except the two Hindu office attendants. Over the past decade we have intentionally sought to attract an interfaith staff. Today of the thirty members more than half are Muslims and Hindus. It was HMI's practice to begin the day's work with prayer. As the staff began to change, I started to feel uneasy about the form of our morning prayer meetings: the reading of a Bible passage, a short reflection, followed by a prayer which starts with "Our Father" and ends with: "... in the name of our Lord and Savior Jesus Christ." How do we pray together in an interfaith context? How does a Muslim participate in a prayer addressed to Jesus? What does reconciliation mean when it comes to the core aspects of our spiritual lives? Do we change? Do we compromise? For some, to deviate from a Christian pattern of prayer meant a betrayal.

For almost a decade we have been struggling to understand what prayer means in a multicultural, multireligious setting. At times the temptation has been strong to say, "Okay, let's give up and begin with a cup of tea instead!" I was not willing to give up, though. If I am serious about taking the message of reconciliation to our troubled streets, the struggle begins at home, in the institute where I work, in my heart. Peace needs to come from within if reconciliation is to be translated into lived experience.

The form that we have adopted at HMI is not perfect, but is often empowering as each of us takes a turn to lead the morning devotion in our own style. Thus we listen, for example to Asma's profound reflections on a Qur'anic passage, Mr. Rao's recitation of a Sanskrit *sloka* "tamasoma jotir gamaya" ('lead me from darkness to light'), Jan's Gregorian chant, "laudate Dominum omnes gentes." The variations in our expressions have been spiritually enriching for many of us. It has made space for diversity: for my Hindu colleague to break a coconut and apply *tilak* (saffron powder) on my forehead or for a Muslim to ask the community to pray for an ailing father or spouse. In my growing understanding of what reconciliation means, I have come to realize that spirituality has no barriers.

Forgiveness as Precondition for Reconciliation

One necessary condition for reconciliation is the ability to forgive on the part of the victim and the desire for forgiveness on the part of the oppressor. I realized how difficult it is to bring *estranged persons* into relationship by a disturbing incident that occurred in the new city of Hyderabad. The relation between Christians and Muslims in the country has been on the whole friendly at least outwardly. There have not been many newspaper headlines signaling open clashes between the two communities. However, most Christians are totally ignorant of Islam, its beliefs and practices, and have profound prejudices against Muslims. Muslims, on the other hand, often distrust Christians, especially organizations like HMI which have missionary histories.

In August 1997 there were headlines in the newspapers and TV broadcasts describing the Muslim-led assault on the principal of Rock Memorial High School and vandalism of the school precincts, including the desecration of some religious statues. Rock Memorial is a Catholic-run school situated in a predominantly Muslim locality. Of the more than thousand students at least 70% are said to be Muslims. The anger of the Muslim community was roused by disrespectful references to the Prophet in the Moral Science textbook for the ninth grade.

The Christian community was highly offended by the attack. All Christian schools were closed for three days, public processions were organized, the bishops and the clergy demanded an immediate apology from the Muslim community. They pressured the government to punish the culprits under the threat of closing down all Christian schools. For their part, Muslims expressed anger and demanded an apology from Christians for the offence to their Prophet. Newspapers carried front-page report of attacks and counterattacks, which were fortunately only verbal.

The roots of conflict in this case go deeper than what appeared on the surface. A few facts help demonstrate this. For example, the textbook in question has been in use in many Catholic schools. Rock Memorial High School had used it for half a dozen years. Why did the conflict come at this particular point? Moreover, the communities involved had been on relatively good terms. In fact, most Muslims in Hyderabad prefer to send their children to Christian schools, well respected for their educational standards. There is a real scramble for seats during admission time. Why then this conflict which almost led to a riot situation?

A close analysis of events revealed a few political agendas operating. The upcoming feast to honor Our Lady of Good Health annually brings huge crowds to the church where the school is located. This provides an opportunity for many small vendors to do a good business. A few weeks earlier the parish priest, who is also the school administrator, announced that unlike in previous years the space for stalls would be auctioned off to the highest bidder. This would make it difficult for the traditional entrepreneurs, most of whom were Muslims, to do business. A related dynamic was that two Muslim political parties were vying to win Muslims over in the area. These deeper issues were important factors contributing to the violence. In HMI's work on this issue we learned that we need to go beyond surface issues if we want to work towards true reconciliation.

Since 1996 as part of its efforts to bring *estranged persons into friendly relationships*, the Institute has invested in learning and training others in third-party mediation techniques. Pastors, teachers, government officials, police officers and ordinary lay people have gone through this training. HMI's Peace Cell has also successfully intervened in a few conflicts. Seeing the tense atmosphere caused by the textbook conflict, HMI invited a select group of Muslims and Christians to come for a series of meetings—first separately and then together. Both communities were well represented and were of one opinion about the causes for the conflict. They made a number of suggestions for follow-up actions, including inviting the parties directly involved to come to the mediation table. However, HMI was unsuccessful in bringing them together even for a first meeting. Frustrating as it was, I realized that reconciliation could not happen unless both parties in conflict are willing to be open to the possibility of healing.

Some Concluding Words

As stated at the beginning of this paper I have narrated some stories to highlight what reconciliation means in practice. I began with a reference to the happy coming together of Hindus and Muslims as a result of HMI's reconciliation efforts. I spoke of HMI's background and of the change in its constitution which has become the foundation for many of its efforts towards reconciliation. I referred to our struggle to define the meaning of reconciliation and to translate that meaning into action—particularly in the aftermath of 1990 riots. I also described HMI's attempt at interfaith prayer in its morning devotions and its efforts to resolve Christian-Muslim conflict.

While trying to capture on paper a decade's experience in practical ways of peace-building, I have come to believe that true reconciliation cannot happen unless I, as an agent of reconciliation, am committed to personal involvement in a process which aims at bringing peace. This process is long, difficult, at times frustrating and even dangerous. I have learnt that to be successful in bringing peace to others I must begin with myself, with an insight into the endemic, inherited and spiral nature of violence. I have also realized that reconciliation cannot happen unless both the victim and the victimizer genuinely desire to forgive and to be forgiven, which requires a long process of inner healing and transformation. It is also true that restoration of lasting peace is possible only when issues of justice are addressed adequately. For healing inner wounds does not happen through empty words.

In conclusion, I must admit that the way to reconciliation is strewn with hurdles which sometimes seem insurmountable. It demands commitment and prolonged struggle. To me as a Christian and to HMI as a Christian organization the mandate is clear: "blessed are the peacemakers for they shall be called children of God" and so is the model: Christ whose death on the cross brought reconciliation. To be a messenger of reconciliation would mean to be ready for the cross.

Bibliography

Diane D'Souza. (1998). *Evangelism, Dialogue, Reconciliation: The Transformative Journey of the Henry Martyn Institute*. Hyderabad: Henry Martyn Institute.

Religion, Conflict, and Reconciliation in Sri Lanka

Nalin Swaris

Introduction

It is common to describe the war in Sri Lanka as the escalation of an ethnic conflict between the Sinhalese and Tamil people. When reporting it, Western news agencies invariably add that the majority of the Sinhalese are Buddhists and that the majority of the Hindus are Tamils. This has created the impression that Sri Lankans are embroiled in a violent religious conflict. This particular reading of the conflict is incorrect and needs to be rectified. In this paper I will present a more realistic explanation. Thereafter, I will discuss the response or rather the lack of response of Sri Lanka's major religions to the great national calamity, that has befallen Sri Lanka.

Three Anglican Gentleman

The first decades of the twentieth century witnessed an extraordinary degree of interethnic unity among the Anglicized elites of the various ethnic groups. The Ceylon National Congress was founded in 1919 to advance the interests of these elites. They elected a Tamil as their first president even though the majority of the Congress membership was Sinhalese. But rifts began to appear as the British began to share the administration with English-educated natives. These divisions took organizational form when the British established a Council of State and handed over the legislature to elected representatives of the indigenous people. Universal adult franchise was granted to the Lankans in 1931 and parties were formed along ethnic lines. The elites of the various ethnic groups wanted to make sure that they would win sufficient seats in the Council and continue to enjoy at least a share of the national cake.

Sri Lanka gained independence ahead of most of the British colonies. The United National Party (UNP) was founded on the eve of the first general elections to Sri Lanka's independent Parliament. This party, founded by D.S. Senanayeke, incorporated most of the membership of the National Congress. It included members from all ethnic groups and it stood for a multi-ethnic policy in Sri Lanka.

The post-Independence politics of Sri Lanka can best be understood if one looks at the careers of three Anglican gentleman, S.W.R.D Bandaranaieke, J.R. Jayewardene and S.J.V. Chelvanayagam. Bandaranaieke, and Jayewardene hailed from families that had a long history of collaboration with Sri Lanka's colonial rulers.

S.W.R.D. Bandaranaieke

Originally from south India, the founding father of the Bandaranaieke dynasty was a late arrival in Sri Lanka. He was Tamil who married a Sinhalese woman and the family gradually became Sinhalized. The name 'Dias' in the family name suggests that it had been Roman Catholic under the Portuguese. The Bandaranaieke clan was Reformed Protestant under the Dutch and Anglican under the British. Bandaranaieke's father's devotion to the British bordered on the sycophantic. When the Bandaranaieke was baptized into the Anglican faith, his father named him, in addition to his own personal name, after the then British governor general of Sri Lanka, West Ridgeway.

Bandaranaieke was raised as if he was the scion of a British aristocrat and as a young man proceeded to Oxford for higher studies. On his return, he realized that the tide was turning against the Anglicized elites. He gave up wearing European clothes in public and donned the national dress. Like his ancestors, who changed their religion according to the political climate of the day, Bandaranaieke embraced the Buddhist faith. During the days of the State Council (1931-47) Bandaranaieke and Jayewardene promoted the parity of status for Sinhalese and Tamil. Both made the motion in the Council that the two languages replace English as the official language. Bandaranaieke also proposed a federal system of government for independent Sri Lanka. Ironically, federalism was opposed by the Tamil politicians.

In the run up to the first general elections Bandaranaieke joined the United National Party (UNP) founded by D.S. Senanayeke and was appointed one of its vice-presidents. He soon realized that his rise to power was hindered by the domination of the party leadership by the Senanayeke clan. In 1951 he left the UNP and founded the Sri Lanka Freedom Party. Bandaranaieke coopted some of the populist policies of the Marxist parties and grafted them on to a nationalist (Lankan, not Sinhalese) political agenda. The party included in its membership Sinhalese, Tamils and Muslims. The founding manifesto of the new party stated in unambiguous terms that it was essential that Sinhalese and Tamil be made the official languages. The UNP also stood for the parity of Sinhalese and Tamil. The SLFP contested the 1952 general elections and Bandaranieke lost to a UNP candidate. After this setback, Bandaranaieke threw principle and statesmanship to the winds and became a blatantly opportunist politician.

As the elections of 1956 drew near, the Sinhala Buddhist Revival Movement, which began in the last quarter of the nineteenth century, had become a formidable social force. Surrendering to the demands of this movement would mean an end to the concept of Lankan nationality, the multi-ethnic policy promoted by the UNP and change the secular character of the state. Enthusiastic popular support for the revival movement provided the political opportunity for which Bandaranaieke was looking to defeat the UNP and come to power. He declared that if elected, he would "within twenty-four hours, make Sinhala Only the official language of the state." The elections were held in an atmosphere of intense religious euphoria among the Buddhists because 1956 was the 2500^h anniversary of the death of the Buddha. The UNP, apprehensive of the nationalist fervor of the Sinhala Buddhists, did a complete turn around, abandoned its two-language policy and also pledged to make the Sinhala Only the official language. Bandaranaieke swept into power.

Riots broke out when Tamils protested the introduction of the Sinhala Only Bill in parliament. Realizing his mistake, Bandaranaieke looked for a compromise formula to address the grievances of the Tamil people. He signed a pact with Chelvanayagam and pledged, among other things, to make Tamil the administrative language in the Northern and Eastern Provinces. When the terms of the agreement were made known, a storm of protest broke out, much of the opposition coming from extremists in Bandaranaieke's own party. Having been defeated at the polls the UNP was anxious to profit from Bandaranaieke's discomfiture. A powerful section in the UNP, led by J.R. Jayewardene, launched a massive protest against the pact as a sellout to the Tamils. Bandaranaieke lost control of the country. When a large group of Buddhist monks began a sit-down strike on the front lawn of his residence Bandaranaieke came out and told them he had abrogated the Pact. Bandaranaieke's political career was brutally ended by the very forces he had unleashed. He was gunned down by a Buddhist monk.

In 1965 the UNP led by Dudley Senanayeke was returned to power. He signed a new pact which was in substance the same as the Bandaranaieke-Chelvanayagam agreement. This time it was the SLFP that raised the cry that the Sinhalese were being sold out to the Tamils. The main Marxist parties had by this time abandoned their call for the parity of languages and joined the SLFP campaign against the Senanayeke–Chelvanayagam pact. With the emergence of the SLFP a two-party system became stabilized and smaller parties, including the Tamil parties, could exercise political influence only by making electoral alliances with either one of them.

S.J.V. Chelvanayagam

This so-called 'Father of the Tamil Nation' was also Anglican. Due to the peculiarities of the Tamil national movement, there was no difficulty for an Anglican in assuming leadership. It is still unthinkable that a Christian could ever become the leader of the Sinhalese or become the head of state. Chelvanayagam was a wealthy landowner who resided in Colombo. He himself owned plantations when he championed the cause of the plantation Tamils. The source of his wealth was his lucrative law practice in Colombo and the profits of the iniquitous plantation system. He began his political career as a member of the Tamil Congress. This party was founded in 1944 by the enormously wealthy Hindu but Anglicized English gentleman G.G. Ponnambalam. He too had a lucrative law practice in Colombo.

In the consultations between the Anglicized elites and the British about the constitution of independent Lanka, Mr. Ponnambalam proposed a fifty-fifty formula of ethnic representation in Parliament: fifty percent of the seats to be reserved for the Sinhalese and the other fifty for the minorities. The proposal was patently unfair because the Sinhalese made up more than 70% of the population. The British rejected it and opted for territorial representation instead. The UNP, led by D.S Senanayeke, won the first general elections of independent Sri Lanka. Senanayeke was dedicated to the concept of a multi-ethnic polity and invited Ponnambalam to join his government. Ponnambalam readily agreed and in exchange for cabinet posts dropped the call for fifty-fifty ethnic representation. One of the first acts of the independent Parliament was to pass a bill excluding the more than one million plantation workers of Indian origin from Lankan citizenship rights. As a result, they lost the franchise they enjoyed under the British in the days of the State Council. The Tamil Congress voted with the UNP to exclude the plantation Tamils from citizenship. Chelvanayagam and some of his supporters left the Tamil Congress and founded the Federal Party. He believed that, by joining the government, the Tamil Congress would compromise the separate interests of the Tamil people. Ostensibly, Chelvanayagam was in favor of a federal system of government. But in Tamil the party was called the *Thamil Arasu Kattchi*, which means The Tamil State or Government Party. This duplicity has been typical of the manner in which the Federal Party and its successor, the Tamil United Liberation Front (TULF), manipulated Tamil sentiment.

Chelvanayagam contested a seat in Jaffna at the elections of 1952 and was defeated by a Tamil UNP candidate. The political influence of the Federal Party soared only after Bandaranaieke made Sinhala the official language. In 1975 Chelvanayagam, realizing that the two main national parties were not taking his demand for regional autonomy seriously, decided to up the ante. He declared openly what was implicit in the Tamil name of his party: the answer to the problems of the Tamil people was the creation of a separate state in the north and the east. He established a natural link between language and territory. After Chelvanayagam's death in 1976 the leadership of the Federal Party was taken over by Amirthalingam. He founded the TULF, which brought the political leaders from the north and east as well of the plantations areas under a single banner. The TULF pledged to establish a separate state for Tamils in the north and east and declared that it would seek a mandate from the Tamil people in the forthcoming general elections to do so.

The TULF won all the seats in the Jaffna peninsula. In the other Tamil districts, including those in the Eastern Province, the UNP won the majority of the seats. The election was in fact a referendum on the question of a separate state. The TULF failed to obtain a convincing mandate from the Tamil people. The party had obtained only 6% percent of the national popular vote. But due to distortions in the pattern of representation created by the Lankan electoral system, the TULF obtained eighteen seats in Parliament. Mrs. Banadaraieke's SLFP won nearly 30% of the popular vote but ended up with only eight seats. For the first time in Sri Lankan history a Tamil party was the main opposition party. The TULF sat in the parliament of the Sri Lankan state, whose authority it rejected. It enjoyed the privileges and perks of national office while maintaining that its avowed aim was to create a separate state for the Tamil. The concept of Sri Lankan nationality was abandoned by the Tamil leadership when it declared that the Tamils formed a distinct nation and that the Northern and Eastern Provinces were the traditional homeland of the Tamil. This enraged Sinhala nationalists because the Northern and Eastern Provinces had been created by the British in 1832.

The Portuguese and the Dutch had secured only a foothold in the maritime regions of the island. The British took the maritime areas over from the Dutch in 1793 and succeeded in annexing the Kandyan Kingdom by fomenting dissension among the Kandyan chiefs. In 1815 a faction of chiefs rose up against the king of Kandy and invited the British to take over the kingdom. The British entered the hill capital, captured the king, and sent him to exile in South India. The Kandyan Kingdom was formally ceded to the British by the pro-British chiefs. But in 1817 open rebellion broke out which continued till 1818. The British were able to quell the rebellion only after a ruthless campaign. Entire villages were burnt down and village cattle destroyed in order to starve the rebels to submission. The British were never sure of the loyalty of the Kandyans. They decided to break up the Kandyan Kingdom and incorporate its outlying regions into four newly created maritime provinces, Northern, Eastern, Western, and Southern. What remained was the hill country nucleus of the old kingdom, which was demarcated as the Central Province. The heart of the Kandyan Kingdom was turned to a landlocked region. The stated objective of the British in effecting this dismemberment was to destroy the political unity of the Kandyan Sinhalese. The claim that the Eastern Province in particular has always been the traditional homeland of the Tamils remains an affront to Sinhala Buddhist sentiments.

July 1983 is a month of shame in Sri Lanka's modern history. Sinhala goons carried out an island-wide pogrom against unarmed Tamil civilians. Tamil homes and businesses were reduced to ashes. Tamil women and girls were brutally raped. According to unofficial sources, the number of civilians killed were as high as 2000. After a silence of four days Jayewardene briefly addressed the nation on television and blamed the victims for provoking the Sinhalese people by the demand for a separate state. However, it is an open secret that the holocaust was organized by senior members of his cabinet. Jayewardene amended the constitution and made it a criminal offence to demand a separate state. All members of Parliament and government officials had to take an oath abjuring separatism. The TULF had no other option but to vacate their seats, leaving the Tamils without any parliamentary representation. In 1983 the cadres of all the young Tamil militants had numbered less than a thousand. After the pogrom Tamil youths by their thousands joined the militant groups and from that time Sri Lanka has been in a state of open warfare.

After the Indo-Lanka Peace Treaty of 1987 the TULF and all the militant groups, except the Tigers, returned to parliamentary politics. Amirthalingam and the leaders of the TULF took up residence in Colombo. He, like Bandaranaieke, fell victim to the forces he had unleashed. From his jungle hideout, the leader of the Tigers sent a delegation of three youths for talks with the TULF leadership. As they sat down for a seemingly cordial conversation, one of the youths coolly pulled out a gun and shot Amirthalingam in the head.

J.R. Jayewardene

J.R. Jayewardene has been called "the evil genius" of Sri Lanka. He, too, like Bandaranaieke was born into the Anglican faith. He too abandoned Western clothes, donned national attire and embraced Buddhism in the years preceding independence.

The founding father of the Jayewardene lineage, according to archival reports, was the offspring of a casual sexual encounter between an itinerant Moorish trader and a Sinhalese village woman. As a boy, he had worked as a domestic servant in the household of Colonel Drieberg, commander of the Dutch army in Colombo. This young man of nondescript origins became a Reformed Protestant and served the Dutch as a native informant. While spying on British troop movements, he was captured by the British. He escaped execution by changing sides and offering to spy for the British against the Dutch. The Jayewardene family, like the Bandaranaiekes, advanced their fortunes by being Dutch Reformed under the Dutch and Anglican under the British. One member of each of these families helped the British take the last king of Kandy and his royal ladies into custody. Both were handsomely rewarded for their services with large holdings and both built large manor houses for themselves and took on the appurtenances of the Kandyan aristocracy.

After the death of Dudley Senanayeke, Jayewardene, by then a septuagenarian, assumed leadership of the UNP. By election year, 1977, the coalition government of the SLFP and two Marxist parties had been become immensely unpopular. Mrs. Bandaranaieke had become increasingly autocratic and ruled during the entire term of her office under emergency regulations. She made no serious attempt to address the problems of the Tamil people. But ethnic consciousness had receded from the consciousness of the Sinhalese people. Their principal concern was the state of economy and the hardships they had to endure due to mismanagement of the country's affairs by the United Front Government.

In its election manifesto the UNP pledged to address the economic problems of the people, ensure the freedom of the press, the independence of the judiciary and of the state bureaucracy. On the Tamil issue, the manifesto said that it viewed the call for a separate state with sympathy and if elected to power the UNP would without delay call for an all-party conference to address the grievances of the Tamil people. These were spelled out in detail. According to well-informed sources this section of the manifesto was written in consultation with Amirthalingam. This shows that, while taking a strident position in public, the leadership of the Federal Party and the TULF have been willing to accommodate themselves to whatever concessions a ruling party would make to safeguard the rights and dignity of the Tamil people. The UNP did not expect to score a decisive victory over the SLFP, which had been in power for seven years, and many state officials were SLFP appointees. If the UNP obtained only a slim majority, its plan was to form a government with the help of the TULF.

The elections of 1977 were remarkably free and fair, unmarred by violence or rigging of votes. Even though the TULF had openly campaigned to establish a separate Tamil state, not a single Tamil was attacked or harmed in any way. The UNP was swept to power winning five-sixths of the parliamentary seats. The SLFP won only eight seats. Not a single Marxist was returned to power. They paid dearly not only for their autocratic attitude while in power but also and most importantly for having given up their struggle on behalf of the working masses and embracing the communalist policies of Mrs. Bandaranaieke.

J.R Jayewardene's election manifesto was calculated to win the support of the Sinhala Buddhists to solve the problems faced by the Tamil people. He promised to create a *Dharmishta* or Righteous Society, and presented himself as a new Ashoka —the Buddhist emperor of ancient India. Ashoka had renounced state violence and pursued a policy of religious tolerance. The majority of Sri Lankans believed that Jayewardene would act as a senior and experienced statesman and usher in an era of peace and justice for all. But the UNP unleashed violence on its rivals as soon as the election results were announced. Using the massive majority in Parliament, Jayewardene introduced a new constitution and made himself an executive president giving himself powers not enjoyed by either the French or American presidents. The most obnoxious feature of the new constitution was the total immunity before the law granted to the executive president. With his great majority in Parliament and uncontrollable executive power, he no longer found it interesting to make any deals with the Tamil political parties. He spent the first term of his office settling old scores with his Sinhalese political rivals, the Bandaranaiekes, the Senanayeke and the leftists. Dormant Sinhalese communalism was aroused by the UNP. Jayewardene encouraged a senior cabinet minister to wage an anti-Tamil campaign using the resources of the state.

The litany of abuses of power, committed by the Jayewardene regime is too long to enumerate in a short paper such as this. When Jayewardene left office at the end his second term, as required by the constitution, the nation was in tatters. The country was convulsed by terrorist insurrections, one led by the Tamil Tigers in the North and the other by Sinhalese youths of the Peoples Liberation Front (JVP). His successor, R. Premadasa, failed in his attempts to make peace with the JVP and turned the full wrath of the state against it. Shadowy death squads raided Sinhalese homes and abducted young men and women suspected of being members of JVP under cover of darkness, brutally tortured and killed them. Female captives were often gang-raped before they were killed. To drive terror into the hearts of the people, the corpses were then piled up in heaps and burnt in public places. More than 60,000 Sinhalese youth were killed or disappeared within a brief period of four months. The number of people killed in the northern war, Tamil militants, Sri Lankan forces and civilians during seventeen years of war is calculated to be about 65,000.

A Paradise Turned into Hell

Because of the breath-taking beauty of the Sri Lankan landscape, its varied climates and topography, since ancient times visitors have hailed it as an earthly paradise. The island has also been blessed with an extraordinarily intelligent and gifted people. The politicians who took over power from the British have turned it into a living hell. At the general election of 1994, a People's Alliance, led by Ms. Chandrika Kumaratunga defeated the UNP by a narrow majority. When she presented herself as candidate for the presidency a wave of hope and optimism swept through the country.

Kumaratunga's credentials with the Tamil were excellent. While in opposition she had valiantly defended the rights of the Tamil people. Euphoria about Kumaratunga was widespread in Tamil areas. Young Tamil women enthusiastically bought bracelets sold on the Jaffna market as 'Chandrika Bangles'. Kumaratunga won the presidency with an unprecedented 62% of the popular vote. It was clear that the majority of the Tamil people had pinned their hopes on her. They yearned for peace and an end to the killings. Children who grew up in Tamil areas after 1983 had known no other reality except war. Kumaratunga promised to abolish the notorious executive presidency within months of coming to power, remove the worst excesses of the unbridled free market policies, introduce a Workers' Charter, end state terrorism and eradicate the corruption which had become a way of life under the UNP. She promised to declare a ceasefire and begin talks with the Tigers. As in 1977 the Lankan people placed their trust in a government which pledged itself to follow non-communalist policies and address the economic woes of the masses.

The hopes of the people have once again been dashed. Kumaratunga continues to rule capriciously, enjoying the powers of immunity given her by the Jayewardene constitution. She has failed to honor any of her election pledges. Corruption is rampant. Her approach to the talks with the Tigers was naive and amateurish. The composition of government delegations to Jaffna was changed at whim. Negotiators were chosen because they were personal friends of the president. They lacked the necessary skills and experience to negotiate with the tough and battle-hardened Tiger delegation. Within months the Tigers broke the ceasefire unilaterally and resumed the war, charging Kumaratunga of duplicity and lack of seriousness. The entire country is now back to square one.

In the war-torn areas of the north and the east there are over a million displaced persons. An equal number of displaced Tamils live in refugee camps in south India. More than half the Jaffna population according to a recent estimate consists of displaced people. Tamils who have the means and the contacts to do so have flown to Western countries and obtained refugees status. The war rages on with no end in sight.

The Response of Religions to Sri Lanka's Tragedy and Moral Crisis

Sri Lanka boasts that it has four major religions of the world, Buddhism, 'Hinduism', Christianity and Islam. Sri Lankan society is intensely religious, even superstitious. On days of observance the Buddhist temples, Hindu kovils, Christian churches and mosques overflow with devotees. However, the great moral crisis in Sri Lankan society seems to elude the concern of its religious leaders. The inertia of the major religions in the face of the great calamity which engulfs the nation is due to the highly devotional and lucrative type of religiosity they offer and foster among their members. The morality inculcated is individualistic and family-oriented. All the major religions promise material blessings through rituals performed by priest and monk and there is always a price tag attached to these services. Attending religious services and giving donations to religious institutions have come to be seen as the hallmark of a virtuous person. Thus, religion, instead of sensitizing the social conscience and moral sensibilities, functions as a mechanism for deflecting awareness away from social realities.

There is no ethnic conflict in Sri Lanka in the sense of Sinhalese and Tamil mobs fighting pitched battles with each other as in the Moluccas. Despite communalist propaganda there is no deep-rooted hostility and suspicion between the ordinary Sinhalese and Tamils as there has been between Protestants and Catholics in Northern Ireland. The great tragedy of Sri Lanka is that it has not produced a single statesman of the calibre of a Mahatma Gandhi, Jawaharlal Nehru or Nelson Mandela. Neither has it produced any religious leader of the moral stature of a Martin Luther King Jr. or a Desmond Tutu to lead all the people of Sri Lanka in a mass non-violent campaign against war and public immorality and to tell the government and the Tigers that enough is enough, that what all Sri Lankans need is a guarantee that they can live in peace in a society which respects the fundamental rights of everyone irrespective of ethnicity or religious affiliation. For this the Sinhalese and Tamil politicians and rabblerousers must be asked to cease their rhetoric about predestined or exclusive homelands. Sri Lanka must be proclaimed the home of all its people and they should have the right to conduct their affairs in their chosen language and the freedom to live and work wherever they wish to do so. What is necessary is to create unity among the people rather than dividing and then uniting territories. This is the principled religious obligation of the moral guardians of Sri Lankan society.

Truth and Reconciliation in Post-Apartheid South Africa

Piet Meiring

Introduction

The South African Truth and Reconciliation Commission (TRC), established by an Act of Parliament in June 1995, received an important mandate: to establish as complete a picture as possible of the apartheid past, to facilitate the granting of amnesty to the perpetrators of gross human rights violations, to allow victims the opportunity to relate their own accounts of the violations they had suffered, and to recommend reparation measures in this respect.

> Before You, in anguish and in shame, we bring the poles of our society—oppressor and oppressed, victim and offender—and we pray for the end to the alienation, for healing and for reparation. Hear our prayer! We looked into the eyes of our children and were overwhelmed. We looked into the eyes of our parents and were dejected. We looked into each other's eyes and turned away. We desire peace! Merciful God, we confess that we never believed what had happened. We tried to escape from reality. We never really listened or heard. We allowed a wedge to be driven between us. We pray for forgiveness!

The large audience in St George's Cathedral in Cape Town—politicians and diplomats, victims and perpetrators, black and white, South Africans from all walks of life, young and old, all who had come to witness the inauguration of the Truth and Reconciliation Commission—bowed their heads in prayer. Candles were lit, hymns were sung. Commissioners were sworn in. President Mandela addressed the hushed gathering. The time had come to remember the past, he said. It may be uncomfortable to many, but we had no other option. Ordinary South Africans were determined that the mistakes of the past would never be repeated. He concluded: "The choice we have is not whether we should disclose the past, but *how* it will be done. It must be done in such a way that reconciliation and peace are promoted." "We do indeed have to face the past," Archbishop Desmond Tutu, newly appointed chairperson of the TRC, concurred, "for if we do not face the past, it may return!" (Meiring 1999: 17).

I was myself a member of the TRC and will in this paper report on the work done by the TRC's three committees and finally I will discuss six important lessons the TRC learned in its search for truth and especially for national reconciliation.

How to Deal with the Past?

For five years—ever since the watershed announcement of President F. W. de Klerk in February 1990 that the ANC and other liberation organizations were to be un-banned, that all political prisoners, among them Nelson Mandela, would be freed, and that democratic elections involving the whole South African population were to be held—the issue of the past had been hotly debated. The debate was on the agenda, too, of the multiparty conference (CODESA) which, prior to the 1994, elections had to struggle, on the one hand, with the plight of the thousands of *victims* of the apartheid years and, on the other, with the urgent needs of the many *perpetrators* of apartheid who were guilty of gross human rights violations in the past. A blanket amnesty would not work—that kind of pardon would have represented a total disregard and dishonoring of the pain and suffering of the victims. On the other end of the scale, Nuremberg-type trials where the victors take the vanquished to court, to be convicted and sentenced, were also not advisable—not if reconciliation was the order of the day. One of the last decisions taken by CODESA was to establish a Truth and Reconciliation Commission. This was not a unique experiment. Between 1974 and 1994 no less than nineteen truth commissions have been established in many parts of the world, in Latin America, Africa, and in Europe.

The South African Truth and Reconciliation Commission (TRC)

The South African TRC was established with high hopes and with an important mandate. Let me quote from the preamble of the *Act on the Promotion of National Unity and Reconciliation* (TRC Report 1998/1: 55-57):

> Since the Constitution of the RSA provides a historic bridge between the past of a deeply divided society characterized by strife, conflict, untold suffering and injustice, and a future founded on the recognition of human rights, democracy, and peaceful co-existence for all South Africans, irrespective of colour, race, class, belief or sex;
>
> And since it is deemed necessary to establish the truth in relation to past events as well as the motives for and circumstances in which gross violations of human rights have occurred, and to make the findings known in order to prevent a repetition of such acts in future;
>
> And since the Constitution states that the pursuit of national unity, the well-being of all South African citizens, and peace, require reconciliation between the people of South Africa and the reconstruction of society;
>
> And since the Constitution states that there is a need for understanding but not for vengeance, a need for reparation but not for retaliation, a need for *ubuntu* but not for victimization;
>
> And since the Constitution states that in order to advance such reconciliation and reconstruction amnesty shall be granted in respect of acts, omissions, and offences associated with political objectives committed in the course of the conflicts of the past;
>
> ... Therefore a National Truth and Reconciliation Commission will be instituted with a fourfold agenda:

1. To establish as complete a picture as possible of the past. The causes, nature, and extent of suffering of human rights violations between 1960 and 1994 have to be established, taking into consideration the following: the circumstances, factors, and context of the violations, the perspectives of the victims as well as the perspectives and motives of the perpetrators.
2. To facilitate the granting of amnesty. After full disclosure of the relevant facts, and if the deed for which amnesty is required complies with the qualifications of the act (specifically the political nature of the act), amnesty may be granted.
3. To establish and make known the whereabouts of the victims, restoring their human and civil dignity by granting them the opportunity to relate their own accounts of the violations they suffered, and by recommending reparation measures in this respect.
4. To compile a report, as comprehensive as possible, on the activities and findings of the TRC, with recommendations of measures to prevent future violations of human rights in the country.

In December 1995 the seventeen commissioners of the TRC were appointed by President Mandela, with the immediate mandate to add another eleven committee members to their ranks, representing the different cultural, racial, political and religious communities of South Africa. The commissioners and committee members were divided into three committees: The Human Rights Violations Committee, the Amnesty Committee, and the Reparation and Rehabilitation Committee. Two directorates, one for Investigations, the other for Research, were added. Four regional offices were established: in Cape Town, Johannesburg, East London, and Durban. The TRC officially commenced with its work on February 1, 1996, and (with the exception of the Amnesty Committee) closed its doors on July 31, 1998. The Final Report was handed to President Mandela on October 29, 1998. The Amnesty Committee's report appeared in early 2001.

The Human Rights Violations Committee (HRVC)
During the two and a half years of its existence the HRVC collected thousands of statements from victims from all over South Africa, many of whom were invited to submit their statements at public hearings conducted in a number of cities and towns in the different provinces. Media coverage was extensive. Night after night the faces of many of the victims appeared on television screens nation-wide: tearful faces of parents who lost their children, of husbands and wives who lost their spouses, bewildered faces of old men and women who carried their sorrows over many years, faces of young comrades, of politicians, of farmers who lost their beloved in land mine explosions, of innocent passersby when a bomb, hidden in a busy street, exploded.

The definition of "gross human rights violations" was rather restrictive. Not everybody who suffered under apartheid, who was forcefully relocated, or humiliated, or discriminated against or wrongfully arrested automatically qualified for making a statement. If that were the case, millions would have joined the queue! Gross human rights violations were defined as murder, manslaughter, kidnapping, rape and severe ill treatment that left permanent scars, mentally or physically. Nobody really knew how many victims to expect. In the end no less than 140 public hearings were held; 21,400 victims submitted statements; the names of 27,000 victims were officially recorded (TRC Report/2 1998: 1-33). To the majority the experience proved to be worth their while, even if it was difficult to take the stand. Tears flowed freely, but those were tears of catharsis and healing.

> An old gentleman from Soweto spoke for many when he remarked at a Johannesburg hearing: "When I was tortured at John Vorster Square my tormentor sneered at me: 'Shout your lungs out! Nobody will ever hear you!' Now, at long last, people do hear me ...." (Meiring 2000a: 190)

Not everybody reacted positively. There were also those who returned home disappointed and frustrated. But they constituted a minority. To thousands of victims it was, indeed, a cathartic experience. Allow me to quote from my diary (East London Hearing, April 16-19, 1996):

> "Was everything worth it?" I asked myself when after one of the morning sessions I walked outside. What one of the Xhosa women—one of the unknown, practically forgotten witnesses—had to say in the hall just now did not only move the archbishop to tears, but left every one of us with a lump in the throat. With effort she put her tale on the table: how she sent her fourteen-year-old son to the local shop to buy bread. There was unrest in the township and somewhere along the way it must have happened that the boy landed in the crossfire. For some reason the Security Police arrested the wounded child and subjected him to brutal torture. Two days later the mother who, panic-stricken, fumbled about to find out what had happened to her son, saw on their neighbour's television set how the boy was being pulled down from a pick-up truck by his ankles, how he was dragged across the tarmac. It was difficult for the mother to relate how the police eventually gave her an address where she could find her son. When she arrived there, it was the mortuary. With her own hands she had to prepare her son's body—with the gaping bullet wound at the back of the head, with the burn marks where he was tortured—for the funeral.
>
> My lunch in my hand, I encountered the woman in the midst of a small group of victims. "Madam," I asked, "you have come such a long way, over so many years, with your story .... You had to travel such a distance to come here. All of us saw how difficult it was for you to tell the story of your son. Please tell me, was it worth it?"
>
> The marks of her tears were still on her cheeks. But when she raised her head and smiled, it was like the dawn breaking. "Oh yes, Sir, absolutely! It was difficult to talk about these things. But tonight, for the first time in sixteen years, I think I will fall asleep immediately. Maybe tonight I will sleep soundly without having nightmares!" (Meiring 1998: 25, slightly abridged)

Apart from the victim's hearings a number of special hearings had been organized to look into specific cases, to try and establish as complete a picture as we could of major instances of protest uprisings of victims of racist oppression in the past: Sharpeville 1960, Soweto 1976, the Boipatong massacres of the early 1990s. Special interest groups were also invited to hearings: prison officials, security police, women, the youth and children, the media, the health sector, business and labor and the legal community. Political parties from across the board made lengthy statements at hearings specially organized for them. A special hearing for the Christian churches as well as for the other faith communities to explain their role in the history of South Africa was held in East London (TRC Report 1998/4: 1-316).

Under Section 29 of the Act the TRC was mandated to subpoena individuals to appear before the Commission if additional information was needed on the incidents mentioned above or on the involvement of certain individuals in these incidents. In the four regional offices Section 29 Hearings became a weekly occurrence. Bit by bit, piece by piece, the jigsaw puzzle of South Africa's recent history was fitted together. When Ms Winnie Mandela appeared before the nation to answer questions on no less than eighteen charges, world attention was focussed on the proceedings—as was the case when former state president P.W. Botha was subpoenaed. Some of the most shocking revelations resulted from the investigation into the involvement of Dr. Wouter Basson ('Doctor Death') and some of his colleagues in the former Defence Force's secret chemical and biological weapons program.

The Amnesty Committee
The second committee, the Amnesty Committee, had an equally arduous task: to receive applications from perpetrators—from all sides of the struggle—who desired amnesty. The offer of amnesty was extremely generous—to some critics far too generous—enabling perpetrators of gross violations, on making a full disclosure of the acts under consideration and by persuading the Amnesty Committee of the political and military nature of those acts, to walk out of the amnesty court with a clean slate. No legal actions or even civil claims could be brought against a perpetrator, once he had received amnesty. The judges and lawyers, together with their legal teams, crisscrossed the country to conduct their hearings. The Committee had been given very strong powers to conduct their business, having the authority of a Court of Appeal.

As was the case with the Human Rights Violations hearings, nobody really foresaw how many perpetrators would come to avail themselves of the amnesty offer. The Amnesty Committee's hearings had a rather slow start, most of the initial applications coming from prisoners who were already serving time on a myriad of purely criminal charges. But then, by the middle of 1996, the small stream turned into a gushing river. In the wake of General Johann van der Merwe, Chief of Police during the last years of the National Party government, a number of policemen—especially from the ranks of the Security Police—made their way to the Amnesty Committee. A smaller number of military officers, as well as politicians representing many parties, followed suit, even though some high profile politicians and senior military officers, to the disappointment of many, refused to do so.

The amnesty process had not been without controversy. From the start spokespersons from the side of the victims, notably a number of well-known victim families, *inter alia* the Biko, Mxenge and Goniwe families from the Eastern Cape, strongly and publicly opposed the amnesty process. It was, to their way of thinking, morally unacceptable to allow perpetrators of heinous crimes to walk away scot free. They should be charged in court and sentenced. Also, the granting of amnesty took away from the victims and their families the possibility of civil suits against their tormentors. Amnesty was costing the victims dearly, they argued.

The first rounds of amnesty hearings dealt mainly with perpetrators from the ranks of the previous regime. Day after day the media carried reports on the criminal acts of police and security police, of people employed by the previous government —fueling the growing perception among some whites that the TRC was little more than a witch hunt, a one-sided action of blacks (the ANC) against whites, with the single purpose of embarrassing the National Party government. Tutu, as well as the members of the Amnesty Committee, did their level best to allay these perceptions and fears, pointing out that the TRC was mandated to work in an evenhanded, unbiased, manner, that perpetrators from all sides of the struggle were called to testify. Not everybody was persuaded. Ironically, at the very end—exactly one day before the Final Report was to be put on the table—the ANC too went to court to request an interdict against the publication of the findings, because the report in their view "criminalized" the ANC's role in the struggle. Perpetrators from the ranks of the liberation movement fighting *against* apartheid operated on a higher moral level than perpetrators from the previous regime who fought to *uphold* apartheid and should be treated with more leniency, the ANC argued.

The Reparation and Rehabilitation Committee

The third committee, called the Reparation and Rehabilitation Committee, received a twofold responsibility. Their *first* task was to see to it that the necessary support systems were put into place to help victims who appeared at the hearings, as well as their families, through the often traumatic process of reliving and dealing with the past. This service was, after some debate, also extended to perpetrators who had applied for amnesty, and their families. The *second* task was to assess the harm suffered by the victims and to make proper recommendations to the government on reparation and rehabilitation. In order to do this, the Reparation and Rehabilitation Committee had to keep proper records of the circumstances of the victims, carefully listing their most urgent needs. Five areas of need manifested themselves: medical, emotional, educational, material and 'symbolic' (the latter referring to such symbolic acts as the erection of tombstones, reburials, expunging of criminal records, the erection of monuments and memorials, special reconciliation ceremonies, etc).

The TRC felt strongly about this matter: the victims of gross human rights violations had a moral and a legal right to proper reparation. If the amnesty process seemed to indicate that the TRC process was 'perpetrator friendly', the reparations proposals were to show that the process was, indeed, a 'victim friendly' process. The very generous offer of amnesty and indemnity to perpetrators was to be counterbalanced by an equally generous reparation program for the victims. Taking into account the needs of the victims, five categories of reparation, were decided upon: *urgent interim reparation* for victims who were old, sick or in dire need; *individual reparation grants* (ranging from R17,000 to R21,000 per person, annually, over a period of six years); the *improvement of community services*; *symbolic reparation*; and *institutional reparation* (TRC Report/5 1998: 170-95, 304-49).

How Successful was the TRC?

The Truth and Reconciliation process was expensive, not only in terms of money but especially in terms of manpower and time. Did it succeed in its task? José Zalaquett, who headed the Chilean Truth Commission once remarked that, based on the collective wisdom of the nineteen similar commissions mandated in the past, *three prerequisites* for success emerged: *firstly*, the nation should own the process; *secondly*, the government should show the political will not only to appoint a commission and to provide for the necessary infrastructure but to implement the proposals made at the end of its course, and *thirdly*, the process cannot go on indefinitely—it needs to come to an end (Meiring 2000a: 194).

Looking at these prerequisites in reverse order: the process in South Africa did end eventually—but not as soon as envisaged in the Act. Instead of eighteen months it went on for thirty. But on October 29 1998 the final report was put on the table —even though the Amnesty Committee at that time was still struggling to finish with its work. Secondly, the South African government did receive and accept the final report. A lengthy debate in Parliament was devoted to the findings, and some reparation interventions have taken place. A lot of pressure was brought to bear on the government during the last quarter of 2000 by civil society, the media, victim support groups, religious organizations, by Truth Commissioners themselves, to start implementing individual reparation grants, which, it was said, would prove that the TRC process had indeed been 'victim friendly'.

As to the *first* prerequisite: did the nation accept ownership of the process? Future historians will have the final say. But a few tentative and preliminary remarks may be made in this regard. For the 21,400 *victims* who submitted their statements and for their families, it was—with some notable exceptions—a healing, cathartic experience. The tears were tears of healing. The words of the Xhosa mother, quoted earlier in this paper, were echoed by many: "Oh yes, it was worth our while." For the more than 7000 *perpetrators* who applied for amnesty, the process also meant a great deal—for those who were granted amnesty it provided a new lease on life.

But how did the general public react? Did the nation own the process? Generally speaking, most black and brown South Africans—the people who were mostly at the receiving end of apartheid—were grateful for and satisfied with the work of the TRC. Critical remarks were made from time to time when Desmond Tutu, for instance, seemed to bend over backwards to accommodate whites—in particular former state president P.W. Botha. The same was unfortunately not true of the white community. While some did enter into the spirit of the process and identified with it and were indeed also healed by the process, others remained aloof and even critical. Being exposed to the horrible past is not a pleasant thing, and having to acknowledge one's own responsibility and complicity—by commission or by omission—does not come easily. A national survey indicated that whereas more than 90% of black and brown

South Africans was satisfied with the TRC process, only one third of their white compatriots is unreservedly positive about it, one third was negative and one third was "undecided" (Institute for Justice and Reconciliation, November 2000).

Was Reconciliation Achieved? Lessons to be Learned

The name of the Commission was the Truth and *Reconciliation* Commission, which leaves one with the question: after the 'truth' was reported, what happened to reconciliation? Was finding the truth done in such a way—to quote Mandela once again —that reconciliation and peace were promoted?

Perhaps the drafters of the TRC Act (all of us involved in the process) were somewhat naïve thinking that once we invited Truth through the front door, Reconciliation would slip in through the back one. What the South African experience taught us is that reconciliation does occur, but it is never to be taken for granted. Reconciliation is a very fragile flower. It does not come cheap. It cannot be arranged or organized. Microwave reconciliation does not last very long.

At least six lessons may be garnered from the South African experience.

Reconciliation needs to be clearly defined. Right up to the end of the process, the commissioners—indeed, most South Africans—were still unclear about how the term should be understood. Whereas the lawyers and politicians in the TRC used a minimalist definition ("Don't expect too much. Simply be glad when people stop the killings, when the dust settles in the streets. Declare that to be reconciliation"), Tutu and the *baruti,* the pastors, favored a far more lofty, maximalist definition. When Tutu spoke of reconciliation, he clothed it in highly religious terminology, often referring to 2 Corinthians 5:11-21: it is only because God had reconciled us to Himself by sacrificing his Son Jesus Christ on the cross, that true and lasting reconciliation between human beings, between communities, became possible. In similar fashion spokespersons for the other faith communities, when they joined in the debate, used deeply religious terminology, referring to the deepest sources of their beliefs (Meiring 2000b: 121-33).

Reconciliation and Truth go hand in hand. Why do we not just close the books and get on with life? was a question asked by many during the TRC years. The answer, of course, was: yes, the time will come when we are able to put our past behind us. But one can only close a book, after it has been properly opened. Finding the truth is a prerequisite for reconciliation. The *victims* needed it; it was an important first step on the road towards reparation and rehabilitation. Zalaquett's comment on the Chilean experience was equally valid in South Africa: "We *owe* the truth to the victims and their families. The truth is at least as important as justice." The *nation*, too, needed to hear the truth, to be shamed by the truth, to wrestle with the truth, to learn to live with the truth and eventually to be set free by the truth (Meiring 1998: 375-76).

Reconciliation requires a deep, honest confession—and a willingness to forgive. Although the TRC Act did not require of perpetrators to make an open confession or ask for forgiveness before amnesty was granted, it has to be stated clearly that lasting reconciliation rests upon the capacity of perpetrators—of a community of perpetrators —to recognize their guilt honestly and deeply towards God and their fellow human beings—the community of victims—and to ask humbly for forgiveness. In South Africa, in spite of a myriad of statements and resolutions by virtually every organization, party and especially by the many churches in the country, we still have a long way to travel on the road of confession—and of forgiveness.

Justice and Reconciliation are two sides of the same coin. For reconciliation to happen, there has to be a sense of justice being part and parcel of the process. Moreover, lasting reconciliation can only flourish in a society where justice is maintained. In South Africa, this brings a number of issues to the fore: not only the issue of proper government reparation to the victims to balance the granting of amnesty to the perpetrators of the past, but wider issues involving every South African: unemployment, poverty, affirmative action, education, restitution, the land issue, economic inequality, redistribution of resources, reparation tax, et cetera.

For Reconciliation, a deep commitment is needed. Reconciliation, history teaches us, is not for the fainthearted. In South Africa God was good to us, providing us not only with the likes of Nelson Mandela and Desmond Tutu, but with thousands of individuals—some well known, others lesser known—who were willing to take up the challenge and, in many cases, to pay the price of reconciliation. The annals of the TRC contain many inspiring stories of ordinary citizens who often reached beyond themselves to facilitate reconciliation.

On the road to Reconciliation: One should expect the unexpected! The road to reconciliation is rocky, full of dangers and disappointments. But it is also full of surprises. "It never ceases to astonish me," Tutu said, "the magnanimity of many victims who suffered the most heinous of violations, who reach out to embrace their tormentors with joy, willing to forgive and wanting to reconcile". A last quote from my diary (21 April 1997):

> "One can see God's influence in what is happening tonight," Mcibisi Xundu, pastor and TRC committee member said, looking at Eric Taylor, former security police officer who had applied for amnesty for his part in the killing of the 'Cradock Four'. "It is God who has led you to take this step towards reconciliation." A few weeks earlier a young DRC pastor Charl Coetzee approached me. One of his parishioners, Eric Taylor, wanted to meet the family of Matthew Goniwe, the activist he had tortured and murdered.
>
> Mrs Goniwe, a strong critic of the TRC process, refused to come, but the rest of the family as well as the families of the rest of the Cradock Four travelled from Cradock to Port Elizabeth for the occasion. Suspicion and anger were in the air. The families of the victims had many questions, needed many answers. Taylor answered as best he could. At the end of a long evening he turned to the Goniwe family and to their colleagues: "I came to ask you to forgive me, if the Lord can give you the strength to do that".
>
> The response was moving. One after another the family members came to the fore to shake Eric Taylor's hand and to assure him of their forgiveness. Many a cheek was wet with tears. The son of Goniwe walked up to the policeman. His

right arm was in plaster, but with his left arm he embraced Eric Taylor. "It is true," he said, "you murdered my father. But we forgive you ...."
When Charl Coetzee reported to me about the meeting, I immediately phoned Desmond Tutu in Cape Town. "I have heard the news," he commented. "Mrs Goniwe told me this morning that the next time she would be there!" When we concluded our conversation Tutu wanted us to pray: "O Lord, we thank You for being the God of surprises, for surprising us every day, for the miracles of reconciliation in our country ...." (Meiring 1998: p 123-27, slightly abridged)

Wounded but Being Healed

Not Cape Town but Pretoria was the venue for the final ceremony of the TRC. On 29 October, 1998, politicians, diplomats, victims and perpetrators, black and white, once again bowed their heads in prayer. Tutu was there, smiling broadly, playfully staggering under the weight of the five volumes of the Final Report. "Not everybody will be happy with the report ..." he remarked. Mandela was there, to receive the report. "I accept the report as it is ... as the TRC's contribution to reconciliation and nation building. Let us accept our responsibility ... to build a better future."

"We have been wounded but we are being healed," the archbishop concluded. "It is possible even with our past of suffering, anguish, alienation and violence to become one people, reconciled, healed, caring, compassionate and ready to share as we put our past behind us to stride into the glorious future God holds before us as the Rainbow People of God." (Meiring 1998: 379)

As if to say 'Amen' to that, which a choir from Soweto intoned, more beautifully than ever, the words of South Africa's new anthem: "Nkosi sikelele i'Afrika:" God bless Africa!

Bibliography

Boraine, Alex. (2000). *A Country Unmasked: Inside South Africa's Truth and Reconciliation Commission*. Oxford: OUP.
Du Toit, C.W. (ed.). (1998). *Confession and Reconciliation: A Challenge to the Churches in South Africa*. Pretoria: UNISA.
Jeffrey, Anthea. (1999). *The Truth about the Truth Commission*. Johannesburg: S A Institute of Race Relations.
Krog, Antjie. (1998). *Country of My Skull*. Johannesburg: Random House.
Meiring, Piet. (1998). *Chronicle of the Truth Commission: A Journey through the Past and Present – Into the Future of South Africa*. Vanderbijlpark: Carpe Diem Books.
———. (2000a). "Truth and Reconciliation: The South African Experience." In: William E. van Vugt and G. Daan Cloete (eds.). *Race and Reconciliation in South Africa*. Lanham: Lexington Books.
———. (2000b). "The *Baruti* vs the *Lawyers*: The Role of Religion in the TRC Process." In: Charles Villa-Vicencio and Wilhelm Verwoerd (eds). *Looking Back, Reaching Forward: Reflections on the TRC of South Africa*. Cape Town/London: UCT Press/Zed Books.
Truth and Reconciliation Commission of South Africa: Report. (October 1998). Volumes 1-5. Cape Town: TRC (Distributed by Juta & Co Ltd, Cape Town).

Tutu, Desmond. (1999). *No Future Without Forgiveness*. London/Johannesburg: Rider.
Van Vugt, William E. and G. Daan Cloete. (2000). *Race and Reconciliation in South Africa*. Lanham: Lexington Books.
Villa-Vicencio, Charles. (2000). *Transcending a Century of Injustice*. Cape Town: Institute for Justice and Reconciliation.
——— and Wilhelm Verwoerd (eds.). (2000). *Looking Back, Reaching Forward: Reflections on the TRC of South Africa*. Cape Town/London: UCT Press/Zed Books.

An Islamic View of Conflict and Reconciliation in the South African Situation

Farid Esack

Introduction

I assume that an Islamic perspective is one which emerges from the textual sources of Islam, the Qur'an and the *Sunnah* (the precedent of Muhammad—peace be upon him). Anyone who is familiar with these, however, would be aware of their discordant impulses on issues of conflict, peace, and reconciliation and that in the final analysis one is left with what the scholar or presenter has decided to present as his or her appreciation of the Islamic perspective (or his or her perspective clothed in the garb of Arabic/Qur'anic expressions and selective invoking of the Qur'an and the *Sunnah*). An additional problem is that my theological heritage—as is the case with everyone—is filled with influences from all sorts of 'alien' intellectual and theological influences. In some ways, we resemble the Nazi who spews forth at the Jews in the secret knowledge or dark fear that he himself is the carrier of Jewish blood. And thus my presentation is an unashamedly Colored/Mulatto/Mezisto one, despite the title.

Second, I assume that we are dealing with conflict and reconciliation in a sociopolitical context. My problem with this is that—if interpreted narrowly—one runs the risk of simplifying the challenges facing our country and of claiming easy victories. If, for example, one were to look at the question of conflict through narrow political lenses then South Africa comes across as a miracle nation that avoided a dirty and bloody racial war at five minutes to midnight. If, however, one observes how domestic violence, rape and murder has escalated in the last few years then a different picture emerges: the war has not been averted—it has merely assumed another character.

Conflict in Apartheid South Africa

South Africa had long been a deeply conflict-ridden society. This conflict assumed a structural nature under colonialism with more pronounced racial undertones during apartheid. The apartheid regime, attempting to obscure its own violent nature, consistently presented any opposition to it as an affront to peace and stability. A series of laws criminalizing opposition to apartheid were, in fact, presented as peacekeeping and stability-ensuring measures. As is the case in most police states in the world 'law and order' were the watchwords. When, on the one hand, peace comes to mean the absence of conflict and when, on the other, conflict with an unjust and racist political order is a moral imperative, it is not difficult to understand that the better class of human beings are, in fact, deeply committed to disturbing the peace and creating conflict. The slogan "No Justice, No Peace" now commonly heard on the streets of Occupied Palestine found a deep resonance in the South Africa of the seventies and eighties—and it was pregnant with meaning. It is a commitment; "We commit ourselves to disturbing the 'peace' for as long as there is injustice." It is a threat: "For as long as there is injustice, we will ensure that you will have no peace." And it is an affirmation of a simple yet profound truth: "For as long as there is injustice, the 'peace', which is evident, is a sham." Along with all other progressive forces in South Africa I affirmed the value of revolutionary insurrection against the apartheid state. I affirmed conflict as a means to disturbing an unjust peace and a path to a just peace. In other words; peace, law and order were of no substantive consequence to us; the fundamental question was: Stability and peace to what end? Our response to the regime's call for peace and stability was to call on people to wage a *jihad* against the apartheid state.[1]

Jihad *in Apartheid South Africa*

Jihad literally means 'to struggle', to 'exert oneself' or 'to spend (energy or wealth)'. For Muslims, the term *jihad* has also come to mean the "sacralization of combat" (Schleifer 1982: 122). Despite its popular meaning as a sacred armed struggle or war, the term *jihad* was always understood by Muslims to embrace a broader struggle to transform both one's self and society. The Qur'an itself uses the word in its various meanings ranging from warfare (4:90; 25:52; 9:41) to contemplative spiritual struggle (22:78; 29:6) and even exhortation (29:8; 31:15). Whatever benign gloss peace activists and Muslim apologists may want to apply to *jihad*, we cannot escape the fact that Muhammad consciously provoked conflict—disturbed the peace, if you will—because the peace was based on injustice. Given the comprehensive use of the term in the Qur'an and the way *jihad* is intended to transform both one's self and society, one may say that *jihad* is simultaneously a struggle and praxis.

The commonly assumed definition of *jihad* in South African Muslim liberatory rhetoric reflects a break with traditional juristic understandings of it. *Jihad*, said a Qibla pamphlet, "is the Islamic paradigm of the liberation struggle ... an effort, an exertion to the utmost, a striving for truth and justice" (*Arise and Bear Witness*, n.d.). Similarly, the Call of Islam argued that, for Muslims "the struggle for freedom and justice in South Africa is a sacred one. Any Muslim who abandons the struggle in South Africa, abandons Islam. *Jihad* in the path of God is part of the *iman* of a Muslim" (Call of Islam pamphlet: *We Fight On* (September, 1985) 2:10) Numerous anecdotes of resistance in the lives of the first generation of Muslims during Muhammad's lifetime as well as the abundant qur'anic texts dealing with *jihad* were regularly

---

[1] I am aware of the contested nature of justice captured particularly in the title of Alasdair Macintryre's work (1988) and that singular interpretations of justice can, in fact, lead to tyranny and even greater injustice.

invoked in support of both the essentially non-violent uprisings as well as the armed struggle. Along with liberation theologians elsewhere, we turned to praxis as "a way of making theology less a false theology, less an academic illusion and less an incoherent abstraction" (Chopp 1989: 37). *The Review of Faith*, a Call of Islam manual for activists, talks about "a dialectical process whereby our jihad will be informed by the Qur'an and our faith as much as our understanding of these will be informed by our jihad" (unpublished).

Violence Now?

We are belatedly discovering that people are not like taps that one can turn on and off at will. While many soldiers of the former *Umkhonto we Sizwe*, the armed wing of the African National Cangress, have been drawn into the new national defence force, not infrequently others emerge as paid assassins willing to kill for less than ten dollars per head. We cannot really say we did not know. We took calculated risks and many of us were aware of the lasting damage that we could be inflicting on our humanity even as we exhorted our people to *jihad*. While apartheid systematically and calculatedly cheapened Black lives; our methods of resisting it—however successful our struggle may seem to have been to us and the world at large—may have contributed significantly to the tainted nature of our victory. Here I want to reflect briefly on how the struggle impacted on young males. One person writes poignantly about a visit to one of the former battlefields of our revolutionary armed insurrection:

> In the early 1990s during the ANC—Inkatha clashes in KwaZulu-Natal I visited an abandoned rural settlement in the Midlands. The residents had fled, leaving behind burned out huts and mealie plants gone to seed.... [S]ome of the fiercest combatants were children, boys as young as nine and ten who patrolled the surrounding hills in groups, armed with guns made from scrap metal and toy guns adapted to shoot real bullets. On the pale blue crumbling wall of a burnt hut, a childish scrawl in red paint exposed the world I had entered: "We are soldiers we kill and rape. Rambo is our hero...."

This writer points out that the boy soldiers' message is

> a disturbing sign of the way many boys in African conflicts try to find empowering identities for themselves by assuming an extreme and destructive form of masculinity.... The destructiveness of such macho messages to adolescent boys at a stage when they are becoming aware of themselves as sexual beings cannot be underestimated.

Thus we see how the country's rape statistics—among the highest in the world gives the lie to the story that we have averted a blood bath. It is just happening in unnoticed and unpublicized drips and drabs. The above writer's comments on the results of this kind of masculinity may as well be applied to society at large and to Muslim society in particular: "The sad end result for the boys who assume a Rambo-type masculinity to produce new powerful social roles for themselves is that in killing one enemy they produce new ones; their violence snowballs to produce other forms of violence." The violence endemic to our society is not only the raw kind exhibited here. A recent opinion poll on South Africa's premier TV breakfast program indicated that 96% of the population supported the death penalty. This call for blood manifested in the rise of calculatedly violent vigilante groups such as *Amatopogo* in the Northern Province and People Against Gangsterism and Drugs (PAGAD) in the Western Cape is another symptom of the violence of our society rather than what the advocates of the death penalty suggest is a solution to it. Some of our public responses to drugs and gangsterism really reflect on us as the prisoners of deep-seated anger and bitterness who have fallen prey to the most atavistic, primordial and revenge cords seen in a long time. We have, in fact, become victims who have internalized the cheapening of the human spirit which the apartheid system had so desperately sought.

Just when we thought that the beast had been slain we find that it had entered our inner being. Desperate to exorcise the beast, we find an enemy 'out there' in the shape of gangsters and drug merchants against whom we direct our venom without fully appreciating the source of the venom. There may well be an enemy out there, as many a victim of gangsterism and drugs may well testify, but that is only one part of the story; we are the Siamese twins born out of yesterday's regime, and the cake cannot now be unbaked nor the sugar separated from the flour. Drug merchants require customers; gangsters require willing customers who will buy their stolen merchandise. And there lies the rub. Blame the collapse of sexual morality on the freedom of the streets, which sex workers seem to be enjoying, if you will, but it takes two to tango. A refusal to recognize the way in which selfhood is tied to the despised other and that the seat of the venom is the self is dangerous because if we do not come to terms with its presence then we will be engaged in an eternal search for external entities on which to unleash it. "What are we going to clean up next?" becomes a driving quest. Yet, venom is like acid; it does more harm to the vessel in which it is stored than to the object on which it is poured.

At a broader South African and more private level, more and more South Africans are resorting to an equally questionable and self-defeating—sometimes literally so—response to the problem of the cheapening of human life. Arm yourself to the teeth. Current estimates suggest that there are seven million guns floating around in the hands of civilians, one for every six South Africans. In 1994 7,000 people were murdered with guns and 17,700 attempted murders involved guns. Given that 15,000 licensed guns are stolen each year and that people are far more likely to be killed by their own guns rather than being protected by them, one shudders at the foolhardiness of it all. In this spectacle of gun-owner falling victim to his (nearly always his) own gun is reflected the symbiotic relationship between self and other and once again the inseparableness of our destinies.

Reconciliation

One of the sources from which these right-wing groups draw their support is the theology of vengeance. Having created God in their image, God has for them become an angry deity of vengeance and they are God's representatives charged with setting the world right through all the righteous venom that they can muster: "Hang the murderers! Kill the merchants." Alas, venom is like acid, it does more damage to the vessel in which it is stored than to the object on which it is poured.

The Qur'an speaks about the time of creation when God breathed into the first created being of his spirit. As a Muslim, I thus believe that every one of us is a bearer of the spirit of the God, that is, in the terminology of the Quakers "everyone is of God." Acknowledging the ever-presence of this spirit, irrespective of how low the bearer has fallen, is for me the basis of human dignity and human rights. More importantly, it is the basis of a theology of compassion. In the Urdu language, we speak of *hamdard* i.e., 'one pain'. To take the pain of the other actually as one's own. The redeeming element in *hamdard* or compassion as distinct from pity or tolerance is that it recognizes one's own propensity to frailty, one's own potential to fall also, to end up also lying in the gutter one day or discovering that one's own child is addicted to crack, that it can happen to the 'best among us'. It is my pain—present or potential—that I recognize in the other. I take a stand for the other not only because the other needs me but equally because I may need the other to take a stand for me. At the same time I do not wish to fall into the language of 'the God of love' that, for much of Western conservative Christianity, has become a strategy for avoiding fundamental issues of social injustice in and poverty in a society that prevents the love of God from being experienced in concrete terms in the daily lives of ordinary people. In this rather sophisticated political love where socio-economic suffering is ignored, the flip side is a deep-seated religious arrogance and hatred that demands the abolition of human rights for prisoners, the restoration of the death penalty and corporal punishment in schools.

There is a path between the apolitical fuzzy love of God and the relentless coldness of a distant transcendent being who only cares via retribution. This, I believe, is what the new South Africa and its constitution is about. We miss the boat when we moan about prisoners living it up in hotels; it is about recognizing that of our God in every one of us—particularly in the least among us. The story is told of a Jewish rabbi whose disciples were debating the question of when precisely 'daylight' commenced. The one ventured the proposal: "It is when one can see the difference between a sheep and a goat at a distance." Another suggested: "It is when you can see the difference between a fig tree and an olive tree at a distance." And so it went on. When they eventually asked the rabbi for his view, he said: "When one human being looks into the face of another and says: 'This is my sister' or 'this is my brother' then the night is over and the day has begun." That is a wonderful story, is it not? I am not entirely convinced. What is the purpose of recognizing the other as my brother or sister? Is this really an 'obvious virtue'? How do we confront the problem of recognizing the humanness of the other when so many of our people have not gone beyond the imperatives of physical survival due to, say, the availability of jobs, food and water or due to the presence of an external force bent on the annihilation of an entire people. Do I really want that an abused woman to wake up in the morning and stare at the face of the man who abused her the previous night and see the face of her 'brother'? Should communities who are dispossessed and marginalized live in harmonious relationships with those who bulldoze their homes or destroy their olive groves, even if the ensuing freedom struggle upsets the onlooking world?

The Truth and Reconciliation Commission

To deal with the challenge of a healing closure of the past, the granting of amnesty for all politically motivated crimes and the task of uncovering the full truth of the last phase of our country's nightmare, the Truth and Reconciliation Commission (TRC) was established by the new constitution. About the work of the TRC let me offer a few brief comments as a Muslim.

a) It is quite fascinating that this mechanism was being hailed by all and sundry in the industrial world—the same world that is vigorously supportive of any move to hound and punish Nazi criminals even if they are well into their eighties. Is the message somehow that Jewish lives are more significant than Black lives, that the savage Blacks cannot be trusted to give free reign to their barbarism but that Whites can be trusted to pursue their killers and exact nothing less than justice?

b) The TRC is the result of party political negotiations, as Desmond Tutu has often reminded us when confronted with some of the inherent weaknesses, such as its predisposition towards reconciliation rather than justice. While the TRC is a genuine attempt to deal with the wounds of the past, it is also an ideological tool of realpolitik where ordinary citizens cannot be allowed to upset an agenda of nation-building and a 'positive investor climate'. Various spokespersons of the Commission have often said that its essential focus is on the victims. We have also seen the remarkable way that they were dealt with; the homage being paid to victims and their families, the way they are being truly heard and the earnest manner in which the Commission pushes the relevant authorities for compensation and other requests to be handled expeditiously. However, in the absence of a clear focus on justice as the other side of the coin, one cannot help but wonder if this talk on focussing on the victims does not have the, even if unintended, effect of allowing the perpetrators to get away.

c) Many families of the victims of the apartheid regime's killing machinery have been reluctant to make submissions to the TRC and their unease or rejection reflects those of many other South Africans. For these families it is not a choice between justice and reconciliation; it is an assumption that reconciliation is premised on justice. If the victims were truly the essential focus of the TRC then why should we not allow the various victims and families to determine their own way of being reconciled? Why should these families be coerced—subtly or otherwise—to become part of what is for many of us a cathartic and very healing process when they insist that this is not the way in which they are going to be healed. If the incredible request for "a bursary for my daughter" or "the return of my husband's hand" is all that is asked by some, why should others be expected to relinquish their quest for justice—even if it is as basic as Mrs. Rebecca Truter's demand that her son's murderer's state pension be stopped "so he can feel how I struggle." Surely the yearning for justice is not any less human than that for reconciliation.

d) While justice is a moral value with intrinsic worth that requires no external—religious, ideological nation-building or whatever—validation, this is not the case with reconciliation. There cannot be any doubt that our country is sorely in need of healing and of the crucial importance of reconciliation in this process. What is called into question is the meaningfulness of reconciliation without justice. Will a process whereby a committee grants amnesty to murderers, often living on huge state pensions, while the families of the victims shed "rivers of tears" in front of the TRC not lead to a new twist to the cruel adage 'finders keepers, losers weepers'? Justice receives such prominence in the Qur'an that it is regarded as one of the reasons why God created the earth: "And we have created the heavens and the earth in Truth so that every soul may earn its just recompense for what it earned and that it may not be oppressed."

e) While the TRC has been careful to avoid casting any aspersions on those families or victims reluctant or unwilling to come forward and never seeking to undermine them, we still need to be aware that a peculiarly Christian version of forgiveness and reconciliation is being played out. It is not a version that finds a resonance in all South Africans, nor even among all Christians. This is a version that seeks stability rather than justice and that derives its strength from a Christ who asks the Father to forgive his persecutors even as he is being crucified.

f) While many may find the idea of unqualified forgiveness truly moving and believe that their own humanity is enhanced by forgiving those who trespass against them, I am skeptical about translating all of this into social and political terms. If truth be told, then the only truths which we were told were those which perpetrators feared were going to come forth in any case. The agents of the apartheid regime confessed only to the barest minimum extent required to get them off the hook. As for reconciliation, those who needed to hear those truths most of all, the whites of South Africa, were essentially absent throughout the proceedings.

g) And the Muslims? Where did we fit into all of this? What did we make of it all?[2] In a single word, our response was one of indifference. Very few of us involved in the struggle for freedom realized that this was really a struggle against all forms of injustice. It was a struggle for "the least," as in the words of Jesus—Peace be upon him: "What you do unto the least of my brothers, you have done unto me." There are, therefore, many Christians who do not understand that Christianity as a privileged religion and discourse must make way for a more humble one which regards all the other faiths of our country as co-equals. I believe that this problem was reflected in the Christianization of the TRC process and that it contributed significantly to Muslims remaining on the sidelines. On the day of my testimony, I spoke

---

[2] There were two exceptions to this indifference. The first was some concerted, albeit largely unsuccessful, efforts by Imam Abdur Rashid Omar of the Claremont Main Rd Mosque to interest the congregation in the TRC and its work and the second was an attempt by *Al Qalam*, to cover the work of the TRC on a regular basis.

critically of the symbolism of having Jews, Muslim and Hindus coming to testify to an all-Christian panel, headed by an archbishop sitting under a huge crucifix in a church hall.

Our challenge is thus to remind the others persistently of our presence and of the value of the religious heritage which we bring with us but to do so in a manner that they would want to embrace us in partners of the reconstruction and reconciliation of our nation.

Bibliography

Chopp, Rebecca S. (1989). *The Praxis of Suffering*. Maryknoll: Orbis Books.
Macintryre, Alasdair. (1988). *Whose Justice? Which Rationality? A Study in Moral Theory*. London: Duckworth.
Schleifer, Abdullah. (1982). "Understanding Jihad: Definition and Methodology." *Islamic Quarterly* 27: 118-31.

On Playing Reconciliation
in a Situation of Racist Conflict

Ton van Prooijen

Introduction

Reading Antjie Krog's *Country of my Skull* (1999) is an unnerving experience. Her book is an account of the two years she reported on the *Truth and Reconciliation Commission* (TRC) for the South African Broadcasting Corporation. The horrifying registration of the victims' stories, including all the repulsive details on the victims' torture and humiliation as well as the personal struggle of a white Afrikaner poet continually exposed to these kinds of revelation, turns *Country of my Skull* into a harsh confrontation with the surreal South African situation. It evokes the image of a society deeply traumatized by unbearable memories, hatred and fear for extreme violence. This paper seeks to offer a Christian view of reconciliation connected to this concrete case (and, accordingly, also connected to the first-hand information in the papers by Piet Meiring and Farid Esack). It focusses on the role churches could play. I will attempt to show the modesty and reserve befitting an outsider. Therefore, this paper does not pretend to offer any final solutions or well-meant advice. It is basically designed to confront some re-echoing South African voices with a Christian perspective on reconciliation.

Impressions

Krog's book leaves the reader with highly ambivalent feelings about the reconciliation process in South Africa. On the one hand, it is a testimony of a unique attempt to reconcile the two sides of a divided nation by telling the truth and granting amnesty, of a fragile but powerful archbishop Tutu who encouraged many people to come forward with their stories, of thousands of victims, relieved after finally being heard, of ordinary people dominating the eight o'clock news, of the "flame of hope" (Krog 1999: 422) keeping alive the idea of a common humanity and a society that prevents such brutal events from happening again.

On the other hand, after reading this book, it can hardly be denied that the whole process ended somehow in disillusion. The TRC failed to get an interim reparation policy off the ground (Krog 1999: 422) and political parties objected to the final report. The African National Congress (ANC) even took the TRC to court in order to prevent the releasing of its report, because it "criminalized the *struggle*" (Krog 1999: 428). The interdict was refused, but its consequences were disastrous. Discussions about political and racial issues undermined the unity of the TRC, its moral authority was damaged and the content of its report was overshadowed by accusations and gossip. In Krog's words: "The taste was gone" (Krog 1999: 432.) A deeply upset Tutu protested against the course of things and declared: "If the oppressed has become the oppressor I will fight them." But, as Krog noted, these words "look flabby, tired—worn out by politics within and outside the Commission" (Krog 1999: 429).

If I understand the South African situation correctly, then the whole issue of reconciliation is dominated by the question of race! Focussing on *human* rights violations, the TRC tried to separate the process of reconciliation from the issue of color (Krog 1999: 87 f.). Attempting to start a process that would create a future for all South Africans, the TRC was compelled to argue that Apartheid had made people lose their humanity. The key question, therefore, was: how could people lose their humanity like that (Krog 1999: 66)? In other words, to create a new nation for all the TRC had to avoid even the semblance of putting forward the issue of racism. That would have been grist to the mill of those accusing the TRC of one-sidedness and a 'witch hunt' among whites. On no account were people to be provoked into thinking that the hidden agenda of the TRC was supporting blacks' attempts to gain the power and positions of the whites in order to exercise the very same values (cf. Krog 1999: 169).

ANC President (and now state President) Thabo Mbeki objected to the TRC policy in his famous "two nation speech," delivered a few months before the presentation of the final report. He declared that South Africa is a country of two nations: a rich white nation and a poor black nation. For Mbeki, reconciliation is not between perpetrators (of all colors) and victims (of all colors) but between the beneficiaries (whites) and the exploited (blacks). In his eyes, the main obstacle is the huge cleft between rich (read: white) and poor (read: black), producing rage among millions of people. Economic power still belongs to whites, he observed. Most of them did not apply for amnesty and they complain about 'affirmative action' policies of the government. The only way to national unity would be a drastic redistribution of wealth and economic resources. Without such an upheaval there was actually no question of reconciliation.

Thus the question seems to be: did the TRC oversee or camouflage the heart of the problem by going beyond racism and is, consequently, its work marginal and irrelevant? Or do people such as Mbeki unjustly overstress the racial issue and is this an instance of stirring up the racial conflict, thus blocking the whole reconciliation process? It is a fact that, despite the work of the TRC, South Africans seems to be further apart than before (Krog 1999: 436, 438). Instead of Tutu's ideal of a "rainbow nation," the South African society is characterized by conflicts and contradic-

---

[1] Among many others, the (black) South African scholar Jonathan Jansen (2000: 36) recently stated that the South African government trivialized the "real" problem (i.e., racism) by focusing on a "peaceful transition." Instead of tackling the deeply rooted problem of racism, the government opted for a political "agreement between elites" "thrown together in a hurry."

tions. In the epilogue of *Country of my Skull* the unavoidable question is asked (Krog 1999: 448): did the TRC process achieve reconciliation? Krog does not answer this question with a straightforward yes or no. What is definitely not visible is reconciliation as a "mysterious Judaeo-Christian process," she holds. If there is any reconciliation between people, it is because the essence of reconciliation is survival. Since survival is part of our "genetic make-up," reconciliation will follow. In other words, reconciliation is unavoidable because it is necessary to survive. This ability to reconcile is, however, not uniquely human. Monkeys and apes engage in reconciliation behavior in the very same way. According to Krog, this "tends to indicate that reconciliation did not originate in the minds of humans and, therefore, it cannot be appropriated by an ideology or a religion."

Outlining a Dilemma for the Churches

The first essay in this book poses the question as to whether religions can and do contribute to understanding and rapprochement in situations of conflict. With TRC member Piet Meiring, this could be specified as such: "Do the churches in our country make a difference? Does it really matter that there are Christians in South Africa?" (Meiring 1999: 111). Regarding the ambivalent role of the churches in the South African history (they were the breeding ground of both ideological foundation of Apartheid and the protest against it), it obviously did matter. However, considering the South African situation as portrayed in the previous section, the question arises as to how churches are and could be involved in the process of reconciliation overcoming the racial conflict at the present time.

There is every appearance that the churches are facing a dilemma. On the one hand, they can follow the line of the TRC, trying to reconcile people on the local level by encouraging and facilitating encounters and by creating possibilities for storytelling and confessing guilt. Then the point of departure would be the idea that all people are dehumanized and, therefore, have to relocate their humanity. It seems that in taking this track churches may run the risk of doing that for which they were blamed during the Apartheid period: hushing up the real conflict by pretending to stand 'above' the conflicting parties.

On the other hand, churches can lay stress on the prophetic protest against the economic domination of whites by demanding expropriation of white property, a change of socio-economic structures, etc. The starting point in that case would be the belief that racism is the very heart of the conflict. Because racism goes far beyond ideologies of individuals and groups, reconciliation is not a matter of converting individuals but of changing structures. Following this line, churches may run the risk of biting off more then they can chew and of slipping back into abstract talk about macrostructures that does not at all affect the daily lives of people.

If the dilemma just sketched is appropriate, churches find themselves between two fires. If they opt for the first line, they will be accused of maintaining the status quo. If they follow the second line, they will be accused of reverse apartheid and of frustrating the reconciliation process.

This paper attempts to explore the openings within Christian theology for an approach in which both positions are integrated. Its purpose is to explore very briefly the Trinitarian theology of the German theologian Jürgen Moltmann in order to find a way in which churches can focus on liberation within 'unfree' structures and on reconciliation within a situation of conflict, without losing the aim of a righteous state in which unjust structures are completely broken down. Within the framework of this theology, Moltmann develops a view on church and reconciliation that does not primarily focus on what churches should do but on what they essentially *are*. After analyzing Moltmann's concept of 'racism',[2] I will outline the theological (Trinitarian) basis of Moltmann's suggestion for overcoming racism. Viewing the 'essence' of churches from that perspective, I will finally indicate what their role could be in a racial conflict.

The Vicious Circle of Racial Alienation

In this section I will attempt to show Moltmann's view on racial conflicts (he only focuses on white-black racism, which is a disadvantage in the complicated South African situation).[3] I first examine the perspective from which the problem of racism is viewed in order to find out what the roots of racial conflicts are. Then I consider Moltmann's analysis of the consequences for both black and white people. Finally, I focus on the way to overcome these conflicts.

In his book *The Crucified God* (1972), Moltmann characterizes the human condition generally speaking as "unfree." He argues that, due to powers that enslave them, humans are not allowed to live a dignified life. In order to find ways to liberate humans, Moltmann indicates that this rather massive idea of the human condition should be dissected into concrete dimensions of the human lack of freedom. Within these dimensions he further locates so-called "vicious circles" that keep humans from being human. In the economic dimension Moltmann distinguishes the vicious circle of poverty and exploitation; in the political dimension that of violence and oppression; in the cultural dimension underlying the previous dimensions that of racial and cultural alienation; in the environmental dimension in which the three dimensions mentioned so far are related that of the industrial distortion of nature; and finally, in the theological dimension enclosing all other dimensions that of meaninglessness and godforsakenness. Moltmann declares that liberation of humans takes place in these concrete vicious circles. Academic debates on general views on the bondage of humans focus-

---

[2] Like Moltmann himself, I am aware of the fact that it will, after all, be a white perspective.

[3] In my analysis of Moltmann's perception of racism, I will focus on the following texts: Moltmann 1971b: 253-257, the sections on vicious circles in Moltmann 1993a, Moltmann 1993b and the section on black theology in Moltmann 2000. These texts are used interchangeably, because I do not see any significant change in Moltmann's opinion on this subject.

sing only on abstract political and economic structures are in his view far from helpful (Moltmann 1993a: 329).

In Moltmann's work, racism is reflected upon from the perspective of the cultural vicious circle. 'Culture' is understood to mean "the sphere of the self-representation of persons, groups and peoples in relation to one another and as a whole before the ground of their existence" (Moltmann 1993b: 182). By focussing on the cultural circle, Moltmann could be accused of neglecting the fact that in situations like that of South Africa, racism is also inherent to political and economic structures. Therefore, it must be stressed that in Moltmann's thinking all dimensions are somehow interrelated (they are dimensions of the same unfree situation of humans). That means, for instance, that liberation from the cultural vicious circle is not completely possible without liberation from poverty. Accordingly, Moltmann does not hold that a change of heart is sufficient to solve the problem of racism. Conversely, however, a redistribution of power will not be possible without liberation of humans from racist mentality (Moltmann 1971b: 253). Thus, the fact that the problem of racism is viewed from a cultural perspective does not imply that Moltmann trivializes the economic and political factors of racism (Moltmann 1971b: 253).[4] However, although cultural self-representation is always bound up with production and consumption as well as political conflicts and associations, it is not totally absorbed by economic and political processes. "It represents a human need of its own as well" (Moltmann 1993b: 182).

Leaving whatever other problems Moltmann's analysis may evoke aside, I will try to consider Moltmann's approach on its own merits now. Having defended the view that cultural self-representation is a relatively independent dimension of the human condition, Moltmann goes on to explain this process of human self-representation. As "questionable beings" that are not at all fixed, humans are continually defining a personality for themselves, he explains. They try to justify their lives and to legitimize the form their life is taking. Basically, Moltmann holds, humans are seeking identity and the recognition of others. He thus argues that the crux of cultural conflicts is the fundamental human quest for identity. It is from this perspective that he surveys the problem of racism.

The basic definition of racism that Moltmann uses was formulated by UNESCO and adopted by the Fourth Assembly of the World Council of Churches at Uppsala in 1968:

> By racism we mean ethnocentric *pride* in one's own racial group and preference for the distinctive characteristics of that group; belief that these characteristics are fundamentally biological in nature and are thus transmitted to succeeding generations; strong negative feelings towards other groups who do not share these characteristics coupled with the thrust to discriminate against and exclude the outgroup

---

[4] Moltmann definitely agrees with those who argue that racism is more than ideology alone.

from full participation in the life of the community. (Moltmann 1971b: 253; 1993b: 183; 2000: 196)

Thus, in racism the characteristics of one's own race are identified with the characteristics of humankind *per se*. In situations of white-black-racism, to be human is to be white and people of different races—'non-whites' (!)—consequently become subhuman.

Moltmann holds that such racial attitudes and ideologies arise because humans perceive persons of another race as a threat to their own identity. In situations where people of different races have to live together, people's inner insecurity can increase, because their previous identity, (unconsciously) legitimized in their own group and race, is called into question. In reaction to this insecurity, whites found the human sense of dignity upon their white skin color. Consequently, 'non-whites' are nonpersons, *Untermenschen* or humans with less capacities.[5]

These practices lead to feelings of superiority of the ruling class and to feelings of inferiority by people of the oppressed class. According to Moltmann, racism always has these two sides: an emotional mechanism for self-justification and an ideological mechanism for the subjection of others (Moltmann 1993b: 183; 2000: 197). These mechanisms destroy humanity on both sides.

In his famous book *Black Skin, White Masks* (1967), Frantz Fanon (1967: 116) writes:

> I am the slave not of the 'idea' that others have of me but of my own appearance.... Shame. Shame and self-contempt. Nausea. When people like me, they tell me it is in spite of my color. When they dislike me, they point out that it is not because of my color. Either way, I am locked into the infernal circle.[6]

This indicates precisely what Moltmann means by the vicious circle of racism. Racism is far more than oppression, discrimination, and exploitation. An inferiority complex caused by people with a superiority complex deeply affects the human soul. Moltmann quotes Malcolm X: "The worst crime the white man has committed has been to teach us to hate ourselves" (Moltmann 2000: 202). For instance, slavery has an immense impact not only on the people involved but also on their offspring. Although slavery and other kinds of white oppression of blacks are much more far-reaching than being imprisoned, Moltmann refers to his own imprisonment after the Second World War to explain what the consequences for the human soul can be (Moltmann 2000: 202).[7] He notes that a hostility is experienced that cannot be re-

---

[5] Moltmann does not overlook the fact that racism mostly serves to safeguard white privileges. He points out that all kind of theories are often primarily developed to legitimize the oppression of 'inferior' races.

[6] Moltmann refers to Fanon as well.

[7] Moltmann was a prisoner in an English prisoner-of-war camp from 1945 till 1948.

sisted. In reaction, people tend to crawl into the shell of their inner self. On the outside they react with indifference. Being 'imprisoned' blocks off people's vital energies. Consequently, they despise themselves in an inner attempt at self-destruction. Extrapolating on his own experiences, Moltmann holds that for the liberation of black people from racism, political rights and economic justice may be of great importance, but it is not sufficient. Equally important is raising up the "bowed-down soul."

As was stated above, Moltmann believes that racism also dehumanizes white people. Being inhumanly proud of his white 'race', the white racist is obsessed by an inhuman fear, he observes. Humans who identify being human with being white thus distort their own humanity. They are forced to convert their fear into aggression towards others, which disturbs their relationship with them. For Moltmann, the racial humiliation of others is basically deadly self-hatred (Moltmann 2000: 197). Centuries of the oppression of blacks made the white soul deeply poisoned with the "disease of racism," even if people are not aware of that today (Moltmann 2000: 195). According to Moltmann, blackness has become a psychopathological symbol for whites. Black symbolizes wickedness, evil and threat. Black is also the irrational, the compulsive, the unclean, the lack of self-control and the sensual. Moltmann holds that this phobia on the part of whites for blacks is nothing else than the projection of "the parts of their own souls they have shut away, and the guilty fear they have suppressed" (Moltmann 2000: 195). In the modern Western world human are taught to control themselves and to suppress their body, their senses and their desires. Moltmann writes that the white suppression of body, senses and instincts is projected on blacks, who, consequently, became the symbol of the uncontrolled and the sensual that has to be dominated by white self-control and enlightenment. In order to be a 'complete' human being, Moltmann believes, whites should be liberated from this narrow-minded idea of superiority.

It could be concluded from Moltmann's analysis that racism is a circle in which superiority and inferiority complexes confirm each other. As long as human identities are constituted on either racial superiority or inferiority, this circle will not be broken. Therefore, Moltmann holds that liberation from racial alienation (as well as other forms of cultural alienation) is only possible if a new human identity is created. With Karl Marx, Moltmann understands this new identity as the "human emancipation of humans" in which humans receive self-esteem and self-confidence in accepting others and in community with others.[8] Moltmann writes:

---

[8] Apparently, this leads to the problem of the relation between integration and identity. Does integration (reconciliation?) with others automatically lead to giving up one's own identity? According to Moltmann, there is not necessarily a contradiction. Real integration cannot lead to faceless masses of identical people, he holds, and real new identity cannot mean complete separation. In other words, liberation from cultural alienation takes place when and in so far as emancipation means *personalization in socialization* and *finding identity in acceptance*.

The human emancipation of men from self-alienation and alienating dealings with each other is only possible when different kinds of people encounter each other without anxiety, superiority or repressed feelings of guilt and regard their differences as fruitful, working together productively. (1993a: 333)

Following James Cone, Moltmann holds that the white man should give up his idea of whiteness as the only right form of being human and risk "the creation of a new humanity" (Moltmann 2000: 215). The only way to overcome racism is to by adopt a liberated, non-aggressive identity "as humans." This would free humans from the compulsion to affirm themselves at the cost of others and enable them to recognize others as persons in their dignity and their rights.

This brief analysis makes clear, that in order to overcome racial conflicts, the vicious circle of racial ideologies, attitudes, and idolatries has to be broken first and that, secondly, a new identity as 'human being' has to be found. So far, the whole process could be described in terms of a person's "I-identity" and "ego-identity" (Moltmann 1993b: 186). Ego-identities are based on the idea of *having* (for instance the membership of race), while the I-identity is founded on the category of *being*. The identity crises mentioned here comes from making a person into a thing. Humans remain uncertain, because they only acquire identity by desperately and aggressively holding fast to what others do not have.

Such psychological phrasing of the problem is very helpful, I believe. It shows that, in order to develop their I-identity, humans should do away with their destructive ego-identity made up of all kind of ideologies and idolatries. However, a few questions arise.

First, the psychological perspective Moltmann offers runs the risk of trivializing the difference between white and black victims of racism. All may be victims in a certain way, but there is a significant difference between sinners and sinned-against. Regarding racism as a vicious circle and all people as its victims, the question of guilt and responsibility fades into the background.

Secondly, what is the content of the new identity "as humans" of which Moltmann speaks? Moreover, what is the guarantee that humans can rely on it? This question Moltmann acknowledges himself. He maintains that for overcoming racial conflicts, its deepest roots must laid bare. To do so, one has to go beyond the diagnosis open to psychology. Moltmann's (implicit) claim is more or less that racial conflicts will not entirely be overcome if the religious dimension of the conflict is not taken into account.

The Theological Dimension

As noted, Moltmann distinguishes a vicious circle of meaninglessness and godforsakenness beneath that of cultural alienation. Theologically speaking, he asserts, cultural alienation turns out to be the problem of the 'godless' person's compulsion to justify himself and substantiate himself over against the ground of his existence which he abandons (Moltmann 1993b: 187). In other words, humans separate themselves from God (their 'ground of being') and, having no longer any ground, they desperately try to become 'gods' themselves. In Moltmann's view this human tendency follows from a deep primal fear of nothingness, which makes people seek constantly for new 'possessions' to which they can cling.

Only if primal fear and insecurity are changed into primal trust, Moltmann holds, can humans find free self-acceptance and free acceptance of people who are different. With Tillich, Moltmann states that theologically speaking this trust is the "acceptance of being accepted by God" (Moltmann: 1971a: 165). "Human life has eternal value because it is loved and accepted by God" (1993b: 187). Because the very being of humans is justified, they are liberated from self-justification through superstitious and idolatrous perversions of humanity. Thus it could be argued that humans' I-identities are founded on the justification of humans by God's grace.

This leads us to the question as to the basis of this justification. Following Moltmann in his argument that to overcome racial conflicts the problem should be tackled at its religious roots, it is necessary to consider the basis of the godless person's justification. Here we come across what Christian theology labels as the reconciliation between God and humans.

If we stick to Gustaf Aulén's terminology (discussed in Cees van der Kooi's paper), Moltmann's view can be labelled as 'objective'. Examining, for instance, a speech delivered at the general meeting of the World Alliance of Reformed Churches (WARC) in Nairobi 1970, there can be no doubt that in Moltmann's thinking reconciliation with God has been brought about by God and by God alone. God is the subject of reconciliation, humans are the objects (Moltmann 1970: 515-20, cf. 517). The reconciliation took place in what Moltmann calls the Christ event (Jesus Christ's death on the cross and his resurrection). This event is exclusive, unique, and irreversible. In Moltmann's theology, 'objective' reconciliation is, thus, the basis and the power of reconciliation between people. "God is in favour of us, therefore we can and should be together and not against each other" (Moltmann: 1970: 517).

So far, Moltmann's view corresponds to the basics of Anselm's theory and to modern representatives of the objective model of reconciliation, for instance Karl Barth. Inadmissibly simplifying Barth's view, God's act in Christ permanently established the reconciliation between God and world. Our concern here and now is to become aware of the fact that although we are still living in a sinful world we are reconciled with God. At this point, Moltmann differs significantly. In order to explore Moltmann's concept, I refer to several books published in the 1970s in which he develops his Trinitarian theology.

Over against the Lutheran *simul iustus et peccator* (humans are both justified and sinner), Moltmann starts with a view that seems basically Calvinistic. As in Calvin's theology, justification and final salvation do not coincide. For Moltmann, the origin of the new order in the Christ event and the final glorification are respectively the beginning and fulfillment of a long process of liberation. Thus our history is put under strain. On the one hand, God's "eschatological reign of freedom and righteousness" has already dawned in God's reconciling act in Christ; on the other hand, this reign is still to be expected.

In Moltmann's opinion, this tension between 'already' and 'not yet' is very fruitful. What happened in God's reconciling act is an eschatological anticipation of our final salvation. Consequently, Moltmann suggests, humans are asked to change the world that is changeable because of God's intervention. In short, they should grasp the freedom offered by God's act of reconciliation in anticipation of the final salvation.

This already-and-not-yet kingdom in which humans can participate challenges churches to criticize existing oppressing structures. Moltmann states that Christians may not preach a form of reconciliation that does not suffer anymore from an unsaved world (Moltmann 1993a: 101). Reconciliation does not allow Christians to withdraw themselves into the enclave of their community of saved people or their redeemed soul. Referring to the *Frankfurter Schule*, Moltmann's notion of this process of liberation can be described as a "critical theory of God" (Moltmann 1993a: 69).

On the other hand, Moltmann also speaks about a real anticipation of God's universal reign of peace and righteousness, which Moltmann describes as a feast open to all humans (cf. Moltmann 1993b: 108 ff.). Therefore, churches should at the same time invite all people to the feast of liberation and reconciliation.

However, if both a 'critical theory' and reconciliation here and now are seriously strived for, there seems to be a problem. How can churches in South Africa both continually and uncompromisingly criticize existing racial structures and propagate universal reconciliation without falling into either unfruitful contradiction or hushing up the racial conflict? Moltmann asserts that to understand how God's process of liberation contains both elements without trivializing one of them, the whole process should be viewed from a *Christological* perspective.

To understand what reconciliation really means, Moltmann holds, one has to look at Jesus' actions first of all: his preaching of the liberating kingdom of God that is near, his message that God can be encountered among the godless, his healing of the sick, his exorcizing of devils, his dinners with sinners and publicans, his standing up for the poor and the oppressed (Moltmann: 1970: 517). These are not the actions of a hero, a powerful man and an adored person. Jesus challenged the existing power structures not by rising above them but by criticizing them from below, among the weak (Moltmann 1970: 519). Only if humans understand this partiality of Jesus will they understand the revolutionary character of the Bible. The Gospel is good news for the poor; for the rich it is painful.

> The message of reconciliation is not the religious honey of the well-to-do society, but the salt of the earth. And salt in the wounds of the earth burns, but it prevents rottenness. When we want to spread the freedom of the Crucified in this chaotic world, we should regain this sharpness of the gospel. (Moltmann 1970: 519)

Jesus' way became the way of the cross. For Moltmann, it is crucial that the anticipation of God's reign is not embodied by some heavenly creature or demigod, but in and by the banished, the rejected, and the crucified one. That means that, according to the gospel, breaking through enslaving structures does not take place by submitting oneself to a God that is even higher, better, and stronger than these structures. Power structures that rule this world are unmasked by the Crucified who took side with the poor and the oppressed. Consequently, Moltmann explains, deactivating these structures is only possible by identification with the Crucified, i.e., being there where he was and becoming engaged with those with whom he was engaged. Therefore, Moltmann can state that concerning the problem of racism the critical question is: Lord, when did we see you black (Moltmann 2000: 215)?

Thus, for Moltmann, it is clear that what distinguishes Christian faith from other religions and revolutions is the reign of the Crucified. The Crucified or the idols of this world—that is the question (Moltmann 1970: 517). Therefore, reconciliation in Jesus' name can never mean 'neutrality'. His mission was for all people, because he firmly took sides with the poor and the suffering. His disarming actions not only challenged the power structures in society, but also human ego-identities. Showing that self-justification by religious idols, law, or political power is enslaving, Jesus also challenged people to stop justifying themselves by clinging to these powers.

While Jesus' identification with the powerless ending in his crucifixion shows us how and where God's liberating process can be experienced, his resurrection shows us the wide horizon of this process. It opens the universal future of freedom. For Moltmann, resurrection is the beginning of salvation in an unsaved world, generating a new community with God and with one another (Moltmann 1970: 216). This community offers the new identity for which humans are desperately searching. If oppressive ego-identities are refuted by following the Crucified, humans find out that they are no longer a Narcissus. They experience themselves as loved, accepted, and reconciled. Humans can become human because the "spirit of reconciliation" liberates them from fear and enables them to stop making a god of themselves. When humans are liberated from enslaving structures, they find their humanity in the acknowledgement that despite their inhumanity they are loved by God.

Moltmann states that the reconciliation of the world in Christ reaches as far as the clouds drift (Moltmann 1970: 518). For the whole world, it opens the wide horizon of salvation, that is: of the reign in which God lives with humans. Salvation means shalom: a new creation of humans as a whole (both body and soul), a new creation of manhood (persons and relations), a new creation of heaven and earth (Moltmann 1970: 518). In short, resurrection generates creative justice, creative freedom, and creative peace (Moltmann 1970: 519).

So basically, reconciliation based upon Christ's resurrection means that the future that has started already in the crucified 'Son of Man' liberates humans from all pride and fear which are the causes of their idolatry. Moltmann calls this freedom 'faith' (Moltmann 1971a: 165). In faith humans find their identity as a human person amidst all inhuman non-identity (Moltmann 1971a: 166). Moreover, they are able to dedicate themselves to the unsaved world with love and patience without fearing to lose themselves again and without the pressure to 'realize' themselves at all costs. In faith humans no longer have to gain identity and, therefore, they can act on the basis of an accepted and loved existence. Experiencing this new humanity, humans cannot be conformed with the existing relationships based upon "like for like." Because otherness is no longer a specter and others are no longer the object of one's own fear, humans can freely love those who are different.

Thus far the question of how the 'Mbeki position' and the 'TRC position' can be integrated has not been answered. At most it has become clearer that genuine reconciliation without change of humans and their relation is cold comfort (Moltmann's message to Christians) and that a change of structures without reconciliation can only lead to terror (this Moltmann holds up to revolutionaries) (Moltmann 1970: 519). How can the message of God's reign of freedom for all be related to prophetic criticism of enslaving power structures? For Moltmann, this problem comes to a head regarding the identification of the Resurrected and the Crucified one[9].

At a certain stage in his thinking, Moltmann came to the conclusion that this identification can only be grasped in a *Trinitarian* theology that differentiates among God as Father, as Son and as Holy Spirit.[10] Without such a Trinitarian framework, belief in the Crucified will necessarily lead to simply a neverending critical attitude,[11] while belief in the Resurrected will end up in the sop of a good life beyond daily reality. Moltmann's conclusion is that to go beyond both options, a 'revolution' in the concept of God must take place. He states that the event of Cross and Resurrection was not only an event initiated by God but also an event that took place "within" God's self." Referring to Philippians 2, Moltmann contends that in the Son, the Father humiliated himself on the cross (Moltmann 1993a: 205). The complete and hopeless godforsakenness of Jesus on the cross not only points to the abandonment (*paradidonai*) of the Son by the Father; in the forsakenness of the Son, the Father also abandons himself (Moltmann 1993a: 243). Moltmann argues that the Son suffers death in godforsakenness, while the Father suffers the death of the Son in the "infinite pain of love." Thus, for Moltmann, the Cross is primarily an event between God and God.

The cross in the middle of God's Trinitarian being (Moltmann 1993a: 207) caused a deep cleft within God's self, but the Resurrection reunified God. Through this process, Moltmann holds, the crucified God took up in himself all godforsakenness, death, damnation, and meaninglessness from which humans suffer (Moltmann 1993a: 246). In other words, the *kenosis* of God created a span within God in which our human history can be included. In Moltmann's own words: "The 'bifurcation' in God must contain the whole uproar of history within itself"(Moltmann 1993a: 246). Thus the history of God that became concrete in the cross includes all abysses of

---

[9] This seems to me the main question in both Moltmann 1967 and 1993a.

[10] I will restrict myself to Moltmann's Trinitarian thinking as developed in the 1970s.

[11] At most this will be a "negation of the negative."

human history. To understand this, the idea of God as a person in heaven above must be abandoned. One should no longer think of God in history but of history in God. Moltmann views God as an eschatologically open history that in a mysterious way goes its own way through our history. It is the history of the love of the Son and the pain of the Father generating the Spirit that liberates humans and opens the future. God is, so to speak, a counterhistory (*Gegengeschichte*), a process of freedom in an unfree world.

How can this Trinitarian process be articulated? If God is a history within our history, God reveals himself necessarily in and through our reality. Accordingly, Moltmann holds that the world is not separated from God nor do we only discover resemblances and equivalents of his coming kingdom. In our reality, synecdochically real presences (*Realpräsenzen*) of God's future reign can be found (Moltmann 1993a: 337). Moltmann describes these real presences of God as the history of God making its way through the dust of our world and as the history of the Spirit that is showered upon all flesh ((Moltmann 1993a: 338). God's presence can be identified with material anticipations, with real symbols (*Realsymbole*) that point beyond themselves just as the real presence of God in the traditional sacraments. Therefore, Moltmann can argue that our reality is not only the material for Christian theology, but also its sacrament. Thus, Trinitarian theology enables us to interpret our reality as the sacrament of God's liberating future, i.e., as a reality qualified by God's word and embraced as the realm of his presence (Moltmann 1993a: 337).

According to Moltmann, liberation from vicious circles takes place by participation in God's liberating Trinitarian history (Moltmann 1993a: 337). In order to trace God's Trinitarian history, we should try to note the identifications (*Identifikationen*) of God in this world. As stated above, the criterion for distinguishing such presences is the history of the Crucified; their fulfilment is in the reign of the Triune God, where God will be "all in all." Concretely, this means that the presence of God can be experienced where the power structures are unmasked in imitation of the rejected and crucified Christ. In other words, participation in the liberating history of God is only possible where enslaving structures that dazzle humans lose their legitimacy. Therefore, Christians may not settle for reconciliation as appeasement within racial conflict. On the other hand, the experience of God's presence in our reality points to a reconciling history that goes far beyond any reconciliation humans could achieve and that is open for everyone. Therefore, Christians cannot agree with those who insist that reconciliation is only possible when all evil structures are dismantled and replaced by other human structures. That would be a denial of God's liberating and reconciling process that can be experienced here and now. Thus, participation in God's Trinitarian history means both the dismantling of power structures and reconciliation here and now.

With this Moltmann actually claims that only if the religious dimension of life (read: the history of the Triune God in our world) is considered, can it be maintained that an ongoing and highly critical protest against racial structures is needed as well as a conciliatory attitude within these structures. Both ways can only be integrated when referred to a God as a history that makes its way though our world and at the same time transcends it.

What does this mean for people imprisoned in the vicious circle of racism? Moltmann holds that by humiliating himself, God unconditionally accepts the whole humanity in order to open humans to participation in God. In other words, God became human to create true humans out of inhuman humans. Consequently, nobody has to keep up appearances to experience community with the living God. On the contrary, all ego-identities should be broken down to experience new identity as human being in God (Moltmann 1993a: 276). The presence of God in the vicious circle of alienation takes place in the experience of identity and acceptance. Where people find themselves in a new identity as human beings (and no longer as whites or blacks), they join in God's reconciling history and, conversely, where they are invited to celebrate the eschatological feast of freedom, they will experience new identity. As said, reality can be seen as the sacrament of God's presence. For Moltmann, concrete events in which humans find identity and acceptance can, therefore, be viewed as a sacrament of God's liberating Trinitarian history (Moltmann 1993a: 336).

The Church as "Messianic Intermezzo"

In Moltmann's theology, ecclesiology is a function of Christology and eschatology. It is not the church that has a mission of salvation to fulfill in the world, but it is "the mission of the Son and the Spirit through the Father" that includes the church and creates a church "as it goes on its way" (Moltmann 1993b: 64). This can be summarized by the following statement of Moltmann: "The Apostles' Creed expresses this truth by integrating the *credo ecclesiam* in the *credo in deum triunum*. And no ecclesiology should think below this level" (Moltmann 1993b: 65).

Consequently, we cannot say what the church *is* in all circumstances, but only *where the church happens*. In the previous section, it was noted that, for Moltmann, those places where humans find identity and acceptance can be regarded as a sacrament of God's liberating counterhistory. When churches are "messianic communities," namely communities in which the eschatological feast of the liberated is celebrated, they could be regarded as such a sacrament. Then churches are an element within the double movement of cross and resurrection, resistance and hope, distorting ego-identities and founding new identity.

This leads us to a twofold question. On the one hand, what does protest and resistance against racial structures mean for a church imbedded in God's Trinitarian history? According to Moltmann, the primary goal of emancipation in the church is not the subversion of earthly structures as such (important though that is for the powerless), but "the 'new man', who no longer acts within the system of lordship or servitude, and hence cannot be the slave of any master or the master of any slave" (Moltmann 1993b: 108). A "church under the cross" (i.e., the church of the Crucified) helps people to dissociate from ego-identities. Moltmann believes that this will influence daily life outside the church. For Moltmann, the basis for changes in society is the confrontation with the liberating history of God.

Storytelling seems to be a very useful way to defuse racial ideologies. Therefore, being a sacrament of God's liberating history churches should help people to "unlock their metaphorical locking devices" (Botman 1996: 39). In South Africa much has been written about the healing influence of storytelling. The South African ethicist Nico Koopman relates it explicitly to the problem of racism. He is convinced that old racial stereotypes can be broken down only if genuine opportunities are created for members of various groups to be exposed to one another (Koopman 1998: 164). "In an atmosphere of openness, honesty and constructive confrontation people can share their deepest pain, hurt, anger, hatred, fear, shame, guilt and feelings of hopelessness which were caused by racism." Although different groups will give different content to this, Koopman holds that "in the end it will become clear how all of us are victims of racism." As a result, people will for the first time look at reality through the eyes of other people and see reality not only as their ideologies portray it. Such meetings will encourage people to develop a common memory that will eventually lead to real community (Koopman 1998: 165).

On the other hand, what does reconciliation mean for a church imbedded in God's Trinitarian history? Basically, it means helping people to find their new identity. Church happens where people experience a new identity as a new human creation, that is, the experience of being free in an unsaved world. Thanks to God's reconciling act, humans are a new creation. In community with Christ they are liberated from the law of the old world, from the fear for its rulers and powers and from sin and death. God's reconciliation is the eternal, living source of liberation for the guilty and the dying, the humiliated, the offended, and the poor. God does not summon humans but invites them (Moltmann 1972: 33). Therefore, the church of the Resurrected is called to invite people to a new future, to freedom, to peace and to justice. They are ambassadors of reconciliation. Meiring states the same: churches are communities of "witnesses of the new creation, the new order on earth that *God* has made possible, of the *shalom*, the peace He brought" (Meiring 1999: 377).

For Moltmann, this gathering of liberated humans is a feast anticipating the future reign of freedom (Moltmann 1993b: 108 ff.). "For a particular time, in a particular space through a particular community, the laws and compulsions of 'this world' become invalid.... An alternative emerges and is presented in festal forms" (Moltmann 1993b: 111). Moltmann writes:

> As an anticipation of what the redeemed life will be in the future it demonstrates the alternatives offered by the creative Spirit. The spell of destiny and the feeling of personal helplessness are lifted where the possibilities and powers of the creative Spirit are experienced in the feast. The helpless discover their power as they are seized by this Spirit. Those who have adapted themselves discover their own personalities as they begin to sing, talk and move within the feast. They discover that they are something and can do something. They "come out of their shells" in a way that surprises themselves. (Moltmann 1993b: 112)

In Moltmann's view, celebrating this feast can never be a flight from the suffering and pain of this world, because it is the feast of the Crucified. In other words, it is the anticipation of the crucified people that is celebrated. Although protest against the unfree situation is absolutely necessary, Moltmann holds that "hope for the coming of the risen one ... forbids us to confine ourselves to a lament over suffering and earthly misery, and keeps us from simply attacking its causes without rejoicing in its future transformation" (Moltmann 1993b: 112).

In his speech for the WARC in Nairobi Moltmann remarked a little provocatively that many people do not believe anymore in a church proclaiming reconciliation because they see churches that are more reconciled with their own privileges in society and the favor of the powerful than with the Crucified (Moltmann 1970: 516). To be liberating communities, churches should free themselves from their slavish obedience towards the powers of this world and be what they essentially are: a sacrament of God's liberating history both by unmasking enslaving structures and by anticipation of the eschatological feast of freedom. Moltmann states: "In this double function of resistance and consolation the liberating feast becomes a 'messianic intermezzo' (A.A. van Ruler) on the risen Christ's way to the new creation of the world" (Moltmann 1993b: 113). In this messianic intermezzo people are never forced or brainwashed by means of all kinds of slogans but are invited to join the reconciling and liberating history of God so that they step by step can learn to 'play' reconciliation themselves.

Conclusion

In this paper I sought to address a dilemma churches seem to be facing in racial conflicts. I confronted South African voices with Jürgen Moltmann's theological approach in which protest and reconciliation are integrated. Therefore I first described Moltmann's analysis of the roots and consequences of racial conflicts. This lead to the conclusion that these conflicts can only be solved by breaking through the vicious circle of racial alienation. Furthermore, it was suggested that the deepest causes of racism can only be understood if the religious dimension is taken into consideration. By outlining Moltmann's Trinitarian approach, I attempted to show that God's process of liberation, grounded in the Christ event and to be fulfilled in the future kingdom, both unmasks existing power structures and offers humans new identity as "humans." Participation in this process encourages people to protest against enslaving power structures without clinging to the idea that reconciliation is only possible and justified after these structures are completely destroyed and replaced by other human-made structures. On the other hand, it inspires people to work on reconciliation without preaching appeasement or feeling obliged to establish never-ending reconciliation themselves.

I am not sure whether Moltmann's ideas fall under what Antjie Krog labelled a "mysterious Judaeo-Christian process." What Moltmann definitely does not have in mind is some wondrous and mysterious activity of God that establishes final and complete reconciliation and peace between all people here and now. Consequently, he would never support people who in God's name put others under moral pressure to confess or forgive. Victims may never be forced to embrace perpetrators because reconciliation must be achieved. For Moltmann, reconciliation is already established by God, but it is a counterhistory in which people are *invited* to participate. Final reconciliation can only be grasped in anticipation of God's eschatological reign. The "Judaeo-Christian process" described by Moltmann is noticed in moments when people find their humanity back and feel reborn and liberated. Could such moments described in Krog's book as well as in Meiring's paper not be interpreted as 'sacraments' of this liberating process? Perhaps Moltmann's intentions are aptly expressed by the words Krog recorded from Cynthia Ngewu, a South African woman whose son Christopher Piet was murdered:

> This thing called reconciliation ... if I am understanding it correctly ... if it means that this perpetrator, this man who killed Christopher Piet, if it means that he becomes human again, this man, so that I, so that all of us, get our humanity back ... then I agree, then I support it all. (Krog 1999: 164)

Does it then matter that there are churches in South Africa? It does not if they cover the real problem with the cloak of charity, nor if they only focus on the subversion of structures. But relating the astonishing examples of people finding their humanity back and Moltmann's view of God's liberating process, it could be concluded that it surely does matter if churches attempt to be what they essentially are: a 'sacrament' of God's liberating process, that is a playing field where liberated people find new identity and recognition and where they are given room to learn the play of reconciliation by trial and error.

Bibliography

Botman, H. Russel. (1996). "Narrative Challenges in a Situation of Transition." In: H. Russel Botman and Robin M. Petersen (eds.). *To Remember and to Heal*. Cape Town.
Fanon, Frantz. (1967). *Black Skin, White Masks*. New York: Grove Press.
Koopman, Nico. (1998). "Racism in the Post-apartheid South Africa." In: Louise Kretzschmar and Len Hulley (eds.). *Questions about Life and Morality: Christian Ethics in South Africa Today*. Pretoria: J.L. van Schaik Publishers. Pp. 153-67.
Krog, Antjie. (1999). *Country of my Skull*. London: Vintage Random House.
Jansen, Jonathan. (2000). "Racisme is hier doodgewoon." *Zuidelijk Afrika* 4: 36-38.
Meiring, Piet. (1999). *Chronicle of the Truth Commission: A Journey through the Past and Present—Into the Future of South Africa*. Vanderbijlpark: Carpe Diem Books.
Moltmann, Jürgen. (1967). *Theology of Hope: On the Ground and Implications of a Christian Eschatology*. London: SCM Press.
———. (1970). "Gott versöhnt und macht frei." In: *Evangelische Kommentaren*. No. 3. Pp. 515-20.
———. (1971a). *Mensch: Christlicher Anthropologie in den Konflikten der Gegenwart*. Stuttgart: Kreuz Verlag.
———. (1971b). "Rassismus und das Recht auf Widerstand." In: *Evangelische Kommentaren*. No. 4. Pp. 253-57.
———. (1972). "Siehe, es ist alles neu geworden." In: *Die Sprache der Befreiung: Predigten und Besinnungen*. Munich: Chr. Kaiser. Pp. 32-40.

———. (1993a). *The Crucified God: The Cross of Christ as the Foundation and Criticism of Christian Theology*. Minneapolis: Fortress Press.
———. (1993b). *The Church in the Power of the Spirit*. Minneapolis: Fortress Press.
———. (2000). *Experiences in Theology: Ways and Forms of Christian Theology*. London: SCM Press.

Seeds of Conflict

Christian-Muslim Relations in Tanzania

Frans Wijsen and Bernardine Mfumbusa

Introduction

On 29 October, 2000, the people of the United Republic of Tanzania held their first democratic elections without the presence of the Father of the Nation, Julius Nyerere. Nyerere had died on October 14, 1999. During the election campaigns it seemed that religious antagonism (*udini*), which had not been present in Tanzania until then, was seeping into the national psyche. Candidates for the presidency and parliament were increasingly defined by their religion rather than who they were as people.

According to political observers, the elections were held in an honest and quiet way. The ruling president, Benjamin Mkapa, was reelected by a greater majority than in 1995 (71.7% of the votes compared to 61.8% in 1995). The press emphasized the chaotic nature of the elections on Zanzibar (5% of the electorate) and the fact that the elections on the mainland, where 97% of the 33 million Tanzanians live, passed off smoothly seemed to be of no interest. Mkapa, a Catholic, had been pushed by Julius Nyerere as the presidential candidate in the 1995 elections after Ali Hassan Mwinyi, a Muslim, had held the office for ten years. The conviction that it would have been Nyerere's will that Mkapa remain in power may have been a factor in his reelection.

But what will happen after Mkapa? Will the foundation laid by Nyerere be solid enough to guarantee harmony in Tanzania in the long run? The 2001 'Zanzibar Riots', in which some 5,000 sympathizers of the Civic United Front (CUF), the main opposition party, contested the outcome of the election on Zanzibar and in which 23 people were shot by the police, may incline one to answer this question negatively. In our view, however, the contest is a regional problem, restricted to 16 out of the 50 Zanzibar constituencies (mainly on Pemba Island, the stronghold of CUF), which comprises only a small although militant minority.

In this contribution our aim is to acquire insight into the dynamics of Islam and into conditions for a dialogue between Christians and Muslims in Tanzania (officially both groups comprise some 33% of the population; exact figures are not available). This paper is an attempt to clarify Islamic grievances in the hope of encouraging mutual understanding and cooperation. It is our presupposition that much of the current misunderstanding between Christians and Muslims has originated from sheer ignorance and fear. To attain our goal we will provide a general description of the situation, interpret and evaluate it and recommend what could be done to make Muslim-Christian relations in Tanzania remain peaceful.

The Muslims' Complaints

In order to assess the extent of religious antagonism (*udini*) the authors conducted fieldwork. We interviewed several religious leaders, both Muslim and Christian in Mwanza, Dodoma, Kondoa, Dar es Salaam and Zanzibar (cf. Wijsen 1997 and 2001). In addition, questionnaires with both structured and open questions were distributed to a random sample in Dar es Salaam in 1998.

We will limit ourselves here to the outcomes of this small-scale survey, because Dar es Salaam is the hotbed of tension. The questionnaires were completed by some religious leaders—Christian and Muslim—and by laypeople. Most ordinary Muslim respondents came from the Kariakoo area in Dar es Salaam. For the Muslim respondents we relied on the help of a Muslim journalist working with one of the newspapers in Dar es Salaam. The outcome is presented here in percentages.

37% of the respondents felt that in Tanzania there is no religious equality, over against the remaining 63% who maintained that it did exist. The question of whether religious conflict posed a future danger for the country was answered in the affirmative by 80% of the respondents. The remaining 20% felt there was no such danger in the foreseeable future.

30% of the respondents held that Muslims are not well-treated in Tanzania. Further, 30% felt that the institution of Islamic Law (*sharia*) would solve Muslims' problems. 55% replied in the negative and the remaining 15% had no opinion. Attendance at religious rallies was admitted by 75%, while the remaining 25% said that they had not attended such rallies. To the further question of whether rallies encouraged tensions 75% said yes, 10% said no and the remaining 15% had no opinion.

Even more interesting were the responses to the open questions. To the question of Muslim rights and the situation in Tanzania, some respondents said that there is no Islamic extremism. "The talk about Islamic extremists," one respondent noted, "is a propaganda gimmick employed by Westerners to discredit Islam." Islamic extremism, according to another respondent, is a "social reawakening," namely "Muslims demanding equal participation in determining the social, economic and political fate of this country."

On Muslim-Christian relations one respondent said: "Christians are employing a variety of tactics—psychological, political and what have you—to maintain the 'status quo' in Tanzania. All evils, bombings, arson, and riots, are blamed on Muslims." On government-Muslim relations some respondents said that the government ignored the plight of Muslims, that the government remained out of touch with Muslims' demands and that Muslims feel they have been excluded from the mainstream politics of Tanzania.

On the question of gender rights some of the respondents said that the government, instigated by the will to adjust to the Western world, is enacting laws to protect women. But "this is a secular state which advocates among other things, freedom of worship," one of the respondents said. "Islam has its own laws on marriage, inheritance, and so on, and the government is turning a blind eye on this fact.

When Muslims fight against this shortsightedness they are castigated as *waislamu wenye imani kali* [Islamic extremists]," this person continued.

When asked why they felt that the religious conflict is likely to flare up in Tanzania, some Muslim respondents answered that the government favored Christians, that Muslims were second-class citizens, that they were used as scapegoats for all evils in the society, that they were discriminated against, and that their rights —such as the right to have Muslim courts or to be members of international Muslims organizations—were violated.

These complaints are not new. The *Baraza Kuu la Jumuiya na Taasisi za Kiislamu Tanzania* (Supreme Council of Islamic Organizations and Institutions of Tanzania) released a circular in which it accused the church of controlling the government. In 1995 the *Baraza Kuu la Waislamu wa Tanzania* (Supreme Council of Muslims in Tanzania) did the same: "The government and the church are one and the same thing." It continued: "Muslims in Tanzania are discriminated and oppressed in two ways. They are denied education and they are denied political power." Though the official position has always been that "all people are equal and so are treated on merit," some think that the government identifies itself with Christianity.

Aboud Jumbe (1995: 122), former vice president of the United Republic of Tanzania, provides school entrance figures to support this thesis. He alleges that Muslims constitute 45% of the Tanzanian population and Christians for 39%. But when it comes to primary school enrolment, 40% of all enrollments are Christians and 40% Muslims. Christians constitute 64% of secondary school enrollments and 86.1% of university enrollments, whereas for Muslims these figures are 35.6% and 13.9% respectively.

According to Jumbe, the government has favored Christians not only with respect to education but also with respect to leadership positions. Quoting the 1993 figures, he says that there were only eight Muslims in the union government compared to sixteen Christians; eight district commissioners were Muslims compared to 113 Christians. The same imbalance applies to leading positions in the Bank of Tanzania, the National Bank of Commerce, postal and telephone services, etc. (Jumbe 1995: 123).

The right to have Muslim courts has been a serious cause of friction between the government and Muslims ever since the government abolished these courts in the 1960s. Some Muslims feel that Tanzania should be declared an Islamic state on the grounds that Muslims are a majority. Some even suggested there should be affirmative action in favor of Muslims joining institutes of higher learning until some kind of a religious 'capillary balance' is attained. This was the purport of the 'Secret Memo' of Kighoma Malima, who was the Minister of Education at the time.

Those who fight for Muslims' rights want the government to adopt the *sharia* (Islamic Law) as a long-term solution to what they say are historical injustices done to Tanzanian Muslims. In November 1998 Alhaj Jumbe formed the Tanzanian branch of the World Muslim League (WML), "to fight for the rights of Muslims." The rioters at Mwembechai Mosque said that they did the same. The Mwembechai riots took place in February 1998, in which four young Muslims were shot by the police (cf. Njozi 2000).

The question of Muslim rights is kept alive by *An-nuur*, a weekly newspaper published in Dar es Salaam. Its basic characteristic seems to be that it is anti-Christian and antigovernment. Some say that one tactic used to demean Muslims is to ignore their positive contribution to the struggle for independence. Mohamed Said is one of those who propose this view. His book (1998) is interesting, not because it has something new to say, but because it tries to separate the contribution of the Tanzanian Muslims from the overall nationalistic struggle.

The persecution complex is not limited to Muslims: Christians seem to be affected by the same complex. The burning of Christian schools, pork butchershops and churches and attacks on Christian doctrines in public rallies have been a cause for concern since the late 1980s. The *Baraza la Maaskofu Katoliki Tanzania* (Tanzania Episcopal Conference) issued a string of letters cautioning the government of the worsening situation in the country. The Christian Council of Churches (CCT) wrote a couple of letters sharing these concerns.

Tanzania in the Post-Cold War Era

It has been suggested that Christian-Muslim relationships have always been adversarial and that this has been caused by the missionary nature of both religions. The latter may be true. But in Tanzania real religious tensions go back to only the mid-1980s. Before that, the ideology of African socialism (in Tanzania called *ujamaa*, family ties) helped relegate religion to churches, mosques and private homes. After the abandonment of the *ujamaa* ideology in 1989, an ideological vacuum emerged that was quickly filled by religious preachers, some of whom had more than a purely missionary agenda. Whether this was inspired by Ali Hassan Mwinyi's rise to power in 1985 or whether it was mere coincidence may never be known.

A cocktail of factors coalesced to make religious antagonism possible. The adjustment to a free market economy in 1989 saw the introduction of videocassette recorders and video cassettes that were used in religious campaigns. Preachers like the late Ali Ngariba recorded videos of debates in which Christians were denigrated. These videos were distributed and shown in public. Christians produced the *Biblia ni jibu* videos in order to combat the Muslims' claims. Also, the emergence of the free press allowed people to express opinions in ways that were not possible before (cf. All Africa Press Service). Sects began to publish newspapers such as the Christian *Haki*, *Injili*, *Lengo* and the Islamic *An-nuur* and *Nyota*. Some of these are also found on the internet (www.islamtz.org/an-nuur/).

The introduction of multiparty politics in July 1992 caused Tanzanians to form political parties and to express their opinions freely. Although strictly forbidden by the Constitution, some of these parties have religious and ethnic bases. The United Democratic Party (UDP), for example, is strong in Mwanza Region and is dominated by the Sukuma ethnic group; the Civic United Front (CUF) is strong on Zanzibar and is linked to Islam. Some politicians, like Rev. Christopher Mtikila, resorted to racial slurs to incite the masses against foreigners, notably Indians. He called them *Gabacholi*, 'thieves', since they control a large share of the economy (cf. Ludwig 1996). It is clear that some movements, both Islamic and Christian, are sponsored by outside agencies. But the religious dynamics within the country are not to be ignored.

The missionary nature of Islam and Christianity may be another factor in the antagonism. Both religions claim divine revelation exclusively for themselves and have instituted programs for converting Africa. The resolution of the Abuja Plan of Action to make sure "that Africa will be an Islamic continent by 2000" has its parallel in the "Evangelization 2000" campaign within the Catholic Church. *Jihad* against Christians is countered by 'Crusades for Christ'.

For some Muslims, the first principle is that the only true source that provides knowledge of God is the Qur'an. The same holds true for Christians and their sacred text, the Bible. But, whereas Muslims believe that Jesus has a place in the salvation history of the world, Christians find it difficult to give Muhammad a place in that history. For Muslims Jesus falls into the category of prophet, whereas for Christians Muhammad does not. This causes an imbalance in the dialogue of arguments between Christians and Muslims.

On the level of the dialogue of life, however, little has changed and relationships between Muslims and Christians remain peaceful (cf. Wijsen 2001). Several scholars have asked themselves whether Tanzanians by nature are more peaceful. Why is Tanzania not racked by social and ethnic strife as Kenya and Uganda are? A study of Tanzania's situation since independence suggests that the feeling of national belonging and unity is a result of deliberate policies adopted by the government of the United Republic of Tanzania. It is not true, as some say, that Tanzania lacks that combustible mixture of ethnic, racial or religious elements that create social unrest in other countries.

Of particular importance was the introduction of Swahili as a national language. This has been an important element in the mass mobilization of the people of this country, facilitating a unique degree of national integration. Another factor that helped promote this unique sense of nationalism in Tanzania was the nationalization of schools after the 1967 Arusha declaration. It led to the creation of the national school system that allowed students of various ethnic groups and religious persuasions to come together. This tended to blend students into a single mass shaped by the same values and ideals.

Likewise, the National Service, a one-year military stint, mandatory for all secondary school students leaving form six, helped create a wide view and greater awareness of matters concerning other ethnic groups. Apart from the physical exercise and basic military training, the National Service was an important area where the youth of the country could meet and where lasting pan-territorial acquaintances were made.

But this heritage is now in serious danger. Except for Swahili, all other unifying factors have been abandoned. One prominent columnist (Mwapachu 1998: 3) noted that the education sector is currently back to where it was at independence, characterized by racial, religious and ethnic divisions. At present there are nursery schools exclusively for Indians, Muslims and Christians. There is even one Arabic Medium University. Such schools are likely to produce people imbued with myopic and fanatic views of other religious groups. This does not augur very well for the future.

Are All People Equal?

The question that concerns us here is to what extent the Muslims' complaints are justified. Most complaints are based on the premise that Muslims form a majority in the Tanzanian society. This premise, however, lacks statistical basis. As part of the deliberate policy of the Tanzania government to create national unity, questions related to ethnicity and religion have not been asked since the 1967 census. Christians also claim that they are the majority (Omari 1984: 5).

The complaint that "the government and the church are one and the same thing" has some foundation. John Sivalon (1992: 24-25), a Catholic priest and senior lecturer in sociology in the University of Dar es Salaam, says that after independence "the leaders of the (Catholic) Church were able to build an alliance between them and the leaders of the Party and the Government." This alliance gave them a "unique opportunity to direct how the *ujamaa* policy was to be understood and implemented by the government leaders." The church leaders "intended to create an alliance with the government leaders in order to be in a good position to protect themselves against the spread of Marxism and Islam."

The major complaint seems to be that Muslims are denied education. It is true that Christians appear to be better educated. But the question is whether the government or the church is to blame. Most schools during the colonial era and immediately after were run by missionaries. Many Muslims were wary of these schools because they feared religious indoctrination. Consequently, they lost the opportunity to become educated.

When Jumbe (1995) appeals to the 1978 school entrance figures to bolster his argument, he seems to forget that Muslims were favored when the Germans were in control of the country. The German colonial administration saw the Muslims as civilized people, those who knew how to read and write. From this historical perspective, the Muslims' complaints seem odd. Nyerere's government made a deliberate effort to favor Muslims when the school system, which was largely church-owned, was nationalized after the 1967 Arusha Declaration. Jumbe and most Muslim commentators do not mention this fact. However, a renowned Mafia Island scholar, Sheikh Yusuf Halimoja, says that there was no conspiracy against Muslims and singled out the nationalization of schools in 1967 as a deliberate act to help give Muslims a fair chance to be educated.

Jumbe and others fail to explain why the Muslims on Zanzibar are as poorly educated per capita as their mainland counterparts. Zanzibar is 99% Muslim and the government there has always been Islamic in all but name. Still, the amount of educated people in Zanzibar is quite low. Towns such as Tanga, Mtwara or Kigoma with a solid Muslim majority do not do any better. The problem may lie in the fact that

Muslims often think that Western education is necessarily secular. Thus, the problem lies with the Muslims' understanding of education and not with the government as such. Some steps being taken to address the problem include the formation of so-called Islamic seminaries.

One needs to pose the question as well as to whether it was a deliberate policy to deny Muslims important posts in the government and to give preferential treatment to the Catholic Church. It seems that no such evidence is available and that it was simply a side effect of the fact that Christians were better educated than Muslims.

It must be admitted, however, that the principle of the government not to mix religion with politics seems to be inspired by a Western, Christian separation of the secular and religious domain. For Muslims (and for African indigenous believers) these two domains are irrevocably one. Yet the majority of African Muslims agree to the secular nature of the state. Moreover, there seems to be an imbalance between the above-mentioned principle and another principle that is invoked: 'play your part'. When the Muslims try to play their part they are branded as 'Islamic extremists'.

The complaint about the violation of Muslims' rights is a serious issue. It is linked to the demand to introduce Islamic Law (*sharia*). The concept of the separation of powers is alien to Islam. Wherever there is a perceived Muslim majority there is pressure to institute *sharia* as the guiding principle of life, thereby relegating other citizens to the status of *dhimmi* or second-class people forced to pay special taxes to an Islamic state.

The present-day frictions reflect an old division between nationalism and pan-Islamism within the Muslim community. African Sunni Muslims constituted the power base of *Tanganyika National Union* (TANU). They favored nationalism in contrast to the more pan-Islamic outlook of Arab and Asian Muslims. This contrast led to the 'Islamic Crisis' in 1968. In that year pro-TANU Muslims sidelined the anti-TANU Muslims within the East African Muslim Welfare Society (EAMWS). The EAMWS, which had pan-Islamic sympathies, was banned by the government, which then established a firm control of the *Baraza Kuu la Waislamu wa Tanzania* (BAKWATA), which was pro-TANU (Westerlund 1980: 179).

Failure to pay attention to these sentiments will have disastrous results. If what is happening in Rwanda and Burundi is any indication, it is clear that the price for perceived or real injustice can be high. In these twin Central African countries, thousands have perished because a group has felt that they have been denied justice and have been transformed into second-class citizens in their own country. Some Muslim groups in Tanzania are registering frightfully similar sentiments today.

Muslims blame the government and Christians for their backwardness. The connivance of the most industrialized countries (G-7), 6 out of 7 of which are 'Christian', is said to be at the root of Muslims' problems. Historical reasons are often advanced. Among these are the identification of Christianity with colonialism and the fact that most post-independence African leaders were Christians. Because most of these leaders engaged in the amassing of wealth, leaving their subjects wallowing in abject poverty, all evils that engulfed Africa were identified with Christianity.

The erosion of morals in African societies today is blamed on the influence of the Western-Christian culture expressed in the omnipresence of TV, video and newspapers. The impression is given that if Christianity is done away with, all will be well. Some Muslims think that Islam is the only religion that will help people solve their problems, basing themselves on the Qur'an when it says: "You are the best of peoples, evolved for mankind, enjoining what is right, forbidding what is wrong, and believing in God" (Sura 3: 110). The reality of backwardness in several Islamic societies sharply contradicts this conviction of the superiority of Islam. Moreover, the Qur'an does not say that the Islam is superior but that believers who do the will of God are superior to those who do not.

What Can be Done?

For most Tanzanians, until the mid 1980s, violence was something that happened elsewhere—in Soweto, Bujumbura or Luanda, something they heard about in the news —far away from their everyday lives. When it finally happened in Dar es Salaam, the aura of peace and harmony that beguiled the country for so long was shattered. The issue of Muslims' complaints in Tanzania is a complex one and needs to be adequately addressed. How can Muslims be appeased and the rest of the population not be antagonized by giving the Muslims preferential help?

Whatever action is taken, the secular nature of the state, to which the vast majority of Tanzanians, Muslims, and Christians assent, should be clearly emphasized. The constitutional separation of the state and religion ought to be protected by legal mechanisms that can be enforced in the court of law. The basic principle should be to foster unity in this pluralistic country. Ministerial, military and other important posts should be ratified by the Parliament to avoid favoritism along religious lines.

The current policy of allowing monoreligious schools should be reviewed. This policy is likely to perpetuate imbalance. Christian schools seem better equipped to offer quality education, which in the long run will create greater imbalance. Interreligious formation must be promoted and religious studies should be included as a subject in the secondary school curriculum, instead of religious instruction. Muslim families could be encouraged to send their children to schools. They should make use of the opportunity provided by so many secular schools in the country. Unfortunately, many Muslims are still wary of so-called secular education.

The teaching of Islam in (Christian) theological colleges and seminaries, which is done from an apologetic point of view, should become less biased. The government should adopt policies that would combat grassroots poverty. Poverty appears to be the main catalyst of 'fundamentalism'. If measures were taken to relieve this problems, this would have an effect on the lessening of other problems as well and people would cease to look for scapegoats.

Offensive rallies and sermons should be discouraged by law. Respect for other religions is a vital aspect of civilized life. It is wrong to brand pious and sincere Muslims as 'fundamentalists'. It is irresponsible of people to set up pork butchershops in predominantly Muslim residential areas, whether they have licenses or not. It is foolish for Islamic preachers to poke fun at biblical teachings rather than propagate the virtues of the Qur'an.

Affirmative action in favor of Muslims should be taken. More Muslims should be encouraged to assume administrative posts in the government, the army and other public sectors to deflect unnecessary rancor. Merit, however, should remain the criterion for giving people responsibility and not religious affiliation alone.

A 'global' theology should be constructed, without neglecting the local context. The work of the Tanzania branch of the World Conference on Religions and Peace is extremely important. Its objectives are

> to share among religious leaders knowledge of the traditions and sanctions each religion has for justice and peace; to identify common religious commitments and principles conductive to the peace of the community; and to undertake actions for peace.

More important still is to promote common ideals and practices. By praying together and fasting together people come to know one another better. Tanzanians at the grassroots level have been living for many years without being conscious of their religious differences. Whenever they were confronted with religious differences, they would say: "Mungu Moja, dini Mbalimbali" (One God, Many Religions). There is no reason why this popular wisdom could not help to maintain peace and harmony in the community in the present-day circumstances.

Conclusion

The international press usually reports on civil wars and religious conflicts, as was the case with the Zanzibar riots in the beginning of 2001, and we may ask ourselves what the causes of those conflicts. That millions of people live together peacefully is not news. In this contribution we focussed on a country with a relatively high level of religious harmony and asked ourselves why harmony is present there and under what conditions it can be maintained.

The lessons to be drawn from the Tanzanian situation are not very clear. Perhaps the tensions are too recent and the situation too ambiguous for that. One lesson could be that religions are not in themselves conflictual but are made conflictual when they are exploited for political gains.

The other lesson could be that, although seeds of conflict are inherent in the missionary nature of both Christianity and Islam, the deliberate policies of the government have so far guaranteed peace in Tanzania. The adoption of Swahili as a national language, the establishment of the national secondary school system and the national service nurtured a sense of national belonging. It has been shown that these policies are now in danger of being neglected. If this remains the case, peace and harmony cannot be guaranteed and the seeds of conflict will grow into serious confrontations.

It is important to acknowledge that Muslim-Christian relations in Tanzania are still more harmonious than in many other countries in Africa. One may not exaggerate the tension between Muslims and Christians. For years Christians and Muslims have coexisted and on the whole continue to coexist peacefully. This peaceful coexistence can be nurtured through trying to understand one another and address mutual problems and grievances. By doing so, the Tanzania experience can be a shining example to other countries in the world that face the same problems.

Bibliography

All Africa Press Service. (1987a). "Muslim-Christian Tension Mounting." *News and Features Bulletin* (June 29).
———. (1987b). "Tanzania Wary of Religious Conflict." *News and Features Bulletin* (July 27).
———. (1989). "Islamic Fundamentalism Worries Churches." *News and Features Bulletin* (August 21).
———. (1992). "Tension between Christians and Muslims Hots up in Tanzania." *News and Features Bulletin* (February 3).
Baraza Kuu la Jumuiya na Taasisi za Kiislamu za Tanzania. (1993). *Madai ya Haki za Waislamu*. Dar es Salaam.
Baraza Kuu la Waislamu wa Tanzania. (1995). *Waislamu na Uchaguzi Mkuu. Kauli ya Maulana*, Dar es Salaam.
Baraza la Maaskofu Katoliki Tanzania. (1993a). *Tamko Rasmi mintarafu Kashfa za Kidini*. Dar es Salaam.
Baraza la Maaskofu Katoliki Tanzania. (1993b). *Ukwelie Utawapa Uhuru (YN & 32). Barua ya Kichungaji*. Dar es Salaam.
Joinet, Bernard. (1998). "A Burning Issue: Muslim and Christian Reactions to the Challenge of Modern Society." *A Letter to my Superiors* No. 20/12.
Jumbe, A. (1995). *The Partnership: Tanganyika-Zanzibar Union. 30 Turbulent Years*. Dar es Salaam.
Ludwig, F. (1996). "After Ujamaa: Is Religious Revivalism a Threat to Tanzania's Stability?" In: D. Westerlund (ed.). *Questioning the Secular State*. London. Pp. 216-36.
Mwapachu, Juma. (1998). "Intellectuals Alarmed by 'Free Fall' of Education Standard." *The African*. (November 28).
Kettani, M. (1985). "Muslims in Tanzania: A Rejoinder." *Journal Institute of Muslim Minority Affairs* 6: 219-20.
Malima, Kighoma. (1988). *Suala la Elimu ya Wanawake na Vijana wa Kiislamu Nchini*. Wizara ya Elimu. Dar es Salaam.
Njozi, Hamza Mustafa. (2000). *The Mwembechai Killings and The Political Future of Tanzania*. Ottawa.
Omari, C. (1984). "Christian-Muslim Relations in Tanzania." *Journal Institute of Muslim Minority Affairs* 5: 373-90.
Said, Mohamed. (1998). *The Life and Times of Abdulwahid Sykes (1924-1968): The Untold Story of the Muslim Struggle against British Colonialism in Tanganyika*. Minerva Press.
Sivalon, John. (1992). *Kanisa Katoliki na Siasa ya Tanzania bara 1953 na 1985*. Ndanda-Peramiho.
Von Sicard, J. (1998). "Tanzania, Muslims in." In: T. Bianquis *et al.* (eds.), *The Encyclopaedia of Islam*. Vol. X. Leiden: Brill. Pp. 194-97.

Westerlund, D. (1980). *Ujumaa na Dini: A Study of Some Aspects of Society and Religion in Tanzania. 1961-1977.* Stockholm.
Wijsen, F. (1997). "Strive in Competition for Good Deeds: Christians and Muslims in Tanzania." *Studies in Interreligious Dialogue* 7: 158-76.
———. (2001). "When Two Elephants Fight the Grass Gets Hurt: Muslim-Christian Relationships in Upcountry Tanzania." In: F. Wijsen and P. Nissen (eds.). *Mission is a Must.* Amsterdam/Atlanta 2001.

Religion, Conflict and Reconciliation in Rwanda

Jan van Butselaar

Introduction

Until fairly recently Rwanda was a country unknown to many outsiders, hidden somewhere in Central Africa. That changed dramatically in the 1990s: a terrible civil war, reaching its low point in the genocide of 1994, gave the country and its people an international reputation for cruelty and tribalism, for hatred and death. Many questions were asked in Christian circles at the time: How could this be? Was not Rwanda one of the most Christian countries in Africa? Was not Rwanda one of the most 'successful' examples of mission—Catholic or Protestant?

The questions were understandable. For although the name of Rwanda as a country drew a blank for the general public, in Christian and missionary circles the country was something of a miracle. In Catholic circles, Rwanda was one of the countries where the White Fathers of Cardinal Lavigerie had worked hard and conscientiously for many long years (Rutayisire 1987) and several of them had even lost their lives (Ntezimana 1979). Rwanda was a special place for the White Fathers. They had tried to realize the dream of their founder, to build a Christian kingdom in Africa, in Uganda—but that had not worked out well: Mwanga, the Ugandan Kabaka, was not exactly the image of a Christian king (Groves 1964: 88 ff.). Thus in 1900 they came to Rwanda. There, through the vicissitudes of history, the country had passed from being a German colony, where Catholics had no special rights, into a Belgian protectorate, where they could count on the cooperation of the authorities. The king, Musinga, seemed to be willing to become a Christian. However, when he hesitated too long, he was dethroned (1930) and replaced by his son Rudahigwa (Heremans 1973: 68). The young king's personal adviser was the 'chief' of the White Fathers and of the Catholic Church in Rwanda, Mgr. Léon Classe. In 1943 the king was finally baptized: the Christian kingdom was in the end realized.

In Protestant circles, the country was also famous for a very special reason: the East African revival. Several missionary organizations had entered the country after the departure of the German Lutheran Bethel mission of Von Bodelschwingh. The Belgians even started their work with the help of the Belgian king (Twagirayesu and Van Butselaar 1982: 84). The Anglicans entered at a later stage, followed by the Baptists and Free Methodists. The number of their followers stayed rather limited for a long time, working as they were not for a maximum of baptisms but for an optimum of Christian education. In the Anglican circles, however, the 1930s witnessed a revival movement that made a big impact on the whole of East Africa (Butler 1976; Warren 1954). Many came to faith in Jesus Christ, moved by the Spirit. Within the churches this movement was not always met with much understanding (Gatwa and Karamaga 1990: 55). Scholars too have to this day always had difficulties in understanding the movement (Longman 1995: 203). But the phenomenon was warmly remembered in evangelical circles worldwide and had made Rwanda renowned as a country of God's favor.

How could this horrifying genocide take place therefore in this Christian context? That was the question that many asked in 1994. And somewhat later: What did the churches do to prevent this ordeal? What did they do to open the road to reconciliation in the country? These are questions that were easily asked—especially by those outside the country. And they are justified. To answer them, it is necessary to put them in historical context. That is hardly possible in this article. Not only is the history of Rwanda a long and complicated one, but also the change of power in 1994 caused a change in the interpretation of history. History textbooks in Rwanda are at the present being rewritten. The history of Rwanda has now become a political issue. To show that a researcher of Rwandese history is staying within the boundaries of science and does not want to play a political role demands more space than is available here. Thus, we can indicate the background of the conflict only in general terms here—and remain open to adjustment and supplementation.

Rwandese History

The key words for understanding Rwandese history seem to be Hutu and Tutsi, the names of the two most important tribes in the country (the third being the small group of Twa). The Hutu constitute the large majority and the Tutsi a considerable minority. Calling them 'tribes' can easily create a wrong impression: in Rwanda, the different ethnic groups do not live in more or less separated areas, with cultural and linguistic differences, as is the case elsewhere in Africa with tribes. Instead, they constitute two groups that share the same country, the same language, the same culture. They also share the same history, a history of conquest of Hutu kingdoms by Tutsi invaders in the sixteenth century, a history of clientship where Hutu were subservient to the Tutsi monarchy and chiefs, a history of colonial masters that first favored the existing Tutsi-dominated social structure and, at the very end of their presence, changed their allegiance to the Hutu majority (Linden 1999; Overdulve 1996; Trouwborst 1998). It is a history of mistrust, of oppression and sometimes of cruelty. It is a history that has deeply influenced the Rwandese culture, where, on the one hand, it is important to please the authorities and, on the other, to avoid giving information—or to use information as a weapon for one's own cause, one's own group (Overdulve 1997).

For many centuries the Tutsi governed the country; the token Hutu that was involved at lower levels of administration did not really change that imbalance of social and political power. Since the 1960s the Hutu took over. That caused violent clashes in that decade caused by Tutsi efforts to gain back their former position and by political manipulations within the Hutu élite. Many Tutsi fled the country. At the beginning of the 1990s they had grown to a population of about half a million people, living in exile in Burundi (where the majority found a place in that Tutsi-led society),

Zaïre, Uganda, Kenya, Europe and the United States. They became more and more frustrated. On the one hand, many of them had gained important positions in intellectual, military or business enterprises. On the other, they never were 'at home', they never really belonged—and in Africa and for Africans that entails suffering (Mbiti 1969: 100 ff.). These feelings became rather strong at the end of the 1980s. In Uganda the Rwandese refugees were increasingly being asked to return home. But the Rwandese government refused—at least, they made it almost impossible for the young Tutsi from Uganda to return home with their cattle and other belongings. Several of these young refugees, who were refused entry into Rwanda, did not want to leave the border post and committed suicide. That probably gave rise to the idea that the Tutsi refugees could only return to their country by force. In 1988 the Rwanda Patriotic Front (RPF) was founded in Kampala, Uganda (Reyntjes 1994: 303).

In the same period, the political and social situation in Rwanda itself deteriorated. The president of the republic, Juvénal Habyarimana, who was also leader of the only legal political party euphemistically called Movement for Development, had since 1973 governed the country and assured its habitants of reasonable peace and economic growth. But by the end of the 1980s the situation had become less favorable. The economic crisis in Europe had its effect on aid-dependent Rwanda; prices for products such as coffee went down drastically. The population growth aggravated the pressure on the available resources. The reaction of the governing group (*akazu*: 'the little house') was to strengthen their own positions and oppress any opposition. Rampant corruption (never fully absent from the country) sprang up, cruel acts against competitors (or assumed competitors) for the country's meager resources were noted. And, as always when a crisis developed in Rwanda, when leaders contested for hegemony, the Hutu-Tutsi question was revived, an old slumbering animosity that was used to keep power or to gain it. It was a beast that, as it turned out, once liberated from its chains, could not be 'managed' as in the 1960s or 1970s.

The time seemed perfect for a first attack by the RPF on the weak country. In 1990 the RPF invaded the country from the north, from Uganda (and with the help of Uganda's President Museveni). It was well-equipped, financed by different sources. In a short time they conquered important parts of the north and stayed there. The Rwandese government troops were not at all prepared to defend their country. It was said that they were better at drinking than at fighting. The Zairian troops, sent by President Mobutu to help his neighbor, added to the problems through their looting rather than helping to push back the RPF rebels. President Habyarimana kindly asked his Zairian brother to withdraw his help. The RPF installed a regime of terror in the 'liberated' part of the country (Niyonsaba 1999: 30). More than 300,000 Hutu fled the region and told their stories to the Hutu in the southern part of the country. It did not help to create trust—already a scarcity in Rwandese culture. And so the war went on. The RPF was winning. The Rwandese government troops would have succumbed to the invaders if a French regiment had not protected the central region of the country, including the capital Kigali. In 1993 efforts were made to overcome the stalemate between the warring parties. In Arusha a peace treaty was drawn up: there would be a sharing of power on a fifty-fifty basis and under the supervision of the UN. That treaty produced the opposite of what it intended. In April 1994 (RPF troops were then lodged in Kigali), President Habyarimana was murdered (together with the Burundese president) when his plane was shot down by what seemed to have been RPF fire (Edwards 2000), UN personnel withdrew after a murderous attack on Belgian paratroopers and genocide took the lives of more than 500,000 people. Many others fled the country: first the endangered Tutsi, later the endangered Hutu (Reyntjes 1995).

Now the RPF showed its strength. In a few months what remained of the Rwandese government was driven from the country into the wilderness of Zaire (where many of them later would be killed by the RPF invasion of that country) and an RPF government was installed. In a short period all responsible authorities in the country were changed and replaced by Tutsi; many leading Hutu who had stayed were kidnapped and disappeared, bishops (seen as friends of the former regime) were murdered and internal refugees killed in their camps. More than 100,000 people were imprisoned, accused of genocide, under inhuman circumstances. The new government showed its strength and received enormous financial help from the West. Not only were they considered by the international community as the 'liberators' of Rwanda who stopped the genocide, but they could also profit from guilt feelings in the West, who had done nothing to intervene in the plight of so many innocent people. According to some, these guilt feelings were rather 'Protestant', since they were mostly evoked in countries as the United States and the Netherlands.

Today there is no war in Rwanda, but neither is there peace. Many are dying in prisons and many are disappearing (Amnesty International). That brings us to the question: what did churches do for peace, for reconciliation? What do churches do? What could they do?

The Role of the Churches in the Past

Before taking up this issue, it is important to know more about the specific relationship between church and state in modern Africa in general, and in Rwanda in particular. Generally speaking, it should be noted that this relationship developed quite differently from what is the norm in Western countries or in South Africa. When, after decolonization, the newly independent countries of Africa were looking for well-educated leadership, it was clear where they could find it: in the mission and church schools and universities. The result was that many of the new political leaders had a 'religious past': they had studied, at least for a period, at seminaries for pastors and priests, present everywhere on the continent. When they discovered that their vocation lay elsewhere, namely in the political field, their friendship with their former classmates and future religious leaders continued, and so a common understanding of life in Africa developed. When these new leaders were later responsible for developing a new society for their countries, it was obvious that they sought counsel with their friends, who by now were bishops and church presidents in offices not far from their own. Without their realizing it, they were continuing an old African tradition.

In former times, the religious practitioner had been one of the most important counsellors of the chief. So what developed between church and state in Africa after independence was not so much a new *corpus christianum* but rather a return to old societal patterns. This gave the church an important role in the newly independent countries. The danger of the situation showed itself when several of the new African leaders turned into old-style dictators. Church leaders found it difficult to dissociate themselves from their friends. They often tried to redress the situation by confidential admonition. But to the public eye, inside and outside Africa, they were often seen as uncritical lackeys of the ruling power. In Rwanda this whole complex of close cooperation and confidentiality between church and state was further strengthened by two factors. First, the Catholic leaders maintained their option of Rwanda as a Christian 'kingdom': that meant that they had to be very close to the ruling power. Second, after the revolution of the early 1960s, most church leaders had a Hutu background. They experienced—the one more than the other—the threat of belligerent Tutsi who would try to regain power in the country. It made the relationship between church and state, between church leaders and public authorities even stronger. Church members generally applauded this attitude: the good relationship between their bishop or church president, with the authorities, could only give an extra protection against abuse of power by those authorities towards the local population. In their understanding, this friendship in high circles was an encouraging copy of the old social pattern.

The concrete result of all this was that the Catholic Archbishop Nsengiyumva (who, together with two of his colleagues, was murdered in 1994 by RPF soldiers) was for many years (until 1985) a member of the central committee of the MRND, the national political movement controlled by the regime. In this way, he had easy access to the president and to other authorities. The president of the Presbyterian Church, Twagirayesu, was a member of the provincial council in his home province of Kibuye. Not a very political man, he probably thought that it was necessary to take up this office so as not to leave all political influence in matters of education to the Catholics. In any case, it was (and is) rather dangerous in Rwandese culture to refuse political functions, once they are offered (Corduwener 2000). For more solid reasons, Twagirayesu also took up the office of president of the semi-official national office for family planning, no Catholic bishop being available for this post.

This typically African situation of understanding between church leaders and public authorities, together with protests in private when needed, did seem to work well for many years. During the upheavals of 1973, when a clash between Hutu and Tutsi tore the country apart, church authorities were able to provide protection for many who were persecuted or endangered. The churches were seen as a 'sanctuary'. That conviction was so strong that twenty years later, when people again felt their lives to be in danger, they automatically took refuge in churches—but now the sanctity of that place was no longer recognized by the mobs.

The Role of the Churches in the Recent Crisis

For the development of church-state relations in recent years in Rwanda and to find out what churches did to build bridges and to work for reconciliation, we will have to divide this period into three episodes: the years 1990-1993 directly after the invasion by the RPF, the terrible year 1994, and the years since the takeover by the RPF. In 1990 the churches found themselves in a difficult position. On the one hand, Archbishop Nsengiyumva had left the central committee of the MRND; the pope no longer allowed his priests to function in political parties or movements. But he still remained friends with the president and his entourage; he even managed to achieve a papal visit to the country. That was a clear sign of 'blessing' of the Habyarimana regime in the eyes of the local population. Also, the invasion of the north and the occupation/liberation of sizable parts of the country had resulted in large streams of internal refugees, who told horror stories about the oppression by the RPF in their territory. Churches had to side with the poor and suffering and chose to side with these refugees. It made them close their eyes (at least in public) to the atrocities that were committed in those days against the Tutsi in several parts of the country, accused of being secret supporters of the invading RPF.

Even before the attack by the RPF, the Catholic bishops had tried to create sensitivity to the dangers that were threatening the country. In a pastoral letter *Le Christ, notre unité* (Evêques Catholiques), they had condemned ethnic conflict, regionalism, nepotism and other evils in society. After the attack, several other pastoral letters followed which expanded on the same theme. But in general, they failed in their aim of setting the different groups on the road to peace and reconciliation. The reason was not so much that they did not name the guilty parties, as Des Forges supposed, but because the church had lost all its credibility in political matters—the archbishop was still seen as a close friend of the ruling regime. One of my sources even spoke of a moral crisis in the country that had been building up since the mid-1980s. The Protestant churches also kept quiet during this first year. Some leaders hoped that, after thirty years of majority rule, the ethnic problem would not trigger a repeat of the massive killings that had taken place in the 1960s and 1970s. They hoped that the generally accepted plan for democratization would end the civil war and bring the RPF as a political party into the political system. That was, as would become clear, somewhat naive. More realistic was the setting up of a 'Contact Committee' of the Catholic and Protestant churches in the first part of 1992 that functioned for a certain time as a liaison between the ruling regime and the RPF (Karamaga 1995: 301). This committee asked the different parties to renounce any form of dictatorship, to reveal their rights and obligations to the public, especially in matters of racism and discrimination, to call for the dismantling of the militia that the different parties had founded, to call the extremist political parties to end their racial propaganda, to call on Christians to refrain from taking part in racist parties.

At the end of the same year the committee declared that it had called on the president and on other authorities not to give any more public speeches, that everyone should respect the political and social rights of others, that they condemned all instigators of persecutions, bandits and terrorists.

This committee met twice with representatives of the RPF in Nairobi and in Bujumbura. That in itself was a courageous act, the RPF being branded as the enemy that was illegally and cruelly occupying a part of the country. In 1993 the church began to take an even more public role. The president of the Presbyterian Church, Twagirayesu, gave a speech at the Protestant Theological Faculty in Butare entitled "Quand les Églises sortent de leur silence," in which he made the position of the churches clear. The same committee was also working to bring the parties together for the peace talks, which were held later that year in Arusha under UN supervision (Reyntjes 1994: 248 ff.). The church leaders were then hopeful that peace could finally be realized. In October 1993 Twagirayesu preached a courageous sermon that was broadcast on national radio, condemning racism and discrimination and calling on the government and the RPF to take the Arusha agreements seriously.

Later that year an encounter on a broader scale was organized in Mombasa to implement the results of the Arusha agreements. Present were representatives of the churches and the warring political groups, as well as the regional ecumenical organization, the All Africa Conference of Churches (AACC). The report of that meeting is not remarkable (*Processus* (1993)), but the fact that parties could sit together and meet each other was an important step forward. It was one of the few occasions when ecumenical bodies like the AACC or the World Council of Churches (WCC) acted in a more helpful sense to find a way for peace and reconciliation in Rwanda. On many other occasions they came out as strong supporters of the RPF. In Nairobi at the time the AACC was even called "the RPF in prayer," since the RPF supporters in high positions in that organization were seen to further the cause of their movement. After the RPF's victory, some of them were given important posts in the new administration. In the WCC the person responsible for the Rwandese question was himself a Rwandese refugee, who made sure that the council reacted favorably to the RPF at key moments. In that way the churches in Rwanda lacked the support of an international mediator, as the San Egidio community had acted in the case of Mozambique (Morozzo della Rocca). The only such action was when, in May 1993, the apostolic nuncio, Mgr. Guiseppe Bertello, left Kigali to visit the RPF authorities in the north of the country (Theunis 1995: 294). But that action was not followed up.

Then came 1994. The situation in Rwanda quickly deteriorated. The agreements of Arusha were not implemented by the regime in Kigali. The different political parties succumbed increasingly to regional divisions and ethnic hatred. The church leaders called once more for a faithful implementation of the peace agreements—this time with the moral support of the diplomatic corps in Kigali. But this time the RPF refused to heed the call of the churches and refused further meetings with them. Church leaders seemed at a loss as to what the next step could be. On April 6 the plane carrying the presidents of Rwanda and Burundi was struck by a missile and both presidents were killed. That triggered a tremendous reaction in Rwanda: all kinds of racist propaganda against Tutsi and moderate Hutu were unexpectedly corroborated by this killing of the symbol of majority rule in Rwanda, which President Habyarimana embodied for many. The horrendous killing began, quickly developing into systematic murder of genocidal proportions. Instead of intervening, foreign troops and UN peacekeepers withdrew from Rwanda—saving only their own citizens. Communications in the country, never very strong, came to a standstill. The churches met with extreme difficulty in responding, it seems, and the members of the Contact Committee could hardly communicate with one another. The Catholic bishops published two statements that month. The first called for support for the new government (i.e., the government that temporarily replaced the one headed by Habyarimana, but in the same line as the former) and asked for a return to the road of peace and security. The second statement, a few days later in April, was more explicit in issuing a strong call to end the bloodshed by all parties concerned (Des Forges 1998: 245). It was more than a month later (May 13) that the leaders of the Catholic and Protestant churches together published a statement condemning the massacres, asking Christians not to take part in them and inviting the warring parties to come back to the negotiating table. The leaders asked to be received by the government and by the RPF in order to call them to stop the war and the killings and to resume the peace talks. The RPF did not answer that call; the prime minister of the temporary government did receive a delegation of the Contact Committee, but they could only conclude that he was hesitant about making a clear commitment concerning the demands of the churches. Moreover, the church leaders received the impression that he was no longer capable of stopping the war or the killings: the real power of the new government being minimal in the crisis situation of the country.

Finally, on June 20, the appeal of the church leaders to the government, the RPF and the international community to help find a solution to the Rwandese problems was not heard by any of the parties. The cruel killings continued, even within church buildings, as the sad example of Ntarama proves. There hundreds of people were burned within the walls of the church where they had sought refuge. The killings were only stopped through the military victory of the RPF. Now a new regime was installed. The hope was strong amongst the population that this regime would be the beginning of a better future for the country. That was not the case. Besides the no less cruel oppression of all opposition or suspected opposition to the new regime (three Catholic bishops were killed shortly after the RPF takeover), their attitude toward Hutu refugees inside and outside the country was without pity: many refugees inside the country were brutally murdered. Outside the country a war was started in Congo, officially to protect the country against the danger of vengeful soldiers and militia of the old regime who had fled to that country. In fact, many thousands of harmless people died in the wilderness of Congo, where they were pushed by the RPF army and its allies. In the prisons of Rwanda 120,000 people awaited trial—many of them without formal charges being made against them. The suffering and killing in those prisons are difficult to describe.

That brings us to the period from 1995 until 'today'. The situation of the churches under the new regime was very different compared with the one before

1994. The new regime started an important action to make public how the churches not only failed to make public the misdeeds of the Habyarimana regime, especially during the genocide, but also how church members, church personnel and church leaders had also taken part in that horrible action. Western researchers, scientists and journalists absorbed the information without question: who would dare to ask questions of a regime that had stopped the genocide, of people who had suffered that much (Meiring 2000; McCullum 1995)?

Another action of the new government was to make sure that the new church leaders were favorable to the RPF regime. In the case of the Protestant churches, this was relatively easy. After the murder of three Catholic bishops by RPF soldiers, it was clear to the remaining church leaders that their lives were in danger; almost all Protestant leaders fled the country. National radio did not stop accusing them of partaking in the genocide—thus blocking the way for them to return. The few who dared to do so felt after a short time that it was impossible for them to function properly: accusations against themselves and threats to their families forced them quickly back on the road to exile.

In the case of the Catholic Church, the replacement of the leaders was more complicated. Here the RPF government took there another course of action, making accusations against the whole body of the clergy, including the hierarchy. That extended from non-cooperation with Catholic church leaders, as exemplified in the refusal to grant a passport to Bishop Sibomana who needed medical treatment, to the accusation of genocide made against Bishop Misago, who in the end was acquitted. In this way, the new government made sure that churches and their powerful international allies would not become independent critics of the country, in whom the majority of the people could place their hope.

The churches themselves were completely devastated after the horrible months of genocide in 1994. Many of their priests and pastors had been killed, had fled or were in prison; many of their buildings were in ruins or desanctified by the killing of innocent people; many of their organizations were suspect in the eyes of the new government. The new church leaders in the Protestant churches were very vocal in condemning the genocide and accentuating the role of the churches in that crime. They even accused former missionaries of having introduced ethnic notions into Rwandese society. No word was heard, however, concerning the inhumane conditions in prisons; no protest was heard when a refugee camp was attacked by the RPF army and the refugees brutally killed; no voice was raised when, during the war in Congo, hundreds of thousands of people were driven into the wilderness to certain death. The Catholic Church was especially quiet in any public statement. The courageous book of Bishop Sibomana, in which he condemned not only the last years of the Habyarimana regime and the genocide but also the violations of human rights by the new regime (Sibomana), certainly did not meet the approval of the government or of the other church leaders.

Thus, the churches in general found it difficult to talk about reconciliation—not only did the word not seem appropriate in the traumatic experiences of many (Van 't Spijker-Niemi 1998) but the churches also had no freedom to act politically. In unison with the state the churches asked for justice, punitive justice (Mulunda-Nyanga 1996: 103). From that point of view, church leaders even opposed the distribution of the Rwandese translation of Bonhoeffer's *Wiederstand und Ergebung* among the Rwandese prisoners: they could get the wrong ideas about justice and reconciliation from it. An even rather moderate critical analysis from the partner churches on the situation in the country was radically rejected (Van Gilst 1998). It was therefore remarkable that the Presbyterian Church tried to make contact with the leadership of the church in exile. With the help of the AACC and European partner churches, a meeting was organized in Namibia, where the old and new leadership of that church met (Krol 1996). Shortly after this event, Rwanda began to give strong support to the (then) rebel movement of Kabila Sr., which led to the disruption of all contact with the Rwandese refugees in Congo/Zaire. The only other actions the churches undertook concerning reconciliation were invitations to all Rwandese pastors and Christians in exile to return to the country. But that call was generally not trusted by those concerned; they wanted rather to wait and see.

In the period after 1994, the churches in Rwanda did not seem to be prepared to work for reconciliation. But that did not mean that the Christian witness, the Gospel, had proved to be without power in that situation. Since churches and church leaders did not call for reconciliation, it was the laity who assumed that mission. That had already become clear during the genocide: the most powerful Christian witness was then given by local, often nameless Christians who put their own lives on the line in order to save others (Deltour 1998). After 1994 the first initiatives came from refugee communities in Africa and Europe. The first, and probably most important, was the initiative of the Detmold group (Rubayiza 1998). Already in December 1996 a group of priests, pastors and lay people from different ethnic backgrounds, coming from Rwanda or from several countries of refuge, wrote a confession wherein they mutually confessed their guilt and promised one another to work for reconciliation, for a better future of the country. The initiative was relatively well received in the churches in Rwanda and among the ecumenical partners of the Rwandese churches.

Delegations of the Detmold group were even able to visit Rwanda and explain the aims of their initiative. Another initiative was even more clearly initiated by the laity. In 1999 a group of people coming originally from Burundi, Congo and Rwanda or still living there, gathered in Machakos, Kenya, in order to study together the problems of the Great Lakes region ("L'initiative de Machakos;" Rukanaira 2001). They were mostly of academic background and had had important responsibilities under the old regime or had these under the new one. Although not officially a 'Christian' meeting nor called by the churches, it became clear that all participants were looking for inspiration from the Gospel and from common prayer. One of the results of this Machakos event, which to the astonishment of many had a peaceful and even meaningful development, was the creation of an internet discussion where participants could exchange views and comment on events in the region. It contributed to breaking down all kinds of myths, such as that those who stayed in Rwanda were all RPF supporters or that those who left the country were all guilty of genocide. An opening was created to listen, to learn and even to plan together for the future. Reconciliation came one step further to realization.

Religion, conflict and reconciliation in Rwanda: the story of Rwanda in the second half of the twentieth century is a sad one, where each time reconciliation between groups of people seemed to be possible, new fuel was thrown on the simmering fire, unleashing yet another round of new hatred, new discrimination, new killings. As Archbishop Desmond Tutu said during a visit to the country: "How long do you think you can go on, each twenty-five years changing the role of oppressor and oppressed" (Tutu 1999: 206-10)?

Concluding Remarks

What have churches done, at least these last ten years, to be 'on the right side', on the side of the poor, the persecuted, the downtrodden? The answer is that they have failed to make their position clear, before, during and after 1994. Before 1994 the churches showed some courage, given the African and Rwandese historical context, in calling the warring parties to peace, in condemning ethnicism, in bringing opposite groups together. However, the problem was that through their (sometimes intimate) relation with the ruling power, they had lost their credibility, their moral power to be truly effective in the situation.

During the genocide, churches failed to be safe havens for persecuted people. That was not always their fault, but in some cases, the priest or pastor was certainly not the first to be killed by the attacking mobs—to say the least. After 1995 church leaders were unable to say more than "We repent" and "We ask for (retributive) justice" (Tutu 1999: 208). No true signs of the will to be reconciled were added. The five challenges Meiring suggests for the churches in Rwanda in view of reconciliation (Meiring 2000: 1039 ff.), are hardly met: (1) the churches led the country in a confession of guilt—but only for crimes against humanity committed by one of the parties involved; (2) churches remain silent in the present situation of the country and refrain today, as before 1994, from true prophetic witness; (3) leadership development and training seem to support only one group in society, thus furthering ethnicism; (4) their pastoral care for the traumatized falls under the same analysis as being rather partial; (5) churches have only been calling for justice and have rejected even the use of the word 'reconciliation'.

Still, the call for reconciliation is not stifled. In Rwanda, this call is heard through the action of individual Christians of all ethnic background who protect the lives of others before, during and after 1994. The call is heard through the action of lay groups who want to confess mutually and to build together a more humane future for the country. It shows the power of the churches in Rwanda, the power of the churches in Africa: in spite of many failures, the Gospel still finds its way into the minds and hearts of many Christians at the grassroots. They give hope for the future.

Bibliography

"Acquittement de Mgr Augustin Misago." (2000). *Dialogue* 217: 89-95.
All African Conference of Churches. (1993). *Processus d'une paix durable au Rwanda: Rapport rencontre de Mombasa*. Nairobi: AACC.
Amnesty International. (2000). *Rwanda: The Troubled Course of Justice*. AFR 47: October.
Bonhoeffer, D. (Forthcoming). *Kuganda no Kuyuboka: Inzandiko níbitekerezo byandikiwe muri gereza*. Yaoundé: CLE.
Butler, B. (1976). *Hill Ablaze*. London: Hodder and Stoughton.
Corduwener, J. (2000). "Wat bezielt Rwanda." *Trouw* (February 15): 13.
Deltour, M. (1998). *Dragers van hoop: Getuigenissen over dood en nieuw leven in Rwanda*. Averbode: Altiora.
Des Forges, A. (1998). *"Leave None To Tell The Story:" Genocide in Rwanda*. New York: Human Rights Watch.
Edwards, S. (2000). "'Explosive' Leak on Rwanda Genocide." *National Post* (March 1).
Evêques catholiques du Rwanda. (1990). *Le Christ, notre unité: Lettre pastorale*. Kigali: Février.
Gatwa, T. and A. Karamaga. (1990). *Les autres Chrétiens rwandais: La présence protestante*. Kigali: Editions Urwego.
Groves, C.P. (1964). *The Planting of Christianity in Africa*. Vol. III. 2nd edition. London: Butterworth Press.
Heremans, P.R. (1973). *Introduction à l'histoire du Rwanda*. 2nd ed. Kigali/Brussels: Editions rwandaises/Editions A. de Boeck.
"L'initiative de Machakos: Rapport du Colloque de la société civile sur la paix, la réconstruction morale et la cohabitation sociale dans les pays des Grands Lacs, Machakos, Kenya, 16-20 Novembre 1999." (2000). *Dialogue* 213: 65-74.
Karamaga, A. (1995). "Les Eglises protestantes et la crise rwandaise." In: A. Guichaoua (ed.). *Les crises politiques au Burundi et au Rwanda (1993-1994): Analyses, faits et documents*. Lille/Paris: Université/Karthala. Pp. 299-308.
Krol, L.R. (1996). *Rencontre de Presbytériens de l'intérieur et de l'extérieur du Rwanda d.d. 22-26 Septembre 1996 à Windhoek en Namibie*. Leusden: De Gereformeerde Kerken in Nederland.
Linden, I. (1999). *Christianisme et pouvoir au Rwanda (1900-1990)*. Paris: Karthala.
Longman, T.P. (1995). "Christianity and Democratisation in Rwanda: Assessing Church Responses to Political Crisis in the 1990s." In: P. Gifford (ed.). *The Christian Churches and the Democratisation of Africa*. Studies of Religion in Africa. Vol. XII. Leiden: Brill. Pp. 188-204.
Mbiti, J.S. (1969). *African Religions and Philosophy*. London: Heinemann.
McCullum, H. (1995). *The Angels Have Left Us: The Rwanda Tragedy and the Churches*. Risk Book Series 66. Geneva: WCC.
Meiring, P.G.J. (2000). "Die kerke in Rwanda: Skandes en uitdagings- en lesse vir Suid-Afrika." *HTS* 56: 1024-42.
Mulunda-Nyanga, N.D. (1997). *The Reconstruction of Africa: Faith and Freedom for a Conflicted Continent*. Nairobi: AACC.
Niyonsaba, A. (1999). *Pastoral Reflection on the 1994 Genocide in Rwanda and the Process of Reconciliation*. Unpublished Thesis, San Francisco Theological Seminary. San Francisco.

Ntezimana, E. (1979). "Recit de la mort du Père Loupias d'après le 'diaire' de la mission de Rwaza." *Etudes rwandaises* XII: 45-59.

Overdulve, C. (1996). *Rwanda - een volk met een geschiedenis*. 3rd edition. Allerwegen XXV, 15. Kampen: Kok.

———. (1997). "Fonction de la langue et de la communication au Rwanda." *Neue Zeitschrift für Missionswissenschaft* LIII: 271-83.

Reyntjes, F. (1994). *L'Afrique des grands lacs en crise: Rwanda, Burundi 1988-1994*. Paris: Karthala.

———. (1995). *Rwanda: Trois jours qui ont fait basculer l'histoire*. Paris/Brussels: L'Harmattan/Institut Africain.

Rubayize, F. (1998). *Guérir le rwanda de la violence: La Confession de Detmold un premier pas*. Paris/Montreal: L'Harmattan.

Rukangira E. (ed). (2001). *Actes du colloque de Mancha Kos*. Brussels.

Rutayisire, P. (1987). *La christianisation du Rwanda (1900-1945): Méthode missionnaire et politique selon Mgr Léon Classe*. Fribourg: Editions universitaires.

Sibomana, A. (1997). *Gardons espoir pour le Rwanda*. Paris: Desclée de Brouwer.

Theunis, G. (1995). "Le role de l'Eglise Catholique dans les événements récents." In: A. Gouichaoua (ed.). *Les crises politiques au Burundi et au Rwanda (1993-1994): Analyses, faits et documents*. Lille/Paris: Université/Karthala. Pp. 289-98.

Trouwborst, A. (1998). "Achtergronden van de conflicten in Midden-Afrika." *Wereld en Zending* XXVII: 4-12.

Tutu, D.M. (1999). *No Future Without Forgiveness*. London: Rider.

Twagirayesu, M. and J. van Butselaar (eds.). (1982). *Ce don que nous avons reçu: Histoire de l'Eglise Presbytérienne au Rwanda (1907-1982)*. Kigali: EPR.

Van Gilst, P.H. (1998). *Verslag van een bezoek aan Rwanda: 21 oktober- 21 november 1998*. Leusden: De Gereformeerde Kerken in Nederland.

Van 't Spijker-Niemi, A. (1998). "Verzoening in Rwanda?" *Wereld en Zending* XXVII: 55-60.

Warren, M. (1954). *Revival: An Enquiry*. London: SCM Press.

Religion, Conflict and Reconciliation in Bosnia Herzegovina

Donna Winslow

Introduction

[T]he peace negotiations between the Orthodox [Christian] Serbs, the Catholic Croats and the Muslim Bosnians had collapsed again. And there is no doubt that the religions that are so involved here had neglected in the period of more than forty years since the Second World War to engage in mourning, honestly confess the crimes which had been committed by all sides in the course of the centuries, and ask one another for mutual forgiveness.... I think there can be no peace among the nations without peace among the religions! (Küng and Kuschel 1993)

In this paper we intend to examine the role of religion and religious institutions in the 1992-1995 war in Bosnia Herzegovina (BH). M. Kaldor (1997: 8) has referred to the Bosnian conflict as an archetypal example of a new type of warfare. By this, she means that the conflict has certain characteristics that are new to violence in the twentieth century, such as a dramatic increase in the number of civilian casualties[1]. 'New wars' can also be contrasted with earlier wars in terms of their goals, the methods of warfare and how they are financed and supported.

According to Kaldor (1997; 1999), the goals of new wars are about identity politics and this is where religion played a role in the Bosnian conflict. In identity politics the claim to power is justified on the basis of a particular identity. Religion has played an important historic role in determining Serb and Croat ethnic identities. As Denitch (1994: 30) has noted:

> Both the churches and the nationalists have labored mightily to get close to a 100 percent fit between religion and ethnic identity among Serbo-Croatian speakers and have tended to reinforce nationalism rather than any sort of "catholic" universalism. The churches are indeed both militant and national in former Yugoslav lands. The two identities thus reinforce each other.

In the 1990s conflict, religious affiliation was piled upon distinctions of dialect, of script (Cyrillic vs. Latin) and of history in order to identify and target specific groups.

The use of identity politics also creates movements of nostalgia preoccupied by (re-)invented idylls of a glorious past. As Anthony Smith (1986: 4-5) has noted in his work on the ethnic origins of nations, communities find themselves in cults of the heroic past in order to reconstruct poetic spaces and golden ages in which the nation

---

[1] According to Kaldor (1997:8) there was a 3 to 1 ratio of military to civilian casualties in world conflicts in the 1970s. In 1990-95 the ratio had changed to 1 to 8.

can locate itself. These cults shape the nation through ethnic maps and the 'moralities' they evoke. In the Serbian case, a cult around the Battle of Kosovo in 1389[2] created a moral space in which Serbs were portrayed as martyrs and victims[3] and Muslim Bosnians equated with 'Turks'[4] and Christ killers, thus making their destruction more justifiable. Mojzes (1995) refers to this as the destructive use of memory. The 1990s conflict was depicted by many Serbian politicians as a form of religious revival: a crusade to expel the 'Turks' once and for all, in order to fulfill "God's will for the national rebirth of the Serbs" (Radovan Karadzic, cited in Hastings 1997: 14; see also Ramet 1998: 174).

For its part, the Roman Catholic Church supported the cult of Cardinal Stepinac—a controversial figure whom Communists had accused of complicity in WW II forced conversions of Serbs to Catholicism and in the genocide of Serbs in Croatia (see Kaplan 1993: 12-21). After the war, Catholic leadership never made strong moves to condemn the deaths of hundreds of thousands of Orthodox Serbs in WW II and at times have tried to minimize the numbers. In this and other ways Mojzes (1995: 138) believes that the Roman Catholic Church contributed to rise of ethnic chauvinism just as much as Serbian Orthodox Church did.

Kaldor (1999: 8) describes the methods of new warfare as techniques of destabilization aimed at sowing fear and hatred.

> The aim is to control the population by getting rid of everyone of a different identity. Hence the strategic goal of these wars is population expulsion through various means such as mass killing, forcible resettlement, as well as a range of political, psychological and economic techniques of intimidation.

Forced conversion to another faith, the targeting of religious monuments, burial sites, and the destruction of places of worship can all be added to the list. This pattern is not new to the Balkans where such events occurred prior to the 1990s. In fact, some

---

[2] The Ottoman Turks conquered what is now Yugoslavia at the Battle of Kosovo in the Field of Blackbirds in 1389. Serbian Prince Lazar could have avoided the conflict by agreeing to pay tribute to Murad I, the Turkish Sultan. However, Lazar and his army rejected this option. They swore the Kosovo Covenant. This committed them to fight to the death of the last man rather than submit to control by a foreign power.

[3] In repeated public pronouncements and published articles in the 1990s, the Serbian patriarchate and bishops stressed the past sufferings of the Serbian people in WW II, ignoring that others had suffered. They thus portrayed the Serbs as guiltless, blameless and innocent victims (Ramet 1998: 174).

[4] During the 1992-95 conflict Bosnian Muslims were referred to by Serbian nationalists and clerics as 'Turks', even though all political ties with Turkey ended after WW I. Sells (1996: 41) believes that this equation with Turks lumped Bosnian Muslims into the symbolic category of killers of the Christ-like Prince Lazar, thus feeding sentiments of revenge.

various means such as mass killing, forcible resettlement, as well as a range of political, psychological and economic techniques of intimidation.

Forced conversion to another faith, the targeting of religious monuments, burial sites, and the destruction of places of worship can all be added to the list. This pattern is not new to the Balkans where such events occurred prior to the 1990s. In fact, some authors (e.g. Bax 1997, Malcolm 1994: 174, Mojzes 1995: 137) believe that the 1990s conflict was a continuation of a WW II revenge cycle.

Another characteristic of new wars is international linkages. Although roving bands and fighting units have always financed themselves through plunder in BH, external assistance has taken on new forms, such as remittances from the Diaspora, taxation of humanitarian assistance, support from other governments[5] or illegal trade in arms, drugs and/or black marketeering. It is not known to what extent religious organizations actually financed the violence of the 1990s. However, it is clear that support was offered and that some members of religious organizations maintained close links with fighting units actively engaged in ethnic cleansing.

In the following pages we will begin with a brief history of the religious communities in Bosnia Herzegovina. We will then go on to examine three characteristics of 'new wars': identity politics, methods and linkages in the Bosnian conflict and look at the role of religion and religious organizations. We will conclude with a brief look at ongoing cleavages between the three major religious communities and reflect upon the possibilities for reconciliation.

The Spiritual Landscape

By the thirteenth century we can identify the presence of three creeds in Bosnia (Bogot 1998: 149). No concerted attempt was made by the political or religious leaders to settle centuries-old religious hatreds. 'Brotherhood and unity' remained fragile and an important opportunity for reconciliation between the ethnic communities was missed.

Communism
At the end of the war, the communists curtailed freedom of religion, restricted the power of the churches and appointed religious leaders who were loyal to the new regime (Duijzings 2000: 111). The Serbian Orthodox Church soon came into direct conflict with the communist regime's policy on nationalities and lost its secular role and influence. The Roman Catholic Church also had uneasy relations with Yugoslavia's Communist regime throughout the postwar period. This was partly because its hierarchy was loyal to Rome and partly because the Catholics supported Croatian nationalism in the early 1970s. In addition, the government's

---

[5] Slobodan Milosevic has admitted to secretly financing Serbian militia forces in Bosnia (see Erlanger 2001:5).

After Yugoslavia's break with the Soviet Union in 1948, religious repression gradually decreased as Tito sought the approval of the West. The state-approved funeral and burial of Stepinac in 1961 signaled a new modus vivendi between the Yugoslav government and the Roman Catholic Church of Yugoslavia. In 1966 Yugoslavia and the Vatican signed a protocol in which Belgrade pledged to recognize freedom of conscience and Rome's jurisdiction over ecclesiastical and spiritual matters for Yugoslav Catholics. In return, the Vatican agreed to honor the separation of church and state in Yugoslavia, including prohibition of political activity by clergy. In 1970 Yugoslavia and the Vatican resumed full diplomatic relations. Nonetheless, opportunities for conflict remained.[7]

Relations of the postwar Communist government with the Islamic community were less troubled than those with the Orthodox or Roman Catholic churches. Yugoslavia's Islamic leaders generally had kept a low profile during WW II, although the authorities condemned the mufti of Zagreb to death for allegedly inciting Muslims to murder Serbs. In the 1960s and 1970s, Tito used Yugoslavia's Islamic community to maintain friendly relations with Arab countries for economic and political reasons. Yugoslavia needed access to inexpensive oil and wanted to play an important role in the Conference of Non-aligned States (Duijzings 2000: 112). A new national category of 'Muslim' was recognized by the Yugoslavian government. This classification was problematic since it finally gave Bosnian Muslims a political voice alongside Catholics and Orthodox but it did so at the cost of reinforcing the identity between religion and nationality (Sells 1996: 14).

Financial contributions from Islamic countries such as Libya and Saudi Arabia helped fund many of the 800 mosques constructed in Yugoslavia after WW II (Sells 1996: 71). Contacts were developed between Islamic clerics and believers in Bosnia and the Middle East, e.g. young Muslims went to the Middle East for Islamic theological training (Ramet 1998 : 42, 165). But after the 1979 fundamentalist revolution in Iran, the Yugoslav government reviewed its policy on potentially destabilizing contacts between Yugoslav Muslims and Middle Eastern governments. The *ulama* responded by disavowing all connection with the pan-Islamic movement.

Political liberalization after Tito's death in the 1980s brought Yugoslavia's religious communities a level of freedom unprecedented in the postwar period. The spring of 1990 marked the beginning of a religious revival throughout the country. On Easter 1990, television stations throughout the country covered Eastern Orthodox and Roman Catholic services for the first time; two weeks later, Belgrade television

---

stand on social issues such as divorce and education to conform with the secular requirements of the communist state of Yugoslavia. Stepinac also had enraged Tito by protesting arbitrary postwar punishment of Catholic clergy.

[7] Franjo Cardinal Kuraric, Primate of Croatia, touched off a major controversy in Serbia in 1981 by proposing rehabilitation of Stepinac; subsequent appeals for canonization of the cardinal met strong government resistance

broadcast prayers marking the end of Ramadan, the Muslim holy month. With the rebirth of Western-style democracy in Yugoslavia, fundamental amendments were expected in laws banning church involvement in politics, education, social and inter-ethnic affairs, and military training. However, this revival was cut short by civil war. As soon as Slovenia and Croatia became independent, it became clear that Bosnia and Herzegovina would also ask for recognition as a sovereign country, and this happened in December 1991. At that time, Bosnia was the only federal unit in Yugoslavia where no single national (or religious) group dominated. According to Kaldor (1999: 32), the 1991 census shows a population of 43.7% Muslim, 31.4% Serb (Orthodox), and 17.3% Croat (Catholic). Around ¼ of the population were intermarried and authors such as Kaldor (1999: 32) maintain that in urban areas a secular pluralistic culture flourished. Other authors such as Duijzings (2000: 10) add more nuance to this observation, noting that the habitat and public spaces of different ethnic groups were often separate and segregated. Even where mixture occurred in towns, ethnic groups were concentrated in particular quarters. By 1992 war had broken out.

Religion and the 1992-1995 Conflict

As Hastings (1997) and Ramet (1992, 1998) have pointed out, ethnicity can be significantly shaped by religion. In the Yugoslavian case we can observe interconnected processes of the politicization of religion and the sacralization of politics where the religious sphere underpins and legitimizes actions and decisions taken in the political sphere.

> The translation of national causes into religious causes and ethnic hatreds into confessional antagonisms not only politicizes religion, but it transforms religion, subtly changing the meaning of its terms of reference and substituting a national ontology for divine ontology as the centerpiece of religious life. (Ramet 1998: 179)

In the following sections we will look at how religious symbolism and ideology were used to justify the violence making the political agenda a spiritual one. Religious sites were specifically targeted in order to erase the memory of an ethnic community's existence. At times, members of the clergy fanned the flames of extreme nationalism thus contributing to the hatred and subsequent violence.

Identity Politics

Identity politics in BH involved the creation of the 'other' using religious symbols. Thus religion was drafted into an active role in the conflict. Hobsbawm (2000: 25) describes how the national myth of Serbia was tied to religion. In particular, the 1389 Battle of Kosovo (see footnotes 2 and 4) became a potent symbol of religious nationalism and a body of epic folk poetry grew up around the Serb leader, Prince Lazar, and the battle.[8] In the nineteenth century this body of poetry was transformed into a supreme national epic (see Malcolm 1998: 80), fusing national and religious identity. By the late nineteenth century it was believed that the myth had inspired Serbs for centuries.[9] Complete with strong religious symbolism it was a perfect myth to infuse a new twentieth-century nationalism[10] and before long Slobodan Milosevic was standing at the Kosovo field telling the crowd that Serbia "was a fortress defending European culture and religion" (quoted in Sells 1996: 154). Hastings (1997: 191) cautions us against the mythologization and commemoration of events such as the Battle of Kosovo which sharpens a sense of 'us and them', with absolute loyalty to the fellowship of 'us' and a moral gap separating us from 'them', who represent a threat to freedom, religion and law.

Sells (1996) refers to the politicization of the Kosovo myth as "Christoslavism," the belief that Muslim Slavs were "Christ killers" (that is, the killers of the Christ-like figure of Prince Lazar). He argues that this is what drove Orthodox Christian Serbs in the frenzy of destruction against a relatively secular Muslim community. Muslims were equated with all that was evil. Once equated with the Devil, their destruction became not only easier but necessary. As Judah (1997: xi) has noted:

> When Serbian peasants from villages surrounding Sarajevo began to bombard the city they did so confusing in their minds their former Muslim friends, neighbors and even brothers-in law with the old Ottoman Turkish viziers and pashas who had ruled them until 1878.

This process of demonization was also stimulated by the Croatian government which also maintained that Muslims of Bosnia Herzegovina were Christ killers who had to be vanquished at all costs (Bax 2000; Sells 1996). Another aspect of "Christoslavism" is the belief that Muslim Slavs betrayed their race by converting to Islam. In fact many Serbs and Croats see Bosnian Muslims as an artificial creation as a nation since they are only Islamicized Serbs or Croats (Duijzings 2000: 15). According to Sells (1996: 45-47) this theme also emerged in nineteenth-century literature. To convert is

---

[8] See Hastings (1997: 132-133) and Duijzings (2000: 182-190) for details of Lazar's portrayal as a Christ-like martyr who had a vision before the battle and chose the kingdom of heaven over that of earth.

[9] Mainstream Serbian historiography maintains that since 1389 the Serbs have suffered centuries of oppression and have fought a never ending battle for the resurrection of their great medieval empire (Duizings 2000: 8) when it would seem that Serbs were in fact Christian cooperators with the Ottoman empire (Hastings 1997: 132).

[10] Serbian theologians in the first half of the 20th century built upon the story of the Kosovo battle to reinforce the Serbian sense of suffering and victimization. Duijzings (2000: 179) describes how they "adapted the mindset of Serbian suffering to the modern conditions of the nation-state, transforming the suffering of the Church into the suffering of the Serbs as a nation."

to betray one's race (since Slavs are naturally Christian) and could only be done out of greed or cowardice—only weak Slavs converted to Islam (Sells 1996: 106).

Another goal of identity politics, according to Kaldor (1997: 12), is to sow fear and discord, to instill unbearable memories of what was once home, to desecrate whatever has social meaning. Conspicuous atrocities, systematic rape, hostage-taking, forced starvation and siege, targeting civilians, use of land-mines to make an area inhabitable and the destruction of religious and historic monuments are all deliberate components of this strategy. When religious sites are destroyed the message is clear. It is a denial of a right to exist as a member of the community through the destruction of one's historical and religious roots. For example, in the Bosnian town of Zvornik after Serbs killed or expelled the Muslim population, destroyed mosques and ploughed them over, the new Serbian mayor declared "there never were any mosques in Zvornik" (Sells 1996: 4). And all three sides were accused of attempting to convert people of other faiths against their will. For example, pressures on non-Muslims to convert to Islam took the form of introducing Koran instruction into the program of the Bosnian Army's 7th Corps. In Croatia, tensions were so high that many of the remaining Serbs changed their names and agreed to have their children or themselves baptized as Catholics in order to prove their confessional and hence political loyalty (Ramet 1998: 173, 176; Duijzings 2000: 35). Similarly, Bosnian Muslims have converted to Serbian Orthodoxy in the Republika Srpska (Duijzings 2000: 35).

Methods
The method of identity politics is ethnic cleansing, rendering an area ethnically homogeneous by using force and intimidation to remove from a given area persons from another ethnic or religious group (Kaldor and Vashee 1997: 141). This means that not only do people have to be physically removed but all evidence of their culture as well. Given the close identification of identity and religion this meant the destruction of religious structures. It is important to note that no religious community was left unscathed. Below are just a few examples of the types of destruction witnessed in the 1992-1995 conflict.

Nationalist militias dynamited the great mosques and churches of Bosnia, including the sixteenth-century Ferhad Pasha Mosque in Banja Luka and the Aladza (Colored) Mosque in Foca, built in 1551 and dynamited in 1993. A parking lot now stands on the site. This was followed by claims that there were never had been mosques in Foca (after they had been eradicated by the Serbs). Serb extremists then renamed Foca Srebinja ('Serb-plac') and the Serbian Orthodox Church Patriarch Pavle in 1996 referred to Foca as Srebinja, thus supporting ethnic extremism. He also authorized the relocation of a Serb monastery to Foca (see Sells 2000 for details). In Baja Luka, Bosnian Serb forces destroyed all 212 mosques and destroyed or seriously damaged 70 out of 75 Catholic churches. As of May 1995 thirty attacks on Catholic nuns had occurred in Banja Luka and seven Catholic priests were held in Bosnian Serb prison camps (Ramet 1998: 177). Survivors of camps tell how they were made to sing Serbian religious nationalist songs (Sells 1996: 89) in order to have water.

Similarly in Stolac the Bosnian Croat militia systematically destroyed non-Catholic sacral sites. Schwartz (1999: 3-4) tells us that when the Bosnian war began in 1992 Stolac was defended against the Serbs by a united Croat and Bosnian Muslim force. However, it was liberated by Croat armed forces in 1993 and 'ethnic cleansing' began almost immediately. While the inhabitants were rounded up and sent to a Croat concentration camp, the recognizably Islamic buildings, including four mosques and the Muslim cemetery were all destroyed (Bax 2000: 27). The Croats also targeted a Serbian Orthodox church and a mourners' shelter at a Jewish sacred site (Schwartz 1999: 3-4).

The 'ethnic cleansing' in Bosnia also involved the systematic destruction of the country's intellectual heritage. In May 1992 the Oriental Institute with the largest collection of Arabic, Turkish, Persian and Aljamiado manuscripts in southeastern Europe went up in flames and in August 1992 the Serb Army burnt down the Sarajevo National Library. Bax (2000: 28) describes how Croatian forces bombed Pocitelj, an Ottoman museum town on the Neretva River and took its population to a camp.

> Not a trace is left of the rich Ottoman tradition. And this indeed was the plan, for Pocitelj was to become a Catholic town, as is demonstrated among other things by the erection of an enormous Franciscan cross on the top of the highest hill of the town.

It is important to note that violence occurred not only between religions but sometimes within them.[11] According to Bax (2000: 28-29), some of the violence in the area of BH in which he worked were not ethnically motivated; in fact, some of the acts of destruction can be traced to ancient vendettas between different parts of the Catholic Church itself (Franciscan friars vs. Diocesan priests).[12] For example, pro-Franciscan military and paramilitary groups blew up the Cathedral at Mostar in 1995. A few chunks of the rooftop now lie as a monument in the Franciscan monastery of Sveti Brgorac. "This trophy is said to have been presented to the monastery by a few militia men from the region" (Bax 2000: 33).

Linkages
In the true tradition of globalization the Bosnian conflict has a transnational character. There are links with other national governments. For example, the Bosnian Serbs and the Bosnian Croats were backed by Serbia and Croatia respectively, not to mention the involvement of Russia, the Arab States and the USA. Local violence formations were also linked to transnational criminal networks (see Kaldor and Vashee 1997 for details). There were also Diaspora links in the conflict. For example, Bax (2000)

---

[11] Duijzings (2000: 112) has also described competition in the Islamic community which officially prohibited the work of dervish orders in BH. Most of the dervish lodges were closed down and handed over to the Islamic Community.

[12] Ramet 1992 also describes the delicate balance between the Franciscans and Diocesans.

mentions that one Croat group that had been purged from an area continued their 'war' from a Roman Catholic refugee shelter in southern Germany.

But what were the links between the religious and violence formations in BH? We know that Muslims were supported by a number of contingents of Mujahidin, veterans of Afghanistan and other countries in the Middle East such as Iran, Saudi Arabia, Yemen, Algeria and Libya.[13] They were a military formation and conducted plainly missionary activities focussed upon establishing a militant and fundamentalist brand of Islam through the distribution of audiocassettes to the local Muslim population, etc.

The Serbian orthodox clergy had jumped onto the nationalist bandwagon as early as 1982 (in the wake of the Albanian riots in Kosovo in 1981). According to Duijzings (2000: 196), the Serbian Orthodox Church took the lead in revitalizing the Kosovo myth after the death of Tito in 1980 and fed the yearning for Christian vengeance. Serbian ecclesiastics used explosive language concerning Serbia as the defender of Europe and Christianity against Islam. However, the Milosevic regime also encouraged the Serbian church's adoption of a siege mentality, both by approving the publication of anti-Catholic propaganda and by increasingly giving Serbian bishops access to public forums for the expression of nationalist sentiments.

> A clear relationship can be detected between the conspiratorial mood that seized the Serbian Church as it worried about a worldwide Vatican-Islamic plot against Serbdom and the Milosevic regime's claims that a Vatican-German-Croatian-Muslim conspiracy existed against the Serbian nation. (Ramet 1998: 172)[14]

When the Serbian Orthodox church endorsed the Serbian military campaign of 1991 it heightened the political profile of the Church and deepened its growing alliance with the Serbian government of Milosevic (Ramet 1992: 180). Church dignitaries began to attend important political meetings while politicians attended huge ceremonies where Serbian victims of WW II were reburied on Church grounds or the remains of Prince Lazar paraded around Serbia and eastern Bosnia (Duizings 2000: 181, 197-98).

As far as Catholicism goes, for decades virtually all Croatian intellectuals, influential politicians and statesmen of the region were educated in the Franciscan monasteries. The monasteries were known as hotbeds of extreme religious nationalism (Bax 2000: 32). Franciscan clergy were thus able to encourage nationalism and use their extensive monastic communication networks to mobilize the adult men into violence formations in which they themselves sometimes occupied a military position.

---

[13] For further information on the influence of hardline Muslims among the Bosniaks see Alibabic-Munja (1996) and Halilovic (1997).

[14] For example, Sells (1996: 81) describes the teachings of a Serb priest who maintains that Croats and Muslims have a genocide plan against Serbs and that "one who forgives is worse than one who did the bad deed in the first place."

"The HOS, the first military formation fighting the Serb-dominated federal army, was mobilized and largely steered by Herzegovinian Franciscans. Through their international networks, these warrior priests also played an active role in supplying arms" (Bax 2000: 29-30).

Bax (2000) describes in detail the relation between the Franciscans and a local thug Z who devoted his energy to manufacturing ammunition.

> He was also experimenting with new weaponry: land mines filled with metal pellets were his first specialty in the region. They were followed by an even more horrific weapon, a grenade filled with metal pellets to be fired from the shoulder. In an empty yard that belonged to the Franciscans ... behind the recently completed Mary Chapel ... Z and some men who lived in the neighborhood, and 'friends' from elsewhere in the region, had started to practice using the murderous weapon they dubbed a "rocket launcher." (Bax 2000: 19)

Z was also a regular and esteemed guest at the local monastery.

> In the course of time, various members of his clan held important positions there. He is said to have been approached by a delegation of young Franciscans from the monastery ... with the request to accompany their families who wanted to return to the land where their fathers were born. The various parties must have reached an agreement, because at the beginning of March 1993, Z and his Rocketeers raided MK and slaughtered virtually the entire population. Only a day later, the young priests from SB planted a Franciscan cross on the smoldering ruins and dedicated the parish to Mary, the Mother of God. (Bax 2000: 23–24)

Similarly, Duijzings (2000: 200) describes the close relationship between members of the Serbian Orthodox Church and Arkan—a paramilitary leader and suspected war criminal who was assassinated in January 2000. Arkan was close to Bishop Amfilohija (a nationalist hardliner) and during the war Arkan maintained that the Serbian Orthodox patriarch, Pavle, was his commander. Poems describe Arkan as being sent from God. Other Serb paramilitary leaders who were active in ethnic cleansing saw themselves as reincarnations of crusaders for a 'Greater Serbia' (see Duizings 2000: 200 for details).

There are other examples of Serb orthodox complicity in violence. For example, in Knezina 60 km east of Sarajevo a Serbian orthodox priest blessed eighteen fighters in a candlelight ceremony where the list of towns they attacked (Srebrenica, Foca, etc.) were read out. Fighters kissed a crucifix and the Bible and were invested with old Serbian title of "military duke."[15]

Sells (1996: 80) also describes how a Serb priest blessed the followers of a warlord after the names of towns associated with atrocities were read aloud. Serbian religious leaders also lauded those Serbian officials responsible for designing and implementing the policy of 'ethnic cleansing'. On Orthodox Easter 1993 the highest

---

[15] See Paul Holmes (Reuters: 15 May 1993), "Serbian Extremists Gather in Bosnia to Honor Fighters."

ranking Serb Orthodox church official in Bosnia, stood between Radovan Karadzic and General Ratko Mladic (later to be condemned as war criminals) and spoke of the Bosnian Serbs under their leadership as "following the hard road of Christ" (Sells 1996: 81-2).

Reconciliation

There is no doubt that the Catholic and Orthodox churches in particular have identified themselves all too much with their own political leadership in the most recent controversies and not made a commitment for peace openly, opportunely and energetically (Küng and Kuschel 1993).

The 1992-1995 war was primarily a conflict between those who supported the continued existence of the country as a multi-ethnic state and nationalist separatists. While the war was not primarily a religious conflict, due to the close association of ethnicity and religion in the country, religion was used to fuel the conflict.[16] As a result, bitterness over the war has contributed to mutual suspicion and hatred among members of all three major religious groups. What possible role is there for religion in reconciliation in Bosnia and Herzegovina? What had occurred since the end of the war?

After the war, Bosnia was further fragmented into two smaller entities: the Republika Srpska (RS) with an orthodox Serb majority and the Federation of Bosnia and Herzegovina where Croats (Catholics) and Bosnians (Muslim) share power. The Constitution provides for freedom of religion and, in general, individuals enjoy this right in their religious majority areas. However, the efforts of individuals to worship in areas in which they are an ethnic/religious minority are still restricted. And this is true for all three ethnic communities.

For example, there were instances of mob violence in RS aimed at preventing Catholics from worshiping. In July 1998, a bomb explosion severely damaged a Roman Catholic church in the central Bosnian town of Kakanj, which had a mixed population before the war but currently has a Bosnian majority. On April 23, 1998, mob violence prevented the holding of a Catholic ceremony in Derventa that had been approved by RS authorities, involving Cardinal Vinko Puljic, the leader of the country's Roman Catholic community. Bosnian Serb protesters set up roadblocks to prevent participants, including Cardinal Puljic, from reaching the church (US Department of State, 1999: 3-4).

Similarly, a Bosnian Serb mob prevented Catholics from Slavonski Brod from attending Mass at the Plehan monastery near Derventa. In Croat-dominated areas of Herzegovina, Muslims felt pressure not to practice their religion in public. In 1998 several incidents of vandalism occurred against Muslim religious sites, including a

---

[16] According to Berger (1999: 15), political movements in Bosnia are not genuinely inspired by religion. Rather, they use religions as a convenient legitimization for political agendas based on quite non-religious interests.

cemetery in Mostar. In July 1998 local government authorities and Serb protestors in Banja Luka, the capital of the RS, prevented the burial of the deceased Muslim religious leader of Banja Luka in that city. Demonstrators broke into an Islamic community building and harassed mourners. In May 2001, angered by plans to rebuild a mosque which had been leveled in 1992, Bosnian Serbs in Banja Luka beat dozens of Muslims. The crowd torched cars, buses and Muslim businesses shouting "This is Serbia, we don't want a mosque."[17] Few of the mosques in the RS destroyed during the war have been rebuilt or repaired, despite requests from the Islamic community for reconstruction (US Department of State, 1999: 3-4).

Thus we can see that methods of intimidation still continue to be used against religious minorities. What about linkages between religious authorities and nationalist politics? In RS, although the constitution provides for religious freedom, it also states that "the Serbian Orthodox Church shall be the church of the Serb people and other people of Orthodox religion" and indicates that the "state shall materially support the Orthodox Church and it shall cooperate with it in all fields" (quoted in US Department of State, 1999: 1). State symbols such as the flag and the hymn are clearly orthodox. In addition, neither the State nor the entity governments have enacted laws clarifying the legal status or ownership rights of religious organizations. Municipal and cantonal authorities have broad discretion regarding disposition of this property. Many use this as a tool of political patronage. This renders religious leaders dependent on the beneficence of nationalist politicians in order to regain lost property. In the RS the symbiosis between Orthodoxy and Serbian statehood continues.

In certain instances, local officials have blocked the return of minority religious leaders by using administrative obstacles. For example, in the spring of 1998 authorities in the Serb-dominated city of Mrkjonic Grad refused to approve the return of the Islamic community leader to the city. In the RS city of Bijeljina, the Islamic community leader has been unable to return since the end of the war in 1995 because local authorities have allowed Serb displaced persons to occupy his home. Officials in the Bosniak-dominated city of Bihac have hindered the return of an Orthodox priest to the city since the end of the war by declining to remove Bosnian IDPs (internally displaced persons) from the Orthodox Church property that previously served as the resident priest's home.

The war resulted in over 270,000 deaths. Furthermore, an estimated 1.4 million citizens remained IDPs or refugees abroad (US Department of State 1999: 3). These people had fled areas where their ethnic/religious community had been in the minority or had ended up in the minority as a result of the war. Administrative and financial obstacles to rebuilding religious structures have discouraged minority returns in many

---

[17] Prayer rugs were also burnt and a pig chased into the mosque. Among the hundreds of people trapped in the compound of the Islamic center was the head of the UN mission to Bosnia, Jacques Klein (see *International Herald Tribune* (May 8, 2001) for details).

areas. Schools do not hire teachers for religious education in minority religions. This also prevents families with children from returning.

Despite the constitutional provisions for religious freedom, discrimination against minorities occurs in virtually all parts of the country. It is significantly worse in the RS than in the Federation. Within the Federation, discrimination against minorities tends to be greater in Croat-majority than in Bosnian-majority areas. Parties dominated by a single ethnic group remain powerful in the country. In the Federation, these include the Bosniak-dominated Party of Democratic Action (SDA) and the Croatian Democratic Union (HDZ), which participate in the entity's ruling coalition government. Alija Izetbegovic, founder of the SDA made an "Islamic Declaration" which recommended the establishment of Bosnia as an Islamic state in which the Muslim majority would rule with the help of the *shari'at* (traditional Islamic) law (quoted in Mojzes 1995: 142). In the RS the Serb Democratic Party (SDS) and the Serb Radical Party (SRS) remain openly opposed to the territory of the RS accommodating a multi-ethnic population. All these parties have identified themselves closely with the religion associated with their predominant ethnic group. For example, at the beginning of every RS assembly session, an Orthodox priest recites a prayer, which leads Bosnian members to feel obliged to excuse themselves. Thus the link between nationalist politics and religion continues to be reinforced.

Conclusions: Forgiveness

The ongoing cleavages in the Balkans can lead one to a very pessimistic view of the future and the potential for reconciliation. Authors such as Mitri (1999: 11) believe that it is possible to promote dialogue between Christians and Muslims and that religion can "draw force from its ability to respond to disillusionment and to the quest of meaning". Others, such as Huntington (1996), predict that religion demarcates the fault lines of the bloody borders of politics. Certainly, religious sentiments and symbols were used as weapons in ethnic cleansing. And in some instances religious authorities were complicit in establishing links with extreme nationalists and in denying the horror.[18]

Is it possible for religious leaders to take an active part in leading the country on the road of forgiveness? Leaders of the Muslim, Orthodox, Roman Catholic and Jewish communities have committed themselves publicly to building a durable peace and

---

[18] For example, the Serbian Orthodox Church's Holy Episcopal Synod stated: "In the name of God's truth and on the testimony from our brother bishops from Bosnia-Herzegovina and from other trustworthy witnesses, we declare, taking full moral responsibility, that [death and detention] camps neither have existed nor exist in the Serbian Republic of Bosnia-Herzegovina" (quoted in Sells 1996: 84).

national reconciliation.[19] Forgiveness does not imply abandoning moral judgment nor does it imply forgetting the evils that have been committed. History must be acknowledged because, beyond all the violence, it ties people together. Indeed the attempts to destroy history through the destruction of religious monuments and particularly mosques were attempts to hide the Bosnian, Serb and Croat common history of cultural plurality.

In order to promote peace the religious leaders need to make a commitment to work together, to take an active role in remembering and morally judging the atrocities of the past. Moreover, they must look at their own complicity and compliance with the violence of the war. The danger of remembering, however, is that it can fuel a lust for revenge. Religious authorities therefore must emphasize forbearance from revenge. According to Donald Shriver (1996), forbearance from revenge is a necessary precondition for forgiveness. This does not mean that forgiveness and some penalty for wrongdoing are not incompatible. Full support for the international war crimes tribunal and its work in prosecuting criminals in The Hague is thus very important. In this light the Serbian Orthodox Church Patriarch Pavle's criticism of the work of the tribunal is particularly disturbing.[20] There needs to be more effort put into creating a sense of shared purpose between the religious communities. Those who make their enemies their friends, as Abraham Lincoln once said, are ultimately more politically successful than those who merely defeat them.

The combination of moral memory, forbearance, empathy, and the relentless intent to nurture reconciliation is formidable. Those who manage to combine these actions have practiced something more than the art of the possible. They have practiced the art of turning enemies into fellow citizens (Shriver 1996).

Forgiveness remains an act of generosity. But if we cannot expect that sense of largesse from our religious leaders, then what hope is there for reconciliation? We must remember what happened in Bosnia and we must remember it morally. Moral leadership is what is required now in Bosnia from all political elements, particularly the religious authorities.

---

[19] Several remarkable statements have been made by religious leaders on their own and in concert with their homologues in other churches. For example, in a 1992 meeting, leaders of the Roman Catholic and the Serbian Orthodox churches stated that to wage war in the name of religion is the greatest crime against religion (Mojzes 1995: 147-49; Ramet 1998: 174). In January 1993 the Pope called for a conference aimed at seeking peace in the former Yugoslavia (Sells 1996: 108).

[20] In 1996 the Pavle issued a statement accusing the tribunal of focussng almost exclusively on crimes by Serbs when the tribunal had begun prosecuting all the members of ethnic communities who engaged in war crimes (see Sells 2000 for details). Interestingly enough, the new President of Serbia, Vijiskav Kostunica, has accused the Hague tribunal of the same thing, saying that it "practices selective justice, which is not justice at all" (Erlanger 2001: 5).

Bibliography

Alababic-Munja, M. (1997). *Bosnu u Kandzama KOS-a* [Bosnia in the Claws of KOS]. Sarajevo: NIP Behar.

Bax, M. (1997). "Mass Graves, Stagnating Identification, and Violence: A Case Study in the Local Sources of 'the war' in Bosnia Hercegovina." *Anthropological Quarterly* 70: 11-19.

———. (2000a). "Warlords, Priests and the Politics of Ethnic Cleansing: a Case-Study of Bosnia Hercegovina." *Ethnic and Racial Studies* 23: 16-36.

Berger, P. (1999). "The Desecularization of the World: A Global Overview." In: P.L. Berger (ed.). *The Desecularization of the World*. Grand Rapids: William B. Eerdmans Publishing Co. Pp. 1-18.

Denitch, B. (1994). *Ethnic Nationalism: The Tragic Death of Yugoslavia*. Minneapolis and London: University of Minnesota Press.

Duijzings, G. (2000). *Religion and the Politics of Identity in Kosovo*. London: C. Hurst and Company.

Erlanger, S. (2001). "Milosevic Admits Funding for Balkan Wars." *International Herald Tribune*. 4 April: 5.

Halilovic, S. (1997). *The Shrewd Strategy* [English translation of *Lukava Strategija*]. Sarajevo: Marsal.

Hastings, A. (1997). *The Construction of Nationhood: Ethnicity, Religion and Nationalism*. Cambridge: Cambridge University Press.

Hobsbawm, E. (2000). *The New Century*. Great Britain: Little Brown and Company.

Huntington, S. (1996). *The Clash of Civilizations and the Remaking of World Order*. New York: Simon and Schuster.

Judah, T. (1997). *The Serbs: History, Myth and the Destruction of Yugoslavia*. New Haven: Yale University Press.

Kaldor, M. (1997). "Introduction." In: M. Kaldor and B. Vashee (eds.). *New Wars*. London: Pinter. Pp. 3-33.

———. (1999). *New and Old Wars: Organized Violence in a Global Era*. Cambridge: Polity Press.

——— and B. Vashee. (1997). "The Political Economy of the War in Bosnia-Herzegovina." In: M. Kaldor and B. Vashee (eds.). *New Wars*. London: Pinter. Pp. 137-76.

Kaplan, R.D. (1993). *Balkan Ghosts: A Journey Through Time*. New York: St. Martin's Press.

Küng, H. and K.J. Kuschel. (1993). *A Global Ethic: The Declaration of the Parliament of the World's Religions*. Internet: http://www.bosnet.org/bosnia/culture/religion. shtml. Accessed January 7, 2001.

Malcolm, N. (1994). *Bosnia: A Short History*. New York: New York University Press.

———. (1998). *Kosovo: A Short History*. New York: Macmillan.

Mitri, T.E. (1999). *The Narrow Path of Genuine Dialogue between Christians and Muslims*. Amsterdam: Inaugural Lecture, Vrije Universiteit.

Norris, H.T. (1993). *Islam in the Balkans*. United Kingdom: C. Hurst and Co.

Mojzes, P. (1995). *Yugoslavian Inferno: Ethnoreligious Warfare in the Balkans*. New York: Continuum.

Ramet, S.P. (1992). *Balkan Babel: Politics, Culture and Religion in Yugoslavia*. San Francisco: Westview Press.

Huntington, S. (1996). *The Clash of Civilizations and the Remaking of World Order*. New York: Simon and Schuster.

Judah, T. (1997). *The Serbs: History, Myth and the Destruction of Yugoslavia*. New Haven: Yale University Press.

Kaldor, M. (1997). "Introduction." In: M. Kaldor and B. Vashee (eds.). *New Wars*. London: Pinter. Pp. 3-33.

———. (1999). *New and Old Wars: Organized Violence in a Global Era*. Cambridge: Polity Press.

——— and B. Vashee. (1997). "The Political Economy of the War in Bosnia-Herzegovina." In: M. Kaldor and B. Vashee (eds.). *New Wars*. London: Pinter. Pp. 137-76.

Kaplan, R.D. (1993). *Balkan Ghosts: A Journey Through Time*. New York: St. Martin's Press.

Küng, H. and K.J. Kuschel. (1993). *A Global Ethic: The Declaration of the Parliament of the World's Religions*. Internet: http://www.bosnet.org/bosnia/culture/religion.shtml. Accessed January 7, 2001.

Malcolm, N. (1994). *Bosnia: A Short History*. New York: New York University Press.

———. (1998). *Kosovo: A Short History*. New York: Macmillan.

Mitri, T.E. (1999). *The Narrow Path of Genuine Dialogue between Christians and Muslims*. Amsterdam: Inaugural Lecture, Vrije Universiteit.

Norris, H.T. (1993). *Islam in the Balkans*. United Kingdom: C. Hurst and Co.

Mojzes, P. (1995). *Yugoslavian Inferno: Ethnoreligious Warfare in the Balkans*. New York: Continuum.

Ramet, S.P. (1992). *Balkan Babel: Politics, Culture and Religion in Yugoslavia*. San Francisco: Westview Press.

———. *Nihil Obstat: Religion, Politics, and Social Change in East-Central Europe and Russia*. Durnham/London: Duke University Press.

Schwartz, S. (1999). *The Rabbi of Stolac*. Internet: http://www.haverford.edu/relg/sells/stolac/stolacrab.htm. Accessed January 8, 2001.

Sells, M.A. (1996). *The Bridge Betrayed: Religion and Genocide in Bosnia*. Berkeley: University of California Press.

———. (2000). *The Human Rights Archives on the Genocide in Bosnia (and the Attempted Genocide in Kosovo*. Internet: http://www.haverford.edu/relg/sells /report.htm. Accessed January 8, 2001.

Shriver, D.W. (1996). *An Ethic for Enemies: Forgiveness in Politics*. Woodstock Theological Center, Woodstock Report No. 45. Internet: http://www.georgetown.edu/centers/woodstock/report/r-fea45.htm. Accessed January 7, 2001.

Smith, A. (1986). *The Ethnic Origins of Nations*. Oxford: Blackwell.

US Department of State. (1999). *Annual Report on International Religious Freedom for 1999:Bosnia and Herzegovina*. Washington, DC: Bureau for Democracy, Human Rights, and Labor (1999). Internet: http://www.state.gov/www /global/human_rights /irf/irf_rpt/1999 /irf_ bosniahe 99.html. Accessed January 7, 2001.

Peace, Reconciliation
and
New Religious Movements

Reender Kranenborg

Introduction

Religions find themselves in an ambiguous position in relation to the establishment of peace and reconciliation. On the one hand, religions can cause wars and conflicts; they may call believers to join in a Holy War or in Crusades. Moreover, many instances of mission work have been a breeding ground for conflicts. On the other hand, during the last few decades religions have promoted peace and reconciliation: peace conferences have been and are organized, believers travel to countries in a state of conflict and efforts are made to reconcile conflicting parties. Religions are increasingly stressing the tremendous importance of peace and reconciliation.

Their efforts in this regard have been very concrete. After all, the task at hand requires more than just words. Peace and reconciliation are the result of action. Efforts can range from organizing peace dialogues to more aggressive action, such as damaging tanks. Every aspect of the peace process calls for concrete action.

As religions strive for peace, they should take the origin of conflicts into account. That is no easy task, since those origins are myriad. Some are historical and others nationalistic. Conflicts can also be religious, resulting in total mutual intolerance between groups or nations. In conducting peace dialogues, religions should discuss these origins in the hope that the different sides will understand and acknowledge the reasons. Religions try to show the consequences of these origins and have taken concrete steps to that end.

We might expect religions to attribute the origin of conflicts to the Fall of humankind or to sin in general. Although that view falls in line with Christian doctrine, it plays no role in the concrete praxis of peace and reconciliation. We could say that religions differ little from non-religious peace organizations in their goal to bring about peace. The motivations may be different, but the praxis is almost identical: peace calls for concrete action.

But the matter is not quite as simple as that. Certain new religious movements have attempted peace and reconciliation using a very different approach. Their method of peacemaking can be described in terms of the 'automatic-energetic' model. This trend can be identified in different movements: Transcendental Meditation, the Brahma Kumaris, the Emissaries of the Divine Light and *A Course in Miracles*.

This article concentrates only on the ideas of Transcendental Meditation, Brahma Kumaris and the *Course* and their ideas concerning reconciliation and the establishment of world peace. Following a discussion of the central ideas of these three groups, I will discuss the reliability of their automatic-energetic model of reconciliation. Does it truly have the potential to help establish peace?

The Automatic-Energetic Model of Reconciliation

Transcendental Meditation[1]

The Hinduistic Advaita Vedanta-oriented movement of Transcendental Meditation (TM) was first introduced into the West in 1958. Through the efforts of Maharishi Mahesh Yogi, the movement's very active leader, it gained worldwide renown. Only a short decade later, in the late 1960s, Maharishi propagated the realization of world peace as the result of the so-called Maharishi effect. In the early 1980s these ideas were discussed and very much propagated—at least in the Netherlands. Two publications are significant in this regard: "The Super Bomb" and "Consciousness as Armament." Although these publications are dated, the ideas they contain still play an important role within the movement.[2]

The central issue in TM is the fundamental alienation of human existence. To understand this alienation it is important to know what 'pure consciousness' is. It is 'the original situation', consciousness as it is, existing in continuous peace and tranquillity. TM sees a close connection here with quantum theories, as reflected in the following statement: "The similarity between the vacuum state in the quantum field theory and the state of pure consciousness is remarkable" (Koornstra 1981: 27). On the one hand, this state is one of tranquillity or a vacuum state. On the other hand, it can be described in terms of potentiality in that it contains all existing possibilities. The quantum state "contains virtual representations of all possible forms of matter and excitation in the form of vacuum fluctuations or 'virtual particles'" or, as expressed in another statement, "The vacuum state can be seen more or less as a non-manifest origin field of creation" (Koornstra 1981: 31). Transcendental Meditation has identified 'pure consciousness' and 'quantum field' with each other.

The next step in this line of thought is the idea that everyone constitutes part of the 'pure consciousness'. Although we may have forgotten it, nonetheless there is a 'Source' within each one of us which is constantly at work and which can be reached. Because 'pure consciousness' and 'quantum field' are analogous, we could say that each human being is a particle within the quantum field. By withdrawing from a state of alienation we seek and establish contact with this 'pure consciousness'. This process takes place through transcendental meditation. Once contact with the Source is established, humans begin to change and the stronger and more intense the medita-

---

[1] See Koornstra 1981 and Ransijn and Schulte 1982.

[2] In: *TM Magazine* 8/1A (March 1999); also in: *Sidhadorp Lelystad* (no date).

tion, the more we change. The belief that people gain power or energy by coming into contact with the Source plays a crucial role in this process of change. In addition, the more we meditate, the more this energy increases. This power is not merely passive but can also be made active. TM has two important consequences. First and foremost, when an individual changes, the whole world changes. This has its parallel in quantum theories: when one particle changes, the entire field changes. Thus, according to TM, when one person changes, all of humankind changes. But one single individual does not constitute many. And his/her influence as a changed person will be very limited. However, when several people change simultaneously, the differences in the field as a whole are considerable. With respect to peace, if TM makes people more peaceful, they, in turn, make the whole world more peaceful. This is the principle of the 'Maharishi effect' and of the 'super bomb'.

> At the transcendental level, the super bomb is so strongly conducive to cohesion and interconnectedness that it nips the destructive tendencies of a potential enemy in the bud. The effect of collective exercises at the transcendental level is so strong that it is estimated that a super bomb, whose nucleus is as big as a square root of 1 percent of the population, is sufficient to transform the enmity of every potential aggressor into kindness. (Koornstra 1981: 41)

According to the author's view, peace could be established if approximately 1000 people in the Netherlands united in meditation.[3]

This brings us to the second consequence. Not only can peace be established by one changed individual or 'particle', as it were, we can also tap into the resulting energy, directing it towards a goal. This is the principle on which the Sidha Village was founded in Lelystad, the Netherlands. A number of people who practice TM meditation collectively produce a power that has an enormous influence on their surroundings and this power can be directed towards specific goals. It is therefore possible to work towards peace. TM regularly sends members to parts of the world plagued by violence in order to meditate there collectively. During meditation, these members direct the flow of energy towards aggressive people and focus on sending them peaceful thoughts. This method is believed to be effective and useful in bringing the world closer to peace. Clearly, the more we participate in TM and are changed by it and the more we send out energy, the greater our progress towards world peace. In fact, in the end we will achieve it.

Brahma Kumaris

This religious movement, whose official name is Brahma Kumaris World Spiritual University, originated in the 1930s in India, based on the revelations of Lekh Raj. In its presentation the movement puts a great deal of stress on raja yoga and 'positive thinking'. Here also we find a kind of 'automatic-energetic' model for reconciliation.

---

[3] In the Netherlands this number has never been reached. It is thus impossible to determine whether there has been any real influence.

The central ideas are as follows: the human being is essentially an eternal soul. In the eternal beginning souls lived together in a non-material world, in harmony with the Supreme Soul, but because of *karma* they left this eternal world, sought the material world and entered into the human body. All souls have a specific role in the material world and therefore need a body in order to express their original positive qualities. Only in the human body can the soul experience life. Aside from its connection to the body, there are three further aspects to the soul: intelligence, conscious mind and unconscious mind. The intelligence is that part of the soul that gives it direction; it determines the thoughts and the conditions of a human being and helps him to be independent and to escape the influence of external factors. The conscious mind is the part of the soul which produces thoughts and ideas; emotions, sentiments and experiences also belong to this part of the soul. It is very important to know why and in which way thoughts are created. If they are created or determined by negative external influences, then spiritual darkness will arise. It is thus very important to know how thoughts arise. The unconscious mind contains the *sanskars*, the impressions and results of all the things one has experienced in past lives and in this life. It is mostly the unconscious mind which influences the origin of the thoughts. The goal of the Brahma Kumaris is to determine the origin of thoughts and thinking in general through orientation to the Supreme Soul. If this contact is established, one will become more liberated and the unclean *sanskars* will be washed away.

In order to come to a realization of these ideas, one has to engage in raja yoga. By doing so, one's connection with the Supreme Soul and with the highest aspect in the soul itself will grow stronger. In actuality, it is a way to the true self, a way which also needs to be expressed in the daily life. Raja yoga implies meditation, which includes the belief that through God one's soul is on the way to a new age. Meditation makes this belief stronger, enlarges one's knowledge and strengthens the connection with the Supreme Soul. This meditation results in humankind as a whole and individual human beings becoming stronger internally. Another result is that one also stimulates others to follow the path of raja yoga to arrive at a genuine purification. Raja yoga is closely connected with 'positive thinking'. For it is, as stated above, important to go to the source of one's thoughts and then to try to engage in positive thoughts on the basis of this source. If one succeeds in thinking these thoughts and making them important in his life, of human being, he will become a positive being who can greatly influence his surroundings. Those thoughts which originate within human beings in this way have a power that can truly change things.

A good illustration of this is the event organized by the Brahma Kumaris, "The Million Minutes of Peace Appeal," during one month in 1986, the year of world peace. The rationale behind this is as follows. As many people as possible were to think each day for some minutes about world peace and the total number of all those minutes would be presented to the United Nations. All these collected minutes were to have such a strong effect that world peace would have been brought closer to full realization.

> If through their participation in the Appeal ordinary individuals start thinking about the meaning of peace and have that experience for even just a minute, then this collective heightened awareness will lead to more positive and practical actions.

Or:

> Modern physics understands that every action, no matter how small, does have an effect in the universe.... Meditation is a profound act. The act of meditation has a strong healing effect on me personally and I take that effect into everything I do.

Or:

> We do not realise enough how much influence thoughts can have.... The power of thoughts is remarkable.... When people radiate inner peace, there will be no room for aggression and violence. Everyone can work on peace on his own by positive thinking, prayer or meditation.[4]

On December 31, 1986, exactly 1,231,975,713 minutes for peace were presented to Perez de Cuellar of the United Nations.

In short, we have here an example of the 'automatic-energetic model' of reconciliation: thoughts have a power and radiation which truly influence and change things. It is not as far reaching as in the case of Transcendental Meditation, so the 'automatic' aspect is not as absolutely strong. Nevertheless, the idea is present that thought is a subtle power which truly has an effect.

A Course in Miracles

A Course in Miracles is a book of 'channelling'.[5] Helen Schucman, the author, heard a voice asking her to write down what she was being told. The result was the *Course*, which became famous in the late 1970s. Steeped in pregnant philosophy on humankind and the world, this book devotes a great deal of attention to forgiveness and reconciliation.

Let us examine the ideas Schucman presents. According to this book, in the beginning humans lived in God's blissful world as his children. At a certain point in time human beings conceived of the notion of 'separation', i.e., separation from God. This idea arose from the individual's ego. We should realize, however, that this notion of separation is, in fact, an illusion caused by a sense of guilt. Building on this illusion and guilt, the ego created the reality in which we live, a reality marked by guilt and by our denial of that guilt. Obviously, this reality based on guilt is also an illusion. Humans are conditioned by this feeling of guilt. Our reaction is twofold: projection and denial. Projection can be described as the tendency to see in someone else things of which we disapprove and to feel threatened by that person, whereas, in fact, all of these feelings stem from our own sense of guilt. Denial involves an

---

[4] These quotes are from documentation given to me by the Brahma Kumaris.

[5] Good presentations of the ideas of this 'Course' can be found in Wapnick 1983 and Dawson 1993.

unwillingness to acknowledge this. In the meantime our guilt continues to plague us, thus causing wars, violence and physical affliction.

The *Course* shows once and for all that specific relations are, in fact, determined by guilt. We need to break free from guilt and can do so, since part of us consists of the 'Holy Ghost'. This part finds its origin in the divine reality. When we realize that we are being controlled by our ego but should be guided by the Holy Ghost, a change occurs: a miracle takes place. Every change in outlook or every time we relinquish part of our ego and give it to the influence of the Holy Ghost, another miracle occurs. Our realization that all reality is an illusion constitutes another miracle. Forgiveness plays a significant role here. Forgiveness occurs when we acknowledge the manifestations of guilt in ourselves and others. As this realization takes root in us, guilt begins to diminish and we begin to forgive others. The more we realize that all is illusion, the more we can be guided by the Holy Ghost. And that, in turn, empowers us to do more: to heal all affliction, including physical affliction, by the power of our minds, thus paving the way for peace in the world. In short, if we follow the *Course*, our guilt will vanish, our relations with our neighbors will improve and we will become more healthy and able to heal all. Finally, we will be able to enter more and more into the loving presence of God. That, too, is a goal, according to the *Course*: at one point—and it will happen through many lives—we will be freed of all illusion and live again in the blissful presence of God.

Various other statements similar in tone and import have been made, such as: "Do not try to change the world, but choose to change your thinking about the world." Or: "Our prayers must not be directed towards changing the world but to changing our view of the world" (Dawson 1992: 127). Every time this happens, the constellation of the world will change, and something of the violence is abolished. Every time we follow this advice, someone will respond differently; he or she will not arouse aggression but radiate peace. The more people forgive, the more the world will change and with it the atmosphere of violence and aggression.

This is not, strictly speaking, the specific 'automatic-energetic' model for reconciliation. There is no mention of a subtle power of energy directed at other people. However, we can say that the transition to peace and reconciliation happens almost automatically, more or less in the same way it does in the theory of TM about particles and quantum fields. When enough people change, the whole world automatically changes.

The Automatic-Energetic Model of Reconciliation: An Analysis

Now that we have examined just three of the countless examples of this automatic-energetic model for reconciliation, let us examine the model itself. There are five basic aspects to the model.

First, the model clearly places great emphasis on the real cause of the conflict or alienation. It is not important to know the specific cause of a particular concrete war or act of violence or aggression. It is important only to see that an all problems, wars and tension have essentially the same universal cause. This cause is the focus of all attention in this model. Regardless of the circumstances, the origin of all evil and misery can be traced to our alienation or separation from our origin. We have lost contact with the Source. We have separated or removed ourselves from the divine reality. That is the real issue and that which forms the basis for this model of reconciliation.

Secondly, according to this model, it is very important that we work to overcome this alienation or separation. We must eliminate it from our lives. Before we try to end conflicts or wars in this world, we must unite with the Source and reestablish contact with the divine reality. The movements discussed offer an opportunity to find and establish that contact and overcome this separation so as to become one with the original Source.

Thirdly, the concept of 'energy' or 'power' plays a key role. The Source is believed to be a real, existing energy or power into which one can tap. This energy is not only spiritual but can be considered to be a 'subtle matter'. What is spiritual is, in fact, also material. The energy attained by this method does not remain passive within us but truly changes us and can also be used by us. It is possible to direct this 'subtle energy' towards the outer world, e.g. towards other people or situations marred by conflict. The effect can be described in terms of 'radiation'. It is also believed that the act of directing energy or bringing about the radiation of energy is very effective and truly succeeds in achieving peace as well as other things.

Fourthly, we occasionally find that the idea of energy exists in combination with the concept of the 'particle'. In other words, if we were to start with the idea of 'unity', an idea which plays an important role in these movements, we would see a very close connection between the part and the whole. The constellation of the parts influences the whole. Together, people form a whole which consists of parts. When a part (particle) changes due to contact with the Source, the whole automatically changes with it. In concrete terms, this means that one individual's attainment of peace will manifest itself in the whole. When enough people change, we will have peace on earth.

This brings us to the fifth aspect. As we can see, there is nothing specific we can do to achieve peace. Peace conferences are not organized. Groups hostile to one another are not brought together. No trips are made to war-afflicted regions or support provided for peace armies. Nor is any effort invested in political activities, sabotage activities for peace or peace marches.[6] Efforts towards peace in this model of reconciliation are purely mechanical. Everyone can contribute on their own or together with people with the same ideas, without actually having to meet the other person or be present in a situation involving violence. Peace is achieved from a distance, while one is sitting on the cushion of meditation.

---

[6] It is sometimes said that TM adherents travel to countries which are at war. But they do not organize activities or conferences; they only want to be there in order to meditate together. This meditation radiates peace and influences the situation.

In his contribution to this volume Cees van der Kooi sketches three models of reconciliation in Christianity: the victorious or dramatic model, the legal or objective model and the subjective model. It is impossible to connect these three models with the ideas proposed by the movements discussed above. None of the three movements endorse any of these models. Thus, it is clear that the three models sketched by Van der Kooi are not generally applicable. I think they can be used in relation to Christianity, but they do not apply to other religions. There are other possibilities with respect to reconciliation, such as the 'automatic-energetic' model.

I have thus called this model the 'automatic-energetic' model for reconciliation. This model gives rise to at least two important questions. The first is: Can we find it within Christian thinking? As we can conclude from the research on this subject in this article this model can be found in Eastern religions, mostly Hinduism. It can also be found in Western esotericism. But can we also find it in Christianity? Even if it does not formally exist, it is—at the very least—possible to come up with a Christian variant. We need only look at the Christian movements that lay great emphasis on prayer and the results of prayer. Some contend that prayer is always effective. (A case in point is the discussion concerning a study in a hospital in the USA which allegedly demonstrated a higher incidence of recovery among patients who had been prayed for than among those who had not). Other examples include specific forms of Christian 'positive thinking' (Norman Vincent Peale) or 'possibility thinking' (Robert Schuller). The ideas of what is called 'spiritual mapping' should also be included here.

The second question also concerns the world religions. Is this model truly essential to Eastern religions? Is this model to be found in all Eastern religions? We can find many beginnings of this model within these religions. In Hinduism the idea of 'subtle matter' or *prana* plays a very important role, at least in Advaita Vedanta Hinduism. *Prana* gives us energy and is also a power we can radiate. Here we should think of the stories of the yogis, i.e., those who had a decisive impact on the situation around them by using the power of their minds. But the use of *prana* in order to establish peace does not actually exist. In this respect, Gandhi's approach is—in my opinion—more representative.

Notions about the 'power of meditation' can also be found in Buddhism. Buddhism does not, however, see meditation as 'subtle matter' and certainly not as a means of establishing world peace. The Buddhist monks who burned themselves to death in order to bring about peace are quite a different story. Within Western esotericism, we find other new movements that can be seen as having some connection to this model. A case in point are the many Western movements that see magic as a real power that can be directed towards others and that truly have an effect. Some of these movements, such as neopaganism, concentrate on the positive use of this magic. Other groups, which are often referred to as Satanic, focus on the negative use of magic. We can also find evidence of this model in Joseph Murphy's 'positive thinking'; according to that belief, everything we think becomes true automatically (Murphy 1981). As a rule, this kind of positive thinking does not have any connection to the realization of world peace.

In short, this automatic-energetic model is not an exception, restricted only to extreme religious movements. It is a way of thinking and living that is found in a wide variety of beliefs. We should, therefore, take it quite seriously.

But if we do, we should ask whether it is actually effective. Does the model work? Can this approach truly achieve world peace? The claims of the adherents are very strong. TM, in particular, strives to prove by scientific research that their meditation and *siddha* exercises have impressive results. Where peace is achieved, it is often attributed to the collective meditations of adherents of TM. With the "Million Minutes of Peace Appeal," however, the Brahma Kumaris did not set out to prove anything by scientific research. Instead, they claim very unequivocally that their actions brought about concrete progress towards world peace. The same is true of those who believe in the power of the prayer or the power of magic. They claim that their actions have a very concrete and effective impact. In their case, however, world peace is not their primary aim. Those who believe in this model have no doubts about it. They see the signs and evidence of its effectiveness everywhere.

I myself respect this belief only as a belief. But I am not convinced by the proofs and signs since they are also subject to very different interpretations. The direct connection between a specific automatic deed and what is claimed to be the automatic result can never be proven but only taken in faith. TM research is not truly scientific and can almost always be falsified. As a rule, concrete results in world peace can be attributed to the concrete actions of nations and some religions. We may see the real cause of the conflict, but we should never attribute the resolution of such a conflict to a subtle energy or radiation of a group in the distance. I would not advise use of this automatic-energetic model as a means of achieving world peace. We would be far better off to continue pursuing a course of concrete action.

Bibliography

Dawson, M. (1993). *Healing the Cause: A Path of Forgiveness.* Tallahassee: Findhorn Press.
Koornstra, P. (1981). *De superbom. Vrede zonder angst.* Laag Soeren: MIU Press.
Murphy, J. (1981). *The Power of Your Subconscious Mind.* New York: Bantam Books.
Ransijn, P. and N. Schulte. (1982). *Bewustzijn als bewapening. Vrede en ontwapening door groei van collectief bewustzijn.* Laag Soeren: MIU Press.
Reinders, P.J. (1989). "De Brahma Kumaris." In: RBN 19. Amsterdam: VU Uitgeverij.
Twyman, J.F. (1996). *Emissary of the Light.* New York: Warner Books.
———. (2000). *The Secret of the Beloved Disciple.* Tallahassee: Findhorn Press.
Wapnick, K. (1983). *A Talk Given on A Course in Miracles.* Roscoe: Foundation for A Course in Miracles.
———. (1976). *A Course in Miracles.* Glen Ellen: Foundation for Inner Peace.

Part IV

The Papers and the Workshops:

Reaping the Harvest

Why Do Religious Groups Become Involved in Conflicts?

André Droogers

When raising the question as to the reasons religious groups become involved in conflicts, it is useful to be aware, in an inductive way, of the concrete cases presented in this volume. It includes essays on Hindu-Muslim relations in India, the conflicts in Sri Lanka and Indonesia, the Rwandan and Tanzanian cases, the South African example of the search for reconciliation, and the case of Bosnia. When comparing these cases, one discovers that they display a number of common as well as idiosyncratic characteristics. In an effort to formulate a provisional answer to the question put to me by the editors, I will raise five sub-questions that can serve as a kind of checklist. In answering these questions, some of the papers included in this volume were helpful, such as Ram-Prasad's, which includes a typology of relationships between religions and reconciliation and Aarsbergen's, which consists of a discussion of Isaiah Berlin's views.

Do the Parties in the Conflict Belong to the Same or to Different Religions?

Though this distinction between the same or different religions may have no influence on the form and intensity of the conflict, the chances for reconciliation may improve if it is possible to rediscover common ground between the parties. In the Asian cases that are included in this book the parties involved belong to different religions. With respect to Africa, Rwanda and South Africa present examples of Christians fighting one another or entering a phase of reconciliation. The Tanzanian and Bosnian cases concern relations between Christians and Muslims.

What Role Does Religion Actually Play?

Religious institutions and leaders may be involved in conflict in differing ways. They may be at the center of the hostilities, either from the start or by being brought into them later, thus making the conflict religious in nature. This conflict may take the form of the defense of one religion against another, or of one faction against another within the same religion. But non-religious interests—social, economic, political, or all three together—may predominate. If secular interests prevail, the role of religion may appear to be more distant. But it is also possible that religion is used to mask secular interests that lie behind the publicly touted religious nature of the conflict. Much will depend on the way the media report such a conflict. The label 'religious' is often used as an attractive didactic simplification of a much more complex problem. In any case, whether the conflict is considered primarily religious in nature or not, religion may serve to legitimize the conflict. Religious messages may contain elements that can be used to make conflicts, even if not directly religious, sacred in nature and therefore plausibly religious. Secular litigants, thus, may therefore use a religious message for strategic purposes or to justify their claims.

Religious leaders and institutions may of course also play a more peaceful role, either passively in abstaining from support of the contestants in a conflict or more actively in seeking a resolution to it. Leaders may use their authority and charisma to facilitate mediation and reconciliation. Violence may be condemned for religious reasons. Again, a religious message may be used for purposes of legitimization—this time for peaceful purposes. In different phases of South Africa's history, the Christian religion and religious leaders have legitimized both conflict and reconciliation. In the case of internal religious conflict there is a chance that the parties involved will more easily accept the task of seeking a solution if they share basic religious views. Yet, usually other, more secular, arguments prevail, such as the struggle for land or other resources. Experiences from religious or secular history, even those that date from a much earlier period, may still represent strong memories that retain their impact. As a rule, it is easier to justify a conflict than its resolution in religious terms. When more than one religion is involved, it will be more difficult to encounter common ground that may serve as a platform for reconciliation.

What Interests Are at Stake?

In our discussion of the role religion may play in conflict, allusion was made to both religious and non-religious interests. Social interests have reference to groups or whole societies and the way they prefer to organize social life. Economic interests regard access to scarce resources. Political interests have to do with a particular scarce resource, namely, power understood as the capacity to influence people's behavior, with a view to achieving certain economic and social interests. Religious interests may influence secular ones, reinforcing or weakening them, as when religion promotes a specific blueprint for the ideal society, or when it justifies a particular way of dealing with scarce resources, including power. Conversely, religion may be influenced by the vicissitudes of secular interests with respect to the positions its adopts.

In order to organize our thinking in terms of this issue, it might be well to distinguish between two possible broad types of religious positions with regard to conflicts. One might be called exclusivist, being an attitude reflecting the interests of a particular religion or religious faction; the other inclusivist, being a stance exhibiting regard for the interests of humanity in all its rich diversity. I have in view here not a dual typology of the world religions but of types of religious positions. The two types of stance may occur side by side within one religion. The types are meant to have both descriptive and normative value, i.e., they may, on the one hand, be helpful in distinguishing between and describing positions; on the other hand, they represent options for taking a stance oneself.

The exclusivist type represents an essentialist and monocultural view of religion, emphasizing tradition as carried across the centuries through the history of the form of religion involved. Those holding this position defend a certain model for the good life and thus for organizing society, a model based on a view of the particular tradition in question. This may take the shape of a religiously-inspired form of nationalism, nationhood, or homeland but also of a theocracy based on an absolute divine law. Within the confines of this position coalitions with political leaders are considered normal, and religion may become the organizing principle of the state. The view on liberty is positive, in Berlin's sense of 'freedom to'—i.e., the freedom to live one's life in a particular way, possibly suggested and facilitated by those in power. Within the exclusivist position there is a strong conviction as to what truth is. Distinctiveness vis-à-vis other communities, with differing views of truth, is thereby emphasized. If a Christian calls Islam satanic, one can be sure that he or she represents an exclusivist position. Accordingly, the more exclusivist type of position may influence views of reconciliation and conflict, with a tendency in the direction of conflict.

The inclusivist type of stance is of a more dialogical and multicultural nature. Tradition is understood as a process of more or less constant reformulation and revision, adapting itself to the demands of the age. A religious group that has assumed this inclusivist position does not so much propose a model for a nation state as for a world society. States are understood to be primarily secular. Representatives of the inclusivist position base such a model on a search for globally applicable universal human values. Coalitions with believers from other religions are possible. In that sense believers operating from the inclusive position behave literally as representatives of the world religions. Their dialogical view of tradition and truth prevents them from propagating—let alone imposing—their own view on a global scale, because their attitude to other views is open and inclusivist. If, for example, a Christian calls the Qur'an the Third Testament, he or she gives specific expression to this open and inclusivist view. The concept of freedom is negative in the above-mentioned sense. Not difference but similarity is cherished. The inclusivist type has consequences for situations of conflict and reconciliation, with a special tendency to seek reconciliation.

What is the Role of Repertoires and Identity?

In talking about repertoires, the implication is that a religion may have a set of prototypes for reflection and behavior in different situations. This set is usually open to interpretation, if not of its basic ideas, at least of its details. Part of its meanings can be latent, becoming manifest only when the demands of the situation correspond to the characteristics of the prototype. But even then, competing prototypes may apply to the same situation. Despite theological efforts at systematization, contradictions may remain. The ongoing debate adds elements to and eliminates others from the repertoire. In addition, the events of history challenge the religions to adapt and change their sets of prototypes.

The cases in this book offer examples of at least three such events. One is an economic crisis, an intensification of the usual scarcity of goods. Such a crisis is often accompanied by a situation of conflict. An appeal to religious repertoires may lead to charity, to justice, but also to a justification of differences. Another example of an influential historical event is the erosion of central political control, such as when for varying reasons influential leaders such as Tito (in former Yugoslavia) or Nyerere (in Tanzania) or Suharto (in Indonesia) stepped down. Within situations of this nature conflicts may emerge in which parts of the religious repertoire play a role. These roles can be either central or marginal or active or passive. A third event regards the transformation of a society, such as in post-apartheid South Africa. Again, the question is: What part of the religious repertoire is activated and for what purposes, but also: How did it change due to events?

Parts of the religious repertoire can be used as markers of religious identity. Conflict and reconciliation entail processes by which identity is made explicit and through which changes in identity are probable. In not a few religions identity is based on a history of conflicts, of battles won or lost, of expansion or reduction.

In the construction and reproduction of identity two strands mingle. On the one hand there is an emphasis on identity as a property, something that transcends time and makes for continuity. This essentialist form of identity corresponds with the exclusivist type of religious stance and with positive freedom as described above. It may also be found in forms of orthodoxy and of fundamentalism. It is like a portrait of a religion, a photograph in a passport. This identity is guarded and controlled. It is reified and regulated by means of disciplinary measures.

But even in its apparently more traditional forms, there is always a dynamic side to the construction of identity as well, if only because tradition must be reproduced and transmitted. This means that identity is also always under construction, its markers may change with the modifications in the repertoire. De-reification may occur. The photograph of essential identity is complemented by the video of dynamic identity. The impact of authority is weakened by a negative view of freedom. Yet dynamism is never total, since in some way continuity must be guaranteed. Otherwise identity would become fully lost.

Events, especially when they are characterized by conflicts, appeal to either an essential or a dynamic strand of identity. Conflicts may arise in order to protect and maintain essential aspects of identity. On the other hand, many a religious movement has engaged in an inevitable internal conflict in order to conquer its own reified identity. In the course of history such an identity, dynamically obtained, may be transformed into an essentialist form of identity, bringing the movement to an institutionalized halt. Some of the world religions are good examples of this trajectory.

Similarly, reconciliation touches on matters of identity-construction. Such a process may contain more elements of the dynamic aspect than of the essentialist dimension of construction of identity. Through such a process enemies may drop their identity as parties in conflict and may come to see each other as kin.

What Role Does Power Play in the Conflict?

There are at least four answers to this question. First of all, religious groups are bound to have some form of organization, which brings with it all kinds of social mechanisms that influence power relations. Wherever two people are together, power is present, at least if power is defined as the capacity to influence other people's behavior. Gender is a good example of this. The exercise of power may lead to conflict as soon as the powers that be are no longer viewed as authoritative. Interests may come to differ in such a way that litigants seek recourse to conflict in order to change power balances. This may take place, for example, especially when glaringly unequal access to scarce resources occurs because of the abusive power. But it is also possible that the religious legitimization of conflict fails to convince, especially if religion itself changes or is secularized.

A second way in which power may manifest itself is through the control of repertoires and identity-construction. Authorities may defend their position and their model of society, appealing to a particular selection from the repertoire, their critics choosing other parts. Sacred texts can be used for contrary goals. A particular identity is then presented as normal and socialization serves to perpetuate this view. Authorities usually see it as important to have legitimate control of the production of the repertoire, including the religious part of it. Socialization and education are viewed as important means of guaranteeing acceptance of the given repertoire of identity. This exclusive control may be contested in a conflict.

A third aspect has to do with the access to power resources. In a way, repertoire and identity construction are part of the scarce resources, just as education is. Knowledge, including sacred, esoteric, ritual or legal knowledge, is power. Religious specialists have this kind of power at their disposal. But one may also think of mundane resources such as weaponry or money. Conflicts may be entered to solve questions of access to power resources, including those of a religious nature. Even when the resources themselves are secular, the struggle for them may be fought with religious means.

Finally, power may play a role when the question arises as to who is allowed to have access to scarce resources in general. A conflict may be initiated in order to guarantee access to those resources. The defense of human rights may lead to such a conflict, just as matters of a just distribution of land and food may, in both cases with a religious justification.

The Meaning of Reconciliation

Victor A. van Bijlert

Introduction

What do we mean when we speak about reconciliation? Is its meaning determined by the context in which we use it, by our upbringing, by our social and cultural background? Is it possible to speak meaningfully about reconciliation across religious and cultural boundaries? Are such boundaries sharply drawn or are they blurry? These are serious issues concerning an important concept. The contemporary world has witnessed a marked increase in violent conflict. Any attempt to understand violence of this kind and restore civil society after the cessation of violence, such as the pursuit of reconciliation, must be welcomed. The idea of reconciliation itself may not be entirely intelligible. It may have different shades of meaning. But this need not prevent us from communicating meaningfully with one another. The various essays in this volume amply bear out the beneficial nature of such communication.

Reconciliation in Christianity

The idea of reconciliation in Christianity stems from the New Testament: "If you are offering your gift at the altar and there remember that your brother has something against you, leave your gift there in front of the altar. First go and be reconciled to your brother" (Matthew 5:23). Here reconciliation between individuals is commanded. The initiative should be taken by the one who realizes that his brother "has something" against him. But in Christianity reconciliation has always connected this closely with the person of Jesus Christ:

> Therefore, if anyone is in Christ, he is a new creation; the old has gone, the new has come! All this is from God, who reconciled us to himself through Christ and gave us the ministry of reconciliation: that God was reconciling the world to himself in Christ. (2 Corinthians 5:16-19)[1]

The crucifixion of Christ is the central symbol of God's reconciliation of the world with himself and we are asked to become emissaries of that reconciliation on this earth. If this is the starting point in Christianity, let us look at what Christian theology itself has to say about reconciliation.

C. van der Kooij discusses three models of reconciliation between God and humankind under the Cross: (1) the victory of Christ over the devil; (2) the objective or juridical model in which Christ has paid to God the punishment for our sins; (3)

---

[1] All New Testament passages are from the New International Version.

the subjective model which appeals to humankind to become reconciled to God, following the example of Christ. All three models can be used as the situation requires. T. van Prooijen shows how Moltmann's theology of the reconciliation of the crucified Christ can help clarify the position of the churches vis-à-vis racism in South Africa. Reconciliation cannot mean neutrality or social peace: it must be an invitation to a new future. Moltmann's theology can help break through the vicious circle of racist alienation. Justice, and not submission to the powers that be, is the goal of reconciliation.

The tragic history of South African Apartheid and the attempt at redemption by way of the Truth and Reconciliation Commission is the main theme of Piet Meiring's contribution. Drawing largely on his personal experience with the Commission, Meiring points to important practical lessons that can be learned from the South African experience. Speaking about the Truth Commission from a Muslim perspective, F. Esack emphasizes that justice should be one of the main objectives of any attempt at reconciliation. The proceedings of the Commission, he stated, were very much colored by Christian concerns.

H.M. Vroom strongly insists on justice in the process of reconciliation. Without justice reconciliation is a flat lie. It ought to be a process involving groups. Absence of conflict may indicate the presence of flagrant injustice. J.D. Gort makes a similar point: Christian reconciliation from an ecumenical perspective ought to go hand in hand with struggles against injustice. Experience, he avers, teaches us that in this regard both utopian enthusiasm and total fatalism should be avoided.

Reconciliation requires making sacrifices and a change of heart must be forced upon us by God; this is the conclusion to which H. Jansen comes in his contribution on Graham Greene's *The End of the Affair*. J. van Butselaar enumerates some essentials of reconciliation: confession of guilt, prophetic witness and the establishment of justice.

Views of Reconciliation

What reconciliation entails or ideally should entail underlies many discussions. There are minimalist, often secular, views of reconciliation which postulate nothing more than that groups of people or individuals who were previously engaged in conflict should be able to be on speaking terms. Such is the position taken by D. Berendsen who links reconciliation to mediation in a legal sense. C. Ram-Prasad opts for secular solutions to Hindu-Muslim conflicts in India. A.A. Engineer hopes Indian Muslims will develop a pragmatic and wise approach to communal problems in India. In the context of 'ethnic' violence in Sri Lanka, N. Swaris stresses the need for unity between the ordinary Sinhalese and Tamils, who do not entertain any deep-rooted mutual suspicions. The cultural anthropologist A. Droogers delineates the frameworks offered by the social sciences for understanding the social and cultural conditions under which reconciliation can take place. R. Kranenborg discusses a special New Age model of reconciliation: the automatic-energetic model which seeks to reconcile two parties through the release of spiritual energies by means of meditation. C.

Aarsbergen writes on Isaiah Berlin's concept of negative liberty as a secular model of reconciliation which implies, among other things, that we should abandon notions of final harmony, for the desire for harmony is the cause of rather than the solution to many conflicts.

In contrast to this stands the strong notion of reconciliation, which should include forgiveness as an integral component. Wrongdoers and their victims need to be reconciled. This is powerfully argued by P. Meiring. Forgiveness seems to be an essential part of the process. This point is asserted from a Buddhist perspective by M. McGhee. Rabbi T. Marx, writing on Yom Kippur, maintains that reconciliation entails conflict resolution between persons, criticism without revenge, right timing, mediation, and the rejection of pious hypocrisy. A. D'Souza, taking an interfaith position, contends that reconciliation is a struggle to bring together estranged persons. D. Winslow regards forgiveness to be an essential part of reconciliation, no matter how difficult it may be to forgive.

Spirituality could play an important part in the process of reconciliation. This position is defended from an enlightened Hindu perspective by Swami Agnivesh, who considers spirituality to be a process in which we transcend our tendencies toward injustice and the exploitation of others. Espousing the cause of Hindu 'liberation theology', S. Gangadaran pleads for the removal of oppressive and unjust social structures. V.A. van Bijlert reviews Vedantic spirituality as a basis for reconciliation on a personal level.

Highlighting the work of the Indonesian Muslim scholar Mukti Ali, H. Beck argues for reconciliation as harmonious coexistence. Mukti Ali promoted comparative religion and interreligious dialogue to further religious and social harmony in Indonesia after the establishment of the New Order. A.R. Widyanto also focusses on the need for harmony in Indonesia. In his view, reconciliation between Indonesian Christians and Muslims is possible only if national unity and the spirit of *Pancasila* can be revived. That dialogue between religions is a road to reconciliation is also put forward by F. Wijsen and B. Mfumbusa in connection with Christian-Muslim relations in Tanzania. Reconciliation between Jews, Christians and Muslims would be viable, according to A. Wessels, if the three faiths would reorient themselves to the faith of Abraham, their common ancestor.

These divergent views seem to indicate that there is a correlation between secular reconciliation, in order to ensure that conflicts will not continue, on the one hand, and religiously-inspired reconciliation, which seeks to establish justice and forgiveness between victims and perpetrators, on the other.

Aims and Possibilities of Reconciliation

Almost half of the authors discuss reconciliation in the context of horrendously violent conflicts: the recent Balkan wars (Winslow); ethnic violence in Sri Lanka (Swaris); the genocides in Rwanda (van Butselaar); Hindu-Muslim communalism in South Asia (Engineer, van Bijlert, Ram-Prasad, D'Souza, van der Burg); ethnic and religious violence in Indonesia (Widyanto); apartheid in South Africa (van Prooijen, Esack,

Meiring). Many authors hold that justice is the principal objective of reconciliation and not simply the quelling of social unrest. Honest relationships between people and between people and God is a common theme running through many of the papers. From an explicitly religious perspective, forgiveness and a radical change of heart often form an integral part of the process of reconciliation. A more secular approach is satisfied with the prevention of revenge.

Is reconciliation possible? On the basis of an analysis of the similarities and differences between two cultural symbols: the Hindu *Bhagavadgita* and Aeschylus' *Seven Against Thebes*, L Minnema answers this question with a qualified 'No'. Minnema warns against superficial and glib notions of reconciliation, for these lead nowhere. C. van der Burg, writing on contemporary Hinduism, does not explicitly hold that reconciliation between, for instance, Hindus and Muslims is totally impossible, but he expresses grave doubts about this. Modern Hinduism has a strong tendency to reconcile differences through one-sided inclusivism. A.A. Engineer remains cautious about the possibility of reconciliation but thinks Indian Muslims should neither hope for too much nor expect too little. D. Winslow has hopes for reconciliation in the Balkans but feels no certainty in this regard. V.A. van Bijlert is not very confident either regarding reconciliation: it may be possible on a personal level, but when large groups of people have been exposed to horrendous and massive violence, how can one expect reconciliation, even of a minimalist kind, to take place?

Reconciliation and Women

An important development in the debate on reconciliation is the position of women in relation to this process. C. Romberg offers a novel analysis of Buddhist texts, and demonstrates how they fail to espouse the issue of equality between men and women. Romberg's findings provide evidence that in the older Buddhist texts women are discriminated against. Only in later Mahayana Buddhism does the situation seem to have improved. And yet, even in ancient Buddhist teaching, gender is not viewed as a real bar to Enlightenment. Modern 'engaged Buddhists', however, are genuinely trying to reconcile traditional Buddhist doctrine with social ethics and a concern for human rights. T. Visser pleads for an Islamic approach to gender issues in the Islamic world. In this connection Visser refers to the writings of the contemporary Arab philosopher Mohammed Abed al-Jabri who argues for a return to the medieval Spanish Muslim philosopher Ibn Rushd. Visser also advocates a rethinking of the gender issue in the light of Rita Gross' androgynous model.

Reconciliation in World Religions

The essays by Van der Kooij, Van Prooijen, Gort, Meiring and Marx express the Christian and Judaic views respectively on reconciliation. Esack presents an Islamic outlook: Muslims are enjoined to struggle for the transformation of themselves and society. This entails the struggle to eradicate injustice and to establish freedom and justice. An important related point in Islam is compassion, the empathetic consciousness of suffering whereby one takes the pain of the other as one's own and seeks to alleviate it in some way. Esack fears that reconciliation (especially in a conservative Christian sense) is often only a tool in the hands of the powerful to suppress social unrest.

Do the beliefs and teachings of non-Abrahamic religions such as Hinduism and Buddhism contain a concept of reconciliation or its equivalent? Almost all authors dealing with these religions ignored this question and tacitly assume that this is the case. What would the Hindu or Buddhist idea of reconciliation look like? Only Van der Burg seems to have posed this question. His answer is that so-called Hindu 'tolerance'—which is, in fact, inclusivism—sweeps all differences under the carpet of Hindu unity and superiority. This then is the Hindu version of reconciliation. Such a view is not explicitly contradicted by Gangadaran's and Van Bijlert's papers. But it is possible to take a less hegemonic view of inclusivism, that is, to understand it as meaning that all the differing religions (including the numerous traditions within Hinduism itself) constitute various aspects or facets of the same divine truth. The idea that different religious traditions are paths leading to the same divine ground of the universe is often articulated by Hindu thinkers. This idea is also expressed in the famous Hindu scripture, the *Bhagavadgita*.[2] According to Swami Agnivesh, reconciliation means the avoidance of conflict through authentic spirituality and the establishment of social justice in a classless and casteless society.

McGhee regards Buddhist reconciliation as the cessation of enmity and as forgiveness. In support of this he quotes *Dhammapada*, verses 3-5. This famous Buddhist scripture declares that enmity only ends when we no longer entertain thoughts about the harm that others have done to us. Among the authors on non-Abrahamic religions, McGhee is the only one who actually refers to and quotes from a specific scripture. This is interesting because it may indicate that many supporters of Hinduism feel little need for scriptural quotations to assert the desirability of a moral value like reconciliation.

---

[2] Cf. *Gita* 4:11: "According as human beings approach Me so do I accept them. All are following My path in every respect." *Gita* 7:21: "If a devoted person wishes to worship with faith a particular form [of the divine], it is still Me Who makes the faith of that devoted person unwavering."

A Blueprint for the Process of Peace and Reconciliation

Josien Folbert

In the case studies published in this volume one can see how people are struggling with everyday reality. In many countries the situations in which groups or individuals find themselves are very complicated: they have to deal with issues of political power, tensions between ethnic and religious groups, upper caste and lower caste people, the rich and the poor, the powerful and the exploited.

The conflicts in the regions in question have very different origins, but almost all instances have a long history of conflict and tension. There have been many attempts to arrive at a solution. Some conflicts have been resolved, while others died down for a time but then flared up again later.

The essays in this volume provide insight into the causes and reasons for conflict and describe their purposes and preconditions as well. In this essay we will follow the process of peace and reconciliation in two countries especially: India and South Africa. In countries such as Tanzania, Indonesia and Rwanda some concrete suggestions will be made and concrete steps described.

There can be no doubt that the achievement of reconciliation and peace takes time. The language of process entails that there is a starting point. But it is impossible to tell where the process will end. Each of the different traditions has its own process, but the authors of the articles in this volume are in agreement the starting point is that justice, peace and reconciliation need to go hand in hand. There can be no peace and reconciliation without justice.

India

A Muslim View

In India a majority of Hindus and minorities of Muslims, Christians and others coexist. In the last decades there have been and are many conflicts which are often called 'religious conflicts'.

In his essay A.A. Engineer states that it was not the case in the past that Hindus and Muslims were always in conflict. Those hostile projections stem from the colonial period of the nineteenth century. There never was a homogeneous Muslim or Hindu community. On the contrary, Muslims often fought against Muslims and Hindus against Hindus.

Partition, i.e., the division of the subcontinent into India and Pakistan, was based on a two-nation theory: a Hindu state and a Muslim state. This partition was to be the solution for the two religious groups, but nothing was further from the truth. Muslims themselves were divided on this concept and up until the present the communal problem has only intensified. The unity of Muslims has been shattered and they now live in three separate countries: India, Pakistan and Bangladesh. "The Muslim masses in all three countries are facing problems of acute poverty, unemployment and illiteracy. If anyone benefited from Partition it was the elite Muslims who created the so-called Muslim 'homeland' in the name of Islam" (242).

In 1950 the new Constitution was drafted and accepted. This Constitution declared that all the citizens of India are "equal in every respect without any distinction of caste, creed or race." Two articles (25 and 30) give special religious and cultural rights to minorities. For Muslims, Christians, Sikhs and others these articles are very important because they provide these groups with the right to establish and administer their own educational institutions and the state may not discriminate on the grounds of religion or language.

After Independence from the British, an Indian form of democracy developed. Unfortunately, however, democracy was used for empowering politicians at the cost of the masses. That power game still continues.

From 1960 onwards, under the government of Nehru, the Congress Party was committed to a secular politics based on a philosophy of Indian freedom. This kind of secularism guaranteed the minorities religious freedom. Adherents of different religions could feel secure, but these positive factors seemed to be only a dream. Riots, destruction and powerful prejudices have frustrated these positive steps in the direction of equal citizenship and freedom.

Engineer sees the following as conditions for peaceful coexistence in India: a just society, freedom of religion, sharing power on equitable basis, better education and a progressive economy, certain necessary changes for women. Engineer's contribution does not show many successful steps towards peace and reconciliation, but he does end his article optimistically with the words: "If the future for Muslims is not bright at this moment, it is not dismal either. Given a little more wisdom and a more pragmatic approach, Muslims can succeed in shaping their future in democratic India, even if its secularism is undulating" (250).

Hindu Views
It is understandable that a Hindu will interpret Indian history differently from a Muslim. C. Ram-Prasad calls the conflicts which exist in India "religion-based" conflicts, but this term stems from a certain reading of the history of the subcontinent after the coming of Islam to India. To overcome this misunderstanding he suggests that the interpretation of history should be changed.

In Ram-Prasad's view the ideal of Indian secularism did not justify the distinct cultural significance of Hinduism nor did it recognize the value and influence of religion in Indian public life. Indian secularism had many negative results: discrimination, distrust, non-identity and disloyalty among Muslims.

It should be clear that Hindu nationalism cannot actually be called religious. It is in essence political, although religious elements do play a role. In his approach to overcoming the problems that exist in India, Ram-Prasad poses the question of managing a religiously pluralistic society: "What are the implications for the management of religious conflict if the instruments of state are in the hands of one of the parties to the conflict" (236)? He pleads for a way of governing that seeks ways of dealing with bilateral and multilateral economic and political entitites and for sound economic management. Conflict resolution that aims at securing fair terms, good deals, mutual confidence, can only be successful if religion becomes irrelevant in a conflict. The government has to manage religious conflict in a neutral way so that peace is secured.

Swami A. Agnivesh pleads for a new approach to the concept of religion. The focus on religion is too often negative and destructive because religion is represented as an ideology of power. He calls religion in essence a culture of peace. To overcome the negative spiral he introduces the term 'spirituality' as a key aspect of peace and reconciliation. In addition to that, it is necessary to come to a reappropriation and reinterpretation of the original vision, i.e., back to the source of the spiritual inspiration. For Hindus this means going back to the Vedas and for Muslims going back to the Qur'an. Conflicts between people of different religions can occur because religiosity instead of spirituality is emphasized too much.

Living out of true spirituality means concern for others and respect for life, commitment to social justice in a spirit of service, empowering people, removing social and economic inequalities and developing a new tolerance for others.

Christian Views
Andreas D'Souza looks at the subject of 'religion, conflict, and reconciliation' within the scope of developments at the Henry Martyn Institute in Hyderabad. After several years this 'International Center for Research, Interfaith Relations and Reconciliation' changed its focus of activities.

In the beginning the Institute functioned as a training institute for missionaries to Muslims, but due to developments in insight into relations between people of different faiths they set out to make a new path through interfaith dialogue. The consequences of the riots exercised great influence in determining the policy of the Institute. In the constitution of the Institute the primary intention is described as "an expression of the Church's ministry of reconciliation" (262).

In the process of reconciliation—a struggle by the people to bring together estranged persons, leading towards transformed relationships and structures based on justice—they discovered the spiral nature of violence: violence always leads to violence. If people want to stop violence, they need first of all to become aware of violence in themselves.

Another big change in the Institute is the consequence of having staff members from religious backgrounds other than Christianity and having to make the requisite changes. Their morning prayers were initially Christian: Bible reading, praying the Lord's Prayer, etc. But what does it mean to pray in a multireligious setting and to talk about reconciliation? They have now found ways through which the faculty and staff of the Institute can be empowered: listening to a reflection on a passage from the Qur'an or a recitation of a Sanskrit *sloka*. D'Souza states: "In my growing understanding of what reconciliation means, I have come to realize that spirituality has no barriers" (267).

The Institute also offers training in mediation techniques for pastors, teachers, government officials, police officers and laypeople. They are enabled to intervene in one way or another in certain conflicts.

Small groups of Hindus, Muslims and Christians are cooperating in a certain way. One of the possibilities for better understanding is telling stories to one another about the painful process of healing injured feelings and of creating mutual trust.

Other initiatives from the Henry Martyn Institute are: fasting on Friday, breaking the fast together and praying for peace; cooking and eating together; starting a tailoring enterprise for Hindu and Muslim women.

Sometimes projects come too early, because people are still too injured. Deep-rooted hatred and desire for revenge cannot be removed without a long process aimed at inner transformation.

South Africa

After oppression, humiliation, rape, exclusion, racism, discrimination, etc. there is no way simply to forget. Nelson Mandela described it in the following words:

> to close our eyes and pretend none of this ever happened would be to maintain at the core of our society a source of pain, division and hatred and violence. Only the disclosure of truth and the search for justice can create the moral climate in which reconciliation and peace will flourish. The choice we have is not whether we should disclose the past, but *how* it will be done. It must be done in such a way that reconciliation and peace are promoted.

P. Meiring, who was very much involved the process of reconciliation after apartheid, writes: "reconciliation is a very fragile flower" (286).

To achieve reconciliation the Parliament of South Africa established the Truth and Reconciliation Commission (TRC). Their agenda was very practical but not easy:

> 1. To establish as complete a picture of the past. The causes, nature, and extent of suffering of human rights violations between 1960 and 1994 have to be established, taking into consideration the following: the circumstances, factors, and context of the violations, the perspectives of the victims as well as the perspectives and motives of the perpetrators.
> 2. To facilitate the granting of amnesty. After full disclosure of the relevant facts, and if the deed for which amnesty is required complies with the qualifications of the act, amnesty may be granted.
> 3. To establish and make known the whereabouts of the victims, restoring the human and civil dignity by granting them the opportunity to relate their own accounts of the violations they suffered, and by recommending reparation measures in this respect.
> 4. To compile a report on the activities and findings of the TRC, with recommendations of measures to prevent future violations of human rights in the country. (See Meiring, 280-81)

To investigate all these points the TRC was divided into three important committees: the Human Rights Violations Committee, the Amnesty Committee and the Reparation and Rehabilitation Committee.

Meiring stated that the committee members represented the different cultural, racial, political and religious communities of South Africa. Nevertheless Farid Esack, a South African Muslim, criticizes the work of TRC because of its Christianization of the TRC process, which resulted in Muslims remaining on the sidelines. Thus many Muslims remained indifferent towards the reconciliation process.

Esack believes that the Qur'an provides a basis for a theology of compassion, because God blew his spirit into his creation. Thus everyone is a bearer of the spirit of God. "Acknowledging the ever-presence of this spirit, irrespective of how low the bearer has fallen, is for me the basis of human dignity and human rights" (294). Another critique by Esack is the content of the words 'forgiveness' and 'reconciliation'. In the South African context these words are too Christian: "This is a version that seeks stability rather than justice ..." (296). From this one can conclude that in a complicated situation of different traditions people have to investigate what these terms mean to all people and not just to one group.

In spite of many mistakes in the reconciliation process Meiring concluded that at least six lessons may be learned from the South African experience (286-88). First, reconciliation needs to be clearly defined. Desmond Tutu often referred to 2 Corinthians 5:11-21, whereas people from other religious communities do not recognize this basis for reconciliation. Second, reconciliation and truth go hand in hand. For the victims it is important that their stories and experiences are heard. Third, reconciliation requires a deep, honest confession—and a willingness to forgive. Fourth, justice and reconciliation are two sides of the same coin: in South Africa this not only entails a balanced amnesty but also the need to deal with issues such as unemployment, poverty, education, restitution, the land issue, economic inequality, etc. Fifth, for reconciliation to occur a deep commitment is needed. Sixth, on the road to reconciliation, one should expect the unexpected, because in a process towards reconciliation there are many negative stories and feelings of hatred. On the other hand, some people do like to express and share their ability to forgive their enemies. Although every situation differs, these points can obtain in other circumstances as well.

After many years of this reconciliation process, feelings remain very ambiguous. People still retain feelings of injustice. In a process such as this one cannot be forced to do something which he or she is not willing to do. Right up to the present many black people are still poor, their children are not being educated and unemployment remains a problem.

Rwanda

In several countries conflicts between adherents of different religions arose, but, as we saw in the previous discussion, that is only one side of the coin. Religion and ethnicity sometimes follow the same path, but in other cases, as, for instance, in the conflict between the Hutus and the Tutsis in Rwanda, ethnicity is itself the cause of conflict. Although the conflict in Rwanda is definitely not a religious conflict, churches and Christianity played an important role. Churches were blamed by the new regime after the genocide because of their failures.

J. van Butselaar states in his essay that "the churches in general found it difficult to talk about reconciliation—not only did the word not seem appropriate in the traumatic experiences of many ... but the churches also had no freedom to act politically" (335-36). The official churches did not seem to be prepared to work for reconciliation; they did not make their position clear during the genocide. Even worse, they failed to be safe havens for persecuted people.

Two initiatives—as steps in the reconciliation process—are worthy of mention. A group of priests, pastors and lay people (the Detmold group) from different ethnic backgrounds wrote a declaration in which they mutually confessed their guilt and promised to work towards reconciliation. Another group of academics (*L'initiative de Machakos*), who had responsible positions under the former regimes created an internet discussion that resulted in a breaking down of all kinds of myths about the several parties.

Tanzania

Tensions between Muslims and Christians in Tanzania arose in the mid-1980s because of political changes and adjustment to a free market. On the level of 'dialogue of life' Muslims and Christians remain peaceful. F. Wijsen and B. Mfumbasa point out that unifying factors such as one language (Swahili), equal opportunities for education and equal positions in the government are important. Tanzania is a secular state and this should be stressed. How is a pluralistic society to be developed? The authors suggest that some initial steps, such as promoting interreligious formation and religious studies, should be included in the secondary school curriculum. Muslim families should be encouraged to send their children to school. Another step is to teach Islam in Christian theological colleges in a less apologetic way. A good education is one of the vehicles of a better understanding between people, but poverty, often used as a catalyst of 'fundamentalism', should also be combatted.

Indonesia

Since Indonesia gained independence there has been an ongoing debate as to whether or not Indonesia would be a Muslim state based on *sharia*. For many years *Pancasila*, the five pillars that formed the basis of the Indonesian state, served this society.

In this short section it is impossible to describe all the new developments in Indonesia. A.R. Widyanto summarizes the complexity in three points: 1) religious tension caused by the politicization of religion; 2) religious tension arising out of a latent suspicion cherished covertly by each religious community toward one another, in particular the suspicion concerning the problem of 'Islamization' and 'Christianization'; 3) religious tension due to confusing or mixing politics and religion.

After the outbreak of conflicts in Aceh, Moluccan, Poso and other areas several groups were formed with the aim of making people more alert and aware of the causes of religious violence. Widyanto pleads for groups that reflect the weak and strong points of their own religion, the practices and ways of approaching others. "[W]e should also cultivate a prophetic attitude, namely, the critical awareness that religion can be turned easily into an ideology for justifying anything we want" (209). Another suggestion by Widyanto is to question if there is unconscious hatred in a religious community itself.

Christians have felt themselves threatened by the revival of Islam since the 1990s, but Muslims feared Christians previously as well, identifying Christianity with modernization, Westernization and secularization. In the past Muslims in Indonesia felt threatened by the Western world. How can this deep-rooted suspicion be overcome?

> [T]he ways toward reconciliation depends on the ability to cultivate the spirit and the national symbols of unity, such as *Pancasila* (the Five Guiding Principles: belief in one God, a just and civilized humanity, national unity, democracy, justice for the people), the common national language and heritage, the common love for the people and the nation. Reconciliation also depends on the ability to uphold the basic foundation of Indonesian society .... (212)

Widyanto provides three points for overcoming this crisis: a) political spirituality means prophetic awareness of the possibility of turning religion into an ideology in order to justify our political claims. Instead of giving higher ethical impulses to politics, religion is degraded into a social mechanism for mobilizing people in order to accomplish political goals devised by the elite leaders; b) political spirituality entails the kind of politics that is always open to something higher than simply the struggle to obtain and to maintain power; c) political spirituality is a spirituality that is able to break through the circle of violence.

Expectations

Human beings are always involved in processes of peace and reconciliation. Are people truly willing to see where they themselves are to blame and to share this with the former enemy? Are people able to abandon political power and interests that damage others?

Pluralistic democracy is one of the conditions for giving space to people of different ethnic and religious backgrounds. A government has to be challenged to manage economic expectations through social development and the negotiation of global liberalization and to secure stability for the sake of the larger whole. This means that a government takes a step outside the conceptual boundaries of religious ideology.

Throughout the articles one can conclude that anyone who is involved in a process of reconciliation
- should be committed to a personal involvement;

- should be aware that it is a process that takes a long time, thereby bringing with it a great deal of frustration and at times danger;
- should pay attention to the signals given by the victims and the victimizers: do they indicate that they are ready to forgive or to be forgiven?
- should have good insight into the endemic, inherited and spiral nature of violence;
- should be aware of the mechanisms that affect relations between people of ethnic and religious groups, such as the distance between the victims and the perpetrators, between the exploited and the beneficiaries, blacks and whites, the poor and the rich, majorities and minorities, etc.;
- should be aware of his/her own prejudices opposing another ethnic or religious group;
- should be able to respect the 'otherness' of the other.

Views of Conflict and Reconciliation

Karel Steenbrink

This brief survey represents an attempt to recapitulate a number of views of conflict and reconciliation outlined in the papers presented at the international, interreligious workshop on Religion, Conflict, and Reconciliation held at Amersfoort, the Netherlands, March 30 – April 1, 2001.

Two Manifestations of Religion

In the oral presentation of his paper André Droogers offered a diagram of two different kinds of religious society.

Exclusive (static)	Inclusive (dynamic)
Specific blueprint for society	General human values and rights
Nationalist	Global
Truth, difference	Dialogical, similarity
Religious state	Secular state
Positive freedom	Negative freedom (= tolerance?)

He stressed that these basic dichotomies are only 'heuristic devices', theoretical models which are never found as such in concrete historic movements or institutions.

It is interesting to see that the theoretical model utilized by Droogers the anthropologist shows close affinity to Isaiah Berlin's philosophical approach. In Berlin's thought, as presented by Connie Aarsbergen, the causes of conflict fit in the left column of the above diagram, while factors leading towards reconciliation fit in the right one. This might lead some to conclude that too much institutionalized religion could engender conflict.

A Secular State and a Modest Role for Religion

When the concrete political and social condition of minorities in India and Sri Lanka was discussed at the workshop, the secular state rather than religious incentives was seen as the major guarantee for a peaceful situation. Writing about Indian Muslims, Asghar Ali Engineer notes that they "dreamt of a secular India." Growing religious consciousness has not improved interreligious relations in India, however, but has resulted in highly resented anti-Muslim tirades and actions. Recent times have not witnessed much improvement in this situation and Muslims decided that "they have to swim even if the ocean is choppy." It is hoped that a dwindling degree rather than an increase of religious fervor will issue in reconciliation, or at least a decreasing amount of conflict and violence.

A similar assessment is made by Chakravarti Ram-Prasad, who identifies two forms of Hinduism: one open and tolerant, promoting multiculturalism, and the other very closed, drawing on "a pathological history of conflict and dominance" and suffering from amnesia regarding the common culture of Muslims and Hindus. Ram-Prasad argues for mediation as a solution to conflict, mediation which would be most effective "when pursued deliberately void of religious motivation." It would seem that he views religious motivation as the dangerous instrument of the sorcerer's apprentice, which must be rendered inoperable or neutralized, even if for a limited time and only in some areas.

In their description of the situation in Tanzania Frans Wijsen and Bernardine Mfumbusa also stress the need for some kind of secular or neutral domain. The *Ujamaa* doctrine, first proposed by Julius Nyerere in the 1960s as a religiously based form of socialism, apparently lost its attractiveness in the 1980s and faded away, together with the more drastic fall of Communism elsewhere. In this paper *Ujamaa* is identified as an ideal of the past. As an antidote to *udini* (the equivalent of what in India is called communalism, the tendency to overstress a group's religious affiliation) a 'global theology' is now being proposed, stimulated strongly by the Tanzanian branch of the World Conference on Religions and Peace. In addition to this global discourse, attempts at tolerance and reconciliation at the grassroots level are adduced as good examples of what is needed. Wijsen and Mfumbasa call attention to the fact that the slogan *Mungu moja dini mbalimbi*: One God, Many Religions, is often employed at local meetings. The question is raised as to why reconciliation is such a difficult matter at the national level. Why do national political leaders use religion to exacerbate divisions, whereas at both the global and the local level methods and means of reconciliation and unity are being proposed and provided?

In his paper Herman Beck makes a case for viewing the discipline of religious studies as a neutral space and safe place where adherents of various religions could meet for academic discourse with an eye to cooling off tensions between their various communities. This is an interesting idea, particularly in light of the common sentiment that scholars have perhaps less influence than moderate and open religious leaders upon the aggressive and hardline sections of religious communities.

Nalin Swaris, discussing Sri Lanka, voices serious doubts about the ability of religions to play a positive role in reconciliation. Notwithstanding the fact that Sri Lankan society is intensely religious, violence continues, often along the boundaries of religious communities. There would seem to be a contradiction between the intense religiosity and the deeply rooted corruption of Sri Lankan society, but, Swaris states, religion in Sri Lanka is usually restricted to individual devotion and ritual and thus is very weak in public affairs and social ethics. Besides this, Sri Lanka lacks great political and religious leaders at the moment.

Jan van Butselaar's paper shows that the Sri Lankan impasse parallels the dilemma of Christian churches in Rwanda. The period of extraordinary violence that broke out in this deeply religious country left individual Christians and churches unprepared to answer questions or to propose solutions leading toward reconciliation. Many experienced a strong desire to seek inspiration from the gospel and from common prayer, but at the same time had to recognize that there was no easy or straightforward way out of the difficulty. Even the familiar religious rule that believers should side with the oppressed was felt to be unreliable in light of South African Bishop Tutu's statement that since the roles of oppressor and oppressed tend to get switched around every twenty-five years or so, we cannot go on following this prescript uncritically.

Arguing against the background of his involvement in the troubles in Hyderabad during the 1990s, Andreas D'Souza upholds the view that religious symbols and acts can function positively in the reconciliation process. As director of the Henry Martyn Institute he found it useful to modify the daily common prayer sessions by refraining from using exclusively Christian formulas. He introduced inclusive prayer language as a means toward religious reconciliation. Besides this, he argues, a most important first step would be for religious communities to prepare themselves for mutual encounter by means of a "process of inner healing and transformation."

Reconciliation and Gender Differentiation

The issue of inclusive language and behavior as preconditions for reconciliation or at least the containment of ethnic and religious conflicts is the specific subject of two workshop papers dealing with the gender issue.

Tirza Visser, reflecting on the clash between Western and Muslim civilizations, emphasizes that the difference between the sexes should be recognized but not exploited. Authority in Islam is commonly related to the male role, but this position, she argues, should be subjected to the critique of the Rushdian dialogue (in reference to the twelfth-century Spanish Muslim philosopher Ibn Rushd), supporting Visser's own advocacy of a harmonious androgynous model of humanity, with continuing diversity for both of its parts.

Claudia Romberg takes a different tack. Objecting to the common perception of traditional Buddhism in which the difference between the sexes is also stressed to the disadvantage of the female half of humankind, she maintains that the best way to effect reconciliation between men and women in Buddhism would be by stressing the equal possibility for all human beings to reach enlightenment, which renders sexual difference unimportant and irrelevant.

Causes of Conflict

In the discussion of the origins of conflicts with religious connotations and overtones it was often stressed that, though such collisions are usually seen as *religious* conflicts, they in fact often result from socio-economic and political causes. Several participants, such as Swami Agnivesh and Ali Engineer, strongly asserted that religions become involved in conflict through misuse by unscrupulous persons or groups.

Jerald Gort argues that though religion itself can sometimes be a direct, primary source of antagonism and enmity among people, religious fanaticism and interreligious ill-will or belligerence do not generally stand alone but are most commonly catalyzed by powerful determinants external to religion itself. The rudimentary agents of human conflict, he contends, are of a chiefly non-religious nature and fall, rather, under the heading of injustice. One could say that Gort takes the position that the adage "If you want peace, work for justice" is of eminent significance in any discussion regarding the relationship between religion, conflict and reconciliation.

While not disagreeing with this, Henk Vroom calls for full recognition of the fact that claims to unique and exclusive truth can give rise to deep-seated dissension and hostility between people of differing faiths, and that the possibility and danger of interreligious clashes inheres in the very formation of religious communities and the varying theological and moral systems they produce. Tensions can run high between coexisting religions.

Preachers of Peace versus Aggressive Activists

In his paper Agus Widyanto describes the conflict between visionary Indonesian religious leaders who plead for peace and young activists who consider these leaders too moderate and seek confrontation. It is often not only the 'other party' which is the victim of interreligious violence but also those *within* the various groups who call for 'accommodation'. In Indonesia as well as Rwanda 'moderates' on both sides fell victim to hardliners. The injunctions to peace urged by well-established religious leaders often lose their power in periods of brutal conflict.

Swami Agnivesh strongly distinguished religion (in the sense of an organized power game) from spirituality. He argued for an ongoing intensive search for ways to make spirituality attractive and imbue it with the power to realize reconciliation.

According to Vincent van Bijlert, reformist Hinduism was characterized by the same search. Sri Ramakrishna, Vivekananda and Sri Aurobindo were all great leaders working to achieve peace. Their doctrines of tolerance and reconciliation present no difficulty. There is no real problem with the these teachings themselves but rather with their socialization and implementation.

Michael McGhee draws the dichotomy even more sharply: in his interpretation of Buddhist ethics the practical work of reconciliation is worldly wisdom and has nothing to do with religion as such. Even though it is an independent human reality, however, this worldly wisdom can become incorporated in a religious tradition.

Anthropological-Philosophical versus Theological Reconciliation

The papers contributed by Desiree Berendsen, Cees van der Kooi and Henry Jansen deal with theological and secular concepts of reconciliation. In the former reconciliation between God and human beings often takes precedence over the more secular, this-worldly notion of reconciliation. Berendsen argues that if reconciliation between human beings takes place, it is a result of the mediation of an additional party. This third party needs to be transcendent to the persons involved in the conflict but does not necessarily need to be divine. In his paper Henry Jansen argues that, given the intransigence of human beings, we need at times to be forced into reconciliation. The agent of this reconciliation is, in his view, God or some version of the Transcendent.

Ton van Prooijen analyzes the concept of reconciliation in the theology of Jürgen Moltmann. Reconciliation (*Versöhnung*) is only possible, according to Moltmann, when good news is brought to the poor, when the rich feel the pain caused by the loss of their privileges. But the this-worldly perspective in Moltmann's thought becomes easily obscured by his interpretation of Jesus' resurrection and the church as a "messianic intermezzo," that is to say, an anticipation of some future reign of freedom. Moltmann's theological elucidation of the concept of reconciliation is fascinating but not clearly related to this-worldly anthropological discourse.

S. Gangaderan takes quite the opposite position, indicating that according to the school of Hindu thought that he represents commitment to and efforts on behalf of this-worldly interhuman reconciliation are prerequisite to authentic faith.

The two papers on reconciliation in South Africa call attention to other important aspects of the workshop discussions.

The Reformed theologian Piet Meiring, who was a member of the South African Truth and Reconciliation Committee, concentrates on reconciliation among human beings in the here and now. The two basic preconditions for reconciliation, truth and justice, are seen as this-worldly qualifications.

In his paper Farid Esack, a South African Muslim, stresses the necessity of working for peace together with adherents of other religious communities. He rejects the "theology of vengeance" of right-wing Muslims, the Pagad. Borrowing from various traditions, he formulates elements of a theology of reconciliation. First, he refers to the Quaker doctrine that "everyone is of God" and then adduces a Jewish rabbinic definition of the beginning of day: "When one human being looks into the face of another and says, 'This is my sister' or 'This is my brother.'"

Conclusion

It was clear from both the workshop papers and discussions that the participants were agreed that religion, like all other human institutions, can become deeply involved in one way or another in situations of conflict. Religion itself produces differences of opinion and varying moral systems, but religion at its best will also bend its efforts to the cooperative building up and maintenance of a peaceful society.

Index of Names

Aarsbergen, C. 145, 367, 374, 385
Abe, M. 32, 34
Abelard 113, 165
Abraham 25, 34, 134-44, 353, 374
Aeschylus 68-70, 74, 80-84, 375
Agnivesh, Swami 66, 251, 374, 376, 379, 387-88
Ahmed, L. 187, 189, 194
Aisha 188-89
Akbar, M.G. 133, 203, 265
al-Jabri, M.A. 186, 192-94, 375
Alexander, J.C. 14, 21
Ambedkar 30, 182
Anselm of Canterbury 109, 165
Arjuna 68, 69, 72, 73, 75, 80, 81
Armstrong, K. 135, 144
Aulén, G. 107, 116, 165, 306
Averroes 186, 192, 193

Bakry, H. 217, 218, 221, 223, 228
Bankim, Chandra Chatterjee 44-48, 50
Barnard, A. 12, 14, 21
Barnard, W. 145
Barth, K. 112, 306
Bauman, Z. 15, 22
Bavinck, J.H. 117, 118, 132
Bendrix, M. 155-60, 162
Berendsen, D. 161, 164, 373, 388
Berger, P.L. 120, 350, 354
Berlin, I. 82, 145-53, 185, 367, 369, 374, 385
Bertello, Mgr. G. 333
Beverley, H. 39, 48
Bhutto, Z.A. 241
Blake, William 90
Bonhoeffer, D. 336, 338
Botha, P.W. 283, 285
Botman, R. 312, 314
Bourdieu, P. 13, 19, 22
Bourdillon, J. 39, 40
Brightman, R. 16, 22, 83

Cain, C. 101
Calvin, J. 120, 165, 306
Carpenter, Joel 119, 120, 132
Castro, E. 125, 126, 129, 132
Chakraborty, S.K. 49, 50
Chethimattam, J.B. 45, 50
Cilliers, P. 16, 22
Classe, Mgr. L. 327, 339
Clifford, J. 16, 22
Cohen, A.P. 16, 17, 22
Cone, J. 305
Cyril of Jerusalem 108

d'Andrade, Roy 19, 22
d'Souza, A. 260, 261, 269, 374, 379, 387
de Klerk, T.W. 280
de Kom, A. 174
des Forges, A. 332, 334, 338
Dogen Zenji 181, 182, 185
Donaghy, H.J. 159, 160, 163
Droogers, A. 11, 367, 373, 385
Drummond, L. 15, 22
du Gay, P. 16, 22
Dumont, L. 40, 50, 53, 58, 82
Duryodhana 68, 69, 73, 76, 78

Eaton, R. 38, 48, 50
Elias, N. 14, 22
Engineer, A.A. 25, 121, 132, 373-75, 377-78, 385, 387
Eriksen, T.H. 16, 22
Esack, F. 161-62, 290, 298, 373-76, 381, 389
Eteocles 69-76, 79-80

Fanon, F. 303, 314

Featherstone, M. 15, 22
Feynman, A. 174
Francis of Assisi 117, 274
Friedman, J. 15, 22
Frye, N. 154, 163

Gandhi, I. 244-46, 249
Gandhi/Gandhiji, M. 57, 64, 122, 240, 246, 248, 249, 278, 363
Gandhi, R. 248
Gangadaran, S. 60, 374, 376
Geschiere, P. 16, 22
Giddens, A. 13, 22
Gort, J.D. 3, 32, 34, 127, 133, 144, 373, 375, 388
Greene, Graham 154-56, 159, 162-63, 373
Gregor, I. 155, 159, 160, 162, 163
Gross, R.M. 185, 186, 190-91, 194, 375

Habyarimana, J. 329, 330, 332, 334-35
Hagar 136-39, 142, 143
Hall, S. 16, 22
Hannerz, U. 15, 22
Harris, M. 12, 22
Harvey, P. 87, 88, 92
Hayek, M. 137, 141-144
Heehs, P. 41, 42, 50
Heesterman, J.C. 40, 50, 75
Heiler, F. 227, 228
Hick, J. 9, 32, 34
Hobsbawm, E. 16, 22, 344, 354
Holland, D. 19, 22
Huntington, Samuel P. 120, 135, 211, 352, 354
Hutchinson, G.O. 70, 74, 83

Irving, J. 157
Isaac 134-40, 143
Isaiah 96, 102, 103, 122, 126, 135
Ishmael 134-43

Jacob (Israel) 134, 139
Jacques, G. 122, 129, 133
Jansen, H. 154, 156, 162, 163, 168, 373, 388, 389
Jenkins, R. 16, 22
Jesus Christ 27, 28, 31, 64, 105-16, 118, 122, 125, 138, 140-42, 211, 266, 286, 296, 306-09, 320, 327, 372, 389

The Crucified 301, 307-13, 315, 373
The Resurrected 309, 312
Jumbe, A. 318, 321, 325

Keesing, R.H. 16, 22, 83
Khadija 187
Khalîl 135
Khoury, A. 24, 34
King, Martin Luther 122, 174, 278
Koeman, R. 174
Koopman, N. 312, 314
Kranenborg, R. 356, 373
Krishna 69, 72, 73, 75, 80, 81, 245
Krog, A. 288, 298-300, 313, 314
Küng, H. 137, 140, 143-44, 340, 350, 354
Kuper, A. 12, 22
Kuyper, Abraham 25, 34

Lavigerie, Cardinal C. 327
Lazar, Prince 341, 344, 345, 348
Lefebure, L.D. 34
Lemmen, M.M.W. 14, 22
Ludwig, F. 3, 320, 325
Luke 26, 113, 114, 138, 262
Lukes, S. 14, 22

Maharishi Mahesh Yogi 357
Malcolm X 303
Malinar, A. 73-76, 83
Mandela, Nelson 174, 278-81, 286-88, 380
Mandela, Winnie 283
Marcus, G.E. 16, 22
Marcuse, H. 120
Marshall, Paul 119, 133
Marx, K. 3, 5, 147 304
Marx, T. 374, 375
Mbeki, T. 299, 309
McGhee, M. 92, 374, 376, 388
Meiring, P. 8, 279, 282, 285, 286, 288, 298, 300, 312, 314, 335, 33-38, 373-75, 380-81, 389
Meyer, B. 16, 22

IINDEX OF NAMES

Mfumbasa, B. 382, 386
Michaels, A. 82, 83
Miles, S. 155, 245
Milosevic, S. 342, 345, 348, 354
Minnema, L. 124, 375
Misago, Mgr. A. 335, 338
Mkapa, B. 316
Mobutu, S.S. 329
Moltmann, J. 131, 133, 301-14, 373, 389
Moore, H.L. 15
Moore, J.D. 12
Muhammad 48, 117, 122, 136, 140-42, 186-88, 239, 251, 290-91, 320
Muhammadiyah 208, 217, 223
Mukti Ali, A. 218-20, 222-29, 374
Murdoch, I. 156, 157
Murphy, J. 363, 364
Museveni, Y. 329
Musinga 327
Mwanga 327
Mwinyi, A.H. 316, 319

Nashat, G. 187, 194
Naudé, B. 122
Nehru, J. 53, 244, 250, 278, 378
Nencel, L. 16, 23
Njozi, H. 319, 325
Nsengiyumva, Mgr. V. 331, 332
Nussbaum, M. C. 70, 71, 80, 84
Nyerere, J. 316, 321, 370, 386

Oldham, J.H. 128
Omari, C. 321, 325
Ortner, S.B. 13, 23

Pandey, G. 39, 50
Paul 109, 111, 114-15, 141, 262
Paul, D. 176-77, 179, 180,
Peale, N.V. 363
Pels, P. 16, 23
Perwiranegara, A.R. 225, 226
Peter 27, 107, 114
Peters, F.E. 136, 138-39, 144, 172, 175
Petersen, R.L. 123-24, 133

Polynices 69, 70, 74, 76

Quinn, N. 19, 23, 83, 84

Rahner, K. 118, 133
Raiser, K. 4, 9, 10, 124, 132, 133
Ram-Prasad, C. 75, 231, 238, 367, 373-74, 378, 386
Rama 56, 57, 64, 75, 236, 248
Ramakrishna 46, 47, 50, 388
Raman, V.V. 79
Rammohun, R. 43
Ranger, T. 16, 22
Rao, N. 248, 267
Ricoeur, P. 26, 34
Robertson, R. 15, 23
Romberg, C. 375, 387
Rosenau, P.M. 16, 23
Rudahigwa 327
Rudolph 12, 23
Rushd, Ibn 186, 192, 375, 387
Rushdie, S. 6, 137, 138, 144

Sagan, E. 78, 84
Samartha, S. 119, 133
Sankara 64
Saradananda, Swami 46, 50
Sarah 134, 136-39
Sarup, M. 16, 23
Schmidt-Leukel, P. 26, 34
Schreiter, R. 122, 124-26, 133
Schuller, R. 363
Scott, J. 20, 23, 58
Seiple, R. 119, 133
Sharma, N. 82, 84, 185
Sibomana, Mgr. A. 335, 339
Siva 60, 62-67
Sivalon, J. 321, 325
Smith, W.C. 219, 228, 340, 355
Sorel, G. 120
Spark, M. 157, 161, 163
Speyer, H. 135, 144
Sri Aurobindo 38, 47-50, 388
Sri Ramakrishna 46, 47, 50, 388
Stepinac, Cardinal 341
Stoffels, H. 24-25, 34
Strauss, C. 19, 22, 23, 83, 84

Suharto 197, 199-202, 205-06, 208, 212-13, 217, 221-23, 370
Sukarno 197, 205, 217, 220-21
Sundermeier, T. 3, 10, 118, 133
Swaris, N. 25, 270, 373, 374, 386
Syadzali, M. 226, 227

Tarmizi, T. 219, 226-27, 229
Thalmann, W.G. 69, 70, 73, 79, 80, 84
Thapar, R. 54, 59, 76-78, 84
Thomas Aquinas 26, 185
Tillich, P. 154, 163, 306
Tirujnana Samabandar 62, 63, 65, 67
Tito 342-43, 348, 370
Tomlinson, J. 15, 23
Tucker, J.E. 187-189, 194
Turner, T. 16, 17, 23
Tutu, Archbishop D. 278-79, 284-89, 295, 298-99, 337, 339, 381, 387
Twagirayesu, M. 327, 331, 333, 339

Uma 65

Van Asselt, W.J. 116, 165, 175
Van Bijlert, V.A. 25, 37, 372, 374-76, 388
Van Butselaar, J. 327, 339, 373-74, 382, 386
Van der Burg, C.J.G. 25, 51, 81, 374-76
Van der Kooij, C. 372, 375
Van Hoogevest 128, 133
Van Langen, E. 174
Van Prooijen, T. 158, 298, 373-375, 389
Van Roermund, B. 166, 168-69, 172, 175
Van Ruler, A.A. 75, 236, 239-40, 247, 313
Visser, T. 186, 375, 387
Vivekananda, Swami 38, 47, 48, 50, 388
Von Bodelschwingh, F. 327
Vorgrimler, H. 118, 133
Vroom, H.M. 31-32, 34, 144, 154, 163, 373, 388

Wach, J. 225, 227-28, 230
Ward, K. 34, 263
Weber, M. 14, 22, 82
Wesley, Charles 117
Wessels, A. 135, 144, 374
Widyanto, A.R. 197, 374, 382, 383, 388
Wijsen, F. 317, 320, 326, 374, 382, 386
Winslow, D. 340, 374-75
Woodward, K. 16, 23

Index of Subjects

Accountability 124, 204, 257
Action
  concrete 356, 364
Agree in disagreement
  concept of 219, 220, 223, 227
Ahimsa 254, 258
Amnesty 279-81, 283-87, 295-96, 298-30, 338, 380-81
An-Nuur 319
Anatta 86, 87
Androgynous model of humanity 186, 191-92, 194, 375, 387
Anglicized elites 270-72
Apartheid 8, 121, 123, 168, 279-81, 284, 285, 290-93, 295-96, 299-300, 314, 370, 373, 374, 380
Approach
  scientific 227
Arabia
  pre-Islamic 136, 187-89, 234, 239
Arbitration 79, 169
Ares 73, 79, 124
Aristocracy 178, 275
Arusha Declaration 320-21, 329, 333
Atonement (*kappara*) 93, 96-100, 103, 107, 112, 116
Authority 4, 14, 23, 24, 40, 55, 73, 75, 76, 117, 131, 170, 187, 205-06, 216, 233, 273, 283, 299, 368, 370, 387
Autonomy 6, 15, 21, 108, 109, 152, 201-02, 212, 273

Babar Mosque 51
Baraza Kuu la Waislamu 318, 322, 325
Bedouins 138, 142
Bengal 37-43, 48, 50
Bhagavadgita 40, 49, 52, 58, 68, 69, 72-76, 80, 83, 84, 375, 376
Bhakti 62, 258

Bhartiya Janata Party (BJP) 57-58, 236-37, 246-50
Black 279, 285, 288, 292, 295, 299, 301, 303-05, 308, 314, 381
Bosnians 340, 341, 350
Brahma Kumaris, the 356-360, 364
British, the 22, 37-43, 48, 54-57, 119, 151, 240, 243, 251, 270-276, 325, 378
Buddhahood 180-81, 183-84
Buddhism 25, 29-30, 37, 45, 47, 49, 63, 87, 90, 92, 118, 176-85, 216, 233-34, 251, 275, 277, 363, 375-76, 387
Byzantine and Sasanian rule 188

Caste 30, 37-39, 42, 48, 55, 58, 61, 62, 69, 75, 176, 235, 239-42, 247-48, 250, 377-78
Catholics 27, 119, 148, 155, 213, 264, 267, 271, 316, 320-22, 327, 331-32, 334-35, 340-44, 346-48, 350, 352-53
Census 38-42, 44, 48, 249, 321, 344
Ceylon National Congress 270
Change in human beings 155-62, 165, 375
Channelling 360
Chesed 118
Choices 99, 108, 119, 146, 150, 174
Christianity 24-28, 30, 32, 44, 45, 49, 64, 106, 123, 128, 130, 135, 140, 142, 144, 154, 176, 205-09, 211-12, 218, 221, 234, 247, 251, 277, 294, 296, 318, 320, 322-24, 338, 348, 363, 372, 379, 382-83
Christianization 198, 207, 209-12, 296, 381-82
Church and state
  separation of 119, 343
Church of the Holy Sepulchre, the 134

Civic United Front 316, 319
Civil supremacy 199, 200
Collective remembrance 124
Colonialism 15, 37-38, 40-41, 48, 50, 53-57, 190, 194, 198, 220, 239-40, 270, 321, 328, 377
Common good 148, 212
Communalism 7, 38, 39, 41-43, 47, 50, 54-56, 58, 59, 90, 118, 151, 197-98, 201-03, 235-37, 240-41, 243-49, 253, 257, 261-65, 276, 373-74, 378, 386
Communism 5, 29, 30, 38, 43, 135, 147, 204-05, 220-21, 223, 225, 245, 342-43, 386
Comparative religion
   study of 216-29, 374
Compassion 3, 7, 32, 34, 65-67, 90-91, 98, 119, 136, 179, 181, 184, 251, 257-58, 294, 375, 381
Conflict *passim*
   rudimentary agents of 120
   civilizational 234
   inner 50, 79-81
   martial model of conflict resolution 252
   religious 29, 31, 43, 51, 65, 120, 198, 206, 208, 231-32, 236-28, 270, 317-18, 325, 350, 368, 379, 382
   resolution 100, 101, 238, 251-52, 254, 262, 374, 379
   social 68, 79-81, 124
   spiritual model of resolution 252
Contact Committee 332, 334
A Course in Miracles 356, 360, 364
Covenant 94, 105, 137-41, 144, 341
Creolization 15-18, 20
Criminal law 166-67, 169, 171, 173, 175
Criticism 9, 100-01, 122, 147, 203, 206, 217, 309, 315, 353, 374
Croatia 341, 343-44, 346-47
Croats 340, 345, 347-48, 350
Crucifixion 165, 173, 308, 372
Crusades 121, 135, 152, 320, 356
Cultural anthropology 14, 16, 17, 22, 23, 83, 84
Culture
   concept of 83
Dar es Salaam 317, 319, 321, 323, 325
Decolonization 330
Dependence 86, 87, 90
Dependent arising 86
Determinism 150, 162
Deterrent 167
Dhimmi 24, 322
Dialogue 4, 7, 10, 25, 28, 31, 33-34, 45, 101, 129-31, 135, 143, 163, 186, 192-93, 219, 221-23, 226, 228-29, 252, 261, 269, 316, 320, 326, 338, 352, 354, 374, 379, 382, 387
   of histories 130
   of life 131, 320, 382
   Rushdian 186, 192, 193, 387
   of spiritualities 131
   of theologies 130
Dictatorship 332
Discipline of quiet patience 125, 126
Disquietude
   existential 118
Djahiliyya period 188
Dukkha 87, 88, 90

Ego-identity 305
Egotism 118, 125, 157
Emissaries of the Divine Light, the 356
Energy 349, 358, 361-64
Engaged Buddhism 176, 177, 182, 184-85
Equivalence 105, 184, 185
Eros 85
Esotericism 363
Eternal salvation 26, 27
Ethics
   establishment 252
Ethnic cleansing 202, 206, 342, 346-47, 349, 352, 354
Evangelism 261, 269

extra ecclesiam nulla salus 26

Failure and rehabilitation 93-97
Fall of humankind 148, 356
Family 68-73, 75-81, 83, 125
Federalism 271
Forgiveness 8, 32, 49-50, 86, 90-91, 94, 98, 111, 124, 132, 156, 165, 168-69, 172-74, 264, 267-68, 279, 286-89, 296, 313, 339, 340, 352-53, 355, 360-61, 364, 374-76, 381, 384
Free market economy 277, 319, 382
Freedom
  civilized 202
  cultural dimension of 11, 301
  economic dimension of 301
  environmental dimension of 301
  political dimension of 301
  theological dimension of 301, 305
  uncivilized 201-03
Functionalism 12, 13
Fundamentalism 21, 58, 144, 238, 252-54, 323, 325, 370, 382
Gender 16, 23, 121, 128, 176, 178, 180, 185-91, 193-94, 198, 317, 371, 375, 387
Gender perspectives 186, 187, 189-90, 193
Genocide 327-28, 330, 335-38, 341, 348, 355, 382
Globalization 15-16, 18, 22-23, 57, 129, 235, 237, 257, 347
God
  conception of 62, 211
  role of in reconciliation 155, 156, 159, 162
  spirit of 381
Grace 27, 60, 62-63, 66, 92, 139, 141, 156, 177, 306
  God's steadfast 118
  of justification 160
  of sanctification 160
Greek philosophy 27, 181
Guilt 8, 70, 73, 74, 93, 98, 100, 106-07, 112, 115-16, 132, 165-66, 168, 172, 287, 300, 305, 312, 330, 336-37, 360-61, 373, 382

Hadith 188
Hall of Isaac, the 134
Harim 189
Harmonious coexistence 3, 7, 9, 13, 17-18, 21, 25, 31, 65, 86, 117, 123-25, 127, 129, 145-49, 152, 198, 216, 220-21, 223-24, 226, 228, 240, 244, 249, 255, 316, 323-24, 359, 374
Hatred 3, 4, 6, 24, 26, 43, 50, 90, 118, 121, 130, 156-59, 162, 181, 182, 206, 209, 239-41, 248, 263-64, 294, 298, 304, 312, 327, 333, 337, 341, 344, 350, 380, 381, 383
  ethnic 118, 333
Heidelberg Catechism 108, 110, 112
Henry Martyn Institute 260-61, 269, 379-80, 387
Hierarchization 53
Hindu-Muslim relations 51, 54, 367
Hinduism 25, 29, 37-40, 43-47, 49, 51-53, 55-57, 61, 64, 216, 233-36, 239, 277, 363, 375-76, 378, 386, 388
Hindutva 56, 57, 243, 246
History
  interpretation of 234, 328, 378
Holy Ghost 361
Holy impatience 126
Holy, encounter with the 118
Homogeneity 39, 82, 83, 240, 346, 377
Human life
  cheapening of 293
Human rights
  violations of 8, 129, 279-81, 283-84, 299, 380-81
Human worth 256-57

'ibada 227
Ideas, clash of 122
Identity 9, 10, 15-17, 21-25, 27-29, 33, 34, 42-43, 55, 59, 85, 94-95, 109-10, 115, 130, 150, 153, 176, 220, 231, 234-36, 239, 242, 247,

250-51, 302-05, 308-09, 311-14, 340-46, 354, 369-71, 378
Identity politics 340, 342, 344, 346
Ijtihad 186
Independence 31, 37, 40-41, 53-54, 57, 176, 197, 207, 234, 242-43, 248, 253, 270, 275, 319-22, 331, 378, 382
India 9, 31, 37, 38, 40, 41, 43, 44, 46-51, 53, 54, 56-60, 66, 68, 75, 78, 176, 182, 231, 233-39, 241-51, 253, 261, 263, 271, 274, 276-77, 358, 367, 373, 377, 378, 385, 386
Indonesia 4, 9, 132, 133, 197-222, 224-30, 367, 370, 374, 377, 382-83, 388
economic development of 224
Industrialization 190
Injustice 4, 5, 8, 30-33, 85, 86, 91, 111, 114, 122-27, 129-32, 151, 166-67, 172, 192, 255-56, 280, 289, 291, 294, 296, 322, 373-75, 381, 388
Interests 3, 4, 8, 12, 13, 19, 32, 39, 42, 54, 105, 108, 121, 128, 147, 149-50, 166, 174-75, 204, 209, 213, 240-41, 244, 251-53, 255, 258, 270, 273, 350, 367-68, 371, 383
Interreligious dialogue 34, 130, 163, 222-23, 226, 228-29, 326, 374
Intolerance 24-28, 148, 252-53, 356
Intransigence of human beings 161-62, 389
Islam 29, 34, 37-40, 43, 45-48, 50, 55, 57, 64, 130, 132, 135-44, 154, 186-191, 193-94, 199, 204-12, 215-19, 225, 228-30, 234, 239, 241-42, 244, 247, 251, 261-62, 267, 277, 290-92, 316-17, 319-25, 345-46, 348, 354, 369, 375, 378, 382-83, 387
Islamization 198, 207, 209-10, 212, 382

Jansangh, the 245-46

Judicial impunity 129
Just war 124
Justice 5, 7, 25, 29-30, 32, 34, 49, 64-67, 71, 103, 104, 109-11, 120, 123-26, 128-30, 133, 146, 167, 183, 191-93, 201, 212, 214, 216, 235, 250, 252, 254, 255, 257, 262-63, 268, 276, 286-87, 289, 291, 295-97, 304, 308, 312, 322, 324, 336-38, 353, 370, 373-77, 379-81, 388-89
restorative 132, 170-73, 175

Kandyan Kingdom 274
Kappara 93, 95-97, 100, 103
Karma 32, 61, 63, 67, 91, 177-78, 182, 359
Kebebasan beradab (civilized freedom) 202
Kebebasan biadab (uncivilized freedom) 202
Kenosis 309
Kingdom of God 32, 105, 129, 148, 307
Kinship 76-78, 253, 259
KKN (corruption, collusion and nepotism) 199, 200, 202
Kosovo 9, 341, 344, 345, 348, 354, 355

Leaders 3, 19, 20, 24, 28, 53, 120, 128, 147-48, 208, 214, 222-23, 225, 240, 242, 244-46, 249-50, 254, 264, 273-74, 277, 317, 321-22, 324, 329-37, 342-43, 349, 351-53, 367-70, 383, 386, 388
Liberation 9, 60, 66, 98, 107-08, 120, 176, 182, 185, 190, 194, 213, 245, 273, 276, 280, 284, 291-92, 301-02, 304, 306-07, 310, 312-13, 332, 374
Liberty
negative 150-53, 374
positive 150, 151
Love 3-5, 7, 25, 26, 28, 31-32, 34, 46, 49, 60, 62, 66, 94, 97, 100-02, 107, 109, 113, 117-18,

124, 126, 155-58, 160, 165, 173, 179, 212, 251-52, 254-58, 294, 308-10, 383
  selfless 158
Maharishi effect 357-58
Mahayana 176, 178-80, 183, 375
Mediation 102, 164, 168-73, 175, 233, 238, 262, 268, 368, 373-74, 380, 386, 388
Mediator 27, 79, 164, 170-71, 173, 333
Medical examinations (of women) 177
Meditation 7, 46, 118, 177, 185, 356-60, 362-64, 373
Messianic Intermezzo 311, 313, 389
Metta 88
Middle East 119, 133, 143, 154, 186, 189-90, 194, 232, 343, 348
Military supremacy 199, 200
Militia 332, 334, 342, 347
Ministry of Religious Affairs (Indonesia) 224, 226
Miracles 159
Modernity 22, 38, 40-41, 43, 47, 49, 50, 53-55, 58-59, 75, 82, 92, 102, 108-09, 112, 120, 123, 126, 130, 132, 145, 152-53, 155, 166, 174, 181, 182-84, 190, 192-94, 200, 224, 228-29, 234, 238, 250, 253, 274, 304, 306, 325, 330, 345, 360, 375
Monism 145, 146, 148, 153
Moral dilemmas 93, 146, 149, 152
Morality
  universal 8
MRND 331-32
Multiparty politics 319
Muslim-Christian Relations 316, 317, 324
Muslims 4, 9, 25, 30, 37-39, 41-49, 51, 54-59, 64, 117, 123, 134-37, 141-43, 188-89, 203-05, 209-11, 213, 216-22, 225, 227, 229-30, 235, 236, 239-50, 260-68, 271, 291, 296, 316-26, 341, 343, 345-46, 348, 350-52, 354, 367, 373-75, 377-83, 385-86, 389
  modernist 205, 217, 220, 223
  traditionalist 205, 220
Mythology
  Greek 124

National Party 270, 271, 283, 284
Nationalism 22, 33, 48, 50, 56, 150, 190, 209, 212, 216, 220, 235-37, 240-41, 320, 322, 340, 342, 345, 354, 369, 378
  religious 54, 55, 59, 236, 344, 348
Nehru period 244
Neo-paganism 8
Neutral space 386
New Age 98, 359, 373
  and Yom Kippur 98
New Left 120
New Order 197, 199-02, 204-07, 209, 212-13, 216-17, 221-23, 225, 306, 312, 374
New Testament 114, 135, 141, 372
Non-whites 303

Orthodoxy 346, 351, 370
  right-wing 24
Ottoman Empire 345
Ottoman Turks 189, 341

Pakistan 9, 37, 41, 43, 57, 219, 234-35, 240-45, 247, 249-50, 377-78
Pancasila 199, 212, 216, 218, 223, 374, 382, 383
Particle 99, 357, 358, 362
Partition 41-42, 235, 241-44, 248, 377-78
Peace 3-5, 7, 9, 18, 25, 29-32, 64, 77, 96, 113, 116-17, 119-20, 123-25, 127-29, 134-35, 143, 149, 153, 166, 206, 208, 214, 216, 226, 237, 244, 249, 251, 254, 258, 260, 262, 264, 266, 268, 274, 276-80, 286, 290-91, 296, 307, 308, 312-13, 323-24, 329-30, 332-34, 337, 340, 350, 352-53, 356-364, 373, 377-80, 383, 386, 388-89

hasty 124, 125
PELITA (five-year plan phases) 200
Persecution 3, 25-26, 28, 48, 133, 207, 221, 319
Plot 156, 160
Pluralism 34, 146, 149, 152, 216-17, 229
Political correctness 182
Positive thinking 358-60, 363, 364
Postmodernism 16, 155, 159, 163
Poverty 5, 57, 61, 122, 128, 130-32, 151, 182, 221, 235, 242, 250, 256, 287, 294, 301-02, 322-23, 378, 381-82
Power 5, 12-14, 17-20, 22, 33, 42-43, 45, 54, 63, 68-69, 73-74, 76-78, 93, 98, 101, 106-09, 111-13, 115, 118, 121-22, 126, 130, 153, 159, 161-62, 176-77, 187-89, 197, 199, 200, 202, 204-06, 208-10, 212-16, 221, 223-25, 231-32, 235-37, 239-41, 245-55, 258, 263, 271-72, 275-77, 299, 302, 306-10, 312-13, 315-16, 318-19, 322, 328-31, 334, 336-37, 340-42, 350, 358-64, 368, 369, 371, 377-79, 383, 388
Priests 31, 48, 93, 97-98, 330, 332, 335, 336, 346-47, 349, 354, 382
Process 11, 13, 14, 16, 18, 19, 21, 29, 33, 34, 45, 78, 108, 377, 379-83
Prophetic attitude 209, 383
Prophetic critique 102
Prophetic protest 32, 300
Protestant 46, 105, 115, 119, 120, 123, 211, 213, 271, 275, 327, 330, 332-35
Protestant Ecumenical Movement 123
Protestantism
 right-wing 24
Public domain 86, 145, 151-53
Punishment 91, 164, 166-68, 170, 175, 294, 343, 372
Pure consciousness 357
Purification 45, 56, 96, 100, 359
Purim 97, 99

Quantum field theory 357
Qur'an
 androcentric interpretation of 191, 194

Race 39, 40, 44, 61, 106-08, 110, 128, 139, 206-07, 242, 280, 288-89, 299, 303-05, 345-46, 378
Racism 122, 128, 132, 299-05, 308, 311-14, 332-33, 373, 380
Reality, ultimate 64, 118
Reality-centered 9, 32
Realpolitik 123, 295
Reconciliation
 concept of 104, 116, 376, 389
 models of 104, 106, 107, 164-65, 173, 363, 372
 dramatic model of 107, 114, 165, 363
 example model of 165
 objective model of 8, 107, 109-10, 113, 116, 165, 306, 363, 372
 ransom model of 165
 sacrifice model of 165
 substitution model of 165
 subjective model of 107, 113, 116, 165, 363, 373
Reform 30, 38, 55, 176, 182, 199, 201-02, 207, 251, 342
Refugees 127-28, 133, 197, 277, 329-30, 332, 334-36, 351
Rehabilitation 93, 94, 114, 281, 284, 286, 343, 381
Relations
 international 119, 120
Relationships
 existential 117
Religions
 Abrahamic 7, 376
 established 20, 119
 non-Abrahamic 376
Religious dynamics 119, 120, 320
Religious symbols 121, 344, 387
Repentance 93, 95, 99, 103, 111, 122, 124, 132, 155, 156
Repertoire 21, 369-71
Resource management 256

Index of Subjects

Responsibility 6, 26, 67, 70, 71, 100, 127, 129, 146-47, 150-52, 172, 175, 177, 188, 222, 254, 256-57, 284-85, 288, 305, 324, 352
Rights 8, 31, 41, 103, 121-22, 127, 129, 133, 166, 177, 182-83, 185-86, 188, 191, 201-02, 205, 207, 211, 214-15, 242, 265, 273, 275, 277, 278-81, 283-84, 294, 299, 304-05, 317-19, 322, 327, 332-33, 335, 338, 351, 355, 371, 375, 378, 380-81, 385
Rock Memorial High School 267
Roman Catholic Church 341-43, 350
Rules
    monastic 177, 179
Rwanda 322, 327-34, 336-39, 367, 374, 377, 381-82, 386, 388
Rwanda Patriotic Front (RPF) 329-35, 337

Sacrifice 40, 73, 75, 113, 134, 137, 160, 165
Sainthood 154, 160-62
Saints of Leiden 173-74
Saiva Siddhantha 60-63, 67
Sakti 62, 64, 66
Sangha 176-178, 181, 182
Satisfaction 88, 107, 109-10, 165-66, 171
Schema 14, 19
Scientific-cum-doctrinair
    concept of 227
Secularism 49, 53, 57-59, 234, 235, 238, 240, 244, 246-48, 250, 253, 378
    Indian 58, 234-35, 244, 247-48, 378
    Nehruvian 246, 247
    Western 31
Secularization 119, 151, 211, 383
Self-denial 99, 150
Self-knowledge 81
Serbia 343-45, 347-49, 351, 353
Serbian Orthodox Church 341, 342, 346-49, 351-53
Serbs 340-41, 343, 345-48, 350-51, 353-54
Sexuality 6, 179, 185
Shabbat 99
Shah Bano judgment 247
Sharia 29, 188, 199, 216, 243, 250, 317-18, 322, 382
Sin 25, 94-97, 100, 101, 109-11, 114, 115, 125, 148, 165, 211, 312, 356
Sinhala Only 271-72
Sinhalese 270-72, 274-76, 278, 373
Social engagement 30
Social pathologies 122
Social sciences 11-14, 17, 18, 21, 23, 373
Solutions
    secular 373
South Africa 8, 154, 168, 238, 279-81, 283, 285-91, 293-94, 296, 298, 299-300, 302, 307, 312, 314, 330, 367-68, 370, 373-74, 377, 380-81, 389
Spirituality 43, 45, 47, 84, 103, 110, 124, 188, 213-14, 234, 251-52, 254-55, 256-59, 267, 374, 376, 379, 380, 383, 388
State
    Islamic 29, 199, 205, 212, 216, 234, 318, 322, 352
    secular 317, 325, 382, 385
    secular nature of the 322, 323
    system of 77
Structure 13-15, 21, 176, 182-83, 188, 193, 208, 213, 328
Substitution 165
Sufis 188, 191
Super bomb 357, 358
Superiority 122, 178, 216-18, 252, 303-05, 323, 376
Supreme soul 359
Swahili 320, 324, 382

Tahara 96, 97
Tamil 60, 270-78
Tamil Congress 272-73
Tamil Tigers 274, 276-78
Tanzania 316-26, 370, 374, 377, 382, 386

Teleology 145, 147-48, 152-53
   antiteleological thinking 145, 147
Telos 146-47
Teshuva 93, 95, 103
Theocracy 29, 369
Theologia crucis 28
Theologia gloriae 28
Therigata 178-79
Time and atonement 100
Timing 101
Tolerance 28, 49-53, 58-59, 130, 193, 198, 206, 212, 219, 222-23, 234, 276, 294, 376, 379, 385-86, 388
Transcendence 8, 22, 33, 75, 83, 89, 155, 159-62, 164, 170, 173-75, 231-32, 252, 294, 389
Transcendental Meditation (TM) 356-58, 360-62, 364
Treaty
   absolute theories of 167
   relative theories of 167
   theories of 167
Trinitarian theology 301, 306, 309-10
Truth and Reconciliation Commission (TRC) 279-80, 295, 298, 380
Truth claims 24, 26, 27, 131, 186

Udini 316, 317, 386
Ujamaa ideology 319, 321, 325, 386
Unfree 301-02, 310, 313
Unilateralism 252
United National Party 270, 271
Upanishads 38, 40, 43, 49, 52
Utopia 53, 126

Values 5, 10, 19, 21-22, 37-38, 40, 42-43, 45-46, 49, 55, 72-73, 76, 78, 81-82, 92-94, 133, 144-52, 183, 189, 194, 205-06, 233, 236-37, 244, 256, 299, 320, 369, 385
Vedanta 37-38, 40, 43-47, 49, 50, 52, 357, 363
Verzoening 116, 166, 175, 339
Violence 3, 4, 14, 19, 25, 28-30, 33-34, 42-43, 51, 53-54, 58-59, 71, 79-80, 85-86, 101, 117, 120, 122-25, 128-29, 202, 208-09, 212, 214-15, 217, 234-36, 238, 243, 244, 246, 249, 253-57, 261, 263, 265, 266, 268, 275-76, 288, 290, 292, 293, 298, 301, 323, 339, 340, 342, 344, 347-50, 353-54, 358, 360-62, 368, 372-75, 379-80, 383-84, 386, 388
   of injustice 122, 123
   retributive 120
   spiral nature of 265-66, 268, 379, 384
Visions of the ideal society 7

White 8, 103, 154, 199, 279, 285-86, 288, 298-301, 303-05, 314, 327
Wider ecumenism 129
Will of God 4, 137, 146, 148, 150, 323
Women, rights of 191
Work culture 257
World Council of Churches (WCC) 10, 67, 123, 125-29, 133, 302, 333, 338

Yom Kippur 93-100, 102, 374
Yugoslavia 198, 341-44, 353-54, 370

Zanzibar 316-17, 319, 321, 324-25
Zen 7, 8, 34, 180-83, 185

Contributors

SWAMI AGNIVESH, Chairperson, U.N. Trust Fund on Contemporary Slavery, Chairperson of Bandhua Mukti Morcha (an NGO), Working President of the World Council of Arya Samaj, Religious Leader and Social Activist, New Delhi, India.

HERMAN BECK, Professor of Phenomenology of Religion, Faculty of Theology, University of Tilburg, The Netherlands.

DESIREE BERENDSEN, Senior Research Fellow in Philosophy of Religion, UFSIA, University of Antwerp, Belgium.

ANDRE DROOGERS, Professor of the Cultural Anthropology of Religion, Faculty of Social Sciences, Free University, Amsterdam, The Netherlands.

ANDREAS D'SOUZA, Director, Henry Martyn Institute: International Center for Research, Interfaith Relations and Reconciliation, Hyderabad, India. Henry Martyn Institute, Hyderabad, India.

ASHGAR ALI ENGINEER, Chairman, Center for the Study of Society and Secularism, Mumbai, India.

FARID ESACK, Former Commissioner for Gender Equality in South Africa, Visiting Professor, Xavier University, Cincinnati, Ohio, USA.

JOSIEN FOLBERT, Project Officer for Muslim-Christian Dialogue, Uniting Dutch Protestant Churches, Utrecht, The Netherlands.

S. GANGADARAN, Professor of Philosophy, Department of Saiva Siddhanta Philosophy, Madurai Kamaraj University, Madurai, India.

JERALD GORT, Associate Professor of Missiology, Faculty of Theology, Free University, Amsterdam, The Netherlands.

HENRY JANSEN, Formerly Senior Research and Teaching Fellow, Faculty of Theology, Free University, Amsterdam, The Netherlands. Currently serving as Pastor in the Reformed Churches of the Netherlands.

REENDER KRANENBORG, Associate Professor of Religious Studies (New Religious Movements), Faculty of Theology, Free University, Amsterdam, The Netherlands.

TZVI MARX, Lecturer in Judaism, Faculty of Theology, Catholic University of Nijmegen, Lecturer at the Crescas Jewish Educational Center and the Netherlands Bible Institute, Fellow of the Folkertsma Institute for Talmud, The Netherlands.

MICHAEL McGHEE, Lecturer in Philosophy, University of Liverpool, United Kingdom.

BERNADINE MFUMBASA, Doctoral Candidate in Mass Communication, Pontifical Gregorian University, Rome.

PIET MEIRING, Professor of Missiology, Faculty of Theology, University of Pretoria, Republic of South Africa.

LOURENS MINNEMA, Associate Professor of Buddhist and Hindu Studies, Faculty of Theology, Free University, Amsterdam, The Netherlands.

CHAKRAVARTHI RAM-PRASAD, Professor of Hindu Studies, Department of Religious Studies, University of Lancaster, United Kingdom.

CLAUDIA ROMBERG, Doctoral Candidate in Buddhism, Faculty of Theology, Free University, Amsterdam, The Netherlands.

NALIN SWARIS, a recent convert to Buddhism, lectured as Roman Catholic priest for many years in Social Philosophy and Methodology of Community Development at the De Horst Academy, Driebergen, The Netherlands.

KARL STEENBRINK, Senior Research Fellow and Lecturer, Interuniversity Institute for Missiology and Ecumenics, Utrecht, The Netherlands.

VICTOR VAN BIJLERT, Associate Professor, Management Center for Human Values, Indian Institute of Management, Calcutta, India.

JAN VAN BUTSELAAR, General Secretary emeritus of the Dutch Missionary Council, Amsterdam, The Netherlands.

CORSTIAAN VAN DER BURG, Associate Professor of Sanskrit and Indology, Faculty of Theology, Free University, Amsterdam, The Netherlands.

CEES VAN DER KOOI, Associate Professor of Systematic Theology, Faculty of Theology, Free University, Amsterdam, The Netherlands.

TON VAN PROOIJEN, Doctoral Candidate in Systematic Theology, Faculty of Theology, Free University, Amsterdam, The Netherlands.

TIRZA VISSER, Doctoral Candidate in Islam, Faculty of Theology, Free University, Amsterdam, The Netherlands.

Contributors

AGUS WIDYANTO, Senior Lecturer in Philosophy, Catholic University in Bandung, Indonesia.

FRANS WIJSEN, Professor Missiology and Director of the Graduate School of Theology, Theological Faculty, Catholic University of Nijmegen, The Netherlands.

HENDRIK VROOM, Professor of Philosophy, Faculty of Theology, Free University, Amsterdam, The Netherlands.

DONNA JEAN WINSLOW, Professor of Social and Cultural Anthropology, Faculty of Social Sciences, Free University, Amsterdam, The Netherlands.

ANTON WESSELS, Professor of Missiology and Religious Studies, Faculty of Theology, Free University, Amsterdam, The Netherlands.

CURRENTS OF ENCOUNTER

GENERAL EDITORS: Rein Fernhout, Jerald D. Gort, Henry Jansen, Lourens Minnema, Hendrik M. Vroom, Anton Wessels

---------- VOLUMES PUBLISHED OR AT PRESS ----------

1 J.D. Gort, et al., eds. *Dialogue and Syncretism: An Interdisciplinary Approach* (copublished with Eerdmans)
2 Hendrik M. Vroom *Religions and the Truth: Philosophical Reflections and Perspectives* (with Eerdmans)
3 Sutarman S. Partonadi *Sadrach's Community and its Contextual Roots: A Nineteenth-Century Javanese Expression of Christianity*
4 J.D. Gort, et al., eds. *On Sharing Religious Experience: Possibilities of Interfaith Mutuality* (with Eerdmans)
5 S. Wesley Ariarajah *Hindus and Christians: A Century of Protestant Ecumenical Thought* (with Eerdmans)
6 Makoto Ozaki *Introduction to the Philosophy of Tanabe, according to the English Translation of the Seventh Chapter of the* Demonstratio *of Christianity*
7 Karel Steenbrink *Dutch Colonialism and Indonesian Islam: Contacts and Conflicts, 1596-1950*
8 A.A. An-Na'im et al., eds. *Human Rights and Religious Values: An Uneasy Relationship?*
9 Rein Fernhout *Canonical Texts: Bearers of Absolute Authority (Bible, Koran, Veda, Tipiṭaka). A Phenomenological Study*
10 Henry Jansen *Relationality and the Concept of God*
11 Wessel Stoker *Is the Quest for Meaning the Quest for God? The Religious Ascription of Meaning in Relation to the Secular Ascription of Meaning*
12 Hendrik M. Vroom and Jerald D. Gort, eds. *Holy Scriptures in Judaism, Christianity and Islam: Hermeneutics, Values and Society*
13 Nelson O. Hayashida *Dreams in the African Church: The Significance of Dreams and Visions among Zambian Baptists*
14 Hendrik Hart et al., eds. *Walking the Tightrope of Faith: Philosophical Conversations about Reason and Religion*
15 Hisakazu Inagaki and J. Nelson Jennings *Philosophical Theology and East-West Dialogue*
16 Christine Lienemann-Perrin et al., eds. *Reformed and Ecumenical: On Being Reformed in Ecumenical Encounters*

17 J.D. Gort *et al.*, eds.   *Religion, Conflict and Reconciliation: Multifaith Ideals and Realities*
18 M. Dhavamony   *Hindu-Christian Dialogue: Soundings and Perspectives*

Volumes in this series are available from Editions Rodopi, Tijnmuiden 7 1046 AK Amsterdam, the Netherlands, or 1 Rockefeller Plaza, Suite 1420, New York, New York 10020